P9-EDW-068

BIOLOGY AND GEOLOGY OF CORAL REEFS

VOLUME II: Biology 1

CONTRIBUTORS

Gerald J. Bakus

Paul R. Burkholder

Leon S. Ciereszko

Joseph H. Connell

A. B. Cribb

Louis H. Di Salvo

Robert Endean

Peter W. Glynn

J. Frederick Grassle

T. K. B. Karns

Leonard Muscatine

Yu. I. Sorokin

Masashi Yamaguchi

BIOLOGY
AND GEOLOGY
OF CORAL REEFS

EDITED BY

O. A. JONES

Department of Geology
University of Queensland
St. Lucia, Brisbane
Queensland, Australia

R. ENDEAN

Department of Zoology
University of Queensland
St. Lucia, Brisbane
Queensland, Australia

VOLUME II: Biology 1

ACADEMIC PRESS   New York   San Francisco   London   1973

A Subsidiary of Harcourt Brace Jovanovich, Publishers

ACADEMIC PRESS, INC.
111 Fifth Avenue, New York, New York 10003

United Kingdom Edition published by
ACADEMIC PRESS, INC. (LONDON) LTD.
24/28 Oval Road, London NW1

LIBRARY OF CONGRESS CATALOG CARD NUMBER: 72-84377

PRINTED IN THE UNITED STATES OF AMERICA
81 82   9 8 7 6 5 4 3

To the Great Barrier Reef Committee, its office-bearers and its many members who have worked unremittingly for fifty years to further our knowledge of the Great Barrier Reef; and to the memory of geologist Professor H. C. Richards, one of its founders, and biologist Professor E. J. Goddard, an early enthusiastic supporter

CONTENTS

1. Microbial Ecology

Louis H. Di Salvo

2. Microbiological Aspects of the·Productivity of Coral Reefs

Yu. I. Sorokin

3. The Algae of the Great Barrier Reefs

A. B. Cribb

4. Nutrition of Corals

Leonard Muscatine

5. The Ecology of Marine Antibiotics and Coral Reefs

Paul R. Burkholder

6. Comparative Biochemistry of Coral Reef Coelenterates

Leon S. Ciereszko and T. K. B. Karns

7. **Population Ecology of Reef-Building Corals**

   Joseph H. Connell

8. **Variety in Coral Reef Communities**

   J. Frederick Grassle

9. **Aspects of the Ecology of Coral Reefs in the
    Western Atlantic Region**

   Peter W. Glynn

10. The Biology and Ecology of Tropical Holothurians

Gerald J. Bakus

11. Early Life Histories of Coral Reef Asteroids, with Special Reference to *Acanthaster planci* (L.)

Masashi Yamaguchi

12. Population Explosions of *Acanthaster planci* and Associated Destruction of Hermatypic Corals in the Indo-West Pacific Region

Robert Endean

LIST OF CONTRIBUTORS

Numbers in parentheses indicate the pages on which the authors' contributions begin.

GERALD J. BAKUS,[*] National Academy of Sciences, Washington, D.C. (325)

PAUL R. BURKHOLDER,[†] Department of Marine Sciences, University of Puerto Rico, Mayaguez, Puerto Rico (117)

LEON S. CIERESZKO, Department of Chemistry, The University of Oklahoma, Norman, Oklahoma (183)

JOSEPH H. CONNELL, Department of Biological Sciences, University of California, Santa Barbara, California (205)

A. B. CRIBB, Department of Botany, University of Queensland, St. Lucia, Brisbane, Australia (47)

LOUIS H. DI SALVO, Naval Biomedical Research Laboratory, University of California, Berkeley, California (1)

ROBERT ENDEAN, Department of Zoology, University of Queensland, St. Lucia, Brisbane, Queensland, Australia (389)

PETER W. GLYNN, Smithsonian Tropical Research Institute, Balboa, Canal Zone (271)

J. FREDERICK GRASSLE, Woods Hole Oceanographic Institution, Woods Hole, Massachusetts (247)

T. K. B. KARNS, Department of Chemistry, The University of Oklahoma, Norman, Oklahoma (183)

LEONARD MUSCATINE, Department of Biology, University of California, Los Angeles, California (77)

YU. I. SOROKIN, Institute of Freshwater Biology, Academy of Sciences of the USSR, Borok, Garoslavl, USSR (47)

MASASHI YAMAGUCHI, The Marine Laboratory, University of Guam, Agana, Guam (369)

[*] *Present address:* Allan Hancock Foundation, University of Southern California, Los Angeles, California.
[†] Deceased.

GENERAL PREFACE

This four-volume work (two volumes covering geological and two biological topics) originated from an article on The Great Barrier Reefs of Australia written by the editors and published in the November 1967 issue of *Science Journal.* The prime aim of this treatise is to publish in one source as many as possible of the major advances made in the diverse facets of coral reef problems, advances scattered in a multitude of papers and published in a variety of journals.

Initially a one-volume work was projected, but the wealth of material available led to this four-volume treatise. Two contain chapters on aspects of geomorphology, tectonics, sedimentology, hydrology, and radiometric chronology relevant to coral reefs, and two accommodate articles on pertinent biological topics.

The task of organizing the contributions by some forty-one authors (situated in eight different countries) on forty-six different topics proved a formidable one. We wish to thank the contributors, all of whom have been as cooperative as their teaching and/or other commitments permitted.

We feel that the material presented in these volumes demonstrates that many major advances in our knowledge have been made in recent years. We realize that the treatment of the topics covered is not complete and that in many cases new problems have been brought to light. It is our hope that the volumes will provide a powerful stimulus to further work on all aspects of coral reefs.

The editors, of course, accept overall responsibility for all four volumes. Dr. Jones is mainly responsible for the editing of the two geology volumes; Dr. Endean for that of the two biology volumes.

O. A. JONES
R. ENDEAN

PREFACE TO VOLUME II: BIOLOGY 1

Coral reefs have long attracted the attention of biologists who have been fascinated not only by the wealth and diversity of the fauna and flora of reefs but also by the multiplicity of problems posed by organisms inhabiting coral reefs. There is the problem of accounting for the great species diversity exhibited by the biota, the problem of accounting for the remarkably high productivity of coral reefs, problems relating to the distribution of organisms (particularly the spacing of sedentary forms) on reefs, problems relating to the biotic control of the structure of reef communities, and problems connected with the growth and recruitment of coral colonies, to name but a few.

Relatively few biologists had the opportunity to work on coral reefs until recently because the reefs were remote from most of the world's leading research centers and were thus not readily accessible. Those that did were frequently restricted in the types of experimental work they could carry out because of a lack of basic research facilities at the reefs visited. If cognizance is taken of this, the work of the pioneers who laid the foundations of our knowledge of coral reef biology becomes especially meritorious. However, since World War II several research institutions have been erected in coral reef areas, and these together with the commissioning of well-equipped research vessels and the introduction of air routes to these areas have enabled increasing numbers of biologists to visit coral reefs. Moreover, these researchers are drawn from a wide range of biological disciplines and utilize a wide variety of modern techniques. As a result, in recent years biological studies on coral reefs have increased markedly, new fields of study have been developed, and work in established fields has been tackled in greater depth and with more sophisticated techniques than previously. In view of this, the time seemed opportune to bring together the results of recent researches in different fields of coral reef biology and to assess the current state of knowledge about coral reef ecosystems.

One formidable task that confronted us was to select from the wealth of information available a representative range of topics which would provide the nonspecialist with an introduction to the major fields of research embraced by modern coral reef biology and which, at the same

xvii

time, would offer stimulating new ideas to those with specialist knowl-edge. Another was to induce leading workers in relevant fields of coral reef biology to write about the topics selected. Although it has not been possible to cover all major facets of coral reef biology, a wide variety of topics and problems relating to the discipline have been in-cluded in the two biology volumes of this treatise.

The approach adopted in this volume is essentially multidisciplinary and involves discussion of information and problems related to several different fields of coral reef biology. However, some integration has been attempted by grouping together related and overlapping topics wherever possible.

Coral reef microorganisms have only recently come under detailed study. In Chapter 1 Dr. Louis H. Di Salvo discusses their distribution and some of their probable roles. It is apparent from his account that microorganisms are of basic importance in coral reef biology. Indeed, in Chapter 2 Dr. Yuri I. Sorokin discusses the marked contribution made by microorganisms to the high productivity of coral reefs. Also, he com-ments on the significance of bacterioplankton as a food source for the marine fauna of coral reefs.

It would seem that as a group the algae of coral reefs in the Great Barrier Reef area have been somewhat neglected. However, in Chapter 3 Dr. Alan B. Cribb gives an interesting account of the algae occurring on certain reefs. Broader issues, such as the competition between algae and corals for space and the roles of algae in reef construction, are also raised.

The food and feeding mechanism of corals, the chief frame-builders of coral reefs, are discussed by Dr. Leonard Muscatine in Chapter 4. Perplexing problems such as the apparent general paucity in coral reef waters of the zooplankton food of corals are raised. An important analysis of the significance of zooxanthellae as active primary producers and the significance of these coral symbionts in other roles are provided.

The late Dr. Paul R. Burkholder provides a fascinating account (Chap-ter 5) of the role of marine antibiotics in coral reef ecology and provides a wealth of background material for those interested in the newly emerg-ing field of chemical ecology. There is a strong possibility that some of the antibiotics produced by coral reef organisms will find a use in medicine, and the search for new pharmaceuticals has attracted workers interested in the chemistry and pharmacology of natural products to coral reefs. Dr. Leon S. Ciereszko and Dr. T. K. B. Karns give a valuable account in Chapter 6 of some of the compounds isolated from coral reef organisms. It would appear that marine pharmacology has a bright future in coral reef areas.

Some of the basic problems relating to the distribution and abundance of hermatypic corals on reefs are discussed in Chapter 7 by Dr. Joseph H. Connell in the light of the interesting results of studies he has carried out in recent years at Heron Island on the Great Barrier Reef. In Chapter 8 Dr. J. Frederick Grassle gives a stimulating account of problems relating to species diversity on coral reefs and provides a theoretical treatment of the reasons for such diversity.

In Chapter 9 Dr. Peter W. Glynn gives a graphic account of the variety of reef structure exhibited by the well-developed coral reefs of the Western Atlantic region. He also discusses some of the major problems associated with coral reefs there and elsewhere.

Toxic materials are produced by holothurians, one of the most conspicuous groups of invertebrates found on coral reefs. In Chapter 10 Dr. Gerald J. Bakus discusses the important role of these toxic materials in the course of an interesting discussion on the general ecology and physiology of coral reef holothurians.

There is a dearth of information on the life histories of most coral reef animals. In Chapter 11 Dr. Masashi Yamaguchi gives a valuable account of the results of his recent studies on the development, feeding, and behavior of the larval stages of several coral reef asteroids. Particular attention is given to the larval and post-larval stages of the crown-of-thorns starfish (*Acanthaster planci*). Some biologists consider that detailed study of these stages might hold the key to an understanding of the remarkable population explosions of this species that have been recorded in recent years on many Indo-West Pacific coral reefs. The recent starfish population explosions and their devastating effects on the hard coral cover of coral reefs are discussed in Chapter 12 by Dr. Robert Endean. Also discussed are possible causes of the population explosions and the apparent need for control of *Acanthaster planci* populations in some areas.

It is hoped that this volume will acquaint readers with some of the exciting new developments in coral reef biology and will provide information which will enable them to assess the present status of research in a variety of different fields. Recent developments have pointed the way toward the solution of some of the perplexing problems associated with coral reef biology and sufficient new problems have been raised to ensure that this broad field will continue to attract workers from a variety of scientific disciplines.

We are indebted to Marian Russell and Ann Cameron for assistance with the indexing of this volume.

R. Endean
O. A. Jones

CONTENTS OF VOLUME I: GEOLOGY 1

1

MICROBIAL ECOLOGY

Louis H. Di Salvo

I. Introduction

There is little information about the microorganisms of coral reefs. However, one cannot conceive of such complex ecosystems functioning without these organisms in their typical roles of (1) organic decomposition, (2) biogeochemical cycling, (3) secondary production, and (4) nitrogen fixation. It is my purpose in this chapter to summarize our fragmentary knowledge of microorganisms on coral reefs, particularly with regard to my own research experience.

The title of the chapter is admittedly ambitious; microbial ecology may encompass the microscopic algae, fungi, and protozoans, as well as bacteria (Wood, 1968). One is even tempted to include the very small metazoan meiofauna in view of their importance at microscopic levels in food webs. In view of the sometimes extensive geomorphological differences between one reef and the next, from Atlantic to Pacific and Indian Oceans, generalizations drawn from the few available data will require extensive documentation in future research.

Although within the realm of microbial ecology, discussions concerning the zooxanthellae have been left to other authors in this volume owing to the highly specialized nature of the relationships between these algae and their metazoan hosts.

1

II. Microorganisms in Waters and Sands

Probably the earliest data relevant to coral reef microbiology were collected during bacteriological studies of waters overlying carbonate banks in the Caribbean Sea and nearby Atlantic Ocean in attempts to explain shoal water deposition of particulate carbonates. Drew (1914) proposed that bacterial ammonia release through denitrification processes caused precipitation of carbonates from carbonate-saturated waters. Subsequent studies on the distribution of bacteria in waters over the carbonate banks failed to substantiate the hypothesis because of the small numbers of bacteria present under normal conditions (Lipman, 1924; Gee, 1932). However, the many bacteria found in the sediments might have been responsible for carbonate precipitation near the bottom (Bavendamm, 1932; see also reviews in Baier, 1937; ZoBell, 1946; Wood, 1962). Waters over the Bahama Banks usually contained less than 10^3 colonies per milliliter as demonstrated by plate count methods (Sisler, 1962). Similar results have been obtained for clear waters near Pacific reefs (Gundersen and Stroupe, 1967; Di Salvo, 1970; J. M. Sieburth, unpublished data), and are within the high range of counts to be expected in pelagic tropical waters. Local blooms near reefs may also be expected as have been reported near Samoan reefs by Lipman (1924).

Bavendamm (1932) and Sisler (1962) found up to 10^{10} bacteria per milliliter in Bahama Banks surface sediments. These authors found high bacterial diversity among the types isolated, including variously pigmented forms, nitrate reducers, organisms active in sulfur cycles, hydrogen releasers, cellulose and agar digesters, and others. Sisler (1962) observed microbiological heating of sediments *in vitro*, suggesting the potential for intense bacterial oxidation of organic matter by fermentative processes. At least one bacterial species from the carbonate sand environment has been shown to require calcium for growth, to adsorb calcium as both living and dead cells, to produce ammonia from nitrates, and to form nuclei for carbonate crystal formation (Greenfield, 1963). Thus laboratory results have suggested that bacteria in the sandy environment may be physiologically active in carbonate dynamics, although supporting field evidence is lacking.

Surface layers of shoal water carbonate sediments may contain diverse microbiological communities of bacteria, algae, and protozoans that in some cases may result in the formation of gelatinous mats (Bathurst, 1967; Garrett, 1970). Blue-green algae are often dominant in these microcommunities and may be active in binding sand grains and in stromatolite formation (Sharp, 1969). Sharp has identified *Schizothrix calcicola*

(Agardh; Gomont) as being the most important species in these processes in Bermuda. This species was identified by Bakus (1967) as being among the major primary producers on exposed intertidal rocky surfaces at Eniwetok Atoll.

Bacteria in the sands may utilize mucopolysaccharides secreted onto sand grains by the blue-green algae (Sharp, 1969) forming bacteria-based food chains similar to those suggested by McIntyre *et al.* (1970). The findings of Lee *et al.* (1966) on nutritional preferences of foraminiferans suggest that microbial production supported forams in sandy back-reef zones at Eniwetok where Odum and Odum (1955) found dry biomass values of these organisms ranging to 48 gm per m² (but could not explain their source of nutrition). Support of forams by sand surface microbial production aids directly in carbonate accretion, as reef sands may be composed of up to 30% foram tests (Stoddart, 1969). Further discussion of the types of microorganisms in the sands is given in Section V.

Numerous species of macroscopic organisms may be supported by the microbiological slime found on sandy flats (Garrett, 1970), and at least one species of commercial importance, *Strombus gigas* (Linnaeus), may be supported by the ingestion of the surface layers of sand containing microorganisms (Randall, 1964). Support of holothurians by passage of reef sands has been well documented (Bakus, 1968).

Bathurst (1967) observed the breakup of subtidal gelatinous mats into flakes on occasion. Do these flakes contribute to "reef snow" (organic aggregates) discussed by Johannes (1967) and Marshall (1965, 1968)? The broad extent of sand coverage near many reefs and the presence of physical (waves, currents) and biological mechanisms (grazing fishes, burrowing organisms, etc.) capable of suspending sand surface films suggests that more attention should be given to the sands as sources of this type of reef organic export.

Upper layers of reef sand are normally oxidized, but may become reduced owing to organic buildup and development of bacteriological sulfur cycles as typically found in sands under Caribbean *Thalassia* beds. The presence of reduced subsurface sand has served as an indicator of sewage pollution near reefs in Hawaii (Johannes, 1971), and at Majuro Atoll (J. M. Sieburth, unpublished). Although Yu. Sorokin (personal communication) was unable to find naturally occurring reduced sands at Majuro Atoll, I have observed an apparently normal occurrence of a reduced zone at the foot of windward oceanic beaches at Eniwetok and Parry Islands at Eniwetok Atoll (Di Salvo, 1970). Gray odoriferous sediments in these regions suggested that plant material

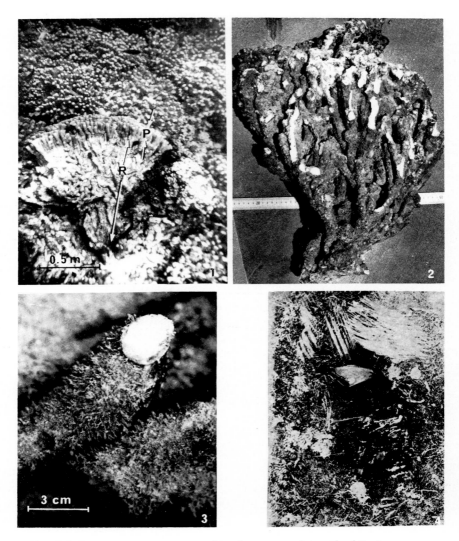

Figs. 1–3. Regenerative structure resulting from upward growth of *Porites compressa* (Dana) at a middle Kaneohe Bay station in Hawaii (1968) and are reproduced by courtesy of the *Canadian Journal of Microbiology,* National Research Council of Canada.

Fig. 1. *In situ* section of coral mass lifted from a continuous formation to demonstrate vertical profile. P, euphotic horizon; R, dysphotic horizon.

Fig. 2. Dysphotic region of corallum to demonstrate internal regenerative surfaces and spaces.

broken from the algal ridge was fermenting anaerobically at the typically high temperatures (ca. 40°C) of the reef flat at low tide. Tides and waves probably transported mineralized nutrients back over the algal ridge in an almost closed cycle of regeneration. The presence of such a local regenerative cycle would help explain the higher primary production recorded for buttress reefs adjacent to atoll islands as compared with the smaller production estimates for interisland buttresses (Marsh, 1970).

III. Bacteria in Complex Reef Environments

Standing coral reefs present a perplexing variety of biogenic structure to the scientist accustomed to more typical two-dimensional benthic environments. Lack of standardized techniques and inadequate laboratory facilities near reefs may explain why so little has been accomplished in the realm of reef microbiology. The following account is presented as a possible method of simplifying somewhat the discussion of reef structure.

As in almost any ecosystem, reefs may be divided into *euphotic* and *dysphotic* life zones on the basis of light penetration as suggested in Fig. 1. The euphotic levels of the reef include sites of primary production either by living corals, calcareous algae, and macroscopic seaweeds; or by microscopic algae (diatoms, blue-greens, etc.) "intimately interwoven with animal and dead skeletal material (Odum and Odum, 1955)." The dysphotic regions of the reef include its internal spaces (Fig. 2), which may exceed the reef horizontal area by a factor of 3 (Odum and Odum, 1955). The internal spaces arise through reef growth and depositional processes, and are further complicated by the activities of the many limestone boring organisms (Bertram, 1936; Otter, 1937; Carriker and Smith, 1969). Biogeochemical processes operating in the internal spaces may result in diagenesis and reef consolidation (Emery *et al.*, 1954; Ginsburg *et al.*, 1967). Reef invertebrates may concentrate in the internal regions because of aversion to light (Kirsteuer, 1969), tendency to avoid living coral surfaces (Gerlach, 1959), and selection pressure exerted by grazing reef fishes (Bakus,

---

Fig. 3. Detail of internal surface to show adherent sediments and hyperamminid forams.

Fig. 4. Photographic film (exposed and developed) that had been placed within regenerative spaces of a Caribbean reef for 10 days in August, 1970. Cleared areas represent grazing by small infaunal organisms where bacteria colonized the gelatin binder on the film. × 1.9.

1964, 1966). Exposed reef surfaces are constantly subject to grazing by fishes and vagile invertebrates that gather and triturate organic materials (Hoskin, 1963) and may eventually deposit some of this matter in the reef as fecal material.

The dysphotic regions of reefs are more favorable as bacterial habitats than are the euphotic regions. In euphotic regions living corals constantly remove bacteria from their surfaces (Di Salvo, 1971c), and preliminary evidence suggests that some reef algae produce antibacterial substances (Doty, 1967). I have referred to the dark internal zones and their transitional euphotic regions as the *regenerative spaces*, and have described what appears to be a sedimentary lining homologous with the benthic surface sediments of flat-bottom environments (Di Salvo, 1970). Figure 3 illustrates an internal sediment surface. As the microbiologist has in the past studied benthic surface sediments from other environments in making generalizations, he may obtain the benthic surface sediments from within reefs as a sampling unit. Table I includes some characteristics of internal reef sediments from Hawaii and Eniwetok Atoll.

Organic enrichment, a carbonate environment, an extensive surface area, and favorable reaeration rates usually provided by reef circulation suggested in advance that internal reef spaces would be favorable to the formation of microorganism communities. Odum and Odum (1955) predicted that essentially all reef surfaces would be bacteria-covered on the basis of bacterial fouling of experimental slides kept submerged for 2 weeks near Eniwetok reefs.

Microscopic observations and enrichment culture of numerous reef substrates proved the extensive coverage of reef surfaces by microorganisms.

Summarization of the distribution and abundance of aerobic heterotrophic bacteria on reefs is presented in Table II. The internal reef sediments showed the highest counts. When dilutions of these sediments were plated in agar or agar enriched with chitin, numerous agar and chitin digesting colonies developed, amounting to 10–20% of comparable counts on media enriched with peptone and yeast extract. Fungi were similarly active on particles of an acid-insoluble (cell-wall) residue of a calcareous alga *Porolithon* sp. (Di Salvo and Gundersen, 1971). The typical inefficiency of the plate count method as used in the determinations suggested that the results represented minimum values. When chitin, paper, and *Porolithon* residue were placed on a reef in test tubes, they were attacked by bacteria and fungi apparently similar to the colonies arising on sediment enrichment plates (Di Salvo, 1970). Reef regenerative surfaces represent interfaces such as those found, for exam-

TABLE I

SOME CHARACTERISTICS OF CORAL REEF REGENERATIVE SEDIMENTS[a]

Station	Distance seaward from shore reef (km)	Terrigenous content[b]	Organic content[c]	N content[d]	Pigment content (ppm) Chlorophyll a	Pigment content (ppm) Pheopigments	Diatom count[e] × 10^4 cells per gm dry sediment
Kaneohe Bay, Oahu, Hawaii Inner bay (south shore reef)	0	25.2 , 24.2(2)[f]	12.4(10)	0.60(3)	20.2	59.4(3)	10(3)
Middle bay	2.6	7.3 , 7.2(2)	7.4(9)	0.35(3)	31.8	25.4(3)	17(3)
Outer bay	5.2	5.3 , 6.7(2)	7.3(10)	0.49(3)	72.6	40.2(3)	118(3)
Eniwetok Atoll, Marshall Islands Lagoon reef stations	—	0.93, 0.74(2)	8.3(30)	0.37(9)	100.5	71.9(11)	—

[a] Di Salvo (1970); Di Salvo and Gundersen (1971).
[b] By decalcification in 50% HCl, percent dry weight.
[c] By ashing at 500°–550°C, percent dry weight.
[d] Total Kjeldhal N, percent dry weight.
[e] Visual count at 100 × magnification.
[f] Number of samples in parentheses.

TABLE II

AEROBIC HETEROTROPHIC BACTERIA FROM CORAL REEF SUBSTRATES

Sample description	No. of samples[a]	Medium	Colonies × 10^6 per gm dry wt Range	Colonies × 10^6 per gm dry wt Mean	References
Eniwetok Atoll, Marshall Islands					
Regenerative sediments from within small ramose dead heads	6	R[d]	77–3820	1790	Unpublished (1964)
Oceanic reef flat, sandy sediment pocket	33	Z[e]	27–2700	282	Di Salvo and Gundersen (1971)
Porites lobata, polyp zone	1	Z	—	4	Di Salvo and Gundersen (1971)
Clionid sponge-invaded coralla	3	R	—	n	Unpublished (1964)
	3	R	—	n	Unpublished (1964)
Kaneohe Bay, Oahu, Hawaii					
Regenerative sediments from within small ramose dead heads	30	Z	35–504	174	Di Salvo and Gundersen (1971)
Discolored Porites lobata corallum	1[b]	Z	—	0.02	Di Salvo (1969)
Clionid sponge-invaded corallum	1[b]	C[f]	—	0.003	Di Salvo (1969)
Porolithon sp. encrusted corallum	1[b]	Z	—	0.03	Di Salvo (1969)
Porolithon sp. encrustation	15	Z	2.1–35.9	9.6	Di Salvo and Gundersen (1971)
	1	P[g]	—	>4	Di Salvo and Gundersen (1971)
			—	>4[c]	Di Salvo and Gundersen (1971)
Fungia scutaria, living surface	n[c]	Z	—	0 to n	Di Salvo (1971c)
Crab carapace, in reef detritus	1	Z	—	1.76	Di Salvo and Gundersen (1971)
	1	C	—	0.50	Di Salvo and Gundersen (1971)
Echinothrix diadema intestinal contents	1	P	—	n[i]	Di Salvo (1970)
Substances placed on the reef in screen-mouthed test tubes					
(1) Porolithon residue	1[b]	P	—	0.36[i]	Di Salvo (1970)
(2) Paper (cellulose)	n	V[h]	—	>10/cm²	Di Salvo (1970)
(3) Crab carapaces	2	C	—	n	Di Salvo (1970)

[a] All plated in duplicate.
[b] Other qualitative samples positive.
[c] n, Numerous.
[d] R, Reuszers' medium (peptone, glucose).
[e] Z, ZoBell 2216E (peptone, yeast ext.)
[f] C, Chitin agar.
[g] P, HCl insoluble residue of Porolithon sp. in agar.
[h] V, Visual examination.
[i] Mycelial clearance.

ple, in trickling sewage filters. Organic breakdown processes mediated by bacteria, fungi, Protozoa, and other microorganisms are probably carried out at rapid rates here as at the sediment–water interfaces of other environments (Seki, 1965).

Laboratory and preliminary field evidence have suggested that reef corals and suspension feeding invertebrates can retain, ingest, and probably assimilate bacteria occurring in circulating waters (Di Salvo, 1971a,c). Most encrusting and vagile infauna are suspension and deposit feeders (Gerlach, 1959) adapted for the recycling of bacterial production within the dysphotic spaces. The evolutionary migration of reef fauna to internal spaces may have been based on trophic considerations and thus may be of great adaptive significance to the development of an internally contained recycling community. Figure 4 illustrates a section of photographic film which had been placed within regenerative spaces of a Caribbean reef for 10 days. Bacteria on the gelatin binder were apparently scraped off by small infaunal organisms, illustrating the high degree of miniature grazing activity on the internal reef surfaces. Thus trophic considerations should be included in speculations concerning the origins of the internally dwelling reef invertebrates as discussed by Bakus (1964, 1966). The trophic significance of bacterial secondary production on reefs is discussed further in this volume by Sorokin (Chapter 2).

Water-soluble phosphate and small molecular compounds derived from proteins (ninhydrin–positive moieties) were abundant in waters used to recover reef regenerative sediments for laboratory study (Di Salvo, 1970). Considering that reefs probably do not allow significant washout of these nutrients under normal conditions (Odum and Odum, 1955; Pomeroy and Kuenzler, 1967), a hypothesis is required to explain the retention of nutrients within reefs. The ability of bacteria to grow on carbon-rich substrates and obtain phosphorus from water (Hayes, 1963; Phillips, 1964), mediated by efficient uptake mechanisms (Wright and Hobbie, 1966), suggests that the bacteria contained throughout reefs may provide an active mechanism for nutrient retention. A role of reef algae in removing inorganic nutrients from reef waters has been postulated by Doty (1958), although the previous references suggest that bacteria are more effective than algae in retaining dissolved phosphorus.

There are indications that a significant quantity of energy is expended on reefs that is unaccountable in terms of the known biomass in the euphotic regions (Kinsey and Kinsey, 1967), and at least one suggestion has been made in the literature implicating bacteria as potentially impor-

TABLE III
OXYGEN METABOLISM OF CORAL REEF REGENERATIVE SEDIMENTS[a]

Station	Distance from south shore[b] (km)	Oxygen consumption		No. samples
		mg O_2/gm dry sediment at zero time[c]	mg O_2/gm dry sediment/hour	
Kaneohe Bay, Oahu, Hawaii				
Inner bay (south shore reef)	0	0.03 ± 0.02	0.06 ± 0.01	5
Middle bay	2.6	0.28 ± 0.05	0.12 ± 0.02	7
Outer bay	5.2	0.83 ± 0.13	0.21 ± 0.04	6
Eniwetok Atoll, Marshall Islands				
Algal ridge	—	1.06 ± 0.18	0.34 ± 0.07	7
Eniwetok interisland reef	—	1.51 ± 0.15	0.50 ± 0.09	4

[a] Sediment-bottle method (Di Salvo, 1971b).

[b] Hawaii stations.

[c] Chemical oxygen demand.

tant consumers of oxygen (Sargent and Austin, 1949). Table III lists the comparative magnitudes of oxygen consumption of reef regenerative sediments from several reef stations. Antibiotic treatment of some Hawaiian sediment samples resulted in a decrease in oxygen consumption of 30–100%, with corresponding reductions in bacterial plate counts of 13–97% (Di Salvo, 1971b). Satisfactory areal estimates of respiratory oxygen demands by regenerative sediments and substrates have so far not been made owing to shortcomings in methodology. In one experiment (Di Salvo, 1971b), two small dead coral heads similar in structure to that in Fig. 2 each respired 240 mg O_2 per m² per hour based on their ideal hemispherical surface area; this fell within the highest metabolic rates for aquatic communities as summarized by Hargrave (1969a).

With the regenerative mass thoroughly populated by bacteria (Table II), it was not surprising that measurements on the internal sediments predicted oxygen balance behavior of intact dead coral heads from corresponding sampling stations. Dead coral heads from a least pollution-stressed region of Kaneohe Bay, Hawaii, and showing the highest rates of sediment metabolism were also the quickest to become blackened internally by sulfate reduction (sulfide precipitation) when held at suboptimal rates of water circulation at the laboratory (Di Salvo, 1971b). I have measured oxygen depletion in internal reef waters *in situ* reaching values as low as 68% below oxygen concentration in circulating waters, suggesting that microaerophiles and facultative anaerobes might occasionally function within the reef spaces. The reaeration rate coupled with the balance of organic matter could regulate chemical cycling in the interiors of coral reefs; reef spaces well oxygenated by photosynthetic and physical processes would tend to conserve phosphate, break down organic matter, and prevent destructive events of the sulfur cycle (H_2S production, oxygen depletion). Naturally occurring oxygen depletion in external waters such as the minimum of 2.1 mg/liter reported by Kinsey and Kinsey (1967) at Heron Island could temporarily reverse the physicochemical trends just mentioned; environmental stress could drive them to extremes and thus kill the internal reef community through anaerobiosis and H_2S poisoning (Banner, 1968; Copeland and Wilkes, 1969).

IV. Microbiological Involvement in Internal Reef Carbonate Dynamics

Although specific evidence is lacking, conditions within reef regenerative spaces appear favorable for $CaCO_3$ precipitation and may eventually explain the origin of "interstitial lime paste" described by Emery *et al.* (1954). Of particular importance is the presence of nitrogenous organic compounds in the internal sediments (Table I) that may release ammonia through bacteriological activity thus driving carbonate equilibria toward precipitation of $CaCO_3$.

A diverse group of microorganisms is associated with the invasion of calcareous substrates (Carriker and Smith, 1969). I have suggested that bacteria may cause coral skeletal breakdown in the process of mineralizing organic skeletal matrix in corals (Di Salvo, 1969). Long-term mineralization of the coral skeletal matrix may explain paleontological observations by Emery *et al.* (1954) where, over geologic periods, buried reef corals disintegrated into aragonite powder without mineralogical changes associated with freshwater intrusion.

Calcareous algae may be attacked by fungi (Bauch, 1936; Kohlmeyer, 1969a) and blue-green algae (Golubic, 1969). Fungi studied by Kohlmeyer were incapable of attacking cell wall materials of calcareous algae, although, as shown in Table II, I found fungi in regenerative sediments that actively broke down *Porolithon* cell wall material *in vitro*. The extent of microbiological breakdown of reef skeletons and the symbioses in these processes by organisms such as the blue-green algae and boring sponges should be investigated in future studies.

V. Microbiological Diversity

There has been little taxonomic work done on the species of micro-organisms of reefs, although J. M. Sieburth's find of *Leucothrix mucor* (Oersted) at Majuro Atoll (unpublished), Kohlmeyer's (1969b) identification of *Lulworthia kniepii* (Kohlmeyer) and other fungi in Hawaii, and Sharp's (1969) identification of *Schizothrix calcicola* in Bermuda suggest that cosmopolitan species occur on reefs although perhaps in previously undescribed niches.

In my work (Di Salvo, 1970) high bacterial diversity of the regenerative sediments was suggested by the presence of bacterial colonies showing diversity of pigmentation, growth rate, and colony morphology. At several stations at Eniwetok Atoll, however, chromogens were few except in two samples of leeward reef internal sediments. Preliminary plating data and informal observations cited above suggested the presence of a full complement of anaerobes in regenerative spaces. W. Weibe (personal communication) has found a predominance of *Vibrio* and *Pseudomonas* spp. (60–70%) in thirty isolates from Bermuda reef sands; remaining types included *Cytophaga*-like, *Bacillus*, and *Achromobacter* spp. Of 33 bacterial isolates obtained at random from within a calcareous algal encrustation from Guam, all were gram positive rods and all were oxidase positive (Di Salvo, unpublished data.). Of these isolates 28 were motile, 27 were nitrate reducers, 30 digested gelatin, 18 digested chitin, and 5 digested agar. Only 7 of the isolates were pigmented. A majority of the isolates (19) showed fermentative utilization of dextrose. Preliminary identification suggested a predominance of *Vibrio* and *Pseudomonas* spp. In transferring isolates it was noted that in several cases large cells (*Bacillus* spp.?) occurred in synergism with smaller-celled isolates, but only the smaller-celled isolates could be obtained in pure culture on the peptone–yeast extract medium employed. It is probable that symbiotic interactions so common among the macroscopic reef organisms are paralleled by biochemical symbioses in the reef microbiota.

Detailed descriptions of microorganisms occurring within reef regenerative spaces, even if available, would be beyond the scope of this chapter. Diatom counts for some Kaneohe Bay, Hawaii, regenerative sediments have been included in Table I. In making these counts it was apparent that diatom diversity was high in the sediments, with pennate types predominant. Preliminary sketches and measurements suggested the presence of 100–200 species in counts of 3000 diatoms.

Essentially all reef sediments I have observed have been well populated by ciliates, blue-green algae, flagellates, and metazoan meiofauna (nematodes, ostracods, copepods, archiannelids, turbellarians, kinorhynchs, and others). One determination of numbers of hypotrich ciliates recovered from regenerative surfaces indicated the presence of about 2.4×10^6 individuals per m^2 (Di Salvo, 1970). This was comparable with other organically rich environments [e.g., Hargrave (1969b) found 2.0×10^6 protozoa per m^2 of lake bottom]. In sampling at Isla Providencia, Colombia (Aug. 1970, unpublished), I found $9-10 \times 10^2$ ciliates per gm coral reef regenerative sediment in four samples. Large flagellates (cryptomonads, dinoflagellates) were almost equally common, and these were, in turn, apparently outnumbered by colorless nannoflagellates. Six samples of reef sand from a depth of 20 m contained 90–400 ciliates per gm, representing about $0.9-2.3 \times 10^6$ ciliates per m^2 (top centimeter). The most easily recognized ciliates in these samples belonged to the genera *Tracheloraphis, Geleia,* and *Litonotus* as described by Fenchel (1969) in his studies of Baltic Sea sands. Numerous holotrich, hypotrich, and peritrichous ciliates were seen but not identified in these samples. Figure 3 has shown that, in addition to the typically free-living reef foraminiferans, regenerative spaces may be populated by ramose sedentary forams (Hyperamminidae). These probably function in roles similar to the related forms found in sea caves (Riedl, 1966), where they were usually associated with bacterial blooms arising from organic decomposition.

The apparently high diversity of all types of microscopic organisms within reefs satisfies the requirements outlined by Johannes (1968) for active nutrient regeneration, where bacteria, Protozoa, and zooplankton function together to promote nutrient regeneration cycles. Monumental research efforts will be required for specific identifications of components, meaningful population estimates, and elucidation of individual functional roles.

In conclusion, the microbial ecology of coral reefs is in its earliest stage of development and promises a challenge equal in complexity to the understanding of macroscopic reef ecology. Indeed, macro- to microscopic interactions are well documented as concerns zooxanthella–coral interactions (Muscatine, Chapter 4), and there are promising avenues of research ahead regarding production of antibacterials (Burkholder and Rützler, 1969). Of further general significance, preliminary data from the R/V Alpha Helix expedition to Eniwetok Atoll in 1971 have suggested the existence of significant nitrogen fixation on those reefs (K. L. Webb and W. D. DuPaul, 1972).

Many of the preceding considerations suggest that the success of coral reefs in nutrient-poor tropical waters has been dependent on their evolution of internal retentive and regenerative systems of microorganisms in effect "managed" by the metazoan infauna. When suitable methodology can be devised and implemented, the metabolism in the dysphotic regions of reefs will probably be shown to account for a large fraction of reef respiration not attributable to organisms in euphotic regions. It follows that systems approaches to the analysis of total reef function will require sophisticated studies of the numerous and varied microscopic reef inhabitants.

References

Baier, C. R. (1937). *Geol. Meere* 1, 75–105.
Bakus, G. J. (1964). *Occ. Pap. Allan Hancock Found.* 27, 1–29.
Bakus, G. J. (1966). *Nature (London)* 210, 280–284.
Bakus, G. J. (1967). *Micronesica* 3, 135–149.
Bakus, G. J. (1968). *Mar. Biol.* 2, 23–33.
Banner, A. H. (1968). *Univ. Hawaii, Inst. Mar. Biol., Tech. Rep.* 15, 1–29.
Bathurst, R. G. C. (1967). *J. Geol.* 75, 736–738.
Bauch, R. (1936). *Pubbl. Sta. Zool. Napoli* 15, 377–391.
Bavendamm, W. (1932). *Arch. Mikrobiol.* 3, 205–276.
Bertram, G. C. L. (1936). *Proc. Zool. Soc. London* pp. 1011–1026.
Burkholder, P. R., and Rützler, K. (1969). *Nature (London)* 222, 983–984.
Carriker, M. R., and Smith, E. H. (1969). *Amer. Zool.* 9, 1011–1020.
Copeland, B. J., and Wilkes, F. G. (1969). *In* "Coastal Ecological Systems of the United States" (H. T. Odum, B. J. Copeland, and E. A. MacMahan, eds.), pp. 1176–1184. Federal Water Quality Admin., Washington, D.C.
Di Salvo, L. H. (1969). *Amer. Zool.* 9, 735–740.
Di Salvo, L. H. (1970). Ph.D. Dissertation, University of North Carolina, Chapel Hill.
Di Salvo, L. H. (1971a). *J. Exp. Mar. Biol. Ecol.* 7, 123–136.
Di Salvo, L. H. (1971b). *Can. J. Microbiol.* 17, 1091–1100.
Di Salvo, L. H. (1971c). *In* "Experimental Coelenterate Biology" (H. M. Lenhoff, L. Muscatine, and L. V. Davis, eds.), pp. 129–136. Univ. of Hawaii Press, Honolulu.
Di Salvo, L. H., and Gundersen, K. (1971). *Can. J. Microbiol.* 17, 1081–1089.
Doty, M. S. (1958). *Proc. Pac. Sci. Congr., 8th, 1957* pp. 923–928.
Doty, M. S. (1967). *Univ. Hawaii, Bot. Sci. Pap.* 3, 1–107.
Drew, C. H. (1914). *Pap. Tortugas Lab.* 5, 7–45.
Emery, K. O., Tracey, J. I., Jr., and Ladd, H. S. (1954). *U.S., Geol. Surv., Prof. Pap.* 260-A, 1–265.
Fenchel, T. (1969). *Ophelia* 6, 1–182.
Garrett, P. (1970). *Science* 169, 171–173.
Gee, A. H. (1932). *Pap. Tortugas Lab.* 28, 67–82.
Gerlach, S. (1959). *Zool. Anz., Suppl.* 23, 356–363.
Ginsburg, R. N., Shinn, E. A., and Schroeder, J. H. (1967). *Program Abstr., Annu. Meet., Geol. Soc. Amer.* pp. 78–79.

Golubic, S. (1969). *Amer. Zool.* **9**, 747–751.

Greenfield, L. H. (1963). *Ann. N.Y. Acad. Sci.* **109**, 23–45.

Gundersen, K. R., and Stroupe, D. B. (1967). *Univ. Hawaii, Water Resour. Res. Cent., Tech. Rep.* **12**, 1–24.

Hargrave, B. T. (1969a). *Limnol. Oceanogr.* **14**, 801–805.

Hargrave, B. T. (1969b). *J. Fish. Res. Bd. Can.* **26**, 2005–2026.

Hayes, F. R. (1963). *In* "Symposium on Marine Microbiology" (C. H. Oppenheimer, ed.), pp. 654–663. Thomas, Springfield, Illinois.

Hoskin, C. M. (1963). *Nat. Acad. Sci.—Nat. Res. Counc. Publ.* **1089**, 1–160.

Johannes, R. E. (1967). *Limnol. Oceanogr.* **12**, 189–195.

Johannes, R. E. (1968). *In* "Advances in Microbiology of the Sea" (M. Droop and E. J. F. Wood, eds.), Vol. 1, pp. 203–213. Academic Press, New York.

Johannes, R. E. (1971). *Mar. Pollution Bull.* **2**, 9–10.

Kinsey, D. W., and Kinsey, B. E. (1967). *Aust. J. Mar. Freshwater Res.* **18**, 23–31.

Kirsteuer, E. (1969). *Mar. Biol. Ass. India Symp. Corals Coral Reefs, 1969* p. 20.

Kohlmeyer, J. (1969a). *Amer. Zool.* **9**, 741–746.

Kohlmeyer, J. (1969b). *Can. J. Bot.* **47**, 1469–1487.

Lee, J. J., McEnery, M., Pierce, S., Freudenthal, H. D., and Muller, W. A. (1966). *J. Protozool.* **13**, 659–670.

Lipman, C. B. (1924). *Carnegie Inst. Wash., Dep. Mar. Biol.* **19**, 179–191.

McIntyre, A. D., Munro, A. L. S., and Steele, J. H. (1970). *In* "Marine Food Chains" (J. H. Steele, ed.), pp. 19–31. Univ. of California Press, Berkeley.

Marsh, J. A., Jr. (1970). *Ecology* **51**, 255–263.

Marshall, N. (1965). *Ecology* **46**, 343–344.

Marshall, N. (1968). *Mar. Biol.* **2**, 50–53.

Odum, H. T., and Odum, E. P. (1955). *Ecol. Monogr.* **25**, 291–320.

Otter, G. W. (1937). *Sci. Rep. Gt. Barrier Reef Exp.* **2**, 87–98.

Phillips, J. E. (1964). *In* "Principles and Applications in Aquatic Microbiology" (H. Heukelekian and N. C. Dondero, eds.), pp. 61–81. Wiley, New York.

Pomeroy, L. R., and Kuenzler, E. J. (1967). *In* "Symposium on Radioecology; Proceedings of the Second National Symposium" (D. J. Nelson and F. C. Evans, eds.), Conf. 670503, Biol. Med. T.I.D. No. 4500, pp. 474–482. U.S. Atomic Energy Comm., Ann Arbor, Michigan.

Randall, J. E. (1964). *Bull. Mar. Sci. Gulf Carib.* **14**, 246–295.

Riedl, R. J. M. (1966). *In* "Biologie der Meereshöhlen. Topographie, Faunistik, und Oekologie eines unterseeischen Lebensraumes," p. 122. Parey, Berlin.

Sargent, M. C., and Austin, T. S. (1949). *Trans. Amer. Geophys. Union* **30**, 245–249.

Seki, H. (1965). *J. Oceanogr. Soc. Jap.* **21**, 25–33.

Sharp, J. H. (1969). *Limnol. Oceanogr.* **14**, 568–578.

Sisler, F. D. (1962). *U.S., Geol. Surv., Prof. Pap.* **350**, 64–69.

Stoddart, D. R. (1969). *Biol. Rev. Cambridge Phil. Soc.* **44**, 433–498.

Webb, K. L., and DuPaul, W. D. (1972). *Program Abstr., Annu. Meet., Am. Soc. Limnol. Oceanogr.*, p. 19.

Wood, E. J. F. (1962). *Proc. Pac. Sci. Congr., 9th, 1957* Vol. 4, pp. 171–173.

Wood, E. J. F. (1968). *In* "Advances in Microbiology of the Sea" (M. Droop and E. J. F. Wood, eds.), pp. 1–22. Academic Press, New York.

Wright, R. T., and Hobbie, J. E. (1966). *Ecology* **47**, 447–464.

ZoBell, C. E. (1946). "Marine Microbiology." Chronica Botanica, Waltham, Massachusetts.

2

MICROBIOLOGICAL ASPECTS OF THE PRODUCTIVITY OF CORAL REEFS

Yu. I. Sorokin

I. Introduction

The enigma of the existence of extremely eutrophic coral reef ecosystems among oligotrophic tropical waters, these ecosystems resembling oases in the oceanic desert, represents one of the most exciting problems of modern marine biology and of general ecology (Odum and Odum, 1955). Other key problems relating to aspects of the ecology and energy balance of the coral reef ecosystem await clarification (Johannes *et al.*, 1970). Such problems include the identification of the sources of the necessary excess organic matter and nutrients that compensate for destruction of organic matter and nutrient loss from the ecosystem. Solution of these problems is hampered to some extent by an incomplete understanding of the nutritional physiology of hermatypic corals. Discussion has proceeded for many years on the relative importance for corals of carnivorous and herbivorous nutrition (Yonge, 1958; Franzisket, 1969; Johannes *et al.*, 1970). Also, although the possibility of filter feeding and osmotic feeding by corals has been discussed (Abe, 1937; Roushdy and Hansen, 1961; Stephens, 1960), the importance of these types of feeding still has to be elucidated. Another serious obstacle to an understanding of reef ecology has been the almost complete lack of any quantitative information on the roles of microbial populations in the metabolism and productivity of the coral reef ecosystem (Wood, 1962, 1967). It has become apparent that the microflora is one of the most important constituents of any natural ecosystem (Kuznetsov, 1969). As a rule, the major portion of the total energy flux in aquatic ecosystems passes through the bacterial part of the food chain (Vinberg, 1970; Sorokin, 1972). Moreover, it is via the participation of the microbial population that "external" organic matter is introduced into the ecosystems of the biosphere (Sorokin, 1971a). Then, too, bacterial protein has been shown to be a normal food for planktonic and benthic animals (Rodina, 1951; Zukova, 1963; Sorokin, 1968). These bacteria play an important trophic role in any aquatic ecosystem. Furthermore, this role is of particular significance in the coral reef ecosystem where suspended organic matter in the form of detritus and organic aggregates is of major trophodynamic importance (Marshall, 1965, 1968; Johannes, 1967). The activity of the bacterial population is responsible for aggregating organic material in seawater and for conferring its high nutritive value upon it (Sieburth, 1968; Parsons and Strickland, 1962; Rodina, 1963; Sorokin, 1971b). In view of all this it is not difficult to postulate that an important role in incorporating allochthonous and autochthonous organic matter in the secondary productivity processes of the coral reef ecosystem is played by the bacterial flora of coral reef sediments, debris, and detritus as well as by the epibiotic microflora of dead corals.

The first important quantitative studies of the microflora as a component of the coral reef ecosystem were made by Di Salvo (1969) in collaboration with E. Odum. Di Salvo worked on the reefs of Kaneohe Bay (Oahu, Hawaii) and Eniwetok Atoll. Since he has contributed data to this book (Chapter 1), I shall discuss these data only briefly. Di Salvo's data indicated the very important role of bacteria in the process of nutrient regeneration in different coral reef environments; they pointed also to the possibility that some reef animals, including corals themselves, feed on bacteria.

We have made the second systematic study of the trophic role of the microflora in different reef communities of the Pacific Ocean. Objects of the study were as follows.

1. Evaluation of the standing stock of bacterial biomass as a food resource and estimation of its rate of production

2. Evaluation of energy sources for bacterial production by estimation

of the quantitative relationships among primary production, bacterial destruction, and production of bacteria

3. Evaluation of the actual nutritional value of microflora as food for the mass of filtering and sediment-ingesting species inhabiting the reefs

The biomass of the microflora was calculated from direct microscopical count of bacteria and by estimation of the average volume of their cells. Volume gives the wet weight, and the biomass in milligrams of carbon is 10% of the wet weight (Sorokin, 1971b). Bacteria production was estimated with the use of ^{14}C (Sorokin, 1971b) using the value of the dark assimilation of CO_2 (Romanenko, 1964). The daily destruction by bacteria was also calculated from the latter value (Romanenko, 1965) using the empirical ratio O_2 consumed/C,CO_2 assimilated = 150 (Sorokin, 1971b). Primary production and the involvement of bacteria in the nutrition of reef animals were also studied by using ^{14}C (Sorokin, 1968, 1971b). To assess bacterial microflora involvement in the nutrition of corals, the natural microflora of water or sediment was labeled with ^{14}C using labeled protein hydrolysate.

II. Biomass and Productivity of the Microflora of Sediments and of Dead Corals

One of the peculiar features of coral reef environments is the presence of vast expanses of solid substrata heavily populated by epibiotic micro- and algoflora (Fig. 1). This is probably one of the main causes of the high productivity of such environments. These substrata are provided by the perforated surfaces of dead corals, by coral debris and coral sands, and by the fine, detrital sediments forming under the "shade" of "internal" reefs and by the so-called "regenerative" sediments (Di Salvo, 1969), which are formed from coral sand, organic aggregates, and coral mucus, and which cover the surface of dead coral heads.

A substantial part of reef sediments is provided by the feces of sand-eating animals that are abundant on coral reefs (Bakus, 1968; Hoskin, 1963; Kornicker and Purdi, 1957). The organic content of the reef sediments examined was 0.2 to 0.4% for the coral sands of Eniwetok Atoll, 0.5 to 1.0% for the reef sediments of Kaneohe Bay, and up to 4.0 to 5.0% for the detrital sediments forming at the polluted reef opposite Coconut Island in the same bay (Di Salvo, 1969). Some of our results of microbiological analysis of reef sediments are shown in Table I and Fig. 2. The total number of bacterial cells in the sediments is usually

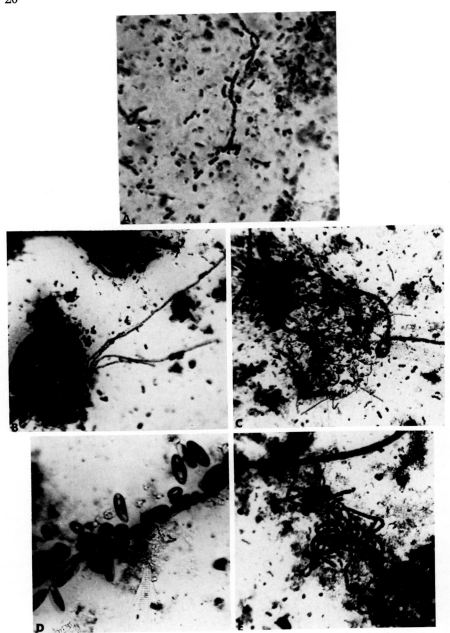

Fig. 1. Microflora in "regenerative" sediment. (A) In coral sand; (B,C), upon the surface of dead corals; (D,E) photomicrographs of Millipore filters stained with erythrosin, ×1200.

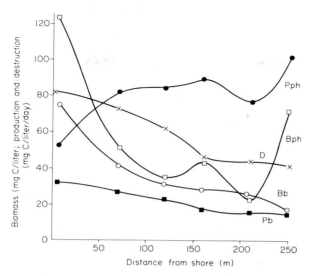

Fig. 2. Biomass (milligrams of carbon per liter of raw sediment) of bacteria (Bb) and of phytoplankton (Bph); production (milligrams of carbon per liter per day) of bacteria (Pb) and phytoplankton (Pph); and rate of destruction (D, milligrams of carbon per liter per day) in the sediments of the external reef at Heron Island, Great Barrier Reef.

about from 1 to 3×10^9 in 1 ml of the raw sediment (1 ml of raw sediment contains 0.5–0.8 gm of dry sediment). These values approximate the value obtained by Di Salvo, 4×10^9 cells per gm of dry sediment. According to his data the number of colonies of heterotrophic bacteria in these sediments on the Kaneohe Bay reefs is of the order of 1 to 3×10^9 per gm of dry sediment and in the sediments on Eniwetok Atoll up to 5×10^8 per gm of dry sediment. Chitinoclastic bacteria represent about 10–30% of this number. The maximum number of heterotrophic bacteria found by Di Salvo occurred in the "regenerative" sediments. Our data showed this also (Table I). In the fine fraction of this sediment, 1×10^{10} cells per 1 ml were found. This number is close to the maximum ever found in bottom deposits (ZoBell, 1946; Kuznetsov, 1969).

It is very peculiar that the sediments of nonpolluted atolls such as Majuro or Fanning contain the same total number of bacteria as do the reef sediments of Kaneohe Bay, which is heavily polluted with the sewage of Kaneohe City (Gundersen and Stroupe, 1967). Di Salvo also noted this peculiarity when he compared data from Kaneohe Bay and Eniwetok Atoll.

The biomass of bacterial flora in the sediments is extraordinarily

TABLE I

BIOMASS, PRODUCTION, AND METABOLISM OF MICROBIAL POPULATIONS IN THE SEDIMENTS OF CORAL ENVIRONMENTS

Position of the station	Characteristics of sediments and of place of sampling	Biomass of bacteria (B)			Production, destruction (mg C/liter/day)				
		Total number of bacteria ($\times 10^9$/ml)	B (mg C/liter)	B (percentage of the total organic carbon in sediments)	Production of bacteria (P)	P/B coefficient	Destruction (D)	Photosynthesis of phytobenthos (Ph)	Ratio D/Ph
Open ocean to the east of Hawaii	Deep sea pelite silt (red clay)	0.022	1.06	0.25	0.032	0.03	0.08	—	—
Mesotrophic lake Punnus-Jarvi (USSR, Karelia)	Brownish soft silt	0.98	47	0.4	8.7	0.18	23	—	—
Internal reefs of Kaneohe Bay around Coconut Is. or close to it (Oahu Is., Hawaii)	Coral sand on the shore reef	2.41	145	4.2	25.0	0.17	71(86)[a]	5.8	12.2
	Coral sand among the living corals near the edge of reef	3.60	222	5.1	39.0	0.18	110(97)[a]	12.3	9.0
	Fine sand and tubes of worms close to the shore of patch reef	1.80	54	2.6	14.3	0.26	41	6.6	6.2
	Coral sand among the living corals near the edge of patch reef	2.60	65	2.2	17.2	0.26	49	7.1	6.7
	Coarse fraction of the regenerative sediment	5.76	81	2.5	54.0	0.66	153	42	3.6

Location	Description								
	Fine fraction of regenerative sediment	9.70	147	3.0	73	0.50	207	96	2.2
External reef of Kapapa Reef, Kaneohe Bay	Coarse coral sand near edge of reef	0.52	7.8	0.5	5.1	0.65	14.5	6.2	2.3
Internal reef of Fanning Atoll, Line Islands	Coral sand among the living corals	1.84	91	4.6	22.6	0.25	56(59)[a]	38	1.5
Internal reef of Majuro Atoll, Marshall Islands	Coarse coral sand among the living corals near the edge of the reef	1.60	21	1.5	7.2	0.34	20	20.5	1.0
	Soft powdery sediment among living corals	3.50	88	2.0	3.52	0.40	100	74	1.4
	Mucoid material and fine soft sediments close to shore	3.80	180	3.2	71	0.39	202	112	1.8
	Coral sand in the intertidal zone of the shore beach	0.86	17.2	0.6	6.8	0.37	17.8	586	0.03
	Material scraped from the surface of dead coral	0.96	28	1.5	14.3	0.57	41	610	0.06
External reef of Majuro Atoll	Dense sediment among the macrophytes near reef edge	1.20	31	2	12.5	0.40	35	42	0.84

[a] Direct estimation of BOD by the usual oxygen-bottle method.

high—up to 150 mg of carbon per liter, that is, about 3% of the total organic content of the sediment. In coral sands and in material scraped from the surfaces of dead corals, the biomass of bacteria is also extremely high—50 to 100 mg of carbon per liter or about 1 gm of raw biomass per liter. These values are equal to or even somewhat higher than those for silts of mesotrophic and eutrophic lakes and are 50–100 times higher than values for the surface layer of pelagic sediments (Table I). The lowest values of microfloral biomass among coral sediments were found in the coarse coral sands on the outer edges of the external reef.

Bacterial production was found to be about 50–200 mg of raw biomass per day per liter of sediment. This corresponds to a P/B coefficient (production per biomass) of around 0.2–0.5, which is somewhat higher than that found in the silt of a mesotrophic lake. In polluted Kaneohe Bay, the production of bacteria in the reef sediments usually exceeded photosynthesis by phytobenthos. This was possibly a consequence of inhibition of the latter by pollution and subsequent sulfate reduction. In the sediments of nonpolluted atolls, photosynthesis by phytobenthos exceeded the production of bacteria (Table I, Fig. 2). But even here the biotic balance is negative. Destruction prevails over photosynthesis. In the sediments of the polluted reef, the ratio of photosynthesis to destruction is about 1:6 to 1:9.

The intensity of photosynthesis in the sediments and in the epibiotic cover of the dead corals is very high. In the coral sand and debris it occurs via the activity of green microalgae and diatoms, while in the epibiotic layers filamentous (often blue-green) algae are mostly responsible. The intensity of photosynthesis per 1 m^2 of the sediment surface is about 0.5–1.5 gm/liter of organic carbon per day in the sediments of a nonpolluted atoll. This is only 3–5 times lower than that of the coral reef itself. The most intensive photosynthesis found was in the coral sands of the intertidal zone and in the dead corals covered with epibiotic algae. Here it is sometimes higher than that of the reef itself. According to Di Salvo (1969), the chlorophyll content in reef sediments ranges up to 100 μg/gm dry weight.

It has been shown then that the intensity of production and of metabolism in the sediments of coral reef communities corresponds with that in the sediments of eutrophic water basins and that it is about 1000 times higher than in tropical deep sea sediments. This high metabolic activity of the microflora of reef sediments provides for a high rate of nutrient regeneration (Di Salvo, 1969). It promotes the high biomass turnover rate of the reef's inhabitants, which is peculiar to the coral reef community (Odum and Odum, 1955).

The high biomass and productivity of the microflora of sediments also provide a rich food resource for the abundant benthic fauna that populates the sediments and the reef surface and may account for the existence of numerous detritus-eating and sand-eating animals in coral reef communities (Bakus, 1968, 1969; Hoskin, 1963). Many gastropods, holothurians, worms, and even fishes feed on coral sands and detrital sediments. Furthermore, part of the organic matter contained in the highly productive coral sediments is constantly being released into the water in the form of bacterial aggregates or detrital particles (marine snow) as a result of wave action and the evolution of oxygen bubbles. Because of this, lagoon waters carry a relatively high concentration of food particles that represent an essential part of the food of an abundance of filtering benthic animals, filtering zooplankton, and probably even of corals. The ability of some corals to filter feed was shown experimentally.

III. Biomass and Productivity of the Microflora Found in Waters of Lagoons

As pointed out above, the presence of a highly productive benthic community must influence the productivity of waters of shallow lagoons and of water passing over reefs. The first analyses carried out revealed that the number of colonies of heterotrophic microflora in lagoon waters is much higher than in the surrounding oceanic waters (Gee, 1932; Bavendamm, 1932). According to Di Salvo (1969) lagoon water at Eniwetok Atoll contains as many as 1000 colonies per ml. Our analysis showed that in lagoon waters the total number, the biomass, and the production of bacterioplankton were 10–20 times higher than in the surrounding waters of the open ocean. Typical data relevant to this are presented in Fig. 3, which contains the results of analyses performed at a transect across Butaritari Atoll from the muddy shore of the lagoon to its center. Close to shore, the biomass of bacterioplankton was about 1.6 gm per m³ of the wet weight. This level of biomass corresponds with that typical of eutrophic basins. In the center of the lagoon, the bacterioplankton biomass was lower by a factor of only 2. This lower level is comparable with that of a mesotrophic lake (Kuznetsov, 1969).

The rate of production of bacterioplankton in the lagoon was about 25 to 40 mg of carbon per m³. The P/B coefficient of the lagoon microflora was 2–4 times lower than that of the open ocean. This is probably a consequence of the benthic origin of a significant part of the lagoon bacterioplankton, in that the microorganisms washed out from the sedi-

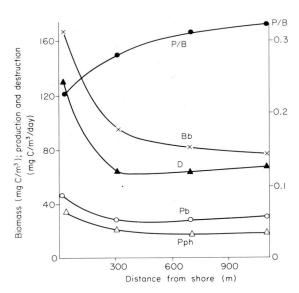

Fig. 3. Biomass of bacterioplankton (Bb, milligrams of carbon per m³); production (milligrams of carbon per m³ per day) of bacterioplankton (Pb) and phytoplankton (Pph); destruction (D, milligrams of carbon per m³); and P/B coefficient of bacterioplankton in the surface samples of water of the cross section from the shore to the center of the lagoon of Butaritari Atoll, Gilbert Islands.

ment cannot multiply in the water column. These new data once again support the contention that the sediments play a significant role in supplying microflora and bacterial aggregates to the water column (Marshall, 1965). The production of bacteria in the lagoons was of the same order as the production by photosynthesis of phytoplankton. Correspondingly, the destruction rate of bacteria was here 3–5 times more than the photosynthesis of phytoplankton.

In the lagoon at Heron Island, Great Barrier Reef, Australia, the maximum value obtained for bacterioplankton biomass was observed in the center of the lagoon when it was filled with water (Fig. 4). In the polluted lagoon of Kaneohe Bay, biomass and production of bacterioplankton are as high as in a mesotrophic lake (Table II). Destruction in the water here exceeded photosynthesis by phytoplankton and had a value of 0.3 mg O_2 per liter per day. In water of the central part of the vast and deep lagoon of Majuro Atoll, the numerical level and the productivity of bacterioplankton approximated those of the open sea. But even in the waters of these reefs, a relatively dense bacterial population was observed in spite of considerable water movements gen-

TABLE II

QUANTITATIVE CHARACTERISTICS OF MICROBIAL POPULATIONS AND THEIR PRODUCTIVITY IN THE WATER OF LAGOONS

Position of stations	No. of cross sections	No. of stations	Total count of bacteria ($\times 10^3$/ml)	Biomass of bacteria (B) (mg C/m³)	Production of bacteria (P) (mg C/m³/day)	Ratio P/B	Rate of destruction (D) (mg C/m³/day)	Rate of photosynthesis (Ph) (mg C/m³/day)	Ratio D/Ph	Percentage of bacterial plankton in aggregates
Kaneohe Bay, Oahu Island, Hawaii	1	1	920	51	32	0.63	91	19.6	4.6	13
		3	630	43	28	0.67	79	36.3	2.2	17
		5	410	21	31	1.47	88	60.6	1.4	22
	2	2	1230	77	43	0.56	122	18.6	6.5	10
		4	1260	63	54	0.86	154	59.1	2.6	23
	3	3	180	7.2	9	1.25	25	12.5	2.0	18
Majuro Atoll, Marshall Islands	2	1	260	6.5	5.6	0.87	16	7.5	2.1	11
		3	490	19	7.5	0.39	21	4.1	5.1	15
		5	1800	29	5.4	0.19	15	12.4	1.2	19
	3	1	66	1.8	2.7	1.50	7.7	10	0.77	16
		3	220	5.6	3.1	0.55	8.8	8	1.1	21
	6	5	92	1.1	0.8	0.73	2.3	6	0.38	24

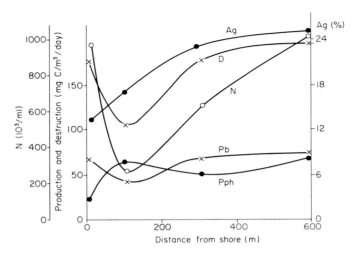

Fig. 4. A cross section from the shore of Heron Island to the center of the lagoon. N, Total number of bacteria in water (10^3/ml), Ag, percentage of bacterioplankton in the aggregates; D, destruction; Pb, production of bacteria; Pph, production of phytoplankton (milligrams of carbon per m^3).

erated by tides. The influence of the reef upon bacterioplankton numbers was detected on even the completely exposed seaward sides of the reefs comprising this atoll.

Data on the vertical distribution of microflora in the water column of a lagoon are presented in Fig. 5. They show a definite increase in

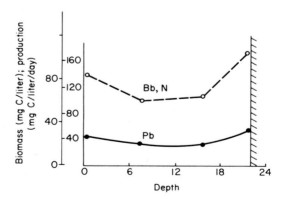

Fig. 5. Biomass and production of bacterioplankton in the water column of the lagoon of Butaritari Atoll. Bb, Biomass of bacteria; Pb, production of bacteria; N, total number of bacteria in water (10^4/ml).

the number and activity of bacteria in the bottom water layers compared with those in the upper layers.

Analyses of the percentage of bacterioplankton in the form of organic aggregates were made by filtration using filters of different pore sizes. The water samples had previously been labeled by insertion of a small portion (30–50 μg of carbon per liter) of a strongly labeled ^{14}C protein hydrolysate (Sorokin, 1971b). This percentage was found to be 20–30% in the water over reefs, and it increased in samples close to the edge of a reef. The abundance of such organic aggregates has been described before (Johannes, 1967; Marshall, 1965, 1968). Indeed, the absolute amount of these aggregates is certainly very high in the water over reefs. However, the relative aggregate content of the water of lagoons is similar to that of the open ocean (cf. Figs. 4 and 15, Tables II and V). It has been shown experimentally that formation of these aggregates is a specific feature of the natural population growth of planktonic bacteria. Formation is not definitely dependent upon the presence of suspended material or even of coral mucus. Such bacterial aggregates form in filtered as well as in nonfiltered water samples (Fig. 6). This process is definitely accelerated by addition of filtered coral mucus. The stability

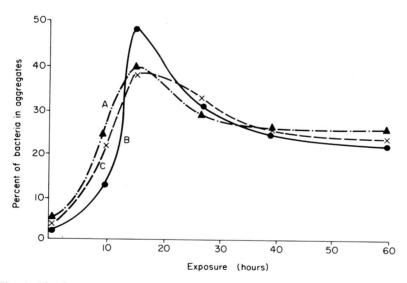

Fig. 6. The formation of bacterial aggregates during the multiplication of planktonic bacteria in the presence of ^{14}C–labeled protein hydrolystate in nonfiltered seawater (A); in water filtered through a filter with pore size 4 to 6 μm (B); and filtered through a filter with pore size 1.2 μm (C).

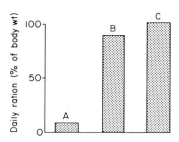

Fig. 7. Consumption by a mixed population of Calanoidae (A) of labeled bacterioplankton from which aggregated cells were previously filtered out, (B) of nonfiltered labeled bacterioplankton, and (C) a suspension of diatoms.

of the bacterial aggregates formed in the presence of coral mucus also increases.

The fact that a significant part of the natural bacterioplankton of seawater is in an aggregated state is of interest from the point of view of its trophic importance. This aggregated state promotes its utilization as food by even crude filter feeders (Fig. 7).

IV. Bacteria as Food of Coral Reef Animals

Di Salvo (1971) showed that the concentration of ^{35}S-labeled bacteria in suspension decreased in the presence of dead coral heads. He assumed that this was a consequence of their consumption by the fauna living on the head. Also, he stated that *Tridacna* can partially filter out bacteria from suspension, and he noted that living corals also possess this ability. Biochemical analyses showed that the organic material consumed by the polyps was digested and assimilated by them. Nevertheless, the author expressed the opinion that the amount of bacterial organic matter being consumed by the coral polyps was too small to prove that bacterial feeding represents a substantial part of their nutrition under natural conditions.

We have made a special study of the bacterial mode of nutrition of the animals of the reef community of Kaneohe Bay. Data on the nutrition of planktonic animals were obtained in collaboration with J. Taylor, T. Petipa, and E. Pavlova. The results of typical experiments designed to estimate the comparative rates of consumption of bacterial food and of planktonic algae by some of the most common animal species are presented in Fig. 8. These data demonstrate marked differences in the ability of different filter feeders to filter out the bacterioplankton.

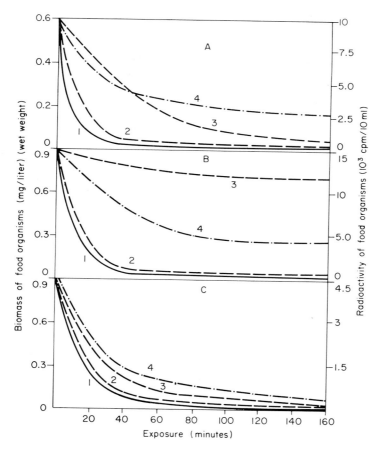

Fig. 8. Consumption of natural bacterioplankton (A), of a suspension of single cells (B), and of a suspension of planktonic algae (dinoflagellates) (C) by the sponge *Toxadocea violacea*, wet weighed 10 gm (1); by 13 specimens of a sabellid worm, total wet weight 3 gm (2); by the tunicate *Ascidia nigra*, wet weight 6 gm (3); and by the oyster *Crassostrea gigas*, wet weight of body 3.4 gm (4). The volume of water in the aquaria was 800 ml. The results presented contain a correction for self-sedimentation of suspended matter.

The sponge and the sabellid worm studied were revealed as very efficient filter feeders on fine particles. They filtered out bacterial cells as small as 0.5 μm from a suspension of single cells. The minimum level to which these animals decreased the bacterial concentration was extremely low, around 0.02 mg per liter of the raw biomass. This value is 20–40 times lower than the bacterial concentration of lagoon water usually observed.

The ascidian *Ascidia nigra* is a crude filtrator. It is capable of filtering out only aggregated bacterioplankton. As a filtrator, the oyster *Crassostrea* occupies an intermediate position, being able to filter out single bacterial cells to a limited extent. Even calanoid copepods and similar filtering planktonic animals, which have been described as unable to feed on bacteria (Fuller and Clarke, 1936), were shown to be capable of feeding on bacterial aggregates, which occur naturally in the bacterial plankton. However, they are unable to filter out single bacterial cells (Fig. 7).

Numerous experiments with the most common coral species of Majuro Atoll and Kaneohe Bay (*Montipora verrucosa, Porites compressa, Fungia scutatia, Pocillopora damicornis, Hydnophora contignato, Pavona* sp.), with the hydroid *Pennaria tiarella,* and with the colonial sea anemone *Palythoa* sp. confirmed Di Salvo's conclusion that coral polyps (as well as other coelenterates) are capable of feeding on and digesting bacterioplankton (Fig. 9, Table III). The ability of these coelenterates to assimi-

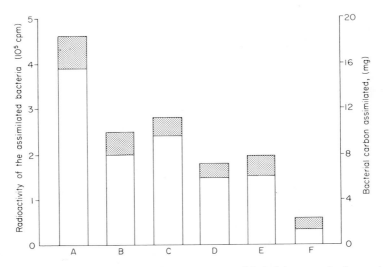

Fig. 9. The nutrition of some coelenterates using labeled bacterioplankton: A, the coral *Montipora verrucosa;* B, the coral *Pocillopora damicornis;* C, the coral *Fungia scutatia;* D, the coral *Porites compressa;* E, the colonial sea anemone *Palythoa* sp.; F, the hydroid *Pennaria tiarella.* The wet weight of corals used ranged from 20 to 30 gm; of *Palythoa,* 1.2 gm; of the colony of *Pennaria,* 0.4 gm. The time of feeding with the labeled food (1.5 mg per liter of raw biomass) was 6 hours; the time of exposure to the nonlabeled media for the collection of metabolic CO_2 was 1 hour. Hatched parts of columns correspond to metabolic CO_2 evolved during the experiment.

TABLE III

THE UTILIZATION OF BACTERIA AS FOOD BY SOME ANIMALS FOUND COMMONLY IN CORAL ENVIRONMENTS

Species	Carbon content of bodies of animals (W)(mg C/sp.)	Radio-activity of consumed bacteria (R_1) (cpm/sp/ 0.5 hours)	Radio-activity of assimilated bacteria (R_2) (cpm/sp/ 0.5 hours)	Amount of consumed bacterial substance (Q) (mg C/sp/ 0.5 hours)	Daily ration percentage of the body carbon $[(Q.48.100)/W)]$	Assimilability of bacterial food $[(R_2 \times 100\%)/R_1]$
Sponge (*Toxadocea violacea*)	122	267,000	220,000	0.086	3.4	82
Ascidian (*Ascidia nigra*)	125	128,500	106,300	0.041	1.6	83
Worm (*Megalomma* sp.)	4.4	22,600	16,500	0.0072	7.8	73
Oyster (*Crassostrea gigas*)	47	68,500	46,600	0.022	2.2	68
Gastropod veligers	0.0012	65	40	0.000013	51	61
Holothurian (*Opheodesoma spectabilis*)	68	487,000	106,000	0.444	10.4	22
Gastropod (*Nerita picea*)	13.6	15,200	74,300	0.0805	9.4	20
Coral (*Pocillopora damicornis*)	0.84(26)[a]	36,200	27,600	0.00095	5.5	76
Coral (*Montipora verrucosa*)	0.90(30)[a]	41,640	34,100	0.00108	5.8	82
Sea anemone (*Palythoa* sp.)	2.4	21,780	12,160	0.00057	1.1	55
Hydroid (*Pennaria tiarella*)	0.17(0.6)[a]	58,600	43,400	0.00154	43.5	74

[a] Colony of organisms, numbers in parentheses indicate its weight.

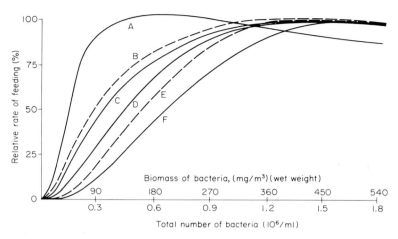

Fig. 10. The dependence of the relative rate of feeding of filtering animals on the concentration of the labeled natural bacterioplankton. A, sponge *Toxadocea violaea;* B, veligers of gastropods; C, serpulid worms; D, coral *Pocillopora damicornus;* E, oyster *Crassostrea;* F, crustacean *Eucalanus attennatus.*

late labeled bacteria was established by measuring the radioactivity of metabolic CO_2 evolved by the animals after a period of feeding on the bacterial suspension. The optimum concentrations of bacterioplankton for the filtering animals ranged from 0.1 gm per m^3 (wet weight) for the fine-particle filtering sponge tested to 0.3 or 0.5 gm per m^3 for the crude filtrators capable of filtering out only aggregated bacteria (Fig. 10). In the lagoons the usual bacterioplankton biomass is around 0.3 to 1.2 gm per m^3. Therefore, it can be concluded that the filtering animals found in reef communities can satisfy their food budget completely using bacterioplankton alone. This storage of bacterial food in atoll lagoons is so significant that we can envisage a positive economic effect from aquacultural enterprises in these rich environments. Bacteria can also serve as a nutrient supply for corals. Recent experiments (Fig. 11) with *Pocillopora* and *Porites* support this contention. Phosphate labeled with ^{32}P was added to samples of shallow water. Some of the samples were enriched with 2 mg per liter of glucose to promote bacterial growth. After most of the phosphate had been taken up by the microflora in the enriched media, coral colonies were placed in the water samples. Some of the coral colonies had been fixed and served as controls. It was found that the rate of uptake by corals of labeled phosphate associated with the microflora was much greater than that of labeled phosphate dissolved in seawater.

The results of the food balance experiments have shown that bacteria are a normal food for many species of reef animals. The capacity to assimilate bacteria possessed by the filtering animals is very high, about 60–80%; the capacity possessed by the sand eaters is up to 20%. When planktonic filtrators were fed bacterial plankton at optimal concentrations, their daily food ration was about 50–100% of the total organic matter of the body (Fig. 12, Table III). Significant values were also obtained in experiments with the sediment-eating animals and with the filtering worm studied. However, the sponge and the ascidian examined assimilated relatively much lower rations, for their bodies possess a large fraction of metabolically inactive tissues. Allowance was made for these tissues during the calculations.

Thus the foregoing data on bacterial feeding by reef animals show clearly that the natural bacterial population of the reef environment can serve as a high quality food, i.e., high percentage of assimilation, for many invertebrates inhabiting the environment and probably even for detritus and sand-eating coral reef fishes. However, coral polyps possess relatively large tentacles covered with mucus as well as cilia; it is possible that they are also able to utilize dissolved organic matter present in coastal waters. Experiments (Fig. 13) designed to investigate

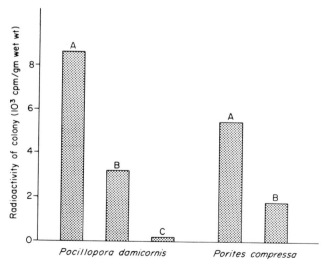

Fig. 11. Rate of consumption of labeled phosphorus by the corals *Pocillopora damicornis* and *Porites compressa*. A, phosphorus is inside bacterial bodies; B, phosphorus is presented as phosphate; C, same, control with previously fixed colony.

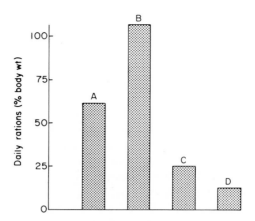

Fig. 12. The daily rations (percentage of the body weight) of labeled bacterio-plankton eaten by fine filtrators, the appendicularian *Oicopleura* (A) and the clado-ceran *Penilia* (B); by an intermediate filtrator, the copepod *Paracalanus* (C); and by a crude filtrator, the copepod *Eucalanus* (D).

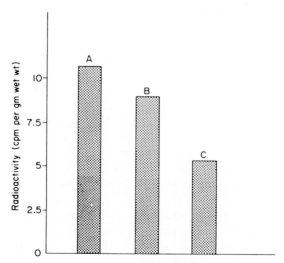

Fig. 13. The relative rate of consumption of labeled protein hydrolysate (0.5 mg C per liter + antibiotic streptomycin to prevent bacterial growth) and particulated labeled food by the coral *Pocillopora damicornis*. A, Hydrolysate; B, bacterioplank-ton; C, algae (*Gymnodinium*).

this possibility were illuminating. It was shown that the common herma-typic coral *Pocillopora damicornis* utilized low molecular weight organic matter such as labeled hydrolysates of algal protein very readily. The rate of uptake at concentrations as low as 0.5 mg of carbon per liter compared favorably with their rate of uptake of labeled bacterioplankton.

V. Effect of Pollution on the Coral Reef Environments

Human population growth, technological progress, and developments associated with expansion of tourism on tropical shores increase the possibility of pollution of coral reef communities. These factors have stimulated interest in studies of the influence of pollution on their ecol-ogy. Microbiological studies of the polluted reefs in Kaneohe Bay made by Di Salvo (1969) have shown that the count of heterotrophic bacteria cannot by itself serve as an indicator of pollution. The number is very high even in nonpolluted coral reef environments. We have found that an excellent indicator of reef pollution is the appearance and extent of sulfate reduction. Reduction of sulfates results in the formation of sulfides, especially the black sulfides of iron, in sediments. The process can be detected readily by the appearance of a dark coloration in the heaps of sediment produced by burrowing worms. Our special studies of this process in Kaneohe Bay revealed a depressing picture of its widespread occurrence in different kinds of sediments (Table IV). The sulfide sulphur content of sediments on the reef itself reached 400 mg per liter in some places, with an Eh (redox potential) of -300 mV even in layers 6–8 cm under the sediment surface (Fig. 14). These character-istics have remarkably high values even in coral sands forming a layer as thick as 8–10 cm at the open windward plateau of the polluted reef opposite Coconut Island, which is subjected to constant wave action. We have never detected this process in the sediments of nonpolluted reefs, even in detritus-like sediments enriched with organic material. For example, signs of sulfate reduction were absent in the coral sands and in the sandy-mucoid sediments enriched with organic detritus both taken from the nonpolluted parts of Majuro Atoll, even when the Eh values were significantly low (-200 mV). But on the polluted reef opposite the village of the same atoll quite obvious sulfide formation was found even when the thickness of the coral sand was only 5–10 cm.

Development of microbial sulfate reduction is one of the most danger-ous consequences of pollution of the coral reef environment. The sulfide so formed is a constant source of a very toxic agent, hydrogen sulfide,

TABLE IV

CHARACTERISTICS OF THE PROCESS OF SULFATE REDUCTION IN SEDIMENTS BY BACTERIA

Region of study	Position of the place of sampling; type of sediment	Depth of sampling of the cores[2-] (cm under the surface)	Number of sulfate-reducing bacteria (colony count) ($\times 10^3$ per ml)	Content of sulfides (mg S^{2-}/liter)
Kaneohe Bay, Ohau, Hawaii	East part of Coconut Reef, close to shore; fine sand	12	148	270
	East part of Coconut Reef, 50 m from shore; coral sand	7	10	110
	West part of Coconut Reef; powdery soft sediment among the dead corals	8	162	410
	Southwest part of open bay, close to place of sewage discharge; brown soft sediment	6	25	130
Majuro Atoll	Internal reef close to Rong-rong Island; coral sand	12	0	0
	Internal reef opposite the village; coral sand	5	12	40

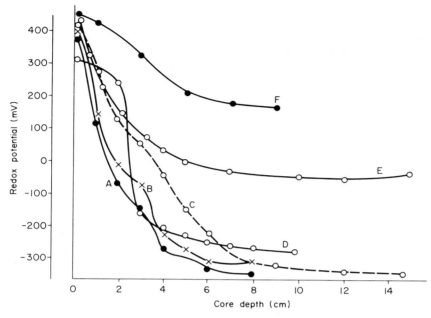

Fig. 14. The redox potential of reef sediments. A, fine sediments among dead corals on the western edge of the reef at Coconut Island, Kaneohe Bay, close to the polluted area; B, coral sand on the internal reef opposite Coconut Island; C, coral sand on the southeastern edge of polluted Coconut Reef (Kaneohe Bay); D, fine, powdery mucoid sediment from the clean part of the internal reef of Majuro Atoll; E, coral sand from Majuro Atoll; F, coral sand from the external Kapapa Reef, Kaneohe Bay.

the presence of which can cause far reaching changes in the reef community. The effect of pollution was also revealed in changes in the ratio between destruction and primary production of the phytobenthos in the sediments (cf. Table I). In polluted sediments the destruction rate was very high and the rate of photosynthesis was suppressed by the pollution. Hence the rate of general destruction exceeds photosynthesis in these sediments several times.

VI. Influence of Coral Reef Ecosystems upon Productivity of Surrounding Oceanic Waters

Estimations of the productivity of microflora and phytoplankton were made on transects off atolls and off barrier reefs towards the open ocean.

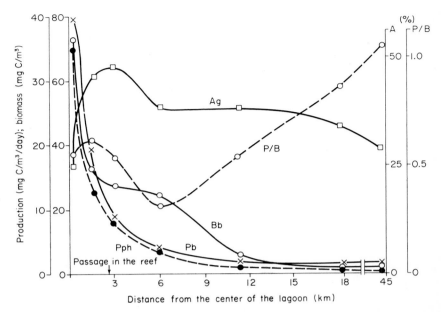

Fig. 15. Characteristics of the biomass and production of bacterioplankton and phytoplankton on a cross section from Heron Island lagoon to the open sea in a northeasterly direction. Ag, Percentage of bacterioplankton in the aggregates; Pb, production of bacteria; Pph, production of phytoplankton; Bb, biomass of bacteria; P/B, coefficient of bacterioplankton.

Typical results are presented in Fig. 15 and Table V. They show that the influence of the rich coral reef communities upon the productivity of the surrounding waters can be readily detected over the shelf area to a distance of 10–12 km from the reefs. Beyond this point, the rate of production and the biomass of bacterioplankton and of phytoplankton decrease 20–40 times in the direction of the open ocean. The influence of reefs on the productivity of surrounding waters is, probably, dependent on the size of the island. Around the big islands this enriched zone can be larger (Doty and Oguri, 1955).

VII. General Conclusions

The data presented prove, quite unequivocally, that microbial populations play an important metabolic and biosynthetic role in the productivity of the coral reef ecosystem. A general scheme illustrating the participation of bacteria in the trophodynamics of this ecosystem is shown

TABLE V

CHARACTERISTICS OF MICROBIAL POPULATIONS IN THE SURFACE WATERS SAMPLED DURING A TRANSECT OF THE LAGOON OF TARAWA ATOLL, GILBERT ISLANDS, IN THE SW DIRECTION

Position of stations	Total count of bacteria ($\times 10^3$/ml)	Biomass of bacteria (B) (mg C/m³)	Production of bacteria (P) (mg C/m³/day)	Ratio P/B	Potential production of bacteria (mg C/m³/day)	Photo-synthesis of phyto-plankton (Ph) (mg C/m³/day)	Destruction (D) (mg C/m³/day)	Ratio D/Ph	Percentage of bacteria in aggregates
Lagoon Passage in the reef	1360	110.0	42.0	0.4	83.0	52.0	111.0	2.1	27
2 km off the passage	890	49.0	14.2	0.3	68.0	28.6	37.4	1.3	35
3 km off the passage	720	21.6	9.2	0.4	56.0	10.8	24.3	2.2	26
6 km off the passage	475	14.1	8.2	0.6	31.0	2.3	21.6	9.3	21
10 km off the passage	78	2.3	5.8	2.5	29.1	2.6	15.3	5.9	18
17 km off the passage	91	2.7	4.1	1.5	15.3	1.1	10.8	9.7	18
23 km off the passage	59	1.8	4.8	2.6	8.9	0.81	12.6	15.2	20
passage	56	1.7	2.6	1.6	10.1	0.51	6.9	13.6	21

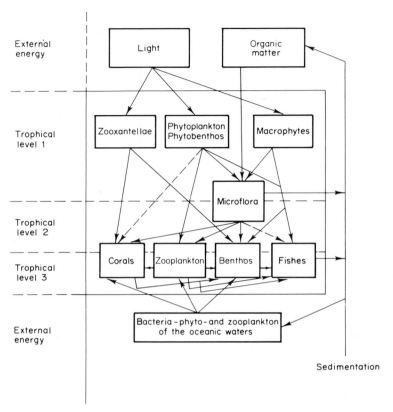

Fig. 16. A general scheme illustrating the participation of the bacterial population in the trophic structure of the reef ecosystem.

in Fig. 16. One of the important functions of microflora in the "internal" metabolism of the reef community is its participation in the process of mineralization and nutrient regeneration. But the microflora do not have a monopoly of this function (Johannes, 1968); it is contributed to by heterotrophic organisms including animals. During their participation in the process of mineralization, bacteria use about 25–30% of the energy of oxidized organic matter for production of the substance of their cells, which provides a fundamental source of food for the animals of the second trophic level.

Together with these "internal" functions, the microbial population of the coral reef ecosystem probably completes important "external" functions. By this I mean the participation of microflora in consumption of "external" energy and nutrients entering the coral reef ecosystem in the state of organic matter carried in oceanic water passing through the reef. Data presented on the ratios between primary production and the rate of destruction occurring in water and in sediments of the coral reef ecosystem show that destruction usually prevails over photosynthesis. Therefore the ecosystem must possess additional mechanisms to compensate for this "essential" destruction and to compensate also for loss owing to removal of organic matter and nutrients. One such mechanism is the predatory feeding of coral polyps, which consume organic matter and nutrients in zooplankton from the "external" waters of the ocean. However, since there is usually a paucity of zooplankton in these waters, this source cannot be accepted as really significant in the organic matter balance (Johannes *et al.*, 1970). Much more significant seems to be the filtering activity of the coral reef fauna which filters bacterioplankton, phytoplankton, and aggregated organic matter out of the incoming oceanic water.

Another possible mechanism recruiting "external" organic matter and nutrients is the utilization by microflora of dissolved organic matter in the oceanic waters passing over the reef. Experiments showed that tropical oceanic water samples taken from different depths contain significant amounts of labile organic matter which has potential for use in the production of microbial biomass (Fig. 17, Table V). Dissolved

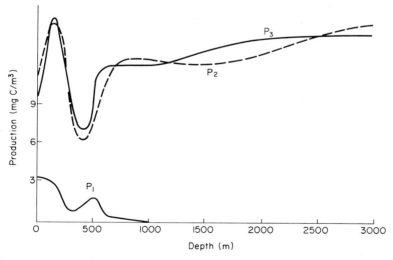

Fig. 17. The actual production of bacteria (P₁) and their potential production in previously filtered water samples (P₂) and in nonfiltered water samples (P₃). Production determined as milligrams of carbon per cubic meter. Open ocean to S–E off Gilbert Islands.

organic matter is of basic importance for this potential production of bacteria. This is shown by experiments involving the prior filtration of water samples (Fig. 17).

A hypothesis can be erected to explain the origin of this labile organic matter. It can be supposed that the organic matter is transported from the regions of the Antarctic convergence to the tropical zone through the advection of the deep and intermediate water (Sorokin, 1971a). Utilization by the microflora of this store of dissolved organic matter in the oceanic waters passing over the reef could be facilitated by the existence on the reef of huge areas densely covered with an epibiotic microflora and by the presence of large areas of dead corals, coral debris, and sands. These surfaces possibly act catalytically, promoting absorption from the water and accumulation and subsequent oxidation of the organic matter by the epibiotic microflora. The existence of the above-mentioned mechanisms of supplying the coral reef ecosystem with "external" energy most probably represents one of the possible answers to the question concerning the causes of the high productivity of such ecosystems. Therefore, further study of the functions of the microbial populations of coral reef ecosystems will have a special importance in elucidating the trophodynamics and bioenergetics of these extraordinarily interesting natural ecosystems.

References

Abe, N. (1937). *Palao Trop. Biol. Stud.* **7**, 469.

Bakus, G. J. (1968) *Mar. Biol.* **2**, 233.

Bakus, G. J. (1969). *Int. Rev. Gen. Exp. Zool.* **4**, 275.

Bavendamm, W. (1932). *Arch. Mikrobiol.* **3**, 205.

Di Salvo, L. H. (1969). Ph D. Thesis, University of North Carolina, Chapel Hill.

Di Salvo, L. H. (1971). *J. Exp. Mar. Biol. Ecol.* **7**, 123.

Doty, U., and Oguri, U. (1955). *J. Cons., Cons. Perma. Int. Explor. Mer.* **22**, 33.

Franzisket, L. (1969). *Naturwissenschaften* **56**, 144.

Fuller, J. L., and Clark, G. L. (1936). *Biol. Bull.* **70**, 242.

Gee, A. H. (1932). *Pap. Tortugas Lab.* **28**, 67.

Gundersen, K. R., and Stroupe, D. B. (1967). *Univ. Hawaii, Natur. Res., Tech. Rep.* **12**, 24.

Hoskin, C. M. (1963). *Nat. Acad. Sci.—Nat. Res. Counc. Publ.* **1089**, 160.

Johannes, R. E. (1967). *Limnol. Oceanogr.* **12**, 189.

Johannes, R. E. (1968). *In* "Advances in Microbiology of the Sea" (M. Droop and E. J. F. Wood, eds.), Vol. 1, p. 203. Academic Press, New York.

Johannes, R. E., Coles, S. L., and Kuenzel, N. T. (1970). *Limnol. Oceanogr.* **15**, 579.

Kornicker, L. S., and Purdi, E. I. (1957). *J. Sediment. Petrol.* **27**, 126.

Kuznetsov, S. I. (1969). "Microflora of the Lakes and its Geochemical Activity." Acad. Sci. USSR, Leningrad.

Marshall, N. (1965). *Ecology* **46**, 343.

Marshall, N. (1968). *Mar. Biol.* **2**, 50.

Odum, H. A., and Odum, E. P. (1955). *Ecol. Monogr.* **25**, 291.

Parsons, T. R., and Strickland, J. D. H. (1962). *Deep Sea Res.* **8**, 211.

Rodina, A. G. (1951). "Transactions of Problem Conference of Institute of Zoology," Vol. 1, p. 21. Acad. Sci. USSR, Leningrad (in Russian).

Rodina, A. G. (1963). *Limnol. Oceanogr.* **8**, 388.

Romanenko, W. I. (1964). *Mikrobiologia* **33**, 679.

Romanenko, W. I. (1965). *Mikrobiologiya* **34**, 391.

Roushdy, H. M., and Hansen, V. K. (1961). *Nature (London)* **190**, 649.

Sieburth, J. Mc N. (1968). *In* "Proceedings of US-Japan Seminar on Marine Microbiology," p. 49. Kyoto.

Sorokin, Yu. I. (1968). *Int. Ver. Theor. Angew. Limnol., Verh.* **16**, 1–41.

Sorokin, Yu. I. (1971a). *Mar. Biol.* **11**, 101.

Sorokin, Yu. I. (1971b). *Int. Rev. Gesamten Hydrobiol.* **56**, 1.

Sorokin, Yu. I. (1972). *In* "Productivity Probability of Freshwaters" (Z. K. Warszawa, ed.), pp. 477–492.

Stephens, G. C. (1960). *Science* **131**, 1532.

Vinberg, G. G. (1970). *Dok. Acad. Nauk SSSR* **186**, 198.

Wood, E. F. J. (1962). *Proc. Pac. Sci. Congr., 9th, 1957* Vol. 7, p. 217.

Wood, E. F. J. (1967). "Microbiology of Oceans and Estuaries." Elsevier, Amsterdam.

Yonge, C. (1958). *In* "Perspectives in Marine Biology," p. 117. Univ. of California Press, Berkley.

ZoBell, C. D. (1946). "Marine Microbiology." Massachusetts.

Zukova, A. I. (1963). *In* "Symposium on Marine Microbiology" (C. Oppenheimer, ed.), p. 699.

THE ALGAE OF THE GREAT BARRIER REEFS

A. B. Cribb

I. The Great Barrier Reefs

On the continental shelf of Queensland a diverse collection of coral reefs stretches from Lady Elliott Island, at lat. 24°5′S, northwards for nearly 2000 km to Torres Strait. This vast assemblage, the largest in the world, consists of barrier reefs, platform reefs, lagoonal platform reefs, and fringing reefs, which may border both continental islands and the mainland coast. It is because of this diversity of reef type and the fact that a more or less continuous barrier reef occurs only north of Cairns that Steers (1937) has recommended for the whole assemblage the term "Great Barrier Reefs," in place of the more widely used but somewhat misleading "Great Barrier Reef." Fairbridge (1950) has given an account of the distribution of the various types of reef, and Maxwell (1968) has discussed their formation.

Phycologically, the area is poorly known, and, of necessity, this account is based on the two widely separated areas where the author has worked. These are the Capricorn and Bunker Groups of reefs at the southern extremity of the Great Barrier Reefs and Low Isles in the northern part of the area.

II. Nomenclature

The nomenclature used here is a variant of that used by Cribb (1965, 1966, 1969), which, in turn, was based on the one proposed by Tracey *et al.* (1955) mainly for Pacific atolls.

The intertidal region can be divided into four main areas, *viz.*, beach, reef flat, reef rock rim, and seaward platform; subdivisions of these areas are discussed below under the appropriate headings.

The beach, the intertidal slope forming the transition between the supralittoral cay and the reef flat, consists of calcareous fragments either as sand and shingle or consolidated as beach rock. Seaward from its base stretches the reef flat, consisting generally of a sand-floored expanse with scattered coral over which, at low water spring tides, water is impounded by the reef rock rim to a depth of mostly 10–80 cm. On

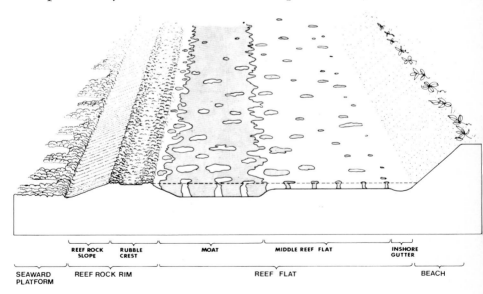

Fig. 1. Diagrammatic representation of part of the intertidal reef, Capricorn and Bunker Groups, not to scale and with vertical heights greatly exaggerated.

some reefs a lagoon occurs, bounded by the reef flat and, in some cases, also in part by the cay. The reef flat terminates at the reef rock rim, a relatively narrow strip, often 50–150 m wide, mostly emergent at low water spring tides and apparent first on a falling tide by a line of surf. The reef rock rim is usually the highest part of the reef, other than the beach, and once the water level of a falling tide drops below its crest it is responsible for damming water over the reef flat. Thereafter, the level of water over the reef flat drops only slightly and slowly until the incoming tide again flows over its crest.

Forming the outermost and lowest part of the intertidal reef is the seaward platform, a relatively narrow strip, 15–45 m wide, of rich coral and lithothamnian growth commonly dissected to form a spur and groove system. It is the seaward platform, reef rock rim, and beach on which surf breaks; the intervening reef flat is largely free from its action.

The various subdivisions of the reef are illustrated schematically in Fig. 1.

III. Capricorn and Bunker Groups of Reefs

Reefs of the Capricorn and Bunker Groups vary in size from approximately 1 to 11 km in greatest diameter. Many are platform reefs. This term is used here to denote a flat-topped, platform-supported reef. Some of the reefs possess lagoons, the largest being that of Lady Musgrave Island, over 1 km long and up to 9 m deep; consistent with the use of the term "platform reef," Maxwell (1968) has used the term "lagoonal platform reef" for these structures. Reefs arising from lagoons are here termed patch reefs in accordance with the nomenclature of Newell (1954, 1956).

A. BEACH

The unconsolidated beach consists of sand or shingle, the latter in some areas being piled up in the mid and upper parts of the beach as ramparts, with the interlocking of the irregular fragments allowing for surprisingly steep slopes, sometimes to 60°.

Sandy beaches are devoid of algae, and it is only near the base of the beach that shingle is colonized by algae, chiefly *Entophysalis deusta* (Menegh.) Dr. and Daily, with some *Enteromorpha clathrata* (Roth) Grev. and *Monostroma* sp. Commonly a darkened, algae-occupied strip occurs along the base of the beach contrasting with the bleached area above. This algal colonization is probably a consequence, in part, of reduced wave action allowing relative immobility of the fragments; the reef flat's damping effect on the waves decreases as the water level over it rises. At higher levels the frequent movement of the fragments prevents algal growth and accounts for the typically brilliant white nature of the major part of these sand and shingle beaches. The appearance of gray-stained shingle, colonized by *Anacystis montana* (Lightf.) Dr. and Daily, clearly marks the upper limit of the intertidal area.

Beach rock, for the formation of which Emery and Cox (1956) could find no thoroughly satisfactory explanation, is lithified beach material, usually dipping seawards at an angle of 5°–10° and, in the Capricorn and Bunker Groups, extending from approximately the reef flat low water level upwards for nearly 2 m to the vicinity of mean high water. Its surface may be smooth and even, particularly where the scouring action of sand may produce an almost polished surface; or, particularly in its upper parts, its surface may suffer solution leaving it deeply pitted or eroded with adjacent depressions separated by irregularly serrated knife-edge ridges. The beach rock is normally colonized throughout by small algae, which commonly are responsible for the appearance of three differently colored bands in downshore succession as follows.

1. Entophysalis deusta Band

Varying in color from pale yellow-brown to gray or almost black, this band is constituted mainly by *Entophysalis deusta*, which forms a microscopically intermittent film over the surface. The basal filaments also penetrate the rock. *Calothrix crustacea* Thuret also may be a common constituent of the band and is responsible for further darkening of the surface.

2. Mixed Cyanophyte Band

This appears as a smooth, closely adherent, leathery "skin," up to 1.5 mm thick, usually very pale pink in color. The layer is made up of several cyanophytic species, entrapping calcareous sediment and covered by a fine, pale pink, calcareous encrustation that appears to be a deposit from solution rather than consolidated surface sediment. The most common algal constituents are usually *Schizothrix arenaria* (Berk.) Gom., *S. tenerrima* (Gom.) Drouet, *Microcoleus lyngbyaceus* (Kuetz.) Crouan, *Calothrix crustacea*, *Kyrtuthrix maculans* (Gom.) Umezaki, *Entophysalis deusta*, *E. conferta* (Kuetz.) Dr. and Daily.

The consolidation of this "skin" is such that the fine parallel scratches made by grazing fish are readily apparent; these were figured by Stephenson and Searles (1960).

3. *Gelidiella bornetii* Band

The general color of this zone during summer is almost white because of the obscuring loosely held sediment, but during winter it may take on a light green appearance due to the more vigorous growth of *Enteromorpha clathrata* at that season. The most consistently present, and usually the dominant alga in this band, is *Gelidiella bornetii* (Weber-van Bosse) Feldmann and Hamel, but numerous other small species occur also.

B. Reef Flat

The reef flat, really an enormous tide pool that stretches seawards from the base of the beach, has a mainly horizontal floor. It can be divided into two or three regions: inshore gutter, middle reef flat, and moat, the first mentioned commonly being absent.

1. *Inshore Gutter*

This innermost and narrowest of the three regions is distinguishable on some cays only, usually bordering beach rock where it forms a strip 2–6 m wide and up to 10 cm deeper than the adjacent part of the reef flat. Along this, gutter water draining from the reef flat at low water escapes relatively rapidly, and the scouring action of the calcareous fragments it carries in suspension is probably responsible for keeping the area mainly free from coral and macroscopic algae.

2. *Middle Reef Flat*

Usually the most extensive of the three areas is the middle reef flat, which may be up to several hundred meters wide and which, in the absence of an inshore gutter, reaches to the base of the beach.

There is a floor of white coral sand, less commonly of coral shingle or reef rock, which, at low water spring tides, is mostly submerged to a depth of 10–30 cm except locally where banks of coral shingle may be emergent. Scattered over this floor are clumps of coral; many of these clumps just break the surface. The density of distribution of the coral varies considerably from reef to reef and from place to place on the one reef, but, in general, the more landward part of the middle reef flat supports widely scattered, small clumps often less than a meter across. The area of unencumbered sandy floor greatly exceeds that occupied by the coral clumps. Here, also, only a small proportion of the coral is living, the extensive dead surfaces supporting a rich growth of macroscopic algae. Seaward, there is a general tendency for an increase in the size of the coral patches with a consequent reduction in the area of sandy floor. Concomitant with this is usually an increase in the proportion of living to dead coral and a reduction in the quantity of macroscopic algae.

The algal layer is usually denser in summer than in winter because of the seasonal growth mainly of species of *Sargassum* and other brown algae. The algal cover may form a fur or mat, a spongy layer of confluent cushions of various species, or a relatively luxuriant growth dominated by *Sargassum* spp. with lax fronds up to 60 cm long. On a falling tide the buoyed, dome-shaped specimens of *Turbinaria ornata* (Turn.) J. Ag. are often the first algae to emerge over the reef flat.

Among the macroscopic species commonly contributing to the flora of the middle reef flat are *Boodlea composita* (Harv.) Brand, *Caulerpa racemosa* (Forssk.) J. Ag. var. *clavifera* (Turn.) Weber-van Bosse, *Chlorodesmis fastigiata* (C. Ag.) Ducker, *C. major* Zan., *Dictyosphaeria versluysii* Weber-van Bosse, *Halimeda discoidea* Dcne, *H. tuna* (Ell. and Sol.) Lamx, *H. opuntia* (L.) Lamx, *Chnoospora implexa* (Her.) J. Ag., *Dictyota bartayresii* Lamx, *Hydroclathrus clathratus* (Bory) Howe, *Lobophora variegata* (Lamx) Wom., *Padina gymnospora* (Kuetz.) Vickers, *Sargassum crassifolium* J. Ag., *S. polycystum* C. Ag., *Turbinaria ornata*, *Amphiroa foliacea* Lamx, *A. fragilissima* (L.) Lamx, *Ceratodictyon spongiosum* Zan., *Gelidiella acerosa* (Forssk.) Feldm. and Hamel, *Hypnea nidulans*, Setch., and *Laurencia obtusa* (Huds.) Lamx. The usually dominant members of the algal fur on dead coral surfaces are *Gelidiella bornetii* and *Herposiphonia tenella* (C. Ag.) Ambronn. While encrusting coralline algae occur here, they tend to be overgrown by noncalcareous species and therefore are less conspicuous than in the moat and seaward platform.

Parts of the under surfaces of coral clumps not in contact with the reef flat floor provide a habitat that supports a flora rather different from that on the upper, exposed surfaces. Encrusting algae, particularly *Peyssonelia* spp. and species of coralline algae are common, the latter including the brittle, foliose fronds of *Lithothamnion simulans* Foslie. Among other species restricted or mainly restricted to this habitat are *Caulerpa brachypus* Harv., *C. sertularioides* (Gmel.) Howe, *Microdictyon obscurum* J. Ag., *Valonia ventricosa* J. Ag., and *Hypoglossum* sp.

Dead coral surfaces moved by storms so that they protrude above the general limit of coral growth carry encrusting colonies of *Ralfsia expansa* J. Ag., which may form an almost unbroken, tarlike layer.

The sandy floor is mainly free from macroscopic algae, only three species being found there. *Halimeda cylindracea* Dcne and *H. macroloba* Dcne, both with massive, embedded, rhizoidal bases, occur sparsely over some reef flats, both usually in small groups of several plants occupying an area of up to a few square meters. *Caulerpa cupressoides* (Vahl.) C. Ag., with its vigorous rhizomes sometimes spreading for a meter or more over the surface, is found particularly near the shore.

3. Moat

Near the seaward margin of the reef flat the increased size of the coral patches leads to their linking up, thus forming a continuous platform enclosing sand-floored pools often channel-like and orientated more or less at right angles to the margin of the reef. This transition from middle reef flat to moat is usually accompanied by an increase in the low water depth to 40–80 cm, thus justifying the term moat which was used by Stephenson *et al.* (1931) for a comparable area at Low Isles. Where best developed, the upper, grill-like surafce of the platform is remarkably even, each contributing branch of coral having ceased growth at approximately the same level, usually 3–5 cm above the extreme low-water level of reef flat waters.

Fleshy algae are poorly developed in the moat but platform surfaces, almost without exception, are coated with a pale pink "paint" of lithothamnia often accompanied by small green flecks of the encrusting *Pseudopringsheimia* sp. Permanently submerged, dead coral branches lining the heavily shaded labyrinthiform cavities beneath the platform surface carry other species of lithothamnia, usually of a deeper pink color, together with dark, dull red crusts of *Peyssonelia* spp. Deposition of coral shingle occurs toward its seaward limit. This becomes progressively heavier, filling the interstices of the platform and finally leading to the obliteration of the moat which is replaced by the reef rock rim.

C. LAGOON

Where a lagoon borders a cay, the sandy beach may shelve gently through a gradually deepening reef flat into the lagoon, or sublittoral shingle at the base of the beach may slope precipitously to almost maximum depth. Commonly the lagoon borders are sharply delimited, the reef flat bounding the lagoon taking the form of an even-topped coral platform, the lagoon coral platform, which descends almost vertically to the lagoon floor. Rising from the floor of the lagoon are patch reefs, which are isolated columns a few to many meters across with their upper surface horizontal and at the same level as the upper coral of the reef flat. The general appearance and algal flora of the lagoon coral platform and of the patch reefs resemble that of well-developed platforms in the moat.

Sublittoral walls of the patch reefs support a high proportion of living coral but, apart from lithothamnia, algae are poorly developed. One of the more frequently encountered species is *Amphiroa crassa* Lamx, but nowhere is it a common alga.

The sandy floors of the lagoons seem to be, perhaps surprisingly, almost devoid of algae. The only algae noted there are occasional clumps of *Halimeda macroloba*. This is in contrast to the lagoon of Kwajalein and Eniwetok where Dawson (1963) described *Halimeda* growing "in such persistent plenty that the lagoon floor sediments are largely built up of the accumulated fragments of these jointed plants."

D. Reef Rock Rim

Enclosing the reef flat, except in some cases on the western, leeward side, is a rim of reef rock, the term reef rock being used here in the sense of MacNeil (1954) and Emery *et al.* (1954) to indicate rock derived from either the growth lattice of organisms or from detrital material. The crest of this reef rock rim, commonly 35–100 m wide, is no more than a few centimeters above the upper limit of coral growth in the reef flat. Here and there, slightly depressed areas allow the further escape of reef flat water after the level has reached the general upper limit of the rim. Typically, this crest is an area of heavy deposition of coral rubble and is termed the rubble crest.

The reef rock of the rubble crest may be horizontal but commonly much of its central area is occupied by a slightly depressed strip, forming a broad, irregular, linear pool, mostly 5–30 cm deep, its floor generally strewn with coral fragments or small coral boulders. The extent, composition and positioning of the rubble varies greatly along the crest. In some cases, it completely obliterates the central depression.

Seaward of the rubble crest the reef rock slopes gently for 20–80 m through a vertical distance of usually 0.5–0.7 m to form the reef rock slope. It is on the reef rock rim that the reef blocks occur. These are massive coral heads or pieces of reef rock up to 2 m high, broken from the outer edge of the reef, and carried on to the reef surface by waves during cyclones. The term reef block is justifiably preferred by Newell (1954) to the less elegant but more commonly used "negro head" or "nigger head."

1. Rubble Crest

The rubble, largely because of the high degree of emergence it experiences, supports an impoverished algal flora. There is typically a yellow-brown stain of *Entophysalis deusta* and, in some places, an inconspicuous, thin, partial encrustation of lithothamnia. A red-brown, bristly fur of *Gelidiella bornetii* occurs on some larger fragments subject to infrequent movement. However, the most characteristic and usually the only prominent species of the rubble is *Yamadaella cenomyce* (Dcne) Abbott, which is almost entirely restricted to this habitat. Its small, pale pink, semiprostrate tufts of repeatedly forked branches suffer a considerable degree of desiccation during low spring tides of calm weather when they may be emergent for up to 4 hours.

2. Reef Rock Slope

Typically, the reef rock slope is shallowly and irregularly terraced. The meandering terraces, mostly not over 5 cm high, commonly link up to form an irregular reticulum. In some areas, rather than terraces, there are numerous potholes or basinlike pools up to 1 m in diameter.

Living coral is virtually absent from this band, which is characterized by the presence of a low, sand-binding algal mat, usually not over 1 cm high, which entraps considerable quantities of calcareous sand that, to a large extent, obscure the constituents. Large numbers of the foraminiferan *Calcarina* sp., which sometimes occur here, further obscure the algal nature of the covering so that, superficially at least, the area may appear to be one only sparsely vegetated. In fact, however, numerous species are found, usually growing so densely that little of the underlying rock is visible.

The most important members of the turf usually are species of *Laurencia*, particularly *L. flexilis* Setch., *L. obtusa* var. *obtusa*, and *L. perforata* (Bory) Mont., with several other dwarf or dwarfed species making smaller contributions. Among the numerous other species usually present are *Boodlea composita* Weber-van Bosse, *Sphacelaria novaehollandiae* Sond., *Ceramium* spp., *Gelidiella acerosa*, *Griffithsia tenuis* C. Ag., *Hypnea* spp., *Jania adhaerens* Lamx, and *Microcoleus lyngbyaceus*. The only relatively large alga commonly found in this area and protruding above the general anonymity of the algal mat is *Laurencia obtusa* var *snackeyi* (Weber-van Bosse) Yam., with its dark olive clumps reaching a height of up to 30 cm.

The few surfaces not occupied by the algal mat mostly carry lithothamnia, often best developed on the lips of the terraces. Pieces of coral shingle in small depressions in this area frequently support bright orange-red to dull blood-red crusts of *Peyssonelia* spp., which provide one of the few splashes of bright color in an otherwise drab expanse.

E. Seaward Platform

The outermost part of the intertidal reef is constituted by the seaward platform. In some places the reef rock slope merges gradually into the seaward platform; in others, particularly in leeward areas, the two are separated by a trough 3–9 m wide carrying water usually 0.1–1.5 m deep at low water.

The seaward platform may dip gently seaward, but usually is more or less horizontal. In some places its seaward edge is elevated 10–20 cm above the general platform level. This elevation is probably the result of the raising here by wave action of the effective low-water tidal level. The general level of the platform is approximately 0.5 m above extreme low-water spring tides, but it is only at and near spring tides during calm weather that its surface is emergent for an hour or two at low water. Coral colonies here, many of them *Acropora* spp., may form an even-topped platform on which one may walk with reasonable ease, although its surface is never planed to the extent found in the moat platforms; however, for the most part, particularly in the more wave-beaten areas, the surface is far more irregular. Its outer edge drops vertically or precipitously and, commonly, is dissected at right angles to its length by gulches mostly 2–4 m wide to produce the spur and groove system well reported for Pacific atolls. Opinions differ as to whether this is a growth or erosion phenomenon. Newell (1954), for instance, has favored the erosion view, while others, including Emery *et al.* (1949, 1954), Goreau (1959), and Yonge (1963) have interpreted it as being constructional in nature and under the influence of wave action. Cloud (1954) considered that there is "probably a complete spectrum of genetic kinds of groove and spur systems—from mainly erosional to mainly construction—" and attributed the spur and groove system at reef fronts to the balanced interplay or erosion and growth. The rich development of coral and lithothamnia on the sublittoral spurs examined certainly suggests growth rather than erosion in the Capricorn and Bunker Groups.

Of the areas of the reef discussed here, this is one of the richest in coral growth and certainly the richest in encrusting, coralline algae and in the coralloid *Lithophyllum moluccense* Foslie. Although in most areas coral is the dominant organism, lithothamnia may predominate locally. Where the development of the latter is most robust, living coral is restricted mainly to a narrow, outermost strip and the greater part of the surface of the seaward platform is covered by the pink to purple-pink smooth to nodulose veneer of these plants. Although several species of lithothamnia are involved, their color and form, superficially at least, show relatively little variation so that they present a generally more uniform appearance than do the corals. Unfortunately, taxonomic work on these algae has not reached a stage where the distribution of the various species in the seaward platform can be profitably considered.

Either coral or algae may overgrow its apparently healthy neighbor although casual observation suggests that the coral is more often the successful competitor. In some cases the two seem evenly matched, and each, at the line of contact, grows upward to form a ridge.

Fleshy algae are poorly developed; in some areas they are virtually absent. However, in the most wave-beaten eastern areas there is often a development of small, closely adherent fleshy species on the dead coral surfaces and, to a smaller extent, over the lithothamnia. Larger fleshy algae are normally absent with the exception of *Chlorodesmis fastigiata, C. major,* and *Bryopsis indica,* which usually occur sparsely.

Wave action along the windward side of the reef makes examination of the sublittoral surfaces of the spurs difficult, and the few examinations made have been mostly along the northern and southern sides of reefs. Here there is a rich growth of coral and lithothamnia, with the former usually predominating. Nonencrusting algae occur only sparsely and include *Halimeda discoidea, Turbinaria ornata,* and *Amphiroa crassa.* However, the roofs of heavily shaded overhangs are commonly festooned with the red fronds of *Plocamium hamatum* J. Ag. or encrusted with *Peyssonelia* spp. The sandy-rubble floors support only occasional plants of *Halimeda discoidea* attached to the larger pieces of rubble. Scouring action here is likely to prevent most algal growth.

IV. Low Isles Reef

A. DESCRIPTION OF THE AREA

Low Isles is the reef on which the Great Barrier Reef Expedition of 1928–1929 spent 1 year and has been described by Yonge (1963) who led the Expedition as "the most intensively studied coral formation in the world." Publications on the biology and topography of this reef include those by Steers (1930), T. A. Stephenson *et al.* (1931), Manton and Stephenson (1935), Fairbridge and Teichert (1947), and W. Stephenson *et al.* (1958).

Although, at first sight, the reef of Low Isles may appear very different
from reefs of the Capricorn and Bunker Groups, much of the basic
pattern found in the latter can be detected also at Low Isles. Probably
the main topographic difference between the two is the marked development at Low Isles of shingle ramparts which, in turn, modify the biota
of part of the reef. These ramparts are essentially the rubble crests
of the Capricorn and Bunker Groups developed to an exceptional degree.
Along the south west side of the Low Isles Reef, the shingle rampart
or rubble crest scarcely exceeds the height of the reef flat it borders,
but eastwards it increases in dimensions and at the weather side reaches
to above extreme high water of spring tides. Behind it here occurs a
somewhat broken line of older ridges. The ramparts drop steeply to
the reef flat, often at an angle of about 45°, while seaward the shingle
spills over the gently dipping pavement of reef rock and in many places
obscures a large part of it. This shingle may be loose or partly compacted
in a sandy-muddy matrix.

The high, windward ramparts thus effectively enclose part of the reef
flat providing a sheltered habitat in which dense mangrove forest, dominated by *Rhizophora*, has become established and which, in turn, provides a muddy and shaded habitat colonized by various algae not normally found on reef flats without mangroves.

The reef flat is floored with sand or reef rock, either of which may
be partly overlaid by calcareous rubble. At low water it may be submerged to a depth of approximately 30 cm or shortly emergent as sand
flat, reef rock, or an irregular mosaic of emergent solid substrata and
shallowly submerged intervening areas.

B. ALGAL VEGETATION

The beach rock vegetation is, in general, similar to that already discussed for the Capricorn and Bunker Groups.

Although the reef flat is divisible into middle reef flat and moat,
the even-topped coral platforms characteristic of the moat in the Capricorn and Bunker Groups are relatively poorly developed, and the vegetational differences between middle reef flat and moat are less marked.
In this brief account, therefore, the two areas are treated as one.

Probably the most striking vegetational differences, as compared with
the reef flats in the Capricorn and Bunker Groups, are the presence
of mangroves and of sea grasses. The mangrove forest, composed of
several species but with *Rhizophora stylosa* Griff. dominant in most
areas, occupies the eastern part of the reef flat extending westwards

as scattered trees, the mangrove park area of Stephenson *et al.* (1931). Associated with the mangroves, both on trunks and aerial roots and on shaded shingle in their vicinity, are algal species that are typically associated with mangroves and which include *Cladophora socialis* Keutz. prox., *Monostroma* sp., *Rhizoclonium capillare* Keutz., *Bostrychia binderi* Harv., *B. tenella* (Vahl) J. Ag., *Caulacanthus* sp., and various cyanophytes.

Sea grasses found on the reef flat are *Halophila ovalis* (R. Br.) Hook., *Zostera capricorni* Aschers, *Halodule uninervis* (Frossk.) Aschers, and *Thalassia hemprichii* (Ehrenb.) Aschers. Of these, *Thalassia hemprichii* is by far the most common and, in some areas in the vicinity of the mangroves, forms an almost unbroken cover supporting a heavy burden of the disclike foraminiferan *Orbitolites complanata* Lamarck.

Although several algal species occurring on the reef flat at Low Isles are not found in the Capricorn and Bunker Groups, the majority are common to both areas and the general aspect of Reef Flat algal vegetation in each is more or less similar.

The shingle forming the rubble crest and overlying much of the pavement of coral rock sloping gently seaward presents a desolate appearance. Although not at first strikingly obvious, four main, intertidal, biotic bands can usually be distinguished in downshore succession as follows.

1. Entophysalis deusta Band. This appears as a yellow-brown to gray-brown stain, often darkest in the upper parts where it may occasionally, in the mass, appear almost black. Particularly where the shingle is stabilized in a sand-muddy matrix, other cyanophytes occur and include *Calothrix crustacea*, *Kyrtuthrix maculans*, *Microcoleus lyngbyaceus*, *Rivularia atra* Roth, and *Schizothrix tenerrima*.

2. Lithothamnion Band. The thin encrustations seldom cover more than half the available surface. When dry the band is distinguished in distant view as a pale, almost white strip that rapidly changes to pale pink on being moistened by a shower of rain.

3. Fleshy Algal Band. Further study will probably justify the subdivision of this band. Its upper part is constituted by a yellow-brown fur of small algae, primarily of *Gelidiella bornetii*, *Gelidium pusillum* (Stackh.) Le Jol., and *Polysiphonia howei* Hollenb. in Taylor. Seaward, these are joined and largely replaced by a dull yellow-brown to fawn mat of numerous species either dwarf or dwarfed, in which species of *Laurencia* usually predominate. It is, in general, similar to the turf of small algae occurring in comparable positions on the reef rock slope in the Capricorn and Bunker Groups except that, particularly in its

lower part, many of the constituents reach greater size, several centimeters in length. Since Low Isles is protected by a barrier reef to the
east, this may be a reflection of the less wave-beaten nature of the
environment.

4. Seaward Platform. Occupying the lowermost intertidal region is
a band of rich coral growth and encrusting lithothamnia emergent for
up to 40 cm at extreme low water spring tides. This is less platformlike
than the comparable region on the Capricorn-Bunker area and resembles
some leeward reefs of that area in descending gradually to deep water
without a sharply marked outer margin. It differs further in the presence
among the coral of several macroscopic fleshy algal species including
Laurencia papillosa (Forssk.) Grev.

V. Factors Influencing Biotic Distribution on the Reef

The reefs of the Capricorn and Bunker Groups, like most coral reefs,
are zoned roughly parallel with the reef margin. While the biotic zonation on the beach rock and on the reef rock rim can be assumed to
be, in large measure at least, determined by tidal phenomena and their
consequences, other factors must be sought to explain zonation over
the reef flat.

The reef flat is, in effect, an enormous tide pool, and over a tidal
range of approximately 3 m there is an interval of perhaps only 5 cm
over which there is a sudden change from permanent submersion to
emergence for periods of up to 4 or 5 hours. It is not surprising that
this emergence, occurring more or less simultaneously over the whole
reef flat, should induce the remarkably sudden biotic cutoff resulting
in the almost planed effect commonly seen on the tops of coral growths.
Kuenen (1933) suggested that accumulation of sediment on the upper
surface of coral colonies plays a part in the formation of micro atolls.
While this may well be so, particularly in nonemergent micro atolls,
on the reef flat the emergence factor alone is sufficient to account
for the cessation of upward growth.

Algae, being dependent on the substratum provided by dead coral,
likewise show a similar, sharp, upper limit. However, even in the presence of substrata elevated by disturbance, there are few algae that can
extend above the limit of coral growth. None of the macroscopic species
of the reef flat occupies these elevated positions, and even the small
species of the beach rock are often absent or sparsely developed, with
their place being taken by the tarlike encrustations of *Ralfsia expansa.*

Possibly the rapid drainage of emergent coral branches in the calm conditions of the reef flat inhibits growth of the beach rock species, while, on the beach rock, *Ralfsia* is probably excluded by competition from the mat-forming, sediment-entrapping species flourishing there on the gentle slope.

Across the reef flat the proportions of fleshy algae to coral show an inverse relationship, with algae best developed near the shore and most sparse in the moat. The reasons for this horizontal zonation are not known with any certainty, but there seem to be several factors that might be concerned with this distribution. Surf breaking on the sandy beach leads to a milky turbidity in adjacent waters, and this relatively high sediment content may have an inhibitory action on coral growth or on the settlement of planulae. At least some species of algae are probably more tolerant of these conditions.

During periods of heavy rainfall coinciding with low water of spring tides, it could be conjectured that fresh water seeping from the cay to the landward part of the reef flat and joining the precipitation over the flat would lower the salinity to a point where coral mortality could occur. Rainford (1925) and Hedley (1925) described almost complete destruction of marine life on reefs near Bowen, Queensland, while Crossland (1928) and Cooper (1966) recorded extensive coral mortality at Tahiti and at Fiji, respectively, following excessive freshwater flooding; Goreau (1964) found widespread expulsion of zooxanthellae from corals following, presumably, less intense flooding in Jamaica. However, lowering of salinity in the vicinity of a sand cay would not be likely to be as severe or prolonged as in the cases noted above and is probably an unlikely cause of coral mortality in view of the finding by Mayer (1915) that at Murray Island "All species of reef corals survive without apparent injury an immersion for 4 to 5 hours in seawater diluted with an equal volume of rain water, and many species can withstand 11 hours of this treatment . . . ." In the event of salinities dropping to dangerous levels, fleshy algae might be no more tolerant of lowered salinities, but their growth rate, being considerably in excess of that of corals, would allow their rapid recolonization.

It might be thought that water flowing over the reef flat on an incoming tide would become progressively depleted of plankton as it flowed over the various plankton consumers. However, Mayer (1918) working at Murray Island did not see evidence of inshore corals being starved. The work at Low Isles reported by Manton and Stephenson (1935), which showed no striking difference in richness of plankton between waters over the reef flat and those beyond the edge of the reef, would seem to support Mayer's view that food supply is not a factor in the distribution of corals.

Some of the herbivorous fish move in over the reef flat on an incoming tide and out again on a receding tide. It might therefore be expected that grazing pressure would be lightest on those areas furthest from the edge of the reef, thus allowing a heavier algal development in the inshore reef waters. Although the larger of the inshore algae, such as *Sargassum* spp., show no obvious indication of being grazed, it is possible that control of some species would be effected at the juvenile phase.

In the atoll environment Palumbo (1962) concluded that temperature variations were "probably not enough to account for the distributional differences of the organism present." Published data on temperature variation over the reef flat in the Capricorn and Bunker Groups are lacking but Mayer (1918) has made interesting observations at Murray Island at the northern extremity of the Great Barrier Reefs. He found that from September to October the range of temperature fluctuation of reef flat waters increased towards the shore, being 12.5°C near the beach. He considered it likely that water temperatures during the hot calms of January would be sufficient to kill all corals within 137 m of the shore. On the basis of experiments on the thermal death points of corals, he concluded that the temperature factor alone was sufficient to account for certain corals being confined to the seaward part of the reef.

The vigorous coral development of the moat is possibly explainable on the basis of greater turbulence, at least as the incoming tide first flows over the rubble crest. However, the smaller temperature fluctuations that could be expected to occur here because of the usually deeper water as compared with the middle reef flat may be a favoring factor.

If once the balance were tipped in favor of either algae or coral, it might be speculated that the favored group might assist in maintaining or increasing its dominance; a vigorous algal development might inhibit settlement and development of coral planulae by occupying available substrata, by shading, or by the mechanical sweeping action of the wave-moved thallus. Antibiotic activity of algae, demonstrated for several marine species, might also inhibit coral development particularly on the reef flat in the shallow, relatively still water occurring at low tide. In this regard, of particular interest is the work of Sieburth and Conover (1965) who showed that tannins in the apical parts of *Sargassum* spp. in the Sargasso Sea retarded fouling of the plants and that hydroids were particularly sensitive to this activity.

On the other hand, increased growth of coral following some favoring influence might possibly lead to progressive reduction of algal growth. Since algal spores do not survive on living coral, it follows that the higher the proportion of living coral the less substratum there is available for algal growth; however, except in some areas of exceptionally rich coral growth, there are always considerable areas of dead coral available for algal colonization, so that unavailability of substratum would seem to be no more than a minor factor in the relative distributions of algae and coral. If the coral itself has any effect on this distribution, it is more likely to be through the production of antibiotic substances. That such a possibility is worthy of consideration seems to be indicated by the work of Ciereszko (1962) who showed that zooxanthellae of two species of gorgonians contained a substance, crassin acetate, which had a toxic action on parrot fish and inhibited the development of sea urchin eggs at a concentration of 10 ppm. The flamingo tongue snail, one of the few predators of the gorgonians, appeared to be resistant to crassin acetate. Ciereszko suggested that the secretion of this and other terpenes by the zooxanthellae may prevent the settlement on the gorgonians of the larvae of other animals. Should the zooxanthellae of corals produce an antibiotic or antibiotics inhibiting the settlement or development of algal spores in their vicinity, this could, in part, explain the relative distribution of algae and coral on the reef. However, antibiotic production by either coral or algae, if it occurs at all, is almost certainly only one of several ecological factors, as yet imperfectly understood, whose interaction determines the distribution of organisms over the reef flat.

The absence of corals from the reef rock slope, except in locally favored positions, is explainable by their lack of tolerance to the degree of emergence experienced at this tidal level. Algae, as a group, survive considerably longer periods of emergence, and numerous species are found here. However, some of the species are present in dwarfed condition and this dwarfing may be caused both by their inability to survive if protruding beyond the mutually protective company of other species in the mat and by the heavy grazing of herbivorous fish, which, unless particularly selective, would be likely to crop any protuberants. However, that the fish do show some degree of selectivity seems to be indicated here by the common occurrence of bushy plants of *Laurencia obtusa* var. *snackeyi*, commonly to 30 cm high, one of the very few algae of such stature to be found on the reef rock slope.

The seaward platform appears to be topographically comparable with the *Lithothamnion* rim or algal ridge of windward Pacific atolls. Powerful surf is a prerequisite for the formation of this latter structure, and it is absent or poorly developed on leeward reefs and, as reported by

Umbgrove (1947), in the land-locked seas of the East Indies. The vigorous growth of lithothamnia of the seaward platform could well be explained on the basis of their metabolism requiring the physiologically rich habitat provided in this area of turbulence where rapid changing of the medium reduces the need for diffusion of either nutrients or waste products and prevents the settlement of sediment. However, it is not so easy to explain the absence or paucity of noncalcareous algae. On the basis of the vegetation found on mainland rocky shores, a vigorous growth of fleshy algae such as *Sargassum* spp. and *Laurencia* spp. could be expected here. The work of Ciereszko (1962) noted above leads to speculation that the usually rich coral development here produces some inhibitory substance or substances that might control the development of fleshy algae, probably in the sporeling stage; lithothamnia would need to show a rather different response. However, the failure of fleshy algae to show a corresponding increase in those areas of the seaward platform only sparsely occupied by coral seems to make the idea of coral-based inhibition untenable as an explanation for the observed biotic distribution. Perhaps the lithothamnia could be considered as a source of some inhibiting substance, but there seems to be, as yet, no evidence of this.

More intensive fish grazing, consequent on its lower tidal level and proximity to large fish populations in the adjacent waters, may be a factor, but seems unconvincing when one considers the dense carpet of algae only a few meters away at a slightly higher level on the reef rock slope where heavy fish grazing is known to occur.

Either coral or lithothamnia may overgrow the other, but hardly anything is known of this struggle. Perhaps confrontations between two particular species usually lead to the same result; perhaps a factor in the environment will favor one competitor of a pair while in a different environment the other member would be successful; possibly some inhibitory substance is produced by one or both competitors, or perhaps the result is decided in some cases by an advantage in growth rate. Although in the Capricorn and Bunker Groups representatives of the two groups often appear fairly evenly matched, with perhaps the advantage more often to the corals, this may not be the case in all areas; at the seaward edge of the reef at the Funafuti Atoll, Finckh (1904) found that "The *Lithothamnion* by no means confines itself to lifeless material, everything that crosses its path is overgrown and overpowered." He concluded that "The only true destroyer of coral, and its great competitor, is the *Lithothamnion*. It kills by smothering." However Setchell

(1924) at Tutuila Island seemed doubtful of Finckh's claim and could find no evidence of living corals being attacked by lithothamnia.

VI. Algae in Destruction of the Reef

Intertidal calcareous material is well known to suffer severe erosion, and on a coral reef much of the carbonate is heavily surface pitted or so penetrated by pores and channels that it is almost spongelike in texture. The causes of marine erosion of carbonates appear to be complex and varied and have been a matter of some debate. Murray (1880) and Gardiner (1931b) considered solution able to account for the formation of atoll lagoons, an idea now generally rejected. Fairbridge (1948) suggested that solution could be explained by the increased solubility of carbon dioxide in the cooler nighttime waters where carbon dioxide would accumulate in the absence of algal photosynthesis. However, Newell and Rigby (1957) stated that "there is no convincing evidence that the circulating water of a lagoon or reef flat becomes undersaturated at night" and concluded that "it has not yet been demonstrated beyond reasonable doubt that surface sea water in the tropics is an effective solvent of limestone." Both Kuenen (1950) and Umbgrove (1947) considered chemical solution to be an important erosive agent in the intertidal area, but Ginsburg (1953) regarded solution by intertidal seawater as unlikely. Ranson (1955a) was more emphatic saying, "L'action chemique de la mer est nulle."

Many authors have stressed the importance of biological agencies, and Ginsburg (1953), who has reviewed the subject, came to the conclusion "that physico-chemical solution is probably not the most important process of intertidal erosion . . . ." Rasping and boring organisms remove significant quantities of calcareous material, and their effect is seen in the thorough perforation of much reef carbonate and in the obvious surface abrasions caused by radular rasping of mollusks and by the grazing of fish. Such surface abrasions have been noted by Stephenson and Searles (1960) on beach rock at Heron Island, and Otter (1937) has given an account of rock destroying animals at Low Isles.

Much of the surface abrasion is indirectly the result of algal colonization, the plants being sought as food by fish and mollusks, with the removal of carbonate substratum being, in a sense, accidental. Cloud (1952) has stressed the contribution made by some herbivorous fish to reef sedimentation, i.e., the layers of calcium carbonate scraped off with algae during feeding being later defecated as clouds of fine sediment.

However, algae are also commonly considered to play a direct part in erosion of calcareous reef material. Duerden (1902) reviewed earlier references to the subject and concluded that penetrating or boring algae played "an important, if not the most important, part in the disintegration of coral masses." Gardiner (1931b) likewise stressed the importance of these algae, regarding them as the chief boring organisms of coral reefs and of major importance in their shaping. Since that time numerous workers have recognized the destructive effect of such algae. Weber-van Bosse (1932) made a detailed systematic study of algae penetrating coral in the East Indies, finding twenty species distributed among the Cyanophyta, Chlorophyta, Phaeophyta, and Rhodophyta.

Ranson (1955a) made the surprising observation that *Porolithon onkodes* (Heydrich) Foslie, generally regarded as the major or one of the major algal reef builders, dissolves calcareous material over which it develops, and remarked, "Ce sont les plus grands ennemis des coraux." In this connection it is interesting that Weber-van Bosse (1932) had earlier found *Porolithon onkodes* in the form of anastomosing strands penetrating coral skeletons, although she was unable to say whether the alga was penetrating in the true sense of removing calcium carbonate or whether it was simply occupying existing cavities in the coral.

In the Capricorn and Bunker Groups, almost all intertidal calcareous material, including the skeletons of living corals, the shells of many living mollusks and the lower parts of lithothamnian crusts, is penetrated by microscopic, filamentous algae. The surface of alga-invaded material is stained brown, gray, or blue-green, and fracturing of the material usually reveals a somewhat brighter green or blue-green subsurface zone, which decalcification reveals to be thoroughly penetrated by algal filaments. In the Capricorn and Bunker Groups, the common penetrating species of the beach rock is *Entophysalis deusta*, while over the reef flat this species is joined by several others including *Mastigocoleus testarum* Lagerh., *Ostreobium reineckei* Born. in Reinb., and the basal, penetrating filaments of *Acetabularia moebii*.

Little is known of the variation in susceptibility to penetration of carbonates from different sources. Echinoderm material has not been examined in the Great Barrier Reefs but was stated by Duerden (1902) to be free from algal invasion, while Ginsburg (1957) reported that boring blue-green algae attack skeletal debris differently, with coral skeleton being more susceptible than the denser lithothamnia.

In spite of the almost universal occurrence of penetrating algae in reef carbonate and the common assumption that they have a role in erosion, there is still little precise information on their quantitative importance or on the mechanism by which they effect erosion. Penetrating algae are generally assumed to cause solution through the production of organic acids or through lowering of the pH as a result of nighttime respiration unaccompanied by photosynthesis. Although this does not seem to have been conclusively demonstrated for boring algae, Emery (1946) has shown erosion of intertidal basins in Californian sandstone stems from solution of calcite cement as a result of nighttime respiration of contained algae and snails; snails then removed the softened surface by radular rasping. Newell and Rigby (1957) considered undercutting of intertidal carbonate in the Bahamas to be caused by mollusks which cut away the surface greatly softened by boring algae.

It would seem reasonable to expect that penetration of the material by numerous algal filaments would result in some weakening of the matrix. However, at the same time, it has been pointed out by Ginsburg (1953) that "All the rock affected by intertidal erosion has a superficial hardening to a depth of a half-inch or less." Emery and Cox (1956) have shown that the surface hardening of beach rock is correlated with the more complete filling of pores by carbonate cement near the surface. It is not yet clear whether this hardening is related in any way to the presence of penetrating algae, but Ginsburg (1953) pointed to the possibility that precipitation of calcium carbonate in pools as a result of algal photosynthesis may not be loosely attached as Emery (1946) claimed but may instead occur as an interstitial cement giving the rock its characteristic surface hardness. However, in view of the work of Goreau (1963), which showed that some algae can calcify rapidly in darkness, the deposition of calcium carbonate by algae is obviously, at least in some cases, more complex than simply the result of utilization of carbon dioxide in photosynthesis leading to a rise in alkalinity.

The green staining commonly observed within the skeletons of living corals is, in the Capricorn and Bunker Groups, attributable to *Ostreobium reineckei*. The role of such algae is largely unknown. Odum and Odum (1955), working on Eniwetok Atoll, estimated that the average living coral colony contained 3 times as much plant as animal tissue and that only about 6% was contributed by zooxanthellae, with the rest contributed by filamentous green algae of the skeleton. These workers suggested that the algae may be in symbiotic relationship with the coral and, rather than weakening the skeleton, may contribute directly to skeleton formation. However, Goreau and Goreau (1960), working in

Jamaica, found that in *Manicina areolata* (L) the content of filamentous boring algae was much less than that estimated by Odum and Odum.

VII. Algae in Construction of the Reef

The destruction of calcareous reef material leads, in turn, to construction through sedimentation, probably the main constructional process in lagoons and reef flats. Examination of sediments and drilling cores have often revealed a high proportion of algal material, particularly of lithothamnia and *Halimeda*. For example, Maxwell (1968) recorded the lithothamnioid algae as comprising 17–40% and *Halimeda* 10–30% of surface sediments in some parts of the Great Barrier Reefs. Finckh (1904) found the lagoon floor at Funafuti Atoll to consist of nearly pure *Halimeda* sand, while lithothamnia and *Halimeda* ranked first and second, respectively, in abundance among reef-forming organisms in the borings. Taylor (1950) remarked on the confirmation provided by the Funafuti borings of what seemed obvious to him on Marshall Islands' reefs. While the proportions of the various constituents in sediments may reflect their proportions on the living reef at the time of deposition, it would be dangerous to assume that this would always be so; account must be taken of the growth rates of the various constituents, of their solubilities, and of the differing effects on them of various destructive agencies.

Among the calcified genera of the Great Barrier Reefs, the most important in reef building on the basis of examination of both sediments and the living plants on the reef, appear to be species of lithothamnia and of *Halimeda*. Lithothamnia contribute to reef building also at their site of growth where they impart both bulk and stability. Several authors, including Howe (1912) and Setchell (1926a, 1928, 1930b), have emphasized this function of lithothamnia in reef building; some, such as Gardiner (1906, 1931a), Finckh (1904), and Setchell (1926a, 1928, 1930a), have suggested that corals can form true reefs only with the stabilizing cooperation of lithothamnia.

The important contribution made by organisms other than coral to the building of calcareous reefs has led some authors to prefer the term "biotic reef" to the better known "coral reef," while the diverse meanings given to the word reef led Cumings and Shrock (1928) and Cumings (1932) to propose the term "bioherm," which, so far, has received only limited acceptance.

The development of lithothamnia varies not only from reef to reef but in different parts of the same reef, showing maximum development commonly at or near the seaward margin of the reef. In windward atoll reefs of the Pacific members of this group, particularly *Porolithon onkodes,* form the main constructional material of the often described *Lithothamnion* rim or algal ridge, which constitutes the seaward edge of the intertidal reef and withstands the crash of the breaking waves where most corals are unable to survive, and where, as Gardiner (1931a) expressed it, "is waged a perpetual struggle between the destructive force of the breakers and the constructive growth of organisms."

In the Capricorn and Bunker Groups, encrusting lithothamnia are common over much of the reef but are best developed in the seaward platform. Although not reaching the degree of luxuriance and dominance reported for the algal ridge in windward atoll reefs of the Pacific, no one who has seen their development even here would be likely to doubt their constructional and stabilizing importance. Although these functions of lithothamnia are widely recognized, there is, as with the destructive algae, a dearth of precise information on the contribution other than that relating to the composition of sediments. Obviously, the algal veneer protects dead coral surfaces from waterborne, physical erosion and from the grazing of fish and mollusks. They are not themselves immune to grazing as is evidenced by the striations frequently seen over their surface, but, presumably, this damage is readily repairable. However, it is not clear to what extent, if any, the algal "skin" gives protection to the underlying material from the activities of boring animals and algae. Certainly the latter are not excluded and may frequently be found penetrating the lower parts of the lithothamnia themselves. The rigid algal casing appears to give considerable added strength to coral branches, probably enabling them to withstand greater wave forces than would otherwise be the case, but the extent of the added strength is unknown. Lithothamnia gives the general impression of frequently being denser and harder than the coral skeletons they envelop, but there seems to be no quantitative information on this aspect. Kuenen (1950) attributed the relatively greater resistance of lithothamnia to solution and mechanical wave action, at least partly, to a higher content (about 18%) of magnesium carbonate. The aragonite of which coral is composed is about 1.5 times more soluble than calcite, the form of calcium carbonate in lithothamnia.

While there have been several studies on the growth rates of corals, little is known of the growth rates of the lithothamnia. Emery *et al.* (1949) suggested that growth of lithothamnia is most rapid in the zone of violent surf; it is probably reasonable to assume most rapid growth where an organism appears most dominant, but no comparative measurements have been made. Umbgrove (1947), also, stated that a coral reef grows more vigorously on the windward side of a reef than on the leeward side, although he was considering corals rather than algae. He attributed the more rapid growth in windward areas to reduced sedimentation. Munk and Sargent (1954) suggested that "windward reef faces may be nearly in equilibrium under conditions of rapid growth and erosion . . . ." However, actual measurements of growth rates are needed; it might be suggested that the dense compact growth on windward reefs is well adapted to the prevailing conditions and is not necessarily rapidly eroded and replaced by correspondingly rapid growth. The only attempt at actual measurement of lithothamnian growth rates in reefs seems to be that of Finckh (1904) who, at Funafuti Atoll, was, in most cases, unable to demonstrate any increase in crustaceous lithothamnia over a period of 5 months; however, some particularly thin, isolated crusts were found to have an average increase in diameter of 2.5 cm in 10 months and a maximum rate of 2.5 cm in 6.56 months. Gardiner (1931b) reported, without explanation, a rate of marginal growth of over 20 mm in 4 weeks for an encrusting form. Setchell (1924, 1926b) suggested an annual increase in thickness of about 0.2–0.3 mm in *Porolithon onkodes*, but this seems to have been based on measurements of growth layers, obvious in vertical sections of some lithothamnia, and the assumption that one layer is produced annually.

It seems clear that algae play an important part in both construction and destruction of coral reefs. However, as yet remarkably little is known of the contributions of the various constructive and destructive factors whose complex interaction results in the approximate equilibrium found on many coral reefs.

VIII. Terrestrial Algae

None of the cays of the Capricorn and Bunker Groups carries natural, permanent fresh water, but subaerial algae are well developed. Almost all coral shingle and boulders above extreme high water of spring tides are stained gray to gray-brown by a layer of blue-green algae, "the first coat of paint Nature gives to the earth" as Baas Becking (1951) described subaerial cyanophytic layers. Ranson (1955b), less romantically, likened this staining in the Tuamotu Archipelago to that of blackened walls in great industrial towns. The principal constituents of this layer are *Anacystis montana* and *Scytonema hofmanni* C. Ag. ex Born. and Flah., with the former showing the greater tolerance of insolation and desiccation. In partially shaded situations other species such as

Nostoc sp., *Trentepohlia lagenifera* (Hildebrand) Wille, and *Hormidium subtile* (Kuetz.) Heering may join these pioneers. Disturbance of the shingle sometimes reveals the shaded surfaces stained green by a thin, encrusting layer of *Pseudendoclonium submarinum*.

Sand immediately above extreme high water, usually supporting strand species such as *Spinifex hirsutus* Labill., *Thuarea involuta* (Forst.) R. and S., and *Lepturus repens* R. Br., is often weakly compacted by algae, mainly *Nostoc* sp. Although usually invisible on superficial examination, slight disturbance of the surface reveals the algae forming a friable, dull-green crust, 2–4 mm thick, in which the fragments are weakly coherent as a result of the presence of numerous microscopic colonies. It seems likely that this stabilization, weak as it is, plays some part in limiting wind-induced sand movement in the area. Little is known as yet of the contribution *Nostoc* and other heterocystous cyanophytes may make to the nitrogen economy of the impoverished substrata of coral cays.

Elsewhere on the cays, sand-inhabiting algae are localized, usually within the *Pisonia grandis* R. Br. forest and mostly in positions stabilized and enriched by excrement from sea birds roosting or nesting in the branches above. Here, species such as *Chlorococcum* sp., *Hormidium subtile*, and various members of the Oscillatoriaceae form small green or blue-green patches, but heterocystous cyanophytes are absent.

The pale, smooth trunks of *Pisonia grandis* support localized, contrasting dark patches of blue-green algae, mainly *Anacystis montana*, often restricted to roughened and presumably more water-retentive areas of the bark; in some cases the trunk base is enveloped in a short black, stockinglike encrustation extending up for 30 cm. On *Pandanus* sp., water trapped in the overlapping leaf bases on the crown and slowly escaping induces, on some trees, the growth of a black streak of filamentous cyanophytes down one side of the trunk.

Brackish pools, mostly not over 30 cm deep, which occur on some cays, carry only a small macroscopic algal flora, which may include *Enteromorpha clathrata*, *Rhizoclonium implexum* (Dillw.) Kuetz., and *Cladophorella calcicola* Fritsch, with the last-mentioned species usually epiphytic on dead stems of marginal vascular plants such as *Sesuvium portulacastrum* L.

IX. Floristics

One used to the rich algal flora of cool temperate shores, might, on first acquaintance with the algae of a coral reef, share the disappointment of Jukes (1847), naturalist on *H.M.S. Fly*, on his first sight of a coral reef in the Capricorn Group. "It looked simply like a half drowned mass of dirty brown sandstone, on which a few stunted corals had taken root; . . . I confess I was much disappointed with the first view of a coral reef, both as to its beauty and richness in animal life."

Jukes' unfavorable impression was a false one with regard to the animal life of the Great Barrier Reefs, which is exceptionally rich and diverse. However, the algal vegetation is relatively meager both as to bulk and number of species. There are no members of the Laminariales, the largest algae being members of the Fucales, *Cystoseira trinode* (Forssk.) J. Ag. and *Sargassum* spp., which occasionally reach 1 m in length but are usually considerably smaller. Foliose rhodophytes are poorly developed and the few which occur, such as *Hypoglossum* sp., are mainly obscured in shaded crevices, the only habitat on the reef where most rhodophytes appear distinctly red. The majority of species do not exceed 6 cm in height and many are considerably smaller. This small size coupled with the generally brownish to dull olive-fawn color and the often partly obscuring sand, sediment, or epiphytic Foraminifera results in the fleshy algae, in general, making a relatively inconspicuous contribution to the biota.

Unfortunately, for most parts of the Great Barrier Reefs floristic lists are not sufficiently complete to allow satisfactory comparisons to be made either with other areas or among different parts of the Great Barrier Reefs. However, for the Capricorn and Bunker Groups it is possible to make a reasonable estimate of the number of species present as being in the vicinity of 230. Without knowing the degree of thoroughness with which areas have been investigated, comparisons of floristic lists are of doubtful value, but comparison of this Capricorn-Bunker figure with the following suggests that the flora of the area is roughly comparable with other tropical, coral reef areas: Dawson (1956), Southern Marshall Islands, 146 (excluding Cyanophyta); Dawson (1957), Eniwetok Atoll, 219; Hackett (1969), Maldive Islands, 320; Howe (1918), Bermuda, 227; Setchell (1926b), Tahiti, 149; Taylor (1950), Northern Marshall Islands, 145 (excluding Cyanophyta); Womersley and Bailey (1970), Solomon Islands, 243. For the whole of the Great Barrier Reefs area the Capricorn-Bunker figure could probably be increased by 100.

The great majority of species known from the Great Barrier Reefs are widely distributed in the tropical Pacific or Indo-Pacific region, and the proportion of endemic species is almost certainly very low, probably no more than 2–3% at the most. This is in striking contrast to the southern Australian region where, in a flora of over 1000 species. Womersley (1959) has found a high degree of endemism amounting to 32%.

Another point of contrast between the southern Australian region and the Great Barrier Reefs is the relatively poor development of Rhodophyta in the latter area. In the southern Australian region the number of rhodophyte species is nearly 8 times the number of chlorophyte species, while in the Capricorn and Bunker Groups there are less than twice as many rhodophytes as chlorophytes.

Wells (1955, 1969) has shown an attenuation southward of the coral fauna of the Great Barrier Reefs resulting from constant subtraction from the maximum variety in the north without any substitution of species; of the 59 genera recorded in the northern part between lat. 9°–17°S, only 25 remain at lat. 24.5°S at the southern end. A careful comparison of northern and southern algal floras of the Great Barrier Reefs is not yet possible, but the majority of species found in the Capricorn and Bunker Groups in the south and at Low Isles in the north are common to both areas. Any loss or gain of species in either direction is very small compared with that recorded for corals. This is perhaps a somewhat surprising condition in view of the distances involved.

References

Baas Becking, L. G. M. (1951). *Proc., Kon. Ned. Akad. Wetensch.*, Ser. *C* **54**, 213.

Ciereszko, L. S. (1962). *Trans. N.Y. Acad. Sci.* [2] **24**, 502.

Cloud, P. E. (1952). *Atoll Res. Bull.* No. 12, p. 1.

Cloud, P. E. (1954). *Sci. Mon.* **79**, 195.

Cooper, M. J. (1966). *Pac. Sci.* **20**, 137.

Cribb, A. B. (1965). *Proc. Roy. Soc. Queensl.* **77**, 53.

Cribb, A. B. (1966). *Univ. Queensl. Pap., Heron Isl. Res. Sta.* **1**, 1.

Cribb, A. B. (1969). *Queensl. Natur.* **19**, 85.

Crossland, C. (1928). *Proc. Zool. Soc. London* No. 27, p. 717.

Cumings, E. R. (1932). *Geol. Soc. Amer., Bull.* **43**, 331.

Cumings, E. R., and Shrock, R. R. (1928). *Geol. Soc. Amer., Bull.* **39**, 579.

Dawson, E. Y. (1956). *Pac. Sci.* **10**, 25.

Dawson, E. Y. (1957). *Pac. Sci.* **11**, 92.

Dawson, E. Y. (1963). *Smithson. Inst., Annu. Rep.* Publ. No. 4551, p. 365.

Duerden, J. E. (1902). *Bull. Amer. Mus. Natur. Hist.* **16**, 323.

Emery, K. O. (1946). *J. Geol.* **54**, 209.

Emery, K. O., and Cox, D. C. (1956). *Pac. Sci.* **10**, 382.

Emery, K. O., Tracey, J. I., and Ladd, H. S. (1949). *Trans. Amer. Geophys. Union* **30**, 55.

Emery, K. O., Tracey, J. I., and Ladd, H. S. (1954). *U.S., Geol. Surv., Prof. Pap.* **260–A**, 1.

Fairbridge, R. W. (1948). *J. Roy. Soc. West. Aust.* **33**, 1.

Fairbridge, R. W. (1950). *J. Geol.* **58**, 330.

Fairbridge, R. W., and Teichert, C. (1947). *Rep. Gt. Barrier Reef. Comm.* **4**, 1.

Finckh, A. E. (1904). *In* "The Atoll of Funafuti. Borings into a Coral Reef and the Results," pp. 125–150. Royal Society, London.

Gardiner, J. S. (1906). *Nature (London)* **73**, 294.

Gardiner, J. S. (1931a). "Coral Reefs and Atolls." Macmillan, New York.

Gardiner, J. S. (1931b). *Proc. Linn. Soc. London, Sess.* **143**, Part 5, 65.

Ginsburg, R. N., (1953). *Bull. Mar. Sci. Gulf Carib.* **3**, 55.

Ginsburg, R. N. (1957). *Soc. Econ. Paleontol. Mineral., Spec. Publ.* **5**, 80.

Goreau, T. F. (1959). *Ecology* **4**, 67.

Goreau, T. F. (1963). *Ann. N.Y. Acad. Sci.* **109**, 126.

Goreau, T. F. (1964). *Science* **145**, 383.

Goreau, T. F., and Goreau, N. I. (1960). *Biol. Bull.* **118**, 419.

Hackett, H. E. (1969). *Proc. Int. Seaweed Symp., 6th, 1968* p. 187.

Hedley, C. (1925). *Rep. Gt. Barrier Reef Comm.* **1**, 35.

Howe, M. A. (1912). *Science* **35**, 837.

Howe, M. A. (1918). *In* "Flora of Bermuda" (N. L. Britton, ed.), pp. 489–540. Hafner, New York.

Jukes, J. B. (1847). "Narrative of the Surveying Voyage of H. M. S. Fly, Commanded by Captain F. P. Blackmore, R. N. ——," Vol. I. T. and W. Boone, London.

Kuenen, P. H. (1933). "Geology of Coral Reefs. The Snellius-Expedition," Vol. 5, Part 2, pp. 1–126. Kemink en Zoon N.V., Utrecht.

Kuenen, P. H. (1950). "Marine Geology." Wiley, New York

MacNeil, F. S. (1954). *Amer. J. Sci.* **252**, 385.

Manton, S. M., and Stephenson, T. A. (1935). *Sci. Rep. Gt. Barrier Reef Exped.* **3**, 273.

Maxwell, W. G. H. (1968). "Atlas of the Great Barrier Reef." Elsevier, Amsterdam.

Mayer, A. G. (1915). *Proc. Nat. Acad. Sci. U.S.* **1**, 211.

Mayer, A. G. (1918). *Carnegie Inst. Wash., Dep. Mar. Biol.* **9**, 1.

Munk, W. H., and Sargent, M. C. (1954). *U.S., Geol. Surv., Prof. Pap.* **260-C**, 274.

Murray, J. (1880). *Proc. Roy. Soc. Edinburgh* **10**, 505.

Newell, N. D. (1954). *Atoll Res. Bull.* No. 36, p. 1.

Newell, N. D. (1956). *Bull. Amer. Mus. Natur. Hist.* **109**, 311.

Newell, N. D., and Rigby, J. K. (1957). *Soc. Econ. Paleontol. Mineral., Spec. Publ.* **5**, 15.

Odum, H. T., and Odum, E. P. (1955). *Ecol. Monogr.* **25**, 291.

Otter, G. W. (1937). *Sci. Rep. Gt. Barrier Reef Exped.* **1**, 273.

Palumbo, R. F. (1962). *Proc. Pac. Sci. Congr., 9th, 1957* Vol. 4, p. 168.

Rainford, E. H. (1925). *Aust. Mus. Mag.* **2**, 175.

Ranson, G. (1955a). *C. R. Acad. Sci.* **240**, 806.

Ranson, G. (1955b). *C. R. Acad. Sci.* **240**, 1007.

Setchell, W. A. (1924). *Carnegie Inst. Wash., Publ.* **341**, 1.

Setchell, W. A. (1926a). *Proc. Amer. Phil. Soc.* **65**, 136.

Setchell, W. A. (1926b). *Univ. Calif., Berkeley, Publ. Bot.* **12**, 291.

Setchell, W. A. (1928). *Science* **68**, 119.

Setchell, W. A. (1930a). *Proc. Pac. Sci. Congr., 4th, 1929* p. 265.

Setchell, W. A. (1930b). *Proc. Nat. Acad. Sci. U.S.* **16**, 781.

Sieburth, J. McN., and Conover, J. T. (1965). *Nature (London)* **208**, 52.

Steers, J. A. (1930). *Sci. Rep. Gt. Barrier Reef Exped.* **3**, 1.

Steers, J. A. (1937). *Geogr. J.* **89**, 1.

Stephenson, T. A., Stephenson, A., Tandy, G., and Spender, M. (1931). *Sci. Rep. Gt. Barrier Reef Exped.* **3**, 17.

Stephenson, W., and Searles, R. B. (1960). *Aust. J. Mar. Freshwater Res.* **11**, 241.

Stephenson, W., Endean, R., and Bennett, I. (1958). *Aust. J. Mar. Freshwater Res.* **9**, 261.

Taylor, W. R. (1950). *Univ. Mich. Stud.* **18**, 1.

Tracey, J. I., Jr., Cloud, P. E., Jr., and Emery, K. O. (1955). *Atoll Res. Bull.* No. 46, p. 1.

Umbgrove, J. H. F. (1947). *Geol. Soc. Amer., Bull.* **58**, 729.

Weber-van Bosse, A. (1932). *Mem. Mus. Hist. Natur. Belg.* **6**, 1.

Wells, J. W. (1955). *Rep. Gt. Barrier Reef Comm.* **6**, 1.

Wells, J. W. (1969). *Micronesica* **5**, 317.

Womersley, H. B. S. (1959). *Bot. Rev.* **25**, 545.

Womersley, H. B. S., and Bailey, A. (1970). *Phil. Trans. Roy. Soc. London, Ser. B* **259**, 257.

Yonge, C. M. (1963). *Advan. Mar. Biol.* **1**, 290.

4

NUTRITION OF CORALS

Leonard Muscatine

I. Introduction

The history of coral physiology spans about 100 years and falls roughly into three stages. The first is characterized by the earliest work on chemical composition, growth, and ecology of corals and culminates in the Great Barrier Reef Expedition of 1928–1929, led by C. M. Yonge. The *Scientific Reports of the Great Barrier Reef Expedition* are still the most comprehensive and detailed source of information on the physiology of reef corals, especially feeding behavior and nutrition. These classical works review earlier literature and have undoubtedly set the stage for the second phase of historical development, carried out in the Dutch East Indies and at Palau in the 1930's and 1940's, and marked by work

77

on feeding, respiration, relationships with zooxanthellae, development and regeneration, tropisms, pigments, and the effects of light and sedimentation on growth of corals. The third and most recent stage of the development of physiology of corals is characterized by the contributions of the late T. F. Goreau on ecology and calcification of West Indian corals and by the contributions of a number of workers on quantitative ecology, general physiology, and biochemistry of corals from a wide range of localities. These efforts have given rise to reviews and monographs treating many aspects of coral physiology, but none has concentrated solely on nutritional physiology in its broadest sense. Consequently this chapter will deal with the feeding and nutrition of reef corals with emphasis on experimental work from 1928 to the present time. The term coral applies here mainly to hermatypic corals of the order Scleractinia, hermatypic implying that they are reef-building species and that they possess zooxanthellae (cf. Yonge, 1968). Since there is scant information on some aspects of scleractinian nutrition, attention is given to relevant studies on other anthozoan corals, especially reef-dwelling gorgonaceans, and octocorals of the order Alcyonacea as well as to relevant studies on other Cnidaria such as sea anemones and *Hydra*. This is done in the hope that such comparisons may help to elucidate obscure features of the nutritional physiology of hermatypic corals. Nutrition is defined here as the acquisition and processing of essential organic and inorganic bodily constituents that are utilized as energy sources and nutrients in promoting growth and maintenance (cf. Darnell, 1968).

II. Feeding Structures, Mechanisms, and Behavior

A. SUSPENSION FEEDING

Coral polyps are carnivorous, usually feeding in typical cnidarian fashion by means of tentacles laden with nematocysts, trapping zooplankton and transporting food to the mouth. When viewed as a colony with polyps expanded, corals present an enormous feeding surface in relation to the bulk of the living tissue, a fact that is thought to contribute to the success of this group (Yonge, 1968). This feeding surface, including the coenosarc between polyps, becomes a sticky, mucus-laden trap for food particles such as Protozoa and nanoplankton too small to be grasped by the tentacles. These particles are transported to the mouth in moving sheets of mucus (Goreau, 1956). For example, colonies of *Siderastrea radians* can "clear" themselves in less than 30 seconds of all food particles dropped on the colony surface (Goreau, 1956). This view of predation by coral colonies, as opposed to predation by individual polyps, has given rise to the erroneous impression that corals are filter-feeders. The careful statement of Yonge (1940, p. 356) that "The distended tentacles of an expanded coral colony constitutes as effective a mechanism for the collection of zooplankton as do the ciliary feeding mechanisms of the members of a bed of lamellibranchs for the collection of phytoplankton" has evolved to the position taken by Goreau (1956, p. 182) who stated that "The weight of the evidence now favors the view that the reef corals are primarily filter-feeders rather than active predators like Actiniaria." Roushdy and Hansen (1961) have described the alcyonacean *Alcyonium digitatum* as a filter-feeder. They introduced ^{14}C-labeled diatoms into the vessels containing *A. digitatum* and, after 30 minutes to 23 hours incubation, the medium showed significant reduction in radioactivity, more so than in controls without animals. Subsequently ^{14}C was detected in various fractions of the animal. Although the results indicate that these animals fed on phytoplankton, they do not conclusively demonstrate that *A. digitatum* is a filter-feeder. Other than the observation that there were "ciliary currents . . . in and out of the polyps," the details of the presumed filtration process were not described. Their statement that "this species can survive for relatively long periods of time in waters deficient in zooplankton" is insufficient evidence on its own from which to conclude that the corals normally feed on phytoplankton. More detailed and sustained efforts will be required to establish with certainty that these alcyonarians filter-feed on phytoplankton.

Filter-feeding may be defined generally as the collection of particulate food of varying particle size by a filtration mechanism consisting of a filter of variable construction, a water current, often produced by the animal itself, a means of recovering the food from the water and transporting it to the mouth, and an exit for the filtered water (Marshall and Orr, 1960). Corals do not, strictly speaking, cause the surrounding water to be passed through a filter that selects particles according to their size and shape. For this reason, they are perhaps better viewed as suspension feeders as defined by Jørgensen (1966). That is, corals rely on the passage of water over the feeding organs, trapping of suspended particulate matter being largely nonselective.

Feeding mechanisms displayed by individual coral polyps are best described by summarizing Yonge's (1930, 1937, 1940) accounts and interpretations together with relevant observations of Abe (1938), Goreau (1956), and others.

1. Tentacular Feeding: Cilia Concerned with Cleansing

Polyp tentacles exhibit a wide range of variation in number, size, and activity. They are arranged generally on the hexamerous plan. Most are of simple hollow construction except in the Siderastreidae where the endocoelic tentacles are bifurcated (Hyman, 1940; Goreau, 1956). Some, such as those of ahermatypic species, are relatively long and prehensile, capable of seizing and delivering prey to the mouth. Others, mostly possessed by hermatypic corals, are relatively short and less agile. These may be arranged in single or multiple circular rows of about 6–30 per row. Tentacles of most corals are retractile, but some are non-retractile as in *Stephanophyllia* and *Fungiacyathus* (Vaughan and Wells, 1943). Tentacles are absent from *Pachyseris* (Yonge, 1930).

Feeding by means of tentacles alone, as in Actiniaria, with cilia concerned only with cleansing, is considered by Yonge to be the primitive condition. This condition is found in solitary corals, mostly ahermatypic species with relatively large polyps and small skeleton (e.g., *Flabellum, Caryophyllia, Lophophelia, Balanophyllia*, and *Dendrophyllia*). Some large hermatypes (e.g., *Isophyllia*, astreids, meandrines except for fungiids) also exhibit raptorial feeding with tentacles. In this type of feeding, prey are trapped and immobilized on tentacles by nematocysts and the inward flexing of the tentacles conveys prey to the mouth (Fig. 1A).

Three basic types of nematocysts are uniformly present throughout the Scleractinia: spirocysts, microbasic mastigophores, and holotrichous isorhizas (glutinants) (Abe, 1938; Hyman, 1940; Goreau, 1956; Werner, 1965; Mariscal, 1971). These may vary in their dimensions and proportions among coral species. Generally, spirocysts, whose function is "enigmatic" (Hyman, 1940) are massed in tentacle batteries especially at tentacle tips, stomodaeal ridges, and the upper, straight portion of mesenterial filaments. Microbasic mastigophores (penetration, adhesion?) and holotrichous isorhizas (function uncertain) are encountered in tentacles and especially in batteries on the convoluted portion of the mesenterial filaments. Abe (1938) noted that microbasic mastigophores predominate in tentacles of those species expanded and showing a feeding response during the day (e.g., *Halomitra, Pavona, Pocillopora, Balanophyllia*), while holotrichous isorhizas seemed most common in tentacles of species expanded and feeding at night (*Herpetolitha, Oxypora, Echinopora, Hydnophora, Tridachophyllia*, and *Caulastrea*). The

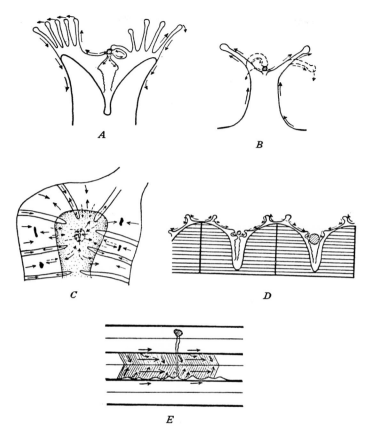

Fig. 1. Diagrams indicating the modes of feeding in hermatypic corals. (A) *Euphyllia*, with large polyps and all cilia beating away from the mouth; (B) *Pocillopora*, with small polyps and cilia carrying particles up the column; (C) *Merulina*, a meandrine with short tentacles and reversal of cilia (resultant current indicated by broken arrows); (D) *Coeloseris*, with all particles carried by cilia over the mouths for ingestion if edible and removal by water movements if not; (E) *Pachyseris*, mouths in rows within parallel grooves; no indication of tentacles but food collected by mesenterial filaments extruded through the mouth. Magnifications vary. From Yonge (1968).

significance of this observation, if true, is not at all clear. However, it is clear that the activity of tentacles in this type of feeding depends largely on the extent to which they are expanded. As pointed out by Yonge, the size of the polyps and calix is not necessarily indicative of the swallowing ability, since polyps with small coelenteron and prominent columella are capable of considerable expansion above the calix. On the other hand, polyps without a columella and possessing a large coelenteron rarely rise to any great height above the skeleton.

The environmental stimuli governing expansion or contraction of coral polyps have not been made clear experimentally. Before a nutritional role of zooxanthellae was established, it was assumed that corals relied solely on zooplankton for their nutrition. It seemed a logical adaptation that with greater availability of plankton at night corals would generally be expanded and feeding at this time. Indeed, Yonge (1930, 1940) and Stephenson (in Yonge, 1940) who give a comprehensive account of species expanded during day or night regarded nighttime expansion as the general rule, noting "exceptions" where daytime expansion was consistently observed (e.g., *Pocillopora*, *Euphyllia*, *Fungia actiniformis*, *Goniopora*). Abe (1938) also observed expansion and daytime feeding of some of these genera and in species of *Pavona* and *Balanophyllia* as well. Kawaguti (1954) attempted to correlate expansion with several factors including flood versus ebb tide, concentration of zooxanthellae, relative porosity of the skeleton, and environmental concentration of ammonia. Goreau (1956) stated that time of day, temperature, oxygen content of the water, presence of plankton or sediment, and hydrographic conditions may influence the state of expansion of corals. He especially noted that more coral polyps were expanded in the reef flats off Jamaica than on the reef slopes, and he correlated this with the warmer water of the flats and cooler water of the slopes. Expansion was also observed in the laboratory in water of low oxygen concentration. In the cases of *Astrangia danae* and *Phyllangia americana*, stirring the water caused expansion of polyps.

From observations on Jamaican corals, Goreau (1956) regarded the effect of light on expansion as "uncertain," since his extensive field and laboratory investigations did not entirely confirm a "negative photo-kinetic behavior" in all corals. Mussid, faviid, caryophylliid, and dendro-phylliid corals in captivity were observed expanded both in day and night under artificial or natural illumination. However, under the same conditions, these corals were contracted if starved. Goreau states that (1956, p. 37) "in the field, corals of nearly all Jamaican species have been observed in the expanded state irrespective of whether the day was dull or sunny, the water clear or turbid."

Wainwright (1967) consistently observed that the polyps of the soft coral *Gorgonia* expanded during the day and contracted at night when zooplankton were most abundant. Since *Gorgonia* possesses zooxan-thellae, daytime expansion was interpreted as an adaptation favoring photosynthesis by the symbiotic algae, presumed to be essential for the well-being of these corals. This interpretation remains as a testable hypothesis to explain the daytime expansion of some species of hermatypic corals, but more difficult to explain, as Yonge (1940) pointed out, is daytime contraction in hermatypic corals.

2. *Ciliary-Mucoid Feeding: Role of Tentacles Variable*

The ectoderm of the oral body wall of a coral consists of a single layer of cells of which four types may be distinguished (Matthai, 1923). One type, called a supportive cell by Goreau (1956), possesses cilia. The abundance of supportive cells in the epidermis of most corals gives rise to ciliary tracts. These tracts, developed to a much greater extent in corals than in Actiniaria, are used, together with mucus secreted from cells in oral disc ectoderm and stomodeum, in feeding and cleansing the surface of the coral (Yonge, 1930). Feeding in the majority of reef corals is aided by regionally specialized ciliary currents. They may run up or down the polyp column, inward near the mouth, and outward near the margin of the oral disc, inward and down at the mouth and pharynx, and from the base to tip on the tentacles (Hyman, 1940).

Ciliary currents in *Seriatopora, Pocillopora, Stylophora, Leptastrea, Cyphastrea,* and *Porites* are upward on the polyp column and outer side of tentacles. The posture of the tentacles then governs acceptance or rejection of particulate matter. In *Psammocora* and *Pavona,* which lack a column, food is captured by nematocysts in the coenosarc and conveyed by cilia to tentacles, which are still active in acceptance or rejection of food (Yonge, 1930; Fig. 1B).

Although tentacles of *Coeloseris mayori* (Agariciidae) capture particulate food, transport to the mouth is accomplished entirely by cilia. Rejected material is rolled into balls and ambient water movements are the principal cleansing forces in this shore-dwelling species (Fig. 1D; Yonge, 1930).

Pachyseris speciosa lacks tentacles entirely and its mouths have only limited ability to expand. Ciliary currents on the ridged surface of this coral convey particles in strings of mucus to the mouths where food is trapped by mesenterial filaments which wrap around prey. Owing to the small size of the coelenteron, digestion and absorption by mesenterial filaments take place outside the coelenteron (Fig. 1E). Finally, where tentacles are too small to bring food to the mouth or reject particles, as in meandrines, *Tridacophyllia lactuca, Merulina ampliata,* and most *Fungia* spp., ciliary currents are thought to reverse, so that the same ciliary tract may at one time act in food collection and at another as a rejection mechanism (Fig. 1C). Yonge (1940) noted that cilia may not assist feeding in such species as *Acropora*, which live at or near the reef surface where water is agitated.

3. *Extrusion of Mesenterial Filaments*

The mesenteries are the sites of digestion, assimilation, and excretion in coelenterates which possess them. The mesenteries in corals, as in other Anthozoa, are radially arranged partitions, each with a free medial side projecting into the coelenteron. This free margin is thickened into a so-called mesenterial filament that bears secretory and cnidoblast cells and extends from the stomodeum to the base of the polyp. The upper portion of the filament is straight while the lower portion is highly convoluted, giving rise to an enormous increase in length and surface area. Filaments of corals consist solely of a cnidoglandular band or filament and lack the lateral ciliated tracts seen in filaments of Actiniaria (Hyman, 1940). Some lateral processes are still evident in coral filaments (Abe, 1938; Goreau, 1956) as a result of hypertrophy of the gastrodermis just behind the septal filament, giving the appearance of lateral lobes but lacking the structure of actiniarian filaments (cf. Fig. 2).

Mesenterial filaments are mobile, undoubtedly owing to ciliary activity, and may creep through the mouth or through temporary openings of uncertain nature in the oral body wall and engage in extracoelenteric feeding activities. Goreau (1956) noted that extrusion is frequently localized at a point where a food particle may contact the ectoderm, the implication being that the stimulus for extrusion of filaments is tactile and chemical. Extrusion of filaments exclusively through the mouth was observed in *Astrangia danae* and *Phyllangia americana*, while extrusion through both the mouth and body wall was seen in many mussid species and in some faviid corals (e.g., *Diploria strigosa, Montastrea cavernosa*, and *Manicina areolata*). A piece of lobster muscle dropped on the oral disc of a polyp of *Mussa angulosa* stimulated the extrusion of filaments within 5–6 minutes. The tentacles remained contracted, but the mouth opened and within 15 minutes the food particles were "covered by a tangled mass of ivory white filaments." Closer investigation revealed that the particle of food gradually became translucent and was enveloped in mucus and "anchored" by nematocysts, which served to prevent it from being swept away by water currents. Even after the particle was removed, the mesenteries remained extruded for over an hour to a length of more than 10 centimeters. When the water was changed in the experimental container, the filaments began to retract and within 20 minutes none was visible. Whereas the impression gained from Yonge's (1930) initial observations is that extrusion of filaments is a

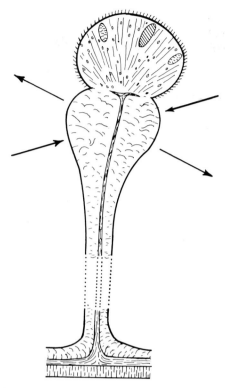

Fig. 2. Diagram of mesentery with terminal filament in transverse section. The filament is ciliated and has enzymatic and mucous glands. Both intake and excretion of particulate matter, as indicated by arrows, occurs in the region of the mesentery adjacent to the filament. From Yonge (1968).

specialized form of feeding in certain corals, his later reviews (1968) and Goreau's (1956) account maintain that feeding by extrusion of filaments, seen most frequently in mussid and faviid species, is more general and that its importance may have been overlooked by previous investigators.

B. Absorption of Soluble Organic Material from Solution

Many dissolved organic substances, ranging from free amino acids in solution to macromolecules, are present in aquatic habitats. Within the past several decades, there has been a resurgence of interest in, and inevitable skepticism about, the extent to which these substances contribute to animal nutrition (cf. Stephens, 1968). Evidence has been marshaled that suggests that corals and other coelenterates may supplement their nutritional requirements by taking up carbohydrates and amino acids present in crystalloidal solution in their environment, rather than similar molecules absorbed on particles. The matter of uptake will be discussed here; its significance will be treated in a later section. Initially, Stephens and Schinske (1961) examined 35 genera representing 11 phyla for their ability to remove amino acids from solution. Among the organisms they tested were several hydroids, anemones, an alcyonacean, and the coral *Astrangia danae*. They found that after 18–21 hours of incubation in seawater containing 2 mM glycine, 19–57% of the initial concentration had been removed from solution. By comparison with appropriate controls it was inferred that uptake stemmed from the presence of the animal. The evidence for absorption was still judged as indirect, since the animals themselves were not and, in fact, could not be analyzed for glycine enrichment. Subsequently, Stephens (1960a,b, 1962) obtained direct evidence by using isotopic tracer that specimens of *Fungia scutaria* of 30–45 gm wet weight could remove [^{14}C]glucose from solutions of which the initial concentrations ranged from 0.37–500 mg/liter. Uptake rates were the same in light or darkness with or without the antibiotic streptomycin. A blank control consisting of a clean skeleton incubated with labeled glucose showed no uptake. At glucose concentrations of 40–500 mg/liter about 1–2 mg of glucose were taken up per hour by a single specimen. Virtually all of the ^{14}C that disappeared from the solution was recovered in sodium hydroxide digests of the animal. Respired ^{14}CO$_2$ was not detected in the incubation medium after 4 hours incubation. Other experiments ruled out absorption by mucus as a possible concentrating mechanism. Plugging the mouth with paraffin did not significantly affect uptake, suggesting that the body wall was the site of uptake. Following this was the observation that 10^{-3} M phlorizin inhibited glucose uptake but not uptake of [^{14}C]glycine. Sucrose, galactose, ribose, and arabinose did not competitively inhibit uptake, and there was no evidence that these sugars themselves were taken up by *Fungia*. The interpretation put forward was that *Fungia scutaria* possesses a specialized mechanism for accumulation of glucose from solution. Stephens also demonstrated that 70–96% of [2-^{14}C]tyrosine, [2-^{14}C]lysine, [4-^{14}C]aspartic acid, and [2-^{14}C]glycine, in concentrations of 0.15–1.2 mg/liter were taken up in 4 hours by *Fungia*. Further, other corals (*Acropora* sp., *Favia speciosa*, and *Dendrophyllia micranthus*) absorbed glycine at significant rates, as did other invertebrates. Stephens carefully pointed out that this investigation established uptake as a fact, but did not reveal the fate of the glucose or its nutritional significance. He did calculate, however, that a concentration of 15 mg glucose per liter would be required to sustain 100% of the maintenance metabolism of *Fungia* as determined by its oxygen consumption. Such concentrations of a single substance such as glucose are unlikely to be encountered under natural conditions, but, as noted earlier, uptake is considered as an auxiliary capability rather than the sole mechanism of nutrient acquisition.

Recently several investigators have confirmed Stephens' work to the extent of verifying uptake of labeled substrates. Lewis and Smith (1971) incubated *Porites divaricata* in the dark in seawater containing low and high concentrations of glucose or glycerol. At low concentrations (1.2 μg/10 ml) uptake was rapid. After 4 hours, 80–90% of the total ^{14}C was removed from the medium while 57–63% was recovered in the coral tissues, the balance presumably lost by respiration. At high concentrations uptake of ^{14}C was apparently slower, resulting in removal of 32–35% from the medium and detection of 16–21% in the tissues after 4 hours. Lewis and Smith pointed out that removal of about one-third of the original glucose or glycerol supplied at high concentration (100 mg/10 ml) means that a 3.5 gm specimen (1.0 gm living tissue) of *P. divaricata* had taken up 30 mg of glucose or glycerol in 4 hours. One may conclude that corals have the ability to remove some substances from solution, but the extent to which this occurs in nature and its significance are not yet known. Observations supporting absorption as a feeding mechanism were made by Goreau (1956). He observed "intense" alkaline phosphatase activity in the ectoderm of corals which regularly display extrusion of mesenterial filaments and extracoelenteric digestion, and showed that these corals have microvilli on their ectodermal cells (Goreau and Philpott, 1956). Such corals may thus have an enormous surface area for absorption of extracoelenteric products of digestion and at least one group enzyme usually associated with membrane transport (see also Goreau *et al.*, 1971).

C. Role of Chemoreception in Feeding Behavior

The conclusion that the recognition of food is mediated chemically is inescapable from field observations on the response of corals and other coelenterates to food and from numerous accounts in the literature describing how food extracts elicit responses generally associated with feeding (e.g., mouth opening, flexing of tentacles). The topic of coelenterate chemoreception and the isolation and identification of the specific

substances in food that activate these feeding responses has been reviewed by Lenhoff (1968). Although particular attention has been given
to *Hydra* and other hydroids, there have been recent studies on anemones
(Lindstedt *et al.*, 1968) and corals (Mariscal and Lenhoff, 1968).

Abe (1938) described a mouth opening response by *Fungia* treated
with clam juice. A control in seawater alone gave no response. It was
not until recently that specific activators of the feeding response in corals,
including *Fungia*, have been identified. Mariscal and Lenhoff (1968)
studied the Hawaiian coral *Cyphastrea ocellina*. After trapping prey
organisms, *Cyphastrea* normally responds with brief contractions of the
tentacles and oral disc, followed immediately by mouth opening. Prey
are conveyed to the mouth by ciliary activity and muscular movements.
This same response could be elicited by one part of aqueous homogenates or extracts of either *Artemia* or plankton in 10,000,000 parts
seawater (Fig. 3). As in previous investigations of a similar nature,
Mariscal and Lenhoff sought to quantify the response in order to obtain
a reproducible bioassay to aid the identification of feeding activators.
They found that the response could be quantified in three ways: (1)
by recording mouth opening ($+$) or not ($-$); (2) by counting the
number of mouths open after an arbitrary time of 15 minutes; (3) by
counting the number of mouths open out of 50 at given intervals after
application of the stimulus. These criteria helped reveal that the constituent of *Artemia* homogenate that elicited a feeding response was heat
stable and soluble in 95% ethyl alcohol. Chromatographic analyses led
to the isolation of two active materials, identified as the imino acid
proline and the tripeptide, reduced glutathione (GSH). The proline
analog, pipecolic acid, proved as effective as proline, while hydroxy-
proline was only about one-hundredth as effective. Similarly, S-methyl
glutathione was equally as potent as GSH. Although the mouth opening
response to proline was one order of magnitude greater than that stimulated by corresponding amounts of GSH, the latter seemed effective
in stimulating extrusion of mesenterial filaments. Much remains to be
learned, however, about the stimuli associated with extrusion of
filaments.

Experiments with *Fungia* were somewhat less consistent. Proline always gave a response, but methionine, tyrosine, and GSH gave a response
only occasionally. Best results were obtained with assays using large
numbers of small stalked specimens. *Pocillopora damicornis* responded
to proline and GSH and occasionally to methionine and phenylalanine.
Mariscal and Lenhoff pointed out that most other coelenterates (e.g.,
Hydra, Cordylophora) for which activators are known respond to only

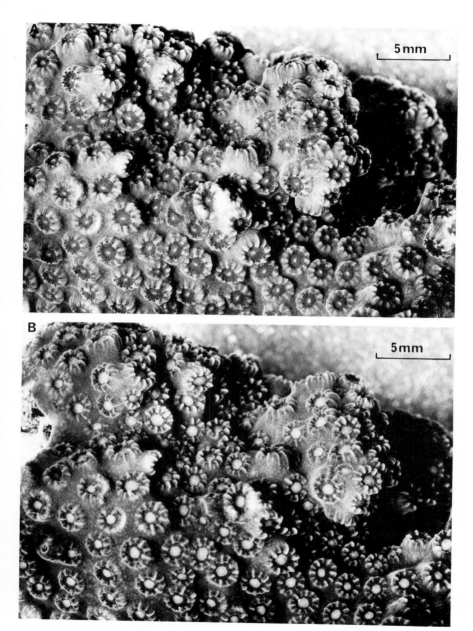

Fig. 3. (A) Photograph of a colony of *Cyphastrea ocellina* in natural seawater in the absence of any feeding activator. (Photo by R. N. Mariscal) (B) Photograph of the same colony of *Cyphastrea ocellina* in 10^{-3} M proline prepared in natural seawater. Note the wide mouth opening of each of the polyps. (Photo by R. N. Mariscal.) From Mariscal and Lenhoff (1968).

one substance. The response of *Cyphastrea* and other corals is the first known instance of a coelenterate responding to both an imino acid and a tripeptide. The behavioral sequence may be summarized as follows. Zooplankton contact the tentacles resulting in nematocyst discharge, trapping the prey, puncturing it, and causing release of body fluids containing proline and GSH. Simultaneously, the tentacles contract and fold in, bringing the prey near the mouth. The side of the mouth near the prey may often move toward it. As soon as the appropriate receptors are activated by proline and GSH, the mouth opens. The prey is moved to the mouth by ciliary activity, and muscular activity of the lips may aid in envelopment and swallowing of the prey. This investigation for the first time brings into sharp focus the general role of chemoreception in prey recognition and feeding by corals.

III. Food of Reef Corals

A. INORGANIC NUTRIENTS

1. Phosphorus, Nitrogen, Calcium

A principle nutrient limiting productivity in the marine environment is phosphorus (Johannes *et al.*, 1970). The manner in which corals acquire phosphorus in a nutrient-poor environment is not thoroughly understood nor are the phosphorus requirements of reef corals known. The experimental observations of Yonge and Nicholls (1931a), Pomeroy and Kuenzler (1969), and Yamazato (1966) show, by colorimetric assays and employment of radioactive isotopes, that corals can take up phosphate ions from the environment. The same techniques also show that phosphorus is excreted. Two factors influence the rate of excretion: metabolic rate and presence of zooxanthellae. Corals are unusual in that they excrete phosphorus more slowly than other invertebrates of comparable tissue weight (Pomeroy and Kuenzler, 1969). The prevailing view is that the presence of zooxanthellae helps to retain phosphorus within the coral possibly by recycling and that phosphorus from zooplankton is required to offset losses through excretion. This role of zooxanthellae is discussed in detail later in this chapter. Nitrogen is available to corals in the form of organic nitrogen (from plankton) and as ammonia, nitrate, nitrite, and dissolved organic nitrogen. Corals can absorb ammonia (Kawaguti, 1953) and organic nitrogen (Stephens, 1962), but their nutritional significance is not known. The possibility of nitrate reduction by zooxanthellae seems unlikely, but it has not yet been investigated. Some nitrogen is lost from corals as free amino acids along with products of protein catabolism presumed to be ammonia (Johannes and Webb, 1972). Zooxanthellae have been shown to release alanine *in vivo* (Lewis and Smith, 1971). This raises the possibility that, if ammonia excreted by the coral is accumulated by zooxanthellae, the nitrogen could be returned to the coral as amino acid. This would have the net effect of conserving nitrogen within the coral (Muscatine, 1971; Lewis and Smith, 1971). Nitrogen fixation and its contribution to nitrogen metabolism of a reef community have not yet been investigated directly. However, the widespread occurrence of blue-green algae in reef communities raises questions concerning nitrogen fixation and its fate.

Corals can absorb calcium from seawater as has been demonstrated using ^{45}Ca (Goreau and Goreau, 1959a). Since calcium is abundant in the environment, corals do not necessarily depend on food as a source of calcium. Similarly, both metabolic and environmental bicarbonate provide a source of carbonate for skeletogenesis. Pearse (1970, 1971), by feeding corals meat labeled with ^{14}C, obtained direct evidence that metabolic carbon dioxide is used in the formation of skeletal calcium carbonate.

B. ORGANIC SOURCES

1. Zooplankton

That reef corals can feed on zooplankton is indisputably supported by numerous laboratory and field observations. For example, specimens of *Fungia, Goniastrea, Psammocora, Galaxea,* and *Cyphastrea* fed by Yonge and Nicholls (1931b) in the laboratory for up to 228 days both in the light and in darkness remained in apparently good condition without diminution of tissues. On the other hand, tissues of starved corals were observed to shrink. Wainwright (1967) observed *Montastrea cavernosa* and *Diploria strigosa* catching and ingesting zooplankton on the reef at night as did Johannes *et al.* (1970) in their nocturnal observations on Bermuda corals. Coles (1969) fed *Artemia* nauplii to *Manicina areolata, Montastrea cavernosa,* and *Porites porites* over 10-hour periods in the laboratory, and then calculated the calories ingested per day (I) and the calories respired per day (R). Observed ratios (I/R) of from 1.6 to 6.6 suggested that these coral species are potentially capable of subsisting entirely on such plankton rations. Along with zooplankton corals can also feed on "dead or moribund" animal material (Yonge, 1968). However, other observations on scleractinians, octocorals, and reef communities question the extent to which zooplankton alone support the energy and nutrient requirements of corals in nature. These observations usually infer a nutritional role of zooxanthellae (treated in a later section), although in most cases there was no experimental evidence for such a role. Early views were summarized by Boschma (1925). For example, Pratt (1905) described the morphological "reduction" of the digestive areas in the octocorals *Lobophytum, Sarcophyton, Alcyonium*, and *Sclerophytum*, correlating this in each species with an increase in numbers of zooxanthellae. Pratt conjectured that the needs of growing colonies of *Sclerophytum* could not be satisfied by the small amount of zooplankton actually captured and that nutrition of these species was supported by zooxanthellae. Gohar (1940, 1948) added members of the family Xeniidae to the species observed by Pratt as having a rich flora of zooxanthellae and also noted that xeniids lacked digestive zones of the mesenterial filaments. These animals were never observed to feed in the laboratory or in the field or to trap and paralyze zooplankters brought into contact with the surface of the animal. Since pulsating colonies ceased to move when placed in the dark but resumed movement when returned to the light, Gohar conjectured that "combustible energy-giving material" is normally supplied by zooxanthellae, rather than zooplankton. Wainwright (1967) reported that *Gorgonia* expanded during the day when plankton was scarce but remained contracted at night showing little feeding activity when zooplankton were most abundant. This was considered to be an adaptation favoring photosynthesis by zooxanthellae during the day, implying a nutritional role for the algae. Taking a more direct experimental approach, Franzisket (1969b) maintained one ahermatypic and four hermatypic species of Hawaiian corals in running seawater in the light for 4 months. During the first 2 months, the water was unfiltered and growth, as measured by increase in fresh weight, was detected in all species. During the last 2 months, plankton was excluded from the water by filtration. Under these conditions growth of the ahermatypic coral ceased, but growth continued at the same rate in the four hermatypic species. Franzisket presented the startling interpretation that the hermatypic species were capable of existing autotrophically, which decidedly minimizes the importance of zooplankton in nutrition of these coral species. It is also liable to a number of criticisms. First, increase in growth may have been solely inorganic, i.e., calcification was sustained while tissues actually diminished in bulk. Organic growth was not measured to test this possibility. Second, corals cannot live autotrophically on carbon alone, and Franzisket's interpretation implies that these corals can obtain sufficient nitrogen and phosphorus solely from seawater. However, Pomeroy and Kuenzler (1969) and Yamazato (1966) suggested that there is a net excretion of phosphorus by corals, and Johannes *et al.* (1970) pointed out that corals thus require a source of phosphorus other than that dissolved in seawater. Similarly, Johannes and Webb (1972) suggested that there may be a net loss of free amino acids by reef corals. If this is true, then nitrogen lost must be replaced from solution or from zooplankton. As pointed out earlier, the extent to which corals can utilize ammonia or other nitrogen sources in seawater is not yet known. More critical data on nutrient budgets will bear heavily on Franzisket's interpretation.

Most estimates of the productivity of atolls in the Pacific (Sargent and Austin, 1949, 1954; Odum and Odum, 1955) and Indian Oceans (Nair and Pillai, 1969) and fringing reefs in Hawaii (Kohn and Helfrich, 1957) range from 1500 to 3500 gm carbon/m^2/year. Gordon and Kelly (1962), calculated a value of 11,680 gm carbon/m^2/year for an Hawaiian fringing reef. In contrast, ambient waters of some of these reefs are virtually devoid of plankton, with gross productivity values of only 21–37 gm carbon /m^2/year for Hawaii (Doty and Oguri, 1956) and 28 gm carbon/m^2/year for Rongelap (Steeman-Nielsen, 1954; data from Stoddart, 1969). The implication is that phytoplankton and thus zooplankton abundance are insufficient to account for the gross productivity of these reefs. The flow respirometry data of Sargent and Austin and Odum and Odum suggest that production of reduced organic carbon on the reef itself, in part by symbiotic algae, may be adequate to meet the respiratory requirements of the reef community. Short-term laboratory investigations employing oxygen electrode techniques are consistent with this idea. Data of Kanwisher and Wainwright (1967), Roffman (1968), and Franzisket (1969a) on scleractinian corals and data of Burkholder and Burkholder (1960) on alcyonarians show photosynthesis : respiration ratios of from 5 to 17. Ratios over a 24-hour diurnal period range from 1 to 4. On the other hand, in similar studies on fringing reefs in Puerto Rico (Odum *et al.*, 1959), the Andaman Islands (Nair and Pillai, 1969) and Hawaii (Gordon and Kelly, 1962), respiration exceeded photosynthesis. Stoddart (1969) suggested that such differences in these ratios may simply reflect the basic differences in metabolism by fringing reefs and oceanic atolls.

The uncertainty existing with respect to zooplankton abundance on coral reefs has been partially satisfied by more rigorous zooplankton sampling programs, especially at night and along the reef front as well as on the reef flat. Emery (1968) surveyed Florida reefs and described an indigenous reef zooplankton fauna. Tranter and Jacob (1969), in preliminary studies of Kavaratti atoll in the Laccadives, reported rich catches of zooplankton in night tows. Biomass outside the lagoon was 336–584 mg/m^3 and 189 mg/m^3 inside the lagoon. Richest catches were made where reef growth was most luxuriant. The investigators speculated that the plankton supply seemed adequate for reef maintenance metabolism. Johannes *et al.* (1970) continuously monitored the concentration of zooplankton drifting over a coral reef community at Bermuda. The zooplankton trapped by a pair of nets anchored at the level of the coral heads and sampled twice daily amounted to a dry weight of about 0.83 mg/m^3 at night and about 0.58 mg/m^3 during the day. The mean respiration rate of four coral species including *Diploria strigosa*, the most common species on the reef, was about 0.96 mg O$_2$/cm^2 of coral surface per day. Assuming that the combustion of 0.7 mg plankton requires the consumption of 1 mg of oxygen, the investigators calculated that corals with a surface area equal to that of the opening one of the nets (1960 cm^2) would require 1300 mg zooplankton daily to offset respiratory requirements. Plankton caught overnight by one net amounted to about 71 mg, or about 5.4% of this requirement. Even after considering a wide range of possible sources of error (e.g., feeding and assimilation efficiencies, plankton net catching efficiencies, estimates of coral energy requirements, sources of energy gains and losses), the supply of zooplankton seemed woefully inadequate to sustain coral energy requirements. From these observations on Bermuda corals, the authors speculated that, although hermatypic corals may grow in the absence of sufficient zooplankton (deriving reduced organic carbon from zooxanthellae), zooplankton are still *essential* to corals as a source of nutrients, especially phosphorus. This hypothesis, still consistent with the observations that corals are carnivores, highly adapted for trapping and digesting zooplankton, may help reconcile a lively and stimulating controversy concerning interpretation of the roles of plankton and zooxanthellae in nutrition of reef corals, reinterpretation of older literature, and planning future experiments.

2. Dissolved Organic Material

As yet, there is no conclusive proof that corals use dissolved organic matter as food. Stephens and Schinske (1961) and Stephens (1967, 1968) discussed the problems that must be overcome in determining the extent of net utilization of a particular dissolved organic substance (see also Johannes *et al.*, 1969). Experiments should be conducted with substances at concentrations consistent with those normally encountered in the environment. Release as well as uptake of total material must be measured in order to ascertain net gain by the organism. Evidence should be sought for participation of the acquired substance in the metabolism of the organism. Until these criteria are satisfied, the problem of utilization or net gain of energy from dissolved organic substances by corals remains a wide open field for investigation.

3. Bacteria

As with the preceding topic, there is virtually no experimental work on utilization of bacteria as a food source other than a preliminary experiment by Di Salvo (1971). He introduced ^{35}S-labeled bacteria to seawater containing living *Fungia scutaria* and clean *Fungia* skeleton as a control. After 40 hours, radioactivity associated with the clean skeleton was almost entirely Trichloroacetic acid (TCA), and alcohol-insoluble, while radioactivity associated with the tissues ranged from 57% to 76% TCA-soluble, suggesting that *Fungia* may be able to digest bacterial protein. The extent to which this occurs in nature and its ecological significance are unknown.

IV. Digestion, Assimilation, Transport, and Excretion

A. DIGESTION

A brief summary of digestion in coelenterates, taking into account the observations from a wide range of species, is instructive as a prelude to consideration of digestion in corals. Early literature on digestion in corals was reviewed by Yonge and Nicholls (1930) and Krijgsman and Talbot (1953), while more recent literature was reviewed by Lenhoff (1968). The digestion process in coelenterates has been studied by following the fate of living prey or furnished substrates such as fibrin, red blood cells, olive oil, crab meat, gelatine, etc., stained with dyes or labeled with radioactive isotopes (Boschma, 1925; Yonge and Nicholls, 1930; Lenhoff, 1961, 1968; Pearse, 1970, 1971).

Being for the most part active carnivores, coelenterates ingest food particles much larger than their digestive cells and immediate phagocytosis is impossible. Some preliminary extracellular digestion within the coelenteron is therefore necessary to produce smaller particles, which can be taken into the digestive cells by phagocytosis; digestion is then completed intracellularly (Yonge, 1937; Krijgsman and Talbot, 1953). The presence of prey in the coelenteron is believed to stimulate secretion of digestive enzymes, particularly proteases in the coelenteric fluid, although this has been shown in only a few species (Lenhoff, 1968; Nicol,

1959). Protein has been suggested as a stimulus for secretion of extra-cellular protease (Nicol, 1959; Philips, 1966, in Lenhoff, 1968), which is thought to be secreted by cells of the glandular margin of mesenteries (Yonge, 1931; Nicol, 1959). The first phase of digestion is marked by relatively rapid enzymatic comminution to small particles and polypep-tides but not to amino acids (Yonge and Nicholls, 1930; Lenhoff, 1961). This process is facilitated in some instances by localization of enzyme in a mucous coating secreted around the prey or by close and repeated contact of mesenteries and prey (Nicol, 1959). In the next and longer phase, particles are taken into food vacuoles by endodermal phagocyto-sis, further reduced to particulate material, or completely solubilized, and the products are then transported to other parts of the polyp either by diffusion, movement in fluid channels in the mesoglea, movement of amoebocytes, or by movement in discrete vesicles derived from food vacuoles (Kepner and Thomas, 1928; Yonge, 1931; Gauthier, 1963; Lunger, 1963). Indigestible food material in the coelenteron is expelled through the mouth, in some cases assisted by the uptake of water in the coelenteron followed by expulsion of the bolus of waste material (Lenhoff, 1961, 1968).

There are so few investigations of digestion in corals that it is impossi-ble to say if they all conform to this general pattern. The studies of Yonge and Nicholls (1930) on digestive enzymes in corals were relatively unsophisticated in terms of modern approaches to digestion and its en-zymology. Much faith was put in the stability of crude extracts during long incubations without temperature control, buffers, or knowledge of cofactor requirements (see Lenhoff, 1968; Barrington, 1962). Yet this work was far ahead of any other similar work on corals during its time, and its main conclusions have not yet been challenged.

Yonge and Nicholls (1930), working with polyps of *Euphyllia*, *Symphyllia*, *Favia*, and *Fungia*, observed the extracellular digestion of copepods, mysids, *Oikopleura*, *Sagitta*, amphipods, and other representa-tive zooplankton. Times for complete digestion ranged from 3 to 14 hours. It is important to note here that Yonge and Nicholls (1930) tested coelenteric fluid of *Fungia danae* and tissue extracts of *Lobo-phyllia corymbosa* for proteolytic activity *in vitro*. The dissolution of fibrin in coelenteric fluid was taken as evidence of proteolytic activity. Two pH optima for this process were discerned, but treatment of fibrin with coelenteric fluid did not result in the liberation of amino acids from the original fibrin substrate. On the other hand, when fibrin was treated with tissue extracts, strong proteolytic activity was observed, including hydrolysis to amino acids. The investigators concluded that corals have at least two proteolytic enzymes, one in coelenteric fluid, which breaks down large particles to smaller ones, and the second which completes hydrolysis intracellularly within food vacuoles of digestive cells. It was also noted that red blood cells introduced into the coelenteron could be degraded by extracellular enzymes and then phagocytized, but they could also be phagocytized directly without any apparent prior digestion. Yonge and Nicholls obtained evidence for intracellular peptidase, weak intracellular lipase, and glycogenase activity. Attempts were made to distinguish enzyme activity originating in tissues from that originating in zooxanthellae. From data available to date, digestion by corals seems consistent with observations on other coelenterates in terms of rapid extracellular enzymatic comminution of proteins, followed by slower intracellular hydrolysis and then egestion and expulsion of unwanted material.

B. Assimilation and Transport

The general problem of assimilation and transport of products of digestion is as poorly understood in most coelenterates as it is in corals. Studies of assimilation by corals have been limited to observations on insoluble products of digestion.

Yonge (1931) fed *Pocillopora* and *Lobophyllia* mollusk meat impregnated with iron saccharate and examined fixed, stained, and sectioned material at various intervals after feeding. Iron was observed exclusively in the absorptive zones of the mesenterial filaments. These zones are composed largely of the same cell type, but the cell boundaries were not clear. Similar results were obtained after feeding red blood cells, meat, india ink, and carmine. Iron appeared in food vacuoles in particulate masses, never in a "diffuse" state. According to Yonge, this is further evidence for an intracellular digestive phase, since, in organisms which digest extracellularly, iron saccharate is found only in a fluid state, never in particulate form. Iron could be detected in the tissues for 2–3 days and thereafter diminished in quantity as particulate iron was discharged from the cells.

While these data establish the site of intracellular digestion in corals, there is little conclusive data on the mechanism of transport of the products of digestion. Pratt (1905) implicated wandering cells in the mesoglea of *Alcyonium*. Yonge (1931) did observe wandering cells with iron particles in the mesoglea after injection of iron into edge-zone tissues, but a definite role of these cells in transport could not be established with certainty. Coelenteric canals or solenia are likely but unexplored avenues of dissemination of products of digestion between polyps. Future investigations might well employ chemical fractionation and isotopic tracers for the study of digestion and synthesis, following the approach taken by Lenhoff (1961) in his study of digestion by *Hydra*.

C. Excretion

Yonge's studies showed conclusively that the site of absorption of particulate material is also the site of its egestion, but there is virtually no information on the excretory products of protein metabolism by reef corals beyond the observations of Kawaguti (1953) who detected an increase in ammonia in beakers of seawater containing corals and inferred that ammonia is one of their excretory products.

V. Role of Zooxanthellae

Zooxanthellae are unicellular algae found without exception in reef-building corals. Their numbers and biomass vary considerably in different tissues in a polyp and among different species. In samples of non-fleshy corals with relatively thin coenosarc, e.g., *Pocillopora damicornis*, the ratios of animal protein to algal protein range from 0.7 to 1.2 and average about 1.00. In other words, such a coral is about one-half plant material (Muscatine and Cernichiari, 1969). The algae occur chiefly within cells of the endoderm. Whether or not the host cells are specialized as "carriers" as claimed by Goreau (1961) requires further investigation as does the contention that zooxanthellae are "intercellular" (Kawaguti, 1964). When cultured *in vitro* a species may give rise to as many as sixteen different morphological forms (Freudenthal, 1962), whereas the symbionts *in vivo* are all encysted vegetative stages about 8–12 μm in diameter. Electron microscopy reveals that the symbionts have a multilayered periplast, a single-lobed chloroplast, stalked pyrenoid, and a large amorphous "assimilation body" that appears to be unique to symbiotic dinoflagellates (Taylor, 1968; Kevin *et al.*, 1969; Trench, 1971a). Kawaguti (1944) first called coral zooxanthellae *Gymnodinium* sp., but whether or not all coral zooxanthellae are congeneric is an open question (see Taylor, 1969). Those from other coelenterates (except *Velella velella* L.) and Tridacna are assigned to the Order Peridiniales (Dinophyceae) and designated *Gymnodinium microadriaticum* (Freudenthal) comb nov. (Taylor, 1971). From *in vitro* studies there is evidence that zooxanthellae from different hosts differ physiologically (Trench, 1971b).

The extent to which zooxanthellae contribute to the nutritional physiology of corals has often been debated. Recent reviews should be consulted for comparative information (Yonge, 1963, 1968; McLaughlin and Zahl, 1966; Smith *et al.*, 1969; Muscatine, 1971). A summary of early observations on reef corals by Vaughan (1930) and Yonge and Nicholls (1931a,b) suggests that: (1) corals feed exclusively on zooplankton, rejecting any form of plant material; (2) there is adequate plankton to support coral nutrition so that zooxanthellae are not essential as a food source; (3) corals have enzymes specialized for a carnivorous diet; (4) starved corals eject their zooxanthellae; (5) corals can live perfectly well in darkness. From these observations, the inference was drawn that zooxanthellae do not contribute substantially to organic productivity of corals. The contention that corals do derive nutriment from their symbiotic algae comes from early studies of Pratt (1905) and Gohar (1940, 1948) on alcyonarians, Boschma (1925) on corals and anemones, and Sargent and Austin (1949, 1954) and Odum and Odum (1955) on reef community metabolism. These investigators inferred a role of zooxanthellae in nutrition based on observations such as reduction of digestive apparatus and concomitant increase in abundance of zooxanthellae, absence of a feeding response to zooplankton; invariable absence of food in the coelenteron, presence of zooxanthellae in digestive zones, dependence of the host on light for normal behavior, and plankton productivity apparently inadequate to support the maintenance metabolism of reef communities. In more direct experiments, Kawaguti (1965) observed that *Oulastrea crispata*, kept for more than 15 months without food, appeared healthy and increased its numbers of polyps as did *Acropora, Hydnophora, Goniopora,* and *Cyphastrea* starved for 3 months. Franzisket (1969b), as noted earlier, showed that hermatypic corals from Hawaii (*Pocillopora, Porites, Montipora,* and *Fungia*) kept in the light continued to gain fresh weight in the absence of exogenous plankton, while ahermatypic controls stopped gaining weight under the same conditions. Franzisket (1970) noted further that corals kept in darkness for 2 months exhibited atrophy and loss of zooxanthellae. When these specimens were placed in the light, still without plankton, they rebuilt their atrophied tissues and regenerated their zooxanthellae. Unfortunately, neither investigator made quantitative measurements of the growth or shrinkage of tissues, at the same time comparing symbiotic and aposymbiotic corals of the same species. This difficult approach seems essential for critical evaluation of the well-being of the host and its correlation with the presence or absence of algae. Muscatine (1961) starved anemones (*Anthopleura* sp.) over a 10-week period and observed that aposymbiotic anemones appeared perfectly healthy and that those with algae ejected them as the tissues diminished in bulk. However, weekly weight measurements revealed that aposymbiotic anemones were losing weight faster than anemones with algae, both in light and in darkness, a fact that was not at all evident from gross qualitative inspection.

All of the foregoing observations have lent insight into the problem of the potential nutritional role of zooxanthellae and its comparative aspects. When ecological, behavioral, biochemical, and physiological data are drawn together, the picture that emerges suggests that zooxanthellae may well be of major importance in primary production, calcification, and conservation of nutrients.

A. ZOOXANTHELLAE AS PRIMARY PRODUCERS

1. Photosynthesis and Primary Production

Zooxanthellae seem to function as efficiently as free-living dinoflagellates. They photosynthesize in the light *in vivo* or *in vitro*, saturating at about 2800–3000 fc (Roffman, 1968; Halldal, 1968; Franzisket, 1969a). Compensation intensities for photosynthesis by zooxanthellae range from 300 to 500 fc (Kanwisher and Wainwright, 1967). Pigments of zooxanthellae from corals have been characterized (Jeffrey and Haxo, 1968), and the action spectrum for photosynthesis by zooxanthellae *in vitro* shows peaks at 440, 490, 640, and 675 nm, denoting the participation in light absorption by chlorophylls a and c and the xanthophyll peridinin (Halldal, 1968). Experimental data on light absorption and photosynthesis by green filamentous algae (*Ostreobium sp.*) found in the skeleton of many species of coral rule out any significant participation by these commensals in primary production (Kanwisher and Wainwright, 1967; Halldal, 1968; Franzisket, 1968).

Zooxanthellae in corals are capable of producing more oxygen than is consumed by the algae and corals combined (Yonge *et al.*, 1932; Sargent and Austin, 1949; Odum and Odum, 1955; Kohn and Helfrich, 1957; Kanwisher and Wainwright, 1967; Roffman, 1968; Franzisket, 1969a). The oxygen evolved is presumably available to the host cells, but, as pointed out by many investigators, its physiological importance to the host is uncertain since few corals and other coelenterates deprived of their zooxanthellae have as yet been reported to suffer from effects attributable to lack of oxygen.

More important to corals than the oxygen produced by the zooxanthellae is the carbon fixed by them. Primary production has been calculated from short- and long-term measurements of photosynthesis both in the laboratory and in the field. From short-term polarographic measurements of oxygen produced by isolated coral heads from Florida, Kanwisher and Wainwright (1967) calculated that gross photosynthesis ranged from 2.7 to 10.2 gm carbon/m^2 per 12-hour day and that the ratio of maximum photosynthesis to respiration (P/R) ranged from 1.9 to 2.8. In all but one experimental observation, production by the species observed exceeded the 24-hour respiratory requirement. The lowest productivity value was said to be higher than that for most values for plankton in the open sea. The highest value "is within a factor of 2 of Ryther's (1959) estimate of the theoretical maximum based on quantum efficiency and available sunlight" (Kanwisher and Wainwright, 1967). Similar P/R ratios (1.7–5.0) were measured by Roffman (1968) for nine species of Pacific corals. Oxygen production by these corals tended to decrease with prolonged observation, suggesting that the corals were deteriorating or that short-term measurements may give rise to maximum estimates of productivity. Diurnal P/R ratios of 2.9–4.3 for Hawaiian corals were reported by Franzisket (1969a) using a flowing system and Winkler titration. The diurnal P/R ratio for *Porites furcata*, calculated from CO_2 consumption, is closer to 1.0 (Beyers, 1966), as is the P/R ratio for reef community metabolism (Odum and Odum, 1955). From the foregoing data, it may be concluded that daytime production is a significant activity of zooxanthellae in reef corals.

Studies on photosynthetic products of zooxanthellae have been detected *in vitro* and *in vivo*. After incubation of *Fungia* zooxanthellae for 1 hour in the light *in vitro*, Trench (1971b) detected ^{14}C in lipid, amino acids, nonamino organic acids, glycerol, organic phosphates, and glucose. A significant amount of ^{14}C was also detected in insoluble products. Similar results were obtained by Muscatine and Cernichiari (1969) with zooxanthellae from *Pocillopora* and by von Holt and von Holt (1968a) for zooxanthellae from the coral *Scolymia*. Products detected after incubation of whole corals in $^{14}CO_2$ are similar to those observed in zooxanthellae incubated *in vitro* (Muscatine and Cernichiari, 1969). However, the distribution of ^{14}C is influenced by the length of incubation, the occurrence of translocation of products to animal tissue, and dark fixation, which amounts to a substantial 10–12% of photosynthesis. Products of zooxanthellae from other coelenterates were described by von Holt and von Holt (1968b) and Trench (1971b), with the observation that prolonged isolation *in vitro* results in definite metabolic changes in zooxanthellae. This raises the argument that algae isolated for prolonged periods or maintained in culture may not represent *in vivo* metabolism as faithfully as those immediately isolated from the host (Trench, 1971c).

2. Fate of Algal Primary Production

Carbon fixed by zooxanthellae is useful to the coral only if available to it. Fixed carbon may be respired, stored, or used in the production of more algae, which, in turn, may be digested or released from the host. Released algae may be returned to the coral via the predator food chain or lost completely. Fixed carbon may also be selectively released *in situ* and translocated to coral host tissue. It also is likely that fixed carbon is cycled through more than one of the foregoing paths over a given time period. As yet, there is insufficient information to state how much fixed carbon is involved in each of these categories under a given set of conditions, although estimates may be made by considering digestion and translocation in detail.

a. Digestion of Zooxanthellae. Digestion of zooxanthellae is usually inferred when fragments of algae or atypical, degenerate algae are observed within host cells. For example, Boschma (1925) presumed that, because zooxanthellae were present in digestive zones of corals and anemones, they were being digested. Kawaguti (1965) showed by electron microscopy that zooxanthellae from the coral *Oulastrea* have a thin plasma membrane covered externally with an accumulation of double membrane fragments (see also Taylor, 1968). These fragments were presumed to be available for assimilation by the host. Fankboner (1971) interpreted degenerative changes in zooxanthellae within amoebocytes in *Tridacna* digestive gland as a digestive process promoted by amoebocyte lysosomes. He conjectured that the degenerate zooxanthellae are utilized nutritionally by the host. However, to demonstrate holozic nutrition at the expense of zooxanthellae, it seems necessary and desirable to show conclusive evidence for digestion, i.e., chemical hydrolysis of algal substrates and the entry of the products into host metabolic pathways. This cannot be done solely by using morphological criteria. Consequently, the idea that corals accumulate nutrients by degradation of insoluble fractions of zooxanthellae, though not ruled out, is still largely speculative.

b. Utilization of Products of Photosynthesis Released by Zooxanthellae. Growth rates of the symbiotic algae *in vivo* are almost certainly reduced as a result of physical restrictions, host-controlled inhibition of algal cell division, or nutrient limitations. Whatever the reason, there is no evidence that their capacity for photosynthesis is reduced. This situation can potentially create a surplus of photosynthetic products (Smith *et al.*, 1969).

Direct evidence that zooxanthellae can release photosynthetically fixed organic compounds comes from studies of algae isolated from the host and immediately incubated with $^{14}CO_2$ for a few minutes to several hours. Zooxanthellae from the coral *Pocillopora damicornis* and the bivalve *Tridacna* release about 5% of the total ^{14}C fixed in 2–4 hours. However, when a homogenate of host tissue is added to the incubation mixture, 30–50% of the total ^{14}C fixed is released to the medium, principally as [^{14}C]glycerol accompanied by small amounts of other labeled compounds such as glucose, alanine, and glycollic acid (Muscatine, 1967). Comparison of intracellular products with those released as extracellular products shows that release is selective and not the result of cell lysis (Fig. 4A,B). It is thus evident that some host tissues contain "factors" that stimulate release of soluble products of photosynthesis. Although the primary effect of host homogenate has not yet been determined, its stimulatory nature has been observed in experiments with zooxanthellae from a wide range of other corals and coelenterates (Trench, 1971c; Muscatine, *et al.*, 1972).

The observation that organic compounds may be released by zooxanthellae *in vitro* has raised the question of whether release also occurs *in vivo*. Evidence that corals acquire soluble organic carbon compounds derived from zooxanthellae comes from a variety of experiments.

Muscatine and Hand (1958) demonstrated that zooxanthellae in the sea anemone *Anthopleura elegantissima* fixed $^{14}CO_2$ into organic molecules whose initial location and subsequent fate were determined by radioautography. Anemones incubated in the dark served as controls for heterotrophic fixation. Translocation was detected in animals incubated with $^{14}CO_2$ for 1–5 weeks. No attempt was made to determine the nature of the translocated material or its quantity. Goreau and Goreau (1960c) performed similar experiments with the corals *Manicina areolata* and *Montastrea annularis*. Evidence for translocation was obtained after 50 hours incubation but interpreted as being able to satisfy "only a very small part of the coral's total nutritional requirement." Although radioautography has the advantage of providing direct evidence for translocation, it is *at best* only a semiquantitative technique, since the solvents used in preparing paraffin sections remove soluble material leaving only insoluble substances. Since the relative proportions of radioactive material in soluble and insoluble material may vary in each preparation, the extent of translocation may easily be misrepresented. In fact, if the translocation process in corals involved soluble

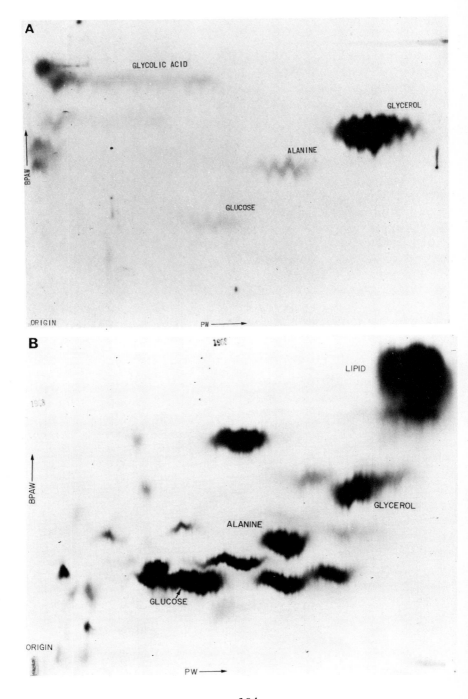

104

materials exclusively, it would be impossible to detect by conventional autoradiography. Since the "total nutritional requirement" of any coral is still unknown, the quantitative interpretation of Goreau and Goreau must be regarded as speculative.

Von Holt and von Holt (1968a) incubated the coral *Scolymia lacera* for 3 hours in the light with $^{14}CO_2$ and determined the amount and nature of the fixed ^{14}C in algae and animal tissue. About 40% of the total fixed ^{14}C was recovered in animal tissue. Of this amount about 80% was alcohol-soluble, justifying caution in interpretation of radioautographic data. About one-half of the translocated ^{14}C was recovered in the lipid fraction and about one-fourth in amino acids. From observations on translocation in *Zoanthus,* von Holt and von Holt estimated that 0.7–1.1 μg of carbon per hour might be acquired by the animal from its zooxanthellae. Muscatine and Cernichiari (1969) incubated *P. damicornis* on the reef for 24 hours with $^{14}CO_2$. Of the total ^{14}C fixed, about 36–50% was recovered in the animal tissue, mostly as lipid and protein. The percentage of fixed carbon translocated *in vivo* is consistent with amounts that have been observed to be released *in vitro*. When labeled animal tissue lipid was deacylated, ^{14}C was detected only in the glycerol moiety. This was taken as evidence that glycerol was released by the algae *in vivo* and utilized by the animal in lipid synthesis. Skeletal carbonate and skeletal organic matrix were also labeled. About 12% of the label in the matrix was ether-soluble and identified as cetyl palmitate (Young, 1971; Young *et al.*, 1971). Lewis and Smith (1971), using information obtained from *in vitro* studies and an "inhibition" technique (see Drew and Smith, 1967; Smith *et al.*, 1969), were able to follow *in vivo* movement of ^{14}C in a wide range of corals from Jamaica. Evidence was obtained for movement in the living coral, in darkness as well as in the light, of the same compounds which are known to be released by zooxanthellae *in vitro*, namely, glycerol, alanine, and glucose. Demonstration of the translocation of alanine is particularly significant since it is the first representation of a movement of nitrogen between symbionts. In comparative studies, Trench (1970, 1971a) has demonstrated the translocation of 20–50% of the carbon fixed by zooxanthellae to the tissues of the zoanthid *Palythoa townsleyi* and the anemone

---

Fig. 4. (A) Radioautograph of chromatogram of medium from zooxanthellae incubated in light with $Na_2{}^{14}CO_3$, for 2 hours, showing labeled soluble extracellular products. (B) Radioautograph of chromatogram of 80% ethanol-soluble extract of zooxantellae treated as in (A), showing labeled intracellular products. From Muscatine and Cernichiari (1969).

Anthopleura elegantissima. In addition, he showed that ^{14}C initially fixed by zooxanthellae in *Zoanthus* sp. later appeared at the surface of the epidermis in newly synthesized mucous cuticle.

Although the detection of translocation of algal products and their utilization by hermatypic corals in protein, carbohydrate, and lipid metabolism are now on a sound experimental basis, further comparative studies and quantitative aspects still remained to be carried out. For example, it would be of great ecological interest to know what proportion of the carbon requirements of the various reef corals can be satisfied by zooxanthellae and what conditions affect this proportion.

The potential significance to coelenterate hosts of the translocation of reduced organic compounds seems primarily nutritional. When food is limited, as in tropical oceanic waters, the algae as "imprisoned phytoplankton" (Yonge, 1940), represent a reservoir of reduced organic carbon and nitrogen. When food is abundant, corals, ensured of a supply of both carbon and nutrients as is often the case in laboratory experiments, would be expected to live perfectly well in darkness or without algae. Quantitative feeding experiments with green hydra support this interpretation (Muscatine and Lenhoff, 1965).

On the other hand, the apparent lack of interest in plankton by xeniid alcyonaceans and their dependence on light suggest greater reliance, perhaps even obligate dependence, on zooxanthellae. This leads naturally to the generalization that the nutritional significance of the zooxanthellae may vary with each association. Franzisket (1970) has observed that corals with large polyps are more efficient at capturing zooplankton, have low metabolic rates, and are therefore less apt to be dependent on zooxanthellae for carbon than corals with small polyps, which are less efficient in capturing zooplankton and which have high metabolic rates. In fact, these corals may depend on nutritional supplementation by zooxanthellae to the extent that the colonies cannot live without light. This is indicated in the preliminary experiments of Connell (unpublished) who excluded light from a section of the Great Barrier Reef by means of an opaque dome without affecting ambient currents and food supply. During $3\frac{1}{2}$ months in the shade, corals expelled their zooxanthellae and all colonies died. Control colonies under transparent domes survived. The relative dependence of corals on zooxanthellae in no way precludes the role of corals as carnivores, especially if zooplankton are indispensable for a supply of nutrients such as phosphorus as hypothesized by Johannes *et al.* (1970). This, however, would appear to leave the xeniid alcyonaceans without a means of obtaining some essential nutrients.

Goreau *et al.* (1971) have attempted to reconcile the unnecessarily polarized views that reef corals are either autotrophs or heterotrophs. They review the evidence that shows that reef corals are carnivorous, possessing tentacles, cilia, and mesenterial filaments adapted for feeding on particulate material. They reiterate that coral nutrition may be supplemented by absorption of dissolved organic substances and that this process is aided by adaptations such as epidermal microvilli and alkaline phosphatase activity in surface epithelia. Their main point is that there are obvious structural adaptations for particulate and absorptive feeding, and that reef boundary waters, "in continuous and dynamic exchange with the reef biota," supply these food substrates. They question the view that reef corals can be wholly (Franzisket, 1969b) or nearly (Johannes *et al.,* 1970) autotrophic and point out that whereas "reef corals have not developed any . . . specializations" for autotrophy, such adaptations do occur in xeniid alcyonaceans, "which have independently evolved a more or less complete nutritional dependence upon their contained zooxanthellae." In taking this viewpoint, Goreau *et al.* (1971) minimize the potential role of zooxanthellae in nutrition of hermatypic corals, pointing out that, although translocation of organic material from algae to coral does occur, its quantitative significance is not yet known. It seems necessary to point out that the force of this argument is diminished somewhat by the fact that, although the gross morphology and behavior of xeniids strongly suggest the potential for an autotrophic nutritional system, there is as yet no experimental evidence that this is actually the case. In addition, the fact that morphological adaptations for obtaining nutrients from zooxanthellae are not discernible in hermatypic corals does not rule out the existence of other kinds of adaptations. For example, adaptations favoring the release and translocation of organic material from zooxanthellae may be biochemical rather than grossly morphological.

B. Calcification

Zooxanthellae play a fundamental role in inorganic growth (skeletogenesis) of reef corals. Goreau and Goreau (1959a) developed a rapid and precise technique for measuring calcium deposition in corals under controlled laboratory and field conditions. Using ^{45}Ca, they observed rates of deposition under various environmental and experimental conditions and measured growth rates in various parts of coral colonies (see also Goreau and Goreau, 1959a,b, 1960a,b). They found that light together with the presence of zooxanthellae significantly accelerated calcification rates in corals, confirming the observations of Kawaguti and

Sakumoto (1948), while an inhibitor of carbonic anhydrase activity decreased the rate of calcium deposition. A working hypothesis was based on the following calcification reaction.

$$Ca^{2+} + 2\ HCO_3 \rightleftharpoons Ca(HCO_3)_2 \tag{1}$$
$$Ca(HCO_3)_2 \rightleftharpoons CaCO_3 + H_2CO_3 \tag{2}$$

Hydrolysis of carbonic acid to the end products water and carbon dioxide was presumed to be catalyzed by carbonic anhydrase. In the ·light, the overall reaction velocity may be increased as zooxanthellae consume carbon dioxide during photosynthesis. This hypothesis is the first to attempt to explain how light accelerates calcium deposition, but it is still inconsistent with the observation that the apical polyps of acroporid corals calcify much faster than lateral ones even though apical polyps have relatively few zooxanthellae (Goreau and Goreau, 1959a; Pearse and Muscatine, 1971). One may also ask how carbonate is supplied for calcification if zooxanthellae remove carbon dioxide from the calcifying milieu.

Only two alternatives to the "carbon dioxide removal" hypothesis have been proposed. (1) If the synthesis of the skeletal organic matrix is a limiting factor in calcium deposition, then zooxanthellae might influence this by supplying more substrate for matrix synthesis. This may occur to a greater extent in the light than in dark as a result of increased photosynthesis and translocation rates. Axial translocation, i.e., toward the apex of a branch, for which there is some evidence, might explain fast calcification of apical polyps in acroporids (Pearse and Muscatine, 1971). (2) Simkiss (1964a,b) and Yamazato (1966) noted that inorganic and organic phosphates act as crystal poisons and interfere with aragonite formation. They suggested that symbiotic algae in corals, as a normal concomitant of their nutritional activities, remove phosphates from the calcifying microenvironment, thus creating a more favorable milieu for calcification. This may explain why corals in darkness with algae calcify significantly faster than those in the dark without algae (cf. Goreau and Goreau, 1959a). Increased removal of phosphate in the light, as has been observed by Yamazato for *Fungia*, may explain how light accelerates calcification. Both of these hypotheses require testing. Efforts by Young (1969) to selectively inhibit matrix synthesis were unsuccessful, but he demonstrated a close correlation between matrix synthesis and carbonate deposition. Taking a different approach, Vandermeulen *et al.* (1972) inhibited light-enhanced calcification in *Pocillopora damicornis* with $5 \times 10^{-4}\ M$ DCMU, a specific photosynthesis inhibitor. This confirmed the idea that light-enhanced calcification is photosynthesis-dependent and not dependent on some other photobiological effect.

Whatever the explanation for increased calcification in the light, the ecological implications are clear. Light is the primary environmental factor controlling vertical distribution of corals, rates of reef building, the form of reefs and atolls, and the shape of individual coral colonies. Corals in dimly lit areas are fragile and do not form reefs. No reef building occurs below 46 m (Wells, 1957). Goreau (1963) suggested that, as light decreases, calcification rates also decrease; but, with an adequate food supply, tissue growth is sustained at normal levels. The result is a flattened, more fragile skeleton. On the other hand, with sufficient illumination, calcium deposition and reef building are accelerated, and the resistance to destructive forces can be developed.

C. NUTRIENT CONSERVATION

Yonge and Nicholls (1931a) measured phosphorus excretion over a 4-day period in the light by *Favia, Porites, Psammocora,* and *Fungia,* and the ahermatypic coral *Dendrophyllia.* All corals excreted phosphorus, but excretion was significantly lower in hermatypic corals than in the control without zooxanthellae. In other experiments, Yonge and Nicholls (1931b) observed that corals with few zooxanthellae excreted more phosphorus over a 10-day period than those with abundant zooxanthellae, whether fed or starved in light or darkness. Furthermore, when three species of hermatypic corals and a *Dendrophyllia* control were kept in seawater to which phosphate had been added, the phosphate concentration declined significantly in the medium containing two of the three hermatypic corals compared with the control. The investigators concluded that the phosphate was taken up by zooxanthellae, and that zooxanthellae in reef corals, especially those in nutrient-poor waters, obtain phosphorus from host metabolic wastes, thus satisfying their own requirements and at the same time assisting the host in waste removal. In this connection, the algae have been described as "performing an intracellular renal function" (Geddes, 1882) or as "automatic organs of excretion" (Yonge, 1940). As a result, the algae were thought to influence favorably the metabolism of reef-building coral communities (Yonge, 1940), presumably by preventing accumulation of toxic wastes. However, the strong unidirectional currents prevalent in reef areas should certainly be sufficient to remove the soluble waste products of coral metabolism. Also, the many species of ahermatypic corals seem to flourish quite well without zooxanthellae. In addition, Yonge and Nicholls (1931b) have shown that corals that have lost their algae live perfectly well. Finally, Slobodkin (1964) noted that "ecological efficiencies" (yield energy/food energy consumed, expressed as percentages) for most animals ranges from 7 to 13%. The figure for *Hydra viridis*, a hydra with endosymbiotic zoochlorellae, lies within this range when the animals are kept in darkness, but, in the light, ecological efficiency is quadrupled. Increased ecological efficiency is difficult to explain merely on the basis of waste removal. The role of photosynthesis as an energy source seems the only reasonable interpretation, especially in view of the wealth of data on translocation of photosynthetic products in alga–invertebrate symbioses. It is suggested, therefore, that the algae be viewed as capable of taking up exogenous or endogenous animal "wastes," with the result that these are conserved and recycled within the symbiotic association existing in a nutrient-poor environment.

Yamazato (1966) found that *Fungia scutaria* actually excretes dissolved phosphorus but that release rates by specimens with zooxanthellae are much slower than those of bleached specimens. Pomeroy and Kuenzler (1969) also observed release of phosphorus by corals, but these release rates were several orders of magnitude slower than those of other marine invertebrates of comparable weight that do not contain symbiotic algae. The implication is that phosphorus turnover by corals is much slower per unit body weight than other organisms owing to recycling by zooxanthellae. If recycling occurs, the translocation of phosphorus in some form from algae to animal is to be expected. Indeed, von Holt (1968) reported that algae from *Zoanthus* release nucleoside polyphosphates *in vitro*, but it is not known if this occurs *in vivo* as well. It is highly likely that nitrogen is treated in a similar fashion. Kawaguti (1953) reported that, after addition of ammonium chloride to seawater containing hermatypic corals, ammonia diminished in quantity over test periods of a few hours in the light. In darkness and without added ammonium chloride, the corals produced ammonia. The coral *Balanophyllia*, which contains no algae, produced ammonia both in light and in darkness. It was concluded that zooxanthellae were responsible for consumption of ammonia in the light. Assuming that the algae tend to accumulate nitrogenous compounds from solution, nitrogen must then be translocated to the host if recycling is to occur. There is some evidence that this is the case. For example, zooxanthellae may accumulate ammonia from solution and use it to synthesize alanine, which is then released *in vivo* (Lewis and Smith, 1971) to the host where it becomes incorporated into protein (Muscatine and Cernichiari, 1969).

VI. Summary

Reef corals may be viewed primarily as carnivores, employing tentacles, nematocysts, cilia, mucus, and mesenterial filaments to remove particulate material from suspension and using chemical cues to govern acceptance or rejection. Whereas ahermatypic and some hermatypic corals feed primarily with tentacles, the majority of hermatypic corals rely on ciliary mucoid feeding mechanisms. The majority of corals expand and feed at night, while others do so during the day. The stimuli governing these behavior patterns are not yet known.

In nature, corals feed primarily on zooplankton and have the capacity to ingest animal detrital material and to absorb dissolved organic substances from solution. Digestion of plankton is rapid, initiated by extracellular proteases which comminute food to small particles. These are phagocytized and digestion is completed in intracellular vacuoles. Little is known of the temporal or chemical aspects of assimilation and transport of the products of digestion, nor is there conclusive information about excretion.

The quantitative significance of zooplankton to the total nutritional requirement of reef corals continues to be evaluated. This is chiefly the result of the apparent paucity of zooplankton in some reef communities and the enigmatic lack of feeding behavior in xeniid alcyonaceans. This, in turn, has stimulated a reexamination of the possible contribution of zooxanthellae to coral nutrition. These symbiotic algae are active primary producers. While there is no conclusive evidence that zooxanthellae are digested by corals, there are experimental data showing that products of photosynthesis may be released by zooxanthellae, possibly as a result of stimulatory properties of host tissue. These soluble products are translocated to host cells and incorporated into animal metabolic pathways. The amount of material translocated in relation to coral nutritional requirements is not yet known. It may be quantitatively less in large, fleshy, solitary polyps with low metabolic rates than in smaller colonial corals with higher metabolic rates or in xeniid alcyonaceans, which apparently do not feed on zooplankton but sustain a rich flora of zooxanthellae. Dependence of corals on zooxanthellae for nutritional supplementation in no way precludes the role of corals as carnivores adapted for feeding on zooplankton. In fact, it is held that zooplankton may be essential as a source of nutrients, such as phosphorus, even though they may be inadequate in some cases as a source of reduced organic carbon.

Zooxanthellae may help conserve nutrients by accumulating host waste products that are then returned to the host in a useful form. The algae definitely play a fundamental role in reef-building by causing corals to calcify at accelerated rates in the light, thereby influencing the growth and form of colonies and entire reefs.

Acknowledgments

I thank Professor Garth Chapman for reading this manuscript and offering many suggestions for its improvement. Preparation of the manuscript was aided by National Science Foundation Grant GB-11940.

References

Abe, N. (1938). *Palao Trop. Biol. Stud.* 1, 469.
Barrington, E. J. W. (1962). *Advan. Comp. Physiol. Biochem.* 1, 1.
Beyers, R. J. (1966). *Arch. Hydrobiol.* 62, 273.
Boschma, H. (1925). *Biol. Bull.* 49, 407.
Burkholder, P., and Burkholder, L. (1960). *Amer. J. Bot.* 47, 866.
Coles, S. L. (1969). *Limnol. Oceanogr.* 14, 949.
Darnell, R. (1968). *Amer. Zool.* 8, 70.
Doty, M. S., and Oguri, M. (1956). *J. Cons., Cons. Perma. Int. Explor. Mer.* 22, 33.
Di Salvo, L. (1971). *In* "Experimental Coelenterate Biology" (H. M. Lenhoff, L. Muscatine, and L. V. Davis, eds.), pp. 129–136. Univ. of Hawaii Press, Honolulu.
Drew, E. A., and Smith, D. C. (1967). *New Phytol.* 66, 389.
Emery, A. R. (1968). *Limnol. Oceanogr.* 13, 293.
Fankboner, P. V. (1971). *Biol. Bull.* 141, 222.
Franzisket, L. (1968). *Zool. Jahrb., Abt. Allg. Zool. Physiol. Tiere* 74, 246.
Franzisket, L. (1969a). *Forma Functio* 1, 153.
Franzisket, L. (1969b). *Naturwissenschaften* 3, 144.
Franzisket, L. (1970). *Int. Rev. Gesamten Hydrobiol.* 55, 1.
Freudenthal, H. (1962). *J. Protozool.* 9, 45.
Gauthier, G. (1963). *J. Exp. Zool.* 152, 13.
Geddes, P. (1882). *Proc. Roy. Soc. Edinburgh* 11, 377.
Gohar, H. A. F. (1940). *Publ. Mar. Biol. Sta. Ghardaqa* 2, 25.
Gohar, H. A. F. (1948). *Publ. Mar. Biol. Sta. Ghardaqa* 6, 1.
Gordon, M. S., and Kelly, H. M. (1962). *Ecology* 43, 473.
Goreau, T. F. (1956). Ph.D. Thesis, Yale University, New Haven, Connecticut.
Goreau, T. F. (1961). *Endeavour* 20, 32.
Goreau, T. F. (1963). *Ann. N.Y. Acad. Sci.* 109, 127.
Goreau, T. F., and Goreau, N. I. (1959a). *Biol. Bull.* 116, 59.
Goreau, T. F., and Goreau, N. I. (1959b). *Biol. Bull.* 117, 239.
Goreau, T. F., and Goreau, N. I. (1960a). *Biol. Bull.* 118, 419.
Goreau, T. F., and Goreau, N. I. (1960b). *Biol. Bull.* 119, 416.
Goreau, T. F., and Goreau, N. I. (1960c). *Science* 131, 668.

Goreau, T. F., and Philpott, D. E. (1956). *Exp. Cell Res.* **10**, 552.
Goreau, T. F., Goreau, N. I., and Yonge, C. M. (1971). *Biol. Bull.* **141**, 247.
Halldal, P. (1968). *Biol. Bull.* **134**, 411.
Hyman, L. (1940). "The Invertebrates," Vol. I. McGraw-Hill, New York.
Jeffrey, S. W., and Haxo, F. T. (1968). *Biol. Bull.* **135**, 149.
Johannes, R. E., and Webb, K. L. (1970). *In* "Symposium on Organic Matter in Natural Waters," pp. 257–273. Univ. of Alaska Press, College, Alaska.
Johannes, R. E., Coward, S. J., and Webb, K. L. (1969). *Comp. Biochem. Physiol.* **29**, 283
Johannes, R. E., Coles, S. L., and Kuenzel, N. T. (1970). *Limnol. Oceanogr.* **15**, 579.
Jørgensen, C. B. (1966). "Biology of Suspension Feeding." Pergamon, Oxford.
Kanwisher, J. W., and Wainwright, S. A. (1967). *Biol. Bull.* **133**, 378.
Kawaguti, S. (1944). *Palao Trop. Biol. Stud.* **2**, 267.
Kawaguti, S. (1953). *Biol. J. Okayama Univ.* **1**, 171.
Kawaguti, S. (1954). *Biol. J. Okayama Univ.* **2**, 45.
Kawaguti, S. (1964). *Proc. Jap. Acad. Sci.* **40**, 545.
Kawaguti, S. (1965). *Proc. Jap. Acad. Sci.* **40**, 832.
Kawaguti, S., and Sakumoto, D. (1948). *Bull. Oceanogr. Inst. Taiwan* **4**, 65.
Kepner, W. A., and Thomas, W. L. (1928). *Biol. Bull.* **54**, 529.
Kevin, M., Hall, W. T., McLaughlin, J. J. A., and Zahl, P. A. (1969). *J. Phycol.* **5**, 341.
Kohn, A. J., and Helfrich, P. (1957). *Limnol. Oceanogr.* **2**, 241.
Krijgsman, B. J., and Talbot, F. H. (1953). *Arch. Int. Physiol.* **61**, 277.
Lenhoff, H. M. (1961). *Exp. Cell Res.* **23**, 335.
Lenhoff, H. M. (1968). *Chem. Zool.* **2**, 158–221.
Lewis, D. H., and Smith, D. C. (1971). *Proc. Roy. Soc., Ser. B* **178**, 111.
Lindstedt, K. J., Muscatine, L., and Lenhoff, H. M. (1968). *Comp. Biochem. Physiol.* **26**, 567.
Lunger, P. (1963). *J. Ultrastruct. Res.* **9**, 362.
McLaughlin, J. J. A., and Zahl, P. (1966). *In* "Symbiosis" (S. M. Henry, ed.), Vol. 1, pp. 257–297. Academic Press, New York.
Mariscal, R. N. (1971). *In* "Experimental Coelenterate Biology" (H. M. Lenhoff, L. Muscatine, and L. V. Davis, eds.), pp. 157–168. Univ. of Hawaii Press, Honolulu, Hawaii.
Mariscal, R. N., and Lenhoff, H. M. (1968). *J. Exp. Biol.* **49**, 689.
Marshall, S. M., and Orr, A. P. (1960). *In* "The Physiology of Crustracea" (T. H. Waterman, ed.), Vol. 1, pp. 227–258. Academic Press, New York.
Matthai, G. (1923). *Quart. J. Microsc. Sci.* **67**, 101.
Muscatine, L. (1961). *In* "The Biology of Hydra" (H. Lenhoff and W. F. Loomis, eds.), pp. 255–268. Univ. of Miami Press, Coral Gables, Florida.
Muscatine, L. (1967). *Science* **156**, 516.
Muscatine, L. (1971). *In* "Experimental Coelenterate Biology" (H. M. Lenhoff, L. Muscatine, and L. V. Davis, eds.), pp. 255–268. Univ. of Hawaii Press, Honolulu, Hawaii.
Muscatine, L., and Cernichiari, E. (1969). *Biol. Bull.* **137**, 506.
Muscatine, L., and Hand, C. (1958). *Proc. Nat. Acad. Sci. U.S.* **44**, 1259.
Muscatine, L., and H. M. Lenhoff (1965). *Biol. Bull.* **129**, 316.
Muscatine, L., Pool, R., and Cernichiari, E. (1972). *Mar. Biol.* **13**, 298.

Nair, P. V. R., and Pillai, C. S. G. (1969). *Mar. Biol. Ass. India Symp. Corals and Coral Reefs,* (abstr.).

Nicol, J. A. C. (1959). *J. Mar. Biol. Ass. U.K.* **38**, 469.

Odum, H. T., and Odum, E. P. (1955). *Ecol. Monogr.* **25**, 291.

Odum, H. T., Burkholder, P. R., and Rivero, J. (1959). *Publ. Inst. Mar. Sci., Univ. Tex.* **6**, 159.

Pearse, V. B. (1970). *Nature (London)* **228**, 383.

Pearse, V. B. (1971). *In* "Experimental Coelenterate Biology" (H. Lenhoff, L. Muscatine, and L. V. Davis, eds.), pp. 239–245. Univ. of Hawaii Press, Honolulu, Hawaii.

Pearse, V. B., and Muscatine, L. (1971). *Biol. Bull.* **141**, 350.

Pomeroy, L. R., and Kuenzler, E. J. (1969). *In* "Proceedings of The Second National Symposium on Radioecology" (D. J. Nelson and F. C. Evans, eds.), pp. 474–482.

Pratt, E. M. (1905). *Quart. J. Microsc. Sci.* **194**, 327.

Roffman, B. (1968). *Comp. Biochem. Physiol.* **27**, 405.

Roushdy, H. M., and Hansen, V. K. (1961). *Nature (London)* **190**, 649.

Ryther, J. (1959). *Science* **130**, 602.

Sargent, M. C., and Austin, T. S. (1949). *Trans. Amer. Geophys. Union* **30**, 245.

Sargent, M. C., and Austin, T. S. (1954. *U.S., Geol. Surv., Prof. Pap.* **260–E**, 299–300.

Simkiss, K., (1964a). *J. Cons., Cons. Perm. Int. Explor. Mer* **29**, 6.

Simkiss, K. (1964b). *Experientia* **20**, 140.

Slobodkin, L. B. (1964). *J. Ecol.* **52**, 131.

Smith, D. C., Muscatine, L., and Lewis, D. H. (1969). *Biol. Rev. Cambridge Phil. Soc.* **44**, 17.

Steeman-Nielsen, E. (1954). *J. Cons., Cons. Perm. Int. Explor. Mer* **49**, 309.

Stephens, G. C. (1960a). *Science* **131**, 1532.

Stephens, G. C. (1960b). *Anat. Rec.* **137**, 395.

Stephens, G. C. (1962). *Biol. Bull.* **123**, 648.

Stephens, G. C. (1967). *In* "Estuaries" (G. H. Lauff, ed.), pp. 367–373.

Stephens, G. C. (1968). *Amer. Zool.* **8**, 95.

Stephens, G. C., and Schinske, R. (1961). *Limnol. Oceanogr.* **6**, 175.

Stoddard, D. R. (1969). *Biol. Rev. Cambridge Phil. Soc.* **44**, 433.

Taylor, D. L. (1968). *J. Mar. Biol. Ass. U.K.* **48**, 349.

Taylor, D. L. (1969). *J. Phycol.* **5**, 336.

Taylor, D. L. (1971). *J. Mar. Biol. Ass. U.K.* **51**, 227–234.

Tranter, D. J., and Jacob, G. (1969). *Mar. Biol. Ass. India Symp. Corals Coral Reefs* (abstr.).

Trench, R. K. (1970). *Nature (London)* **227**, 1155.

Trench, R. K. (1971a). *Proc. Roy. Soc., Ser. B* **177**, 225.

Trench, R. K. (1971b). *Proc. Roy. Soc., Ser. B* **177**, 237.

Trench, R. K. (1971c). *Proc. Roy. Soc., Ser. B* **177**, 251.

Vandermeulen, J. H., Davis, N., and Muscatine, L. (1972). *Mar. Biol.* (in press).

Vaughan, T. W. (1930). "The Oceanographical Point of View," pp. 40–56. Contrib. Mar. Biol., Stanford Univ. Press, Stanford, California.

Vaughan, T. W., and Wells, J. W. (1943). *Geol. Soc. Amer., Spec. Pap.* **44**, 1–363.

von Holt, C. (1968). *Comp. Biochem. Physiol.* **26**, 1071.

von Holt, C., and von Holt, M. (1968a). *Comp. Biochem. Physiol.* **24**, 73.

von Holt, C., and von Holt, M. (1968b). *Comp. Biochem. Physiol.* **24**, 83.

Wainwright, S. A. (1967). *Nature (London)* **216**, 1041.
Wells, J. (1957). *In* "Treatise of Paleontology" (R. Moore, ed.), Vol. F, pp. 328–443.
Werner, B. (1965). *Helgolaender Wiss. Meeresunters.* **12**, 1.
Yamazato, K. (1966). Ph.D. Thesis, University of Hawaii, Honolulu.
Yonge, C. M. (1930). *Sci. Rep. Gt. Barrier Reef Exped.* **1**, 14.
Yonge, C. M. (1931). *Sci. Rep. Gt. Barrier Reef Exped.* **1**, 83.
Yonge, C. M. (1937). *Biol. Rev. Cambridge Phil. Soc.* **12**, 87.
Yonge, C. M. (1940). *Sci. Rep. Gt. Barrier Reef Exped.* **1**, 353.
Yonge, C. M. (1963). *Advan. Mar. Biol.* **1**, 209–260.
Yonge, C. M. (1968). *Proc. Roy. Soc., Ser. B* **169**, 329.
Yonge, C. M. and Nicholls, A. G. (1930). *Sci. Rep. Gt. Barrier Reef Exped.* **1**, 59.
Yonge, C. M., and Nicholls, A. G. (1931a). *Sci. Rep. Gt. Barrier Reef Exped.* **1**, 135.
Yonge, C. M., and Nicholls, A. G. (1931b). *Sci. Rep. Gt. Barrier Reef Exped.* **1**, 177.
Yonge, C. M., Yonge, M. J., and Nicholls, A. G. (1932). *Sci. Rep. Gt. Barrier Reef Exped.* **1**, 213.
Young, S. D. (1969). Ph.D. Thesis, University of California, Los Angeles.
Young, S. D. (1971). *Comp. Biochem. Physiol.* **40B**, 113.
Young, S. D., O'Connor, J. D., and Muscatine, L. (1971). *Comp. Biochem. Physiol.* **40B**, 945.

5

THE ECOLOGY OF MARINE ANTIBIOTICS
AND CORAL REEFS

Paul R. Burkholder

I. Introduction

In connection with studies of antagonisms existing among marine plants and animals, the author has enjoyed the unusual privilege of scuba diving on the magnificent coral reefs of Australia, the Philippines, Palau, and many islands in the Caribbean Sea. The splendor of the gigantic Swain reefs off the coast of Queensland, diversity of species in the coral communities of the Palau Islands, and the beautiful stone architecture of the inner reefs at Anegada, British Virgin Islands, provide thrilling examples of the great natural wonders of tropical seas. Other natural wonders of the world, such as lofty mountains, deep canyons, high waterfalls, and ramifying caverns, are the results of physical and chemical forces of erosion and disintegration acting through geological history,

117

but the great barrier reefs and atolls are the architectural creations built up by vast arrays of living plants and animals, working together over long periods of time. Their work is never ending; generation after generation, their growth and reproduction are accompanied by the continual fashioning of these beautiful undersea cathedrals of coral, many of which are older than mankind.

It is hoped that information in this chapter and in this entire book will serve further to acquaint many people in all lands with diverse knowledge about the dynamic reef communities, and to show how countless assemblages of flora and fauna carry on their ways of life together while constantly bathed in the common seawater from which we have all come. Can it be possible that, if the primitive builders of coral cathedrals were sufficiently well understood to be appreciated, man would not wantonly destroy them for temporary material gain or condemn them as places for the disposal of wastes? Only time will tell how far the consequences of pollution can go and what havoc will be caused by exploitation and the pressures of an everexpanding human population. As Plutarch once said, "Though the boys throw stones at frogs in sport, yet the frogs do not die in sport but in earnest."

II. The Concept of Antibiosis

Where numerous kinds of plants and animals live together, as in tropical marine ecosystems, many types of interactions constantly occur. One of the most powerful of all coactions is that special kind of interference among living organisms known as *antibiosis*. While symbiosis connotes mutual benefit derived from an association of organisms living together, antibiosis signifies a relationship that is harmful or against certain kinds of life (*anti*, against; *bios*, life). We can envisage antibiotic substances as a natural means for protection of organisms producing such substances, to be used against others that would do them harm.

The narrow concept of antibiotics, as those special compounds produced by microorganisms cultivated under laboratory conditions and having the capacity in low concentrations to inhibit growth and destroy other microorganisms (Waksman, 1945), has in recent years been broadened in scope to include substances derived not only from microorganisms growing in culture media but also substances produced in nature by fungi, plankton, higher plants, and even animals. Biologists now regard antibiosis as a phenomenon in which special products of certain organisms severely limit the life activities of other organisms.

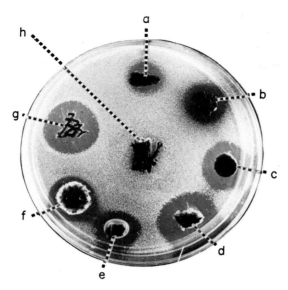

Fig. 1. Growth inhibition of a marine bacterium (No. 13) in nutrient agar when tissues of gorgonids are placed on the agar surface: (a,b) *Eunicea calyculata;* (c) *Plexaurella dichotoma;* (d) *Muricea elongata;* (e) *Eunicea succinea;* (f) *Plexaurella porosa;* (g) *Gorgonia ventalina.* No inhibition is shown by the piece of black coral (*Antipathes* sp.) placed in the center of the petri dish(h).

This approaches the original concept of antibiosis as the term was first used by Vuillemin (1889) to describe the opposition of one organism to the life of another. In Fig. 1, various gorgonids collected from a depth of 10 m cause distinct zones of growth inhibition of marine bacteria seeded into seawater nutrient agar, while the black coral, collected at a depth of 170 m in the Virgin Islands, exhibits no antibiotic activity against these bacteria. This example shows that some kinds of marine animals, but not all, produce substances that inhibit growth of marine microorganisms taken from the same environment. The inhibiting substances are considered to be antibiotics.

This chapter will be devoted chiefly to antimicrobial substances produced by marine organisms and their possible ecological significance in the sea. Much of the discussion concerns organisms living on coral reefs or in nearby waters. A few references are taken from the general literature on antibiotics and toxic substances produced by marine organisms in other areas of the ocean, because they seem to contribute significantly to the subject. Many aspects of the overall topic of biological activity belonging strictly in the realms of medicine and pharmacology are not included. Extensive and detailed information concerning marine toxins, venoms, drugs from the sea, and marine pharmacology in general can be found in many excellent treatises on these special topics (Jackson, 1964; Halstead, 1965, 1967; Russell, 1965; Baslow, 1969; Der Marderosian, 1969ab, 1970; Burkholder, 1968; Burkholder and Sharma, 1970).

III. Growth Inhibitors in Seawater

The evidence for ecological effects of antibiotics in the sea is derived chiefly from observations concerning localized phenomena among the flora and fauna of coral reefs, in plankton communities, and in mangrove lagoons, rather than from studies in the open ocean. Nevertheless, in recent years marine microbiologists have come to recognize the presence of growth-inhibitory properties in raw or filtered seawater, as compared with artificial or autoclaved seawater. Thus, it has been found that the pollution bacterium *Escherichia coli* and the marine *Serratia marinorubra* are inhibited by natural seawater, as compared with artificial seawater used as a control (Jones, 1963). The antibacterial activity increases with depth in the sea down to 1000 m. Gram-positive bacteria of terrestrial origin seem to be most susceptible (Saz *et al.*, 1963), and this is said to lend support to the explanation that gram-negative bacteria are more common in ocean waters, possibly because they have become more resistant to the antibacterial properties of seawater. The inhibitory substances appear to be diminished by ultrafiltration, are thermolabile, and are destroyed by autoclaving (Jones, 1963; Pramer *et al.*, 1963).

In addition to the antibacterial action of raw seawater, observations have shown that in a short time seawater can inactivate viruses suspended in it (Magnusson *et al.*, 1966). It seems possible that the virus-inactivating properties may be related to special substances derived from certain kinds of marine bacteria (Gundersen *et al.*, 1967). It is not entirely clear whether microbial antagonism observed in some samples of raw seawater is caused by organic substances of an antibiotic nature, or whether some toxic effects of metals may be involved. A good review of the literature is given by Baslow (1969).

IV. Bacteria as Producers of Antibiotics

Among a total of 1600 described species of bacteria, about 12% are found in the sea. Most kinds and greatest numbers appear to be close to land where suitable nutriment is provided by the plankton and benthic plants and animals. Numerous kinds of marine bacteria can be readily isolated from the sea by using convenient plating methods (Burkholder, 1970) with samples obtained from marine grass meadows, algal beds, and sediments taken from coral reefs or other likely areas. Some marine bacteria possess pigments of many diverse colors; others digest agar or show luminescence in the dark, and some produce antibiotic substances. Investigators of antibiotic phenomena have oftentimes used terrestrial assay cultures of microorganisms or pathogenic strains in their screening for antibiotic cultures isolated from the sea. Antimicrobial substances produced by marine microbes actually may be inhibitory for various kinds of organisms derived from either the land or the sea. It is relatively easy to demonstrate antibiotic action of marine bacteria by streaking suitable cultures near each other on the surface of a nutrient agar plate (Fig. 2). After a few hours, the inhibiting effects of an an-

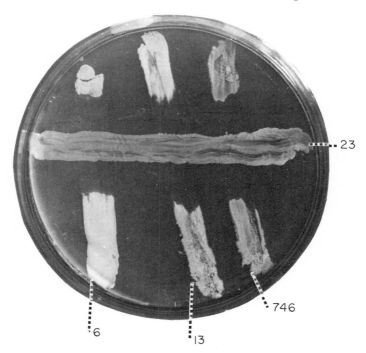

Fig. 2. Antibiosis is demonstrated by streaking sensitive marine bacteria (such as Nos. 6, 13, and 746) across the surface of a nutrient agar plate and then cross streaking an antagonistic culture (No. 23) over the indicator streaks. After incubation for a few hours, the antagonistic culture (No. 23) has inhibited growth of the others where antibiotic substances have been excreted into the substratum.

tagonistic organism will be seen where growth of susceptible organisms is prevented by diffusion of an antibiotic substance into the agar.

The first investigations of marine antibiotic-producing bacteria were carried out by Rosenfeld and ZoBell (1947) who reported that nine of their isolates inhibited *Bacillus* and *Micrococcus* test cultures. Later, Grein and Meyers (1958) found that more than half of the seventy cultures of actinomycetes that they isolated from coastal areas were active against gram-positive and gram-negative bacteria. There is considerable doubt, however, that these actinomycetes were true marine organisms with an obligate requirement for seawater. In another study, less than 4% of bacterial isolates obtained from the sea gave evidence of antibiotic production (Buck *et al.*, 1962). One marine *Pseudomonas*, isolated from amphipods, showed marked selective ability to inhibit growth of yeasts of both terrestrial and marine origins (Buck *et al.*, 1963; Buck, 1968). The marine yeast *Rhodotorula minuta* was markedly inhibited by culture products of the *Pseudomonas*. Few or no pink yeasts were observed in amphipod communities from which the pseudomonad was isolated. A summary of this work was published by Buck (1968).

Krasil'nikova (1962) tested 326 isolates of marine bacteria taken from the sea in a worldwide study and found that 124 cultures showed some degree of activity against laboratory strains of bacteria, yeast, and some fungi. Baam *et al.* (1966a) isolated 60 cultures from the sea near Bombay and demonstrated antagonism against *Staphylococcus aureus, Salmonella typhosa, Alginomonas* sp., and many other bacteria. In further studies (Baam *et al.*, 1966b), these authors observed pronounced effects of 11 different kinds of media upon antibiotic production.

Until now, the only structurally known antibiotic substance derived from marine bacteria is 2-(3,5-dibromo-2-hydroxyphenyl)-3,4,5-tribromopyrrole, obtained from a new species *Pseudomonas bromoutilis*, which was isolated from *Thalassia* (turtle grass) in Puerto Rico (Burkholder *et al.*, 1966). Lovell (1966) elucidated the structure and Hanessian and Kaltenbronn (1966) synthesized the compound (Fig. 3). P.

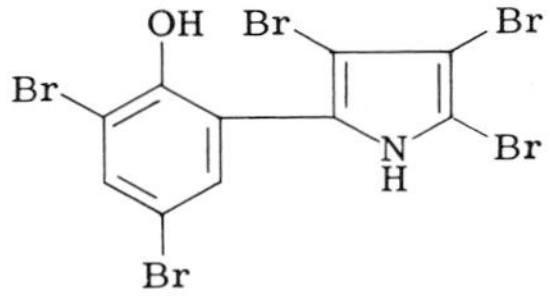

Fig. 3. This antibiotic, 2-(3,5-dibromo-2-hydroxyphenyl)-3,4,5-tribromopyrrole, is produced by the marine bacterium *Pseudomonas bromoutilis*.

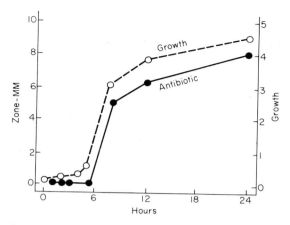

Fig. 4. Growth and excretion of an antibiotic substance into nutrient seawater medium by the red-pigmented marine bacterium P 9. After Burkholder (1963).

bromoutilis has a requirement for seawater, and it inhibits numerous kinds of terrestrial gram-positive bacteria and cultures derived from the sea. In a screening experiment, 11 out of 15 marine isolates were found to be susceptible to the antibiotic produced by the marine *P. bromoutilis*. Two of the four resistant strains turned out to be the same species, *P. bromoutilis*.

It has been our experience that some marine bacteria produce and liberate antibiotics into the surrounding seawater medium during their active phase of growth (Fig. 4). Other antibiotic producers, e.g., *Pseudomonas bromoutilis*, grow and synthesize antibiotics best on solid substrates such as nutrient seawater agar (Burkholder *et al.*, 1966). There seems to be no good reason why laboratory observations of microbial activities cannot be regarded as suggesting the types of natural activities that may occur in the sea. A strain of *Alginovibrio aquatilis*, which decomposes alginates and other polysaccharides, has recently been discovered to make a broad spectrum antibiotic that is especially active against smooth strains of *Pseudomonas aeruginosa* (Doggett, 1968).

Investigations by Gauthier (1969a), conducted at the Centre d'Etudes et de Recherches de Biologie et d'Océanographie Médicale (CERBOM) in Nice, have revealed that many truly marine bacteria possess the power to inhibit terrestrial and marine microorganisms. A group of 26 antibiotic cultures, including species belonging in the genera *Pseudomonas*, *Achromobacter*, *Flavobacterium*, *Xanthomonas*, *Chromobacterium*, and *Vibrio*, showed pronounced antagonism against gram-positive bacteria. Certain species of *Achromobacter* and *Flavobacterium* also inhibited the growth of *Escherichia coli, Pseudomonas aeruginosa,* and *Proteus vulgaris.*

It has been observed that products of the diatom *Skeletonema costatum* stimulate growth of *Pseudomonas* populations in Narragansett Bay, Rhode Island (Sieburth, 1968a). An inverse relationship between *Arthrobacter* species and the appearance of phytoplankton blooms and *Pseudomonas* suggested that either the diatoms or the pseudomonads might be inhibiting the arthrobacters. Marked inhibition of *Arthrobacter* sp. by dominant pseudomonads was readily demonstrated in cross-streak plates in the laboratory. Graphic representation of the percent of bacterial isolates of the two genera in the Bay plotted against time from January to June, 1964, showed clear and consistent inverse relationships between pseudomonads and arthrobacters (Fig. 5).

Additional experimental data concerning antibiotic-producing marine bacteria have been obtained recently in our laboratories by making tests of marine microbial products against numerous bacterial isolates (96) obtained from coral reef areas near La Parguera, Puerto Rico (see Fig. 6). In one experiment, 11 antagonistic cultures were grown on the surface of nutrient seawater agar in petri plates. After 3 days, small cylin-

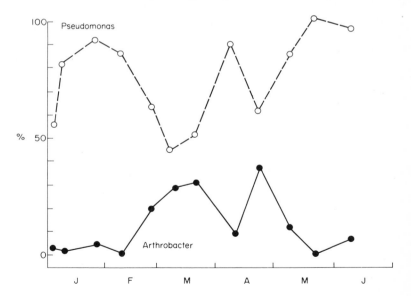

Fig. 5. Inverse relationship in fluctuating populations of *Pseudomonas* sp. and *Arthrobacter* sp. in Narragansett Bay. After Sieburth (1967).

Fig. 6. Near La Parguera, Puerto Rico, shallow lagoons protected by surrounding mangroves often support luxuriant growths of *Thalassia testudinum, Lyngbya majuscula* (prominent mats), and other algae. In this kind of habitat, many marine organisms can be found for antibiotic and other studies. Some of the bacteria used in experiments reported in Figs. 7 and 8 were isolated from the Enrique reef area shown in this photo.

ders of agar were punched out with a sterile cork borer, one-quarter inch in diameter, and the small pieces of agar were then placed upon the surface of plates, each of which had been streaked with a cotton swab containing a culture of test bacteria. After incubation for 24 hours, the inhibition zones (Fig. 7) were measured and recorded in millimeters of radius outside the edges of the agar cylinders. Some representative results are plotted in Fig. 8. The percent of test cultures that were inhibited to different extents by antibiotic cultures Nos. 6, 23, and 81 show three typical kinds of statistical distribution. Number 6 is a marine

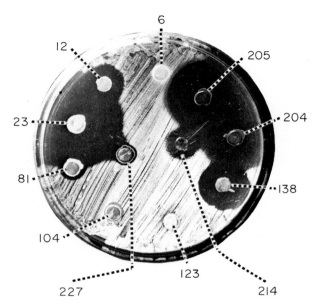

Fig. 7. Antibiotic zones caused by marine bacteria Nos. 12, 23, 81, 138, 204, and 205 when tested against a sensitive marine bacterium (No. 24) seeded in the agar plate. Note that Nos. 6, 104, 123 and 227 show little or no antibiotic action.

isolate (pink in color) that possesses relatively weak powers of antagonism, about 80% of the test cultures being uninhibited by its fermentation products, and the rest showing small zones of inhibition in the assay plates. Isolate No. 81 (colorless) failed to inhibit approximately one-third of the test cultures and showed weak inhibition against the others. Isolate No. 23 (a yellow culture), quite distinct from the other antibiotic bacteria, showed a flattened distribution curve of inhibition in all groups, from 0 (about 15%) through the 1–2, 3–4, and to the 15–16 mm zone. Some of these antibiotic marine cultures were observed to inhibit other antibiotic-producing bacteria, and certain older cultures were found capable of inhibiting young, growing cultures of the same species. Thus, we find examples of both auto- and heteroinhibition among the matched pairs of antagonistic cultures. The results of these tests indicate the presence of diverse and selectively acting antibiotics among marine bacteria. Some of the active isolates, which show little or no inhibition against the majority of test bacteria, e.g., No. 6, nevertheless may inhibit cultures that are resistant even to generally more potent cultures, such as No. 23. Some of our cultures appear to be identical with antimicrobial bacteria reported by Gauthier (1969b) in the Mediterranean. Isolation and characterization of active compounds produced by marine bacteria would provide new and significant knowledge.

Some of these antibacterial substances are secreted into the surrounding seawater medium by growing cells. Centrifugation or filtration of liquid cultures in the exponential phase of growth provided solutions that showed good zones of inhibition when tested against sensitive marine isolates. Bacteria and phytoplankton appear to secrete antibiotics into their environment, but it is difficult to demonstrate secretion of antagonistic compounds by living, marine, multicellular plants and animals, such as sponges, zoanthids, and gorgonids. In these larger organisms, antibiotic substances appear to be retained normally within the living tissues, but the activity can be released upon injury to the cells.

It is not known whether any marine viruses are inhibited by products of marine bacteria, but recent evidence suggests that *Vibrio marinus* possesses virus-inactivating properties against poliovirus (Gundersen *et*

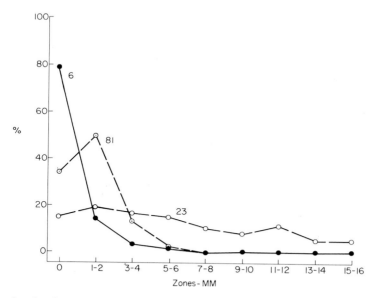

Fig. 8. The frequency (as %) of antibiotic zones of different sizes produced in 96 sensitive bacteria seeded in agar plates, when the beers of antagonistic cultures No. 6, 23, and 81 were applied to the surface of the agar. Note how culture No. 23 inhibits about 85% of all the test bacteria, with zones varying from 1–2 to 15–16 mm radius. See Fig. 7 and text discussion.

al., 1967). It should be mentioned that sponges and other invertebrates apparently harbor a variety of viruses, some of which have been studied by Vago and Bergoni (1968). Lysis of *Escherichia coli* by certain kinds of marine bacteria, forming large plaques, has been reported by Mitchell *et al.* (1967). The influence of *Bdellovibrio* in autopurification of polluted estuaries has been studied by Daniel (1969). Apparently this small parasitic vibrio, which lyses *E. coli,* is often present in polluted marine areas. Parasites of gram-positive bacteria have also been reported from polluted waters (Guelin *et al.*, 1968). Purification of unclean estuaries, therefore, cannot always be attributed to the possible action of antibiotics, in view of the presence of other organisms and processes that can destroy pollution microorganisms.

Very little is known about the antibiotic properties of marine fungi. In tests which we conducted on about fifty cultures of marine fungi, supplied by Dr. Jan Kohlmeyer, only two showed slight evidence of having antibiotic activity. The broad-spectrum antibiotic cephalothin was derived from a species of *Cephalosporium* isolated from the sea off Sardinia (Brotzu, 1948; Crawford *et al.*, 1952, Abraham, 1962), but this organism may not be regarded as a true marine fungus.

V. Phytoplankton and Microalgae

Excretion products of phytoplankton have long been recognized to have ecological significance from the viewpoints of both nutrition and antagonism (Burkholder, 1963). The earlier literature has been reviewed by several authors (Lucas, 1947, 1955; Schwimmer and Schwimmer, 1955; Jorgensen, 1959; Nigrelli, 1958, 1962; Fogg, 1962; Lefevre, 1964) who have pointed out various facts and theories concerning regulating substances implicated in the periodicity and succession of marine organisms. Considerable interest has developed in regard to the possibility that marine antibiotics may interfere in the determinations of primary productivity in the ocean with the ^{14}C technique (Steeman-Nielsen, 1955a,b; Steeman-Nielsen and Jorgensen, 1961; Jorgensen, 1962). The animal exclusion hypothesis of Hardy (1965) was proposed to explain the occasionally observed absence of grazing animals from dense stands of phytoplankton, where antibiotic substances of a deterrent nature may be present. Other microalgae, such as microbenthic blue-greens and the symbiotic zooxanthellae living abundantly in many invertebrates of coral reefs, appear to be capable of making antibiotic substances along with numerous other bioactive compounds. Excretion of glycerol, glycolic acid, amino acids, and other unknown substances appears to be a common phenomenon among microalgae (Hellebust, 1965). Identification and significance of various growth factors and inhibitory substances can be determined with appropriate bioassay and chemical procedures (Bentley, 1960; Hartman, 1968).

A discussion of some specific contributions in the recent literature concerning antagonistic properties of marine microalgae will now be presented. In temperate and polar seas, antibiotics can be produced by the planktonic *Phaeocystis, Skeletonema,* etc. (Sieburth, 1959, 1960; Sieburth and Pratt, 1962), and, in the tropics, different antimicrobial substances are formed by other kinds of plankton, especially dinoflagellates and blue-green algae. Among the first observations of antibiosis in tropical phytoplankton was the report of antibacterial and antiyeast compounds produced by *Goniodoma,* a dinoflagellate which sometimes blooms abundantly in mangrove lagoons of Puerto Rico, Jamaica, and elsewhere (Burkholder *et al.,* 1960). This red-tide organism was at first thought to be *Gonyaulax,* but later studies by Dr. Estela Silva indicated that it is a species of *Goniodoma.* Repeated collections of this phytoflagellate exhibited both growth-promoting and growth-inhibiting properties when tested against laboratory cultures and bacteria isolated from the sea. A novel compound called goniodomin was isolated from material filtered from shallow waters near La Parguera, Puerto Rico (Sharma *et al.,* 1968a). The compound inhibits growth of many kinds of yeast and fungi. Its molecular formula appears to be $C_{43}H_{58}O_{11}$, and it probably contains a dihydrogeranyl radical. The chemistry of other antibiotics present in *Goniodoma* is not known.

Antimicrobial activity has been demonstrated in red tides caused by *Cochlodinium* sp. in the headwaters of Phosphorescent Bay, Puerto Rico. Cultures of *Gyrodinium cohnii* are also antibiotic. Toxicity and other biological properties of *Amphidinium carteri* have been observed by Louzon (1964). This organism produces extensive blooms in coastal waters of the temperate zone. Antibiotic blooms of peridinians have been reported from the Mediterranean by Aubert *et al.* (1967).

Marine dinoflagellates are represented by about 1100 species. Some of them form red tides that can cause mass mortality of marine animals (Connell and Cross, 1950; Howell, 1953; Grindley and Taylor, 1964). Others synthesize toxic materials that are lethal for many kinds of organisms (Abbott and Ballantine, 1957), and, after entering into food chains, may cause paralytic shellfish poisoning in man. Numerous studies of toxins in various dinoflagellates, including species of *Gonyaulax* and *Gymnodinium,* have been reviewed by Halstead (1965) and Russell

(1965, 1967). The toxins and antibiotics of Pyrrhophyta could be produced in mass cultures for further valuable studies of their chemistry and biomedical relationships. Satisfactory methods for cultivating marine flagellates have been compiled from the literature by Aaronson (1970).

Production of antibiotic compounds by zooxanthellae (see Fig. 9), symbionts in alcyonarians and other invertebrates, has been suggested

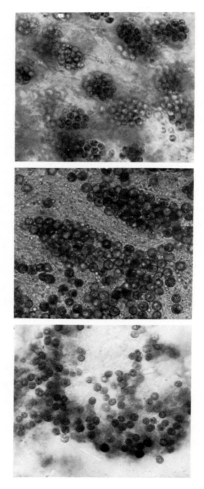

Fig. 9. Zooxanthellae, symbionts in various species of Cnidaria, may be the producers of antibiotics and other special substances isolated from these animals. Top, symbionts from *Cassiopea frondosa;* middle, from *Zoanthus sociatus;* bottom, from *Briareum asbestinum.*

by Ciereszko (1962) to explain the antagonistic properties of the plant–animal complexes. Further discussion of this concept will be found in the consideration of substances observed in various Cnidaria.

Diatoms, which often occur as plankton blooms, may also produce antibiotic substances. Thus, the diatom *Skeletonema costatum* shows anticoliform activity as well as other direct and indirect ecological effects (Sieburth and Pratt, 1962). Burkholder (1963) observed selective inhibition by aqueous extracts of *Skeletonema* tested against several kinds of marine bacteria. Antibacterial activity of the marine diatoms, *Asterionella japonica, Chaetoceros teres*, and other species growing in the Mediterranean Sea, has been studied by Aubert and colleagues (1966a; Aubert and Gauthier, 1966a). Concentrates of active principles prepared on Sephadex G-25 columns (Aubert and Gauthier, 1966b) appear to contain nucleotides and fatty acids. All together, the antibacterial activity of 45 kinds of diatoms and 11 other species of phytoplankton have been screened in the laboratories of the CERBOM in Nice, with the result that over 25% appear to have activity against bacteria (Aubert and Gauthier, 1967). The potency of some diatoms, such as *Asterionella japonica, Gyrosigma spenceri*, and *Chaetoceros affinis*, was lost after sterilization in the autoclave (Aubert *et al.*, 1966b; Aubert and Gauthier, 1966a,b). Isolation and chemical characterization of more active compounds produced by oceanic plankton are needed because their influence in marine ecology appears to be exerted through regulation of bacterial and algal growth (Gauthier, 1969a) over wide geographic areas.

An interesting study of antibiotic production by marine phytoplankton grown in axenic culture was carried out by Duff *et al.* (1966). Cell extracts of 14 species, belonging to 6 algal classes, were tested against 9 marine isolates and 14 strains of terrestrial saprophytes. The phytoplankters most active against marine bacteria were *Phaeodactylum tricornutum, Skeletonema costatum* (diatoms); *Coccolithus huxleyi, Isochrysis galbana, Monochrysis lutheri* (chrysophytes); *Cryptomonas* sp., *Hemiselmis virescens, Rhodomonas lens* (cryptophytes); and *Amphidinium carteri* (dinoflagellate). The cultures of blue-green algae that were tested failed to show significant inhibition of marine bacteria. Lecithinase toxin was demonstrated in *Monochrysis lutheri* (Antia and Bilinski, 1967), and antibacterial chlorophyll derivatives were observed in *Isochrysis galbana* (Bruce and Duff, 1967). The commonly observed algal antibiosis against gram-positive strains of terrestrial bacteria suggests that inhibitory substances may prevent such organisms from becoming dominant in the sea, where the level of organic nutrients anyhow is usually limiting for microbial growth.

The antibiotics, toxins, and growth-regulating substances in Chryso-phyta have been discussed by Sieburth (1964), Shilo (1967), and Baslow (1969). The ichthyotoxins from *Prymnesium* and *Ochromonas* (Reich and Spiegelstein, 1964) can readily serve as exemplary model systems to suggest future studies on different toxigenic algae and methods for their control.

Some species of planktonic and benthic blue-green algae show antibiotic activity on a vast scale. The blue-green *Trichodesmium erythraeum*, found frequently near the surface in tropical seas, has been reported to make antibacterial substances (Ramamurphy and Krishramurphy, 1967). A species of *Trichodesmium* (named *Skujaella thiebautii* in the new nomenclature) is abundant in waters of the Lesser Antilles (Hargraves *et al.*, 1970), and, in view of its ability to fix atmospheric nitrogen, doubtless contributes much to organic productivity and special substances elaborated in seawaters of relatively low fertility. Vast areas of the Coral Sea off Australia are frequently covered with *T. erythraeum*, which can be readily seen from an airplane north from Townsville as long windrows floating near the surface. Baas-Becking (1951) has described the death of corals caused by masses of *Trichodesmium* driven onto the reefs by the wind.

Other tropical blue-green algae, such as *Lyngbya majuscula* and *Hydrocoleum comoides*, inhibit various kinds of bacteria (Burkholder *et al.*, 1960). That this alga can grow abundantly in tropical reef areas is illustrated in Fig. 6. *Lyngbya majuscula* also has antifungal activity (Welch, 1962). Cytotoxic and antiviral properties have been shown in collections of blue-green algae made in Hawaii and Puerto Rico (Starr *et al.*, 1962, 1966). *Lyngbya* produces a toxin causing dermatitis in swimmers (Banner, 1959; Chu, 1959) and has been incriminated as a possible source of ciguatoxin in poisonous fish (Habekost *et al.*, 1955; Randall, 1958; Banner *et al.*, 1960). The alga is worldwide in distribution, occurring commonly in the benthos of reefs and nearby areas, and often breaks free to form loose floating masses in estuaries. Sometimes it is found in unusual places (Fig. 10). From personal observations of the author in Puerto Rico, it is difficult to implicate *Lyngbya* in ciguatera poisoning. At La Parguera, *Lyngbya* is dominant in the harbor where small snappers, grunts, and other fish feed on the algae. Fish caught in the harbor are eaten freely by the local residents, but only occasional outbreaks of ciguatera are known to occur in the area.

A recent study by Moikeha (1968) confirmed many of the previously known antimicrobial properties of *Lyngbya majuscula*. The review of ecology, physiology, and biochemistry of blue-green algae by Holm-Han-

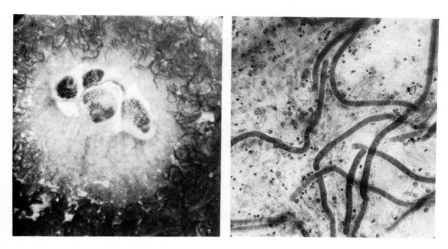

Fig. 10. The blue-green alga *Lyngbya majuscula* grows sometimes in unusual places. Left, shown around the mouth of *Zoanthus sociatus.* ×10. Right, filaments of *Lyngbya.* ×100. This blue-green has antibiotic properties and has been implicated in the food chain leading to ciguatera toxicity.

sen (1968) is very informative and gives a brief discussion of their toxins. The antimicrobial activities of blue-green algae have not yet been demonstrated to be caused by specific compounds. Antialgal, antibacterial, and toxic substances that can kill animals have been demonstrated in freshwater blue-green algae such as *Microcystis aeruginosa, Nostoc muscorum, Oscillatoria princeps,* and *O. splendida* (see Jackson, 1964; Schwimmer and Schwimmer, 1955).

Fukada (1968) extracted an antiviral agent from *Chlorella* cells. Thus green algae, as well as bacteria, appear to possess virus-inactivating capacity (see Magnusson *et al.,* 1966).

VI. Macroalgae

A review of the principal observations on antibiotics of marine macroalgae will be presented, as they seem to have significance for the ecology of organisms in tropical ecosystems. Samples of algae may be prepared for testing antibiotic potency by grinding them to fine slurries in water or by extraction in organic solvents, such as methanol, chloroform, or acetone. A discussion of the pharmacological aspects of studies on green, brown, and red algae can be found in the reference book by Baslow (1969). Slurries or extracts are usually assayed in filter paper discs placed upon the surface of agar plates seeded with appropriate test microorganisms. The radius of inhibition zones around the paper discs indicates the relative degree of antibiotic activity in the sample. By means of such simple procedures, the screening of crude materials for antibiotic activity can be accomplished rapidly.

The first investigation of this kind was carried out by Pratt et al. (1951) who reported on the antibiotic activity of various seaweed extracts. Chesters and Stott (1956) assayed the ether extracts from 17 algal species against bacteria in seeded plates and found that *Polysiphonia fastigiata* gave the widest spectrum of activity among the active organisms. In a similar way, Roos (1957) surveyed numerous kinds of algae obtained from the North Sea, but the results can have only indirect bearing in the general considerations of our subject because of the geographic, climatic, and other differences between northern and tropical seas. Turning the attention to tropical environments, Burkholder et al. (1960) screened 150 marine algae in Puerto Rico, and found 66 with antimicrobial activity against laboratory strains of bacteria and yeasts, and also isolates of marine bacteria. At about the same time, Allen and Dawson (1960) reported that some of the algae from the Pacific Ocean off Central America were active against gram-positive bacteria and *Mycobacterium,* but ineffective against gram-negative organisms.

Antibiotic properties of the algae along the Venetian coast have been reported by Fassina (1962). Olsen et al. (1964) studied methods of solvent extraction and made some microchemical tests of tropical seaweed antibiotics separated by chromatography. The work of Starr et al. (1962) and of Kathan (1965) demonstrated antiviral activity in seaweeds and agar preparations derived from marine algae. Extracts of the green alga *Pithophora* sp. inhibited growth of *Mycobacterium tuberculosis* (Klein, 1964). Possibly in the future, it may be feasible to test antibiotic activity against pathogens that cause diseases of marine animals and eventually to investigate utility of antibiotics for marine animal protection. So far, the screening and physiological observations of seaweed antibiotics have been concerned chiefly with effects upon laboratory cultures of terrestrial origin.

Significant contributions to the whole subject have been made through investigations of the chemical nature of antibiotic substances derived from the algae of the sea. Thus, fatty acids (Fig. 11) and carbonyl and terpene fractions have been demonstrated in *Porphyra, Enteromorpha, Digenea, Laminaria, Sargassum, Codium,* and *Ulva* (Kamimoto, 1955; Katayama, 1962). The antibiotic activity in *Iridiophycus* may be

(a) $CH_3(CH_2)_8COOH$

(b) $CH_3(CH_2)_{10}COOH$

(c) $CH_3(CH_2)_{12}COOH$

(d) $CH_3(CH_2)_{14}COOH$

(e) $CH_3(CH_2)_{16}COOH$

(f) $CH_3(CH_2)_7CH{=}(CH_2)_7COOH$

(g) $CH_3(CH_2)_4CH{=}CHCH_2CH{=}CH(CH_2)_7COOH$

(h) $CH_2{=}CHCOOH$

Fig. 11. Fatty acids are present in many algae, and apparently account for some of the antibiotic properties reported in the literature. The saturated fatty acids shown above are: (a) capric; (b) lauric; (c) myristic; (d) palmitic; and (e) stearic. The unsaturated fatty acids are: (f) oleic; and (g) linoleic. Acrylic acid (h) has been demonstrated in many algae, where it is contained in dimethyl-β-propiothetin.

due to acrylic acid (Pratt *et al.*, 1951), as is the case for *Phaeocystis* (Sieburth, 1960). Antibacterial activity is not always the result of some specific substance. For example, in the alga *Desmarestia* and in some tunicates, restricted growth effects may be accounted for by the stored sulfuric acid causing very low pH values (Roos, 1957; Eppley and Bovell, 1958), which are inimical to many bacteria.

In *Symphocladia gracilis* and *Rhodomela larix*, the activity has been considered to be caused by brominated phenolic compounds (Mautner *et al.*, 1953; Saito and Sameshima, 1955). In *Polysiphonia morrowii*, Saito and Ando (1955, 1957) found 5-bromo-3,4-dihydroxybenzaldehyde. The chief phenolic constituent in *Polysiphonia fastigiata* appears to be a dipotassium salt of 2,3-dibromobenzyl alcohol 4,5-disulfate (Hodgkin *et al.*, 1966) (see Fig. 12). In *Rhodomela larix* and *Odonthalia corymbifera*, bromobenzyl methyl ethers have been reported (Katsui *et al.*, 1967; Craigie and Gruenig, 1967). The compound 5,6-dibromoprotocatechualdehyde also occurs in *Rhodomela larix*. Craigie and Gruenig (1967) identified 3,5-dibromo-*p*-hydroxy benzyl alcohol in *Odonthalia* dentata and *Rhodomela confervoides*. From *Laurencia glandulifera*, the compounds laurencin ($C_{17}H_{23}O_3Br$) and laurene ($C_{15}H_{20}$) (see Fig. 13), and, from *Laurencia nipponica*, laureatin ($C_{15}H_{20}O_2Br_2$) have been isolated (Irie *et al.*, 1965a, 1968). A brominated sesquiterpenoid, laurinterol ($C_{15}H_{19}OBr$), was obtained from *Laurencia intermedia* (Irie *et al.*, 1966). Possibly the compounds aplysin and aplysinol found in sea hares (Yamamura and Hirata, 1963) are derived from red algae of the genus *Laurencia* (Irie *et al.*, 1965b, 1969) upon which the animals feed (Fig. 13).

Demonstration of the occurrence of acrylic acid, $CH_2{=}CH{-}COOH$,

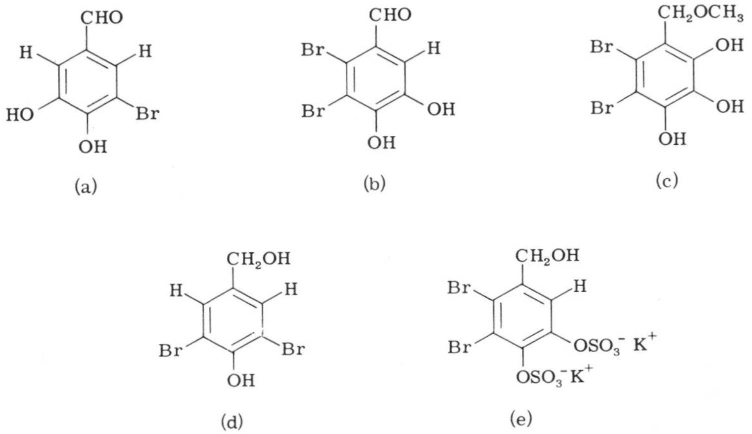

Fig. 12. Some brominated compounds found in red seaweeds: (a) 5-bromo-3,4-dihydroxybenzaldehyde; (b) 2,3-dibromo-4,5-dihydroxybenzaldehyde; (c) 2,3-dibromo-4,5,6-hydroxybenzyl methyl ether; (d) 3,5-dibromo-*p*-hydroxybenzyl alcohol; (e) 2,3-dibromobenzyl alcohol-4,5-disulfate, dipotassium salt.

in blooms of *Phaeocystis pouchetii* in Antarctica (Sieburth, 1960) stimulated renewed interest in the biological activity of this and related compounds. The peculiar odor of certain kinds of marine algae influenced Haas (1935) to discover that dimethyl sulfide is produced by *Polysiphonia fastigiata*. The precursor of $(CH_3)_2S(DMS)$ was isolated from this red alga by Challenger and Simpson (1948) and demonstrated to be dimethyl-*p*-propiothetin (DMPT). By enzymatic hydrolysis the thetin

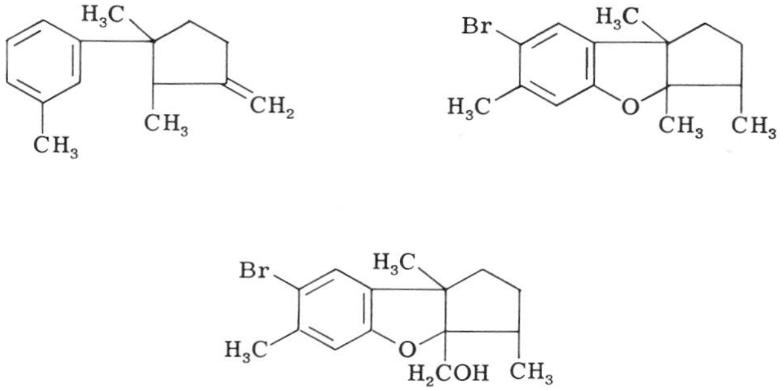

Fig. 13. Laurene (top, left), aplysin (top, right), and aplysinol (below) occur in the red alga *Laurencia glandulifera*. The sea hare *Aplysia kurodai* also contains the compounds aplysin and aplysinol, possibly because the animal feeds upon the red alga.

compound, $(CH_3)_2$—S—CH_2COOH is split to form $(CH_3)_2S$ and CH_2=CH—COOH (Bywood and Challenger, 1953; Cantoni and Anderson, 1956; Greene, 1962). DMPT has been found in many marine algae (Challenger *et al.*, 1957; Katayama, 1962). A substance resembling DMS was detected in cultures of the diatom *Phaeodactylum tricornutum* (Armstrong and Boalch, 1960).

It has been pointed out by Sieburth (1964) that the marked antibiotic activity of *Polysiphonia fastigiata* (Chesters and Stott, 1956) and of *Ulva, Enteromorpha,* and other DMS-evolving algae is probably due to liberation of free acrylic acid. The presence of DMPT in several species of multicellular algae has been well documented (Challenger, 1959), and its occurrence in 14 species of cultured unicellular marine algae has been demonstrated by gas–liquid chromatography of DMS evolved from cold alkali-treated cells (Ackman *et al.*, 1966a,b). *Syracosphaera carterae* contained as much as 2.9% of DMPT in the wet cells. It is also of interest to note that the diatom species, *Skeletonema costatum* and *Phaeodactylum tricornutum,* and the flagellate *Amphidinium carteri,* reported to have strong antibacterial potency (Duff *et al.*, 1966), all contain appreciable concentrations of DMPT in the range from 0.30 to 0.68% of the wet weight (Ackman *et al.*, 1966b). DMPT produced by phytoplankton and macroalgae can be transferred either directly to fish that eat algae, or indirectly via zooplankton to fish, where its hydrolytic products, DMS and acrylic acid, can persist (see Sieburth, 1968b). Occurrence of DMS and acrylate in the food chains of marine birds, fish, and shellfish is now recognized, and the aesthetic implications of these smelly compounds in raw fishery products can be surmised.

In some instances it appears that water soluble chlorophyll derivatives may have antibacterial activity (Smith, 1944). Oxidation products of chlorophyllides from certain kinds of green algae have been reported to inhibit bacterial growth (Blaauw-Jansen, 1954; Jorgensen, 1962).

A few examples of the ecological implications of algal antibiotics can be discussed briefly. Inhibition of algal growth by antibiotic substances produced by marine algae has been demonstrated by McLachlan and Craigie (1966). Certain yellow substances, with ultraviolet absorbance, were demonstrated in the brown alga, *Fucus vesiculosus* (McLachlan and Craigie, 1964). The compounds lanosol and 5-bromo-3,4-dihydroxy-benzaldehyde inhibit *Skeletonema, Monochrysis,* and *Amphidinium* at concentrations of 0.03 to 0.30 mmole/ml (McLachlan and Craigie, 1966). It has been suggested (Antia and Bilinski, 1967) that the potent lecithinase C found in *Monochrysis lutheri* may be a toxic and protective agent against possible predators. It has been pointed out that naturally occurring bromophenols may exert ecological effects by regulating or preventing growth of epiphytes and endophytes as a result of their anti-algal activity (McLachlan and Craigie, 1966; Craigie and Gruenig, 1967). Possibly some protection against fungal epiphytes and parasites could be envisioned as a result of the works of Mautner *et al.* (1953), Welch (1962), Burkholder *et al.* (1960), and others who have observed antifungal properties of seaweeds (see Table I).

Antibiotics of *Chondria littoralis* and *Sargassum natans* have been studied by Martínez-Nadal *et al.* (1964, 1965, 1966). Two broad spectrum substances were separated by chromatographic techniques and designated Sarganin A and B. Polyphenols occur to the extent of 9% of the dry weight of some brown algae (Haug and Larsen, 1958). Sieburth (1968a) and Sieburth and Conover (1965) have considered the probability that phenolic compounds exert antifouling action in seaweeds, some of which contain large concentrations of this class of compounds in the older parts of the plants.

Denaturing effects of phaeophyte polyphenols on the epifauna (hy-

TABLE I

ANTIFUNGAL ACTIVITY OF SOME MARINE ALGAE[a]

Species	Inhibition of assay fungi					
	Rhizopus	*Mucor*	*Asper-gillus*	*Peni-cillus*	*Candida*	*Crypto-coccus*
Red algae						
Amphiroa fragilissima	3	1	5	4	0	1
Hormothamnion						
enteromorphoides	3	2	5	0	2	2
Laurencia obtusa	8	6	5	5	0	2
Wrangelia argus	10	5	3	6	10	8
Green algae						
Caulerpa racemosa	0	0	0	6	6	8
Halimeda opuntia	3	0	4	2	0	3
Udotea flabellum	2	0	1	0	0	2
Brown algae						
Dictyota bartayresii	0	0	0	1	0	2
D. divaricata	2	1	4	3	0	1
Padina gymnospora	1	0	2	1	1	2
Blue-green algae						
Lyngbya majuscula	0	0	0	6	2	10

[a] Values are given as millimeters width of zone at the edge of paper disks.

droids), encrusting old segments of *Sargassum,* is an example of algal–microfaunal relationships. These compounds from brown algae appear to be active against zooplankton in tidepools (Conover and Sieburth, 1964, 1966) and show toxic effects on *Acartia tonsa,* trochophores, veligers, and nereid worms. These authors point out the possibility that ecologically significant activity of phenolic substances is likely to occur in lagoons, bays, and other protected environments of coastal waters.

Though antibiosis is a common phenomenon in marine algae (see Table II), marked seasonal and geographic fluctuations occur in the degree of activity shown at different times and places. *Ascophyllum nodosum* apparently shows greatest activity in the summer months (Vacca and Walsh, 1954). Algae in the North Sea varied in their antibiotic contents on a monthly basis, and each species seemed to have its own seasonal variation (Chesters and Stott, 1956; Roos, 1957), showing either summer or winter maxima. Antibacterial activity of *Laurencia obtusa* in Puerto Rico was greatest during the winter months, whereas *Halimeda opuntia* exhibited no clear-cut seasonal activity (Almodóvar, 1964).

That biologically active substances of algae may exert influences upon animals that consume algae as food can be envisioned from publications concerning habitats and food preferences of marine animals. The location of many mollusks in beds of algae would suggest selective influences of special substances or favorable physical conditions (Warmke and Almodóvar, 1963). Feeding habits of herbivorous fishes, which are known to consume mixtures of many kinds of seaweeds (Randall, 1967), suggest adaptation to balanced diets of algal species that have antibiotics (Table III). Thus, the stomachs of sea chubs contained 37 kinds of algae (13 of which are known to have antibiotic activity); damselfishes contained 32 species (8 antibiotic); parrot fishes, 22 (7 antibiotic); blue tang, 30 (8 antibiotic); black durgon, 26 (7 antibiotic); ocean surgeon, 26 (4 antibiotic); and french angel fish, 15 (3 antibiotic). If algal antibiotics persist in the alimentary tract of fishes, as is the case in marine birds (Sieburth, 1961), then it can be possible that they exert some ecological effects in food chains.

The antihelminthic agent occurring in the red alga, *Digenea simplex,* inhibits many kinds of worms. The active substance is kainic acid (see Fig. 14) $C_{10}H_{15}O_4N$—H_2O, and it has been synthesized (Ueno *et al.,* 1957). Other algae having antihelminthic properties include *Corallina officinalis* and *Alsidium heminthochorton* (Benigni *et al.,* 1962). A compound related to kainic acid was isolated from *Chondria armata* and named domoic acid (Fig. 15) (Takemoto *et al.,* 1966).

TABLE II

SUMMARY OF THE ANTIBACTERIAL PROPERTIES OF MARINE ALGAE

Algae	Gram +[a]	Gram −	Remarks	References
Cyanophyta				
Lyngbya	X	X	Antiviral, antifungal	Burkholder et al., 1960; Starr et al., 1962
Rhodophyta				
Grateroupia, Plocamium	0	X		Kamimoto, 1955
Callophyllis	X	X		Pratt et al. 1951
Chondria	X	X		Burkholder et al., 1960
Chrysmenia	X	X		Kamimoto, 1955
Delesseria	X	X		Roos, 1957
Digenea	X	X	Antihelminthic	Katayama, 1962
Falkenbergia	X	X		Burkholder et al., 1960
Gloiopeltis	X	X		Kamimoto, 1955
Gelidium	X	X	Antiviral	Kamimoto, 1955; Gerber et al., 1958
Holosaccion	X	X		Pratt et al., 1951
Murrayella	X	X		Burkholder et al., 1960
Iridiophycus	X	X	(Acrylic acid)	Pratt et al., 1951
Laurencia	X	X	Antifungal	Burkholder et al., 1960
Porphyra	X	X	Fatty acids, terpenes, etc.	Katayama, 1962
Polysiphonia	X	X	Acrylic acid, dibromo benzyl alcohol	Chesters and Stott, 1956; Hodgkin et al., 1966; Roos, 1957; Sieburth, 1964
Rhodomela	X	X	Brominated phenol	Mautner et al., 1953; Roos 1957; Saito and Sameshima, 1955
Wrangelia	X	X		Burkholder et al., 1960
Ceramium, Cystoclonium	X	0	Antifungal	Roos, 1957
Gracilariopsis	X	0		Allen and Dawson, 1960
Phycodrys	X	0		Roos, 1957
Spyridia	X	0		Allen and Dawson, 1960

Pyrrophyta				
Cochlodinium, Goniodoma	X	0	"Goniodomin," antialgal, anti-yeast	Burkholder et al., 1960; Burkholder, 1968
Amphidinium	X	0		Sharma et al., 1968a
Gyrodinium	X	0		Duff et al., 1966
Zooxanthellae	X	X	Terpenes, hydrocarbons	Sharma et al., 1968b; Burkholder and Burkholder, 1958; Ciereszko, 1962
Bacillariophyta				
Asterionella	X	0	Fatty acids, nucleotides	Aubert et al., 1966c
Chaetoceros, Skeletonema	X	X		Aubert and Gauthier, 1966a; Sieburth and Pratt, 1962
Nitzschia	0	X		Steeman-Nielsen, 1955a
Gyrosigma	X	0		Aubert and Gauthier, 1967
Cyclotella	X	X		Aubert et al., 1966b
Licmophora, Rhizosolenia, etc.	X	X		Duff et al., 1966; Aubert and Gauthier, 1967
Phaeophyta				
Ascophyllum	X	X	Acrylic, fatty acids, terpenes, antiviral	Vacca and Walsh, 1954
Egregia	X	X		Pratt et al., 1951
Laminaria	X	X		Saito and Sameshima, 1955; Roos, 1957; Katayama, 1962; Kathan, 1965
Macrocystis	X	X		Pratt et al., 1951
Postelsia	X	X		Pratt et al., 1951
Undaria	X	X		Saito and Sameshima, 1955; Kamimoto, 1955
Sargassum	X	X	Sarganins, tannin	Katayama, 1962; Kamimoto, 1955; Conover and Sieburth, 1964; Martínez-Nadal et al., 1964, 1965
Chorda	X	0		Roos, 1957
Cymopolia	X	0		Burkholder et al., 1960
Desmarestia	X	0	H_2SO_4	Roos, 1957

TABLE II (*Continued*)

Algae	Gram +[a]	Gram −	Remarks	References
Dictyota	X	0	Antifungal	Allen and Dawson, 1960; Starr *et al.*, 1962
Dictyopteris	X	0	Polyphenols in fucus	Burkholder *et al.*, 1960
Fucus	X	0	Polyphenols in fucus	Roos, 1957; Craigie and Gruenig, 1967
Halidrys, Pelvetia	X	0	(Acrylic acid)	Chesters and Stott, 1956; Challenger *et al.*, 1957
Padina	X	0	Antifungal	Allen and Dawson, 1960; Burkholder *et al.*, 1960
Ectocarpus	X	0		Roos, 1957
Chrysophyta				
Phaeocystis	X	X	Acrylic acid	Sieburth, 1960
Coccolithus	X	X		Duff *et al.*, 1966
Chlorophyta				
Codium	X	X	Fatty acids, terpenes, etc.	Katayama, 1962; Kamimoto, 1955
Enteromorpha	X	X	Acrylic acid, terpenes	Roos, 1957; Allen and Dawson, 1960; Starr *et al.*, 1962; Katayama, 1962
Cladophora	X	X		Starr *et al.*, 1962
Derbesia, Cladophoropsis	X	0		Allen and Dawson, 1960
Dunaliella	X	0	Antialgal	Accorinti, 1964
Spongomorpha	X	0	Acrylic acid	Roos, 1957; Challenger *et al.*, 1957
Ulva	X	X	Acrylic, fatty acids, terpenes	Pratt *et al.*, 1951; Roos, 1957; Challenger *et al.*, 1957; Katayama, 1962; Kamimoto, 1955
Cryptophyta				
Rhodomonas	X	X		Duff *et al.*, 1966
Hemiselmis	X	0		Duff *et al.*, 1966

[a] X Signifies inhibition of growth; 0 indicates no inhibition.

TABLE III

OCCURRENCE OF ANTIBIOTIC ALGAE IN THE STOMACHS OF FOURTEEN KINDS OF TROPICAL FISH[a]

Kind of antibiotic algae in stomach	Yellow damsel	Night surgeon	Yellow tail damsel	Bermuda chub	Dusky damsel	Redhn parrot	Queen parrot	French angel	Ocean surgeon	Doctor fish	Blue tang	Black durgon	Scrawled filefish	Trunkfish
Acanthophora spicifera	X						X							X
Amphiroa fragilissima		X										X		X
Caulerpa racemosa					X			X						
C. sertularioides					X			X						
Ceramium byssoideum	X								X					
C. nitens	X	X		X	X	X					X	X	X	
Chondria littoralis	X	X		X							X	X		
Coelothrix irregularis	X	X			X	X	X				X			
Dictyopteris delicatula								X				X		
D. plagiogramma				X	X								X	
Dictyota bartayresii				X		X		X		X			X	
D. divaricata	X	X			X	X	X		X				X	X
Digenea simplex				X				X						
Halimeda opuntia		X				X			X	X		X		
Laurencia obtusa		X			X	X	X	X	X	X	X	X		X
L. papillosa	X		X	X		X								
Lyngbya majuscula	X	X	X		X	X	X		X	X	X		X	X
Padina gymnospora		X	X	X		X	X	X	X	X	X	X	X	
Polysiphonia ferrulacea	X	X			X	X			X	X		X		
Sargassum sp.				X				X	X	X		X		
Spiridia filamentosa	X	X		X					X	X		X		
Wrangelia argus	X		X		X									
Percent of algae in total stomach contents	99.3	94.0	89.3	99.5	56.2	92.6	94.0	74.8	91.8	93.9	92.8	70.8	34.2	4.9

[a] Data from Randall (1967).

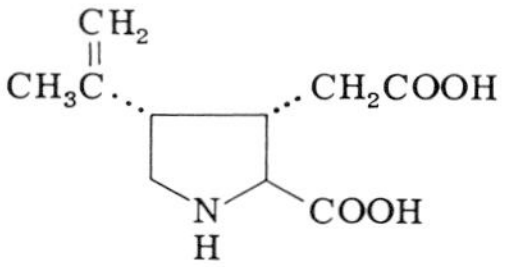

$$CH_3C \overset{\overset{\displaystyle CH_2}{\|}}{\ldots} \quad \ldots CH_2COOH$$

Fig. 14. α-Kainic acid (digenic acid) was isolated from the red alga *Digenea simplex*. The compound is an active antihelminthic.

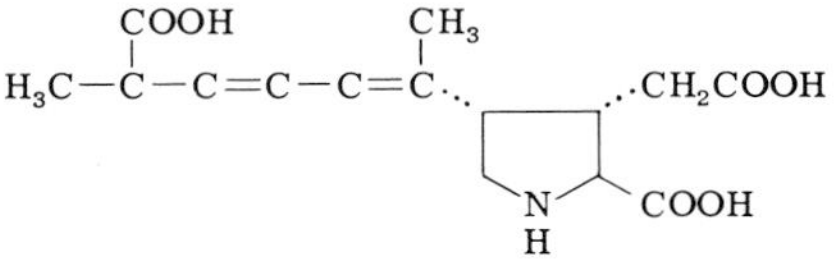

$$H_3C-\overset{\overset{\displaystyle COOH}{|}}{C}-C=C-C=\overset{\overset{\displaystyle CH_3}{|}}{C} \ldots \quad \ldots CH_2COOH$$

Fig. 15. Domoic acid occurs in the red alga *Corallina officinalis* and is related closely to α-kainic acid.

Although some antibiotics and other products of marine algae show little toxity for animals, e.g., the sarganins (Martínez-Nadal *et al.*, 1966), other algal compounds can be toxic (Habekost *et al.*, 1955; Doty and Aguilar-Santos, 1966). Reference has already been made to the toxic properties of *Lyngbya*. Possible contributions of toxic materials to food chains and ciguatera poison in fishes poses serious problems needing further investigation: The antiviral and cytotoxic effects of marine algae have been reported in a series of papers by Starr and colleagues (1962, 1966; Starr and Halterman, 1967). The toxic substances, caulerpin and caulerpicin, obtained from species of the green alga *Caulerpa* (Doty and Aguilar-Santos, 1966; Aguilar-Santos and Doty, 1968) would be expected to have some ecological effects in turtles and fish which eat *Caulerpa* and possibly also contribute to the chain of events leading to ciguatera intoxication (see references in Baslow, 1969). *Caulerpa*, nevertheless, continues to be part of the daily diet of many Philippine people who eat this seaweed as a delectable raw salad.

VII. Sponge Antibiotics

Sponges are relatively simple multicellular animals whose cells are held together under the influence of specific aggregating factors of a protein nature (Gasic and Galenti, 1966; Fry, 1970). Numerous kinds of colorful sponges grow in coral reef areas, where they are often attached to the stony structures of dead corals. Different species occur at different depths down to a hundred meters or more. Other kinds grow on the submerged roots of mangroves or in meadows of *Thalassia*.

It is necessary to limit our discussion chiefly to the antimicrobial substances of sponges, although the pigments, toxic substances, morphogenetic factors, and many other aspects of sponge life make them attractive for study.

A special interest in the chemical constituents of sponges was stimulated by the investigations of graduate students of Professor Werner Bergmann at Yale University in 1950, when the group isolated some unusual nucleosides from sponges, e.g., spongothymidine and spongouridine from *Cryptotethya crypta* (Bergmann and Feeney, 1950) (Fig. 16). Other compounds were isolated and synthesized too (Bergmann and Stempien, 1957). Reports of such unusual metabolites suggested further research and synthesis of novel compounds of medicinal value, such as D-arabinosylcytosine and others with antiviral and antitumor properties (see Baslow, 1969).

The discovery of antibiotics in sponges is credited to Nigrelli *et al.* (1959) who isolated a white crystalline material from ethyl ether extracts of the red beard sponge *Microciona prolifera*. Antibiotic substances were reported also in other sponges (Jakowska and Nigrelli, 1960; Nigrelli *et al.*, 1961). Active extracts from the fire sponge *Tedania ignis* (Fig. 17) yielded eight antibiotic fractions after chromatography in propanol, acetic acid, and water. Active fractions obtained from the Caribbean sponge *Haliclona viridis* (Fig. 17) and the Hawaiian sponge *Haliclona magnicanulosa* are soluble in water, thermostable, and nondialysable (Baslow and Read, 1968). There is reason to believe that peptides may be present in one of the chromatographed active spots (Nigrelli *et al.*, 1961). Crude, toxic extracts have been prepared from *Haliclona viridis* (Baslow and Turlapaty, 1969). Aqueous extracts of the sponge *Toxadocia violacea* from Hawaii have shown hypotensive and paralytic activities (Baslow *et al.*, 1967).

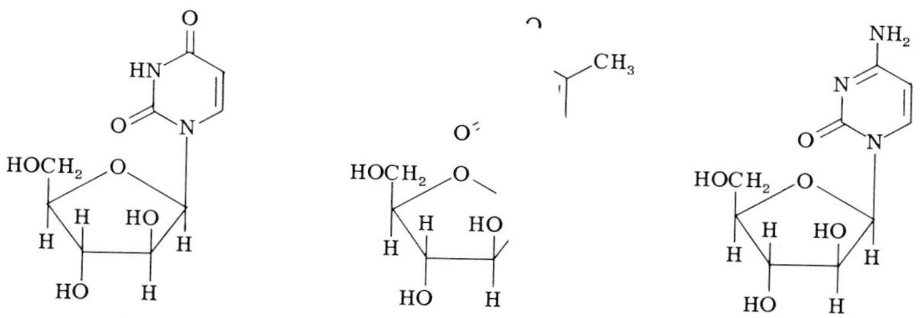

Fig. 16. Spongouridine (left) and spongothym center) were isolated from the sponge *Cryptotethya crypta* and served as n. or synthesis of D–arabino-sylcytosine (right), which has antiviral and other . ical properties.

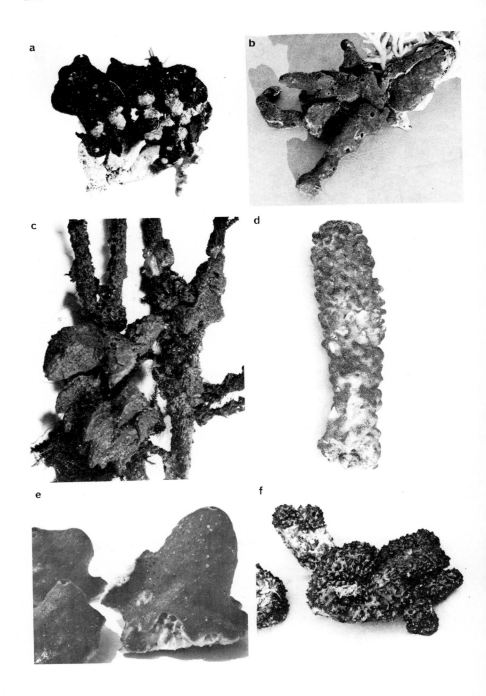

Fig. 18. An antibiotic substance, dihydroxyindole, having either the 4,6-dihydroxy (left) or the 6,7-dihydroxy configuration (right), is produced by a sponge, *Agelas* sp.

Varying degrees of antimicrobial activity have been found in extracts obtained from the Caribbean sponges, *Halichondria panicea* (crumb of bread sponge), *Cliona celata* (sulfur sponge), *Tedania ignis* (fire sponge), *Haliclona viridis* (green sponge), *Dysidea etheria* (heavenly sponge), and *Oligocera hemorrhages* (bleeding sponge), according to the group of investigators at the Osborn Laboratories of Marine Sciences in Brooklyn (Jakowska and Nigrelli, 1960; Nigrelli *et al.*, 1967). Apparently the antimicrobial principle in *Haliclona viridis* acts as a bacteriostatic agent in low concentrations up to 50 μg/ml, and becomes bactericidal above 80 μg/ml (Baslow and Read, 1968). Water, acetone, and methanol extracts of species in the genera *Haliclona, Axinella, Verongia, Agelas, Homaxinella, Callyspongia, Plakortis,* and *Ianthella* inhibit gram-negative bacteria (Stempien, 1966; Nigrelli *et al.*, 1967). Extracts of *Ianthella* sp. were found to inhibit the yeast *Rhodotorula marina* (Buck and Meyers, 1965). Species of *Agelas, Verongia, Homaxinella,* and other genera obtained from the Mediterranean Sea showed good inhibition when tested against gram-negative bacteria (Nigrelli *et al.*, 1967).

Much effort has gone into the collecting and screening of antibiotic sponges (see Tables IV and V). Less success has been attained in isolating and determining the chemical structure of the sponge antibiotics. The antibacterial principle of *Agelas* sp. collected in Jamaica appears to be a dihydroxindole (Fig. 18) (Stempien, 1966).

Broad surveys of antibiotic activity in sponges have been carried out in our laboratories with a very simple technique of placing cut portions

---

Fig. 17. Some common antibiotic sponges of the Caribbean region: (a) *Pellina carbonaria* growing on *Porites* coral; (b) *Haliclona viridis* collected from a *Thalassia* meadow; (c) *Tedania ignis* (fire sponge) growing on roots of mangrove; (d) *Verongia lacunosa* growing at a depth of about 50 ft on the face of a coral reef; (e) a maroon-colored sponge collected in 60 ft of water at the edge of the Puerto Rican shelf south of La Parguera; (f) *Ianthella ardis* grows at about 30 ft on the sides of coral reefs.

TABLE IV

SOME REPRESENTATIVE TYPES OF ANTIBIOSIS IN FIFTEEN SELECTED SPONGES

		Antimicrobial activity		
Sponge	Source	Gram +	Gram −	Candida
Hymeniacidon sp	Palau	+	+	+
Dysidea herbacea	Palau	+	0	0
Tedania ignis	Bahamas	+	+	+
Haliclona viridis	Bahamas	+	+	+
Dysidea etheria	Bahamas	+	+	0
Oligocera hemorrhages	Bahamas	+	+	0
Phakellia flabellata	Australia	+	+	+
Verongia aerophoba	Mediterranean	+	+	0
Verongia fistularis	Puerto Rico	+	+	0
Crambe crambe	Mediterranean	+	+	+
Cinachyra cavernosa	Puerto Rico	+	+	+
Speciospongia vesparia	Puerto Rico	+	+	+
Homaxinella sp.	Jamaica	+	+	+
Pellina carbonaria	Puerto Rico	+	+	+
Ianthella ardis	Puerto Rico	+	0	0

of tissue upon nutrient agar plates seeded with microbes and incubating for a few hours to observe the growth inhibition responses. As is usual in such tests, growth inhibition is indicated by clear zones where antimicrobial substances have diffused out from the tissues into the surrounding medium and interfered with life processes of the indicator microorganisms.

In recent years we have gathered, for antibiotic studies, numerous sponges and other animals from the Caribbean Sea, Great Barrier Reef of Australia, Phillipine Islands, Palau, and the Mediterranean Sea. Preliminary screening has been done with seeded agar plates using gram-

TABLE V

RESULTS OF SCREENING MARINE ANIMALS FOR ANTIMICROBIAL ACTIVITY

		Antimicrobial activity (%)		
Region	No. of samples	Gram +	Gram −	Candida
Caribbean	777	35	15	10
Great Barrier Reef	464	39	12	11
Palau	50	46	12	14
Philippines	100	35	19	25

positive and gram-negative bacteria and the yeast *Candida albicans.* Fresh or frozen tissues were used directly or, if deemed necessary, ground in a mortar and neutralized to pH 7.0, and then small amounts were placed on test plates to determine the effects upon microbial growth. Some overall results of these tests have been summarized in Table V. It can be seen that more animals inhibit gram-positive than gram-negative bacteria or yeast. Possibly the gram-negative types have become resistant to the compounds represented in these animal sources. There are some species of sponges, however, which inhibit growth of gram-negative *Proteus, Pseudomonas, Escherichia,* and many kinds of marine bacteria. Activity of some Mediterranean sponges against *E. coli* is summarized in Table VI. These data are taken from the papers of Nigrelli *et al.* (1967) and Burkholder and Ruetzler (1969).

In a series of papers, Sharma *et al.* (1968a,b, 1970a,b; Sharma and Burkholder, 1967a,b) have reported some of their work with antibiotic substances of sponges. Purification and chemical properties of a new bromine-containing antibacterial substance isolated from *Verongia cauliformis* and *V. fistularis* were published, and later the structure was elucidated and synthesis of the compound reported (Sharma and Burkholder, 1967a,b). The structure represented in Fig. 19 is 2(3′,5′-dibromo-1′-hydroxy-4′-ketocyclohexadien-1′-yl)acetamide. It has activity against gram-positive and gram-negative bacteria but does not inhibit fungi. A related

TABLE VI

ANTIBIOTIC ACTIVITY OF SOME MEDITERRANEAN
SPONGES AGAINST *E. coli* IN SEEDED AGAR PLATES[a]

Species of sponge	Relative size of zones
Aplysilla sulfurea	++[b]
Axinella damicornis	++
Crambe crambe	++
Haliclona viscosa	++
Hemimycale columella	++
Homaxinella rudis	++++[c]
Placospongia decorticans	++
Verongia aerophoba	++++
Verongia archeri	++++
Verongia fistularis	++++

[a] Data from Nigrelli *et al.* (1967); Burkholder and Ruetzler (1969).

[b] Zones less than 22 mm radius.

[c] Zones greater than 22 mm radius.

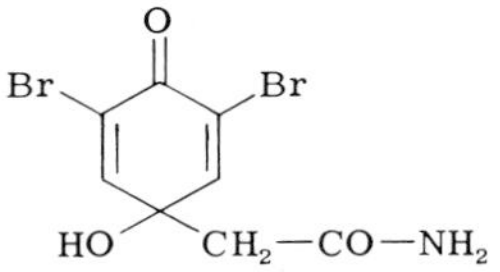

Fig. 19. This antibiotic is 2-(3',5'-dibromo-1'hydroxy-4'keto-cyclohexadien-1'-yl) acetamide, isolated from *Verongia fistularis* and *V. cauliformis.* The substance inhibits growth of gram-positive and gram-negative bacteria.

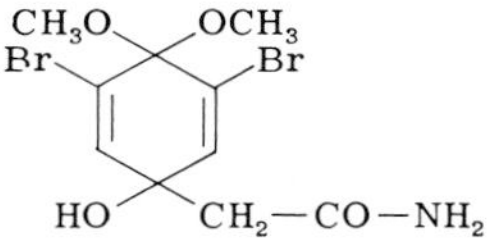

Fig. 20. A second bromine-containing antibiotic isolated from the sponges *Verongia fistularis* and *V. cauliformis.* This compound is the dimethyl ketal relative of the keto form shown in Fig. 19.

compound has the keto group substituted by a dimethyl ketal group (Fig. 20) (Sharma *et al.*, 1968b).

The compound called aeroplysinin-1 (Fattorusso *et al.*, 1970a,b) is closely related to these antibacterials. The total structure of aeroplysinin has been determined from spectral and chemical data (Fulmor *et al.*, 1970). A (−)-isomer mp 112°–116°, [α]D − 198 (c. 0.5 in acetone) was obtained from *Ianthella ardis*, and a (+)-isomer, [α]D + 182 (c. 0.5 in acetone) was isolated from a different species, *Ianthella compressa*, and also from a species of *Verongia.* Occurrence of each enantiomorph in different genera of invertebrates is unusual. Both isomers are equally potent *in vitro* against gram-positive and gram-negative bacteria in the range of 20 to 100 gamma per ml by agar dilution assay. The structure of aeroplysinin is shown in Fig. 21. Fattorusso *et al.* (1970b) have also isolated a tetrabromo compound, aerothionin, from the sponges *Aplysina aerophoba* and *Verongia thiona.*

An antiyeast agent was demonstrated in methanol extracts of *Plakortis*

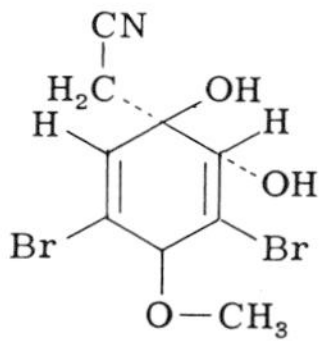

Fig. 21. Structure of aeroplysinin, obtained from species of *Ianthella* and *Verongia.*

sp. The compound appeared as a viscous oil when isolated by column chromatography. After methylation, a number of compounds could be separated by gas chromatography, but the antiyeast activity was lost. From a new species of *Homaxinella,* a product active against *Bacillus* and *Escherichia* was isolated and later found to be a mixture of three antibiotics. A water-soluble compound showing anti-*Candida* activity was prepared from *Pellina carbonaria* (Sharma *et al.,* 1968b).

The sponge *Dysidea herbacea,* obtained from the Western Caroline Islands, contains a series of diphenyl ether compounds that inhibit gram-positive and gram-negative bacteria. All of these compounds appear to be brominated products of 2-phenoxyphenol. Five of the isolated structures are represented in Fig. 22. The structures proposed for penta-bromo and dibromo compounds have been confirmed by synthesis (Sharma *et al.,* 1970a).

Two novel bromine-containing alkaloids, monobromophakellin and di-bromophakellin, have been isolated from a marine sponge, *Phakellia flabellata* (Sharma and Burkholder, 1971), obtained from the Great Barrier Reef of Australia. These compounds exhibit only mild antibacterial

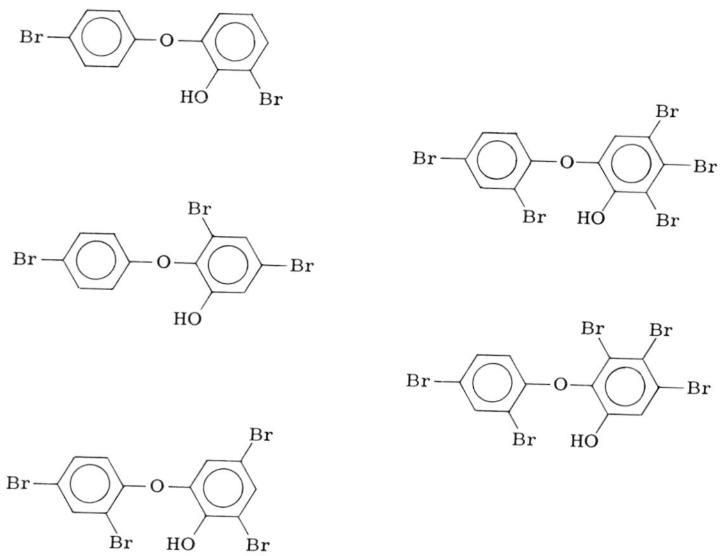

Fig. 22. A series of diphenyl ethers has been isolated from the sponge *Dysidea herbacea* collected at Koror, Palau. The number and position of the Br atoms vary in the five compounds isolated. These substances inhibit gram-positive and gram-negative bacteria.

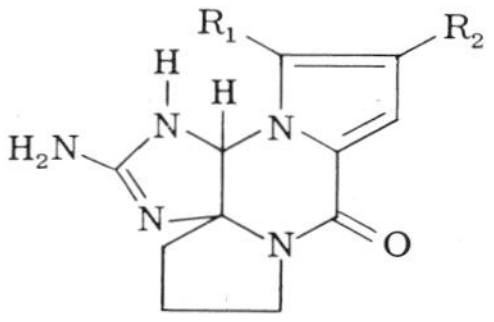

Fig. 23. Antibacterial phakellins have been isolated from the sponge *Phakellia flabellata* collected in the Great Barrier Reef of Australia. Dibromophakellin has R_1 and R_2 = Br; monobromophakellin has R_1 = H and R_2 = Br.

activity against *B. subtilis* and *E. coli* as well as other bacteria. Their structure is shown in Fig. 23.

Research on sponges indicates that the group possesses a wealth of biologically active materials, including antibiotics, ichthyotoxic, and morphogenetic substances. The accompanying Table VII, taken from the published work of the Osborn Laboratories of Marine Sciences, serves to indicate the types of physiological activity shown by some species of sponges collected from the sea around Jamaica (Stempien *et al.*, 1970). Among 10 species, antibacterial activity against gram-negative organisms occurred in 6, 4 were toxic to killifish, and 9 exhibited some kind of morphogenetic effect in developing sea urchin eggs and plutei.

The toxicity of marine sponges to animals has been reviewed by Baslow (1969). Halstead (1965) listed 12 toxic marine sponges. Baslow and Read (1968) reported that extracts of *Haliclona viridis* and *H. magnicanulosa* were toxic to carp, goldfish, and killifish, when placed

TABLE VII

Some Physiological Activities of Ten Sponges from Jamaica[a]

Sponge	Gram − antibiosis	Ichthyo-toxin	Activity in sea urchins
Agelas sp.	+ +	0	No effect
Haliclona erina	+ +	+	Clumping of eggs
H. rubens	+ +	+	Parthenogenesis
Hemectyon sp.	0	+	Inhibits ciliary action
Iotrochota birotulata	0	+	Radialization
Verongia sp.	+ +	0	Ciliary inhibition
Halichondria melanodocia	+ +	0	Radialization, animalization
Homaxinella rudis	+ +	0	None
Mycale laevis	0	0	Animalization
Speciospongia vesparia	0	0	Radialization

[a] Stempien *et al.* (1970).

in the water with the fish. One of the symptoms of injury was loss of response to tactile stimulation. According to Jakowska and Nigrelli (1960), extractives from *Haliclona viridis* can kill fish at concentrations as low as 10 μg/ml of water. This material is bactericidal for *Aerobacter aerogenes* at 80 μg/ml, lethal for the protozoan *Paramecium caudatum* at 50 μg/ml, and kills sea urchin larvae at 1 μg/ml.

We have observed the toxicity of several Caribbean sponges to squirrel fish when sponges and fish were placed together in small seawater containers in the laboratory. In the aquarium at Green Island, Australia, valuable fishes were lost unintentionally by placing the pretty orange sponge *Phakellia flabellata* in the same container. It is fairly well known now that certain kinds of sponges cannot be kept along with fishes in exhibit aquaria.

The relationships existing among sponges and bacteria in nature have often been the object of investigation. Within the mesoglea and cells of sponges, bacteria sometimes are present in large numbers. How do these bacteria exist in the presence of antibacterial substances? Are bacteria the source of antibiotics found in sponges? To answer such questions, Jakowska and Nigrelli (1960) isolated and studied bacteria taken from the canal system of an antibiotic sponge and from the surrounding seawater. Since the bacteria were able to grow well on nutrient agar containing extract from the same sponge, the microorganisms appeared to be resistant to the effects of the antibiotic substance. When pure cultures of these resistant bacteria were streaked across the test cultures of cocci susceptible to extracts from the sponge, no inhibition of the indicator cocci was observed. The authors concluded that the bacteria isolated from the sponge represented strains adapted to tolerate the sponge antibiotic, but the bacteria taken from the sponge were not the source of the antimicrobial activity. Such experiments lend support to the idea that the sponge is the actual producer of the antimicrobial material.

In order to gain information concerning the antimicrobial potency of coral reef animals against marine bacteria isolated from widely scattered sources, we tested 20 species of Puerto Rican sponges against representative bacteria selected from nine computer groups sorted in a numerical taxonomy program (Pfister and Burkholder, 1965). Two additional marine isolates, one from Sapelo Island and another from Woods Hole, were also included in the list of test bacteria. The results are shown in Table VIII. It can be seen that the sensitive vitamin-requiring bacteria, Sa 123 and WH 302, were inhibited by 12 and 15 species of a total of 20 sponges, respectively. Cultures of the various computer

TABLE VIII

ANTIBIOTIC ACTIVITY SHOWN BY TWENTY SPECIES OF PUERTO RICAN
SPONGES TESTED AGAINST ELEVEN MARINE BACTERIA
REPRESENTING DIFFERENT COMPUTER GROUPS

Computer group	Type of organism	Geographic origin	Number of sponges inhibiting each type
I	Micrococcaceae	South Georgia	9
II	Gram + cocci	South Georgia	6
III	Pseudomonads	South Orkney	11
IV	Pseudomonads	Puerto Rico	10
V	Achromobacters	South Georgia	6
VI	Flavobacterium	South Orkney	8
VII	Pseudomonads hydrolize starch	South Orkney	8
VIII	Pseudomonads do not hydrolyze starch	South Pacific	4
IX	Pseudomonas	South Pacific	6
Sa 123	Requires biotin and thiamin, gram −	Sapelo Island	12
WH 302	Requires B_{12}, gram −	Woods Hole	15

groups were inhibited by 4 to 11 kinds of sponges, indicating susceptibility and resistance among the diverse types of marine bacteria from widely scattered geographic areas. Within the different clusters of Pseudomonadaceae, sensitivity to sponge antibiotics does not seem to be related merely to geographic origin but rather depends upon the specific metabolism of the microorganisms.

The sedentary habit, apparent passiveness, and long life of sponges have raised questions concerning their methods of protection against enemies. It seems that various aspects of adaptation and protection in the community life of sponges are fulfilled by elaboration of chemical compounds and through mechanical activities. Large specimens of *Ircinia*, which produce peculiar and odoriferous substances, commonly provide the lifelong home for many crustaceans, mollusks, and worms. The fire sponge is known to be covered at times with numerous bryozoans of the genus *Loxosomella* (Ruetzler, 1968). Sponges and other invertebrates are supposed to harbor viruses (Vago and Bergoni, 1968). Claus *et al.* (1967) believe that certain sponges can filter, and use for food, quantities of bacteria, and in this way act as a natural system for disposal of pollution microorganisms. Apparently, sponges can resist bacterial infection and show remarkable ability to repair injuries

(Connes, 1967). It seems reasonable to suppose that, in sponges which produce powerful antimicrobial substances, these substances may serve to inactivate microbial prey, as a preliminary to their digestion and use as food. The habitat and feeding of certain nudibranchs on selected species of sponges are examples of protective coloration and perhaps specific adaptation to the presence of toxin in the diet (MacGintie and MacGintie, 1968). Both toxic and nontoxic sponges are eaten by certain kinds of fish (Randall and Hartman, 1968). Possibly the toxins are destroyed in the acid pH of the stomach. It is known that the toxic extracts of *Haliclona viridis* rapidly lose activity when kept at pH 3.

Actually only a few kinds of fish concentrate on sponges as their main diet (Randall and Hartman, 1968). Sponges comprise over 95% of the food of angelfishes in the genus *Holocanthus*, over 70% in the related genus *Pomacanthus*, and more than 85% in the filefish *Cantherhines macrocerus*. Among 212 species of West Indian reef and inshore fishes studied by Randall and Hartman (1968), in only 11 species did sponge material comprise 6% or more of the stomach contents. The small number of fishes selecting sponges as their food suggests that defensive properties of sponges, such as spicules, tough fibers, and noxious chemical substances may be highly effective in discouraging predation. Sponge-eating fish do, indeed, ingest antibiotic species of sponges, as for example members of the following genera: *Agelas, Ircinia, Ianthella, Haliclona, Tedania, Plakortis, Verongia,* and *Cinachyra*. Fishes, whose diet consists chiefly of sponges, tend to consume a wide variety of sponge species, thus diluting the possible toxic substances, and avoiding the chance of taking in only material of low nutritive value. *Holocanthus ciliaris* (queen angelfish), with a diet consisting of 96.8% sponge material, was found to be eating a mixture of 40 species of sponges. Included were antibiotic species of *Ianthella, Ircinia, Verongia, Tethya, Tedania, Haliclona,* and others. Any special physiological effects of such a peculiar diet can only be surmised.

VIII. Coelenterates

The phylum Cnidaria (coelenterates) embraces many antibiotic and toxic animals belonging to the groups of hydroids, jellyfish, sea anemones, corals, etc. Various aspects of toxicity in some 70 species have been reviewed by Halstead (1965), Russell (1967), and Baslow (1969). We cannot include most of the interesting phenomena described in the voluminous literature, because most of the substances and bioactivities are not known to be truly antibiotic in the more precise (but arbitrary) sense, i.e., they have not been demonstrated to affect life processes in microorganisms. Historically, it is very interesting to recall that diiodotyrosine (iodogorgoic acid) was isolated from *Gorgonia cavollini* in 1896 (Drechsel, 1896), and dibromotyrosine was obtained from the gorgonid *Primnoa lepadifera* by Morner (1913). Marine biochemistry is not entirely of the present generation.

Antimicrobial activity of alcyonarians was first reported by Burkholder and Burkholder (1958) who found moderate effects in sea whips, sea fans, and plexaurid types (see Figs. 24 and 25). It has been suggested that nonlipid substances, such as crassin acetate and eunicin, may account for the observed antibiotic activity (Ciereszko *et al.*, 1960;

Fig. 24. Underwater scene at a depth of 30 ft on a reef at St. Thomas, U.S. Virgin Islands. Among the common antibiotic octocorals growing in this habitat are: *Pseudopterogorgia americana, Gorgonia ventalina, Briareum asbestinum,* and *Plexaura homomalla.* Additional species are listed in Table IX.

Fig. 25. Small portions of eighteen species of gorgonids tested for antibacterial activity against *Bacillus subtilis* (above) and against the marine bacterium No. 746 (below). Some gorgonids inhibit many kinds of marine bacteria but not the more resistant types. See also Table IX.

Ciereszko, 1962) of some octocorals. Several different lactones have been isolated and characterized from species of gorgonians. Crassin acetate, from *Pseudoplexaura crassa,* is a diterpene lactone cembranolide (Weinheimer *et al.,* 1968) (Fig. 26). Mammosin is a diterpene lactone isolated from *Eunicea mammosa* (Marsico, 1962). Ancepsenolide, obtained from *Pterogorgia anceps,* is a bis butenolide compound (Schmitz *et al.,* 1966) (Fig. 27). Eunicin, from *Eunicea mammosa,* is considered to be a sesquiterpene lactone. Crassin acetate is said to be toxic to developing sea urchin eggs and parrot fish at levels of 10 ppm (Ciereszko, 1962), and inhibitory for *Endamoeba* at 20 μg/ml. Single unsaturated lactones appear in many natural products, and a number of antibiotics are derivatives of these lactones, e.g., penicillic acid. Possibly gorgonids may eventually be utilized as a source of antibiotics and other fine chemicals.

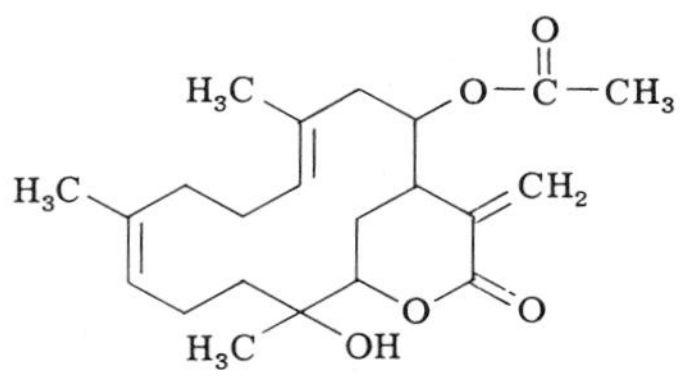

Fig. 26. Crassin acetate has been isolated from gorgonids, *Pseudoplexaura crassa* and *Pseudoplexaura wagenaari*. The substance inhibits some kinds of bacteria and protozoans.

The presence of special compounds with biological activities suggests a basis for our general observations that gorgonids are seldom eaten by marine animals.

Two new prostaglandins, which are different from the mammalian prostaglandin in C-15 configuration, have been reported recently from *Plexaura homomalla* (Weinheimer and Spraggins, 1970). Doubtless this class of compounds will be found to exert important physiological effects in marine animals. It has been surmised that at least some of the substances that we have mentioned, as well as many other terpenes, etc., may be produced by the zooxanthellae which live within the bodies of numerous species of octocorals and other cnidarians (Ciereszko, 1962). The data presented in Table IX suggest that many Caribbean gorgonids contain antibacterial substances. What is the role of the symbiotic microalgae in the production of these substances? It is within the realm of possibility to grow the zooxanthellae axenically and to test their powers to produce physiologically active compounds.

Among the stony corals that are so active in reef building, we have observed antibiotic activity against gram-positive bacteria. This was found especially in the Philippine reefs where gorgonids are relatively scarce, and more effort was directed toward testing the abundant stony corals. No data are available to permit evaluation of the possible role of antibiotics in the life of reef-building corals. It would appear, however, that their stony structures and abundant slime secretions would offer effective mechanisms for protection against fouling organisms and predators.

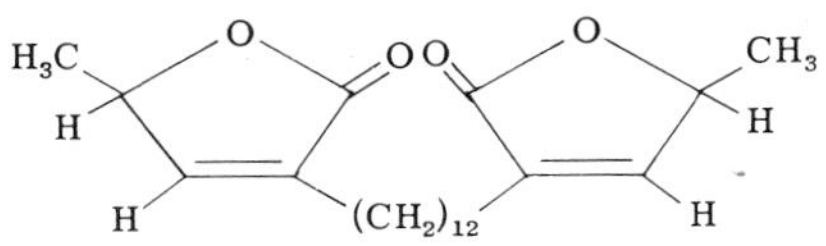

Fig. 27. Ancepsenolide was obtained from the gorgonid *Pterogorgia anceps.*

TABLE IX

Antibiotic Activity of Some Gorgonians Collected
near St. Thomas, U.S. Virgin Islands

Gorgonians	B. subtilis[a]	E. coli[a]	Candida[a,b]	Marine bacteria No. 13	No. 24	No. 20
Briareum asbestinum	0	0	0	0	5	0
Eunicea asperula	10	11	5	12	12	10
Eunicea calyculata	7	8	2	5	10	4
Eunicea laciniata	11	10	3_p	7	15	8
Eunicea laxispica	3	2	0	5	6	4
Eunicea mammosa	4	7	2_p	6	12	4
Eunicea succinea	3	7	1_p	5	8	3
Gorgonia ventalina	8	10	4	9	11	5
Muricea atlantica	10	10	8	10	12	8
Muricea elongata	7	9	3_p	8	13	6
Muriceopsis flavida	3	7	2	4	7	2
Plexaura homomalla	9	12	3	9	15	12
Plexaurella dichotoma	6	10	1_p	5	12	3
Plexaurella porosa	3	4	0	3	5	3
Pseudoplexaura crucis	4	7	1_p	5	7	3
Pseudoplexaura flagellosa	6	2	0	3	8	3
Pseudoplexaura wagenaari	5	9	1	5	7	3
Pseudopterogorgia americana	5	12	3	9	9	4
Pseudopterogorgia acerosa	4	8	3	5	9	5
Pterogorgia guadalupensis	8	10	2	7	11	4

[a] Inhibition zones in agar test plates are indicated in millimeters radius.
[b] Subscript p indicates partial inhibition, i.e., some growth within the inhibition zone.

Scattered observations concerning antibiotic properties of various coelenterates should be mentioned. The ctenophore *Beroe cucumis* appears to have a substance that inhibits growth of the bacterium *Pseudomonas heterocea* (Chentsov, 1964). The siphonophore *Porpita,* collected in the South Pacific, showed activity against gram-negative bacteria (see Burkholder, 1968). Growth-promoting and growth-inhibiting substances and regulators of morphogenetic activity among hydroids have been suggested in recent publications (see review by Baslow, 1969).

IX. Antibiotic Worms

Many kinds of marine worms, belonging to unrelated groups, are known to contain toxic and antibiotic substances. Thus, proboscis worms,

Bonellia sp., peanut worms, *Goldfingia* sp., and the annelid *Lumbriconereis*, all possess toxic materials (Baslow, 1969). Crude extracts of *Bonellia* are toxic to protozoans and other animals (Baltzer, 1925; Ruggieri and Nigrelli, 1962). Nereistoxin is lethal to flies and killifish (Okaichi and Hashimoto, 1962).

Antifungal and antiprotozoal substances have been observed in parasitic nematodes of the genus *Ascaris* (Morishita and Kobayashi, 1963; Przyjalkowski, 1964a,b), but little information is available concerning the ecological role of antibiotics produced by marine nematodes.

X. Mollusks

Many substances produced by mollusks exhibit antibiotic activity and show effects upon the neuromuscular tissues of animals. A toxic choline compound, murexine, various extracts from cone shells, and toxins from sea hares, have certain pharmacological and ecological significance. Some *Conus* venoms kill fish, as in the case of piscivorous *C. geographus*. The poison of *C. planorbis* paralyzes polychaete worms, and *C. marmoreus* immobilizes other gastropods but has little effect on fish (Endean and Rudkin, 1963, 1965). Possible effects of cone venoms upon marine protozoans and other microorganisms are not known. It would be interesting to know more about the antibiotic properties of toxins and venoms. Some compounds present in cone venom are shown in Fig. 28.

Several substances derived from sea hares (*Aplysia* sp.) have considerable ecological importance as examples of how special substances may be transported through food chains. Two brominated sesquiterpene compounds, aplysin and aplysinol, were isolated by Yamamura and Hirata (1963) from *Aplysia kurodai* (Fig. 13). A similar substance, laurene,

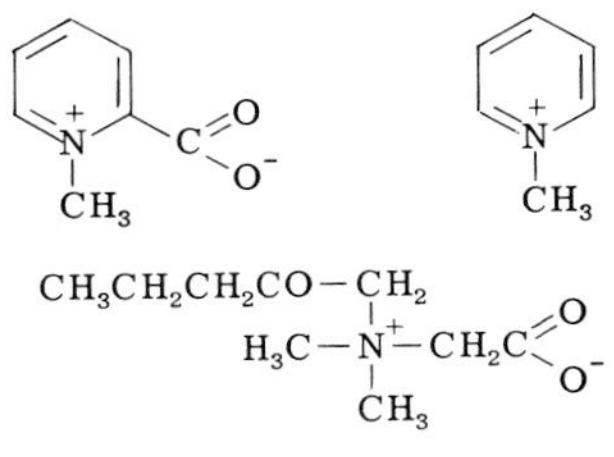

Fig. 28. The venoms of cone shells contain homarine (upper left), N-methyl pyridinium (upper right), and γ-butyrobetaine (bottom), along with toxic proteins and polypeptides.

is present in the red alga, *Laurencia glandulifera,* upon which *Aplysia kurodai* feeds (Irie *et al.,* 1965b). Recently the aplysin substances have also been demonstrated to be present in a species of *Laurencia* (Irie *et al.,* 1969).

Of considerable interest are the reports concerning antimicrobial substances, paolins obtained from abalone (*Haliotis*), queen conch (*Strombus*), and topshell (*Tegula*). Paolins are said to be mucoproteins having antibacterial and antiviral properties (Li *et al.,* 1962a,b, 1965). It is not obvious what effects, if any, may be exerted in the sea by the antitumor substance, mercenene, extracted from clams (*Mercenaria*) and whelks (*Busycon*) by Schmeer (1966) and Schmeer and Huala (1965).

Detailed discussion of shellfish poisons and pharmacological aspects of mollusk toxins is beyond the scope of this paper. The contributions of dinoflagellate plankters and symbionts to formation of antibiotics and toxins in bivalve mollusks is an important area for further ecological and pharmacological investigations. The presence of antiviral and antitumor agents in shellfish poses interesting questions concerning the chemical nature and biological roles of the active compounds (see discussion in Baslow, 1969).

XI. Arthropods

Toxic substances are present in some arthropods, but true antibiotics have not been reported in marine species of this group. The serum of a freshwater decapod, *Paracheraps bicarenatus,* has been reported to contain antibiotic activity that is inactivated by trypsin (Schwab *et al.,* 1966). Bactericidin can be induced in the spiny lobster *Panulirus argus* by injections of bacteria derived from the intestinal flora of the animal (Evans *et al.,* 1968). The induced substance is not a true antibiotic in the usual sense.

XII. Echinoderms

Some starfish and their relatives show antibiotic activity when their tissues are applied to the surface of seeded agar plates. In Philippine waters, we observed very large zones of inhibition caused by an unidentified starfish tested against bacteria and *Candida.* While some species of starfish inhibit both gram-positive and gram-negative bacteria, the giant star *Acanthaster planci* shows only slight antibiotic effects upon gram-positive bacteria. Toxic agents of starfish often turn out to be

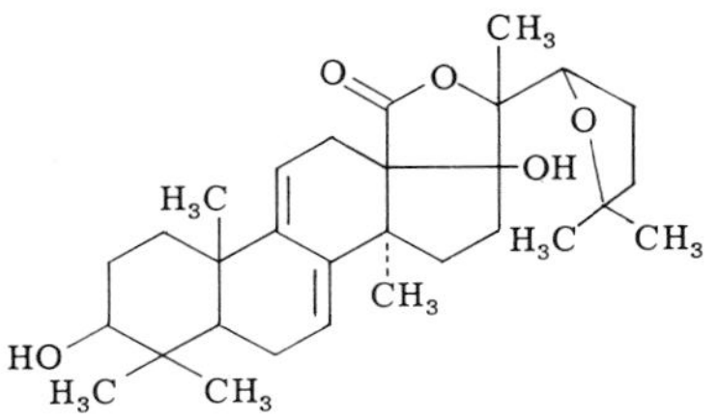

Fig. 29. Holothurins isolated from sea cucumbers contain sugars and "genins," of which the above 22, 25-oxidoholothurinogenin is typical. One of the fractions in holothurin A has D-quinonose, 3-O-methyl glucose, D-glucose and D-xylose attached in a linear series to the steroid hydroxyl at the C-3 position on the left side of the diagram.

saponins (Rio *et al.*, 1965). Saponins are injurious to fish and may serve some function in the food habits of the echinoderms.

Certain kinds of steroid glycosides called holothurins (Fig. 29) are

Fig. 30. The sea cucumber *Holothuria mexicana* produces an antifungal substance that appears to be different from holotoxin. Many species of holothurians are known to inhibit fungi.

produced by sea cucumbers (see Chanley *et al.*, 1966). These substances are toxic to protozoans and many other animals (Nigrelli and Zahl, 1952). Holothurin A preparations, obtained from the Cuvierian organs of *Actinopyga agassizi*, are toxic to *Amoeba proteus* and *Paramecium caudatum*(Nigrelli and Jakowska, 1960). A saponin preparation from *Stichopus japonicus*, exhibiting antifungal activity, has been called holotoxin (Shimada, 1969). Many other sea cucumbers, such as the Caribbean *Holothuria mexicana* and numerous species collected in the Philippines, show antifungal activity, which may confer upon the animals some protective value against microbial enemies that might be present in the sediments where holothurians commonly live (Fig. 30).

XIII. Tunicates

Several years ago we tested 42 species of tunicates in Jamaica for antibacterial activity. The well known *Ascidia nigra* showed marked inhibition of many bacteria, but, when the very acid extracts of this ascidian were neutralized, the antibacterial activity disappeared. At least one of the colonial tunicates of the genus *Didemnum* exhibits marked antibiotic action against many test microorganisms, but the active substance appears to be toxic to animals but without chemotherapeutic power, and hence has not seemed to warrant further attention of organic chemists. From the viewpoint of ecology, the production of so powerful a substance by the tender *Didemnum* suggests the possible value of this antibiotic in survival of the animal that produces the compound.

XIV. Hemichordates and Chordates

Halogenated compounds are found in some hemichordates in sufficient amounts to cause disinfection (Ashworth and Cormier, 1967; De Jorge *et al.*, 1965). The compound 2,6-dibromophenol has been isolated from the acorn worm *Balanoglossus biminiensis* (see Fig. 31). We have shown

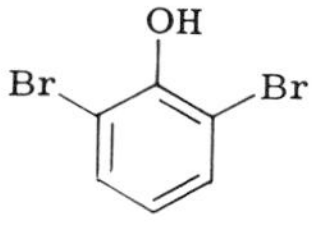

Fig. 31. 2,6-Dibromophenol is an antiseptic substance isolated from the hemichordate *Balanoglossus biminiensis*.

that a *Saccoglossus* sp. also possesses antibacterial and anti-yeast properties (Burkholder, 1968). It has been calculated that acorn worms produce ample amounts of bromophenol to provide protection against possible bacterial infection. The iodine content of mucus secreted by *Balanoglossus gigas* is reported to be about 8 μg/ml (De Jorge *et al.*, 1965), which seems to be ample to exert physiological effects.

Among the marine vertebrates, toxins and venoms of certain kinds of fishes and the venoms of sea snakes are well known to biologists (Halstead, 1965; Bucherl *et al.*, 1968, 1970; Russell and Saunders, 1967; Werler and Keegan, 1963). Most of these venoms have not been studied for antimicrobial activity. We have looked for, but failed to find, any antibacterial activity in potent preparations of poisonous puffer fish. A toxic material from golden striped bass *Grammistes sexlineatus* is said to inhibit growth of *E. coli* (Liguori *et al.*, 1963).

XV. Miscellaneous Observations

Many types of diverse patterns of growth inhibition and promotion are often seen in tests of antibacterial activity in seeded agar plates (Burkholder, 1944). Some examples of the reactions shown by marine bacteria in response to substances present in an unidentified maroon sponge are illustrated in Fig. 32. Clear zones of inhibition are sometimes surrounded by areas of enhanced growth, in situations where nutriment has diffused from the crude test materials outward beyond the diffusion zone of the antibiotic. Conversely, when the antibiotic moves rapidly through the agar beyond the area containing growth-promoting substances, little or no growth stimulation is observed. Potent antibiotics, such as are present in some species of the tunicate *Didemnum*, the anthozoan *Parazoanthus*, and certain species of sponges, usually cause large inhibition zones with sharp boundaries at the perimeter and remaining free from resistant colonies within the zones. Any evaluation of phenomena shown in this kind of test must take into consideration the kinds and numbers of microorganisms and their growth rate. Rapidly growing cultures of test organisms tend to form smaller zones of inhibition because growth takes place before the inhibiting substances have time to diffuse out into the agar. Sometimes resistant or dependent colonies are formed within the clear areas of inhibition (Fig. 32). Such phenomena suggest that one of the consequences of antibiosis is the selection of resistant organisms that are capable of surviving the toxic action of the substances causing lethality or growth stasis in susceptible

Fig. 32. Examples of different kinds of inhibition zones caused by placing small pieces of a maroon sponge upon agar plates streaked with four kinds of marine bacteria. Note the rings of growth promotion outside some of the inhibition zones. A thin ring surrounding the sponge on bacterial plate No. 131 (upper right) resembles an Auchterlony type of precipitin reaction. Resistant colonies growing within the areas of inhibition are shown in cultures 2, 3, and 124. Growth of resistant colonies near the piece of sponge (lower right) suggests some physiological stimulation by poriferan substances.

organisms. This principle can have important implications for the evolution of susceptibility and resistance in the interrelationships of parasites and their hosts, as well as in competitive interactions in general.

The phytoplankton of the ocean produces organic substances that form the base of a vast food pyramid. It seems probable that some degree of antibiotic selection may be exerted upon the many kinds of bacteria that may be competing for planktonic nutriment. Some of the relationships concerned with growth promotion and inhibition can be illustrated here with two examples of experiments conducted with plankton, one with a dinoflagellate *Goniodoma*, and the other with the diatom *Skeletonema*. For the purpose of demonstrating effects of *Goniodoma* upon a marine growth factor-requiring bacterium, an agar media was prepared with only seawater and 1.5% washed agar. The heterotrophic bacterium No. 746, requiring thiamine, biotin, and cobalamine, was seeded into the agar and poured into a petri plate. Some *Goniodoma* cells, containing their antibiotics, were placed in the center of the plate, and the bacteria were then allowed to incubate for 24 hours (Fig. 33). Both nutrients and antibiotics diffused outward into the petri plate culture causing an inner zone of growth inhibition and an outer ring of growth promotion beyond the diffusion zone of the antibiotics. No growth was possible outside the ring of growth because of the lack of organic nutrients and B vitamins in the plain seawater agar.

Availability of nutriment for growth of marine bacteria in the presence of naturally occurring antibacterial substances contained in the same test materials has been studied with marine bacterial cultures and substances extracted from a bloom of the diatom *Skeletonema costatum* (Burkholder, 1963) collected in Long Island Sound. Aqueous extracts

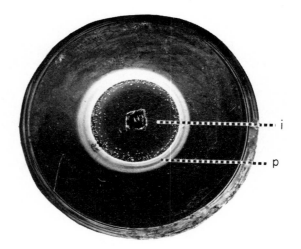

Fig. 33. Cells of the dinoflagellate *Goniodoma* placed in the center of seawater agar plate (without nutriment), seeded with a marine bacterium (No. 746) requiring B vitamins, causes growth inhibition (i) and an outer ring of growth promotion (p). A few antibiotic-resistant colonies can be seen growing within the inhibition zone.

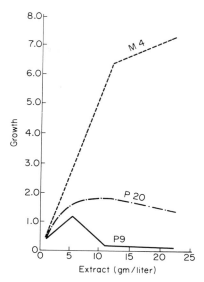

Fig. 34. Growth of three marine bacteria in response to extracts of the diatom *Skeletonema costatum*. Note the promotion of M4 and the marked inhibition of cultures P9 and P20 by increasing amounts of extract After Burkholder (1963).

of the diatom were prepared at different concentrations in seawater to provide growth media. The media were sterilized by Seitz filtration, placed in Ryan flasks, and then inoculated with pure cultures of several kinds of marine bacteria. During 3 days of incubation at room temperature the turbidity was measured as an indication of growth. Some of the resulting data are plotted in Fig. 34. Growth of the culture M-4, resistant to the antibiotic action of *Skeletonema*, was proportional to the amount of extractives available in the media. This bacterium had been isolated actually from the bloom water of the *Skeletonema*. In the antibiotic-susceptible cultures, which originated from a different geographic source (Puerto Rico), some growth occurred only at the lower levels of nutrient supply, but marked inhibition took place in the presence of greater amounts of extract. Further studies of susceptibility and resistance of the naturally occurring microbial associates of antibiotic and nonantibiotic plants and animals should be rewarding.

In considering whether or not antibiosis is a character conducive to fitness in the marine environment, one would not expect that all organisms should produce antibiotics for "purposes" of self-protection. Survival does not usually depend upon one character alone; adaptability to diverse conditions and rapid rates of growth and efficient methods of dispersion may, for some organisms, exceed the value of any capacity for antibiotic production. It is quite clear from the evidence presented in this chapter that occurrence of antibiotics in bacteria, phytoplankton, and the symbiotic condition (zooxanthellae) is commonplace in the sea. Moreover, the antibiotic spectrum of activity is selective; only some organisms are inhibited in the presence of antibiotics. Some antibiotic bacteria inhibit each other with their toxic substances. Occasionally an old culture of bacteria may prove to be harmful for young cultures of the same species. This was the case for the red-pigmented bacterium P9 (see Fig. 4), which produces a prodigiosinlike compound (pyrrole) and tends to die off rapidly in aging cultures after 3–5 days. The marine *P. bromoutilis*, which produces a brominated pyrrole, also is short-lived in agar slant tubes and must be transferred twice weekly to preserve the culture. The same is true of *Chromobacterium marinum*. Thus, in microenvironments in the laboratory and possibly also in microhabitats in the sea, antibiotics may exert powerful and selective influences on survival of both producers of these substances and associated organisms.

Another aspect of the antibiotics-for-survival concept is possibly found in the host–zooxanthellae relationships, which are not very different in principle from the kind of organization found in terrestrial lichens. Both symbiont associations, i.e., of invertebrates and lichens, consist of auto- and heterotrophic partners; antibiotics are commonly made in numerous kinds of such associations. It is possible that specific action of antibiotics is one factor in selecting and maintaining the natural algal components in association with the terrestrial lichen fungus or the marine inverte-brate host. We have pointed out earlier that perhaps successful symbiosis may be enhanced by the antibiotic properties of the complex organiza-tion of animals and algae in gorgonians (Burkholder and Burkholder, 1958).

One of the remarkable characteristics of many marine plants and ani-mals is their freedom from fouling and encrustation by epiphytes and epizoons. Whereas many inanimate objects, as well as turtle grass and some mollusks, etc., are covered with numerous kinds of small and large organisms, the mucus-producing and antibiotic-producing corals, sea anemones, gorgonids, etc., seem usually to be relatively clean. Quantita-tive studies of the bacteria in washings from antibiotic gorgonids have shown almost complete absence of bacteria from many of these animals. Apparently the excretions of alcyonarians are effective in keeping them free from microbes and larger epiphytes and hydroids which might be expected to cover them.

In order to test the ability of gorgonids to resist fouling in a polluted lagoon, we placed both killed (by drying out) and living specimens in the sea at the dock of the marine laboratory in La Parguera, Puerto Rico. After 3 weeks had elapsed, the skeletons of the killed gorgonids were covered with living algae, hydroids, tunicates, and debris, whereas the living gorgonids were free from all these things. The photographs shown in Fig. 35 illustrate how a living gorgonid can remain relatively clean under severe fouling conditions, while a nonliving specimen is at the same time completely covered by pollution and opportunistic flora and fauna. The views of Sieburth on antifouling properties of *Sargassum* and other plants, which produce sarganins, antimicrobial tannins, etc., have been mentioned elsewhere in this chapter.

Fig. 35. A dead gorgonid (a) becomes covered with detritus, algae, and hydroids when transfered to a polluted estuary, while the living gorgonid (b) remains clean, even under conditions conducive to fouling.

The phenomena of phytoplankton periodicity and succession have sometimes been explained on the basis of excretion products called ecto-crines by Lucas (1947, 1955), which include vitamins, toxins, antibiotics, and diverse nutriments produced and secreted into the sea. Is it possible that metabolic products of a plankton species may exert profound growth-promoting and growth-inhibiting action on other kinds of plank-ton, thus encouraging the onset of certain blooms or preventing others? What effects may antibiotics produced by certain kinds of diatoms and flagellates have upon other kinds of phytoplankton? There has been much speculation in the literature concerning these problems. To help answer such questions, we have examined the influence of *Goniodoma* cells (obtained from a bloom and filtered in a Buchner funnel) upon motility and survival of other species of phytoplankters. The living motile flagellates, serving as indicators, were transferred in a drop of seawater to a microscope slide, and then a small amount of *Goniodoma* cells was placed at one edge, and the preparation was sealed with a cover glass. Microscopic observation soon revealed cessation of flagellate move-ment adjacent to the *Goniodoma* cells, with the result that the dead flagellates accumulated in the region near the source of toxin. A photo-graph of dead *Peridinium* cells, which swam from remote areas in the drop of seawater to their death among the cells of *Goniodoma*, is shown in Fig. 36. Whether the lethal substance is goniodomin (Sharma *et al.*, 1968a) or some other dinoflagellate toxin is not known. Similar obser-vations have been made with other species of test flagellates belonging in the genera *Cochlodinium* and *Glenodinium*.

A different method of demonstrating the antiflagellate activity of sponges and of phytoplankton consists of placing the donor cells or tissues in the bottom of small test tubes of seawater containing the motile test flagellates. After mixing to provide contact with the suspected antibiotics from the donor tissues, the flagellate suspensions are allowed to stand in a room with overhead illumination. In the control tube, without any antibiotic additions, the flagellates promptly swim to the surface showing their usual phototactic response. In the presence of antibiotic sponges such as *Pellina carbonaria, Haliclona viridis,* and the plankter *Goniodoma,* the test flagellates (*Peridinium,* etc.) disappear.

A statistical study of the antibiotic effects of some marine animals upon growth of selected cultures of marine bacteria can be presented as experimental evidence of the ecological impact of antibacterial sub-stances upon marine microbes. Species of *Parazoanthus* (Fig. 37) and selected sponges (Fig. 17) provide good experimental materials, as is indicated in some current investigations conducted in our laboratories.

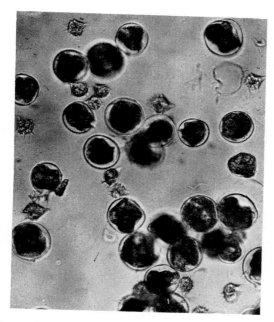

Fig. 36. The larger dinoflagellate *Goniodoma* sp. shows antibiotic activity against the smaller *Peridinium* sp. by causing cessation of its swimming movements and eventually death.

In one experiment, five kinds of *Parazoanthus* and the sponges upon which they grow among the coral reefs of Puerto Rico were assayed for antibiotic activity against 82 cultures of marine bacteria isolated from nearby waters. This group of bacteria included many diverse species, some of which were pigmented, others luminescent, and a few were agarolytic. Small pieces of sponge tissue or isolated zoanthids were placed on the surface of nutrient seawater agar plates, seeded with actively growing bacteria taken from stock culture agar slants. After incubation overnight, the zones of inhibition were measured in millimeters radius from the edge of the tissue to the outer periphery of the zones. For each test animal, the percent of bacterial cultures showing zones of 0, 1–2, 3–4, and so on up to 15–16 mm radius was recorded. Representative data are presented in Fig. 38. The statistical curves for *Parazoanthus swiftii* and *P. parasiticus* are very different. *P. swiftii* exhibited inhibition against all marine isolates, while *P. parasiticus* seemed to lack antibiotic activity against 94% of the bacteria tested. Likewise, differences in potency of the various sponges were manifested by the

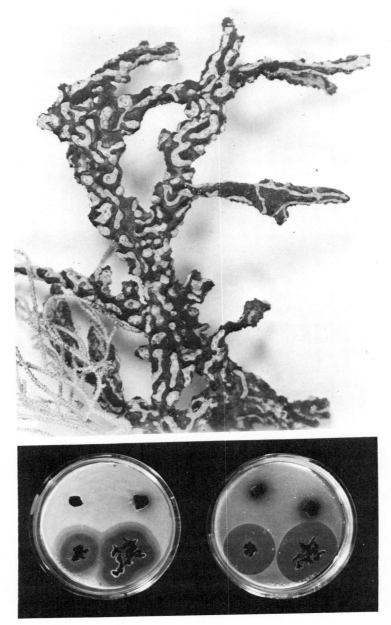

Fig. 37. Parazoanthus swiftii growing on the sponge *Lotrochata birotulata* (above). The *P. swiftii* collected from two species of inactive sponges shows antibacterial

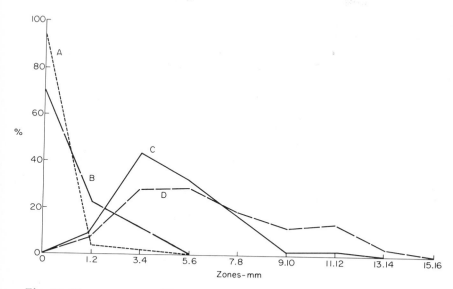

Fig. 38. The percentage of bacterial cultures showing different sizes of inhibition zones in millimeters, under influence of antibiotics from zoanthids and sponges placed on seeded agar plates. A, *Parazoanthus parasiticus;* B, Xestospongia (basket sponge); C, a maroon sponge; and D, *Parazoanthus swiftii*. Note that *P. swiftii* inhibits all cultures with varying zones sizes up to 15–16 mm radius.

distribution curves, indicating high activity in the unidentified maroon sponge and low degrees of activity in the basket sponge (*Xestospongia* sp.) and brown sponge (*Agelas* sp.). All of these animals were collected from the same reef environment, located at a depth of 10–27 m, near La Parguera, Puerto Rico. It is thought that the observed antibiotic inhibitions represent inherent differences in the biochemical properties and physiological activities of the epizootic zoanthids and the reef sponges. It appears to be a mere coincidence that, in nature, the antibiotic zoanthid *P. swiftii* grows on the surface of a nonantibiotic sponge, while the nonantibiotic *P. parasiticus* lives on an antibiotic sponge. Other different combinations have also been found.

In the maroon sponge, discussed above, it was observed that only the exterior tissues (to a depth of about 1 mm) contain the antibiotic material; samples taken from successive layers inward show no activity

activity against *Bacillus subtilis* (lower left) and a marine bacterium, No. 746 (lower right). The pieces of sponge in the upper areas of the petri plates show little or no antibiosis.

when tested against sensitive bacteria in seeded plates. The presence of powerful deterrent substances on the surface of a sponge appears to provide a mechanism of resistance to potential pathogens or predators. In contrast with this situation, the secretion of active substances into the media by growing cells of microorganisms suggests that their "needs" for survival may better be served by having protective compounds present in the environment where selective influences may be exerted in such phenomena as parasitism, competition, and symbiosis. In multi-cellular organisms, toxic substances appear to be conserved within the tissues, where they are available as deterrents against predators, parasites, and various other enemies.

Sometimes special types of antagonistic action are observed unexpectedly in antibiotic experiments. As an example, a delayed type of inhibition was observed after 1 week when five kinds of *Parazoanthus* were kept in contact with 96 indicator cultures of bacteria. Three bacterial cultures out of the whole lot showed delayed susceptibility to diffusible substances from the species of *Parazoanthus*. During the first day, the usual inhibitory action of *P. swiftii* was observed (Fig. 39), while the other zoanthids appeared to be without antibacterial activity. After 1 week, a delayed reaction developed with five out of six zoanthids that had remained in constant contact with the bacteria. The activity appeared to involve lysis of the three cultures after their growth had taken place.

The roles of antibiotics in the sea have been discussed primarily from

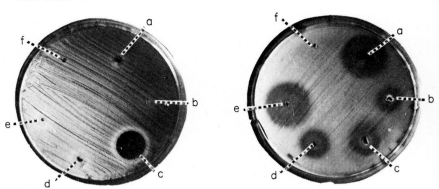

Fig. 39. Immediate and delayed types of inhibition are shown in antibiotic tests with six kinds of *Parazoanthus*. Left, the prompt, commonly occurring inhibition of marine bacteria (No. 20) by *P. swiftii* (c); the others fail to show immediate antibiosis. Right, delayed inhibition (or lysis) of marine culture (No. 130) by five out of six kinds of *Parazoanthus* after an incubation period of 7 days.

the general viewpoint of growth-inhibitory substances active against microorganisms. In most instances, the specific mechanisms involved in the various effects of antibiotics upon microbes and higher plants and animals in the sea are unknown, and further research is needed to provide a more complete picture. Accelerated efforts in the isolation and characterization of marine natural products would greatly stimulate further investigations and applications in the areas of physiology, pharmacology, and biomedicine. Because of the restrictions imposed by the formal definition of antibiotics given at the beginning of this chapter, the scope of our discussion has seldom ventured out of bounds into the fascinating areas of marine toxins, venoms, or growth-regulating substances. Evidence for antibiotic phenomena in the sea has been presented with reference to sources of activity and indicating marine organisms that are sensitive to crude materials or purified compounds. Antibiotic agents are produced by many kinds of marine microbes and occur in the tissues of many algae, sponges, coelenterates, etc., but the small amounts of these substances, which may be secreted into the surrounding seawater, are so diluted that activity in the water usually falls below the minimal threshold for detection in ordinary test systems. In the restricted environments of test tubes, petri plates, and small aquaria, the biological action of marine antibiotics becomes more apparent.

Antibiotic interactions among species of marine bacteria and different kinds of phytoplankton, and the effects of substances derived from sponges and coelenterates upon the life processes of bacteria, microalgae, and Protozoa, point to the potential significance of antibiosis for these organisms in the sea. If the simple coaction analyses, so easily demonstrated in systems of microbes, could be extended with appropriate techniques to include macroorganisms, the role of antibiotic substances would be much better understood in relation to survival, succession, colonization, competition, and other activities of the larger marine flora and fauna. The various phenomena of selective antibiosis discussed in this chapter seem to be compatible with the view that the capacity to produce antibiotics is a characteristic related to protection and conducive to fitness in the environment.

Acknowledgment

The valuable cooperation of Dr. John Webb and generous support contributed by Lederle Laboratories, a division of the American Cyanamid Company, is gratefully acknowledged. Certain aspects of the study were enhanced by financial aid contributed by the U.S. National Science Foundation Grant GB-6419 and by the U.S. National Institutes of Health Grant GM-11735-04.

References

Aaronson, S. (1970). "Experimental Microbial Ecology." Academic Press, New York.

Abbott, B. C., and Ballantine, D. (1957). *J. Mar. Biol. Ass. U.K.* **36**, 169.

Abraham, E. P. (1962). *Pharmacol. Rev.* **14**, 473.

Accorinti, J. (1964). *Phyton* **21**, 95.

Ackman, R. G., Tocher, C. S., and McLachlan, J. (1966a). *J. Fish. Res. Bd. Can.* **23**, 355.

Ackman, R. G., Tocher, C. S., and McLachlan, J. (1966b). *Proc. Int. Seaweed Symp., 5th, 1965* pp. 235–242.

Aguilar-Santos, G., and Doty, M. S. (1968). *In* "Drugs from the Sea" (Hugo D. Freudenthal, ed.), pp. 173–176. Marine Technology Society, Washington, D.C.

Allen, M. B., and Dawson, E. Y. (1960). *J. Bacteriol.* **79**, 459.

Almodóvar, L. R. (1964). *Bot. Mar.* **6**, 143.

Antia, N. J., and Bilinski, E. (1967). *J. Fish. Res. Board Can.* **24**, 201.

Armstrong, F. A. J., and Boalch, G. T. (1960). *Nature (London)* **185**, 761.

Ashworth, R. B., and Cormier, M. J. (1967). *Science* **155**, 1558.

Aubert, M., and Gauthier, M. (1966a). *Rev. Int. Oceanogr. Med.* **4**, 33.

Aubert, M., and Gauthier, M. (1966b). *Rev. Int. Oceanogr. Med.* **2**, 63.

Aubert, M., and Gauthier, M. (1967). *Rev. Int. Oceanogr. Med.* **5**, 63.

Aubert, M., Aubert, J., Gauthier, M., and Daniel, S. (1966a). *Rev. Int. Oceanogr. Med.* **1**, 9.

Aubert, M., Aubert, J., Gauthier, M., and Daniel, S. (1966b). *Rev. Int. Oceanogr. Med.* **1**, 27.

Aubert, M., Gauthier, M., and Daniel, S. (1966c). *Rev. Int. Oceanogr. Med.* **1**, 35.

Aubert, M., Aubert, J., Gauthier, M., and Pesando, D. (1967). *Rev. Int. Oceanogr. Med.* **6–7**, 43.

Baam, R. B., Gandhi, N. M., and Freitas, Y. M. (1966a). *Helgolaender Wiss. Meeresunters.* **13**, 181.

Baam, R. B., Gandhi, N. M., and Freitas, Y. M. (1966b). *Helgolaender Wiss. Meeresunters.* **13**, 188–191.

Baas-Becking, L. G. M. (1951). *Proc. Kon. Ned. Akad. Wetensch., Ser. C* **54**, 3.

Baltzer, F. (1925). *Mitt. Naturforsch. Ges. Bern* **8**, 98.

Banner, A. H. (1959). *Hawaii Med. J.* **19**, 35.

Banner, A. H., Scheuer, P. J., Sasaki, S., Helfrich, P., and Alender, C. B. (1960). *Ann. N.Y. Acad. Sci.* **90**, 770.

Baslow, M. H. (1969). "Marine Pharmacology." Williams & Wilkins, Baltimore, Maryland.

Baslow, M. H., and Read, G. W. (1968). *Proc. West. Pharmacol. Soc.* **11**, 117.

Baslow, M. H., and Turlapaty, P. (1969). *Proc. West. Pharmacol. Soc.* **12**, 6.

Baslow, M. H., Read, G. W., and Dormer, K. (1967). *Amer. Zool.* **7**, 738–739.

Benigni, R., Capra, C., and Cattorini, P. E. (1962). *In* "Piante Medicinali-Chimica Farmacologia e Terapia" (R. Benigni, ed.), Vol. 1, pp. 394–395. Inverni and Della-Beffa, Milan, Italy.

Bentley, J. A. (1960). *J. Mar. Biol. Ass. U.K.* **39**, 433.

Bergmann, W., and Feeney, R. J. (1950). *J. Amer. Chem. Soc.* **72**, 2809.

Bergmann, W., and Stempien, M. F. (1957). *J. Org. Chem.* **22**, 1575.

Blaauw-Jansen, G. (1954). *Proc., Kon. Ned. Akad. Wetensch., Ser. C* **57**, 498.
Brotzu, G. (1948). "Richerche su di un nuovo antibiotico." Lav. Inst. Ig. Univ. Cagliari.
Bruce, D. L., and Duff, D. C. B. (1967). *J. Gen. Microbiol.* **48**, 293.
Bucherl, W., Buckley, E. E., and Deulofeu, V. (1968). "Venomous Animals and Their Venoms," Vol. 1. Academic Press, New York.
Bucherl, W., Buckley, E. E., and Deulofeu, V. (1970). "Venomous Animals and Their Venoms," Vol. 2. Academic Press, New York.
Buck, J. D. (1968). *In* "Drugs from the Sea" (Hugo D. Freudenthal, ed.), pp. 127–133. Marine Technology Society, Washington, D.C.
Buck, J. D., and Meyers, S. P. (1965). *Limnol. Oceanogr.* **10**, 385.
Buck, J. D., Meyers, S. P., and Kamp, K. M. (1962). *Science* **138**, 1339.
Buck, J. D., Ahearn, D. C., Roth, F. J., and Meyers, S. P. (1963). *J. Bacteriol.* **85**, 1132.
Burkholder, P. R. (1944). *Amer. J. Bot.* **31**, 555.
Burkholder, P. R. (1963). *In* "Symposium on Marine Microbiology" (Karl Oppenheimer, ed.), pp. 133–150. Thomas, Springfield, Illinois.
Burkholder, P. R. (1968). *In* "Drugs from the Sea" (Hugo D. Freudenthal, ed.), pp. 87–112. Marine Technology Society, Washington, D.C.
Burkholder, P. R. (1970). *In* "Food-Drugs from the Sea" (Heber W. Youngken, Jr., ed.), p. 255. Marine Technology Society, Washington, D.C.
Burkholder, P. R., and Burkholder, L. M. (1958). *Science* **127**, 1174.
Burkholder, P. R., and Ruetzler, K. (1969). *Nature (London)* **222**, 983.
Burkholder, P. R., and Sharma, G. M. (1970). *Lloydia* **32**, 466.
Burkholder, P. R., Burkholder, L. M., and Almodóvar, L. R. (1960). *Bot. Mar.* **2**, 149.
Burkholder, P. R., Pfister, R. M., and Leitz, F. H. (1966). *Appl. Microbiol.* **14**, 649.
Bywood, R., and Challenger, R. (1953). *Biochem. J.* **53**, 26.
Cantoni, G. L., and Anderson, D. G. (1956). *J. Biol. Chem.* **222**, 171.
Challenger, F., Bywood, R., Thomas, P., and Hayward, B. J. (1957). *Arch. Biochem. Biophys.* **69**, 514.
Challenger, R. (1959). "Aspects of the Organic Chemistry of Sulphur." Butterworth, London.
Challenger, R., and Simpson, M. I. (1948). *J. Chem. Soc., London* **3**, 1591.
Chanley, J. D., Mazzetti, T., and Sobotka, H. (1966). *Tetrahedron* **22**, 1857.
Chentsov, B. V. (1964). *Ref. Zh., Biol.* No. 8D, p. 237; (1965) *Biol. Abstr.* **47**, 1544 (abstr. 18718).
Chesters, C. G., and Stott, J. A. (1956). *Proc. Int. Seaweed Symp.* 2nd, 1956, p. 49.
Chu, G. W. T. C. (1959). *Proc. Hawaii. Acad. Sci.* p. 19.
Ciereszko, L. S. (1962). *Trans. N.Y. Acad. Sci.* [2] **24**, 502.
Ciereszko, L. S., Gifford, D. H., and Weinheimer, A. J. (1960). *Ann. N.Y. Acad. Sci.* **90**, 917.
Claus, G., Madri, P., and Kunen, S. (1967). *Nature (London)* **216**, 712.
Connell, C. H., and Cross, J. B. (1950). *Science* **112**, 359.
Connes, R. (1967). *Vie Milieu* **18**, 281.
Conover, J. T., and Sieburth, J. M. (1964). *Bot. Mar.* **6**, 147.
Conover, J. T., and Sieburth, J. M. (1966). *Proc. Int. Seaweed Symp.* 5th, 1965, p. 99.

Craigie, J. S., and Gruenig, D. E. (1967). *Science* **157**, p. 1058.

Crawford, K., Heatley, N. G., Boyd, P. F., Hale, C. W., Kelly, B. K., Miller, G. A., Smith, N. S. (1952). *J. Gen. Microbiol.* **6**, 47.

Daniel, S. (1969). *Rev. Int. Oceanogr. Med.* **15**, 61.

De Jorge, F. B., Sawya, P., Peterson, J. A., and Ditadi, A. S. F. (1965). *Science* **150**, 1182.

Der Marderosian, A. H. (1969a). *J. Pharm. Sci.* **58**, 1.

Der Marderosian, A. H. (1969b). *Lloudia* **32**, 438.

Der Marderosian, A. H. (1970). *In* "Food and Drugs from the Sea" (Heber W. Youngken, Jr., ed.), p. 211. Marine Technology Society, Washington, D.C.

Doggett, R. G. (1968). *J. Bacteriol.* **95**, 1972.

Doty, M. S., and Aguilar-Santos, G. (1966). *Nature* (*London*) **211**, 990.

Drechsel, E. (1896). *Z. Biol.* **33**, 85.

Duff, D. C., Bruce, D. L., and Antia, N. J. (1966). *Can. J. Microbiol.* **12**, 876.

Endean, R., and Rudkin, C. (1963). *Toxicon* **1**, 49.

Endean, R., and Rudkin, C. (1965). *Toxicon* **2**, 225.

Eppley, R. W., and Bovell, C. R. (1958). *Biol. Bull.* **115**, 101.

Evans, E. E., Painter, B., Evans, M. L., Weinheimer, P., and Acton, R. T. (1968). *Proc. Soc. Exp. Biol. Med.* **128**, 394.

Fassina, G. (1962). *Arch. Ital. Sci. Farmacol.* **12**, 238.

Fattorusso, E., Minale, L., and Sodano, G. (1970a). *Chem. Commun.* **12**, 751.

Fattorusso, E., Minale, L., and Sodano, G. (1970b). *Chem. Commun.* **12**, 752.

Fogg, G. E. (1962). *In* "Physiology and Biochemistry of the Algae" (R. A. Lewin, ed.), p. 475. Academic Press, New York.

Fry, W. G., ed. (1970). "The Biology of the Porifera." Academic Press, New York.

Fukada, T. (1968). *Appl. Microbiol.* **16**, 1809.

Fulmor, W., Van Lear, G. E., Morton, G. O., and Mills, R. D. (1970). *Tetrahedron Lett.* p. 4551.

Gasic, G. J., and Galenti, N. L. (1966). *Science* **151**, 203.

Gauthier, M. (1969a). *Rev. Int. Oceanogr. Med.* **15–16**, 41.

Gauthier, M. (1969b). *Rev. Int. Oceanogr. Med.* **15–16**, 103.

Gerber, P., Dutcher, J. D., Adams, E. V., and Sharman, J. H. (1958). *Proc. Soc. Exp. Biol. Med.* **99**, 590.

Greene, R. C. (1962). *J. Biol. Chem.* **237**, 2251.

Grein, A., and Meyers, S. P. (1958). *J. Bacteriol.* **76**, 457.

Grindley, J. R., and Taylor, F. J. R. (1964). *Trans. Rey. Soc. S. Afr.* **37**, Part 2, 11.

Guelin, A., Lepine, P., Lamblin, D., and Sisman, J. (1968). *C. R. Acad. Sci., Ser. D.* **226**, 2508.

Gundersen, K., Brandberg, A., Magnusson, S., and Lycke, E. (1967). *Acta Pathol. Microbiol. Scand.* **71**, 281.

Haas, P. (1935). *Biochem. J.* **29**, 1297.

Habekost, R. C., Fraser, J. M., and Halstead, B. W. (1955). *J. Wash. Acad. Sci.* **45**, 101.

Halstead, B. W. (1965). "Poisonous and Venomous Marine Animals of the World," Vol. 1. U.S. Govt. Printing Office, Washington, D.C.

Halstead, B. W. (1967). "Poisonous and Venomous Marine Animals of the World," Vol. 2. U.S. Govt. Printing Office, Washington, D.C.

Hanessian, S., and Kaltenbronn, J. S. (1966). *J. Amer. Chem. Soc.* **88**, 4509.

Hardy, A. (1965). "The World of Plankton," see p. 216. Houghton, Boston, Massachusetts.

Hargraves, P. E., Brody, R. W., and Burkholder, P. R. (1970). *Bull. Mar. Sci.* **20**, 331.

Hartman, P. A. (1968). "Miniaturized Microbiological Methods." Academic Press, New York.

Haug, A., and Larsen, B. (1958). *Acta Chem. Scand.* **12**, 650.

Hellebust, J. A. (1965). *Limnol. Oceanogr.* **10**, 192.

Hodgkin, J. H., Craigie, J. S., and McInnes, A. G. (1966). *Can. J. Chem.* **44**, 74.

Holm-Hansen, O. (1968). *Annu. Rev. Microbiol.* **22**, 47.

Howell, J. F. (1953). *Trans. Amer. Microsc. Soc.* **72**, 153.

Irie, T., Suzuki, M., and Masamune, T. (1965a). *Tetrahedron Lett.* No. 17, p. 2091.

Irie, T., Yasunari, Y., Suzuki, T., Imai, N., Kurosawa, E., and Masamune, T. (1965b) *Tetrahedron Lett.* No. 40, p. 3619.

Irie, T., Suzuki, M., Kurosawa, E., and Masamune, T. (1966). *Tetrahedron Lett.* No. 17, p. 1837.

Irie, T., Izawa, M., and Kurosawa, E. (1968). *Tetrahedron Lett.* No. 17, p. 2091.

Irie, T., Suzuki, M., and Hayakawa, Y. (1969). *Bull. Chem. Soc. Jap.* **42**, 843.

Jackson, D. F., ed. (1964). "Algae and Man." Plenum, New York.

Jakowska, S., and Nigrelli, R. F. (1960). *Ann. N.Y. Acad. Sci.* **90**, 913.

Jones, G. E. (1963). *In* "Symposium on Marine Microbiology" (Karl Oppenheimer, ed.), pp. 572–579. Thomas, Springfield, Illinois.

Jorgensen, E. G. (1959). *Carnegie Inst. Wash., Yearb.* **58**, 341.

Jorgensen, E. G. (1962). *Physiol. Plant.* **15**, 530.

Kamimoto, K. (1955). *Jap. J. Bacteriol.* **10**, 897.

Katayama, T. (1962). *In* "Physiology and Biochemistry of Algae" (R. A. Lewin, ed.), pp. 467–473. Academic Press, New York.

Kathan, R. H. (1965). *Ann. N.Y. Acad. Sci.* **130**, 390.

Katsui, N., Suzuki, Y., Katamura, S., and Irie, T. (1967). *Tetrahedron* **23**, 1185.

Klein, S. (1964). *Bot. Mar.* **6**, 247.

Krasil'nikova, E. N. (1962). *Microbiology* **30**, 545.

Lefevre, M. (1964). *In* "Algae and Man" (D. F. Jackson, ed.), pp. 337–367. Plenum, New York.

Li, C. P., Prescott, B., and Jahnes, W. B. (1962a). *Proc. Soc. Exp. Biol. Med.* **109**, 534.

Li, C. P., Prescott, B., Jahnes, W., and Martino, E. C. (1962b). *Trans. N.Y. Acad. Sci.* [2] **24**, 504.

Li, C. P., Prescott, B., Eddy, B., Caldes, G., Green, W. R., Martino, E. C., and Young, A. M. (1965). *Ann. N.Y. Acad. Sci.* **130**, 374.

Liguori, V. R., Ruggieri, G. D., Baslow, M. H., Stempien, M. F., and Nigrelli, R. F. (1963). *Amer. Zool.* **3**, Abst. 302.

Louzon, F. (1964). M.S. Thesis, University of Rhode Island, Kingston.

Lovell, F. M. (1966). *J. Amer. Chem. Soc.* **88**, 4510.

Lucas, C. E. (1947). *Biol. Rev.* **22**, 270.

Lucas, C. E. (1955). *Deep-Sea Res.* **3**, Suppl., 139.

MacGintie, G. E., and MacGintie, N. (1968). "Natural History of Marine Animals," p. 115. McGraw-Hill, New York.

McLachlan, J., and Craigie, J. S. (1964). *Can. J. Bot.* **42**, 287.

McLachlan, J., and Craigie, J. S. (1966). *J. Phycol.* **2**, 133.

Magnusson, S., Hedstrom, C. E., and Lycke, E. (1966). *Acta Pathol. Microbiol. Scand.* **66**, 551.

Marsico, W. E. (1962). *Diss. Abstr.* **23**, 1928.

Martínez-Nadal, N. G., Rodríguez, L. V., and Casillas, C. (1964). *Antimicrob. Ag. Chemother.* p. 68.

Martínez-Nadal, N. G., Rodríguez, L. V., and Casillas, C. (1965). *Antimicrob. Ag. Chemother.* p. 131.

Martínez-Nadal, N. G., Rodríguez, L. V., and Iguina-Dolagaray, J. (1966). *Bot. Mar.* **9**, 62.

Mautner, H. C., Gardner, G. M., and Pratt, R. (1953). *J. Amer. Pharm. Ass.* **42**, 294.

Mitchell, R., Yankofsky, S., and Jannasch, H. (1967). *Nature (London)* **215**, 891.

Moikeha, S. N. (1968). Univ. Microfilms, Ann Arbor, Michigan. Order No. 68-11, p. 937; *Chem. Abstr.* **70**, No. 1005a, 126 (1969).

Morishita, T., and Kobayashi, M. (1963). *Jap. J. Exp. Med.* **33**, 107.

Morner, C. T. (1913). *Hoppe-Seyler's Z. Physiol. Chem.* **88**, 138.

Nigrelli, R. F. (1958). *Trans. N.Y. Acad. Sci.* [2] **20**, 248.

Nigrelli, R. F. (1962). *Trans. N.Y. Acad. Sci.* [2] **24**, 496.

Nigrelli, R. F., and Jakowska, S. (1960). *Ann. N.Y. Acad. Sci.* **90**, 884.

Nigrelli, R. F., and Zahl, P. (1952). *Proc. Soc. Exp. Biol. Med.* **81**, 379.

Nigrelli, R. F., Jakowska, S., and Calventi, I. (1959). *Zoologica* (New York) **44**, 173.

Nigrelli, R. F., Baslow, M., and Jakowska, S. (1961). *Antimicrob. Ag. Chemother.* pp. 83–84.

Nigrelli, R. F., Stempien, M. F., Ruggieri, G. D., Liguori, V. R., and Cecil, J. T. (1967). *Fed. Proc., Fed. Amer. Soc. Exp. Biol.* **26**, 1197.

Okaichi, T., and Hashimoto, Y. (1962). *Bull. Jap. Soc. Sci. Fish.* **28**, 930.

Olsen, P. E., Maretzki, A., and Almodóvar, L. R. (1964). *Bot. Mar.* **6**, 224.

Pfister, R. M., and Burkholder, P. R. (1965). *J. Bacteriol.* **90**, 863.

Pramer, D., Carlucci, A. F., and Scarpino, P. V. (1963). *In* "Symposium on Marine Microbiology" (Karl Oppenheimer, ed.), pp. 567–571. Thomas, Springfield, Illinois.

Pratt, R., Mautner, R. H., Gardner, G. M., Sha, Y., and Dufrenoy, J. (1951). *J. Amer. Pharm. Ass.* **40**, 575.

Przyjalkowski, Z. (1964a). *Wiad. Parazytol.* **10**, 209.

Przyjalkowski, Z. (1964b). *Wiad. Parazytol.* **10**, 301.

Ramamurphy, V. D., and Krishramurphy, S. (1967). *Ann. Sci.* **36**, 524.

Randall, J. E. (1958). *Bull. Mar. Sci.* **8**, 236.

Randall, J. E. (1967). *Stud. Trop. Oceanogr.* **5**, 665.

Randall, J. E., and Hartman, W. D. (1968). *Mar. Biol.* **1**, 216.

Reich, K., and Spiegelstein, M. (1964). *Isr. J. Zool.* **13**, 141.

Rio, G. J., Stempien, M. F., Nigrelli, R. F., and Ruggieri, G. D. (1965). *Toxicon* **3**, 147.

Roos, H. (1957). *Kiel Meeresforsch.* **13**, 41.

Rosenfeld, W. D., and ZoBell, C. E. (1947). *J. Bacteriol.* **54**, 393.

Ruetzler, K. (1968). *Proc. U.S. Nat. Mus.* **124**, 1.

Ruggieri, G. D., and Nigrelli, R. F. (1962). *Amer. Zool.* **2**, 252.

Russell, F. E. (1965). *Advan. Mar. Biol.* **3**, 255.

Russell, F. E. (1967). *Fed. Proc., Fed. Amer. Soc. Exp. Biol.* **26**, 1206.

Russell, F. E., and Saunders, P. R. (1967). "Animals Toxins." Pergamon, Oxford.

Saito, K., and Sameshima, J. (1955). *J. Agr. Chem. Soc. Jap.* **29**, 427.

Saito, T., and Ando, Y. (1955). *Nippon Kagaku Zasshi* **76**, 478.

Saito, T., and Ando, Y. (1957). *Chem. Abstr.* **51**, 17810i.

Saz, A. K., Watson, S., Brown, S. R., and Lowery, D. L. (1963). *Limnol. Oceanogr.* **8**, 63.

Schmeer, M. R. (1966). *Ann. N.Y. Acad. Sci.* **136**, 211.

Schmeer, M. R., and Huala, C. V. (1965). *Ann. N.Y. Acad. Sci.* **118**, 605.

Schmitz, F. J., Kraus, K. W., Ciereszko, L. S., Sifford, D. H., and Weinheimer, A. J. (1966). *Tetrahedron Lett.* No. 1, p. 97.

Schwab, G. E., Reeves, P. R., and Turner, K. J. (1966). *Brit. J. Exp. Pathol.* **47**, 266.

Schwimmer, M., and Schwimmer, D. (1955). "The Role of Algae and Plankton in Medicine," p. 85. Grune & Stratton, New York.

Sharma, G. M., and Burkholder, P. R. (1967a). *J. Antibiot.*, Ser. A **20**, 200.

Sharma, G. M., and Burkholder, P. R. (1967b). *Tetrahedron Lett.* No. 42, p. 4147.

Sharma, G. M., and Burkholder, P. R. (1971). *Chem. Commun.* pp. 151–152.

Sharma, G. M., Michaels, L., and Burkholder, P. R. (1968a). *J. Antibiot.* **21**, 659.

Sharma, G. M., Vig, B., and Burkholder, P. R. (1968b). *In* "Drugs from the Sea" (Hugo D. Freudenthal, ed.), pp. 119–126. Marine Technology Society, Washington, D.C.

Sharma, G. M., Vig, B., and Burkholder, P. R. (1970a). *In* "Food-Drugs from the Sea" (Heber W. Youngken, Jr., ed.), pp. 307–310. Marine Technology Society, Washington, D.C.

Sharma, G. M., Vig, B., and Burkholder, P. R. (1970b). *J. Org. Chem.* **35**, 2823.

Shilo, M. (1967). *Bacteriol. Rev.* **31**, 180.

Shimada, S. (1969). *Science* **163**, 1462.

Sieburth, J. M. (1959). *Limnol. Oceanogr.* **4**, 419.

Sieburth, J. M. (1960). *Science* **132**, 676.

Sieburth, J. M. (1961). *J. Bacteriol.* **82**, 72.

Sieburth, J. M. (1964). *Develop. Ind. Microbiol.* **5**, 124.

Sieburth, J. M. (1967). *J. Bacteriol.* **93**, 1911.

Sieburth, J. M. (1968a). *In* "Advances in Microbiology of the Sea" (M. Droop and E. J. F. Wood, eds.), p. 63. Academic Press, New York.

Sieburth, J. M. (1968b). *In* "Drugs from the Sea" (Hugo D. Freudenthal, ed.), pp. 67–68. Marine Technology Society, Washington, D.C.

Sieburth, J. M., and Conover, J. T. (1965). *Nature (London)* **208**, 52.

Sieburth, J. M., and Pratt, D. M. (1962). *Trans. N.Y. Acad. Sci.* [2] **24**, 498.

Smith, W. L. (1944). *Amer. J. Med. Sci.* **207**, 647.

Starr, T. J., and Halterman, O. A. (1967). *Nature (London)* **216**, 600.

Starr, T. J., Deig, E. F., Church, K. K., and Allen, M. B. (1962). *Tex. Rep. Biol. Med.* **20**, 271.

Starr, T. J., Kajime, M., and Piferrer, M. (1966). *Tex. Rep. Biol. Med.* **24**, 208.

Steeman-Nielsen, E. (1955a). *Deep-Sea Res.* **3**, Suppl., 281.

Steeman-Nielsen, E. (1955b). *Nature (London)* **176**, 553.

Steeman-Nielsen, E., and Jorgensen, E. G. (1961). *Physiol. Plant.* **14**, 896.

Stempien, M. F. (1966). *Amer. Zool.* **6**, 363.

Stempien, M. F., Ruggieri, G. D., Nigrelli, R. F., and Cecil, J. T. (1970). *In* "Food-Drugs from the Sea" (Heber W. Youngken, Jr., ed.), pp. 295–305. Marine Technology Society, Washington, D.C.

Takemoto, T., Diago, K., Kondo, Y., and Kondo, K. (1966). *Yakugaku Zasshi* **86**, 874.

Ueno, Y., Tanaka, K., Ueyanagi, J., Nawa, H., Sanno, Y., Honjo, M., Nakamari, R., Sugawa, T., Uchibayashi, M., Osugi, K., and Tatsuoka, S. (1957). *Proc. Jap. Acad.* **33**, 53.

Vacca, D., and Walsh, R., (1954). *J. Amer. Pharm. Ass., Sci. Ed.* **43**, 24.

Vago, C., and Bergoni, M. (1968). *Advan. Virus Res.* **13**, 247.

Vuillemin, C. (1889). "Notes et mémoires," 18th Sess., pp. 525. C. R. Ass. Fr. Avance. Sci., Paris.

Waksman, S. A. (1945). "Microbial Antagonisms and Antibiotic Substances." Commonwealth Fund, New York.

Warmke, G. L., and Almodóvar, L. R. (1963). *Malacologia* **1**, 163.

Weinheimer, A. J., and Spraggins, R. L. (1970). *In* "Food-Drugs from the Sea," (Heber W. Youngken, Jr., ed.), pp. 311–318. Marine Technology Society, Washington, D.C.

Weinheimer, A. J., Karns, T. K. B., Sifford, D., and Ciereszko, L. S. (1968). *Amer. Chem. Soc., Abstr.* p. 171.

Welch, A. M. (1962). *J. Bacteriol.* **83**, 97.

Werler, J. E., and Keegan, H. L. (1963). *In* "Venomous and Poisonous Animals and Noxious Plants of the Pacific Region" (H. L. Keegan, ed.), pp. 219–294. Macmillan, New York.

Yamamura, S., and Hirata, Y. (1963). *Tetrahedron* **19**, 1485.

6

COMPARATIVE BIOCHEMISTRY OF CORAL REEF COELENTERATES

Leon S. Ciereszko and T. K. B. Karns

I. Introduction

The coral reef coelenterates must be considered among the most successful of organisms, and, because of their symbiotic zooxanthellae, are large producers of organic matter in waters poor in essential nutrients. Many of the animals are large and showy. Being attached to the bottom they have the problem of protection against predators in a medium in which animals are always hungry. They also have the problem of warding off potential settlers, the larval forms of other sessile forms, which might encrust and smother them, in the intensive competition for "space," the solid substrate to which the larva must attach to develop into the mature form.

The primary productivity of coral reefs is far greater, on an areal basis, than all other marine environments studied, except for rather specialized turtle grass communities (Kohn and Helfrich, 1957). Kanwisher and Wainwright (1967) concluded that reef corals are among the most productive organisms known, and in Florida corals the boring green algae contribute little to this productivity. The chlorophyll content of both horny and stony reef corals is very high, certainly as high or higher than that of calcareous algae and approaching that of turtle grass (Burkholder and Burkholder, 1960). Bergmann and Lester (1940) have called attention to coral reefs as one of the possible sources of petroleum, pointing out that a significant portion of the organic matter becomes trapped in the ever-growing inorganic mass and hence is removed from circulation. They regarded reefs as vast accumulators of materials that may be considered as potential precursors of petroleum and referred to the Leduc oil field as an example of a commercial oil pool associated with an ancient reef.

The contributions of zooxanthellae to the nutrition of their hosts are becoming clearer as a result of the studies of Muscatine (1967; Muscatine and Cernichiari, 1969; Smith *et al.*, 1969) and von Holt (von Holt and von Holt, 1968a,b). There appears to be a rapid transfer of newly synthesized organic substances from plant to animal, as well as a reverse movement of such substances as glycine, which are required for the biosynthetic activity of the symbionts (von Holt, 1968).

That some reef coelenterates possess chemical defenses against microorganisms is indicated by the observation of the antimicrobial activity of horny corals by Burkholder and Burkholder (1958) and by Ciereszko (1962).

The biosynthetic versatility of reef coelenterates is indicated by the growing list of novel compounds recently isolated from horny corals (gorgonians): prostaglandins; sterols and secosterols with unusual side chains; a family of butenolides containing lactone rings joined by a polymethylene chain; a variety of sesquiterpene hydrocarbons; a series of diterpenes, including cembranolides and organic chlorine compounds; and taurobetaine and its analogs. The occurrence of these novel compounds poses biosynthetic problems and offers clues to biosynthetic pathways as well.

Many of the new compounds found in coelenterates occur in relatively high concentration, often 1% or more of dry weight which is largely calcium carbonate. What is the biological function of the prostaglandin which makes up 1% of the gorgonian *Plexaura homomalla*? What do the cembranolides contribute to the economy of the animals in which they can be observed in crystalline form? Why do the diterpenes and sesqui-terpenes present in related species differ in small but significant detail? Why should the coelenterates produce such a variety of sterols? Why should taurobetaine [$(CH_3)_3N^+$—$CH_2CH_2SO_3^-$] occur in *Briareum*, but its analog choline sulfate [$(CH_3)_3N^+$—CH_2—CH_2—O—SO_3^-] in the closely related *Erythropodium?*

Sessile organisms not only require defenses against predation and against settling by encrusting forms, but must have means of communi-cation, pheromones, for synchronization of release of sexual products and to serve as repellents and attractants. Perhaps a requirement for precision in communication demands the secretion of different but re-lated chemical "signals" by related forms.

The field of natural products derived from marine invertebrates has now become more attractive to the chemist because of the recent devel-opment of means of separation of closely related substances, the advent of automated x-ray diffraction equipment and the powerful tools for determining structural features of complex molecules, such as nuclear magnetic resonance and mass spectrometry.

The coral reef offers tantalizing prospects for an ecological biochemis-try and a mine for novel compounds of potential value as drugs or as tools for pharmacological research.

II. Lipids

The reef coelenterates have a very high lipid content when calculated on the basis of the organic matter of the animals rather than on the total weight, which often is largely calcareous matter (Cary, 1918). The unsaponifiable and steroid fractions of coelenterates make up an unusually large proportion of the lipids (Bergmann, 1949; Marsh, 1965; Ciereszko et al., 1968). The unsaponifiable matter contains fatty alcohols, sterols, α-glyceryl ethers, and hydrocarbons.

A. Fatty Acids, Including Prostaglandins

The fatty acids of reef coelenterates have not been extensively ex-amined. Myristic acid (51%), palmitic acid 31%, stearic acid 3%, and behenic acid 3%, have been found in the sea anemone *Condylactis gi-gantea* (Bergmann et al., 1956). The myristic acid was found as the wax myristyl myristate and the symmetrical triglyceride palmityldimyris-tin. Palmitic, stearic, and oleic acids have been found in all the coelenter-ates examined by Marsh (1965). Fox et al. (1969) have found an inter-

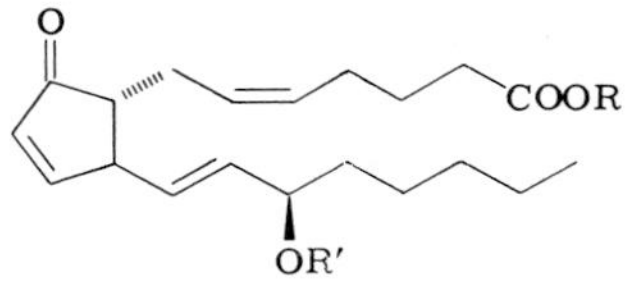

I. R, R' = H
II. R = Me. R' = Ac

Fig. 1. Prostaglandins from *Plexaura homomalla.*

esting mixture of fatty acids, including C_{15} and C_{17} members, in the calcareous microspicules of the fan coral *Eugorgia ampla* Verrill.

That a systematic study of the fatty acids of coelenterates might be very rewarding is made evident by the finding that prostaglandins make up 15% of the lipids of the gorgonian *Plexaura homomalla* (Esper). Spraggins (1970) found that the prostaglandin 15-*epi*-PGA₂, 15(R)-hydroxy-9-oxo-5-*cis*-10,13-*trans*-prostatrienoic acid (I), and its diester, methyl 15(R)-acetoxy-9-oxo-5-*cis*-10,13-*trans*-prostatrienoate (II) make up 0.2 and 1.3% of the total dry weight of cortex of *P. homomalla* (Weinheimer and Spraggins, 1969). (See Fig. 1.)

Some forms of *P. homomalla* contain esterified derivatives of (15S)-PGA₂ and (15S)-PGE₂ identical with the prostaglandins derived from mammalian sources (Schneider *et al.*, 1972) and a new naturally occurring prostaglandin 5-*trans*-PGA₂ (Bundy *et al.*, 1972).

B. WAXES AND FATTY ALCOHOLS

The lipids of reef coelenterates contain much wax. Cetyl palmitate is easily isolated from the zooanthid *Palythoa mammilosa* (Bergmann *et al.,* 1951), the staghorn coral *Acropora cervicornis* (Lester and Bergmann, 1941), the elkhorn coral *Acropora palmata* (Ciereszko, unpublished), the gorgonians *Pterogorgia anceps* (Pallas)(Kind and Bergmann, 1942), *Briarium asbestinum* (Pallas) and *Plexaurella nutans* (Duchassaing and Michelotti)(Schmidt, 1960), and the soft coral *Sclerophytum capitale.* Myristyl myristate is the major wax of the sea anemone *Condylactis gigantea* (Bergmann *et al.,* 1956). There is considerable evidence that other waxes occur in coelenterates.

Many coelenterates contain cetyl and stearyl alcohol (Kind and Bergmann, 1942; Marsh, 1965), as well as myristyl alcohol.

C. α-GLYCERYL ETHERS

The first isolation of batyl alcohol from a coelenterate, the gorgonian *Plexaura flexuosa* Lamouroux, was reported by Kind and Bergmann

(1942). The α-glyceryl ether content of coelenterates is high, usually 10–21% of the unsaponifiable fraction (Marsh, 1965). The major α-glyceryl ether is batyl alcohol. This is usually accompanied by much chimyl alcohol and none or very little of the unsaturated selachyl alcohol.

D. Sterols

The sterols have been the most intensively studied lipids of invertebrate animals largely because of the work of Bergmann (1962) and his students. It early became evident that the sterols of coelenterates were varied and that they occurred as complex mixtures. Bergmann *et al.* (1943) identified cholesterol in the unsaponifiable lipids of the gorgonian *Xiphigorgia* (*Pterogorgia anceps*) and clearly presented evidence for the occurrence of a hitherto unrecognized sterol in *Plexaura flexuosa*. Bergmann called the new sterol gorgosterol after its occurrence in the gorgonian, and correctly suggested that the unusually high-melting levorotatory sterol had a C_{30} skeleton with an unusual side chain. The occurrence of gorgosterol was confirmed by Ciereszko *et al.* (1963, 1968), who established its molecular formula as $C_{30}H_{50}O$ and showed it to occur in a large number of coelenterates containing zooxanthellae, including the jellyfish *Cassiopea xamachana*, the coral *Manicina areolata*, the alcyonacean *Lobophytum* sp., and a large number of gorgonians from both the Caribbean and the Pacific.

The side chain of gorgosterol has recently been shown to contain a cyclopropyl ring (Hale *et al.*, 1970; Gross, 1969) by a combination of spectral and degradative methods (see Fig. 2). The stereochemistry of the gorgosterol molecule (III) has been established by x-ray crystallography (Ling *et al.*, 1970), which shows it to be (22R,23R,24R)-22,23-methylene-23,24-dimethyl-cholest-5-en-3β-ol.

A second example of a sterol with a cyclopropyl side chain is the lower homolog of gorgosterol, the C_{29} sterol, 23-desmethylgorgosterol (V), identified by Schmitz and Pattabhiraman (1970) as one of the sterols in the purple and yellow sea fans *Gorgonia ventalina* and *G. flabellum*. It would appear that the cyclopropane methylene is introduced at C-22,C-23 before methylation at C-23.

The Δ^7-isomer of gorgosterol, named acansterol, has been isolated from crown-of-thorns starfish *Acanthaster planci* (Sheikh *et al.*, 1971). Although Δ^7-sterols are typical of starfish (Bergmann, 1962), it is likely that the C_{30} skeleton of acansterol is derived from the reef corals upon which *Acanthaster* feeds.

Two C_{30} secosteroids related to gorgosterol have been found to occur in *Pseudopterogorgia americana* (Gmelin). These have been identified

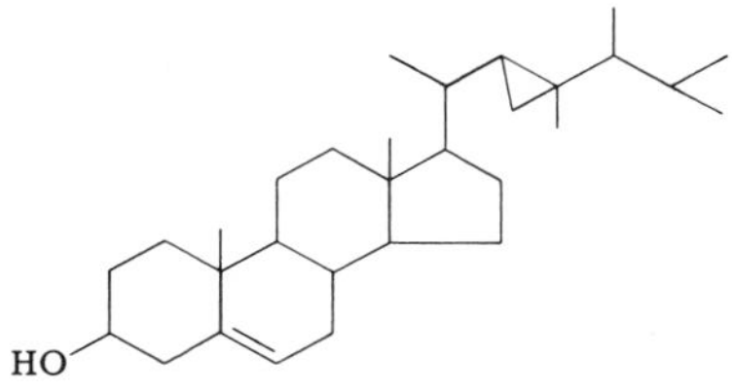

III

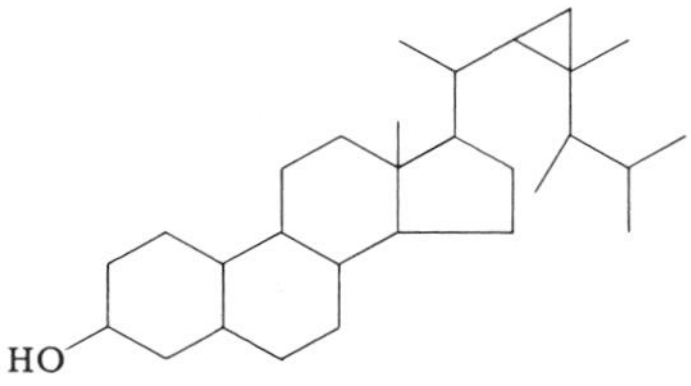

IV

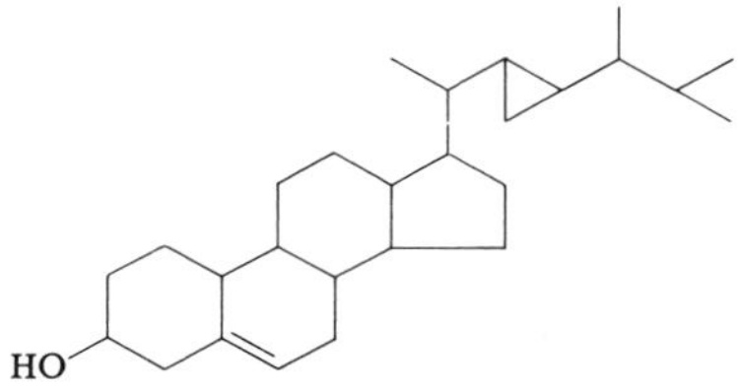

V

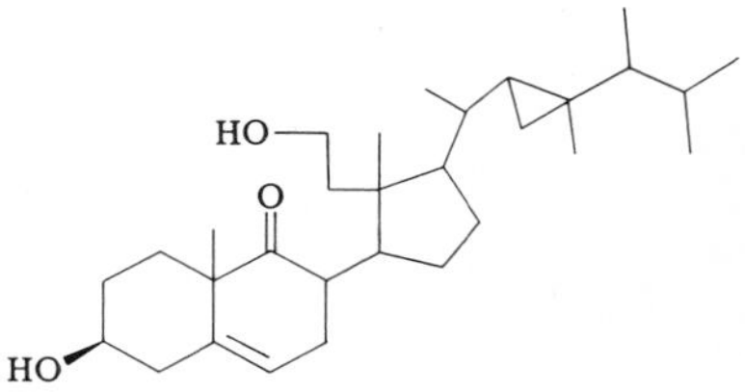

VI

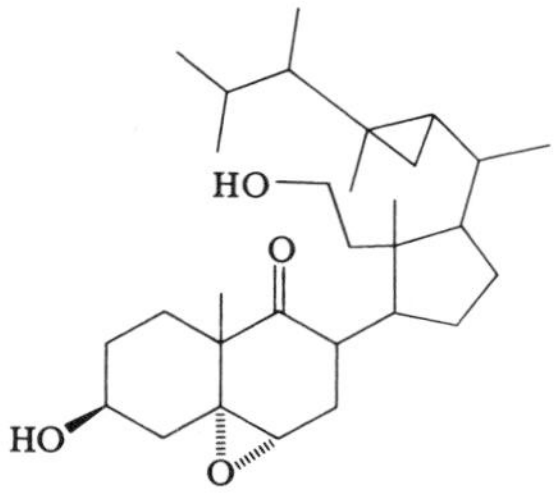

VIA

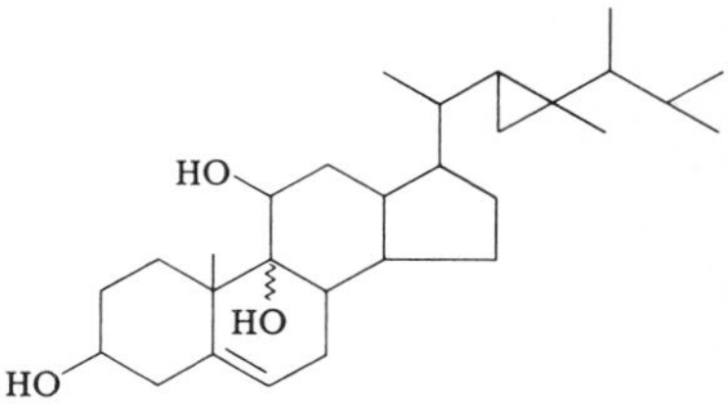

VII

Fig. 2. Gorgosterol derivatives.

by Spraggins and Weinheimer as the two novel compounds Δ^5-9,11-secogorgosten-3,11-diol-9-one (VI) and its epoxide (VIA) (Spraggins, 1970). A possible precursor of the secosteroids is the dihydroxy derivative of gorgosterol gorgost-5-en-3,9,11-triol (VII) found in extracts of *Pseudopterogorgia americana* by Haertle (1971).

Enwall *et al.* (1972) have determined the structures and absolute configurations of 23-desmethylgorgosterol (V) and of the secosteroid (VI) by single crystal X-ray diffraction studies on their *p*-iodobenzoate derivatives.

Wolf (1963) found the sterols of gorgonians to occur as complex mixtures showing as many as seven components by gas–liquid chromatography. Gupta and Scheuer (1969) have shown the "palysterol" isolated from *Palythoa* by Bergmann *et al.* (1951) to be a complex mixture. The sterols of *Palythoa tuberculosa* from Eniwetok include cholesterol, gorgosterol, brassicasterol (24β-methylcholesta-5,22-dien-3β-ol), 22,23-dihydrobrassicasterol (new in nature), and β-sitosterol. The sterol mixture isolated from *P. mammilosa* from Jamaica by Silberberg (1971) has a similar composition, but 24-methylenecholesterol appears to be the sole sterol in a *Palythoa* from Tahiti (Gupta and Scheuer, 1969).

Another zoanthid, *Zoanthus confertus*, analyzed by Gupta and Scheuer, contains cholesterol, 24-methylcholesterol, 24-methylenecholesterol, and brassicasterol (major sterol).

Bergmann (1951) found 24-methylenecholesterol (chalinasterol) to be the major sterol of *Zoanthus proteus* as well as of *Condylactis gigantea*, a sea anemone, from Bermuda.

Schmitz *et al.* (1969b) have tentatively identified cholesterol, brassicasterol, neospongosterol, poriferasterol, clionasterol, gorgosterol, and a sterol with a molecular weight of 384 in three species of the gorgonian *Pterogorgia*.

E. L. Biersmith has found that the sea pansy *Renilla reniformis* from the Gulf of Mexico and the hydrozoan *Distichopora violacea* from Eniwetok, both of which appear to have no zooxanthellae, contain a complex mixture of sterols, tentatively identified by gas–liquid chromatography as containing no gorgosterol, but including 23-desmethylgorgosterol, β-sitosterol, stigmasterol, campestrol, brassicasterol, cholesterol, a "384" sterol, and a C_{26} sterol with MW 370. Silberberg (1971) has examined the sterol fractions of a variety of coelenterates by mass spectrometry and gas chromatography. He found the C_{26} sterol with molecular weight 370, 22-*trans*-24-norcholesta-5,22-dien-3β-ol, first reported from the scallop *Placopecten magellanicus* by Idler *et al.* (1970), to be present in all his samples.

A new C_{28} sterol, 25-hydroxy-24ξ-methylcholesterol, in addition to cholesterol, 24α-methylcholesterol, and gorgosterol, has been isolated from a "soft coral" (Alcyonacea), probably *Nephthea* sp., by Engelbrecht *et al.* (1972).

In spite of the complexity of sterols in coelenterates all of those identified appear to be derivatives of cholesterol.

So far gorgosterol has not been identified in coelenterates without zooxanthellae, although its lower homolog has been identified. It is possible that the zooxanthellae may be involved in the methylation of the C_{29} sterol 23-desmethylgorgosterol to gorgosterol.

Gorgosterol is readily reduced to dihydrogorgosterol (IV) under anaerobic conditions (Ciereszko *et al.*, 1968). The reduction occurs in a few days in thick suspensions of zooxanthellae prepared by breaking the cortex of the fresh animal in a blendor and concentrating the zooxanthellae by repeated suspension in fresh water and decantation.

The gorgonians mentioned above were classified according to Bayer (1961).

E. *n*-Alkane Hydrocarbons

Higher *n*-alkanes occur in the unsaponifiable matter of gorgonians (Koons *et al.*, 1965). The *n*-alkane distributions show very little odd-number preference, as compared with the distributions in land plants, and in this respect resemble the higher *n*-alkane distributions in petroleums.

F. *n*-Alkyl Disulfides

n-Alkyl disulfides are formed under the same anaerobic conditions which lead to the reduction of gorgosterol to dihydrogorgosterol in the "sediment" from the gorgonian *Pseudoplexaura porosa* (Houttuyn) (Ciereszko *et al.*, 1968). Youngblood (1969) has identified the main components of the disulfide mixture as: *n*-hexadecyl disulfide $[CH_3(CH_2)_{14}CH_2—S—S—CH_2(CH_2)_{14}CH_3]$, *n*-hexadecyl *n*-octadecyl disulfide $[CH_3(CH_2)_{14}CH_2—S—S—CH_2(CH_2)_{16}CH_3]$, and *n*-octadecyl disulfide $[CH_3(CH_2)_{16}CH_2—S—S—CH_2(CH_2)_{16}CH_3]$. This is the first report of the occurrence of long-chain disulfides in material derived from living organisms. No disulfide was isolated from the fresh animal indicating the possible presence of labile S-alkyl compounds in the animal or in its symbiotic zooxanthellae (Ciereszko and Youngblood, 1971).

G. Polymethylene Butenolides

Examination of *Pterogorgia anceps* (Pallas), a gorgonian from Bimini, led to the discovery of the novel bisbutenolide ancepsenolide, which was shown to be a dodecan, 1,12-dilactone (VIII), by Schmitz *et al.*

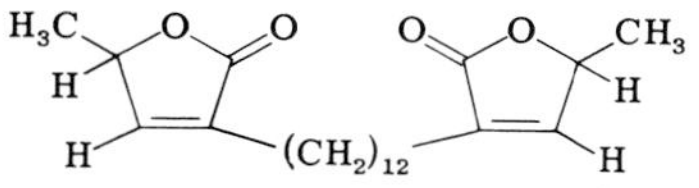

Fig. 3. Butenolides from *Pterogorgia* sp.

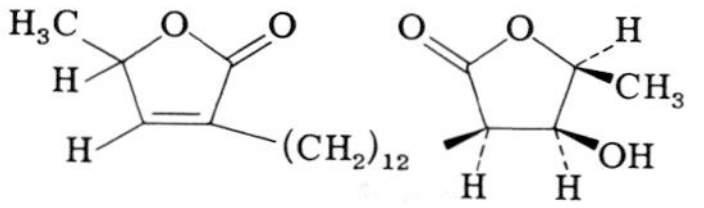

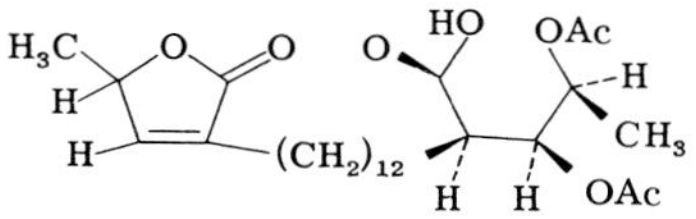

(1966) and the related hydroxyancepsenolide (IX) (Schmitz *et al.*, 1969a). (See Fig. 3.)

The value of looking at related species was demonstrated by the finding of the related monobutenolide guadalupensic acid diacetate [2-(13-carboxy-14,15-diacetoxyhexadecanyl)-2-pentene-4-olide] (X) along with ancepsenolide in *Pterogorgia guadalupensis* Duchassaing and Michelin (Schmitz *et al.*, 1969b; Schmitz and Lorance, 1971). The yields of the butenolide lactones are large, 3% ancepsenolide and 1% guadalupensic acid diacetate in *Pterogorgia guadalupensis*, which contains well over half its dry weight of calcareous spicules. The existence of dodecane butenolides poses an interesting problem in biosynthesis.

III. Terpene Compounds

A. SESQUITERPENE HYDROCARBONS

Many gorgonians have an odor which one would call aromatic, readily noticed shortly after the animals are taken out of the sea. This odor can be quite strong. The particularly sweet odor of *Eunicea mammosa* Lamouroux led us to make extracts of the dried animal and to subject the extracts to steam distillation. The steam distillate of both *E. mammosa* and *Pseudoplexaura porosa* (Houttuyn) contained oily material characterized as sesquiterpene hydrocarbons (Ciereszko *et al.*, 1960a). (See Fig. 4.) The sesquiterpene hydrocarbon from *E. mammosa* obtained at Bimini has been identified as (−)-germacrene-A (XI), an elusive sesquiterpene, previously unreported but long sought in nature,

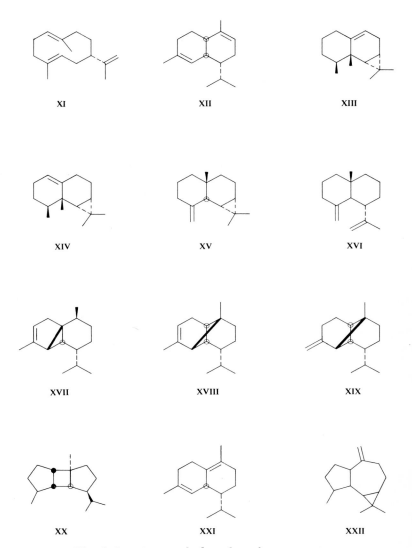

Fig. 4. Sesquiterpene hydrocarbons from gorgonians.

which readily isomerizes to β-elemene (Youngblood, 1969; Weinheimer *et al.*, 1970).

Eunicea mammosa from the Florida Keys also contains germacrene-A but the major hydrocarbon (80%) is (+)-α-muurolene (XII). Specimens from Jamaica contain the latter hydrocarbon to the extent of 99% of sesquiterpene content. There are other chemical differences, noted below in connection with the diterpene lactones, which may be associated with the symbiotic zooxanthellae present in the animals.

Over 95% of the sesquiterpene hydrocarbon fraction of *Pterogorgia americana* (Gmelin) is accounted for by the four compounds: (+)-9-aristolene (XIII); (−)-1(10)-aristolene (XIV); (+)-γ-maaliene (XV), previously unknown in nature; and (+)-β-gorgonene (XVI) (Washecheck, 1967; Weinheimer *et al.*, 1968b). (+)-β-Gorgonene possesses a new isoprenoid skeleton having a "misplaced" isopropenyl residue and forms a crystalline complex with silver nitrate, whose structure has been determined by Hossain and van der Helm (1968).

The genus *Pseudoplexaura* (Youngblood, 1969) is characterized by a complex mixture of sesquiterpene hydrocarbons which have been consistently found in *P. porosa* (Houttuyn), *P. wagenaari* (Stiasny), and *P. flagellosa* (Houttuyn) from well-separated geographical locations: (+)-α-cubebene (XVII), (+)-α-copaene (XVIII), (+)-β-copaene (XIX), (+)-β-epi-bourbonene (XX), (+)-α-muurolene (XII), (−)-δ-cadinene (XXI), and an alloaromadendrene (XXII). Within the gorgonian, these sesquiterpenes are distributed between the zooxanthellae and the animal portion of the symbiotic complex. Furthermore, though broken cell preparations derived from pure zooxanthellae will not form labeled sesquiterpenes from biosynthetic labeled farnesol pyrophosphate, in an identical incubation mixture, particulate preparations which are derived solely from gorgonian tissue will catalyze substantial conversion of this substrate to a number of *Pseudoplexaura* sesquiterpenes (D. G. Anderson, unpublished).

Eunicea palmeri Bayer from Miami contains (+)-α-muurolene (XII) and (+)-β-copaene (XIX) (Youngblood, 1969).

Three species of *Plexaurella* (*P. dichotoma* (Esper), *P. grisea* Kunze, and *P. fusifera* Kunze) contain (+)-α-muurolene (XII), (−)-α-curcumene (XXIII), (+)-β-curcumene (XXIV), (+)-α-bisabolene (XXV), and (+)-β-bisabolene (XXVI). (See Fig. 5A.)

It is worth noting that each of the sesquiterpenes isolated from the marine coelenterates is the optical antipode of the form found, where known, in terrestrial plants.

A new benzofuran, furoventalene (XXVII), a nonfarnesyl sesquiterpene, has been obtained as an artifact from the purple sea fan *Gorgonia ventalina* L. by steam distillation of the total lipid extract (Washecheck, 1967; Weinheimer and Washecheck, 1969).

The sesquiterpene hydrocarbons make up an appreciable proportion of the lipid extracts of some gorgonians (0.8% dry weight of *E. mammosa*,

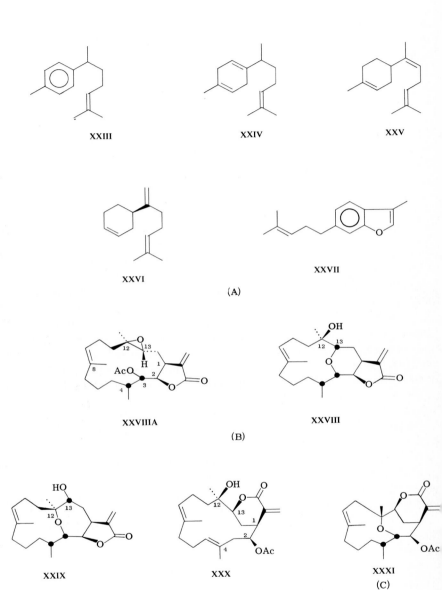

Fig. 5. (A) Sesquiterpenes from gorgonians. (B) Cembranolides isolated from gorgonians. (C) Tentative formula of cueunicin acetate, a cembranolide from Curaçao *Eunicea.*

0.12% *P. porosa*, 1% *P. americana*, 0.3% *P. dichotoma*). No appreciable amount of sesquiterpenes has been found in the three species of *Pterogorgia* examined.

B. DITERPENES

1. Cembranolides

Extraction of dried *Eunicea mammosa* Lamouroux from Bimini with ether or pentane led to the easy isolation of the crystalline lactone eunicin (Ciereszko *et al.*, 1960b), whose structure (XXVIII) was elucidated both by chemical degradation (Middlebrook, 1966; Weinheimer *et al.*, 1968a) and x-ray diffraction (Hossain *et al.*, 1968). (See Fig. 5B.)

Jeunicin (XXIX) (Weinheimer *et al.*, 1967), an isomer of eunicin, was found admixed with varying proportions of eunicin in *E. mammosa* from Jamaica but not from Bimini.

A related lactone, recently named eupalmerin acetate, was found by Ciereszko in *E. succinea* from Florida. Rehm (1971) has found it to occur in *Eunicea palmeri* collected near Miami, but not in specimens collected in the Florida Keys which yield eunicin. Eupalmerin acetate occurs along with eunicin in *E. mammosa* from Puerto Rico. The structure of eupalmerin acetate (XXVIIIA) has been elucidated by Rehm (1971). Eupalmerin acetate can be looked upon as the biosynthetic precursor of both eunicin and jeunicin, yielding one or the other by reaction of the epoxide group with the hydroxyl group released by hydrolysis of the acetate group. The carbon skeleton of the three lactones, XXVIII, XXVIIIA, and XXIX, is a 14-membered ring related to cembrane and the compounds may be classed as cembranolides.

The cembranolide crassin acetate (XXX) occurs in three species of *Pseudoplexaura: P. porosa, P. wagenaari*, and *P. flagellósa*. It has been isolated from specimens of *Pseudoplexaura* collected at Bermuda, Bimini, Jamaica, Florida, British Honduras, Puerto Rico, and the Virgin Islands, in yields of 1–2%. A new cembranolide, cueunicin (XXXI), has been obtained from *Eunicea* collected in Curacao (Fig. 5C). Preliminary nuclear magnetic resonance data indicate that it has the seven-membered ether ring of jeunicin, the six-membered lactone ring of crassin acetate, and occurs as the acetate ester.

The consistent finding of crassin acetate in *Pseudoplexaura* sp. and the variation in the diterpene lactone content of *Eunicea* from different locations leads us to suggest the possibility that the biosynthesis of the diterpenes in the gorgonians involves their symbiotic zooxanthellae and that these differ in their identity and therefore metabolic capability in the different specimens of *Eunicea*. The same consistency in sesquiterpene hydrocarbons in *Pseudoplexaura* sp. and inconsistency in sesquiterpene hydrocarbons in *Eunicea* sp. support the suggestion that the zooxanthellae symbiotic with gorgonians from different locations are not the same.

Anderson (Rice *et al.*, 1970), at the University of Miami, has undertaken a study of the biosynthesis of crassin acetate. He found incorporation of labeled acetate and carbon dioxide into crassin acetate in *P. porosa*. Anderson has observed crystalline crassin acetate in homogenates of fresh *Pseudoplexaura* made in a blender. We have observed crystals of crassin acetate, eunicin, and ancepsenolide (?) in the juice freshly expressed from live *Pseudoplexaura porosa*, *Eunicea mammosa*, and *Pterogorgia anceps*, respectively. These lactones are poorly soluble in water. Anderson found the crystals of crassin acetate extracellular to the zooxanthellae, but associated with gorgonian endoderm containing zooxanthellae, suggesting that crassin acetate is a product of host–zooxanthella interaction. Preliminary results following the incorporation of radioactive mevalonic acid into crystalline crassin acetate indicate that soluble preparations derived from isolated zooxanthellae of *P. porosa* are capable of forming crassin acetate without any intermediary action by gorgonian tissue (C. Papastephanou and D. G. Anderson, personal communication).

The biological function of the diterpene lactones, which occur in high concentrations in gorgonians, has puzzled us. We have suggested that they may have a protective function against larval forms of sessile animals which might otherwise settle and encrust the gorgonian (Ciereszko, 1962). Donald L. Perkins of the University of Oklahoma has evaluated the effect of crassin acetate on the growth and mobility of axenic *Tetrahymena pyriformis*. The effects depend upon concentration of crassin acetate and include increased generation time (0.027 mM), decreased population density, decreased motility, and death (0.133 mM). Eunicin and jeunicin are more active in affecting motility and survival. *Tetrahymena* colonies resistant to the action of the lactones were developed.

High concentrations (0.133–0.266 mM; 50–100 mg/liter) of crassin acetate are lethal to aquatic metazoa such as *Asplanchna*, anuran larvae, *Diaptomus*, gastropod mollusks, and *Tebistes*.

2. Other Diterpenoid Derivatives

The structure of a diterpenoid, eunicellin (XXXII), obtained from the gorgonian *Eunicella stricta* in 0.005% yield has been determined

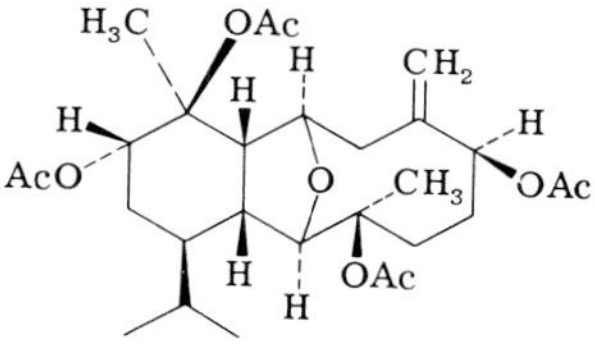

Fig. 6. Eunicellin.

by x-ray analysis. It has a ten-membered carbon ring, an ether oxygen bridge, and four acetate groups (Kennard *et al.*, 1968). (See Fig. 6.)

Gross (1969) has carried out a preliminary study of a diterpene isolated by Ciereszko from the soft coral *Sclerophytum capitale*. Mass spectral data coupled with elemental analyses indicate the molecular formula $C_{23}H_{34}O_7$. The compound appears to be a fully substituted conjugated diene, carrying the following groups: isopropyl, hydroxyl, tertiary methyl, vinyl methyl, acetate, a five-membered ring containing a methylenedioxy group, and a lactone ring. Other diterpene compounds occur in *Briareum asbestinum* and *Erythropodium caribbeorum*. These occur as mixtures of highly oxygenated, acylated compounds containing organically bound chlorine (Hyde, 1966).

IV. Nitrogen Compounds

A variety of nitrogen compounds have been identified in reef coelenterates. Welsh and Prock (1958) have found tetramine, homarine, trigonelline, and zooanemonine in the gorgonian *Plexaura flexuosa*, using paper chromatography. Creatine has been found in nine gorgonians examined by Odense (1958; Ciereszko *et al.*, 1960b).

Examination of the dipolar ion fraction of three gorgonians has led to the isolation of taurine, $+NH_3CH_2CH_2SO_3^-$, from *Pterogorgia anceps*; taurobetaine, $(CH_3)_3N^+—CH_2CH_2SO_3^-$, from *Briareum asbestinum* (Ciereszko *et al.*, 1960b); but choline sulfate, $(CH_3)_3N^+CH_2CH_2O—SO_3^-$, from *Erythropodium caribbeorum* (Schmidt and Ciereszko, 1969). The finding of two different but analogous compounds, taurobetaine and choline sulfate, in the closely related species of gorgonians, in high concentration (0.5–0.6%) is one of the chemical curiosities which keep turning up in reef coelenterates. Taurobetaine has also been crystallized from methanol extracts of the sea rod *Pseudoplexaura porosa* from Bermuda, the hard coral *Porites furcata* from Puerto Rico, and the soft coral *Sarcophyton tro-cheliophorum* from Australia (Ciereszko *et al.*, 1972). The extracts of *Sarcophyton* contained taurine as well as taurobetaine.

Glycine has been found as the principal free amino acid in the two zoanthids studied, *Zoanthus* (von Holt, 1968) and *Palythoa* (Schmidt and Ciereszko, (unpublished). Sheikh (1969) has isolated *m*-tyramine, homarine, anemonine, and histamine from extracts of toxic *Palythoa*.

Wainwright (1962) has found chitin in the Hawaiian reef coral *Pocillopora damicornis*. The axial skeleton of gorgonians contains much protein, which is rich in iodine and bromine bound to tyrosine (Roche, 1952; Schmidt, 1960). Young (1971) found the usual protein amino acids in hydrolysates of acid decalcified skeletons of all fourteen species of stony corals he examined. A collagenlike protein has been reported to occur within the calcareous spicules of the gorgonian *Briareum asbestinum* (Silberberg *et al.*, 1972). The spicules contain 0.9% of material insoluble in dilute hydrochloric acid.

The aminophosphonic acids were first discovered in ciliates. Kittredge and Hughes (1964) found a new amino acid, α-amino-β-phosphonopropionic acid, in the zoanthid *Zoanthus sociatus*. Quin and Shelburne (1969) reported the presence of 2-aminoethanephosphonic acid in the gorgonian *Leptogorgia virgulata*. The occurrence of aminophosphonic acids in nature has been reviewed by Kittredge and Roberts (1969).

Keezer (1969) has surveyed a variety of coelenterates for indole compounds. He found large concentrations, 200 ppm, of serotonin (XXXIII) and *O*-serotonin sulfate (XXXIV) in the zoanthids *Palythoa mammilosa* and *P. caribbeorum*. (See Fig. 7.)

Zoanthids of the genus *Palythoa* have been found to contain a toxic substance now called palytoxin (Scheuer, 1964; Ciereszko and Attaway, 1961). Palytoxin as currently isolated is an amorphous hygroscopic solid of relatively high molecular weight. It contains nitrogen but is not a protein. It tends to concentrate at lipophilic surfaces, although it is highly polar and insoluble in most organic solvents. It is under study

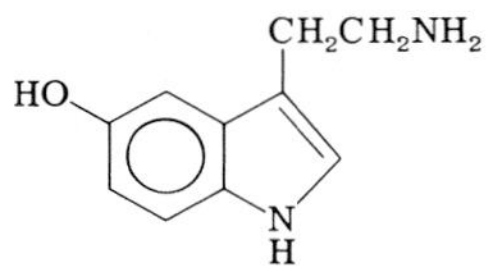

XXXIII 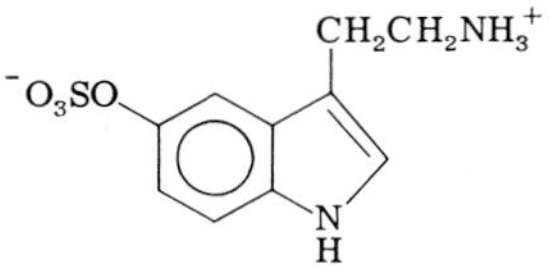   XXXIV

Fig. 7. Serotonin and serotonin sulfate.

at the University of Hawaii (Scheuer, 1969; Sheikh, 1969; Moore and Scheuer, 1971) and at the University of Oklahoma (Attaway, 1968).

V. Carbohydrates

Little work has been done on the carbohydrates in coelenterates. Johannes (1967) has observed a marked increase in the concentration of suspended particulate organic aggregates in oceanic water as it crosses the windward coral reef at Eniwetok Atoll and enters the lagoon. He presented evidence that these aggregates consist of mucus released by corals and suggested that aggregates of mucus may be an important food source for zooplankton in the vicinity of coral reefs.

Mizelle (University of Oklahoma) has examined the gorgonian *Pseudopterogorgia americana* which secretes considerable slime. He has obtained almost 7% of the dry weight of the animal as sulfated polysaccharide containing arabinose, fucose, and galactose.

Mizelle examined zooxanthellae, the symbiotic algae of various reef animals, for cellulose and was unable to detect the polysaccharide.

Scyllitol, one of the inositols, has been isolated from *Briareum asbestinum* and from *Erythropodium caribbeorum* in yields of more than 0.5% of dry weight (Schmidt and Ciereszko, 1969).

VI. Pigments

Coelenterates are often highly colored. In many cases, part of the color is attributable to the presence of symbiotic zooxanthellae. Jeffrey and Haxo (1968) have analyzed the pigment composition of zooxanthellae from various corals collected from the Great Barrier Reef of Australia, by chromatography. In coral zooxanthellae the chlorophyll c content was only about one-tenth that of chlorophyll a. Burkholder and Burkholder (1960) had found a higher ratio of chlorophyll c:a, 0.5:1, in alcyonarian corals (gorgonians) from the Caribbean area. The carotenoids found by Jeffrey and Haxo in coral zooxanthellae are identical with those in the dinoflagellate *Amphidinium* and include β-carotene, peridinin, neoperidinin, dinoxanthin, neodinoxanthin, diadinoxanthin, and three minor xanthophyll fractions not previously described.

Strain *et al.* (1971) have shown peridinin, probably the principal carotenoid of the zooxanthellae of reef coelenterates, to be a unique tricyclic carotenoid with a C_{37} skeleton, including allenic and butenolide units in the polyene chain (XXXV). (See Fig. 8A.)

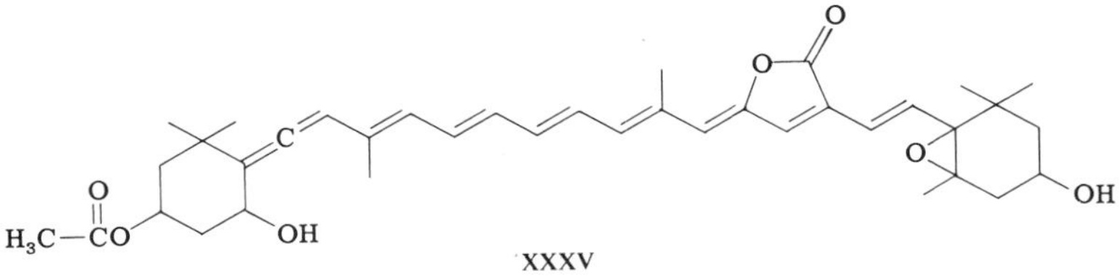

XXXV

(A)

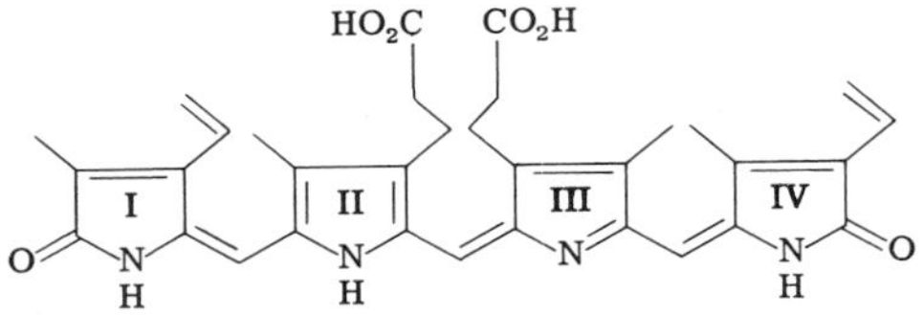

XXXVI

(B)

Fig. 8. (A) Peridinin, from Strain *et al.*, 1971. (B) Biliverdin-IX,α.

Rudiger *et al.* (1968) have isolated biliverdin-IX,α (XXXVI) as the principal pigment of the calcareous skeleton of the blue coral *Heliopora coerulea* Pallas (see Fig. 8). A number of gorgonians contain calcareous spicules with a yellow, red, or purple color.

"Eugorgiaenoic acid" has been proposed as the name for the principal yellow compound isolated from the orange-yellow calcareous spicules of *Eugorgia ampla* by Fox *et al.* (1969).

Eugorgiaenoic acid appears to be a nonfluorescing, chemically unstable, nonaromatic, polyene-chained acid with properties suggestive of a dihydrobixin.

We have been unable to extract the purple color from the spicules found in many gorgonians with any solvent. The purple color vanishes when the calcareous spicules are dissolved in acid. The purple color also vanishes upon irradiation with x rays, but returns after some time.

VII. Halogen Compounds

The gorgonians incorporate the halogens chlorine, bromine, and iodine into organic compounds. The skeletal proteins usually contain bromine and iodine bound to the tyrosyl residues (Roche, 1952; Schmidt, 1960).

Briareum asbestinum and *Erythropodium caribbeorum*, two related scleraxonians, have yielded mixtures of highly acylated diterpenes containing chlorine. These compounds are currently being investigated at the University of Oklahoma and have also been studied by B. Tursch of Brussels.

Acknowledgments

The work on the chemistry of coelenterates at the University of Oklahoma has been supported by the National Institutes of Health and the Petroleum Research Fund of the American Chemical Society. We are particularly grateful for Research Training Grant HE-5675 from the National Heart Institute. We dedicate this paper to the late Professor Werner Bergmann of Yale University, an inspiring teacher, and a successful pioneer in the chemistry of marine invertebrates.

References

Attaway, D. H. (1968). Ph.D. Dissertation, University of Oklahoma, Norman.

Bayer, F. M. (1961). "The Shallow-water Octocorallia of the West Indian Region." Nijhoff, The Hague.

Bergmann, W. (1949). *J. Mar. Res.* **8**, 137.

Bergmann, W. (1962). *Comp. Biochem.* **3**, Part A, 103–162.

Bergmann, W., and Lester, D. (1940). *Science* **92**, 452.

Bergmann, W., and Lester, D. (1941). *J. Org. Chem.* **6**, 120.

Bergmann, W., McLean, M. J., and Lester, D. (1943). *J. Org. Chem.* **8**, 271.

Bergmann, W., Feeney, R. J., and Swift, A. N. (1951). *J. Org. Chem.* **16**, 1337.

Bergmann, W., Creighton, S. M., and Stokes, W. M. (1956). *J. Org. Chem.* **21**, 721.

Bundy, G. L., Daniels, E. G., Lincoln, F. H., and Pike, J. E. (1972). *J. Amer. Chem. Soc.* **94**, 2124.

Burkholder, P. R., and Burkholder, L. M. (1958) *Science* **127**, 1173.

Burkholder., P. R., and Burkholder, L. M. (1960). *Amer. J. Bot.* **47**, 866.

Cary, L. R. (1918). *Carnegie Inst. Wash., Dep. Mar. Biol.* **12**, 185.

Ciereszko, L. S. (1962). *Trans. N.Y. Acad. Sci.* [2] **24**, 502.

Ciereszko, L. S., and Attaway, D. H. (1961). *6th Annu. Rep. Res., Petrol. Res. Fund, Amer. Chem. Soc.* p. 107.

Ciereszko, L. S., and Youngblood, W. W. (1971). *Geochim. Cosmochim. Acta* **35**, 851.

Ciereszko, L. S., Sifford, D. H., and Weinheimer, A. J. (1960a). *Ann. N.Y. Acad. Sci.* **90**, 917.

Ciereszko, L. S., Odense, P. H., and Schmidt, R. W. (1960b). *Ann. N.Y. Acad. Sci.* **90**, 920.

Ciereszko, L. S., Attaway, D. H., and Wolf, M. A. (1963). *8th Annu. Rep. Res., Petrol. Res. Fund,* Ameri. Chemi. Soc. pp. 33–34.

Ciereszko, L. S., Johnson, M. A., Schmidt, R. W., and Koons, C. B. (1968). *Comp. Biochem. Physiol.* **24**, 899.

Ciereszko, L. S., Mizelle, J. W., and Schmidt, R. W. (1972). *In* "Food-Drugs from the Sea" (L. R. Worthen, ed.), in press. Marine Technology Society, Washington, D.C.

Engelbrecht, J. P., Tursch, B., and Djerassi, C. (1972). *Steroids* **20**, 121.

Enwall, E. L., van der Helm, D., Hsu, I Nan, Pattabhiraman, T., Schmitz, F. J., Spraggins, R. L. and Weinheimer A. J. (1972). *Chem. Commun.* p. 215.

Fox, D. L., Smith, E. V., Grigg, R. W., and Macleod, W. D. (1969). *Comp. Biochem. Physiol.* **28**, 1103.

Gross, R. A. (1969). M.S. Thesis, University of Oklahoma, Norman.

Gupta, K. C., and Scheuer, P. J. (1969). *Steroids* **13**, 343.

Haertle, W. R. (1971). M.S. Thesis, University of Oklahoma, Norman.

Hale, R. L., Leclercq, J., Tursch, B., Djerassi, C., Gross, R. A., Weinheimer, A. J., Gupta, K., and Scheuer, P. J. (1970). *J. Amer. Chem. Soc.* **92**, 2179.

Hossain, M. B., and van der Helm, D. (1968). *J. Amer. Chem. Soc.* **90**, 6607.

Hossain, M. B., and van der Helm, D. (1969). *Rec. Trav. Chim. Pays.-Bas* **88**, 1413.

Hossain, M. B., Nicholas, A. F., and van der Helm, D. (1968). *Chem. Commun.* p. 385.

Hyde, R. W. (1966). Ph.D. Dissertation, University of Oklahoma, Norman.

Idler, D. R., Wiseman, P. M., and Safe, L. M. (1970). *Steroids* **16**, 451.

Jeffrey, S. W., and Haxo, F. T. (1968). *Biol. Bull.* **135**, 149.

Johannes, R. E. (1967). *Limnol. Oceanogr.* **12**, 189.

Kanwisher, J. W., and Wainwright, S. A. (1967). *Biol. Bull.* **133**, 378.

Keezer, W. S., Jr. (1969). Ph.D. Dissertation, University of Oklahoma, Norman.

Kennard, O., Watson, D. G., Riva di Sanseverino, L., Tursch, B., and Bosmans, R. (1968). *Tetrahedron Lett.* p. 2879.

Kind, C. A., and Bergmann, W. (1942). *J. Org. Chem.* **7**, 424.

Kittredge, J. S., and Hughes, R. R. (1964). *Biochemistry* **3**, 991.

Kittredge, J. S., and Roberts, E. (1969). *Science* **164**, 37.

Kohn, A. J., and Helfrich, P. (1957). *Limnol. Oceanogr.* **2**, 241.

Koons, C. B., Jamieson, G. W., and Ciereszko, L. S. (1965). *Amer. Ass. Petrol. Geol., Bull.* **49**, 301.

Lester, D., and Bergmann, W. (1941). *J. Org. Chem.* **6**, 120.

Ling, N. C., Hale, R. L., and Djerassi, C. (1970). *J. Amer. Chem. Soc.* **92**, 5281.

Marsh, M. E. (1965). M.S. Thesis, University of Oklahoma, Norman.

Middlebrook, R. E. (1966). Ph.D. Dissertation, University of Oklahoma, Norman.

Moore, R. E., and Scheuer, P. J. (1971). *Science* **172**, 495.

Muscatine, L. (1967). *Science* **156**, 516.

Muscatine, L., and Cernichiari, E. (1969). *Biol. Bull.* **137**, 506.

Odense, P. H. (1958). Ph.D. Dissertation, University of Oklahoma, Norman.

Quin, L. D., and Shelburne, F. A. (1969). *J. Mar. Res.* **27**, 73.

Rehm, S. J. (1971). Ph.D. Dissertation, University of Oklahoma, Norman.

Rice, J. R., Papastephanou, C., and Anderson, D. G. (1970). *Biol. Bull.* **138**, 334.

Roche, J. (1952). *Experientia* **8**, 45.

Rudiger, W., Klose, W., Tursch, B., Houvenaghel-Crevecoeur, N., and Budzikiewicz, H. (1968). *Justus Liebigs Ann. Chem.* **713**, 209.

Scheuer, P. J. (1964). *Fortschr. Chem. Org. Naturst.* **22**, 265.

Scheuer, P. J. (1969). *Fortschr. Chem. Org. Naturst.* **27**, 322.

Schmidt, R. W. (1960). Ph.D. Dissertation, University of Oklahoma, Norman.

Schmidt, R. W., and Ciereszko, L. S. (1969). *Proc. Okla. Acad. Sci.* **48**, 258.

Schmitz, F. J., and Lorance, E. D. (1971). *J. Org. Chem.* **36**, 917.

Schmitz, F. J., and Pattabhiraman, T. (1970). *J. Amer. Chem. Soc.* **92**, 6073.

Schmitz, F. J., Kraus, K. W., Ciereszko, L. S., Sifford, D. H., and Weinheimer, A. J. (1966). *Tetrahedron Lett.* p. 97.

Schmitz, F. J., Lorance, E. D., and Ciereszko, L. S. (1969a). *J. Org. Chem.* **34**, 1989.
Schmitz, F. J., Lorance, E. D., and Ciereszko, L. S. (1969b). *In* "Food-Drugs From The Sea" (H. B. Youngken, ed.), pp. 315–318 Marine Technology Society, Washington, D.C.
Schneider, W. P., Hamilton, R. D., and Rhuland, L. E. (1972). *J. Amer. Chem. Soc.* **94**, 2122.
Sheikh, Y. M. (1969). Ph.D. Dissertation, University of Hawaii.
Sheikh, Y. M., Djerassi, C., and Tursch, B. (1971). *Chem. Commun.* p. 217.
Sifford, D. H. (1962). Ph.D. Dissertation, University of Oklahoma, Norman.
Silberberg, M. S. (1971). Ph.D. Dissertation, University of Oklahoma, Norman.
Silberberg, M. S., Ciereszko, L. S., Jacobson, R. A., and Smith, E. C. (1972). *Comp. Biochem. Physiol.* **43B**, 323.
Smith, D., Muscatine, L., and Lewis, D. (1969). *Biol Rev.* **44**, 17.
Spraggins, R. L. (1970). Ph.D. Dissertation, University of Oklahoma, Norman.
Strain, H. H., Svec, W. A., Aitzemüller, K., Grandolfo, M. C., Katz, J. J., Kjøsen, H., Norgård, S., Liaaen-Jensen, S., Haxo, F. T., Wegfart, P., and Rapoport, H. (1971). *J. Amer. Chem. Soc.* **93**, 1823.
von Holt, C. (1968). *Comp. Biochem. Physiol.* **26**, 1071.
von Holt, C., and von Holt, M. (1968a). *Comp. Biochem. Physiol.* **24**, 73.
von Holt, C. and von Holt, M. (1968b). *Comp. Biochem. Physiol.* **24**, 83.
Wainwright, S. A. (1962). *Experientia* **18**, 18.
Washecheck, P. H. (1967). Ph.D. Dissertation, University of Oklahoma, Norman.
Weinheimer, A. J., and Spraggins, R. L. (1969). *Tetrahedron Lett.* p. 5185.
Weinheimer, A. J., and Washecheck, P. H. (1969). *Tetrahedron Lett.* p. 3315.
Weinheimer, A. J., Schmitz, F. J., and Ciereszko, L. S. (1967). *In* "Drugs From The Sea," pp. 135–140. Marine Technology Society, Washington, D.C.
Weinheimer, A. J., Middlebrook, R. E., Bledsoe, J. O., Jr., Marsico, W. E., and Karns, T. K. B. (1968a). *Chem. Commun.* p. 384.
Weinheimer, A. J., Washecheck, P. H., van der Helm, D., and Hossain, M. B. (1968b). *Chem. Commun.* p. 1070.
Weinheimer, A. J., Youngblood, W. W., Washecheck, P. H., Karns, T. K. B., and Ciereszko, L. S. (1970). *Tetrahedron Lett.* p. 497.
Welsh, J. H., and Prock, P. B. (1958). *Biol. Bull.* **115**, 551.
Wolf, M. A. (1963). M.S. Thesis, University of Oklahoma, Norman.
Young, S. D. (1971). *Comp. Biochem. Physiol.* **40B**, 113.
Youngblood, W. W. (1969). Ph.D. Dissertation, University of Oklahoma, Norman.

7

POPULATION ECOLOGY OF
REEF-BUILDING CORALS

Joseph H. Connell

I. Introduction

This chapter will review what is known about the detailed population ecology of those stony corals which build reefs. I will restrict myself to those aspects which concern their distribution and abundance and will not discuss their contribution to overall reef morphology or productivity. One purpose of this chapter is to point out the many gaps in our knowledge of the population ecology of corals.

II. Reproduction

After the larvae settle from the plankton on to a hard substrate, corals have a period of development and growth before reaching sexual maturity. I have found only two estimates of how long this might take. Marshall and Stephenson (1933) at Low Isles, Great Barrier Reef, lat.

16°S, found that most *Favia doreyensis* over 10 cm in diameter had "numerous" gonads, whereas smaller ones seldom did. Stephenson and Stephenson (1933) measured growth over 8 months during the warm seasons (September to May) when growth should have been fastest; 13 *Favia* between 4 and 14 cm in diameter grew (median value) 0.8 cm in that time. There is no trend shown in these rather variable data between growth rate and size. Assuming that this rate holds for the whole year, *Favia* will grow about 1.3 cm in diameter per year. Thus it probably takes at least 8 years for *Favia* to reach sexual maturity at Low Isles. Abe (1937) studying *Fungia actiniformis* at Palao, lat. 7°N, found that only individuals greater than 7 cm in diameter liberated larvae. Growth of *Fungia actiniformis* at Palao is about 7.8 mm/year (Tamura and Hada, 1932) so that again this species probably requires about 10 years to reach sexual maturity. As will be shown later, most branching corals grow much faster than these massive ones, and possibly die sooner. Therefore, it is probable that they reach sexual maturity earlier. Unfortunately, I could find no published data to test this hypothesis.

In some species, individual polyps are known to contain ripe eggs and sperm at the same time, so that self-fertilization is a possibility. These are *Pocillopora brevicornis* (Fowler, 1885); *Manicina areolata* (Wilson, 1888; Duerden, 1902); *Diploria labyrinthiformis* (*Meandrina labyrinthia*),* *Favia fragum* (Duerden, 1902); *Favia doreyensis*, and *Lobophyllia* sp. (Marshall and Stephenson, 1933). In others only eggs or sperm have been seen, suggesting either that each colony is unisexual or that a colony changes sex as it ages, as suggested by Gardiner (1902). The species in which only eggs have been seen are *Acropora durvillei*, *Turbinaria* sp., *Sphenotrochus rubescens* (Fowler, 1885, 1887, 1888, 1890); *Coenopsammia* sp. (Gardiner, 1900); *Acropora palmata*, *Isophyllia sinuosa* (*dipsacea*), *Montastrea cavernosa* (*Orbicella radiata*), *Siderastrea radians* (Duerden, 1902); and *Symphyllia recta* (Marshall and Stephenson, 1933). Only testes were found in a colony of *Pavona cactus* seen extruding sperm in a pool (Marshall and Stephenson, 1933). If we presume that further examination of all these species will reveal the other sex, then cross-fertilization is evidently the rule.

Fertilization is probably usually internal, the sperm released from a neighboring colony being drawn into the polyp where the eggs are fertilized. However, fertilization may sometimes be external. Duerden (1902) found that in the laboratory eggs and sperm of *Manicina areolata*

---

* If, in the original publication a scientific name is used which is now superseded, the older name has been placed in parentheses.

and *Favia fragum* were occasionally extruded, but he considered this to be abnormal since both species often had developing larvae in their gastric cavities.

Favia doryensis at Low Isles may have external fertilization. Marshall and Stephenson (1933) examined 24 colonies about once a month between August and the following June. Most had ripe gonads in early December but the gametes were gone in early January. Since no planulae were ever seen it is probable that the eggs and sperms were released during December and fertilized externally. The alternative interpretation of internal fertilization followed by very rapid development and release of planulae, all within a month, is possible but seems less likely. Of the 10 species studied by Marshall and Stephenson larvae were seen in only 2, *Porites haddoni* and *Pocillopora bulbosa*. Since hundreds of colonies were sampled over 9 months, this indicates that the individuals of many species do not breed every year or, since no collections were made of these species in July, September, or October at Low Isles, that a spawning period may have been missed. However, the periods missed were during the winter and spring months when less reproductive activity is to be expected, judging from the species which were observed breeding. It is clear that histological examination of gonads in collections made every 2 weeks over at least a year would be necessary to resolve these alternatives. However, in those species which produce larvae in quantity, much information has been gained.

The reproductive activity of corals was seasonal in some places and species, and in others continued through the year. Gonad development of *Favia doryensis* took about 6 months at Low Isles, with a sudden diminution in early summer. Since no gonads developed during the following 6 months it is probable that this species spawns only once a year. *Porites* released planulae in summer and autumn but *Pocillopora bulbosa* did so in every month in which collections were made. In the Atlantic, *Agaricia fragilis* in Bermuda (Mavor, 1915) and *Manicina* (*Maeandra*) *areolata* in Tortugas (Yonge, 1935) released planulae only in the summer. At Hawaii, planulae were released every month of the year by *Pocillopora damicornis* and *Cyphastrea ocellina* (Edmondson, 1946). At Palao, five species of coral released larvae every month that observations were made, which in most instances extended throughout the year (Abe, 1937; Atoda, 1947a,b, 1951a,b). Marshall and Stephenson (1933) found a very marked lunar periodicity in the rate of release of planulae from *Pocillopora bulbosa*. Curiously, in summer and autumn most larvae were released at the time of the new moon, whereas in winter the spawning had shifted to the full moon.

Fecundity (the number of eggs or larvae produced by an adult) can be estimated very roughly for a few species. Those with large polyps have many eggs per polyp. A transverse section through the fertile region of a polyp of *Favia doreyensis* from Low Isles contained 93 eggs (Marshall and Stephenson, 1933, Fig. 2). Since all eggs were probably not cut in the section, this is a minimum estimate. In the same paper counts of larvae liberated by known numbers of colonies are given. In *Porites haddoni* 6 to 250 planulae were released per colony and from *Pocillopora bulbosa* 1 to 100 from a group of branches collected from a colony. Edmondson (1929) found that a colony of *Cyphastrea ocellina* with 1850 polyps liberated 600 planulae. If these very scanty data be used as a basis, it would appear that a moderate-sized colony may produce up to a few thousand eggs or planulae in a breeding season. Some species may have several such liberations in a year. It is clear that at this time it is impossible to construct an age-specific fecundity table for any reef coral. For a species known to breed once a year, such as *Favia doreyensis*, this could and should certainly be done.

So far in this discussion we have treated each colony as an individual. In population ecology it is important to define what is meant by an individual, since this is the unit counted in calculating rates of recruitment or mortality. There is some evidence for regarding small parts of the colony or even individual polyps as independent units. The separate polyps are similar, showing no obvious polymorphisms such as hydroids do. If small parts of a colony are broken off each is capable of founding a new colony; parts of a colony often die without affecting the rest. Many species exhibit no regular form in their growth pattern, although this may be the result of local differences in the environment rather than evidence of independence of parts of the colony.

On the other hand, there seems to be some integration between the parts of a single colony. For example, Stephenson and Stephenson (1933) found that out of 93 colonies in which growth was unequal on the two diameters, 63 grew more on the lesser diameter than on the greater diameter, tending to bring the colony toward a circular shape. If there was no integration of growth within the colony one would expect that in uncrowded colonies such as these the growth would as often be greater in the larger as the smaller diameter. The departure of the observations from this expectation was significant (chi-square of 11.6, $p < 0.001$), implying some sort of integration. That there is some transfer of energy-rich material between adjacent parts of a colony has been shown experimentally by Pearse and Muscatine (1971). Lastly, there is the suggestion that colonies of at least two species evidently require years to reach sexual maturity. If this is supported by future observations two alternative hypotheses are suggested. First, the size of the whole colony determines whether some of its energy is to be diverted into the production of gametes. Alternatively, each polyp requires a certain amount of time to develop to maturity after which it continues to be sexually mature for many years. The first hypothesis might be tested by dividing a large mature colony into many smaller pieces of different sizes and determining the breeding condition for several years. If small pieces continue to produce gametes the first hypothesis will be rejected.

For the purpose of this paper I will define an individual as any colony growing independently of its neighbors. Only in those cases where an individual colony has clearly been separated into two or more portions by the death of the intervening parts, such as the dead bases of branches, will I include the separate portions as part of a single individual. In many instances the records of separate portions of an original colony cannot be combined, either because the growth form was irregular, or because the parts have been moved to new locations by currents or under their own power, as in *Fungia*. Therefore, it is probably best to regard separated colonies as individuals. Separation of a colony into parts can then be regarded as a form of asexual reproduction.

III. Larval Dispersal and Settlement

Coral larvae spend some time drifting in the plankton but there is no direct information on how far they are carried before they settle down. In the laboratory newly released planulae first swim upward or toward light, or both; some swim toward strong light and away from weak light (Edmondson, 1929; Abe, 1937; Kawaguti, 1941; Atoda, 1947a,b, 1951a,b). However, all workers have found that most planulae soon change their behavior and swim down to the bottom where they attach, usually within the first 2 days. A very few remain swimming longer, up to 3 weeks or, in one instance, 2 months (Atoda, 1951b). These latter will obviously be important in the zoogeographic distribution of the species to which the planulae belong but this is beyond the scope of this paper.

If this sort of behavior seen in the laboratory also occurs in the field the vast majority of planulae, representing the normal recruitment to coral populations, must settle within about 2 days of release. One bit of evidence supporting this is that few planulae are ever collected from the plankton. Even collections taken just above corals known to be capable of releasing larvae seldom catch any planulae (Marshall and Stephenson, 1933). In plankton tows taken several times a month for a year at Low Isles, planulae were caught only in December, even though some species liberated planulae every month in the laboratory (Russell and Coleman, 1934). The nets had very small mesh sizes, so that planulae, which are usually at least 0.25 mm in diameter, would be caught. (The mesh size of 77/cm would have a hole about 0.13 mm across.)

Considering only recruitment to local populations, the question is how far are larvae carried in about 2 days? Some evidence indicates that there is wide dispersal and mixing, whereas other evidence suggests that dispersal is rather limited. For example, the current patterns in lagoons of atolls tend to keep larvae within the lagoon. At Bikini Atoll, the trade wind drives the surface water across the lagoon. The volume of surface water moved is too great to be exhausted through the leeward passages or over the edge of the reef so that some sinks and returns upwind along the bottom (von Arx, 1948). This bottom current carries more water than the surface current but moves more slowly. This partially closed circulation would tend to keep organisms within the lagoon. In addition many plankton organisms in Bikini lagoon migrate vertically; the bulk of the planktonic population remains in the deeper two-thirds of the lagoon which moves slowly upwind (Johnson, 1949). Besides this wind-driven circulation, tidal changes cause currents to flow back and forth over the edge of a reef so that some larvae swept away from the reef may be carried back by the next tide. Johnson (1954) found that the plankton was two to four times more abundant within the lagoon than in the waters just outside the reef. He attributed at least part of this concentration to the ebb and flow of these countercurrent patterns.

Even though planulae may not be carried great distances by currents the chances are slight that they will be brought back near their parents. Tidal currents are sometimes very fast and mixing must be intense. Only if larvae were released at slack water and settled down almost immediately would they attach close to their parents. However, Duerden (1902) pointed out that it is a common occurrence to find a few young polyps of the same species adhering to the lower, dead surfaces of colonies of *Manicina* and *Favia*. He suggested that they had settled there soon after release from the parent. If further observations confirm that young polyps are usually more common on or near adults of the same species than further away, the following three hypotheses in addition to Duerden's need to be considered and, if possible, tested. First, the planulae may spend some time in the plankton but be stimulated to attach by contact with their own species, as in oysters, barnacles, and tube worms (Knight-Jones, 1953). Second, they may settle randomly but survive better if attached to their own species. Last, larvae of each species may settle only in response to particular physical conditions which would lead them to settle only near others of the same species.

The settlement of coral planulae has been studied only in the laboratory. No observations or experiments on choice of substrate or habitat have been made. Edmondson (1946) found that planulae in Hawaii could attach in light or dark, and under slightly altered temperature and pH. An interesting observation made by several authors (Duerden, 1902; Boschma, 1929; Stephenson, 1931; Abe, 1937; Edmondson, 1946) is that several planulae settling close together in the laboratory may grow together into a single colony. These were always of the same species, but no information was given as to whether the planulae came from the same or different colonies. Unless there is a very dense settlement of planulae it is unlikely that such fusion would happen under natural conditions. Therefore, it is probably safe to conclude that most coral colonies on a reef have grown from a single larva, although some instances of fusion undoubtedly occur.

IV. Recruitment of New Colonies

Although the settlement of planulae has not been studied in the field, the combined effects of settlement and early survival have been followed in two cases. Stephenson and Stephenson (1933) placed logs, pieces of sandstone, earthenware, glass, and clamshells on the reef at Low Isles as settling surfaces. Of 36 colonies found after periods of up to 11 months, 26 were *Pocillopora bulbosa*, 7 *Porites*, 1 *Cyphastrea*, and 2 unknown. These species are evidently among the pioneers in colonizing newly vacated surfaces.

In my own work at Heron Island, Great Barrier Reef, I have marked out permanent quadrats and taken color photographs at intervals since 1962. The corners of the quadrats were marked by driving in steel rods; no corals were disturbed in any quadrats. All colonies over 1 cm in diameter are clearly visible in these photographs, so that I have records of all new colonies which have survived to this size. In this area, most corals can grow to this size in about a month. Therefore, these records miss any corals which attach but die before they reach this age. The

TABLE I

ABUNDANCE, RECRUITMENT, AND MORTALITY OF CORALS ON HERON ISLAND, 1962–1970

Species	Interval recruited	No. of each age group present					Deaths per age group	Total	
		Jan 1963	Aug 1965	Feb 1967	Aug 1969	July 1970		Deaths per species	Recruits per species
Area 1. Square Meter A, South Outer Reef Crest									
Acropora squamosa	Pre-1963	14	12	10	9	8	6	20	24
	1963–1965	—	14	11	6	4	10		
	1965–1967	—	—	3	1	1	2		
	1967–1969	—	—	—	7	5	2		
Acropora hebes	Pre-1963	3	3	3	3	3	0	4	4
	1963–1965	—	3	2	0	0	3		
	1965–1967	—	—	1	0	0	1		
Acropora digitifera	Pre-1963	3	3	3	3	3	0	4	10
	1963–1965	—	7	4	3	3	4		
	1965–1967	—	—	1	1	1	0		
	1967–1969	—	—	—	1	1	0		
	1969–1970	—	—	—	—	1	—		
Acropora cuneata	Pre-1963	3	3	2	2	2	1	1	2
	1963–1965	—	1	1	1	1	0		
	1967–1969	—	—	—	1	1	0		
Acropora surculosa	Pre-1963	2	1	1	1	1	1	3	3
	1967–1969	—	—	—	3	1	2		
Montipora foliosa	Pre-1963	2	2	2	2	2	0	1	7
	1963–1965	—	2	2	2	2	0		
	1965–1967	—	—	2	2	2	0		
	1967–1969	—	—	—	3	2	1		

Pocillopora damicornis	Pre-1963	2	2	1	1	1	6	8
	1963–1965	—	3	3	2	2	2	5
	1965–1967	—	—	3	1	0	0	2
	1967–1969	1	1	1	1	1	—	—
Porites lutea	Pre-1963	1	1	1	2	1	2	5
	1963–1965	—	1	0	1	0	0	—
	1967–1969	—	1	1	0	3	6	—
Porites annae	Pre-1963	1	1	1	4	1	1	2
	1965–1967	—	—	1	1	1	—	—
	1967–1969	—	—	1	1	1	—	—
Leptastrea purpurea	Pre-1963	1	1	1	1	0	0	0
Montipora hispida	1965–1967	—	—	3	1	1	3	6
	1967–1969	—	—	1	2	2	2	—
Acropora acuminata	1963–1965	1	1	1	1	1	0	2
	1967–1969	—	—	2	1	1	0	—
Acropora quelchi	1963–1965	—	2	2	1	0	2	2
Total present		32	63	65	73	60	47	75
Deaths per interval		3	12	18	14			
Recruits per interval		34	14	26	1			
Deaths per year, mean		1.2	8.0	7.2	15.6		6.3	10.0
Recruits per year, mean		13.2	9.3	10.4	1.1			

Area 2. Square Meter No. 4, South Inner Reef Flat

		Dec 1962					
Porites annae	Pre-1962	16	14	12	10	10	10	9
	1962–1965	—	4	2	1	1	6	
	1965–1967	—	—	4	3	3	3	
	1967–1969	—	—	—	1	1	0	

TABLE I (Continued)

Species	Interval recruited	No. of each age group present					Deaths per age group	Total	
		Dec 1962	Aug 1965	Feb 1967	Aug 1969	July 1970		Deaths per species	Recruits per species

Area 2. Square Meter No. 4, South Inner Reef Flat

Species	Interval recruited	Dec 1962	Aug 1965	Feb 1967	Aug 1969	July 1970	Deaths per age group	Deaths per species	Recruits per species
Porites lutea	Pre-1962	10	6	5	5	5	5	13	16
	1962–1965	—	11	5	4	4	7		
	1965–1967	—	—	1	0	0	1		
	1967–1969	—	—	—	4	4	0		
Acropora formosa	Pre-1962	2	2	2	2	2	0	0	3
	1962–1965	—	1	1	1	1	0		
	1965–1967	—	—	1	1	1	0		
	1967–1969	—	—	—	1	1	0		
Acropora bruggemanni	Pre-1962	1	1	1	1	1	0	0	0
Leptastrea purpurea	Pre-1962	1	1	0	0	0	1	1	0
Seriatopora hystrix	Pre-1962	1	0	0	0	0	1	1	0
Total present		31	40	34	34	34		25	28
Deaths per interval		7	12	6	6	0			
Recruits per interval		16	6	6	0	0			
Deaths per year, mean		2.6	8.0	2.4	0	0		3.3	
Recruits per year, mean		6.0	4.0	2.4	0	0			3.7

Area 3. Square Meter NW North Outer Reef Crest

	March 1963							
Acropora digitifera Pre-1963	12	11	8	6	6	6	9	6
1963–1965		2	1	0	0	2		
1967–1969				4	3	1		
Porites annae Pre-1963	9	4	2	2	1	8	10	4
1963–1965		2	2	1	1	1		
1967–1969				1	1			
Pocillopora damicornis Pre-1963	6	5	3	0	0	6	9	7
1963–1965		1	1	0	0	1		
1967–1969				4	4	2		
1969–1970				1	2			
Acropora cuneata Pre-1963	3	3	3	3	2	1	1	0
Acropora hebes Pre-1963	3	2	1	0	0	3	4	2
1967–1969				2	2	1		
Acropora squamosa Pre-1963	2	2	2	2	1	0	0	0
Acropora humilis Pre-1963	1	1	1	1	1	0	0	0
Acropora hyacinthus Pre-1963	2	2	2	1	0	1	1	0
Acropora nasuta Pre-1963	2	2	1	0	0	2	2	0
Acropora valida Pre-1963	2	2	1	0	0	2	2	0
Leptoria gracilis Pre-1963	1	1	1	1	0	0	0	0
Stylophora mordax 1967–1969				2		2	2	2
Total present	43	40	29	31	24		40	21
Deaths per interval	8	11	12	9				
Recruits per interval	5	—[a]	14	2				
Deaths per year, mean	3.3	7.3	4.8	10.0			5.5	
Recruits per year, mean	2.1	—[a]	5.6	2.2				2.9

[a] Recruitment on the north crest between 1965 and 1967 was difficult to estimate accurately since the area had been damaged, with fragments of corals scattered over it, when the photographs were taken 2 weeks after a hurricane in February 1967.

study areas were all near low-tide level, where they were either exposed
to air for short periods at extreme low tide (these were on the outer
reef crest) or just below that level and so never exposed (an area on
the inner flat near the island and another in a pool just inside the outer
edge on the leeward side of the reef). Since the colonies were small
(seldom exceeding 30 cm in diameter), photographs of a few square
meters included a large number of colonies and species. Their accessibil-
ity and large numbers allow more detailed observation and experimentation than in deeper areas at Heron Island where colonies tend to be
much larger. Whether the information obtained can be applied to these
corals in deeper water will only be discovered with further study. The
present analysis includes only a small portion of the total area photographed; the results should be regarded as preliminary ones for the
purpose of illustrating trends and suggesting hypotheses which need
to be tested.

The rate of recruitment (of colonies more than a month old) for
each species between 1962 and 1970 is shown in Table I. For all species
the average rate varied between 0 and 13 new colonies per square meter
annually, with an average of about 5. Area 1 had more recruits than
the other areas, and the rate was greater during the first $6\frac{1}{2}$ years than
during the last one. There is no obvious explanation for these general
variations in space and time.

In all areas the commoner species had high rates of recruitment and
mortality and maintained their abundance. Some less common species
also had high rates of recruitment and mortality (e.g., *Pocillopora damicornis,* area 1), while in others recruitment exceeded mortality (e.g.,
Acropora digitifera and the two species of *Montipora* on area 1).

There were great differences in recruitment of individual species between areas 1 and 2 which were only 300 m apart. The same two species
of *Porites* lived in both areas yet their recruitment was greater on area
2, even though the rate for all species combined was higher on area
1. Both areas were suitable for older *Porites,* though the abundance
and also the recruitment and mortality rates were all greater on area
2. The simplest explanation for the greater recruitment on area 2 is
that, although the larval settlement might have been similar at both
places, the mortality in the first month, before the colonies grew large
enough to identify, was higher on area 1. Alternative hypotheses are
that planulae are not carried far in the plankton, or that they choose
to settle near others of the same species.

Another form of recruitment occurs when parts of larger colonies
are broken off and carried away in storms. If the living tissue is not

too badly damaged and if the piece lodges in a suitable place it will continue to grow. If the storm is long or very severe the tissues will probably be too badly damaged, so that this form of recruitment probably happens in a moderate storm rather than after a severe hurricane. This may account for the observation by Stephenson *et al.* (1958, p. 286) that after the moderate hurricane of 1954 at Low Isles, fragments of *Acropora* were washed into pools, became imbedded in sand and rubble, and so founded flourishing colonies. In one of my plots a branched piece of large staghorn coral, 22 × 31 cm, arrived in this way and grew to a size of 26 × 51 cm in the next 2 years. Dr. Peter Glynn has told me that small pieces of *Porites* are sometimes broken off and washed into new places on the reef in Puerto Rico, starting new colonies. Dr. John Wells has pointed out to me that corals are sometimes found on floating pieces of pumice and that colonies may have been carried between island groups in sailing canoes which always seem to have water in the bottom.

V. Growth, Occupation of Space, and Estimation of Age

The growth of corals has been studied very extensively, mainly with the aim of estimating the geological growth of whole reefs. Stoddart (1969) has reviewed this work, emphasizing the ecological conditions controlling the rate of growth of corals and reefs. In this chapter I will consider two other aspects of growth: the rate of occupation of the space available and the use of growth to estimate age.

Space in the light seems to be critical for reef-building corals. Goreau and Goreau (1959) found that calcification rates varied directly with amount of light, being twice as fast on sunny as on cloudy days, for example. I shaded corals with opaque plastic domes on the reef crest so that they received less than 10% of ambient illumination but had the same water circulation as controls under clear plastic domes. The corals in the heavy shade died after 2 to 6 months; the controls flourished (Connell, 1972).

There are instances of certain species growing in deep water or in shaded places, which might be taken to indicate that these species avoid stronger light. However, it is possible that these species might grow even faster with increased light but would lose in competition with species normally living there. Until suitable transplanting experiments are done to show whether some species are harmed by stronger light it is probably safe to assume that most species need to acquire and

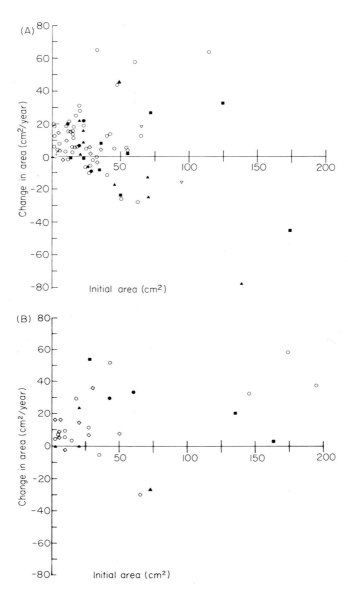

Fig. 1. Change in area of living tissue in individual corals on a square meter at area 1, south reef crest, Heron Island, over three successive periods: Oct. 1963–Aug. 1965, Aug. 1965–Feb. 1967, Feb. 1967–Aug. 1969. (A). *Acropora* species. The following three records of *A. surculosa* were not plotted for reasons of space;

hold space in the light. To measure the rate of occupation of space I took photographs of areas of corals from directly above, mounting the camera tripod on a frame 1 m sq. I measured the horizontal area occupied by projecting the color transparency onto paper, tracing the outline of each colony and measuring its area with a planimeter. Although this measures only the horizontal extent of each colony, this is probably the best estimate of its success in acquiring the essential space in the light. Other methods would need to be used for corals growing on steep slopes.

Figure 1 shows the annual change in area of all the colonies on a square meter on the southwestern reef crest at Heron Island in three successive intervals over 6 years. Corals between 1 and 25 cm² in area grew about 10 cm²/year. After this the change in area occupied was very variable, sometimes decreasing, and showing no consistent trend with increasing size. The fact that larger corals increased about the same amount in absolute size as smaller ones means that, like all other organisms, they grow proportionately more slowly as they age. Stephenson and Stephenson (1933, p. 176) showed this clearly, as have other workers. Goreau and Goreau (1960) found that the absolute calcification rate was much faster in smaller colonies.

The consequence of this process on this particular area is that once a coral reaches a size of about 25 cm², at the age of about 2–3 years, it has about the same absolute capacity to acquire new space as older colonies. In colonies between 25 and 100 cm², almost as many lost as gained space, so that corals of this size are evidently vulnerable to partial damage by accidents or natural enemies. Fewer of the corals greater than 100 cm² lost space, but only one gained ground at a significantly greater rate than any smaller one.

Under certain circumstances it is possible to estimate the age of a colony from its rate of growth. The necessary conditions are (1) that growth continue throughout the life of the colony; (2) that growth be appreciable in comparison with the variation between individuals, to reduce error; and (3) that the environmental conditions affecting growth during the period of measurement be similar to those occurring in the earlier life of the colony.

(initial area/change): (381/+ 40), (459/+ 190), (745/+ 143). (○) *A. squamosa;* (◇) *A. cuneata;* (▲) *A. hebes;* (■) *A. digitifera;* (●) *A. quelchi.* (B). Species other than *Acropora.* The following two records for *Montipora foliosa* were not plotted for reasons of space: (290/ + 48), (361/ − 20). (○) *Montipora foliosa;* (◇) *Pocillopora damicornis;* (●) *Porites annae;* (▲) *Porites lutea;* (■) *Leptastrea purpurea.*

Taking these conditions in order, does growth continue throughout life? Vaughan (1915) and Tamura and Hada (1932) suggested that it did not, that corals ceased growing after reaching a certain size. However, those published data which include both the initial size and the increment added do not support this conclusion consistently. Vaughan (1915) followed individual colonies for several years in Florida and the Bahamas; his colonies were small, usually less than 10 cm diameter and less than 10 years old. As shown in Table II, growth between the first two yearly measurements was significantly faster than in the next interval in *Favia fragum* and *Porites asteroides*. After that the growth rate re-

TABLE II

EFFECT OF INCREASING AGE ON GROWTH OF COLONIES MEASURED INDIVIDUALLY FOR 5 YEARS AT TORTUGAS, FLORIDA[a,b]

	Growth increments between measurements in the following years (mean diameter, mm)			
	1910–1911	1911–1912	1912–1913	1913–1914
Favia fragum				
No. of measurements	26	21	14	7
Median increment	7.7	3.5	3.5	4.0
Range of increments	0.5–16	0.5–9	0.5–9.5	0–8
Wilcoxon test: No. of pairs		21	14	7
p		<0.01	>0.05	>0.05
Porites astreoides				
No. of measurements	14	14	12	12
Median increment	14	8	7.5	13
Range of increments	10–24	1–15	3–36	7–18
Wilcoxon test: No. of pairs		14	12	12
p		<0.01	>0.05	>0.05
Maeandra areolata				
No. of measurements	5	5	5	5
Median increment	15.5	14	7	5
Range of increments	12–19	9–16.5	4–9.5	1–8
No. of instances in which the earlier increment was greater than the later one:		3	5	3

[a] From Vaughan (1915).
[b] The Wilcoxon matched-pairs signed-ranks test was used to compare growth increments of the same colony in successive pairs of years.

mained about the same. In *Manicina* (*Maeandra*) *areolata* too few colonies were measured to judge the statistical significance of the change in rate with age. However, in 11 of the 15 possible comparisons between successive increments the growth was faster in younger colonies. Thus the growth seems to be faster at first, then to continue at a rather constant lower rate.

Between Vaughan's observations and my own, evidently no one has followed the growth of individual colonies over several years. Instead, colonies of various sizes have been measured at the beginning and end of the period of study. Since there is no information about age in such studies, the original question must be changed to: do larger corals grow more slowly than smaller ones? To answer this question I have summarized other data of Vaughan (1915) as well as those of Mayor (1924), Edmondson (1929), Tamura and Hada (1932), and Stephenson and Stephenson (1933), the only authors who have published both the initial and final size of growing colonies. Since few colonies were measured within a single species in one locality, I have simply calculated the Spearman rank correlation coefficient of increment grown versus initial size. If larger corals grow slower than smaller ones, there should be a negative correlation between growth rate and initial size. As shown in Table III, there was only 1 significant negative correlation in 38 sets of records; there were about the same number of positive as negative correlations. It is obvious that these records leave much to be desired, there being few replicates and in some cases, a limited range of sizes. However, the existing evidence does not support the hypothesis that corals stop growing at a certain size.

One interesting record of continued growth of very large colonies exists. Mayer (1918) at Thursday Island, Queensland, in 1913 measured three colonies which had been originally measured in 1890 by Saville-Kent (1893). A *Goniastrea* 2.4 m in diameter had not grown, but a *Symphyllia* grew from 0.8 to 1.8 m and a 5.8 m *Porites* grew to 6.9 m. Thus even very large old colonies may continue to grow. Some massive colonies (such as the *Goniastrea* above), may grow so slowly after they reach a certain size that they may, for all practical purposes, be regarded as having stopped growing.

It is clear that an experiment could be designed to test specifically the hypothesis that coral growth is determinate. What is needed is a large number of replicates within each species, with a wide range of sizes. Until this is done, we may accept the evidence that most stony corals continue to grow throughout their life, and, after an early phase of rapid growth, that the rate of increase in diameter is rather constant.

TABLE III

EFFECT OF INITIAL SIZE OF COLONY ON GROWTH[a,b]

Species	Location	Period	No. of colonies	Ranges (cm)		Correlation coefficient, r_s
				Initial diam.	Increase in diam.	
Vaughan (1915): Andros Island, Bahamas (period in years)						
Orbicella annularis	Golding Cay	2	5	4.4–9.0	0.6–2.7	+0.70
Acropora palmata	Golding Cay	2	5	3.4–7.8	4.4–16.5	+0.60
Mayor (1924): Samoa (period in years)						
Acropora hyacinthus	Samoa (Table 2)	1	5	3.7–9.3	5.1–19.6	+0.70
Pocillopora damicornis	Samoa (Table 2)	1	4	5.4–8.8	2.6–8.1	−0.60
	Samoa (Table 3)	1	5	3.6–12.7	2.8–7.2	−0.60
Acropora leptocyathus	Samoa (Table 5)	1	4	8.3–13.7	2.0–4.8	+0.40
Porites sp aff. *lutea*	Samoa (Table 6)	1	7	7.5–44.8	3.3–4.2	−0.01
Porites andrewsi	Samoa (Table 2)	1	4	5.9–11.2	3.5–5.3	−0.25
Edmondson (1929): Hawaii (period in months)						
Fungia scutaria	(Detached)	20	5	2.6–5.8	0.1–0.7	−0.14
	(Attached)	11.5	14	0.5–1.9	1.1–2.6	−0.01
Tamura and Hada (1932): Yap Island and Palao (period in days)						
Acropora abrotanoides	Yap A	92	6	6.8–12.0	2.6–3.9	+0.21
	Yap B	102	7	14.6–30.7	0.3–4.4	−0.45
Acropora pulchra	Yap A	60	6	9.2–16.3	3.5–4.1	+0.26
Acropora digitifera	Yap A	118	7	8.0–11.2	0.3–0.6	−0.53

Acropora polymorpha	Yap B	102	9	8.8–17.5	0.1–0.5	+0.26
Porites nigrescens	Yap A	118	5	8.8–10.5	0.5–1.2	+0.05
Stylophora mordax	Yap	86	6	5.3–10.2	0.2–0.6	−0.38
Pocillopora malokensis	Yap B	102	9	12.1–17.2	0.3–1.7	+0.45
Porites convexa	Yap A	117	6	6.3–9.4	0–0.4	−0.35
Porites lutea	Yap A	85	4	6.9–9.4	0.3–0.5	−0.15
Montipora verosa	Yap A	102	9	8.0–12.0	0–5.0	+0.54
Fungia fungites	Yap B	102	10	10.1–22.0	0.1–0.3	+0.53
Fungia echinatus	Yap A	102	9	10.1–16.1	0–0.5	−0.05
Fungia sp.	Yap A	102	9	12.6–16.7	0.2–0.8	−0.03
Fungia actiniformis	Palao	110	18	7.7–17.3	0–0.5	−0.35
Fungia costulata	Palao	94	6	4.8–10.1	0–0.7	−0.79
	Palao	94	4	6.4–9.0	0–0.1	0

Stephenson and Stephenson (1933): Low Isles, Queensland; Experiment I (period in weeks)

Acropora squamosa	Anchorage	29–30	7	8.6–22.7	3.8–9.1	+0.20
	Moat	33–35	4	4.2–12.7	2.5–7.1	−1.00
Acropora quelchi	Anchorage	26–30	5	7.9–15.7	4.1–7.0	−0.60
Acropora quelchi var. 1	Moat	32–33	4	4.7–9.5	2.9–5.1	+0.80
Acropora pulchra	Anchorage	27–30	4	9.0–27.0	6.1–11.6	−0.40
Porites sp.	Moat	32–35	5	6.8–11.0	0.5–3.0	+0.62
Pocillopora bulbosa	Moat	31–35	13	6.2–20.6	3.5–5.6	+0.01
Favia doryensis	Moat	31–33	4	6.5–15.4	0.8–1.2	+0.35
Favia sp. 1	Moat	32–35	4	7.0–13.8	0.7–1.0	−0.20
Symphyllia recta	Moat	32–34	5	5.2–19.2	0.2–0.9	+0.25
Psammocora gonagra	Moat	31–35	9	5.7–16.7	2.5–3.3	+0.08

[a] The Spearman rank correlation coefficient was calculated for increment of growth on initial size (mean diameter, cm). All species in which at least four colonies were measured are included.

[b] p is not significant in all cases except for *Acropora squamosa* from Low Isles, Moat, for which $p = 0.05$.

The second condition, that variation in growth rate be minimal, is difficult to contend with, since the number of replicates is usually few. There is certainly great variation in growth rates between colonies and between years for the same colony. This means that precise estimates of age simply cannot be made with any great confidence.

Finally, there remains the question of whether the measurements were made in a period of "normal" environmental conditions and so representative of average growth. Obviously, the longer the period of observation, the greater the probability that the sample is representative: Mayer's measurements after 23 years are to be preferred to Tamura and Hada's after 3 months. However, I have found no published data which could be used to estimate the degree of variation in growth among years, independently of size and age. Until a series of experiments is performed to estimate such variation, the existing data must be presumed to be representative.

VI. Mortality

Mortality in early life must be very heavy. Large numbers of planulae are released but by the time they have weathered the hazards of the plankton and the first month of settled life, only about $5/m^2$ survive to be recruited to the population each year at Heron Island (Table I). After this, the mortality rate is much lower and continues to decrease, as shown in Table IV.

The higher mortality rate of smaller colonies suggests the following hypothesis to explain the cause of mortality of part or all of a colony of coral. If the living tissue on a small portion of a large colony is destroyed, the exposed part of the skeleton is quickly covered by regeneration from the surrounding coral tissue (Stephenson and Stephenson, 1933). This is probably because materials and energy are contributed at a rapid rate by the large amount of live tissue surrounding it. If, on the other hand, the same amount of damage is done to a very small colony regeneration is less rapid owing to the low rate of supply of energy from the small area of living colony remaining. This hypothesis could be tested by removing living pieces of varying size from a colony, damaging each to the same degree, and measuring the rate of regeneration. The consequence of this process would be a greater probability of permanent damage to a part of a small colony and so a greater chance of complete mortality of the whole colony.

To determine the cause of death is difficult, except after catastrophes. Past workers have shown that corals are killed by long exposure to

TABLE IV

EFFECTS OF SIZE ON MORTALITY RATES OF CORALS OF ALL SPECIES
COMBINED, AT HERON ISLAND, OVER TWO SUCCESSIVE INTERVALS
OF 3.4 YEARS EACH

Area of colony, at start of interval (cm^2)	South Crest		South Inner Flat		North Crest	
	No. at start	Mortality (%)	No. at start	Mortality (%)	No. at start	Mortality (%)
October 1963–February 1967						
1–40	24	42	20	55	16	50
41–80	10	10	4	25	11	54
81+	4	0	11	0	13	8
February 1967–July 1970						
1–40	49	45	12	33	12	75
41–80	7	29	12	17	3	33
81+	10	0	12	17	14	29

air, either in the sun or in heavy rain, by floods of fresh water, especially if accompanied by heavy sedimentation, by stoppage of normal water circulation, and by severe wave action during storms (Stoddart, 1969).

In these catastrophes all or most of the colonies were killed, often over large areas. However, on my study area at Heron Island, individual colonies died, in whole or in part, while their neighbors survived. The two most likely causes of this local mortality are competition and natural enemies. A discussion of the ways these forces act may suggest hypotheses which can be tested.

A. COMPETITION

Space in the light seems to be as essential for corals as it is for green plants and probably for much the same reasons (Muscatine and Cernichiari, 1969). Thus we should expect that corals would compete with each other for that space. If two colonies meet, interference should take either the indirect form of one colony growing above the other, cutting off the light or reducing the flow of water, or a more direct form of interference.

One of the first examples of such an indirect effect was an experiment cited by Darwin (1842, p. 77). In Madagascar in 1830, Dr. Allan had transplanted colonies of 20 species of corals to a pool and staked them down, either separately or in clumps. In 7 months, some of the corals in the clumps had grown over each other. The most vigorous grower was believed to have been *Madrepora* (*Acropora*), although this could not be confirmed, the collection having been lost by shipwreck. Brugge-mann (1877) described a museum specimen of the ramose *Porites porites* (*P. clavaria*) growing over an encrusting *Porites astreoides;* the latter was dead under the former.

By photographing the corals in the same area over several years I have observed branched colonies of *Acropora* gradually extending out above encrusting species such as *Montipora*. When some of the branching colonies were destroyed in a hurricane it was revealed that the portion of the encrusting colony which had been under the overhanging branches was dead. I interpret this as indirect interference, the upper colony preventing the lower one from acquiring some requisite, such as light or zooplankton food.

Corals may compete for space with other organisms, such as the larger algae. From the photographs, I have observed a large fleshy alga, *Hydroclathrus clathratus*, growing over a living branch of *Acropora*. After a period of time the alga disappeared and the branch was revealed to be dead. Whether this interference was indirect or direct, I do not know.

If faster growing organisms such as algae or branching corals can grow over and so kill slower growing encrusting or massive corals, how do these latter species persist? One answer is that the slow-growing species may interfere directly with neighboring colonies which threaten to encroach on their living space. This was apparently first described by Gravier (1910) on a reef in French Somaliland. He noticed that those portions of colonies of *Favia* and *Cyphastraea* which were within 1 or 2 cm of the edge of an adjacent colony of *Hydnophora* ("*Hydrophorella*") were dead. He felt that the *Hydnophora* was killing the other colonies as it grew, its effect being felt at a distance. Similarly, the polyps of a colony of *Porites* were dead in a band some millimeters around the edge of a basal plate of a colony of *Pavona*. Likewise a colony of *Montipora* had begun to indent a branch of *Acropora*. He felt that the massive "globular" forms were succumbing to the encrusting or foliaceous ones.

Taking my cue from these very original early observations, I searched for such effects on Heron Island. On several of the marked plots, I had noticed that branching *Acropora* never extended over massive colonies such as *Leptoria* in the 7 years I had been observing them. In fact, the underside of the tips of the *Acropora* surrounding one

Leptoria were dead, with filamentous algae growing on them. I then examined every massive colony I could find on the adjacent reef crest and in every case the adjacent *Acropora*, or in one instance *Montipora*, did not encroach closer than 1 or 2 cm to the massive colony. In one instance, shown in Fig. 2, a fast-growing *Acropora* in a pool had stopped growing only in a zone which accurately followed the irregular contour of the adjacent massive colony.

The cause of this inhibition of growth has been discovered by Lang (1970). She has found that certain species will extend their mesenterial filaments and digest any living coral tissue from a colony of another species which they can touch, up to about 2 cm away. The species can be arranged in an aggressive hierarchy, each species attacking all others below it in the hierarchy and being attacked by all ranked higher. In general, the massive species of the families Mussidae, Meandrinidae, and Faviidae rank higher than those of other families. This agrees with my findings that slow-growing massive colonies were not overgrown by the faster growing branching ones. In some instances, as found by Gravier, foliaceous species may inhibit massive species.

Extrusion of mesenterial filaments in response to disturbance or to

Fig. 2. A colony of *Acropora hyacinthus,* above, being inhibited in its outward growth by a colony of a massive species below, in a pool on the north reef crest, Heron Island, Queensland.

feed on food too large to engulf has been described by Carpenter (1910), Yonge (1968), and others. Catala (1964, Pl. 1, Fig. 4) noted the response to adjacent coral colonies which he interpreted as "reciprocal cannibalism." As Lang (1970) has shown, no colony ever attacked another of the same species and the aggression was never reciprocal.

In summary, fast-growing species may grow so as to extend out over others below them which then are killed. However, if the slower growing species can touch the fast-growing one, it may be able to protect itself from being overshadowed by killing the encroaching edge of its competitor.

B. Natural Enemies

Living corals are harmed by their natural enemies in two ways: either living tissues is removed or the skeleton is bored into and weakened. If a small amount of living tissue is removed the coral may be able to regenerate it. If the skeleton is exposed tissue may grow over it, as happens when the end of a branch is broken off (Stephenson and Stephenson, 1933). However, if a large area of living tissue is eaten, the remaining coral evidently cannot cover the exposed skeleton with tissue quickly enough to prevent other organisms from colonizing it and that part of the colony must then be regarded as dead.

Thus attacks on living corals resemble the process of grazing on plants rather than of predation on animals. Only when the colony is small enough so that all or most of the tissue is eaten in a short period, can the colony be said to have been killed by a predator. The only animals which have been shown to act in this way are the starfish *Acanthaster planci* (Mortensen, 1931; Goreau, 1964) and certain fish (Motoda, 1940). A single starfish can kill a small colony, and several individuals together may kill a large colony. However, parts of a large colony are sometimes left uneaten.

The other species which eat living corals may slash the tissues, suck off bits, or eat whole polyps or groups of polyps. This sort of attack may result in the death of very small colonies and of parts of larger ones. Natural enemies which act in this way include echinoids (Pearse, 1969), annelid worms, crustaceans (copepods, cirripedes, crabs), gastropod mollusks and fish (see the comprehensive review by Robertson, 1970). In a special category is the aggressive attacking of one coral by another, described above.

To assess the effects of natural enemies requires either observation over long periods or experiments in the field. This has seldom been done. Motoda (1940) transplanted colonies of *Goniastrea aspera* from the reef flat to the edge and found that the upper parts both of the tissues and skeletons were quickly bitten off, presumably by fish. Fish also graze other species of corals but their effect has not been measured. Many fish graze on attached algae which are potential competitors of corals. Cages excluding or containing certain species of fish would elucidate their effect on corals. Adjacent cages with openings allowing fish to enter would be necessary to control for the effects of the cage on currents, light, etc.

The predatory starfish *Acanthaster planci* has recently been noticed in high numbers in certain areas and has killed over 90% of the corals on parts of some reefs (Goreau, 1964; Chesher, 1969a,b; Pearson and Endean, 1969). Several large-scale surveys have recently been made which illustrate the distribution and abundance of this predator in the Pacific region. The abundance is usually estimated as the number counted in a known interval of time. As shown in Table V, *Acanthaster* is very patchily distributed, being very abundant and causing high mortality of corals on certain reefs in three regions: the central Great Barrier Reef (but not to the north or south); certain of the Fiji Islands; and in three areas of Micronesia, namely four islands in the southern Marianas and two groups of islands in the Carolines, Truk with adjacent Kuop and Ponape with nearby Ant Island. In many other regions of the Pacific *Acanthaster* was either rare or, if common, was having no effect on the corals. Surveys of damage by *Acanthaster* are being carried out in other areas at present. When the results of these are published the picture will be more complete and perhaps different.

Although there has been some controversy on this point, it is clear that there has been an increase in numbers of *Acanthaster* on certain reefs with resultant great mortality of corals; this is true for certain reefs in the central Great Barrier Reef, in the southern Marianas, and in certain of the Carolines. In most other areas, however, little damage evidently has been caused to the corals even when the starfish is common. High numbers of *Acanthaster* have occurred in the past, on the Great Barrier Reef and the Solomon Islands (Vine, 1970) and on Christmas Island (Pacific Ocean), the Philippines, Palao and Java (Dana, 1970). Several hypotheses have been suggested to explain the recent increases (see references cited); none has been tested experimentally.

Acanthaster often occurs in groups or even large herds, apparently moving in a group and eating most of the corals in their path. The genera of corals which are evidently attacked more frequently are

TABLE V
DISTRIBUTION AND ABUNDANCE OF *Acanthaster planci* ON CORAL REEFS IN THE PACIFIC OCEAN

Pearson and Endean (1969), Table 2

	Count/20 minutes		
	>40	10–40	<10
Great Barrier Reef, central (lat. 14° to 19°)			
No. of reefs	24	16	35
No. of censuses	52	36	113
Great Barrier Reef, southern (lat. 19° to 24°)			
No. of reefs	0	0	17
No. of censuses	0	0	37

Chesher (1969b), Standardized surveys

	Abundance and coral damage		
	Common, great damage (conditions 3, 4, 5)	Common, no damage (conditions 2, 6)	Few, no damage (condition 1)
Micronesia (Table 1, p. 27)			
Mariannas			
No. of islands	4	0	0
Other areas			
No. of islands	4	5	6
Island of Hawaii (p. 74)			
No. of islands/no. of censuses	0	0	1/17
Other Hawaiian Is. (pp. 74–75)			
No. of islands/no. of censuses	0	1/1	4/27

Weber and Woodhead (1970), Table 1

	Categories of abundance			
	Abundant	Common	Rare	None
Great Barrier Reef, northern				
No. of reefs	0	0	0	6
Great Barrier Reef, central				
No. of reefs	1	0	1	6
Great Barrier Reef, southern				
No. of reefs	0	2	1	16

TABLE V (*Continued*)

	Categories of abundance			
	Abundant	Common	Rare	None
Australian east coast south of Great Barrier Reef				
No. of reefs	0	0	0	3
Fiji Islands				
No. of reefs	11	2	0	3
Eight other areas in South Pacific				
No. of reefs	0	3	5	15
Total no. of reefs	12	7	7	49

Vine (1970), Table 1

	Count/20 minutes		
	>5	1–5	0
Great Barrier Reef, northern			
No. of reefs	0	0	21
Great Barrier Reef, central			
No. of reefs	2	8	8
Great Barrier Reef, southern			
No. of reefs	0	0	6
Fiji Islands			
No. of reefs	2	0	2
Other reefs in South Pacific			
No. of reefs	0	4	30
Total no. of reefs	4	12	67

Acropora, Montipora, Seriatopora, and *Stylophora* (Weber and Wood-head, 1970). Large smooth heads of *Porites* and the genera *Pocillopora, Fungia,* and the hydrozoan corals *Millepora* and *Heliopora* are evidently eaten less frequently (Pearson and Endean, 1969; Chesher, 1969a; Barnes *et al.,* 1970; Weber and Woodhead, 1970). The tube feet of *Acanthaster* tend to withdraw quickly after they make contact with living coral; paradoxically, they withdraw less quickly from the genera which *Acanthaster* avoids eating (*Porites, Millepora,* and *Heliopora*), than from *Acropora,* a common food (Barnes *et al.,* 1970). These authors found that *Acanthaster* seldom attaches its tube feet to living coral, presumably because they are stung by the nematocysts; it clambers onto the colony on the tips of its many spines using its muscular arms. The reason why it selects or avoids certain corals is not known. In the laboratory, *Acanthaster* extended its stomach if extracts of *Acropora* or *Pocillopora* were injected into its mouth, but when *Porites* was used, most *Acanthaster* withdrew the tube feet around the mouth and closed the ambulacral grooves (Brauer *et al.*, 1970). Thus certain corals such as *Acropora* have strong nematocyst defenses but are easily climbed and eaten; others, such as *Porites*, have weak nematocyst defenses but their large smooth surfaces may be difficult to climb and they also may have chemical defenses.

Another sort of defense which corals enjoy is the presence of commensal crustaceans and fish. Xanthid crabs attacked an *Acanthaster* crawling onto a colony of *Pocillopora* in an aquarium (Pearson and Endean, 1969). Crabs and small fish drove the starfish off *Stylophora* and *Acropora* on the reef at Fiji (Weber and Woodhead, 1970). These observations illustrate the complex interactions which occur in coral communities. They suggest the hypothesis that large aggregations of *Acanthaster* can kill most of the corals in an area only when the populations of commensal crustaceans and fish are greatly reduced. Preliminary tests of this hypothesis could be made by comparing the abundance of commensals in places where *Acanthaster* was heavily damaging the corals with those where *Acanthaster* was common but not killing much coral.

The other sort of attack by natural enemies is the weakening of the skeleton by boring organisms, principally sponges, worms, and mollusks. Sponges excavate the older basal portions of colonies and may extend into the living branches. They greatly weaken the attachment at the holdfast so that waves may easily detach them or, on steep slopes, colonies may break off under their own weight (Goreau and Hartman, 1963). Boring mollusks, especially species of the bivalve *Lithophaga*, were very common in living corals in the Red Sea (Soliman, 1969), and at Heron Island. This is contrary to the observation of Otter (1937) who stated that living coral was infrequently bored by mollusks at Low Isles. The opening to the burrow is usually surrounded with living coral tissue. Since this is the only opening, it seems clear that the larval mollusk must somehow penetrate the coral tissue to begin to burrow into the skeleton, unless it finds a small exposed part of the skeleton, such as a place where a branch has broken off, or a fish has grazed off the tissue. Larval mollusks are evidently capable of searching over the surface of a living coral without being eaten. Soliman (1969) placed veligers of a boring gastropod directly on the surface of a live coral, and they lived there unaffected for several days. Another mytilid bivalve,

TABLE VI

BORING ORGANISMS IN SAMPLES OF FOUR SPECIES OF CORALS FROM FOUR LOCALITIES ON THE REEF AT HERON ISLAND, GREAT BARRIER REEF[a]

Lithophaga

	Outer crest of reef				Inner reef flat			
	North		South		North		South	
	No. samples with Lithophaga/total no. samples	Avg. no. Lithophaga/sample	No. samples with Lithophaga/total no. samples	Avg. no. Lithophaga/sample	No. samples with Lithophaga/total no. samples	Avg. no. Lithophaga/sample	No. samples with Lithophaga/total no. samples	Avg. no. Lithophaga/sample
Acropora palifera	11/11	5.9	8/10	3.6	3/14	0.5	1/10	0.1
Pocillopora damicornis	9/10	2.1	5/10	0.8	4/20	0.2	1/10	0.1
Porites lutea or *P. andrewsi*	0/10	0	0/10	0	0/9	0	0/9	0

Boring Sponges and Polychaete Worms
(No. samples having at least one borer/total no. samples)

	Outer crest of reef				Inner reef flat			
	North		South		North		South	
	Sponges	Worms	Sponges	Worms	Sponges	Worms	Sponges	Worms
Acropora palifera	2/10	3/10	4/10	2/10	0/14	3/14	3/10	2/10
Pocillopora damicornis	1/10	0/10	3/10	0/10	0/20	0/20	0/10	1/10
Porites lutea or *P. andrewsi*	1/10	2/10	0/10	1/10	1/10	0/10	0/9	0/9

[a] Each sample was either a connected group of branches about 10 cm long (*Acropora* and *Pocillopora*) or a colony about 10 cm in diameter (*Porites*).

Fungiacava eilantensis, has recently been found excavating the skeletons of living fungid corals (Goreau *et al.,* 1969).

To assess the rate of attack of boring organisms on living corals at Heron Island, I examined samples of living corals of three species from the reef crests and from the inner reef flat. As shown in Table VI, the branching corals *Acropora* and *Pocillopora* had many more *Lithophaga* than the more massive *Porites.* The incidence of attack by *Lithophaga* was much greater on the reef crest than on the inner flat. The branching species had a slightly higher incidence of attack by sponges and worms than *Porites,* and the rate of attack was slightly greater on the reef crest. I suggest that the rate of attack by borers is an inverse function of the density of the skeleton. Fast-growing species probably construct a less dense skeleton which is more easily bored. Branching species usually grow faster and have more borers than massive ones. Whether this accounts for the difference between the reef crest and the reef flat cannot be decided at present. J. Lang and P. W. Frank have pointed out to me that, although some massive or branching species in the Caribbean (e.g. certain *Porites*) grow slowly, they have less dense skeletons and are heavily bored.

One other form of attack should be mentioned. In the photographs of October, 1963, on area 1 on the south crest of the reef at Heron Island, I observed whitish material covering some of the branches of several colonies of *Acropora hebes.* These branches were living in July, 1963, but in the next set of photographs in August, 1965, these particular branches were dead and covered with encrusting coralline algae. They seemed to be the only branches dead in their colonies at that time. What the material consists of and whether it was the cause of mortality, I do not know. This was the only species affected, and I have not observed it again. I have not since returned in October so that, if it only occurs in these spring months I would not have had the opportunity to see it. It did not occur in any of my other study areas at the same time.

VII. Longevity and Age Distribution

In a few instances it is possible to reconstruct the age structure of a population of corals. The problems of estimating age from the rate of growth were discussed earlier. If the hypothesis of Wells (1963) is confirmed, it may be possible to estimate age from periodic growth rings. At this stage in our knowledge only very rough etimates are possible, but they may serve as guides for future work.

The only data on both the size of all corals in an area and their rates of growth are those from the Great Barrier Reef Expedition of 1928 and my own measurements at Heron Island. Manton (1935) published several maps showing all colonies greater than about 3 cm in diameter on areas of 6–8 m². The rates of growth of colonies measured by Stephenson and Stephenson (1933) were used to calculate the mean annual increment of each colony. Since there were few replicates, species of similar life form were grouped and the median increment calculated for the group. The size (mean of two diameters) of each colony was measured from the map (Plate IX, Manton, 1935) and divided by the appropriate median annual increment to give an estimate of its age. Table VII shows the age distribution of colonies in each group, with the median annual increment used to estimate the ages.

To obtain the age distribution of corals from my study areas at Heron Island, I had records of new recruits for $7\frac{1}{2}$ years (see Table I) as well as older colonies which were present at the beginning of my study. To estimate the age of these older colonies, I measured their growth from the periodic photographs and, as before, used the median of the annual increments for groups of species of similar growth form. Thus for colonies less than $7\frac{1}{2}$ years old the estimates were made directly from my records but for colonies older than this the estimates are subject to the inaccuracies discussed earlier.

In Table VII the ages of the nonmassive forms such as *Acropora*, *Montipora*, and the branching *Porites*, may be underestimated since it is sometimes difficult to judge the extent of a single colony. As they ramify over a hard surface, the older parts may die and only the younger edge of the colony may survive, sometimes in separate living patches. In most cases, the original size can be judged from the shape of the living portion. The records over several years were helpful in making these decisions. Without some knowledge of the past history of such colonies, it is probably unwise to attempt to estimate their ages. On my study areas, about half of the colonies had attached during the $7\frac{1}{2}$ years I had been observing them, so that the median ages shown are accurate. At Low Isles, most of the colonies in the western moat were massive species which grow in a well-defined convex form so that there was no ambiguity about their size.

Table VII shows the age structure of three populations from Heron Island and one from Low Isles. These were all relatively young assemblages, with median ages of less than 10 years. At Heron Island, the corals on the inner flat were mainly massive *Porites* with an older age structure than the corals on the outer reef crest. In the western

TABLE VII

Age Distribution of Corals at Heron Island and Low Isles[a,b]

Coral[c]	Growth diameter (cm/year)	Age (years)							Total no.	Median age
		0–4.9	5–9.9	10–14.9	15–19.9	20–24.9	25–29.9	30–34.9		
Area 1. Outer Reef Crest (July 1970)										
Acropora (6)[d]		10	15	7					32	6.5
Montipora (2)		8	3	1					12	4.5
Porites (2)		4	1	1					6	4
Pocillopora (1)[d]		1	3						4	5.5
All species		23	23[e]	9					55	5.5
Area 2. Inner Reef Flat (July 1970)										
Acropora (1)[d]	2.0	2	1	1	2				6	5.5
Porites (2)	2.0	8	6	4	6	3			27	9.5
All species		10	7	5	8	3			33	9.5
Area 4. Outer Reef Crest Pool (August 1965)										
Acropora (5)[d]	4.1	7	5	3					15	5
Porites (2)	1.1	6	3	1					10	3.5
Pocillopora (1)[d]	1.1	2	5	1					8	8
Other (2)			2						2	—
All species		15	15	5					35	5.5

Low Isles, Western Moat[f]

Acropora (1)[d]	4.6	7						7	2.5
Montipora (1)[d]	8	5	1		1			7	2.5
Porites (1)	2.7		2	2			1	5	11.5
Pocillopora (1)[d]	6.7	1						1	—
Psammocora (1)	4.6	2	1					3	4.5
Massive species (11)	1.3	25	22	14	8	4		73	7.5
All species		40	26	16	9	4	1	96	7.5

[a] From Manton (1935).

[b] The number of colonies in each age group was calculated either from the sizes and growth rates as shown or, at Heron Is., from records kept since Dec. 1962.

[c] Numbers in parentheses indicate species included in each taxonomic category.

[d] Fragile, easily broken species.

[e] Includes one colony of *Leptastrea purpurea* which was not tallied separately.

[f] See Manton, Plate IX. No colonies less than 3 cm in diameter were mapped at Low Isles, so the numbers in the group less than 5 years of age were probably underestimated.

moat at Low Isles most of the species, being of the massive growth form, also had a somewhat older age structure.

The age distributions given in Table VII are probably representative of the shallow-water areas of these reefs. The other maps of Manton (1935), both from Low Isles and from Yonge Reef on the outer barrier, show a similar size distribution of corals, as do the other areas which I have photographed at Heron Island.

From these distributions one can get an idea of the size of the breeding population. At Low Isles, about one-third of the massive colonies were more than 10 years old, which, as discussed earlier, is about the age of sexual maturity. The faster growing species may reach maturity sooner, although no direct data exist to support such a judgment. Only about a quarter of the colonies of *Acropora* and a smaller proportion of *Pocillopora* and *Montipora* were over 10 years old at Heron Island. Since they grow about 3 to 6 times as fast in diameter, and thus 9 to 36 times as fast in area as the massive species, the few branching colonies which reach 10 years of age could produce great numbers of larvae. However, it is impossible at this stage to construct an age-specific fecundity and mortality table for any coral. Such tables will probably differ greatly between the branching species, which have high rates of recruitment, growth, and mortality and the massive species, with low rates.

Although none of the colonies in Table VII was older than 32 years, corals can live much longer. A few measurements of the growth of very large colonies have been made and, under the assumptions discussed earlier, their age can be estimated. The only published data I have found on large colonies growing under natural conditions are those of Mayer (1918), who remeasured Saville-Kent's colonies at Thursday Island after an interval of 23.3 years and his measurements at Samoa and Fiji (Mayor, 1924).

I have measured the diameter of a series of microatolls on the reef flat at Heron Island. They were sampled by measuring every microatoll touched by a line stretched across the inner reef flat. A line northeast of the island crossed mainly colonies of *Acropora palifera*, whereas a line south of the island sampled mainly *Porites annae*. The annual growth increments were estimated from the periodic photographs at area 2, which is on a microatoll on the inner reef flat south of the island. These estimates can only be regarded as very approximate, since there is no unequivocal way to be sure that each microatoll represents the growth of only one colony.

The estimates of the ages of these older colonies are given in Table

TABLE VIII

AGE OF LARGE COLONIES GROWING NATURALLY ON REEF FLATS IN SAMOA, FIJI, AND ON THE GREAT BARRIER REEF

Authority	Location	Species	Annual increment to diameter (cm)	Age of individual colonies (years)
Mayer (1918)	Thursday Island, Queensland	*Symphyllia* sp.	4.3	41
Mayor (1924)[a]	Samoa	*Porites* sp.	4.9	140
		Porites sp. aff. *lutea*	3.3	16, 20, 30, 31, 63, 86
Mayor (1924)[a]	Fiji	*Porites* sp. aff. *lutea*	2.8	54, 88, 95
Present paper	Heron Island	*Acropora palifera*	2.0	7–130, median 50[b]
	Heron Island	*Porites annae*	2.0	23–140, median 50[c]

[a] Table 7.
[b] 30 colonies.
[c] 15 colonies.

VIII. The oldest, 140 years, probably does not represent the maximum age attainable by corals. However, these are the only reasonable data available at present. The most accurate estimate is probably still that of Mayer (1918); in this, as in other aspects of the population ecology of corals, the most useful data are to be found in some of the early publications.

It would be of interest to know the age structure in other parts of the reef, such as in the deeper areas of the outer slope. Are the thickets of staghorn *Acropora* off the edge of the reef at Heron Island very old assemblages? Some of the populations of large massive *Diploria* and *Montastrea annularis* and the *Acropora cervicornis* and *A. palmata* which have very thick and heavy branches, as shown in photographs off Jamaica in Goreau (1959), may have a much older age distribution. Such questions cannot be answered until the individuals are measured and aged.

VIII. Variations in Abundance

As a result of variations in rates of recruitment, growth, and mortality, the abundance of corals varies in space and time. These variations on permanent quadrats in my four study areas over $7\frac{1}{2}$ years are shown

TABLE IX

CHANGES BETWEEN 1963 AND 1970 IN NUMBERS AND AREA (M²) OF LIVING
CORALS ON FOUR PERMANENT SQUARE METER QUADRATS
AT HERON ISLAND, GREAT BARRIER REEF[a,b]

	Locations of m² quadrats			
	South		North	
	1	2	3	4
		Reef		Outer
	Crest	flat	Crest	pool
	(sq. A)	(sq. 4)	(sq. NW)	(sq. 2)
No. of colonies in 1963	32	31	43	43
No. of 1963 colonies surviving in 1970	23	18	14	0
No. of colonies attaching between 1963 and 1970 which were alive in 1970	37	16	10	31
Total no. of colonies in 1970	60	34	24	31
Area of colonies in 1963	0.27	0.28	0.55	0.29
Area of 1963 colonies surviving in 1970	0.30	0.07	0.63	0
Area of colonies attaching between 1963 and 1970 which were alive in 1970	0.13	0.03	0.04	0.09
Total area of colonies in 1970	0.43	0.10	0.67	0.09

[a] A hurricane in January 1967 destroyed the corals at area 4.

[b] A colony was counted as being in the square meter if at least half of its area was inside. The area calculations include all living cover, including parts of colonies which were not counted as described.

in Table IX. With the exception of the complete destruction during a hurricane on area 4, the numbers of colonies varied by about a factor of 2, while the area covered by living coral varied by a factor of between 2 and 3. The colonies present in 1963 continued in 1970 to hold the greater proportion of the space occupied; only at area 1 on the south crest did later recruits acquire much space. These records indicate that variations in abundance were not very great on the upper parts of the reef, even during a period which included a hurricane. Only in pools near the leeward edge and on the slope below were many corals destroyed by the hurricane (P. Woodhead, personal communication). In most such storms massive corals survive better than branching ones, although in all instances so far observed branching corals survived in some places (Stoddart, 1969).

On the quadrats at area 4, in pools near the north edge of the reef at Heron Island, stony corals covered 57% of the surface in August 1965

Almost all were destroyed in a hurricane in January 1967. In $2\frac{1}{2}$ years after the hurricane, few corals had attached; after $3\frac{1}{2}$ years about 10% of the surface was occupied, and after $4\frac{1}{2}$ years, about 20%.

Restoration of a coral reef ecosystem after it has been destroyed may take a very long time for several reasons. Initial recolonization of corals depends mainly upon two factors: the degree of mortality caused and the availabilty of a source of larvae. If some colonies survive within the area of destruction, they will continue to grow and to produce larvae which may colonize the surrounding depopulated regions. However, if almost no corals have survived all new colonies must be founded by the settlement of planktonic larvae produced outside the damaged region. Since the only existing data indicate that most planulae settle within the first few days after they have been released from the parent, the distance to the source of larvae and the relevant current patterns are critical. If all corals are killed on a reef which is isolated by distance or adverse current patterns from others, or if a large stretch of continuous reef is destroyed, recruitment from the distant intact reefs may be very slow. The type of substrate produced after the destruction is important. If a soft substrate is maintained, or if a mat of algae develops because grazing animals are killed, settlement of planulae will be prevented.

Even after larvae have settled and colonies are growing, no larvae will be produced in the damaged area for a long time. First, corals take up to 10 years to reach sexual maturity. Second, cross-fertilization seems to be the rule, so that even after the colonies reach maturity, no larvae will be produced until the population density of a species becomes high enough to ensure successful mating.

Under normal conditions at Heron Island establishment of new colonies occurred at an average rate of $5/m^2/year$ (Table I). However, about half of these young colonies died within a year. (Table IV). Colonies which attached between 1963 and 1970 covered an area of only about 0.1 m^2 in 1970 (Table IX).

Coral reef ecosystems are characterized by great complexity. There are many species, with different life forms, of different ages, all intermingled in a complex mosaic. In the early years of recovery the assemblage will tend to be much less complex. If a few species survive the destruction their larvae may contribute disproportionately to the early colonization, resulting in a less diverse species assemblage. Also, most of the colonies will be young, so that the complexity afforded by a mixed-age distribution will be missing.

All these factors tend to delay the restitution of the full complexity and diversity characteristic of a mature coral reef ecosystem.

IX. Summary

There are many gaps in our knowledge of the population ecology of reef-building corals. As the name implies, most previous work has been directed toward their role as reef-builders, little toward understanding their population dynamics. Most of the best work was done before 1940.

There appears to be a prereproductive period of 8–10 years in the two species where data on this aspect exist. Sexes may be separate, or sex may change with age; other species are hermaphrodite. Fertilization may occur externally or inside the polyp; larvae are often brooded in the polyp. Gonad development and release of gametes or larvae tends to be less seasonal at lower latitudes. A mature colony may produce up to a few thousand eggs or larvae in a breeding season. Suitable data on reproduction are very sparse; no age-specific fecundity information exists.

Once released, larvae swim for a short time and then settle onto suitable surfaces. Indirect evidence suggests that they are usually dispersed away from their parents. In the laboratory, several settled larvae may fuse into one colony; this probably seldom happens in the field. No study of choice of substrate by larvae has been made.

Since newly settled colonies are seldom seen in the field, recruitment of new colonies to the population can be measured only after some early mortality has occurred. The rates of recruitment at Heron Island varied from 0 to 13 colonies/m²/year, averaging about 5. The commoner species all had good recruitment, as did some less common ones. If a species was common in one area and rare in another, the recruitment reflected this difference. This tended to maintain the relative abundance of the different species in an area. Recruitment also occurred when pieces of colonies were broken off and washed into an area.

Space in the light seems to be critical for many corals. At Heron Island they grew from 10 to 20 cm²/year at first, then the rate of occupying space was variable. Larger colonies often lost space when part of the colony died. Growth (in diameter) was faster at first, but then slowed to a rather constant rate; growth was indeterminate and even very large colonies continued to grow. This makes it possible to estimate the approximate age of colonies.

Mortality of the entire colony was heavy at first, then decreased; parts of larger colonies often died. Various physical catastrophes kill corals over large areas, but the cause of death of individual colonies is not known. Competition for light may cause death if one colony overshadows another. Some slower growing species can prevent a faster growing one from shading them by direct aggression, attacking and killing the edge of the encroaching colony by using their mesenterial filaments.

Attack by natural enemies can remove tissue from part or all of a colony. Large predators, such as fish or starfish, can kill an entire colony, but smaller predators usually kill only part of it. A recent increase in numbers of the starfish *Acanthaster* has caused much mortality of corals in three particular regions of the Pacific. It either has not increased or, if common, has not damaged much coral in many other regions. Corals may be defended from such attacks by commensal fish or crustaceans. Organisms which bore into the skeleton of living corals also increase their mortality. Such attack was commoner on the reef edge than on the reef flat at Heron Island, and in branching than in massive species. No quantitative estimates of the effect of natural enemies on mortality of corals have been made.

The age distribution of some coral populations in shallow water indicates that they are young assemblages, with median ages of less than 10 years. Individual colonies can live much longer; estimates range up to 140 years at least. About one-third or fewer of the colonies in an assemblage appear to be large enough to be sexually mature. However, the data are as yet too sparse to construct tables of age-specific fecundity and mortality for any species. Older colonies have continued to hold most of the space over the $7\frac{1}{2}$ years of my study. When most colonies were destroyed by a hurricane recolonization by fast-growing species was not appreciable for at least 3 years. Recovery of the coral ecosystem on badly damaged reefs may require many years.

Acknowledgments

I would like to thank the officers and members of the Great Barrier Reef Committee for permission and facilities to work at the G.B.R.C. Research Station, Heron Island. Many people helped me in countless ways; I want to thank especially I. Bennett, J. Choat, T. Dana, R. Endean, P. Frank, G. French, P. Glynn, F. Grassle, M. Hopkins, J. Lang, R. Manning, S. Marshall, P. Mather, R. McMahon, P. MacWilliam, V. B. Pearse, D. Potts, W. Stephenson, D. Stoddard, J. Tracey, L. Webb, P. Woodhead, and C. M. Yonge. Particular thanks are due to J. W. Wells who identified the large collection of coral specimens. The study was supported by a fellowship from the John Simon Guggenheim Foundation and grants from the National Science Foundation.

References

Abe, N. (1937). *Palao Trop. Biol. Stud.* 1, 73–93.
Atoda, K. (1947a). *Sci. Rep. Tohoku Univ., Ser. 4* 18, 24–47.
Atoda, K. (1947b). *Sci. Rep. Tohoku Univ., Ser. 4* 18, 48–64.
Atoda, K. (1951a). *J. Morphol.* 89, 1–15.
Atoda, K. (1951b). *J. Morphol.* 89, 17–35.
Barnes, D. J., Brauer, R. W., and Jordan, M. R. (1970). *Nature (London)* 228, 342–344.
Boschma, H. (1929). *Carnegie Inst. Wash. Publ.* 3, 129–147.
Brauer, R. W., Jordan, M. R., and Barnes, D. J. (1970). *Nature (London)* 228, 344–346.
Bruggemann, F. (1877). *Kosmos* 1, 161–162.
Carpenter, F. W. (1910). *Proc. Amer. Acad. Arts Sci.* 46, 49–162.
Catala, R. L. A. (1964). "Carnival Under the Sun." R. Sicard Paris.
Chesher, R. H. (1969a). *Science* 165, 280–283.
Chesher, R. H. (1969b). "*Acanthaster planci.* Impact on Pacific Coral Reefs," Final Report. Research Lab., Westinghouse Electric Co., Pittsburgh, Pennsylvania.
Connell, J. H. (1972). In preparation.
Dana, T. F. (1970). *Science* 169, 894.
Darwin, C. (1842). "The Structure and Distribution of Coral Reefs." Smith, Elder & Co., London.
Duerden, J. E. (1902). *Mem. Nat. Acad. Sci.* 8, 401–649.
Edmondson, C. H. (1929). *Bull. Bishop Mus. Honolulu*, 58, 1–38.
Edmondson, C. H. (1946). *Occ. Pap. Bishop Mus.* 18, 283–304.
Fowler, G. H. (1885). *Quart. J. Microsc. Sci.* 25, No. I.
Fowler, G. H. (1887). *Quart. J. Microsc. Sci.* 27, No. II.
Fowler, G. H. (1888). *Quart. J. Microsc. Sci.* 28, Nos. III and IV.
Fowler, G. H. (1890). *Quart. J. Microsc. Sci.* 30, No. V.
Gardiner, J. S. (1900). *Willey Zool. Results* IV.
Gardiner, J. S. (1902). *Proc. Cambridge Phil. Soc.*, 11, Part 6, 463–471.
Goreau, T. F. (1959). *Ecology* 40, 67–90.
Goreau, T. F. (1964). *Sea Fish. Res. Sta. Haifa, Bull.* 35, 23–26.
Goreau, T. F., and Goreau, N. (1959). *Biol. Bull.* 117, 239–250.
Goreau, T. F., and Goreau, N. (1960). *Biol. Bull.* 118, 419–429.
Goreau, T. F., and Hartman, W. D. (1963). In "Mechanisms of Hard Tissue Destruction," Publ. No. 75. pp. 25–54. Amer. Ass. Advance Sci., Washington, D.C.
Goreau, T. F., Goreau, N., Soot-Ryen, T., and Yonge, C. M. (1969). *J. Zool* 158, 171–195.
Gravier, C. (1910). *C. R. Acad. Sci.* 151, 955–956.
Johnson, M. W. (1949). *Trans. Amer. Geophys. Union* 30, 238–244.
Johnson, M. W. (1954). *U.S., Geol. Surv., Prof. Pap.* 260–F, 301–314.
Kawaguti, S. (1941). *Palao Trop. Biol. Stud.* 2, 319–328.
Knight-Jones, E. W. (1953). *J. Exp. Biol.* 30, 584–598.
Lang, J. C. (1970). Ph.D. Thesis, Yale University, New Haven, Connecticut.
Manton, S. M. (1935). *Sci. Rep., Gt. Barrier Reef Comm.* 3, 273–312.
Marshall, S. M., and Stephenson, T. A. (1933). *Sci. Rep., Gt. Barrier Reef Exped* 3, 219–245.

Mavor, J. W. (1915). *Proc. Amer. Acad. Arts. Sci.* **51**, 485–511.

Mayer, A. G. (1918). *Carnegie Inst. Wash., Pap. Dep. Mar. Biol.* **9**, 1–48.

Mayor, A. G. (1924). *Carnegie Inst. Wash., Pap. Dep. Mar. Biol.*, **19**, 51–72.

Mortensen, T. (1931). *Kgl, Dan. Vidensk. Selsk., Skr. Naturv. Math., Ser. 9*, **4**, 1–39.

Motoda, S. (1940). *Palao Trop. Biol. Contrib.* **36**, 61–104.

Muscatine, L., and Cernichiari, E. (1969). *Biol. Bull.* **137**, 506–523.

Otter, G. W. (1937). *Sci. Rep., Gt. Barrier Reef Exped.* **1**, 323–352.

Pearse, J. S. (1969). *Bull. Mar. Sci.* **19**, 323–350.

Pearse, V. B., and Muscatine, L. (1971). *Biol. Bull.* **141**, 350–363.

Pearson, R. G., and Endean, R. (1969). *Fish. Notes, Queensl. Dep. Harbours Mar.* **3**, 27–55.

Robertson, R. (1970). *Pac. Sci.* **24**, 43–54.

Russell, F. S., and Colman, J. S. (1934). *Sci. Rep., Gt. Barrier Reef Exped.* **2**, 159–201.

Saville-Kent, W. (1893). "The Great Barrier Reef of Australia: Its Products and Potentialities." Allen, London.

Soliman, G. N. (1969). *Amer. Zool.* **9**, 887–894.

Stephenson, T. A. (1931). *Sci. Rep., Gt. Barrier Reef Exped.* **3**, 113–134.

Stephenson, T. A., and Stephenson, A. (1933). *Sci. Rep., Gt. Barrier Reef Exped.* **3**, 167–217.

Stephenson, W., Endean, R., and Bennett, I. (1958). *Aust. J. Mar. Freshwater Res.* **9**, 261–318.

Stoddart, D. R. (1969). *Biol. Rev.* **44**, 433–498.

Tamura, T., and Hada, Y. (1932). *Sci. Rep. Tohoku Univ., Ser. 4* **7**, 433–455.

Vaughan, T. W. (1915). *Carnegie Inst. Wash., Yearb.* **14**, 220–231.

Vine, P. J. (1970). *Nature* (*London*) **228**, 341–342.

von Arx, W. S. (1948). *Trans. Amer. Geophys. Union* **29**, 861–870.

Weber, J. N., and Woodhead, P. M. J. (1970). *Mar. Biol.* **6**, 12–17.

Wells, J. W. (1963). *Nature* (*London*), **197**, 948–950.

Wilson, H. V. (1888). *J. Morphol.* **2**, 191–252.

Yonge, C. M. (1935). *Carnegie Inst. Wash. Publ.* **452**, 185–198.

Yonge, C. M. (1968). *Proc. Roy. Soc., Ser. B* **169**, 329–344.

8

VARIETY IN CORAL REEF COMMUNITIES

J. Frederick Grassle

I. Introduction

The most obvious characteristic of the fauna and flora of coral reefs is variety. This variety is reflected in large numbers of species, many scales of species distribution, and many kinds of interspecific relationships. The main thesis of this discussion is that the apparent variety—referred to as species diversity, pattern diversity, or complexity of organization—can be explained independently of high productivity, spatial heterogeneity, or any absolute characteristic of the environment. The variety results from specialization on particular spatial and biotic features—the responses over time to the relative predictability of the environment.

247

Specialization is frequently divided into two categories largely based on methods of study: food specialization and specialization with respect to microhabitat. In sessile invertebrates, microhabitat specialization is the result of small population size. Population size determines scale of response to the physical configuration of the environment. In even the most apparently homogeneous medium, the ability to resolve microhabitat differences for animals of similar size is a function of local abundance or patch size. The fidelity of species to narrowly defined habitats has been noted in tropical rain forests by MacArthur *et al.* (1966), Janzen (1967), and Ashton (1969). Such fidelity is also a major feature of tropical coral reefs.

Feeding specialization is also a characteristic of coral reefs (Kohn, 1971). In food specialization, individuals are responding to particular components of the possible food resources as they move through an area (or process a medium, in the case of filter-feeders). Depending on the configuration of these resources, specialization is still related to population size, but it is less profitable to define the resources in spatial terms. Specialized response to widely distributed resources, which results in increased abundance, should not be thought of as specialization. In a spatially heterogenous environment, the extent to which species can specialize in smaller and smaller microhabitats is determined by the least number of individuals required for survival. No environment is unchanging in time; local disturbances insure that no habitat is completely homogeneous. The topographic variety seen on coral reefs may be thought of as a fine scale temporal mosaic produced by the localized occurrence of disturbance in relatively predictable climatic regimes.

The least number of individuals required for survival is directly related to the predictability of the environment (Grassle, 1972), which, in turn, determines the spectrum of species abundance measured as species diversity. Relative environmental predictability in parts of coral reefs and the strong environmental gradients across these features make coral reefs ideal places for observing the processes involved with species diversity. After a more detailed discussion of the theoretical framework, some quantitative data and general characteristics of reef populations such as long-lived larvae, asexual reproduction, longevity, and localized disturbance, will be discussed in the context of maintenance of variety in relatively predictable environments.

A. Environmental Predictability

Environmental changes that reduce predictability occur sporadically and without autocorrelation once to many times within the life span of an average adult individual of a species. The changes must differ sufficiently from the mean to result in differential mortality or viability. A change included within the physiological tolerance of every individual of a species would not affect predictability. A change that locally killed all the individuals of a species would also not affect predictability. This means that for most species predictability is reduced by sudden large deviations from the mean monthly range of any environmental variable, which occur with a frequency of one to several times in a hundred years. In most comparisons between areas, the variance and severity of sporadic changes in the environment are adequate measures of predictability.

B. GENETIC VARIATION

The only way to adapt to a capricious or unpredictable environment is through variation per se. At the population level, the requisite variety for species survival, or homeostasis, is the variety represented by differences among individuals. By maintaining these differences there are always some individuals relatively better adapted or specialized for each new circumstance. Populations with a high genetic variability will have a greater mean fitness of offspring than populations with low genetic variability in either new environments or environments that vary unpredictably. The population survives through a genetic elite, which varies from place to place and time to time. An important component of this kind of adaptation is high mortality. Over short periods of time, this allows selection for new optima as the environment changes. The relative role that mortality plays in adaptation may be defined as the degree of opportunism of the species. The corollaries of high mortality are high reproductive rate, short generation time, and large maximum population size. High mortality is the parameter most relevant to adaptation at the population level, for the adaptive significance of the life history phenomena depends on frequent intense selection. Ranking species on a continuous scale of opportunism, defined by mortality rates, has the additional advantage that it pinpoints the critical period for adaptation, the high mortality stages.

Three main explanations for the high genetic variability found in relatively opportunistic species are some form of balancing selection (Prakash *et al.*, 1969) and random mutation in the absence of selection (Kimura, 1968). Selection in an unpredictably varying environment (cf. Lewontin, 1966) is considered balancing selection but is less frequently discussed, probably because there are fewer possibilities for precise description and experimental analysis. In an unpredictable

environment, characters that appear to be neutral or somewhat disadvantageous may be maintained with the possibility that they may be
strongly selected for during some future period. Haldane and Jayakar
(1963) have shown mathematically that selection need only favor a
particular gene once in a number of generations for the gene to be
maintained in the population. This explanation has the advantage that
the adaptive significance of differences among individuals and the life
history phenomena associated with maintaining the variation are accounted for. Recent experimental studies have shown that temporal variation of the environment leads to greater genetic variability (Beardmore
1970; Powell, 1971).

C. Population Size

The amount of genetic variation that can be maintained in a population depends on the population size. Even without selection, genetic
variation decreases by one-half every $1.4\ N$ generations, where N is
the effective population size (Wallace, 1968). There are two major components that contribute to effective population size: (1) local (neigh-
borhood) population size, and (2) the rate of dispersal of individuals
or gene flow, among local populations. In the subsequent discussion
these components will be considered separately in sections on local patch
size and density and long-distance dispersal by means of planktonic
larvae.

Reduced population size and increased inbreeding enable species to
become relatively specialized and thereby maintain maximum competitive advantage over neighboring species. Species with larger population
sizes are relatively well-adapted to unpredictable events but cannot compete with relatively more specialized species. Lang (1970) provided
an interesting example of competition in corals. She found that slower
growing species inhibit the growth of faster growing species by digesting
the coral tissue. Perhaps it is not surprising that faster growing species
have larger population sizes but are restricted from the most predictable
portions of the environment by the slower growing species.

D. The Mosaic Nature of the Environment

In an environment where the slow-growing species control population
size of the faster growing (and relatively opportunistic) species, succession will proceed very slowly. Any disturbance such as heavy sedimentation or the breaking up or abrasion of coral by wave action, will start

a highly localized succession. The relatively opportunistic species are likely to be the first to settle and grow. With time, a locally high diversity may develop before much competition has occurred (Slobodkin and Sanders, 1969). Eventually, the slower growers would grow over the area reducing local diversity (although over a larger area diversity would be high). Localized denudation of reef surfaces can in this way produce a temporal mosaic of microsuccessional states. In the most predictable areas the relatively opportunistic species will be limited to sites of localized catastrophes, and in the less predictable environments the rare species are excluded and the environment becomes dominated by relative opportunists. The mosaic of coral distributions observed at Heron Island may be interpreted in this way.

E. BIOTIC RELATIONSHIPS

The specializations of reef organisms are most obvious in the many close relationships among species. No quantitative studies exist on the comparative importance of symbiotic and parasitic relationships in predictable and unpredictable environments. In unpredictable environments, predation is likely to be the most frequently encountered type of biotic relationship. Species having a high mortality as an important component of the adaptive strategy are most likely to be prey species. For such species, predation that results in population oscillations may not be disadvantageous (cf. Carson, 1968). Specialized biotic relationships such as the interactions between cleaner fish and their mimics and other fish (Feder, 1966), or the relation of anemone fish to anemones (Mariscal, 1970), are more common on tropical reefs than elsewhere. Similarly, symbiotic and parasitic copepods are more commonly associated with benthic organisms on tropical reefs (Humes and Ho, 1968a–e) than in other benthic communities. Of course, the symbiotic relationship between zooxanthellae and corals is a fundamental feature of tropical reefs. Some other examples of biotic interrelations are given by Gotto (1969) and Utinomi (1954). Since a greater number of species have populations that are relatively constant, there are increased possibilities for biological accommodation (Sanders, 1968).

F. RELATIONSHIPS WITH THE PHYSICAL ENVIRONMENT

In addition to biotic specializations, species may become more specialized on physical features of the environment as, for example, the underside of coral boulders thrown up by storms along parts of the inner edge of reef crests. Such close coupling to topographic features of the environment is possible in only the most predictable circumstances.

II. Measurements of Patterns of Distribution

To learn about patterns of distribution, I studied the larger epifaunal organisms in 3 m × 30 m areas on the inner reef flat, seaward reef margin or reef crest, and reef slope at Heron Island on the Great Barrier Reef. The reefs at Heron Island have been described by Endean *et al.* (1956), Cribb (1966), and Maxwell (1968). All of the study areas were located with the long axis perpendicular to the shore of the island. The reef-flat area was located SE of the Heron Island Research Station, 100 m east of the seawater intake, and 50 m from the outer margin of the gutter separating the intertidal sand and beach rock from the beginning of the subtidal reef flat. The subtidal reef crest area was NNE of the Research Station near the start of a rubble area about 20 m from the outer edge of the reef (the outer margin of the reef that is exposed at very low tides). The reef slope area was SE of the reef-flat plot and extended from about 9 m depth to 15 m depth. In the 2-year period from July, 1967, to July, 1969, the maximum monthly temperature variation on the reef slope was 7.1°C. The maximum daily temperature range was found to be 5.0°C in a 1-year study (P. Woodhead, personal communication; Frank, 1969). The range of temperatures on the reef crest north of the island is somewhat more variable, and the reef flat is the most variable, with a maximum monthly temperature range of 16.6°C in October, 1967. Glynn (1968) has described the effects of temperature extremes on a reef flat and crest in Puerto Rico. As at Heron Island, the reef flat was most variable, the crest less so, and the slope least variable. Manton (1935) noted that the reef flat (called the moat) at Low Isles "provides the greatest extremes of temperature, exposure, etc., on the reef."

Cartesian coordinates of centers and area of coverage were recorded for each individual or colony of the common large species (all species on the reef flat). A pattern analysis (Greig-Smith, 1964) using density data (number of individuals/area) for the ten most common species on the reef crest revealed more than one scale of aggregation for all species. For the analysis, the 30 m transect was divided into 64 lengths 3 m wide (block size 1 = 0.46 m × 3.0 m). Quadrats of successively larger area were used to analyze the different scales or quadrat sizes in which aggregation occurred. Table I shows the block size where

TABLE I
PEAKS INDICATING MAXIMUM MEAN SQUARE AT
SUCCESSIVELY LARGE QUADRAT SIZES[a]

Group	Species	Block size[b]					
		1	2	4	8	16	32
A	*Millepora platyphylla*	P			P		P
	Lunella argyrostoma	P			P		P
B	*Codium spongiosum*		P			P	
	Holothuria leucospilota		P			P	
C	*Halimeda opuntia*		P				P
	Acropora corymbosa		P				P
	Pocillopora damicornis		P				P
D	*Halimeda discoidea*			P		P	P
	Acropora cuneata			P			P
	Xenia elongata			P			P

[a] Method described in Greig-Smith (1964).
[b] P indicates a peak in mean square.

maximum mean squares (equivalent to variance/mean ratios) appear.
There are four types of aggregation indicated by groups A–D. The peak
at the largest block size for most of the species indicates an environmental gradient across the transect, which is probably the result of
larger coral rocks at the seaward end of the transect. The initial peaks
at block sizes 1, 2, and 4 are probably related to the tendency of offspring
to settle near the first colony established in the area. The large scale
(block size 4) of the initial peak of the last three species, or group
D, indicates that these are likely to be the most rapidly propagating
species. They are also the most abundant species in the area. Conversely,
the coral *Millepora platyphylla* and the gastropod *Lunella argyrostoma*
are the least abundant species. The abundance of these species appears
to be relatively high or low in alternate one-eighth transect segments.
Covariance analysis (Greig-Smith, 1964) of pairs of species shows strong
associations between (1) *M. platyphylla* and *L. argyrostoma* at block
sizes 1 and 4 ($p < 0.001$), (2) the holothurian *Holothuria leucospilota*
and the alga *Halimeda discoidea* at block size 8 ($p < 0.01$), and (3)
the hard coral *Acropora cuneata* and the soft coral *Xenia elongata* at
block size 4 ($p < 0.01$). These and all pairs of species within each
group show negative associations at some block sizes and positive associations at others. A close inspection of the data indicates that no biotic
associations are involved. The associations are best interpreted as coinci-

TABLE II

PATTERN ACROSS THE THREE ADJACENT 1 M × 30 M REEF CREST TRANSECTS FOR ALL SPECIES AND COVARIANCE OF TOTAL MEAN SQUARE WITH MEAN SQUARE FOR EACH OF THE THREE ADJACENT 1 M × 30 M TRANSECTS AND COVARIANCE BETWEEN EACH OF THE TRANSECTS

	Block size[a]					
	1	2	4	8	16	32
Pattern						
All species transect 1			P	P		P
All species transect 2				P		P
All species transect 3			P			P
All species transects 1, 2, and 3			P			P
Covariance						
Covariance total spp./tr. 1 spp.	0.67**	0.74**	0.59	+	0.99*	+
Covariance total spp./tr. 2 spp.	0.65*	0.37	0.73	0.83*	+	+
Covariance total spp./tr. 3 spp.	0.35	0.82**	0.54	+	+	+
Tr. 1 spp./tr. 2 spp.	+	−	+	+	+	+
Tr. 1 spp./tr. 3 spp.	+	0.51	−	+	+	+
Tr. 2 spp./tr. 3 spp.	−	+	+	−	+	+

[a] P indicates a peak in mean square. Where figures are given $p < 0.05$, * indicates $p < 0.01$; ** indicates $p < 0.001$; + indicates nonsignificant positive association; − indicates nonsignificant negative association.

dence at the various block sizes of small-scale response to the environment. In a study of four coral species on a reef crest in Barbados, Lewis (1970) also found very patchy distributions using 80 m² quadrats randomly distributed over a large area.

Table II shows heterogeneity across the transect. The differences between the middle 1 × 30 transect and those on either side suggest that similar clumping on several scales of pattern might have been located in a transect parallel with the shore. The covariance shown in part B of Table II confirms the lack of coincidence in pattern between the adjacent meter wide strips. A more detailed pattern analysis using all three areas, and more species, is planned.

In a study of tropical rain forest species, Ashton (1969) used pattern analysis to show that clumping was most pronounced in species lacking or having unreliable means of dispersal. He concluded that populations of these aggregated individuals "will conform to Wright's ideal conditions for rapid and sustained evolution and will be able to evolve into locally specialized habitats." The evidence suggests that this is also true of the highly aggregated reef forms.

Even fish, the most motile reef species, show a remarkable attachment to particular spatial configurations of the environment and tend to be found in the same area for their entire adult life (H. Choat, personal communication). This helps to explain why fish diversity is related to the spatial heterogeneity of the environment (Talbot and Goldman, 1969).

A. CORALS

Table III shows the abundance of the most common species of hard corals (scleractinian corals and the hydrozoan *Millepora platyphylla*) in each of the three areas. The species show much greater dominance on the reef flat than on the crest, with 9 species occurring more than 20 times in the 90 m² study area. On the reef crest only 5 species are

TABLE III

CORALS WITH GREATER THAN 20 COLONIES IN EACH OF THE 3 M × 30 M AREAS

Species	No. of colonies	Total coverage (cm²)	Average coverage (cm²)
Reef flat			
Acropora cuneata	251	14,037	55.9
Acropora squamosa	28	9,701	346.5
Porites andrewsi	88	7,343	83.4
Pocillopora damicornis	52	3,453	66.4
Porites annae	115	2,646	23.0
Goniastrea benhami	48	2,582	53.8
Leptastrea purpurea	210	2,273	10.8
Acropora pulchra	23	1,418	61.7
Porites lutea	35	732	20.9
Reef crest			
Acropora cuneata	70	4,509	64.4
Acropora corymbosa	60	5,512	91.9
Millepora platyphylla	23	1,620	70.4
Pocillopora damicornis	79	1,379	17.5
Stylophora pistillata	36	419	11.6
Reef slope			
Acropora formosa	77	196,897	2,557.1
Montipora sp. A	123	65,676	534.0
Acropora hyacinthus	45	36,090	802.0
Seriatopora hystrix	86	5,263	61.2
Pocillopora damicornis	47	2,247	47.8
Montipora sp. B	109	1,930	17.7
Stylophora pistillata	32	919	28.7

as common, and none is represented by more than 70 colonies. The data for the reef slope are less easily interpreted since the colonies of the three most common species, *Montipora* sp. A, *Montipora* sp. B, and *Acropora formosa*, and possibly *Acropora hyacinthus*, each appear to have been one or two large colonies. Other species have settled between the branches and in dead portions of these large colonies. If these species are. considered as only a few colonies, then 4 species have an abundance of greater than 20. These results suggest a larger effective population size for the reef-flat species than for either the crest or slope species. The large coral heads (bommies) of the slope would have a very low effective population size.

A complete inventory of the corals was made in the 90 m² reef-flat transect and 24 species were found (913 colonies). Although all species were not surveyed in the crest transect, a single m² quadrat nearby had 13 species (one-third coverage, 66 colonies). Transects larger than 3 m × 30 m are unlikely to add significantly to the number of species on the reef flat, but this is not true of either the reef crest or reef slope. The line transect method using very long transects would be most appropriate for comparing diversities in the three areas. Loya and Slobodkin (1971) used this method and found that diversity increased with depth (and increased environmental predictability) on reefs near Elath in the Red Sea. The reef slope at Elath has many relatively small colonies. At Heron Island the existence of many very large colonies and a number of isolated individuals of rare species (the large coral bommies) makes the sampling problems on the reef slope more difficult. A 1-yard wide traverse across the leeward reef at Low Isles yielded a maximum number of species on the flat of 7 spp./yard² (10 colonies/yard²), 14 spp./yard² (17 colonies/yard²) near the crest (the actual crest was somewhat different from Heron Island) and 21 spp./yard² (29 colonies) at 3–5 m depth on the reef slope (Manton, 1935). Although calculations are not possible with the data presented, the diversities may be highest on the reef slope at Low Isles.

Table IV shows a comparison of abundance, coverage, and average colony size in each of the three areas for hard corals, soft corals, and an alga, which are common in more than one area. The two corals, *Pocillopora damicornis* and *Stylophora pistillata*, and the alga, *Chlorodesmis comosa*, are common to the three areas and have smaller colonies on the crest. The two soft corals common to the reef crest and reef slope also show smaller colony size on the crest. Only the flat encrusting varieties such as *Acropora cuneata* and *Millepora platyphylla* have similar colony sizes on both the crest and slope. This

TABLE IV

Number of Colonies, Total Area Covered, and Average Area Covered for Each Species Common in More Than One of the 3 M × 30 M Study Areas on the Reef Flat, Reef Crest, and Reef Slope

Species	No. of colonies			Area (cm²)			Average coverage/colony (cm²)		
	Flat	Crest	Slope	Flat	Crest	Slope	Flat	Crest	Slope
Pocillopora damicornis	52	79	47	3453	1379	2247	66.4	17.5	47.8
Stylophora pistillata	8	34	32	166	419	919	20.8	12.3	28.7
Acropora cuneata	251	70	—	14,037	4509	—	55.9	64.4	—
Millepora platyphylla	5	23	—	312	1620	—	62.4	70.4	—
Palythoe sp.	—	29	3	—	392	86	—	13.5	28.7
Alcyonium sp.	—	7	9	—	198	392	—	28.3	43.6
Chlorodesmis comosa	61	1287	255	514	9193	4213	8.4	7.1	16.5

suggests that the small average colony size is the result of destruction of colonies by wave action and abrasion before they reach a large size. All of these species that have a smaller colony size on the reef crest also consistently have a greater number of colonies there. These most common species may be thought of as the relatively opportunistic species favored in the unpredictable parts of the reef. Heavy wave action in storms and cyclones (cf. Glynn et al., 1964) results in a mosaic of microsuccessional states, with some areas frequently scoured by rocks occupied by the more opportunistic species and other areas where more specialized species are favored. A completely denuded section of reef may develop a particularly high diversity over a small area. The relatively opportunistic species are the first to settle, but a great variety of species may have settled before any are eliminated by competitive exclusion (Slobodkin and Sanders, 1969). Lang's work (1970), indicating that slow-growing species are superior competitors, suggests that the winnowing process may be very slow. This process is likely to result in a uniform diversity over the affected area. The large scale variation in reef topography results from the differences in lengths of time following localized destruction of the reef surface. The temporal mosaic of microsuccessional states develops on several scales of pattern depending on the size of the areas affected. The most specialized species survive because there are always some areas that have not been disturbed. The best examples are the large coral heads, or bommies, which are probably hundreds of years old. These species may occasionally occur in disturbed areas but only because some portion of their environment is highly predictable over long periods of time. The adaptive strategies of species evolve over very large areas on a time scale in which small scale successional effects may be of little importance.

B. GASTROPODS

Kohn (1968) reported that in species of the genus *Conus* high population density is associated with low species diversity in intertidal rock areas, whereas in subtidal reef-crest areas species are less abundant and a greater diversity is found. This diversity–density relationship appears to be true of all gastropods at Heron Island, with the reef flat intermediate between the intertidal beach rock and the reef crest.

Frank (1969), in a study of growth rates and longevity at Heron Island, marked many common gastropods in these three areas north and south of the island. The only common species excluded from the study because of the thickness or roughness of the shell were *Haliotis asinina* and *Lunella argyrostoma* on the reef crest and *Planaxis sulcatus* and *Cerithium moniliferum* on the intertidal beach rock. Of the species studied by Frank, the intertidal species *Nerita albicilla* had the highest density of 1.6/m² in randomly spaced quadrats. I estimated that *P. sulcatus* and *C. moniliferum* were also very abundant at the eastern and western ends of the beach rock. These species have a very patchy distribution with maximum densities of 997/m² (*P. sulcatus*) and 1246/m² (*C. moniliferum*). Several 1 m vertical transects were taken across the intertidal beach rock with maximum numbers of 1198 *P. sulcatus* and 2137 *C. moniliferum* per transect. Careful examination of the whole length of the Heron Island intertidal beach rock yielded only seven species of gastropods.

In the much smaller 3 m × 30 m area of the reef crest, 17 species were collected. Table V gives the abundance of each species. These results agree well with those of Frank who found a maximum for any of the reef crest species of 4 individuals per 10 m². The sandy areas of the reef flat are less favorable for gastropods, and the 3 m × 30 m area yielded only one stromb and one cowrie. The stromb *Strombus luhuanus* is more common on the reef flat south of the island near

TABLE V

NUMBERS OF INDIVIDUALS OF GASTROPODS COLLECTED FROM THE 3 M × 30 M
AREA ON THE REEF CREST

Species	No. of individuals
Lunella argyrostoma	53
Monetaria annulus	5
Trochus maculatus	5
Pleuroploca filamentosa	4
Trochus pyramis	3
Astraea rhodostoma	3
Rhizoconus miles	2
Conus suturatus	2
Conus catus	2
Conus lividus	1
Conus coronatus	1
Ravitrona caputserpentis	1
Lunella necnivosus	1
Haliotis asinina	1
Mancinella tuberosa	1
Latirolagena smaragdula	1
Peristernia australiensis	1

the gutter just below the beach rock. *S. luhuanus* reaches its greatest density north of the island in a kidney-shaped patch, which has its long axis running east-west nearly the length of the island. The density data of Frank (1969) (0.3 individuals/m²) gives an estimate of population size in this patch of about 45,000. The most common reef crest species, *Monetaria annulus* and *Lunella argyrostoma,* are restricted to areas with loose coral rocks. This fact, coupled with Frank's observation of very restricted movements in *M. annulus,* suggests a much smaller effective population size for the reef-crest species than for the reef-flat or intertidal species. The small number of juveniles (<2%) in the *M. annulus* populations and, more particularly, the highly localized and sporadic recruitment in *Trochus, Conus, Vasum,* and *Latirolagena* indicates that the small effective population sizes represented by the adult populations are unlikely to be greatly affected by larval dispersal (Frank, 1969).

No gastropods were seen in the slope 3 m × 30 m transect, but the rarer species of molluscivorous and piscivorous cones are most likely to be found on the slope. Thus, as with the corals, species with the most specialized habitats may only be found on the relatively predictable slope.

Highly specialized species characteristic of predictable environments may also be expected to be long-lived (Frank, 1968). At Heron Island all of the species studied by Frank were found to live several years or more. There is a suggestion that the more common species have shorter average life spans, but the data are not conclusive (Frank, 1969). As Frank pointed out, even without the gastropod data, the slow growth and large size of massive corals support the generalization that reef forms are long-lived.

C. Algae

The bright green alga *Chlorodesmis comosa* shows the same trends in abundance as the relatively opportunistic corals, *Pocillopora damicornis* and *Stylophora pistillata.* The macroscopic algae as a group, excluding the very small algal fur species (Cribb, 1966), are more abundant on the reef flat than on the reef crest. The reef-slope algae are confined to isolated patches where some disturbance such as broken coral branches is evident. The relationship of the algae to relatively disturbed environments is supported by the occurrence of large fields of algae on the windward reef slope which receives heavy wave action. Table VI lists the species in order of abundance. All species with an

TABLE VI

Most Common Algae from the Reef Flat, Reef Crest, and Reef Slope[a]

Reef flat	Reef crest
Sargassum crassifolium	*Turbinaria ornata*
Sargassum polycystum	*Chlorodesmis comosa*
Chnoospora implexa	*Halimeda opuntia*
Hydroclathrus clathratus	*Halimeda discoidea*
Padina gymnospora	*Codium spongiosum*
Pocockiella variegata	Reef slope
Halimeda discoidea	*Pocockiella variegata*
Halimeda opuntia	*Chlorodesmis comosa*
Caulerpa racemosa	
Boodlea composita	
Chlorodesmis comosa	

[a] Listed in order of abundance.

abundance approaching that of *Chlorodesmis comosa* on the reef flat are listed. These results agree well with previous studies by Cribb (1966) at Heron Island. The algae near the crest tend to be found in the rubble areas and the most favorable substrata on the reef flat are the burned-off tops of coral heads. The abundance of algae depends on the number of spaces available to opportunists.

On the reef flat, algal species abundance has been determined in randomly distributed quadrats in a 100 m × 100 m grid on the inner reef flat SSE of the Heron Island Research Station. The area was sampled by measuring coverage in each 10 cm × 10 cm subdivision of a permanent 3 m × 3 m quadrat and randomly placed 2 m × 2 m quadrats. A total of 30–37 meter squares were studied in each of the sampling periods in April, August, and November. All quadrats were used to estimate total coverage of rocky substratum. About 28.0% of the total surface area consisted of coral rock. Table VII gives the percentage of coverage of each of the three most common species during the three sampling periods. Total coverage per hectare is calculated from the proportion of rocky surfaces covered using 28% rock coverage for all three sampling periods. Collections of *Sargassum* spp. for wet and dry weights were taken from three m² quadrats in which both algal and rock coverage had been estimated. Average wet weight was 28.9 gm/100 cm² coverage (range 27.2–30.1), and the average dry weight was 6.1 gm/100 cm² coverage (range 5.9–6.3). The turnover of *Sargassum* spp. amounts to about 1.1×10^6 gm/ha/yr (1835 m²/ha/yr). With *Chnoospora implexa* and *Hydroclathrus clathratus* the turnover is 705 m² and

TABLE VII

PERCENTAGE COVERAGE OF ROCK SURFACES AND TOTAL COVERAGE
IN A 100 M × 100 M AREA DURING TWO SUMMER PERIODS AND
ONE WINTER PERIOD ON THE INNER REEF FLAT

	Permanent 9 m² quadrat (% rocky surface)	Total area (% rocky surface)	Total coverage (m²/ha)
April (37 m²)			
Sargassum spp.	76.8	75.7	2117.3
Chnoospora implexa	<0.1	0.4	11.2
Hydroclathrus clathratus	0	0.1	2.8
August (34 m²)			
Sargassum spp.	11.3	10.1	282.5
Chnoospora implexa	33.0	25.6	716.0
Hydroclathrus clathratus	17.7	21.8	609.8
November (30 m²)			
Sargassum spp.	67.0	69.7	1949.5
Chnoospora implexa	11.6	19.9	556.6
Hydroclathrus clathratus	0.1	2.4	67.1

607 m² coverage per year. Although only wet weights were measured, the thick growths of C. implexa have nearly twice the weight of Sargassum per area, suggesting that Chnoospora and Hydroclathrus contribute at least as much to yearly turnover as Sargassum. The minimum yield from these three species is, therefore, about 2×10^6 gm/ha/yr. Most of these algae become detached with the change of season and are transported to the reef slope. In areas other than the reef flat there is very little seasonal turnover of algae. Such excess production of organic matter may be a characteristic of the most opportunistic species.

D. INFAUNAL ASSEMBLAGES FROM CORAL ROCK

In addition to the conspicuous epifauna, reefs support an abundant and varied infauna. The dead parts of corals or coral rock contain a fauna that is, for the most part, undescribed. The first study of the extensive community associated with the dead portions of corals was made by McCloskey (1970) on *Oculina arbuscula,* a species from North Carolina which is not a reef-builder. I studied the polychaete component of a similar community from the dead portions of coral heads from Heron Island.

The coral heads were collected by covering each head with a muslin bag before removal from the substratum, so that some small epifaunal species may have been included. After collection, the living and dead portions were weighed separately and then broken into small pieces. As the coral was broken up it was repeatedly washed over a 0.25 mm screen. All material retained by the screen was carefully sorted under a microscope.

A single head of *Pocillopora damicornis* from 5 m depth on the reef slope south of the Research Station weighing 4.7 kg (1.6 kg living) contained 1441 polychaete individuals belonging to 103 species. Syllids were by far the most abundant family with 921 individuals. Capitellids were next most abundant with 102 individuals followed by terebellids (68), nereids (62), lumbrinereids (56), sabellids (44), and phyllodocids (32). Most of the larger individuals belonged to the Eunicidae. Approximately two-thirds of the macrofaunal animals removed from the coral were polychaetes. The other major groups, in order of abundance, were tanaids, amphipods, and isopods. A number of sipunculids, oligochaetes, decapods, and ophiuroids were also present.

The number of species from this single coral head is surprising when it is considered that extensive collections at Eniwetok Atoll have yielded only 97 species (Hartman, 1954; Reish, 1968). In a study of a number of areas in the Solomon Islands, Gibbs (1971) obtained 2000 individuals belonging to 220 species. The only other quantitative study is that of McCloskey (1970). In a shallow subtidal area at Cape Lookout jetty off North Carolina (lat. 34°37′N), heads containing 797 and 1517 individuals contained 30 and 37 species, respectively. Heads in deeper water (about 15 m) contained 8267 and 3916 individuals and 50 and 57 species, respectively. These results provide further support for the generalization that tropical areas support particularly high diversities of species. An estimate of species diversity of polychaetes using Sanders' rarefaction method gave a diversity for the head of *P. damicornis* equal to that measured from the most diverse sample of both polychaetes and bivalves collected from soft sediments in a shallow tropical area (Sanders, 1968).

E. Differences among Taxa

As has already been shown, the abundance spectrum of the major reef taxa varies from area to area. If abundance can be equated with degree of opportunism, then the most opportunistic corals are *Acropora cuneata, Leptastrea purpurea, Porites annae,* and *Pocillopora damicornis.* The commonness of these species does not nearly approach the abundances of the more ubiquitous algae, which are *Sargassum crassifolium,*

Sargassum polycystum, Chnoospora implexa, and *Hydroclathrus clathratus.* Of the common large reef animals, echinoderms and mollusks rank next in maximum abundance. The holothurian *Holothuria atra* was the most common echinoderm on the reef flat. Although its density is 2.9/10 m², compared with 3.2/10 m² for the most common gastropod, *Strombus luhuanus* (Frank, 1969), *H. atra* is likely to have a larger breeding population size since it is evenly distributed over a much larger area than the stromb. Some of the reef-crest species also reach high densities but are common only in small areas.

The number of individuals required for survival in the most exposed portions of the reef flat depends on the regulatory abilities of an average individual. If every individual in the population can withstand the whole range of changes in the environment, then the species can survive with a small population size. Algae are likely to have less individual homeostatic ability than corals, corals less than echinoderms, and echinoderms less than gastropods. The ability of the average individual to withstand changes in the environment is not simply physiological tolerance. Behavioral adaptations that enable all the individuals of a species to avoid the extremes of the environment would contribute to this resistance.

In the most biologically diverse areas we would expect the most opportunistic species to be excluded since they could not compete with the more specialized species. This is likely to be the reason algae are excluded from areas of maximum coral growth. Manton (1935) found evidence to suggest that the abundance of algae was inversely related to the variety of corals.

III. Life History

A. Reproduction

There have been a number of discussions of the adaptive significance of sexual and asexual reproduction (Crow and Kimura, 1965; Maynard Smith, 1968, 1971), but little attempt has been made to relate the importance of these two types of reproduction to the range of species found in different environments. Information available on reproduction on coral reefs suggests that asexual reproduction may be of greater importance in this environment. The common algae reproduce primarily asexually and asexual reproduction is of obvious importance in corals (although the frequency of sexual reproduction is unknown). The overwhelmingly abundant polychaete family on coral reefs, the Syllidae, is well known for its high incidence of asexual reproduction compared with other families. Many of the individuals collected could be seen to be budding. All species of the most common tropical genus of asteroids, *Linckia,* are known for their ability to reproduce asexually (Edmondson, 1935; Hyman, 1955). Asexual reproduction is also a common phenomenon in tropical ophiuroids and holothurians (Grassé, 1948; Swan, 1966). The only two asexually reproducing sipunculids are also tropical species (Rice, 1970).

Asexual reproduction is likely to be important in species that need less genetic variation for survival. Maynard Smith (1971) considered two principal reasons for sexual reproduction: "it accelerates evolutionary adaptation" and "by producing more variable progeny it increases the chance of producing some offspring of very high fitness." These are the same two arguments that may be given for maintaining a high degree of genetic variation through large population size. Maynard Smith argued for the traditional view that populations with sexual reproduction (or with higher genetic variability) can evolve faster (Fisher, 1930). He contended that sex would be of immediate advantage only in instances where the environment was unpredictable to the extent that "correlations between selectively relevant features of the environment commonly change sign between one generation and the next." This is precisely what occurs in unpredictable environments as I have defined them.

The theory of genetic variation as a mechanism to maintain maximum evolutionary potential may be rejected using another line of evidence. Stehli *et al.* (1969) and Stehli and Wells (1971) have found that rates of evolution are higher in the tropics (including coral reefs) despite life histories that might be thought to retard rates of evolution according to Maynard Smith's first hypothesis. If the higher genetic variabilities conferred on temperate populations through large population size (as well as the high incidence of sexual reproduction) do not result in increased rates of evolution, then the short-term or second explanation is favored, i.e., high genetic variability increases the possibility of some individuals being highly adapted to the unpredictable circumstances encountered each generation.

B. Larval Dispersal

Length of life, mortality, and conditions for settlement of reef larvae are poorly known. These areas of ignorance are the main obstacles to an understanding of life histories of these organisms. Large numbers of reef species have planktonic larval dispersal. In less predictable environments, larvae can colonize unexploited areas and act as agents for free gene exchange between widely separated populations.

High larval densities are found in the plankton in unpredictable environments (Schram, 1970). Many reef species do not regularly produce large numbers of larvae. For example, attempts to collect coral larvae have not been very successful, and only a few species are known to produce larvae regularly (Marshall and Stephenson, 1933; Edmondson, 1946; Atoda, 1947a,b, 1951a,b). Most of these are commonly found in the most unpredictable parts of reefs. This limited information, together with the observation of sporadic settlement for gastropods (Frank, 1969), suggest that larvae may serve a somewhat different function on reefs.

Scheltema (1972) found that tropical species tend to have long-lived larvae. Those species known to have very long-lived larvae (42–320 days), occurring in plankton collections from stations throughout the North Atlantic, were mostly reef species (Scheltema, 1968, 1971). The zooanthid larvae of *Palythoa* live long enough to cross the Atlantic. All larvae of the ten gastropod species considered in detail have small adult populations in comparison with temperate forms. Certain snails such as *Phillipia krebsii* have very specialized habitats (Robertson *et al.*, 1970). Rather than serving to increase effective population size, the dispersal phase in such forms may enable the species to locate the widely separated features of the environment on which they may be specialized. This kind of dispersal would be especially important for a species associated with another species of narrow distribution.

IV. Toxicity and Color Polymorphism in Common Reef Species

The idea that species cannot attain large population size because of the intense predation pressure in relatively predictable environments (Paine, 1966; Janzen, 1970) is not consistent with the many means by which abundant species avoid predation. The majority of toxic invertebrates are limited to the tropical and warm temperate regions (88% of the echinoderms and 80% of the gastropods according to Halstead, 1965). There is insufficient information to say whether species in which the toxicity constitutes a defense mechanism are the most common reef species.

One of the conspicuous features of coral reefs that contributes to the impression of variety is the color polymorphism in species such as the bivalve *Tridacna crocea* and the polychaete *Spirobranchus giganteus*.

In the Red Sea reefs near Elath, the morph ratios of S. *giganteus* were the same at widely separated collecting areas, at different depths, and in different species of coral (Grassle, in preparation). In these species conspicuous polymorphism appears to be a means for avoiding predation, with selection favoring rare against common morphs. The variety of colors prevents predators from forming a search image for the whole species. In fish, color polymorphism may be more important for individual recognition within the species.

The phenomenon has been demonstrated for the North Atlantic brittle star *Ophiopholis aculeata* and the clam *Donax variabilis* (Moment, 1962). Color polymorphism as a means of avoiding predation has also evolved in the Red Sea gastropods *Nerita forskalii* and *Nerita polita* (Safriel, 1969), as well as Heron Island species of *Nerita*. Owen (1969), from studies of African insects and land snails, noted that "conspicuous colour polymorphism tends to occur much more frequently in common terrestrial animals than in rarer species." The reef species exhibiting color polymorphism are generally the more common, relatively opportunistic species.

V. Conclusions

Reef variety results from specialization. Relatively specialized species have small effective population sizes, are generally long-lived, and have low reproductive rates. Since larval dispersal is important in locating specialized habitats, the reproductive rate is best measured in terms of larval recruitment, which may be infrequent and sporadic. The life history characteristics of specialized species result in increased homoselection (Carson, 1959) or inbreeding. Under optimal circumstances, single genotypes are favored and asexual reproduction plays an important role. Homoselected or specialist species are likely to have increased rates of speciation (Carson, 1959), and the paleontological data for this conclusion have been presented (Stehli *et al.*, 1969; Stehli and Wells, 1971).

Less predictable areas on reefs have relatively opportunistic species. They are species that adapt to the environment through short-term selection measured by rates of mortality. All species utilize this mechanism of adaptation to a certain extent, but the more opportunistic species maintain higher degrees of genetic variability through increased effective population size. In this way, they can adapt to a wider range of unpredictable conditions.

Specializations may be on biotic or physical characteristics of the environment. Patterns of distribution depend on the immediate history of the area considered, and on the long-term evolutionary history that molded the spectrum of adaptive strategies found throughout the area. Zones of the reef have been compared in terms of the predictability of the environment. Within these zones, a temporal mosaic exists as a result of different time spans elapsing after the creation of small open spaces following disturbances. The size of these areas and how frequently they appear are measures of environmental unpredictability. The relatively opportunistic species are best able to respond to appearance of these spaces by rapidly establishing themselves, but subsequently these species are not able to compete with more specialized species.

A framework has been presented for relating features of the coral reef environment to one another. In all instances the data are insufficient. Hopefully, this discussion will stimulate more detailed quantitative studies of the natural history of reef organisms.

Acknowledgments

E. Hegerl and R. Robertson helped to collect data on the 3 m × 30 m slope transect. A student group from the University of Queensland led by M. Thorne assisted with the estimates of numbers of beach rock gastropods. I am indebted to J. Walker of the CSIRO Woodland Ecology Unit for the pattern analysis of common reef crest species. The work was greatly aided by identifications of algae by A. Cribb and corals by P. Woodhead. I am grateful to the University of Queensland and the Great Barrier Reef Committee for assisting in a number of ways and providing facilities during the course of the research. The work has benefited greatly from discussions with H. Choat, J. Connell, P. Frank, H. Sanders, W. Stephenson, and P. Woodhead. Y. Loya, H. Sanders, and A. Scheltema read and commented on the manuscript. J. Grassle assisted with all phases of the work. The Red Sea reef observations were accomplished with support from the Hebrew University-Smithsonian Institution grant to study "Biota of the Red Sea and Eastern Mediterranean" awarded to W. Aron and D. Por. The research in Australia was done during the tenure of a U.S. Government Grant awarded under the Fulbright-Hays Act, and was aided by grants from the Society of the Sigma Xi and The Cocos Foundation. Compilation of the data and preparation of the manuscript were supported by National Science Foundation Grant GA-31105.

References

Ashton, P. S. (1969). Biol. J. Linn Soc. 1, 155–196.
Atoda, K. (1947a). Sci. Rep. Tohuku Univ., Ser. 4 18, 24–47.
Atoda, K. (1947b). Sci. Rep. Tohuku Univ., Ser. 4 18, 48–64.
Atoda, K. (1951a). J. Morphol. 89, 1–15.
Atoda, K. (1951b). J. Morphol. 89, 17–35.

Beardmore, J. (1970). *In* "Essays in Evolution and Genetics in Honor of Th. Dobzhansky" (M. Hecht and W. Steere, eds.), pp. 299–314. Appleton, New York.

Carson, H. L. (1959). *Cold Spring Harbor Symp. Quant. Biol.* **24**, 87–105.

Carson, H. L. (1968). *In* "Population Biology and Evolution" (R. C. Lewontin, ed.), pp. 123–137. Syracuse Univ. Press, Syracuse.

Cribb, A. B. (1966). *Univ. Queensl. Pap.* **1**, 1–23.

Crow, J. F., and Kimura, M. (1965). *Amer. Natur.* **99**, 439–450.

Edmondson, C. H. (1935). *Occas. Pap. Bishop Mus.* **11**, 1–29.

Edmondson, C. H. (1946). *Occas. Pap. Bishop Mus.* **18**, 283–304.

Endean, R., Stephenson, W., and Kenny, R. (1956). *Aust. J. Mar. Freshwater Res.* **7**, 317–342.

Feder, H. M. (1966). *In* "Symbiosis" (S. M. Henry, ed.), Vol. 1, pp. 327–380. Academic Press, New York.

Fisher, R. A. (1930). "The Genetical Theory of Natural Selection." Oxford Univ. Press (Clarendon), London and New York.

Frank, P. W. (1968). *Ecology* **49**, 355–357.

Frank, P. W. (1969). *Oecologia* **2**, 232–250.

Gibbs, P. E. (1971). *Bull. Brit. Mus.* (*Natur. Hist.*), *Zool.* **21**, 99–211.

Glynn, P. W. (1968). *Mar. Biol.* **1**, 226–243.

Glynn, P. W., Almodóvar, L. R., and González, J. G. (1964). *Carib. J. Sci.* **4**, 335–345.

Gotto, R. V. (1969). "Marine Animals, Partnerships and other Associations." Amer. Elsevier, New York.

Grassé, P.-P., ed. (1948). "Traité de Zoologie," Vol. XI, pp. 231–232 and 260–261. Masson, Paris.

Grassle, J. F. (1972). *Arch. Oceanogr. Limnol.* (in press).

Greig-Smith, P. (1964). "Quantitative Plant Ecology," pp. 54–93 and 110–111. Butterworth, London.

Haldane, J. B. S., and Jayakar, S. D. (1963). *J. Genet.* **58**, 237–242.

Halstead, B. W. (1965). "Poisonous and Venomous Marine Animals of the World," Vol. I. U.S. Govt. Printing Office, Washington, D.C.

Hartman, O. (1954). *U.S., Geol. Surv., Prof. Pap.* **260-Q**, 617–644.

Humes, A. G., and Ho, J.-S. (1968a). *Bull. Mus. Comp. Zool., Harvard Univ.* **136**, 353–413.

Humes, A. G., and Ho, J.-S. (1968b). *Bull. Mus. Comp. Zool., Harvard Univ.* **136**, 415–459.

Humes, A. G., and Ho, J.-S. (1968c). *Proc. Biol. Soc. Wash.* **81**, 635–692.

Humes, A. G., and Ho, J.-S. (1968d). *Proc. Biol. Soc. Wash.* **81**, 693–750.

Humes, A. G., and Ho, J.-S. (1968e). *Proc. U.S. Nat. Mus.* **125**, 1–41.

Hyman, L. H. (1955). "The Invertebrates," Vol. IV, pp. 310–313. McGraw-Hill, New York.

Janzen, D. H. (1967). *Amer. Natur.* **101**, 233–249.

Janzen, D. H. (1970). *Amer. Natur.* **104**, 501–528.

Kimura, M. (1968). *Nature* (*London*) **217**, 624–626.

Kohn, A. J. (1968). *Ecology* **49**, 1046–1061.

Kohn, A. J. (1971). *Limnol. Oceanogr.* **16**, 332–348.

Lang, J. C. (1970). Ph.D. Thesis, Yale University, New Haven, Connecticut.

Lewis, J. B. (1970). *Nature* (*London*) **227**, 1158–1159.

Lewontin, R. C. (1966). *BioScience* **16**, 25–27.
Loya, Y., and Slobodkin, L. B. (1971). *Symp. Zool. Soc. London* **28**, 117–140.
MacArthur, R., Recher, H., and Cody, M. (1966). *Amer. Natur.* **100**, 319–332.
McCloskey, L. R. (1970). *Int. Rev. Gesamten Hydrobiol.* **55**, 13–81.
Manton, S. M. (1935). *Sci. Rep. Gt. Barrier Reef Exped.* 3, 273–312.
Mariscal, R. N. (1970). *Univ. Calif., Berkeley, Publ. Zool.* **91**,1–43.
Marshall, S. M., and Stephenson, T. A. (1933). *Sci. Rep. Gt. Barrier Reef Exped.* 3, 219–245.
Maxwell, W. G. H. (1968). "Atlas of the Great Barrier Reef," pp. 91–151. Elsevier, Amsterdam.
Maynard Smith, J. (1968). *Amer. Natur.* **102**, 469–473.
Maynard Smith, J. (1971). *J. Theor. Biol.* **30**, 319–335.
Moment, G. B. (1962). *Science* **136**, 262–263.
Owen, D. F. (1969). *J. Zool.* **159**, 79–96.
Paine, R. T. (1966). *Amer. Natur.* **100**, 65–76.
Powell, J. R. (1971). *Science* **174**, 1035–1036.
Prakash, S., Lewontin, R., and Hubby, C. (1969). *Genetics* **61**, 841–858.
Reish, D. J. (1968). *Pac. Sci.* **22**, 208–231.
Rice, M. E. (1970). *Science* **167**, 1618–1620.
Robertson, R., Scheltema, R. S., and Adams, F. W. (1970). *Pac. Sci.* **24**, 55–65.
Safriel, V. (1969). *Isr. J. Zool.* **18**, 205–231.
Sanders, H. L. (1968). *Amer. Natur.* **102**, 243–282.
Scheltema, R. S. (1968). *Nature (London)* **217**, 1159–1162.
Scheltema, R. S. (1971). *Biol. Bull.* **140**, 284–322.
Scheltema, R. S. (1972). *Proc. Eur. Symp. Mar. Biol., 4th, 1969* (in press).
Schram, T. A. (1970). *Nytt. Mag. Zool.* **18**, 1–21.
Slobodkin, L. B., and Sanders, H. L. (1969). *Brookhaven Symp. Biol.* **22**, 82–93.
Stehli, F. G., and Wells, J. W. (1971). *Syst. Zool.* **20**, 115–126.
Stehli, F. G., Douglas, R. G., and Newell, N. D. (1969). *Science* **164**, 947–949.
Swan, E. F. (1966). *In* "Physiology of Echinodermata" (R. A. Boolootian, ed.), pp. 397–434. Wiley, New York.
Talbot, F. H., and Gòldman, B. (1969). *Symp. Corals Coral Reefs, Mandapam Camp. India (M.B.A.I.), 1969* Abstr. 33, p. 24.
Utinomi, H. (1954). *Proc. Pac. Sci. Congr., 7th, 1949,* Vol. 4, pp. 533–536.
Wallace, B. (1968). "Topics in Population Genetics," pp. 99–117. Norton, New York.

9

ASPECTS OF THE ECOLOGY OF CORAL REEFS IN THE WESTERN ATLANTIC REGION*

Peter W. Glynn

I. Introduction

The interest generated over the past decade in the tropical waters of the western Atlantic Ocean has resulted in numerous significant insights regarding our understanding of coral reef communities in this region. One result that has emerged is that several generally recognized views of reef structure and function are in need of revision and others will require substantiation if they are to be of any further use. To a large extent, models of Atlantic coral reefs have been fashioned from studies in the Bahamas and Florida, areas near the marginal limits of coral reef development. This has lead to the conclusion that Atlantic reefs are poorly developed, have a low rate of constructional growth

---

* This chapter is dedicated to the memory of Thomas F. Goreau, who contributed so substantially to our knowledge of coral reef biology.

and therefore represent weak counterparts of Indo-Pacific reef communities. Recent studies in the Caribbean Sea, where the marine climate is more nearly comparable with that of other regions in the lower latitudes, reveal a greater unity in the organization of these ecosystems than had previously been supposed. To focus briefly on this subject, it is necessary to cite only a few examples at this time.

The meticulous exploration of Jamaican reefs by Goreau and associates has revealed the presence of 62 species of scleractinian corals (Goreau and Wells, 1967), greatly exceeding the former maximum number of 42 species reported from a single tropical American area, namely, Florida (Vaughan, 1916a; Smith, 1948, *in* Goreau, 1959). In terms of coral diversity, Goreau and Wells believed that the north shore Jamaican reefs compare favorably with many Indo-Pacific reefs. Studies of the morphology of coral reefs over wider geographic areas along western Atlantic shores have demonstrated that the generalized plan of reef structure for the Bahamas (Wells, 1957; Newell, 1959; Yonge, 1963) does not always represent an adequate description of reefs in this region.

Cognizance should be taken of the following findings: (1) subaerial exposure of reef flats is commonplace (Glynn, 1968); (2) calcareous algae are often an important element on reefs (Goreau, 1963; Boyd *et al.*, 1963; Kempf and Laborel, 1968) and can even form an algal ridge under appropriate conditions; (3) the structural framework of modern reefs can be massive, leading to the development of thick deposits (up to 10 m) over basement rock; (4) reef-building does often occur along the margins of continental (British Honduras) and insular shelves (Jamaica: Goreau and Wells, 1967; Lesser Antilles: Macintyre, 1967); and (5) flourishing coral communities occur to depths of 70 m (Goreau and Wells, 1967). Improved methods for measuring coral growth rates (Shinn, 1966) have shown that these were probably underestimated in Florida and the Bahamas (Vaughan, 1916a). The growth of corals in the Caribbean Sea, compared with the earlier values which have been frequently quoted as typical for this region, was found to exceed that of their northerly congeners by factors of approximately 3 and 4 for massive and ramose species, respectively (Lewis *et al.*, 1968). This constructional activity rivals the most vigorous growth reported for Indo-Pacific reef corals. Finally, it is now evident that the supposed virtual immunity of corals from predators[*] (e.g., Yonge, 1963) no longer applies for many widely separated Atlantic reef areas. A number of different vertebrate and invertebrate predators, some feeding

---

[*] For convenience, a predator is herein defined as an animal that usually consumes or otherwise kills entire polyps.

habitually on live coral, is currently known. Much of the present chapter will be devoted to the above-mentioned subjects, especially in the context of an ecologically oriented survey of the nature of western Atlantic coral reef communities.

Other areas of inquiry currently receiving greater attention are the contribution of plankton to the benthos and the interactions of reef populations as agents modifying community structure. The vigorous controversy relating to the trophic relations of coral reef communities, i.e., their degree of autotrophy, has found substance in investigations which still claim conflicting results. For example, some data indicate that plankton is of little importance, whereas other lines of evidence suggest a substantial utilization of this resource. The richness, maturity, and apparent stability of coral reef ecosystems are all attributes related to complex and relatively well-regulated interactions. [Considering the influence of sea-level changes on coral reef development—modern Atlantic reefs are no older than ca. 5000 years (Goreau, 1969)—the marked damage caused by storms and the important effects of *Acanthaster* in certain areas of the Pacific, it is likely that coral reef communities undergo severe perturbations and successional changes more frequently than is often assumed.] The influence of several kinds of biotic control on the structure of reef assemblages, e.g., their composition, spacing, patterns of growth, and rates of accretion, are now receiving rigorous documentation. Herbivorous invertebrates and fishes can produce very marked effects over short periods of time. A conspicuous strip of sand separating fringing reefs and grass flats, for example, was shown experimentally to be the result of intensive fish grazing (Randall, 1965). An example of an interference strategy employed for reducing competition for space is the recent discovery of extracoelenteric feeding exhibited by many solitary, massive, and branching corals, whereby subordinate species are excluded from the area of influence of superior predators (Lang, 1970). Many different sessile populations offer evidence of direct competition for space through interference interactions in conformity with Miller's (1969) model. In short, it appears that community structure in warm seas is regulated to a greater extent by biotic factors than is the case in colder waters (Jones, 1950); therefore, this aspect will require careful attention.

While major emphasis will be placed on the hermatypic scleractinian component of reef framework construction, frequent reference to other bioconstructional forms such as coralline algae, foraminifers, sponges, hydrocorals, and vermetid mollusks should help to reveal the fuller meaning of the term coral reef. The recent discovery of high population densities of sclerosponges, an unsuspected constructional element in the subreef framework (Hartman and Goreau, 1970), adds a new dimension to an assessment of the relative contribution of different reef-building agents. Also, submarine cementation from the surface to depths of 70 m is now known to be an important factor in solidifying reef materials (Land and Goreau, 1970). An effort will be made to restrict the use of the term coral reef to organically produced limestone structures of Recent age that typically provide a base for continued growth.

II. General Character of Western Atlantic Coral Reefs

A. SCLERACTINIAN SPECIES

In 1967 Goreau and Wells produced a list of 62 extant scleractinian coral species found on Jamaican reefs, exceeding by far the maximum number previously reported for any other single area in the tropical American region. At that time, 42 species were known from Florida (Vaughan, 1916a; Smith, 1948), 41 from Jamaica (Goreau, 1959), and 37 were listed for Cuba (Duarte Bello, 1961). These were among the most complete faunal inventories available. The hermatypes in Jamaica are represented by 48 species distributed among 25 genera and the ahermatypes by 14 species in 11 genera. With respect to the entire West Indian–Caribbean region, with 53 currently recognized scleractinians, this represents an increase of 9 species, augmenting the regional diversity by 14%. Eight of the Jamaican species were new, and as yet undescribed, and three represented new records for the West Indian–Caribbean region (including two of the undescribed species). This sudden increase in the number of coral species is a result of the careful study of Jamaican reefs by Goreau and co-workers designed to provide quantitative data on the composition of the various reef zones to the greatest depths of coral growth. Four of the new hermatypic species reported occur at a minimum depth of 25 m or greater, indicating the importance of extending collections to deeper waters.

There is no reason to assume that the rich coral fauna of Jamaica should be unique. The marine biota of Jamaica belongs to the Caribbean–West Indian biogeographic province. Furthermore, extensive shelf areas with favorable ecological conditions for coral growth occur widely throughout this region. A preliminary study of the coral fauna of the Rosario Islands, Colombia, reported the occurrence there of 48 scleractinian species (Pfaff, 1969). Limited collecting along the south coast of Curaçao (Netherlands West Indies), to 75 m depth, produced 45 scleractinians, of which 39 are hermatypes (Lang, 1970). Preliminary surveys of the Panamanian coral fauna, from Galeta Island east to San

Blas, have disclosed the presence here of 49 hermatypic and 16 ahermatypic species (Porter, 1972). The hermatypes not yet found living in Panama, following Goreau and Wells' (1967) list, are two undescribed species of *Madracis, Oculina valenciennesi* Milne-Edwards and Haime, *Solenastrea hyades* (Dana), and *Dendrogyra cylindrus* Ehrenberg. Fragments of *D. cylindrus* have been collected, but it is possible that these represent fossil remains. In summary, these data indicate that the coral fauna in the entire Caribbean area may be richer than formerly suspected. Moreover, the abundance of coral species near large land masses suggests a comparable diversity on continental and island shores (contrary to Vaughan and Wells, 1943).

Recently, ethological criteria used to differentiate certain closely related coral species of the suborder Faviina suggest the existence of cryptic species groups that had hitherto been treated as ecovariants or formae (Lang, 1969, 1970). The first clue leading to the rediscovery of *Scolymia cubensis* (Milne-Edwards and Haime) came from the distinctive differences in feeding behavior displayed by this species and *S. lacera* (Pallas), with which it was formerly confused. Subsequent study of the skeletal structure and ecology has corroborated the distinctness of these species on the basis of behavioral differences (Lang, 1971; Wells, 1971). No less than three formae of *Mycetophyllia lamarckana* Milne-Edwards and Haime also show distinctive feeding interactions, indicating the probable occurrence of a cryptic species complex in this genus as well.

It is expected that the number of scleractinian coral species will increase with continuing exploration to greater depths and the development of new techniques for discriminating among species which display such great variance in morphology. The Brazilian coral fauna, treated in greater detail in the next section, contains at least 20 species (Laborel, 1967, 1969a) with approximately one-half occurring in the Caribbean Sea. Taking these into account, it is seen that the entire western Atlantic reef fauna contains over 70 species of scleractinian corals. It must be cautioned that intensive field work in the Indo-Pacific region, on a scale comparable with the Jamaican effort, would probably also provide significant additions to the coral faunas presently known there, so that current regional comparisons of species numbers should be viewed on a provisional basis.

B. Distribution and Regional Development of Reefs

Although the taxonomy of reef corals has not reached a definitive stage, it appears at present that the tropical and subtropical areas of the western Atlantic region contain a relatively homogeneous faunal assemblage of hermatypic scleractinian species. This is particularly true of the shores and shallow banks of the Caribbean Sea, the Greater and Lesser Antilles, the Gulf of Mexico, the Bahamas, southern Florida, and Bermuda. The only significant departure, aside from the attenuating effects of unfavorable environmental conditions and isolation, occurs in southern waters along the Brazilian coast, where several endemic elements are commingled with a depauperate assemblage of Caribbean species. The occurrence of particular species suites and their development into coral reef communities is dependent on the availability of suitable substrata and their relief, the thermal and light regimes, variations in salinity, sedimentation, and other factors. The following brief survey of reef types and their distribution is related in a general way to the influence of the physical environment and the regional differences known to exist in the western Atlantic region.

Major coral reef formations of high species diversity and varying structure are widespread in the Caribbean Sea (e.g., Goreau, 1959; Lewis, 1960a; Stoddart, 1962a; Almy and Carrión Torres, 1963; Roos, 1964; Milliman, 1969). From the reports of others, Darwin (1842) rated the barrier reef off British Honduras as one of the preeminent reef systems in this region. It extends 240 km along the coastline and is 12–40 km wide with a lagoon ranging in depth from 3 to 30 m. The seaward slope descends abruptly to 180 m and depths of 900 m occur not far offshore (Thorpe and Stoddart, 1962).

Fringing reefs of impressive dimensions are developed on the edge of the narrow insular shelf along the north coast of Jamaica (Goreau, 1959). Offshore cays (patch or bank reefs) are present on the south coast shelf of Jamaica off Kingston and are also common along the Caribbean side of Puerto Rico (Kaye, 1959; Almy and Carrión Torres, 1963). Coral reefs are absent from the north coast of Puerto Rico. Kaye (1959) has proposed a combination of factors to explain this, all related to river runoff or the detrimental effects of high seas. Goreau and Wells (1967) have stressed the importance of the morphology of the substratum; they found most active coral growth along the edges of terraces where sediment drainage is most efficient and the plankton food supply possibly in greatest abundance. In Panama, high coral diversity and biomass are often found on bottom areas subject to moderate sedimentation and pronounced river drainage.

Small fringing coral reefs occur in Barbados (Lewis, 1960a) and St. Vincent (Adams, 1968), Lesser Antilles. These reefs are confined in distribution to the leeward or western sides of the islands. The east coast of Barbados is subject to a strong influx of Tertiary quartz sand. Volcanic sediments appear to have a controlling influence on reef development in St. Vincent.

On the basis of geomorphic criteria, atoll reef structures also occur in the Caribbean Sea, having been described in some detail off British Honduras and Nicaragua (Stoddart, 1962a; Milliman, 1969). It is possible that subaerial processes, perhaps karst erosion, were involved in the formation of the antecedent basin-like platforms of some of these reefs. Smaller, basin-shaped patch reefs resembling atolls occur commonly in some near-shore areas. An exceptionally fine series of such structures, in all stages of transition from completely submerged reefs and mangrove cays to shore areas with strand vegetation, are present along the southwestern coast of Puerto Rico (Welch, 1962). Another form of basin or cup reef was described at Cozumel Island, Mexico (Boyd et al., 1963). While the principal framework is predominantly coral, an algal rim outlines the periphery.

Among some of the major meteorological and hydrographic factors directly or indirectly affecting reef development in the Caribbean are the latitudinal distribution of pressure belts (which control rainfall and the paths of cyclonic disturbances), condition of the sea, tidal patterns, and currents and centers of upwelling (see Fig. 1). Considerable evidence is available indicating the destructive effect of hurricanes on patch and bank reefs situated on the leeward sides of islands (Goreau, 1959; Glynn et al., 1964). Even minor storms passing at relatively great distances can generate high seas which are destructive to ramose corals of erect growth posture, such as *Acropora palmata* (Lamarck). Hurricanes of high intensity, e.g., Hattie, which passed across the barrier reef of British Honduras (Stoddart, 1962b), can completely obliterate shallow reef structures formed in moderately high-energy environments. Nearly complete coral destruction, including massive buttress formations, occurred over a 43-km front in this region. A resurvey of the affected area conducted 4 years later (Stoddart, 1969a) indicated no regeneration. Evidence adduced from this study suggests that recovery may require up to 20–25 years.

A physiographic feature of coral reefs often related to exposure to high seas, i.e., the algal ridge, will be considered later. A reversal in the timing of diurnal tides, resulting in midday low-water exposures in the spring and summer seasons, can cause significant mortalities in populations that colonize reef flats during the remainder of the year (Glynn, 1968). Microatolls and the dead upper stratum of large tracts of branching corals probably result from such periods of emersion.

278

PETER W. GLYNN

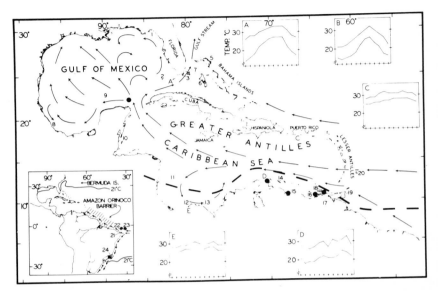

Fig. 1. West Indian–Caribbean region illustrating direction of prevailing surface currents, annual variations in sea surface temperature at selected localities, and the southern limit of hurricane occurrences. The surface circulation depicts only the major patterns (U.S. Navy Oceanographic Office, 1965, 1969). Temperature plots represent the long-term maximum and minimum values (C&GS, 1968) observed at A, Key West, Florida; B, Ferry Reach, St. Georges Is., Bermuda; C, Magueyes Is., Puerto Rico; D, Amuay, Venezuela; E, Cristóbal, C. Z., Panama. Solid circles along the Venezuelan coast, Campeche Bank, and in the inset map of Brazil indicate areas of upwelling. Minor upwelling has also been reported off the north coast of Cuba (Cushing, 1971). Hurricanes occur frequently, ca. 4.5 storms per annum, north of the heavy broken line, indicating their approximate southern limit (data for period 1901–1963, Cry, 1965). Inset shows the distribution of tropical waters over the entire western Atlantic Ocean. The location of the 21°C surface isotherm is indicated for the coldest month of the year (U.S. Navy Hydrographic Office, 1954). The countercurrent along the Brazilian coast develops over the period March–August. Limits of Amazon–Orinoco barrier from Laborel (1969b). The numbered areas identify the following localities. 1, Aucilla River, Florida; 2, Dry Tortugas (Ft. Jefferson, Loggerhead Cay); 3, Key Largo; 4, Carysfort Lighthouse; 5, Abaco Is.; 6, Andros Is.; 7, Bimini Is.; 8, Veracruz, Mexico; 9, Alacrán Reef; 10, British Honduras barrier reef; 11, Courtown and Albuquerque Cays; 12, Galeta Is., C. Z., Panama; 13, San Blas, Panama; 14, Curaçao, Netherlands West Indies; 15, La Guaira, Venezuela; 16, Cumaná, Venezuela; 17, Carúpano, Venezuela; 18, Margarita Is., Venezuela; 19, Trinidad; 20, Barbados; 21, Cabo São Roque; 22, Fernando de Noronha; 23, As Rocas; 24, Cabo Frio.

The predominantly westerly moving surface currents could theoretically lead to isolation and the development of impoverished reef communities at outlying localities, e.g., the Lesser Antilles. Lewis' (1960a) study of the fringing coral reefs of Barbados suggests that this factor, at least with respect to the Scleractinia, may not be as important as previously suspected. A coral fauna of 34 species was found there at shallow depth. On the other hand, many shore invertebrates do show adaptations in their reproduction and larval development to restrict the time exposed in the water (Lewis, 1960b).

Detailed field studies of the coral fauna off the northeastern coast of Venezuela have been initiated recently (Antonius, 1969, 1972) and these indicate that reef development is greatly attenuated in this region of periodic upwelling and high productivity. In the Gulf of Cariaco coral growth is limited to depths shallower than 15 m; 21 hermatypic Scleractinia are known from the area but only two species, *Porites porites* (Pallas) and *Siderastrea siderea* (Ellis and Solander), contribute significantly to the total coral cover. Minimum sea surface temperatures of 18°–21°C have been recorded at four different shore stations centered between 63.5°W and 70°W (C&GS, 1968). This low thermal influence apparently extends as far offshore as Los Roques Islands. Here a strong vertical thermal gradient was observed at 40 m, at which depth coral growth ceased abruptly (Antonius, personal communication). Further study is needed to determine if the modest coral fauna thus far known from eastern Venezuela (Antonius, 1969; Wells, 1944; Rodríguez, 1959) is characteristic of this region and causally related to the suboptimal conditions observed here.

Smith's (1954) account of the distribution of corals in the Gulf of Mexico and his distinction between structural reefs and coral communities is very useful. Coral reefs are present in the lower reaches of the Gulf, beyond the southernmost limits of influence of the 21°C isotherm. Along the Mexican coast they first begin to appear between Tampico and Veracruz, and extend eastward offshore on the Campeche Bank. Along the easternmost margin of the Gulf, flourishing reefs are found on the Florida Cays and along the northwestern coast of Cuba. Coral aggregations are fairly common on suitable offshore bottom areas in the upper Gulf. According to Work (1969), a disjunct distribution of West Indian elements exists from north of Clearwater, Florida to near the Aucilla River mouth. Six hermatypic coral genera and several other groups with tropical affinities occur commonly in this area.

Rigby and McIntire (1966) claim that Isla de Lobos and two similar reefs southeast of Tampico, centered near 21°30′N, represent the north-

ernmost coral reefs along the western margin of the Gulf of Mexico.*
Several well-defined structural reef zones are present here, including
a *Lithothamnion* ridge of low elevation. The reefs off Veracruz are built
on banks of calcareous bioclastic debris, predominantly of Recent coral
materials (Emery, 1963). The coral fauna in both areas is impoverished,
however, consisting of 14 to 16 species (Moore, 1958; Rigby and Mc-
Intire, 1966; Villalobos Figueroa, 1968). Alacrán Reef, on the Campeche
Bank, is a large complex of reefs with at least 18 species of hermatypes
(Kornicker *et al.*, 1959; Kornicker and Boyd, 1962). Five other emergent
reef structures are present along the western margin of the Yucatán
shelf (Busby, 1966; Logan *et al.*, 1969). These have developed on non-
reefal limestone banks, on which occur in addition numerous submerged
reef–coral communities and biostromal deposits. The thermal climate
is typically warm in this area of vigorous coral growth (Fuglister, 1947),
in contrast with the eastern shoulder of the shelf which experiences
cold-water upwelling with bottom temperatures of 17°–18°C (Cochrane,
1961). Logan *et al.* (1969) suggested that the absence of coral reefs
on the eastern sector of the shelf is due to this low thermal influence.

    Well-developed coral reefs and coral communities occur in southern
Florida and the Bahamas (Newell *et al.*, 1951, 1959; Voss and Voss,
1955; Squires, 1958; Shinn, 1963; Ginsburg, 1964; Storr, 1964), although
local distributions are markedly affected by the patterns of circulation.
The largest reefs in this area, e.g., along the Florida reef tract and
off Great Abaco and Andros Islands, are mostly confined to the windward or eastern margins of the banks; patch reefs frequently occur leeward of the reef barriers but are rare along the inner shoreline. Diminished coral growth on the western flanks of shallow banks and near
shore has been attributed to the inimical effects of shoal water, which
is driven westward by the prevailing easterly winds (Newell *et al.*,
1959). Moreover, reef growth is most luxuriant on the seaward sides
of islands which provide protection against cross-platform currents
(Ginsburg and Shinn, 1964).

    The effect of a cold front on shoal water may amount to as much
as a 5.8°C difference between the surface temperature of the sound
and bank (Busby and Dick, 1964). Ginsburg (1964) noted a more
northerly occurrence of reefs in the Bahamas and correlated this with
the higher minimum temperatures observed there. Recorded minima
at Fowey Rocks, Florida (Vaughan, 1918) and off the Little Bahama
Bank were 15.6° and 22.8°C, respectively. According to Ginsburg and
Bayer (personal communication) the northernmost outpost of flourishing

---

* See note added in proof on p. 324.

Acropora reefs is at Carysfort Reef. The hermatypes *Solenastrea* and *Siderastrea* reported off the North Carolina shelf, where bottom temperatures descend to 10.6°C, occur as isolated colonies (Macintyre and Pilkey, 1969).

Despite the marginal character of Bermuda and its distance from the West Indies proper, this outpost contains a multitude of flourishing coral reefs. Currently, the coral fauna is considered to contain 19 hermatypes (Laborel, 1966; Ginsburg and Stanley, 1970). Some of the principal genera contributing toward reef growth are *Montastrea, Porites, Siderastrea,* and *Diploria. Acropora palmata* and other species of *Acropora,* the former an important primary framework builder in the West Indies, are absent. Dissection of the lagoon reefs indicates that these are modern, actively growing structures (Frazier, 1970). There are well over 1500 of these in the central lagoon, representing fringing, knoll, cellular, pinnacle, and mesa-type reefs (Garrett *et al.,* 1971). The important role of early diagenetic processes has been clearly elucidated in these reefs by Ginsburg and Schroeder (1971). These workers described a series of features—broadly classified as (1) cavity-lining growths, (2) internal sediment, and (3) cement—which alter the original framework structure, some few centimeters below the living surface. While Stanley and Swift (1967) maintained that the outer reef front at 18 m depth shows evidence of only minor accretion, other workers (Land, personal communication) believe that constructional coral growth may occur to depths of 40 m.

The significant tropical affinities of the Bermudian biota are due to the influence of the warm Gulf Stream. Winter temperatures do descend to 14°C (C&GS, 1968), however, and this has often been cited as an explanation of the observed attenuation of the tropical biota in this area. Another important factor is the isolating effect of Bermuda's location, ca. 1700 km from the Little Bahama Bank (following the path of current flow). The maximum life of the planulae of four corals found in Bermuda is 17–23 days (Vaughan, 1916b). Under ideal conditions, a particle moving at a mean velocity of 2.5 knots (Boisvert, 1967) would reach Bermuda in about 15 days. Information on the larval lives of coral species absent from Bermuda would be useful in connection with this distributional problem. Also, further knowledge of the composition and distribution of the coral fauna in the Venezuelan center of upwelling should provide an additional basis for distinguishing between the effects of long-distance larval transport and marginal thermal conditions.

Laborel's (1967, 1969a) recent inventory of the coral fauna of Brazil confirms that this southern tropical area cannot be regarded as an impoverished extension of the Caribbean region. Only one-half of the

Brazilian corals also occur in the Caribbean region, illustrating the significant degree of endemism that has developed. The Brazilian *Mussismilia*, with three species, does not occur in the Caribbean and 21 Caribbean genera are absent south of the equator, including, for example, *Acropora, Diploria, Colpophyllia,* and *Dichocoenia*. At least one of the three hydrocorals, viz., *Millepora nitida* Verrill, is also apparently restricted to the southwestern Atlantic region (the coasts of Bahia and the Abrolhos reefs). Evidence from the distributions of other marine groups, e.g., mollusks (Marcus and Marcus, 1967; Work, 1969; Vermeij and Porter, 1971), octocorals (Bayer, 1961), and isopods (Glynn, 1970b), indicates that the Brazilian coast should be treated as a distinctive subregion of the western Atlantic province. Verrill (1901) and Laborel (1969b) believed that the Amazon–Orinoco river systems have served as a partial hydrographic barrier, tending to isolate the two areas. The similarity of Brazilian coral endemics to the European Miocene fauna has lead Laborel (1969b) to conclude that the barrier has existed since this time.

No less than six zoogeographic subregions were recognized by Laborel, with flourishing coral reefs restricted to the shelf between Natal and the Arquipélago dos Abrolhos in the south. This represents a latitudinal spread of about 12° as opposed to 18°–20° in the northern hemisphere. The relatively narrow distribution of reefs in South America is evidently due to the unfavorable conditions associated with this large continent. The northern impoverished subregion extends from the state of Maranhão, and probably much farther north, to Cabo de São Roque. The absence of coral reefs here is considered due to improper substrate conditions, turbidity, and unfavorable currents (from source areas that would allow an influx of colonizing species) rather than freshwater dilution. Modern reef construction in the Cape São Roque subregion is poor. Hermatypic corals are present in the third subregion, the oceanic islands of Fernando de Noronha and As Rocas, but most active organic accretion is due mainly to crustose coralline algae and vermetid mollusks. Corals contribute to the construction of pinnacles along the leeward side of Fernando de Noronha; observations have not yet been made on the windward side of the island. The northeastern coastal and central subregions contain numerous coral reefs, increasing in richness to the south. The São Francisco River and a barren sandy stretch to the south serve to divide these two areas for a distance of nearly 400 km. Salvador south to the Abrolhos islands represents the region of greatest reef development, which may have acted as a refugium during low sea-level stands in Quaternary time. Coral reefs diminish in number with a concomitant reduction in other tropical elements south of Abrolhos to Santos. The effects of the southern thermal barrier are pronounced beyond Cabo Frio.

Our present meager knowledge of the West African coast would suggest that coral reefs are either absent or few in number. This is the result of a combination of conditions associated with heavy river drainage and the compressed thermal structure characteristic of eastern boundary currents. The early accounts of Gravier (1909) and Thiel (1928) include eight hermatypic scleractinian genera. Chevalier (1966) lists 19 Scleractinia from the West African region, but only 4 of these are hermatypes. It is now possible to add *Madracis decactis* (Lyman), which occurs on a southern route to Africa from Brazil (Laborel, personal communication). Because of problems in synonymy and the uncertain identity of some of the early collections, it would be premature to attempt an assessment of the faunal diversity based on these studies. Although the scleractinian fauna is heterogeneous, containing Caribbean–West Indian, Brazilian, Indo-Pacific, and Mediterranean elements, the hermatypic coral species of West Africa, including the Cape Verde Islands, belong to Caribbean–West Indian genera.

III. Structure, Zonation, and Species Composition

In spite of the broad range of environmental conditions under which coral reefs develop, there are often present distinctive zones or species associations that can be recognized over wide geographic areas. Also, notable regional variations in reef structure are evident, especially where there exist qualitative differences in the composition of the hermatypic species. This section will be concerned with a general survey of the major known features of coral reef structure. The algal ridge and reef flat habitats, considered by many to be absent in the western Atlantic region, will be given more detailed treatment. Biological modification of the environment, e.g., degradation of reef structures through the erosive effects of boring organisms, will also be referred to in this discussion.

A. Reef Shores

In the Caribbean Sea coral reefs are often evident above the high-water line or exposed during periods of low water. These subaerial sections may represent the remnants of fossil reefs, ancient limestone shorelines, recent beach rock formations, unconsolidated bioclastic debris or the products of modern coral framework construction. In the hurricane belt, cays frequently contain large amounts of coral rubble and bioclastic sand that provide support for the development of strand vegetation. Cays formed along protected shores often contain sediments of predominantly fine texture with mangrove forests present over much of their surface area. *Rhizophora mangle* (Linnaeus), a pioneer sometimes found far offshore, is succeeded by *Avicennia germinans* (Linnaeus) and other mangrove species where soil conditions are more suitable along the coast. A transitional series of littoral communities, indicative of the major trends of succession, have been described along the south coast of Puerto Rico (Margalef, 1962; Welch, 1962). An example of the progressive development of these toward a terrestrial sere would include intermediate communities of corals (*Porites* reef), epiphytic and sediment trapping algae, *Halimeda, Thalassia,* and mangrove forests.

A distinctive fauna is usually present on the mangrove cays. Several species of shore birds nest here; some, for example, the Cattle Egret, *Bulbulcus ibis* (Linnaeus), and Brown Pelican, *Pelecanus occidentalis* Gmelin, establish large rookeries. Local phosphate enrichment can reach significant proportions (Lund, 1957), and the extent this may affect the surrounding reef biota is worthy of attention. The supralittoral island floor often harbors dense populations of the scavenging hermit crab *Coenobita clypeatus* (Herbst). The brachyuran decapod *Aratus pisoni* (Milne-Edwards) and mesogastropod *Littorina angulifera* (Lamarck) are found on the prop roots or in the canopy of *R. mangle.*

Numerous species with high population densities inhabit the rock surfaces of the supralittoral splash and intertidal zones. Among some of the more common invertebrates are the prosobranch gastropods *Tectarius muricatus* Linnaeus, *Nodilittorina tuberculata* Menke, and *Littorina ziczac* Gmelin at relatively high levels on the shore; centered at lower horizons are *Nerita tessellata* Gmelin, *N. versicolor* Gmelin, *N. peloronta* Linnaeus, *Astraea caelata* Gmelin, and *Cittarium pica* Linnaeus. Amphineurans (*Acanthopleura granulata* Gmelin, *Chiton tuberculatus* Linnaeus), decapods [*Grapsus grapsus* (Linnaeus), *Microphrys bicornutus* (Latreille)], and echinoids [*Echinometra lucunter* (Linnaeus), *Eucidaris tribuloides* (Lamarck)] also abound in the intertidal zone. All of these species are herbivores which scrape or abrade algal encrusted surfaces. The effects of grazing by three species of *Nerita* in controlling the height of a blue-green algal turf was demonstrated experimentally by Blasini de Austin (1968). Under normal grazing conditions, the algal mat attains a height of about 10 mm; removal of *Nerita* allowed plant growth to reach nearly 40 mm in 70 days. Upon introduction of the snails, rapid cropping reduced the height of the algal mat to near normal level within a week.

The many different kinds of organism active in the erosion of tropical Atlantic shores have been reviewed by Ginsburg (1953) for the Florida area. Data now available on the destructive effects of a few species substantiate earlier views on the importance of biologically induced erosion (Ginsburg, 1953; Newell and Imbrie, 1955). For example, populations of *Chiton tuberculatus*, with a mean dry weight biomass of 41 gm/m², were found to void a comparable amount of inorganic material in 38 days. *Acanthopleura granulata* defecates its own mass in fine sediment, 69 gm/m² in 55 days. Relating the mass of sediment production to the rock volume and adjusting for surface irregularities in the substratum, it follows that the surficial planation resulting from each chiton species amounts to approximately 0.18 mm/year. Estimates of erosion due to physicochemical solution, in the range of 0.012 mm/year, are an order of magnitude below that determined for chitons. Other potentially important agents in the bioerosion of reef shores are presented in Table I. Clionid sponges can effect a remarkable rate of degradation; for example, *Cliona lampa* de Laubenfels in the subtidal notch on Bermudian shores can erode 22–26 kg substratum/(m² year) (Neumann, 1966). The activities of these few species indicate the desirability of obtaining data on the combined effects of all organisms active in rock destruction, including endolithic algae, polychaetes, sipunculans, cirripeds, etc. Moreover, it is now apparent that the penetrating effects of certain lower plants, e.g., bacteria into coral skeletons (Di Salvo, 1969) and fungi into barnacle and mollusk shells (Kohlmeyer, 1969), may also play a role in the disintegration of intertidal carbonate substrata.

B. Shoal Reef Formations

1. Algal Ridge

While several workers have emphasized the importance of red calcareous algae along the seaward edge of reefs, particularly members of the Corallinacae (Newell *et al.*, 1951; Zans, 1958; Kaye, 1959; Kornicker and Boyd, 1962; Boyd *et al.*, 1963; Rigby and McIntire, 1966; Milliman, 1969), it is still generally held that an emergent algal ridge is not present in the West Indian–Caribbean region (Newell, 1959; Stoddart, 1969b). Recent study of an offshore barrierlike reef on the Atlantic side of Panama conclusively confirms the existence of an algal ridge formation in this part of the Caribbean Sea. The ridge is exposed at

TABLE I

RATES OF EROSION OF SOME HERBIVORE POPULATIONS INHABITING INTERTIDAL LIMESTONE SUBSTRATA

Species	Locality	Population density (no./m²)	Mass of rock removed gm/(m² year)	Substratum	Source
Cliona lampa	Bermuda	Abundant	22,000–26,000	Calcarenitic country rock	Neumann, 1966
Chiton tuberculatus	Puerto Rico	22	394	Coral rubble mod. indurated	Glynn, 1970a; Glynn, unpublished
Acanthopleura granulata	Puerto Rico	8	478	Coral rubble mod. indurated	Glynn, 1970a; Glynn, unpublished
Nerita tessellata	Barbados	220	154	Beachrock mod. indurated	McLean, 1967
Echinometra lucunter	Bermuda	25	7,000 (wet wt)[a]	Eolianite	Hunt, 1969

[a] Preliminary estimate based on short-term observations.

low water along the eastern end of the reef front and is also emergent at high water on certain sections of the reef. A brief description of this impressive physiographic feature, where it reaches a high degree of development on the Holandés Cays, is presented here for the first time.

The appearance of the emergent section of the windward reef edge is shown in Fig. 2. The algal ridge has its greatest elevation where wave action is strongest and decreases in height to leeward in the direction of diminishing wave turbulence. This apparent adjustment in growth form is good evidence of an active seaward extension of this zone. The ridge is terraced and descends in steplike fashion to a shallow moat. The algal ridge zone has a mean width of about 15 m, but may extend up to 30–40 m seaward as spurs. Crustose coralline algae, particularly

Fig. 2. Views of the reef front and algal ridge, eastern section of Holandés Cays, August 5, 1970. (A) Seaward extending spurs and terraced algal ridge; (B) moat and limestone parapet.

members of the Mastophoroideae form a veneer of pavement on exposed surfaces [e.g., *Neogoniolithon* sp., *Hydrolithon børgesenii* (Foslie) Foslie, *Porolithon pachydermum* (Foslie) Foslie, *Porolithon* sp.] or frequently assume an erect, arborescent growth form [e.g., *Lithophyllum congestum* (Foslie) Foslie] in sheltered situations, as along the sides of channels or beneath overhangs. Dissection of a portion of one terrace, to a depth of 0.5 m, showed this to be formed predominantly of coralline laminae and vermetid tubes. Shallow pools are common on the terraced ridge and contain a variety of large fleshy algae, such as *Turbinaria turbinata* (Linnaeus) Kuntze, *Laurencia papillosa* (Forsskål) Greville, *Sargassum polyceratium* Montagne, and *Padina gymnospora* (Kützing) Vickers. Accretion also appears to be taking place on the back side of the ridge, a result of the growth of the vermetid *Dendropoma* (*Novastoa*) aff. *D. (N.) irregulare* (Orbigny). Water movement over the ridge is vigorous, but intermittent at low tide, at which time breaking waves cascade from the terraces to the shallow moat. Blow holes, which spout in rhythm with the advancing breaker line, suggest the presence of subsurface room and pillar structures. The moat acts as a temporary catchment basin, containing a thin layer of coarse, bioclastic sediment. A sinuous, limestone parapet divides the moat from the broad, leeward reef flat. This structure is a lithified conglomerate of corals (*Diploria, Montastrea,* etc.) and bioclastic detritus (*Halimeda, Homotrema,* etc.). Its position on the reef corresponds with the boulder zone present on Indo-Pacific atoll reefs (Stoddart, 1969b). Four sources of evidence indicate that the parapet is an erosional feature, probably a remnant of an older reef structure. Weathering of the surface appears pronounced, living hermatypic populations are absent, the detrital calcareous material has been partly recrystallized, and a lithified coral fragment gave a ^{14}C date of 2115 ± 125 years BP. Newman *et al.* (1970) examined exposed fossil coral outcrops on leeward islands of the Holandés Reef and speculated that these emergent 3–4 m platforms correspond in age to the dated 120,000–130,000-year Sangamon reefs present in Jamaica (Land and Epstein, 1970), southern Florida (Hoffmeister *et al.,* 1967), and elsewhere in the western Atlantic and Indo-Pacific regions. The major physiographic features of the windward reef and patterns of biotic zonation are presented diagrammatically in Fig. 3.

The extent of development of the algal ridge in Panama is generally related to the degree of exposure of the coastline. Along more protected shores the ridge has a lower elevation, though it is typically exposed at low water; under such conditions *Millepora complanata* (Lamarck) and zoanthids (*Palythoa, Zoanthus*) tend to assume a relatively greater

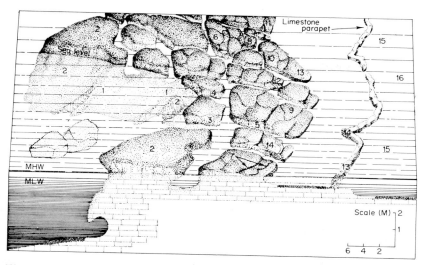

Fig. 3. Schematic view of algal ridge zone, Holandés Cay, Panama, reconstructed from surveys conducted at various points along the reef and from aerial photographs. Foreground, cross-sectional view; background, simplified three-dimensional view ~50 m along the reef. The locations of some major species populations: 1, *Porites* and *Agaricia;* 2, Crustose mastophoroid algae; 3, *Chiton marmoratus;* 4, *Cittarium pica;* 5, *Lithophyllum congestum;* 6, Fleshy algae; 7, Vermetid-*Laurencia* rim; 8, *Thais haemastoma;* 9, *Acanthopleura granulata;* 10, *Echniometra lucunter;* 11, *Purpura patula;* 12, *Fissurella nodosa;* 13, *Nerita* spp.; 14, *Littorina ziczac;* 15, *Porites* spp.; 16, *Thalassia*.

role in this zone. The growth form of the hydrocoral is often quite sturdy and effective in withstanding the force of breaking waves. On some reefs *Millepora* grows as continuous, submerged banks along the reef front, effectively forming a sill.

As expected, the innominate zone of the seaward slope has all the appearances of a high-energy environment subject to appreciable scouring. The predominant organic growth along the submerged seaward face of the algal ridge consists of filamentous and encrusting calcareous algae. Caves, ledges, and fissures abound on this section of the reef. Limited coral growth does occur in some areas, with *Porites astreoides* Lesueur and foliose colonies of *Agaricia agaricites* (Linnaeus) the main species present. *Acropora palmata* was not seen in the breaker zone, but further seaward at greater depth (4–6 m). This is evidence of a deep wave base and the attendant rigorous growth conditions imposed on the reef front at shallow depth. Windward reefs elsewhere in the Atlantic often contain populations of *A. palmata* reaching upward to within 1 m of the surface (Newell *et al.*, 1951; Goreau, 1959; Stoddart, 1962a; Shinn, 1963). A series of subsurface views across the windward reef is shown in Fig. 4.

An impressive contribution of crustose coralline algae and vermetids to the framework structure of the seaward crest of Brazilian reefs has been reported by several workers. The concretional deposits of these

Fig. 4. Subsurface views across the Holandés Cays illustrating some important physical features and biotic zones (August 5 and 6, 1970). (A) Seaward slope, *Acropora palmata*, 5 m deep; (B) reef front, groove and spur formation, 4 m deep, note ripple marks and *Acropora* debris on sand bottom and undercutting along base of spur; (C) reef front, exposed face of algal ridge, 3 m deep; (D) reef front, protected face of algal ridge with live coral growth, 2 m deep; (E) windward reef flat behind moat, *Porites astreoides* abundant, 1 m deep; (F) windward reef flat nearer reef island, *Porites furcata* and *Thalassia testudinum* abundant, 1 m deep.

organisms form a prominent algal ridge on the offshore islands of Fernando de Noronha (Kempf and Laborel, 1968) and As Rocas (de Andrade, 1960). The algal ridge is best developed along the eastern and southern shores of both islands, facing the strong seas which buffet this area (U.S. Navy Hydrographic Office, 1948). The eolianite tidal terraces and "boilers" in Puerto Rico (Howe, 1912; Kaye, 1959) and Bermuda (Iams, 1970) also contain thick deposits of crustose coralline algae, but these are not generally associated with coral reef formations.

It is instructive to propose an explanation for the development of an algal ridge at Panama's low latitudinal position. In the Pacific Ocean this feature usually occurs on coral reefs in the trade-wind belt, under conditions of strong winds and high seas. A valid clue to this problem, perhaps, is the relatively deep wave base alluded to above. The highest seas in the Caribbean Sea and Gulf of Mexico have been observed near Panama's geographic position, when the Intertropical Convergence zone migrates to the south, from about December through March (U.S. Navy Oceanographic Office, 1963). During this season the swells are at least 3.7 m in height for 3–5% of the time. Compared with the north coast of Jamaica, rough to high seas (>1.5 m) persist 3.6 times longer in Panama over a year's period. Other coastal and island localities subject to extreme high seas are largely confined to the northern coast of South America, indicating a limited area suitable for the formation of an algal ridge elsewhere in the Caribbean Sea. More importantly, the presence of an algal ridge in Panama suggests that present-day Caribbean reef communities have the potential to develop similar structures as Indo-Pacific reefs under comparable meteorological and hydrographic conditions.

2. Reef Flat

Emergent reef flats do occur on Caribbean and Brazilian coral reefs. The fossil sections of fringing reefs along the Caribbean shores of Panama form a broad reef flat (50–100 m in width) that is exposed at low water. Living corals are present on the flat in water-filled depressions and above the mean low-water spring level along the windward edge of the reef crest. During extreme low water, several coral species are exposed and often survive these periods of tidal emergence. Some of the more resistant corals are *Agaricia agaricites* forma *agaricites*, *Siderastrea radians* (Pallas), *Porites astreoides*, *Diploria clivosa* (Ellis and Solander); and the hydrocoral *Millepora complanata*. Milliman (1969) reported intermittent exposure of reef flats on Nicaraguan atolls. All of the major shoal coral species were exposed at low water, including, in addition to those named above, *Acropora palmata, A. cervicornis* (Lamarck), *Porites porites,* and *Montastrea annularis* (Ellis and Solander). The summits of hemispherical massive corals, such as *Diploria* and *Siderastrea,* are often dead and eroded centrally. This is presumably a result of subaerial exposure and not from resumption of growth around the colony base after overturning (Kornicker and Boyd, 1962). In Puerto Rico, heavy mortality of reef flat populations has been related to extreme, midday low-water tidal stands in the spring and summer seasons (Glynn, 1968). Several reefs in this locality contain large tracts of recently killed *Porites furcata* Lamarck in original growth position, between 3 and 8 cm below mean low water (MLW).

Low-water exposure of extensive areas is a characteristic feature of the linear reefs situated along the continental shelf of Brazil (Laborel, 1969b). Living corals, however, are largely confined to subtidal habitats; organisms tolerant of tidal exposures are fleshy and crustose algae, zoanthids (*Palythoa*), and vermetids. Unlike the emergent sections of Caribbean reefs, which represent remnants of ancient reefs or recently formed deposits of coral, van Andel and Laborel (1964) have obtained convincing evidence that Brazilian reefs have undergone an emergence during the last few thousand years. Radiocarbon dating of vermetid limestone at 2.6 m elevation revealed a higher relative sea level stand between 1190 and 3660 years ago.

Numerous workers have suggested that an absence of emergent reef flats in the more marginal areas may be due to low atmospheric temperatures which limit the upward growth of corals. However, Vaughan (1919) noted long ago that some corals, notably *Montastrea,* can survive exposure on Florida reefs. The great time differences in the origin of bioclastic materials contributing to the development of reef flats, e.g., contemporary in Puerto Rico or Modern (ca. 1000–4000 years) in Brazil, suggest that such reef zones are not entirely dependent on present-day coral growth at intertidal levels.

3. Subtidal Associations

Moderately protected bottom areas receiving adequate circulation frequently provide support for sea grasses and corals. A characteristic suite of photophilous corals found with *Thalassia* includes *Oculina diffusa* Lamarck, *Cladocora arbuscula* (Lesueur), *Porites porites, P. divaricata* Lesueur, and *Manicina areolata* (Linnaeus). Also present at shallow depth, but more dependent on the availability of firm substrata, are *Agaricia agaricites, Porites astreoides, P. furcata, Siderastrea siderea, S. radians,* and *Favia fragum* (Esper). Kissling (1965) has shown how the population densities of several of these coral species are determined by the availability of supporting vegetation or firm substrata.

These corals contribute substantially toward the formation of a variety of shoal, coral reef structures. For example, patch reefs of basin-like design have been described in the Bahamas (Newell *et al.*, 1951) and Puerto Rico (Welch, 1962). Coral growth occurs along the peripheral edge and most actively on the windward or upcurrent side. A centrally located, shallow depression is essentially devoid of corals, but usually contains a dense mat of phanerogams or algae. In Puerto Rico the circular ridge is exposed at extreme low-water tidal stands. A suggested mode of formation of this kind of reef is dependent on the upward growth of *Porites* hillocks (Welch,. 1962). The windward crest grows more rapidly and eventually interferes with current movement across the central portion of the reef. Reduced circulation impedes leeward coral growth, but leads to conditions favorable for the proliferation of sea grasses (*Thalassia, Syringodium*) and calcareous algae (*Halimeda, Amphiroa*) in the central basin.

On the leeward edge of reef flats, or in other partially protected habitats, ramose *Porites* often forms extensive beds, sometimes covering an area of several hundred square meters (see Fig. 4F). Stephenson and Stephenson (1950) have called attention to the occurrence of equivalent coral associations (composed of ramose *Montipora* and other massive corals) on the reef flats at Low Isles, Great Barrier Reef, Australia. The population density, biomass, and species diversity of the associated biota of such assemblages in the Caribbean region can be very high. Some preliminary results of quantitative sampling of the macrofauna are given in Table II, indicating the relative importance of benthic algae, *Homotrema* (foraminifer), crustaceans, mollusks, echinoderms, and other animal groups.

Shallow, seaward, reef zones subject to moderate wave action often contain a variety of corals, some of which assume resistant growth forms in response to the conditions of this high energy environment. A few of the more common species found on the windward reef face are *Acropora palmata, Diploria strigosa* (Dana), *D. labyrinthiformis* (Linnaeus), *Agaricia agaricites, Porites astreoides, Montastrea annularis*, and *Colpophyllia natans* (Müller). Buttresses are often present at 0.5–6 m depth in the *Acropora* zone. These have been shown to form through the active seaward growth of *A. palmata* which, after crowding and death in the initial formative stage, are grown over by other hermatypic species (Shinn, 1963). The slightly deeper buttress zone (1–10 m) along the north coast of Jamaica (Goreau, 1959) is also a result of recent·

TABLE II

PRELIMINARY DATA ON THE NUMERICAL AND BIOMASS DENSITIES
OF THE MAJOR COMPONENTS OF THE MACROBIOTA
IN A REPRESENTATIVE M^2 AREA OF *Porites* REEF[a]

Group	No. species	No. individuals	Biomass (gm dry wt)	Protein (gm) All species	Protein (gm) Suspension feeders
Algae (benthic fleshy forms)	12	—	1,022.1	32.5	—
Foraminifera, *Homotrema rubrum* (Lamarck)	1	13,700	135.6	1.8	1.8
Porifera	5	Several colonies	11.8	5.8	5.8
Scleractinia, *Porites furcata* (living branches)	1	Several colonies	12,022.3	285.5	285.5
Zoanthidea, *Zoanthus sociatus*	1	2 colonies	1.1	0.4	—
Polychaeta	27	23,160	6.7	3.2	0.1
Sipunculida	3	20	0.9	0.7	—
Crustacea	32	2,668	40.3	14.9	0.6
Mollusca	25	137	59.4	10.0	4.5
Echinodermata	20	2,002	263.3	52.6	—
Pisces	9	15	6.1	3.6	1.8
Totals	136	41,702	13,569.6	411.0	300.1

[a] The proportion of known suspension feeders in protein biomass is also indicated.

coral growth. *Montastrea annularis* is the dominant framework species, whose growth is oriented normal to the prevailing seas. Interdigitating valleys develop into canyons as lateral growth proceeds, and eventually these are obliterated by the roofing over of adjacent framework structures.

Shallow coral growth on the windward, seaward face of Holandés Reef, Panama, which is periodically exposed to exceptionally high seas, contrasts markedly with that described above. *Acropora* grows sparsely and is present at a greater depth zone, 4–6 m (Fig. 4A). *Montastrea* occurs at 6–15 m depth, but not as a series of buttresses. In general, corals occur at a low numerical density and are poorly developed in the seaward spur and groove zone (Fig. 4A–D). By contrast, vigorous coral growth is taking place on the leeward reef shelf and slope, with nearly complete coverage of high species diversity from MLW to depths of 45 m (Fig. 5). This structural reef bears a striking resemblance to the rich leeward lagoon reef and slope communities described on western Pacific atoll reefs (Wells, 1957). Evidence from elsewhere in the western Atlantic region, e.g., Bermuda (Ginsburg and Stanley, 1970), the Bahamas (Storr, 1964), and Brazil (Laborel, 1966, 1969b), also contradicts the tenet that coral growth is most active on the windward, seaward, shallow sections of reefs. Stoddart *et al.* (1966) and Barnes *et al.* (1970) draw attention to the sparse coral growth observed at shallow depths on the seaward slopes of reefs in the Indian Ocean. Particular conditions associated with these high-energy environments, e.g., wave activity, sediment load, and scouring, need to be investigated as they affect the production of structural materials by the coral component.

The formation of coral buttresses appears to be confined largely to the West Indian–Caribbean region. The upper and lower *A. palmata* zones (vide Goreau, 1959) are represented by an algal ridge and *Millepora* zone, respectively, in Brazil (Laborel, 1966, 1969b). Also, pinnacles of *Mussismilia* are found at the buttress zone level on Brazilian reefs. *Acropora* is also absent from Bermuda and massive corals (e.g., *Montastrea* and *Diploria*), while active in reef construction, do not form buttresses.

Fig. 5. Constructional reef composed of dense coral growth on the leeward platform of Holandés Cays, maximum depth 3 m, August 6, 1970.

C. Deep Coral Formations

1. Biotic Province

Goreau's (1959) earliest contribution toward a description of Jamaican coral reefs, to depths of about 25 m, was planned as an initial phase of a comprehensive ecological study. Continued exploration beyond the reef crest, buttress and fore-reef environments, however, revealed abundant coral growth down to 70 m, significantly exceeding the previously accepted depth penetration to about 50 m. The discovery of these deep coral associations has added an important dimension to our understanding of the coral reef ecosystem.

While coral diversity and biomass can be quite high in the 30–70 m depth range, rigid framework construction is much reduced here owing to lower rates of calcification, a reduced coralline algal flora (important in cementation processes) and the intense erosive activities of boring sponges (Goreau and Hartman, 1963). Recent work, however, has shown extensive lithification to depths of at least 70 m, a process which may be relatively more important in binding reef sediments at greater depths (Land and Goreau, 1970; Goreau and Land, 1972). Several features shared by deep-growing corals seem to render them more susceptible to bioerosive destruction, viz. (1) flattened colony form and less dense skeleton, (2) relatively weak attachment to substratum, and (3) heavier encrustation of skeleton by associated sessile forms. The flattened growth form of deep-living corals, formerly considered an adaptation to maximize exposure to low light levels, must be related as well to the difficulties of maintaining an upright posture on unstable sections of the reef (Goreau and Hartman, 1963). Eroded massive corals that become detached are more apt to be transported to unfavorable depths than are those of prostrate growth form.

A sill reef, composed principally of *Montastrea annularis* with a flattened growth form, is often present on the upper fore-reef slope (ca. 40 m). Additional abundant coral growth on the sill reef includes *M. cavernosa, Madracis* spp., *Stephanocoenia* spp., *Scolymia lacera,* and *Helioseris cucullata* (Ellis and Solander). At least four species of *Agaricia,* with *A. undata* (Ellis and Solander) often forming the dominant population, contribute importantly to the composition of the hermatypic coral fauna of the lower fore-reef slope (ca. 45–60 m) and the deep fore-reef slope (ca. 70–100 m). At least two undescribed species of *Madracis* and one new *Mycetophyllia* are largely confined to this deeper reef zone (Lang, personal communication). However, *Montastrea cavernosa* also extends to at least 90 m and forms large flattened colonies along the upper edge of the deep fore-reef slope. Other common groups of the macrobenthos include fleshy sponges, *Halimeda* spp. (Goreau and Graham, 1967), and gorgonians, frequently of very large size (Goreau, 1965, 1967). Often the principal substrates material is talus, derived from the upper, more actively growing reef zones. The slope is usually of a steep gradient, ranging from about 30° (fore-reef slope) to 90° (deep fore-reef slope). This results in the mass transport of materials into deeper water by way of slides, avalanches, sediment flow, etc. Sediments accumulate where the angle of repose is not exceeded by the slope gradient; the growth of epibenthic forms is inhibited under such conditions. Coral abundance is greatest on projecting structures, such as the upper and deep sills and small to giant nunatak-like pinnacles. The reader is referred to Goreau and Hartman (1963), Goreau (1965), and Goreau and Wells (1967) for further information on the structure of these deep reef zones.

Preliminary studies of deep reef formations elsewhere in the western Atlantic indicate that rich hermatypic coral populations may be common-place at relatively great depth. A recent reconnaissance of the lower fore-reef slope at Glover's Reef, British Honduras, showed significant coral coverage at 50–70 m depth (Fig. 6). Exploration of the Andros Island barrier reef escarpment by means of a manned submersible has similarly disclosed luxuriant coral growth to a depth of 60 m, diminishing in extent and finally disappearing below 107 m (Busby *et al.*, 1966; U.S. Navy Oceanographic Office, 1967).

Subreef habitats, such as caves, tunnels, and the undersides of ledges, are often free from burial by sediments when present on relatively steep slopes. Coralline sponges were recently found to comprise an important element of the cryptofauna inhabiting this environment, and where these animals are abundant they contribute substantially to limestone accretion at the reef base (Hartman and Goreau, 1970). The new class Sclerospon-giae has been proposed to accommodate this group, as well as the extinct order Stromatoporoidea. The six species of sclerosponges investigated in Jamaica extended over a bathymetric range of 8–92 m. More re-cently they have been found just below the intertidal zone at a depth of 1 m. While the majority of these sponges are true cavernicoles, at least one species, *Ceratoporella nicholsoni* Hickson, occurs out in the open beyond 60 m depth. *Ceratoporella* may grow to a large size, up to 1 m in diameter, and can attain a population density of 5–12 colonies (diameter > 10 cm) per square meter. In the deeper reef zones (beyond 70 m depth), *Ceratoporella* sometimes competes for space with the hermatypes *Madracis* n. sp. and *Montastrea cavernosa* (Linnaeus), and

Fig. 6. Agaricia buildup of ca. 1 m height (left-hand side of photograph) at 50 m depth, lower fore-reef slope off seaward side of Southwest Cays, Glover's Reef, British Honduras, November 10, 1971.

appears to approach their growth rates. The lithified walls of caves and tunnels often contain a large quantity of the remains of *Cerato-porella*. Although they are found mainly in the deeper reef zones, it is suspected that optimal conditions for the growth of sclerosponges occur at shallow depth where presumably greater food resources are available.

Sill reefs, pinnacles, and long, steep-sided, linear ridges are widespread throughout the western Atlantic region between depths of 18 m and 160 m (e.g., Jordan and Stewart, 1959; Goreau, 1961; Goreau and Burke, 1966; Goreau and Wells, 1967; Macintyre, 1968, 1972; Ballard and Uchupi, 1970). A submerged bank reef at 25 m depth off the south coast of Puerto Rico is shown in Fig. 7. Recent study of these structures indicates that many of them are best interpreted as drowned or submerged coral reef bioherms and not cemented beach and dune formations (cf. Newell, 1962). Macintyre (1968, 1972) concludes, on the basis of the following evidence, that the submerged barrier or bank reefs commonly centered at the 40- and 80-m depth levels in the eastern Caribbean were formed through active organic growth: (1) the ridges usually occur on the outer flanks and upper slopes of platforms where conditions are often most favorable for coral growth; (2) their steep slopes indicate formation through active framework construction rather than the accumulation of sediments; (3) seismic reflection profiles of shelf-edge ridges show these to consist of thick (up to 30 m) unstratified accumulations of calcareous material; (4) the presence of abundant living coral populations indicates that organic accretion is still taking place. The sill structures developed at 40 m depth along the south coast of Jamaica were found by Goreau and Burke (1966) to represent submerged coral reefs. Their evidence rested largely on examination of the surface morphology, which reveals a complex of characteristic reef features, including systems of spurs and grooves. Certain features of the fore-reef and reef slope morphology were investigated on the north coast of Jamaica by excavating with explosives and drilling, to depths of 1.8 m into the reef structure, in order to determine the thickness of bioclastic materials and their rate of deposition (Goreau and Land, 1972). The major relief features were found to have resulted from recent reef growth unconformably superimposed on the edges of drowned Pleistocene terraces.

Fig. 7. Submerged bank reef present along outer edge of insular shelf off La Parguera, Puerto Rico (ca. 67°01'W, 17°53'N), April 9, 1967. Summit of reef approximately 20 m deep, sand channel 25 m deep.

The hermatypic members of these deep coral reef communities, below ~40 m depth, are not presently undergoing significant framework construction. Indeed, the relative abundance of the Scleractinia diminishes in the deeper reef zones with a concomitant increase in sponges and antipatharians as compared with the fore-reef or buttress zone.

2. Late Quaternary Sea Level Changes

Because of the high degree of variability present in eustatic sea level curves constructed for the period covering the last 35,000 years (e.g., Milliman and Emery, 1968) and the wide depth range over which submerged coral reefs occur, efforts to correlate pauses in sea level with the initiation and growth of reefs at such times must be undertaken with great care. Macintyre (1967, 1968, 1972) has reviewed data on the depth distribution of submerged upper slope reefs (75 m–90 m deep) in the Caribbean Sea, suggesting that these may have formed during the early Holocene still stand (16,500–15,000 years BP) proposed by Curray (1965). If future work corroborates this time relationship, it will be necessary to acknowledge extensive coral reef growth during a period when relatively low thermal conditions prevailed. In the tropical waters of the western Atlantic Ocean this may have amounted to a decline in the mean surface temperature of at least 3° C (Olausson, 1965, 1967) and possibly as much as 5°–6°C (Emiliani, 1970).

IV. Associated Plankton Community

Measurements of total community metabolism (Odum et al., 1959) or the gross photosynthesis of major component coral populations (Kanwisher and Wainwright, 1967) reveal a very high level of productivity on western Atlantic coral reefs, similar to that demonstrated for reef ecosystems in the western Pacific Ocean. In Puerto Rico the gross productivity of near-shore coral reef communities was 6–24 gm carbon/(m² day) (Odum et al., 1959). Some of these measurements showed that respiration exceeded photosynthesis. Shallow reef communities composed of Porites and Thalassia revealed a net respiratory loss of −1.4 and −3 gm carbon/(m² day). Nonautotrophy has also been observed on a Hawaiian fringing reef, leading Gordon and Kelly (1962) to suggest a fundamental trophic difference between open ocean reefs and those present on large island and continental areas. A central problem now demanding attention is that of defining the pathways of energy flow through this highly productive system. Benthic algae, sea grasses, and corals contribute significantly to reef production and have been shown to enter the food web in varying degrees. Another potential energy source is plankton, which is available to some reef communities in high abundance.

Often a major difficulty in assessing the contribution of plankton is the presence of an abundant benthic component that alters the composition of plankton through feeding, release of sexual products, etc. This fact demands that volumetric or numerical measurements of plankton across selected reef segments must be combined with analyses of the species composition in order to determine that fraction actually removed. In applying such methods, Tranter and George (1969) have succeeded in demonstrating the extent to which zooplankton is utilized by the reef populations of two atolls in the Laccadive archipelago. Since numerous workers have shown that the quantity of offshore plankton is greatly diminished in the lagoon, Emery (1968) has argued that this must have been removed by the reef community over which it passed.

An attempt to determine the quantity of plankton utilized by one coral reef assemblage, the reef flat biotope dominated by *Porites furcata,* was carried out on a Puerto Rican reef (Glynn, 1973) similar to those studied by Odum *et al.* (1959). The appearance of such a *Porites* community in Panama is shown in Fig. 4F. Currents moving across the reef flat are normally unidirectional and quite vigorous, generated by the local wind field, solitary waves, and possibly tidal effects. The total volume flow across a 1-m-wide path varied between 39,900 m^3/month in March to 68,700 m^3/month in June. This current flux resulted in the transport of 735 gm suspended dry matter/(m^2 month) in March and 1344 gm/(m^2 month) in June. Numerical density differences across the reef at the species level, used to indicate the magnitude of gain by the reef community, were detected in the net plankton component only. This amounted to a filtering efficiency by the reef of 91% for diatoms and 60% for zooplankton. In terms of biomass, the zooplankton component usually contributed far greater amounts than did the diatoms.

Equated on the basis of carbon, and allowing for seasonal and diel variations in abundance, the total net plankton gain ranged between 0.075 and 0.290 gm C/(m^2 day), or 65.4 gm C/(m^2 year). Relating a mean daily gain of 0.18 gm C/(m^2 day) to a nonautotrophic system, with respiratory losses of -1.4 and -3 gm C/(m^2 day), it is seen that energy from plankton could theoretically satisfy between 6 and 13% of the total community expenditures.

If this represents a close approximation of community consumption, it would not appear excessive considering the high population densities of suspension feeders present in this coral assemblage. For example, the aggregate numerical density and protein biomass of known invertebrate plankton consumers (computed from the proportion of these feeding types presented in Table II), exclusive of the Scleractinia, can amount to 38,930 individuals/m^2 and 12.8 gm/m^2, respectively. The feeding activities of planktivorous reef fishes can also be appreciable. Several individuals of *Apogon conklini* (Silvester), often abundant on *Porites* patch reefs, were observed to ingest an average of 51 zoea larvae in 30 minutes. While it is fairly clear that plankton is an important food resource for many reef animals, its role as an energy source in the hermatypic corals is still unresolved. Johannes *et al.* (1970) present evidence from Bermuda, based on laboratory measurements of respiration, that only a small fraction of the energy requirements of corals, something less than 5.4%, is satisfied by zooplankton consumption.

Owing to the prevalence of pelagic larvae among reef-associated species, the plankton community assumes an additional important role in the recruitment of the benthos. Annual cycles in phytoplankton abundance and productivity have been demonstrated by several workers in the tropical western Atlantic region (see Sournia, 1969, for pertinent references). Fluctuations in neritic plankton populations appear to be influenced by local meteorological and hydrographic conditions which control the nutrient enrichment of surface waters. The annual cycles characteristic of particular areas have been correlated with upwelling, wind-induced mixing, river runoff, and currents. Such seasonal fluctuations in the plankton can be expected to affect the benthic community through recruitment, variations in the food supply available to suspension feeders, and the reproductive periodicities of species with planktotrophic larvae.

To gain some impression of the annual variations in recruitment on a Puerto Rican reef, screened enclosures were suspended in the current passing over a *Porites* reef flat assemblage. The larvae which settled and metamorphosed in these enclosures were harvested monthly, thus providing a measure of the intensity of predator-free recruitment in this habitat. Synoptic plots illustrating the rate of settlement for a 1-year period are presented in Fig. 8A–E. Generally, recruitment was greatest in the spring and late summer to fall seasons. Polychaetes, ascidians, and mesogastropod mollusks underwent a heavy settlement from March through June; mesogastropod and tectibranchiate mollusks, and ophiuroids and echinoids appeared abundantly at different times between August and December.

While many animal groups comprising coral reef communities appear

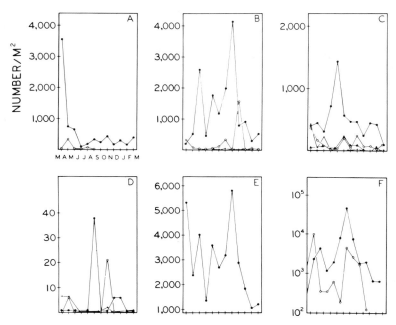

Fig. 8. Seasonal patterns of recruitment into enclosures suspended over a *Porites* patch reef community, Laurel Reef, La Parguera, Puerto Rico, March 1967–March 1968. (A) Polychaetous annelids (●) and ascidians (○); (B) Mollusca, mesogastropods (●), tectibranchs (○), bivalves (+); (C) Crustacea, brachyurans (●), amphipods (○), isopods (+), carideans (▲); (D) Echinodermata, ophiuroids (●), echinoids (○), holothuroids (+); (E) total recruitment in all groups; (F) numerical density of diatoms (cells/liter) at Laurel Reef, 1963–1964 (●), 1964 (○).

to be long-lived and produce larval stages relatively advanced in development, attributes of species constituting mature ecosystems (Margalef, 1968), it should be clear that a very important species component also exists with quite different life history characteristics. A mean monthly accrual approaching 3000 individuals per square meter, representing 7.2% of the standing stock, is indicative of a high turnover rate. Many of the polychaetes, crustaceans, and mollusks reach sexual maturity and bear eggs in a minimum period of 30 days. Moreover, evidence is available that these so-called fugitive species produce large broods throughout the year, many with planktotrophic larvae of long life which are well adapted for long-distance dispersal. The prevalence of species with life history strategies of this nature is not surprising in view of the frequent disturbances which occur in the reef flat environment, viz., unpredictable periods of low-water exposure, storm effects, etc.

The seasonal maxima in the standing crop of diatoms in Puerto Rico appear to show a close correspondence with the most active periods of recruitment (Fig. 8E and F). Additional data on species with planktotrophic larvae indicate a peak breeding period in this area centered around the fall season (Glynn, 1970a). It is tempting to infer a causal connection between these phenomena, with breeding synchronized to the seasons of greatest phytoplankton production. An area perhaps appropriate to the investigation of this apparent relationship is that along the northeastern coast of Venezuela, where seasonal upwelling is pronounced. Information on the degree of accommodation of tropical species to a relatively low thermal regime and concomitant increase in the plankton food supply should allow a more rigorous interpretation of the relative importance of these two parameters. Most available data on the breeding and recruitment of littoral populations in the Caribbean Sea indicate a significant seasonal aspect in these activities (e.g., Allen, 1957; Lewis, 1960b, 1966; Goodbody, 1961; Erdman, 1965). The environmental factors influencing or regulating these patterns and their effects on the benthic communities are questions of fundamental theoretical significance.

V. Coral and Coral Reef Growth Rates

The prevalent notion that the constructional activity of western Atlantic coral reefs is significantly less than that of Indo-Pacific reefs (e.g., Wells, 1957; Helfrich and Townsley, 1963) stems largely from growth data obtained under quite different thermal conditions in the two regions. The often-quoted comparative assessment of reef growth made by Vaughan (1916a) was based on growth rates of corals in the Florida–Bahamas area and in the Indo-Pacific at the Cocos-Keeling Islands and Torres Straits. The Atlantic study sites are situated near the 21°C winter isotherm, whereas the lowest thermal influence in the two Indo-Pacific localities is that of the 25°C isotherm (Hydrographic Office, 1944). While Vaughan and Wells (1943) emphasized the effect of the thermal environment on growth rates, data from the northern limit of coral distribution in the western Atlantic have continued to be used as a basis for comparisons between the two regions. Growth rate data obtained recently in the Caribbean Sea, where the minimum mean monthly sea surface temperature is near 26.5°C, reveal coral growth rates comparable with those observed in the center of the tropical Pacific and Indian Ocean regions.

Before reviewing the data for the western Atlantic region, it must be cautioned that the variance in measurements of coral growth can be high and therefore care should be exercised in comparing the data obtained by different workers in different areas. For example, within given species populations individual colony growth has been shown to depend on age (Vaughan and Wells, 1943), location of polyps on the corallum, light intensity, and the condition of the symbiotic algae (Goreau and Goreau, 1959). Food supply, sedimentation, salinity, and the various destructive agents, both physical and biological, must also affect growth.

Hoffmeister and Multer (1964), repeating in much the same manner Vaughan's growth measurements of *Montastrea annularis* in Florida, found this species (multilobulate growth form) to undergo a mean annual height increment of 1.07 cm (Table III). This represents a 1.6-fold increase over the earlier maximum value observed. Shinn (1966), performing *in situ* measurements on the Florida reef tract, obtained an optimal annual growth rate of 11.5 cm for *Acropora cervicornis*. Vaughan's maximum observed growth for this species was 4.53 cm, only about 39% of the more recent value. The mean growth rate of transplanted corals subjected to suboptimal conditions was only one-half that of the control populations. The effects of temperature were well illustrated by the group relocated at a near-shore station. Growth was vigorous initially at relatively high stable temperatures, decreased upon bleaching at extreme high temperatures and finally ceased when the corals succumbed at 13.3°C. The natural control group showed accelerated growth during the warm summer season. Shinn's method of measurement in the natural habitat, never removing or touching the animals as formerly practiced, is a decided improvement and probably in part accounts for the higher growth values obtained.

The relatively slow growth of corals observed in Bermuda by Iams (1969) was probably related to their advanced age and uncertain date of establishment—all data are from corals growing on submerged structures 25–107 years old—as well as to the lower thermal conditions in this area. The mean annual growth estimates of *M. annularis* are near those observed in Florida, but *Diploria strigosa* was considerably less. The growth rates of corals in the Caribbean Sea are clearly greater than their congeners further north (Lewis *et al.*, 1968). The greatest mean growth in diameter of *M. annularis* observed by Vaughan in Florida was surpassed by factors ranging from 1.8 in Barbados to 2.4 in Jamaica. In like manner, the highest growth rate yet observed for

TABLE III

COMPARATIVE GROWTH RATE DATA ON SELECTED HERMATYPIC CORAL SPECIES FROM THE WESTERN ATLANTIC REGION

Locality	Species	Annual growth increment (cm)[a]		Growth rate relative to Vaughan's data[b]	Author	Mean monthly sea-surface temp. for coldest month of year (°C)
		Height	Diameter			
Florida Loggerhead Key	*Montastrea annularis*	0.68(0.53)	0.90(0.69)	1	Vaughan, 1916a	20.2[c]
	Porites furcata	2.28(0.9)	3.93(3.15)	1		21.1
Ft. Jefferson		1.60	4.48			
	Diploria strigosa	1.00(0.35)	1.98(1.12)	1		
Bahamas Golding Cay, Andros Is.	*Acropora cervicornis*	4.53	—	1		
Florida Carysfort Lighthouse and near Key Largo	*Montastrea annularis*	*1.07*	—	1.6	Hoffmeister and Multer, 1964	21.5[c]
Florida Key Largo	*Acropora cervicornis*	*11.5*	—	2.5	Shinn, 1966	20[d]
Bermuda Shipwrecks along northern edge of Bermuda platform	*Montastrea annularis*	*0.81*	*1.26(0.36)*[e]	0.9	Iams, 1969	17.3[f]
	Diploria strigosa	*0.32*	*0.36(0.27)*	0.2		

Barbados, West Indies						
West coast	*Montastrea annularis*	*1.9 ± 0.4*	*1.6 ± 0.3*	2.8(h)	1.8(d)	Lewis *et al.,* 1968	26.4
	Porites porites	*3.7 ± 0.7*	—	—		
	Acropora cervicornis	*14.5 ± 3.1*	—	3.2		
Jamaica, West Indies						
Mouth of Kingston Harbour, Port Royal	*Montastrea annularis*	*2.5 ± 0.7*	*2.2 ± 0.9*	3.7(h)	2.4(d)	Lewis *et al.,* 1968	27.2
	Porites porites	*4.1 ± 0.6*	—	—		
	Acropora cervicornis	*26.6 ± 8.2*	—	5.9		

[a] Mean in italic type with confidence limits at 95% level, maximum values in roman type, minimum values in parentheses.
[b] Calculations based on Vaughan's maximum values.
[c] Temperature records from Vaughan, 1918.
[d] Minimum recorded temperature.
[e] Maximum radial dimensions.
[f] C.&G.S. Pub. 31-1, 1968.

A. cervicornis in Florida (Shinn, 1966) was exceeded in Barbados and Jamaica, respectively, by factors of 1.3 and 2.3. Within the Caribbean, *Acropora* displayed a significantly higher growth rate in Jamaica ($0.01 > p > 0.001$), a difference not presently understood.

Without entering into detailed comparisons of coral growth rates, consideration of only a few of the highest Indo-Pacific values is enough to dispel the supposed significant regional differences often cited. Ramose *Porites* undergoes an annual height increment of 3.0 cm in Samoa (Mayor, 1924) and 3.8 cm in the Cocos-Keeling Islands (Guppy, 1889); *Acropora* 12.0 cm in Samoa (Mayor, 1924) and 10.1–17.2 cm at Yap (Tamura and Hada, 1932). It is also evident that the relatively high growth values for various massive Indian Ocean species, 2.0–2.9 cm per annum (Vaughan, 1916a), are in close agreement with *M. annularis*, the only Caribbean species carefully studied to date.

Several attempts have been made to determine the long-term growth of coral reefs from known coral growth rates (e.g., Vaughan, 1915; Hoffmeister and Multer, 1964). Elucidation of the numerous factors contributing to reef growth, however, such as the diverse assemblage of hermatypic species of varying abundance and rates of accretion, the extent of physical and biological erosion, and degree of lithification, to name a few, underscores the uncertainties inherent in this approach. Estimates of reef growth derived from growth rates of corals are at best measures of gross levels of skeletal formation by this one particular group. One of the best methods now available for measuring the net growth of reefs entails the radiometric dating of sections representative of the major axis of accretion.

Modern reef growth estimated by means of ^{14}C dating indicates accretionary rates of 1200 *B* (the Bubnoff Unit *B* represents a geologic increment of 1 mm/10^3 years) for cup reefs (Ginsburg and Schroeder, 1969) and 1900 *B* for shoal reefs (Frazier, 1970) in Bermuda. The only measurements available in the Caribbean Sea at this writing are those of Goreau and Land (1972) from Jamaica. These indicate a rapid growth of 1200 *B* at 25 m depth. The growth of Yucatán shelf reefs, computed from the relative elevation of the reef base above the glacial stage terrace with the Holocene transgression, suggests a rate of accretion of ~2000–4000 *B* (Logan, 1969). The much higher estimates of reef growth inferred from the growth of individual corals stand out in marked contrast with the former values (Table IV). While the present data on net coral reef accretion are admittedly few, they are more in line with the expected rate of growth relative to the sea-level curve now established for the past 5000–7000 years.

TABLE IV

Estimates of Coral Reef Growth in the Western Atlantic Region

Locality	Author	Method	Nature of reef	Estimated growth	
				Original data	B (1 mm/10³ years)[a]
Florida Keys	Hoffmeister and Multer, 1964	Extrapolated from growth rate of *M. annularis*	Pleistocene Key Largo coral reef <10 m depth?	7 ft/250–500 years	4300–8500
Bermuda	Ginsburg and Schroeder, 1969	¹⁴C dating of dissected reef	Cup reefs of algae, vermetids and *Millepora*; located on rim of Bermuda platform; 3–9 m above sea floor	Sample from 3.5 m depth 2980 ± 160 years BP	1200
Bermuda	Frazier, 1970	Correlation of sea level transgression with age of harbor channel	Coral shoal reef, Castle Harbor, 6 m above sea floor	6 m/3200 years BP	1900
Jamaica	Goreau and Land, 1972	¹⁴C dating of dissected reef	Near base of fore-reef escarpment, 25 m depth	1.2 m/1000 years BP	1200
Yucatán, Mexico	Logan, 1969	Inferred from depth of reef base and rate of Holocene transgression	Emergent bank and knoll coral reefs	60–120 ft/9000 years BP	1800–3700

[a] B represents the Bubnoff Unit as defined by Fischer (1969).

VI. Biotic Interactions at the Community Level

A number of boring organisms were alluded to earlier that erode and weaken the skeleton of corals, thereby affecting directly or indirectly, through sediment production, the growth of individual colonies and even the character of deeper coral communities. While it is not practical here to develop the subject of bioerosion, it must be recognized that the destructive activities of organisms can proceed with great rapidity and are to a large extent responsible for many of the major physiographic features of structural reefs. In this section consideration will be given to the effects of reef animals on the living parts of corals, mainly with reference to their interference with survival and growth and thus their potential role as modifiers of community structure.

Some general remarks will first be made on foraging fish populations and how their activities can act as a repressive influence on the development of the benthos. A survey of the known predators of corals is followed by a discussion of their presumed chronic effects, largely inferred from the appearance of corals invaded and overgrown by alien forms. Several reef organisms come into direct competition with one another for space. Examples of this are examined in the extracoelenteric feeding behavior of certain scleractinians and among other organisms exhibiting the capacity to invade and subdue their neighbors.

A. Feeding Intensity of Herbivorous Reef Fishes

Coral reef communities lack abundant, massive algal growths that typically occur in the littoral zone of temperate shores or in terrestrial environments of high productivity. The high photosynthetic activity of coral reefs derives from a low growth of filamentous algae, an endolithic flora, crustose coralline and other calcareous algae, and symbiotic dinoflagellates or free chloroplasts in the tissues of a variety of animal species. A flora of this character, often present in combination with benthic animal populations of extensive coverage, might well lead to a situation where herbivores are resource-limited. Perhaps an obvious expression of this is the intense feeding activities of herbivorous reef fishes, involving frequent scraping, grazing, and browsing of virtually all exposed surfaces (Bakus, 1966, 1969). Conclusive evidence that browsing fishes control the development of the flora on intertidal reef surfaces was first provided experimentally by Stephenson and Searles (1960) at Heron Island, Great Barrier Reef, Australia. Though only limited data are now available from the western Atlantic region, these do clearly illustrate the range of influence of the feeding activities of fish herbivores.

The fish populations associated with Atlantic coral reefs are present at a high biomass density, as are those on Indo-Pacific reefs, possibly significantly higher than the standing stocks reported for many shallow temperate areas. The mean standing stock of omnivores (primarily herbivores) on a Bermudian reef was estimated by visual counts to attain 0.016 kg/m² (Bardach, 1959) and on natural reefs in the Virgin Islands, by direct census procedures, 0.039 kg/m² (Randall, 1963). In Bermuda it was estimated that 0.23 kg calcareous material/m² is passed through the alimentary tract of reef fishes in 1 year (Bardach, 1961). On coral reefs in Panama, where very accurate measurements are now available for several large schools of *Scarus croicensis* (Bloch), it has been found that a population of 3500 individuals feeding in a 5300-m² area can defecate a dry weight mass of 2.41 kg/(m² year) (Ogden, personal communication).

Other indications of the influence of fishes on the benthos are the nicks frequently seen on the substratum and the rapid growth of algae in exclosures. Moreover, naturally protected surfaces, for example, the nonliving basal branches of ramose corals such as *Porites* spp., *Eusmilia fastigiata* (Pallas), and *Acropora cervicornis*, which provide shelter from foraging fishes, often contain abundant growths of bivalves, cirripedes, bryozoans, and even young corals. Newman (1960) observed a general paucity of Cirripedia in the intertidal zone on western Pacific reefs and attributed this to the side effects of rasping fish herbivores. An additional example provided by Randall (1965) shows how herbivorous fishes crop sea grasses adjacent to reefs, thus producing a conspicuous band of sand. It was also found that given adequate shelter, herbivorous fishes attained higher densities on seagrass flats than on reefs. This observation suggests population control through a limited food resource on reefs and from predation away from reef structures.

The majority of workers agree that the feeding range of fish herbivores is generally restricted to the upper 10-m depth levels (Bakus, 1969). It can be deduced from the foregoing observations that plant-covered reef substrata are continuously reworked by fishes and that this activity must profoundly affect the survival and growth of benthic reef populations at shallow depth. Goreau's (1967) perceptive observation that the greater abundance of fleshy animal groups and their tendency to attain gigantic proportions in the deeper reef zones are an expression of the diminished influence of foraging fishes, offers a plausible hypothesis for explaining many of the major differences in community structure along the depth gradient.

B. Coral Predators and Their Effects

It was observed by Robertson (1970) that the number of animals specialized to feed on the Scleractinia has been underestimated (Wells, 1957; Yonge, 1963). Some of the observed effects also go far beyond the negligible damage claimed by Yonge (1968). Since many of the known coral predators have been described only relatively recently, it is likely that continued study will add to our knowledge of this feeding habit. The following review will no doubt soon be supplemented by new discoveries.

In Randall's (1967) survey of the food habits of reef fishes small volumes of coral were found in the alimentary tracts of four species: *Scarus coelestinus* Cuvier and Valenciennes and *Sparisoma aurofrenatum* (Cuvier and Valenciennes) [Scaridae], *Chaetodipterus faber* (Broussonet) [Ephippidae], and *Microspathodon chrysurus* (Cuvier and Valenciennes) [Pomacentridae]. The only specific coral identification noted was that of *Oculina diffusa*, a fragment consumed by *C. faber*. In some localities coral consumption by fishes appears greater than indicated by Randall's (1967) study. For example, in Panama (Bakus, 1969) and Bermuda (Gygi, 1969), the rasping of live corals by scarids is commonplace. *Scarus guacamaia* Cuvier rasps *Siderastrea siderea* with fair regularity along much of the north coast of Panama. The summits of large hemispherical colonies are commonly scraped to depths of 2–3 mm (Fig. 9B); such feeding is often performed by relatively small schools of *S. guacamaia* (5–15 individuals) which appear to range over extensive areas. *Microspathodon chrysurus*, though predominantly herbivorous on epontic diatoms and filamentous algae, frequently feeds on *S. siderea* as well. Juveniles and adults of this fish bite the surface of the corallum vigorously, removing primarily the extended polyps. Corals preyed upon in this manner can be distinguished by the characteristic circular lesions left behind (Fig. 9A). Juveniles of *Microspathodon* commonly feed on the hydrocoral *Millepora* in Florida (Ciardelli, 1967) and both juveniles and adults attack *Millepora complanata* in Panama. Other corals observed in Panama with deep rasping marks, similar to those produced by *S. guacamaia*, are *Montastrea annularis*, *Acropora palmata*, *A. cervicornis*, *Agaricia agaricites*, and *Porites furcata*. Mixed schools of *Scarus croicensis*, *Acanthurus chirurgus* (Bloch), *Chaetodon capistratus* Linnaeus, and other species occasionally feed

Fig. 9. (A) Circular lesions on the surface of *Siderastrea siderea*, the result of feeding by *Microspathodon chrysurus*, 2 m deep, Galeta Island, Panama, July 10, 1970. (B) Deep rasping marks on the surface of S. *siderea*, the result of feeding by *Scarus guacamaia* Cuvier, 3 m deep, Galeta Island, Panama, October 16, 1969.

on *A. cervicornis*. Such incidental feeding forays can lead to coral rasping by the scarid and selective removal of polyps by the latter two species (Ogden, personal communication). On one occasion a scarid, possibly *Scarus vetula* Bloch and Schneider, was observed to bite off a terminal 2-cm tip of *Porites porites*. On some areas of the reef, *Porites* colonies commonly have many of their terminal branches broken off. This feeding habit was reported long ago in Haiti by Beebe (1928), who observed that scarids (most likely *S. guacamaia*) break off and ingest the terminal branches of corals. The effects of fish predators on *Porites astreoides* have not been reported in the Caribbean, but according to Gygi (1969) *Sparisoma viride* (Bonnaterre) commonly feeds on this coral at Bermuda, removing up to 200 mg with each bite.

To account for the recognized greater feeding on corals by Indo-Pacific (Hiatt and Strasburg, 1960; Talbot, 1965) as compared with Atlantic reef fishes, Randall (1967) suggested that Indo-Pacific reefs carried a more extensive coral cover than Atlantic reefs and that the extensive coral cover reduced the quantity of plant food available to fishes on Indo-Pacific reefs. Reef fishes on the Pacific side of Panama consume larger quantities of living coral than do those present on the Atlantic side. All of eight commonly occurring scleractinian species on eastern Pacific reefs (Las Secas and Las Contreras Islands) showed signs of having been consumed and over 50% of the colonies of four coral species had been frequently preyed upon (Glynn *et al.*, 1972). One possible explanation for this difference is the absence of marine phanerogams around the reefs studied in the Pacific areas. Intense predation on the depauperate eastern Pacific coral fauna is not consistent with Bakus' (1969) contention that the utilization of corals seems more evident on western Pacific reefs because of the greater number of species present there.

As Yonge (1963) suggested, nematocysts must certainly deter some fishes from feeding on corals. That *Microspathodon* regularly consumes large amounts of the hydrocoral *Millepora*, however, indicates that certain species can cope with this potent means of defense. Possibly another effective deterrent that would tend to discourage fish predators is the presence of sharply projecting septa, often with serrated edges, on the corallites of *Mussa*, *Scolymia*, *Isophyllastraea*, *Mycetophyllia*, *Isophyllia*, and *Eusmilia*. It may therefore be significant that the coral species most often consumed by large fishes have relatively smooth and unobtrusive surfaces.

Five invertebrate coral predators have been discovered in the Caribbean region since 1962. These include the amphinomid polychaete *Hermo-*

dice carunculata (Pallas), the majid decapod *Mithrax* (*Mithraculus*) *sculptus* (Lamarck), and the gastropod mollusks *Coralliophila abbreviata* Lamarck, *C. caribea* Abbott, and *Calliostoma javanicum* Lamarck. *Hermodice* was first described by Marsden (1962a) to be an habitual predator of *Porites porites* and subsequently observed to feed on *P. astreoides* by Marsden (1962b) and on *Acropora palmata* by Glynn (1962). Usually, the upper tips of ramose *Porites* are selectively attacked but the worm can also feed on flat surfaces as on *Acropora palmata*. Ebbs (1966) notes that coral browsing may occur in all Atlantic members of the Amphinomidae. Both *P. furcata* and *P. porites* are attacked by *Mithrax*, which severs the polyps with its chelae. This feeding habit, first observed in Puerto Rico (Glynn, 1962), was recently confirmed in Panama, where *Mithrax* commonly preys upon ramose species of *Porites*. Ward (1965) believed that the mode of feeding of *Coralliophila abbreviata*, involving the dissolution and ingestion of soft tissues, can lead to the death of polyps and eventual destruction of the colony of *Montastrea annularis*. On the other hand, Robertson (1970) maintains that this species is a well-adapted parasite, causing little damage to the polyps. One may infer from Robertson's (1970) collecting records that *C. abbreviata* derives sustenance from several different corals, including *A. palmata*, *Diploria clivosa* (Ellis and Solander), and *Favia fragum*. Miller (1970) found *Coralliophila abbreviata* and *C. caribea* associated with 14 hermatypes at Discovery Bay, Jamaica, and suggests that the gastropods may feed on plankton ingested by the corals. *Calliostoma javanicum* feeds on *Mussa angulosa* in the laboratory and on *Agaricia* spp. in the laboratory and field (Lang, 1970), with a preference for the latter group. Small circular lesions are produced, but it is not yet known which of the soft parts of the coral are consumed.

From the foregoing, it is obvious that several reef animals are adapted to feed on the Scleractinia. Though the actual quantities of coral consumed appear to be slight, there is good evidence that the damaged areas of the corallum that do not undergo regeneration are invaded by other organisms which may overgrow and eventually smother the entire colony. Continuing observations of the rasped surfaces of *Siderastrea siderea* have shown that, while repair normally takes place rapidly (2–3 months), some areas suffer irreparable damage. The latter are often invaded initially by a variety of filamentous algae, including members of the Cyanophyceae, Chlorophyceae, Rhodophyceae, and Phaeophyceae, and epontic diatom growths. Large colonies of *Montastrea annularis* with their surfaces in various stages of invasion provide a concrete example of the course of destruction. Scarid nicks often contain mixed growths of filamentous algae and these can be traced through a successional continuum to surfaces highly eroded by boring clionid sponges. Zoanthids (*Palythoa*) and sponges (e.g., *Chondrilla nucula* Schmidt and clionids) also commonly occur on *Siderastrea* in various stages of invasion. The frequent location of such growths, away from peripheral areas, indicate a probable invasion through previously damaged areas. *Chondrilla* can also be found encrusting the truncated (presumably due to scarids) upper branches of *Porites porites*, in relative isolation from surrounding areas.

Direct evidence of the ability of alien growths to expand from injured sites over undamaged coral surfaces is available. This was obtained from sections of *Cliona* (in the beta stage of development) that were transplanted from infected *Siderastrea* to the algal-covered scars of uninfected colonies. The implanted sponges began to grow immediately, and expanded 2 cm peripherally in a 9-month period, killing the underlying coral.

The destruction of *A. palmata* by *Hermodice*, over areas up to 150 cm^2 in extent, may also prevent regeneration of the coral; this is in need of further study. In addition, it would be useful to know to what extent the constant feeding on soft parts by *Microspathodon* and *Mithrax* affects coral growth.

C. COMPETITION FOR SPACE

There is a good deal of evidence from the field indicating that competition for living space is acute among the long-lived benthic populations of coral reefs. It appears that many groups of reef organisms have evolved body morphologies which tend to maximize the area of exposure to light and currents. Certain minimum levels of exposure are necessary for both photosynthetic and suspension feeding forms. Therefore, it is not surprising to find that a variety of strategies are employed to ensure the acquisition of space and access to the surrounding medium, and a subsequent hold on this resource once obtained.

1. Extracoelenteric Feeding in the Scleractinia

To the rapid and spreading mode of growth employed by many corals as a means of reducing competition for space and light, must now be added the newly discovered adaptation of extracoelenteric feeding (Lang, 1970). This behavior is best developed in members of the Mussidae, Meandrinidae, and Faviidae in the suborder Faviina. It is a normal feeding response, where closely growing subordinate corals are attacked by more active species. The fleshy areas of prey species within reach are digested in an extracoelenteric manner by the extruded mesenterial filaments. In the western Atlantic, competitive interactions appear to be best developed among species which normally extrude the mesenterial filaments in feeding and produce relatively strong ciliary feeding currents. The Caribbean populations investigated by Lang (including data from thesis and subsequent studies) demonstrated the following hierarchical ranking in feeding behavior: *Mussa angulosa* (Pallas) = *Scolymia lacera* > *Isophyllia sinuosa* (Ellis and Solander) = *Mycetophyllia* sp. 1 = *Meandrina meandrites* (Linnaeus) > *Mycetophyllia* sp. 2 > *Mycetophyllia* sp. 3 > *Mycetophyllia lamarckana* > *Scolymia cubensis* = *Isophyllastraea rigida* (Dana) > *Montastrea annularis* > other faviid spp. > acroporids > *Agaricia* spp. = *Helioseris cucullata* (Ellis and Solander) > other fungiid spp. > astrocoeniid spp. (Numerals refer to taxa presently being described.)

While such competitive interactions can be observed among adult corals, they probably also play an important role among young growing forms. An active feeder, for example, would preclude the establishment of subordinate species within its feeding radius. Competitive exclusion by means of predatory interactions occurs most noticeably in the densely populated buttress zone (1–10 m deep), fore-reef (10–30 m deep), and fore-reef slope (30–60 m deep) zones. *Montastrea annularis,* one of the principal reef-building species, is moderately active in extracoelenteric feeding and perhaps owes its presence in the buttress zone and along the seaward slope in part to its ability to compete successfully with more rapidly growing ramose and foliaceous forms.

2. Interactions between Corals and Other Sessile Organisms

Careful observation of benthic reef populations reveals frequent instances of unrelated organisms approaching each other in growth and then one overgrowing and excluding its neighbor. While certain corals can coexist for long periods in close contact with alien species, for example, the beneficial association of *Montastrea annularis* with the sponge *Mycale laevis* (Carter) reported by Goreau and Hartman (1966), it appears that there is a tendency for some of the larger algae, sponges, octocorals, and zoanthideans to displace coral growth. This seems to take place in the absence of any detectable preexisting damage to the coral as noted earlier for destruction initiated through the activities of predators. Some examples follow.

Among algae, *Halimeda opuntia* (Linnaeus) Lamouroux, *Caulerpa racemosa* var. *macrophysa* (Kützing) Taylor, and *Peyssonnelia rubra* (Irgebille) J. Agardh are commonly found covering large areas of *Porites furcata*. The brown alga *Lobophora variegata* (Lamouroux) Womersley often proliferates over extensive populations, up to 20 m², of *Agaricia* spp. and other corals between 15 and 30 m depth. *Chondrilla nucula*, an encrusting sponge, can overgrow large tracts of *Porites furcata* and entire colonies of *Siderastrea siderea* and *Diploria clivosa*. *Porites* is usually invaded from below, by way of the dead basal branches, and the massive corals from peripheral areas. The octocoral *Briareum asbestinum* (Pallas) also invades ramose *Porites* from below. Kinzie (1970) gives evidence of various forms of interaction, however, from a modification of the growth pattern of corals by gorgonians to the suppression of the polyp areas of gorgonians from the physical contact of corals. Rützler (1971) has found that adociid poriferans, members of the genus *Siphonodictyon*, can burrow directly into the living and undamaged colonies of several corals. *Stephanocoenia michelinii* (Milne-Edwards and Haime), *Siderastrea siderea*, *Porites astreoides*, *Diploria strigosa*, and *Montastrea annularis* are attacked in the lower buttress, fore-reef, and fore-reef slope zones. *Palythoa*, a zoanthidean often dominating shallow surfaces, can overgrow and exclude *Siderastrea siderea* and *Diploria clivosa*.

It would seem that competitive interactions of this intensity should come into play at particular life history stages, otherwise coral populations would assume a more limited role on reefs than appears to be the case. The evidence presented here suggests that the older members among iteroparous species are more vulnerable to replacement. The form of competition observed seems to be well accommodated by the interference strategy postulated by Miller (1969) for competitive interactions in highly evolved communities. Generally, the population attributes of species which compete through interference, such as large body size, long generation time, and low replacement rate, seem to be shared by the major populations alluded to.

These preliminary findings underscore the great influence of particular biotic interactions in coral reef communities. Now it remains to be learned to what extent community structure is controlled by the differential effects of predation and competition. And how do the various anti-predator adaptations and superior competitive qualities of certain sessile reef populations relate to the success of these groups? These are challenging questions amenable to observational and experimental analysis.

Acknowledgments

Much of the original data presented here was obtained through the technical assistance of F. Fernández, C. Glynn, D. Quintero, and F. Robison. Species identifications were provided by W. Adey (coralline algae), A. Myra Keen (vermetid gastropods), and J. Redemske Young (fleshy algae). J. C. Lang, J. Ogden, J. W.

Porter, and R. Stewart have offered valuable companionship in the field and in discussions of the biology of coral reefs. Of outstanding assistance in providing library materials was J. Marcquardt of the Smithsonian Institution Libraries. I am particularly indebted to several workers, acknowledged in the text of this chapter, who allowed extensive reference to their unpublished data. My experience with coral reefs in the American seas has been due largely to support provided by grants from the University of Puerto Rico, the National Science Foundation and the Research Awards Program of the Smithsonian Institution. Appreciation is also expressed for the critical comments offered by several people in the preparation of this chapter, notably T. Dana, R. Endean, J. C. Lang, J. McCosker, J. W. Porter, and J. W. Wells.

References

Adams, R. D. (1968). *J. Geol.* **76**, 587.
Allen, M. J. (1957). *Biol. Bull.* **113**, 49.
Almy, C. C., Jr., and Carrión Torres, C. (1963). *Carib. J. Sci.* **3**, 133.
Antonius, A. (1969). *Abstr., 8th Meet., Carib. Ass. Isl. Mar. Lab.*, Mimeo.
Antonius, A. (1972). *Bol. Inst. Oceanogr. Univ. Oriente* (in press).
Bakus, G. J. (1966). *Nature (London)* **210**, 280.
Bakus, G. J. (1969). *Int. Rev. Gen. Exp. Zool.* **4**, 275.
Ballard, R. D., and Uchupi, E. (1970). *Bull. Mar. Sci.* **20**, 547.
Bardach, J. E. (1959). *Limnol. Oceanogr.* **4**, 77.
Bardach, J. E. (1961). *Science* **133**, 98.
Barnes, J., Bellamy, D. J., Jones, D. J., Whitton, B. A., Drew, E., and Lythgoe, J. (1970). *Nature (London)* **225**, 268.
Bayer, F. M. (1961). "The Shallow-Water Octocorallia of the West Indian Region, A Manual for Marine Biologists." Nijhoff, Netherlands.
Beebe, W. (1928). "Beneath Tropic Seas." Halcyon House, New York.
Blasini de Austin, S. (1968). M.S. Thesis, University of Puerto Rico.
Boisvert, W. E. (1967). TR-193, p. 92. U.S. Navy Oceanographic Office, Washington, D.C.
Boyd, D. W., Kornicker, L. S., and Rezak, R. (1963). *Univ. Wyo., Contr. Geol.* **2**, 105.
Bright, T. J., and Pequegnat, L. H., eds. (1973). "Fauna of the West Flower Garden Coral Reef, Texas," Gulf Publ. Co., Houston, Texas (in press).
Busby, R. F. (1966). TR-187, p. 1. U.S. Navy Oceanographic Office, Washington, D.C.
Busby, R. F., and Dick, G. F., Jr. (1964). TR-174, p. 1. U.S. Navy Oceanographic Office, Washington, D.C.
Busby, R. F., Bright, C. V., and Pruna, A. (1966). TR-189, p. 1. U.S. Navy Oceanographic Office, Washington, D.C.
C&GS (1968). Publ. 31-1. U.S. Govt. Printing Office, Washington, D.C.
Chevalier, J. P. (1966). *Bull. Inst. Fondamental Afr. Noire, Ser. A* **28**, 912.
Ciardelli, A. (1967). *Bull. Mar. Sci.* **17**, 845.
Cochrane, J. D. (1961). *In* "Oceanography and Meteorology of the Gulf of Mexico" (H. J. McLellan, ed.), Rep. 61-15 F, pp. 5–6. Texas A & M University, College Station.
Cry, G. W. (1965). *Weather Bur., Tech. Pap.* **55**.
Curray, J. R. (1965). *In* "The Quaternary of the United States" (H. E. Wright,

Jr. and D. G. Frey, eds.), pp. 723–735. Princeton Univ. Press, Princeton, New Jersey.

Cushing, D. H. (1971). *Advan. Mar. Biol.* **9**, 255–334.

Darwin, C. (1842). "The Structure and Distribution of Coral Reefs." Univ. of California Press, Berkeley (1962 reprint).

de Andrade, G. O. (1960). *An. Div. Hidrografia* **18**, 203.

Di Salvo, L. H. (1969). *Amer. Zool.* **9**, 735–740.

Duarte Bello, P. P. (1961). "Corales de los Arrecifes Cubanos." Acuario Nacional, Marianao, Cuba.

Ebbs, N. K., J. (1966). *Bull. Mar. Sci.* **16**, 485.

Emery, A. R. (1968). *Limnol. Oceanogr.* **13**, 293.

Emery, K. O. (1963). *Geofis. Int.* **3**, 11.

Emiliani, C. (1970). *Science* **168**, 822.

Erdman, D. S. (1965). *Carib. J. Sci.* **5**, 103.

Fischer, A. G. (1969). *Geol. Soc. Amer., Bull.* **80**, 549.

Frazier, W. J. (1970). In "Seminar on Organism-Sediment Interrelationships" (R. N. Ginsburg and S. M. Stanley, eds.), Spec. Publ. No. 6, pp. 63–72. Bermuda Biological Station for Research, St. George's West.

Fuglister, F. C. (1947). *Pap. Phys. Oceanogr. Meteorol., Mass. Inst. Technol. Woods Hole Oceanogr. Inst.* **10**, 3.

Garrett, P., Smith, D. L., Wilson, A. O., and Patriquin, D. (1971). *J. Geol.* **79**, 647.

Ginsburg, R. N. (1953). *Bull. Mar. Sci. Gulf Carib.* **3**, 35.

Ginsburg, R. N. (1964). *Guideb. Geol. Soc. Amer. Field Trip* No. 1, p. 35.

Ginsburg, R. N., and Schroeder, J. H. (1969). *Bermuda Conf. Carbonate Cements, 1969* Mimeo., pp. 1–14.

Ginsburg, R. N., and Schroeder, J. H. (1971). *Abstr. 8th Int. Sedimentol. Cong, 1971* p. 35.

Ginsburg, R. N., and Shinn, E. A. (1964). *Bull. Amer. Ass. Petrol. Geol.* **48**, 527.

Ginsburg, R. N., and Stanley, S. M., eds. (1970). "Seminar on Organism-Sediment Interrelationships," Spec. Publ. No. 6, p. 109. Bermuda Biological Station for Research, St. George's West.

Glynn, P. W. (1962). *Abstr., 4th Meet., Carib. Ass. Isl. Mar. Lab. 1962* p. 16.

Glynn, P. W. (1968). *Mar. Biol.* **1**, 226.

Glynn, P. W. (1970a). *Smithson. Contrib. Zool.* **66**, 1.

Glynn, P. W. (1970b). *Mem. Soc. Cient. Nat. La Salle* **30**, 5.

Glynn, P. W. (1973). *Mar. Biol.* (in press).

Glynn, P. W., Almodóvar, L. R., and González, J. G. (1964). *Carib. J. Sci.* **4**, 335.

Glynn, P. W., Stewart, R. H., and McCosker, J. E. (1972). *Geol. Rundschau* **61**, 483.

Goodbody, I. (1961). *Proc. Zool. Soc. London* **136**, 403.

Gordon, M. S., and Kelly, H. M. (1962). *Ecology* **43**, 473.

Goreau, T. F. (1959). *Ecology* **40**, 67.

Goreau, T. F. (1961). Final Progr. Rep., Contract Nonr (G)-0003-60, pp. 1–14. Biology Branch, Office of Naval Research, Washington, D.C.

Goreau, T. F. (1963). *Ann. N.Y. Acad. Sci.* **109**, 127.

Goreau, T. F. (1965). *Abstr. Annu. Meet., Geol. Soc. Amer. 1964* p. 76.

Goreau, T. F. (1967). *Abstr., 7th Meet., Carib. Ass. Isl. Mar. Lab., 1966* p. 26.

Goreau, T. F. (1969). *Micronesica* **5**, 323.

Goreau, T. F., and Burke, K. (1966). *Mar. Geol.* **4**, 207.

Goreau, T. F., and Goreau, N. I. (1959). *Biol. Bull.* **117**, 239.
Goreau, T. F., and Graham, E. A. (1967). *Bull. Mar. Sci.* **17**, 432.
Goreau, T. F., and Hartman, W. D. (1963). *In* "Mechanisms of Hard Tissue Destruction," Publ. No. 75, pp. 25–54. Amer. Ass. Advance. Sci., Washington, D.C.
Goreau, T. F., and Hartman, W. D. (1966). *Science* **151**, 343.
Goreau, T. F., and Land, L. S. (1972). *Soc. Econ. Paleontol. Mineral., Spe. Publ.* (in press).
Goreau, T. F., and Wells, J. W. (1967). *Bull. Mar. Sci.* **17**, 442.
Gravier, C. (1909). *Ann. Inst. Oceanogr.* **1**, 1.
Guppy, H B. (1889). *Scot. Geogr. Mag.* **5**, 573.
Gygi, R. A. (1969). *In* "Seminar on Organism-Sediment Interrelationships" (R. N. Ginsburg and P. Garrett, eds.), Spec. Publ. No. 2, pp. 137–143. Bermuda Biological Station for Research, St. George's West.
Hartman, W. D., and Goreau, T. F. (1970). *Symp. Zool. Soc. London* **25**, 205.
Helfrich, P., and Townsley, S. J. (1963). *In* "Man's Place in the Island Ecosystem" (F. R. Fosberg, ed.), pp. 39–56. Bishop Museum Press, Honolulu.
Hiatt, R. W., and Strasburg, D. W. (1960). *Ecol. Monogr.* **30**, 65.
Hoffmeister, J. E., and Multer, H. G. (1964). *Geol. Soc. Amer., Bull.* **75**, 353.
Hoffmeister, J. E., Stockman, K. W., and Multer, H. G. (1967). *Geol. Soc. Amer., Bull.* **78**, 175.
Howe, M. A. (1912). *Science* **35**, 837.
Hunt, M. (1969). *In* "Seminar on Organism-Sediment Interrelationships" (R. N. Ginsburg and P. Garrett, eds.), Spec. Publ. No. 2, pp. 35–40. Bermuda Biological Station for Research, St. George's West.
Hydrographic Office. (1944). Publ. No. 225. United States Navy, Washington, D.C.
Iams, W. J. (1969). *In* "Seminar on Organism-Sediment Interrelationships" (R. N. Ginsburg and P. Garrett, eds.), Spec. Publ. No. 2, pp. 65–76. Bermuda Biological Station for Research, St. George's West.
Iams, W. J. (1970). *In* "Seminar on Organism-Sediment Interrelationships" (R. N. Ginsburg and S. M. Stanley, eds.), Spec. Publ. No. 6, pp. 91–98. Bermuda Biological Station for Research, St. George's West.
Johannes, R. E., Coles, S. L., and Kuenzel, N. T. (1970). *Limnol. Oceanogr.* **15**, 579.
Jones, N. S. (1950). *Biol. Rev.* **25**, 283.
Jordan, G. F., and Stewart, H. B., Jr. (1959). *Amer. Ass. Petrol. Geol., Bull.* **43**, 974.
Kanwisher, J. W., and Wainwright, S. A. (1967). *Biol. Bull.* **133**, 378.
Kaye, C. A. (1959). *U.S., Geol. Surv., Prof. Pap.* **317-B**, 49.
Kempf, M., and Laborel, J. (1968). *Rec. Trav. St. Mar. End. Bull.* **43**, 9.
Kinzie, R. A., III (1970). Ph.D. Thesis, Yale University, New Haven, Connecticut.
Kissling, D. L. (1965). *Bull. Mar. Sci.* **15**, 599.
Kohlmeyer, J. (1969). *Amer. Zool.* **9**, 741–746.
Kornicker, L. S., and Boyd, D. W. (1962). *Amer. Ass. Petrol. Geol., Bull.* **46**, 640.
Kornicker, L. S., Bonet, F., Cann, R., and Hoskin, C. M. (1959). *Publ. Inst. Mar. Sci., Univ. Tex.* **6**, 1.
Laborel, J. (1966). *Bull. Mus. Hist. Natur., Paris* **38**, 281.
Laborel, J. (1967). *Postilla* **107**, 1.
Laborel, J. (1969a). *Ann. Inst. Oceanogr.* (Paris) **47**, 171.

Laborel, J. (1969b). *Ann. Univ. Abidjan, Ser. E* **2**, 1.

Land, L. S., and Epstein, S. (1970). *Sedimentology* **14**, 187.

Land, L. S., and Goreau, T. F. (1970). *J. Sediment. Petrol.* **40**, 457.

Lang, J. C. (1969). *Abstr., 8th Meet., Carib. Ass. Isl. Mar. Lab.* Mimeo.

Lang, J. C. (1970). Ph.D. Thesis, Yale University, New Haven, Connecticut.

Lang, J. C. (1971). *Bull. Mar. Sci.* **21**, 952.

Lewis, J. B. (1960a). *Can. J. Zool.* **38**, 1133.

Lewis, J. B. (1960b). *Can. J. Zool.* **38**, 391.

Lewis, J. B. (1966). *Bull. Mar. Sci.* **16**, 151.

Lewis, J. B., Axelsen, F., Goodbody, I., Page, C., and Chislett, G. (1968). *Mar. Sci.* **10**, 26.

Logan, B. W. (1969). *Amer. Ass. Petrol. Geol., Mem.* **11**, Part 2, 129.

Logan, B. W., Harding, J. L., Ahr, W. M., Williams, J. D., and Snead, R. G. (1969). *Amer. Ass. Petrol. Geol., Mem.* **11**, Part 1, 1.

Lund, E. H. (1957). *Econ. Geol.* **52**, 582.

Macintyre, I. G. (1967). *Can. J. Earth Sci.* **4**, 461.

Macintyre, I. G. (1968). *5th Carib. Geol. Conf., St. Thomas, Virgin Isl., 1968* pp. 1–17.

Macintyre, I. G. (1972). *Amer. Ass. Petrol. Geol., Bull.* **56**, 720.

Macintyre, I. G., and Pilkey, O. H. (1969). *Science* **166**, 374.

McLean, R. F. (1967). *Bull. Mar. Sci.* **17**, 551.

Marcus, E., and Marcus, E. (1967). "American Opisthobranch Mollusks." University of Miami Press, Coral Gables, Florida.

Margalef, R. (1962). "Comunidades Naturales." Inst. Mar. Biol., Univ. of Puerto Rico, Mayagüez.

Margalef, R. (1968). "Perspectives in Ecological Theory." Univ. of Chicago Press, Chicago, Illinois.

Marsden, J. R. (1962a). *Nature (London)* **193**, 598.

Marsden, J. R. (1962b). *Can. J. Zool.* **41**, 165.

Mayor, A. G. (1924). *Carnegie Inst. Wash., Publ.* **340**, 51.

Miller, A. C. (1970). OTS Mar. Biol. Course, Miami.

Miller, R. S. (1969). *Brookhaven Symp. Biol.* **22**, 63–70.

Milliman, J. D. (1969). *Atoll Res. Bull.* **129**, 1.

Milliman, J. D., and Emery, K. O. (1968). *Science* **162**, 1121.

Moore, D. R. (1958). *Publ. Inst. Mar. Sci., Univ. Tex.* **5**, 151.

Neumann, A. C. (1966). *Limnol. Oceanogr.* **11**, 92.

Newell, N. D. (1959). *Natur. Hist., N.Y.* **119**, 227.

Newell, N. D. (1962). *In* "Study of the Earth" (J. F. White, ed.), pp. 121–136. Prentice-Hall, Englewood Cliffs, New Jersey.

Newell, N. D., and Imbrie, J. (1955). *Trans. N.Y. Acad. Sci.* [2] **18**, 3.

Newell, N. D., Rigby, J. K., Whiteman, A. J., and Bradley, J. S. (1951). *Bull. Amer. Mus. Natur. Hist.* **97**, 1.

Newell, N. D., Imbrie, J., Purdy, E. G., and Thurber, D. L. (1959). *Bull. Amer. Mus. Natur. Hist.* **117**, 177.

Newman, W. A. (1960). *Veliger* **2**, 89.

Newman, W. A., Curray, J. R., Dana, T. F., and Crampton, P. J. S. (1970). *In* "ALPHA HELIX Research Program: 1969–1970," p. 39. Univ. of California Press, San Diego.

Odum, H. T., Burkholder, P. R., and Rivero, J. (1959). *Publ. Inst. Mar. Sci., Univ. Tex.* 6, 159.

Olausson, E. (1965). *Progr. Oceanogr.* 3, 221.

Olausson, E. (1967). *Progr. Oceanogr.* 4, 245.

Pfaff, R. (1969). *Mitt. Inst. Colombo-Aleman Invest. Cient.* 3, 17.

Porter, J. W. (1972). *Proc. Biol. Soc. Wash.* (in press).

Randall, J. E. (1963). *Carib. J. Sci.* 3, 31.

Randall, J. E. (1965). *Ecology* 46, 255.

Randall, J. E. (1967). *Study Trop. Oceanogr.* 5, 665.

Rigby, J. K., and McIntire, W. G. (1966). *Brigham Young Univ. Geol. Stud.* 13, 3.

Robertson, R. (1970). *Pac. Sci.* 24, 43.

Rodríguez, G. (1959). *Bull. Mar. Sci. Gulf Carib.* 9, 237.

Roos, P. J. (1964). *Stud. Fauna Curaçao* 20, 1.

Rützler, K. (1971). *Smithson. Contrib. Zool.* 77, 1.

Shinn, E. A. (1963). *J. Sediment. Petrol.* 33, 291.

Shinn, E. A. (1966). *J. Paleontol.* 40, 233.

Smith, F. G. W. (1948). "Atlantic Reef Corals. A Handbook of the Common Reef and Shallow-Water Corals of Bermuda, Florida, the West Indies and Brazil." Univ. of Miami Press, Coral Gables, Florida. (1971 rev. ed.)

Smith, F. G. W. (1954). *U.S., Fish Wildl. Serv., Fish Bull.* 55, 291–295.

Sournia, A. (1969). *Mar. Biol.* 3, 287.

Squires, D. F. (1958). *Bull. Amer. Mus. Natur. Hist.* 115, 219.

Stanley, D. J., and Swift, D. J. P. (1967). *Science* 157, 677.

Stephenson, T. A., and Stephenson, A. (1950). *J. Ecol.* 38, 354.

Stephenson, W., and Searles, R. B. (1960). *Aust. J. Mar. Freshwater Res.* 11, 241.

Stoddart, D. R. (1962a). *Atoll Res. Bull.* 87, 1.

Stoddart, D. R. (1962b). *Nature (London)* 196, 512.

Stoddart, D. R. (1969a). *Atoll Res. Bull.* 131, 1.

Stoddart, D. R. (1969b). *Biol. Rev.* 44, 433.

Stoddart, D. R., Davies, P. S., and Keith, A. C. (1966). *Atoll Res. Bull.* 116, 13–42.

Storr, J. F. (1964). *Geol. Soc. Amer., Spec. Pap.* 79, 1.

Talbot, F. H. (1965). *Proc. Zool. Soc. London* 145, 431.

Tamura, T. and Hada, Y. (1932). *Sci. Rep. Tohoku Univ., Ser. 4* 7, 433.

Thiel, M. E. (1928). *In* "Beiträge zur Kenntnis der Meeresfauna Westafrikas" (W. Michaelsen, ed.), Vol. 3, pp. 253–350. L. Friederichsen & Co., Hamburg.

Thorpe, J. E., and Stoddart, D. R. (1962). *Geogr. J.* 128, 158.

Tranter, D. J., and George, J. (1969). "Symposium on Corals and Coral Reefs (Abstract)." Mandapam Camp, India.

U.S. Navy Hydrographic Office. (1948). Publ. No. 799B. Washington, D.C.

U.S. Navy Hydrographic Office. (1954). Publ. No. 225. Washington, D.C.

U.S. Navy Oceanographic Office. (1963). Publ. No. 700. Washington, D.C.

U.S. Navy Oceanographic Office. (1965). Publ. No. 700. Washington, D.C.

U.S. Navy Oceanographic Office. (1967). Spec. Publ. No. 94. Washington, D.C.

U.S. Navy Oceanographic Office. (1969). Publ. No. 106. Washington, D.C.

van Andel, T. H., and Laborel, J. (1964). *Science* 145, 580.

Vaughan, T. W. (1915). *J. Wash. Acad. Sci.* 5, 591.

Vaughan, T. W. (1916a). *Carnegie Inst. Wash., Yearb.* 14, 220.

Vaughan, T. W. (1916b). *Proc. Nat. Acad. Sci. U.S.* **2**, 95.
Vaughan, T. W. (1918). *Carnegie Inst. Wash., Publ.* **213**, 319.
Vaughan, T. W. (1919). *Smithson. Inst., Annu. Rep.*, p. 189.
Vaughan, T. W., and Wells, J. W. (1943). *Geol. Soc. Amer., Spec. Pap.* **44**, 1.
Vermeij, G. J. and Porter, J. W. (1971). *Bull. Mar. Sci.* **21**, 440.
Verrill, A. E. (1901). *Trans. Conn. Acad. Arts. Sci.* **11**, 169.
Villalobos Figueroa, A. (1968). *Abstr. Symp. Invest. Res. Carib. Sea Adj. Reg. Prep. CICAR, Curaçao. 1968*, p. 39.
Voss, G. L., and Voss, N. A. (1955). *Bull. Mar. Sci. Gulf Carib.* **5**, 203.
Ward, J. (1965). *Can. J. Zool.* **43**, 44.
Welch, B. L. (1962). Ph.D. Thesis, Duke University, Durham, North Carolina.
Wells, J. W. (1944). *J. Paleontol.* **18**, 429.
Wells, J. W. (1957). *In* "Treatise on Marine Ecology and Paleoecology" (J. W. Hedgpeth, ed.), Vol. 1, pp. 609–631. Waverly Press, Baltimore, Maryland.
Wells, J. W. (1971). *Bull. Mar. Sci.* **21**, 960.
Work, R. C. (1969). *Bull. Mar. Sci.* **19**, 614.
Yonge, C. M. (1963). *Advan. Mar. Biol.* **1**, 209–260.
Yonge, C. M. (1968). *Proc. Roy. Soc., Ser. B* **169**, 329.
Zans, V. A. (1958). *Geol. Surv. Dep., Jam., West Indies, Occas. Pap.* **3**, 1.

Note added in proof: Since this was completed I have learned from Bright and Pequegnat (1973) of the Flower Garden banks south of Galveston, Texas. The West Flower Garden bank is located at 93°49.0′W; 27°52.6′N. The Flower Gardens are considered to be the northernmost extant shallow water coral reefs bordering the eastern continental region of North America. Like the outlying Bermudian reefs, the occurrence of flourishing reef coral populations in the upper Gulf is attributed to the influence of the warm Gulf Stream.

10

THE BIOLOGY AND ECOLOGY OF
TROPICAL HOLOTHURIANS

Gerald J. Bakus

I. Introduction

There are approximately two dozen important articles on the ecology of tropical holothurians. This conclusion is based on an evaluation of more than 1500 publications on echinoderms. With the exception of relatively few papers, there is a conspicuous lack of emphasis on ecology evolution, or experimentation. In particular, there is a lack of ecological observations in much of the taxonomic literature, which comprises the bulk of our knowledge of holothurians. The most significant contributions in large part have been examined; those aspects that have not been studied or emphasized herein were discussed by Hyman (1955, 1959) and Pawson (1966a). The lengths of the forthcoming sections in some cases reflect the biases of the author rather than the available knowledge

Because there is little information on "genuine" coral reef species, liberty has been taken to include literature on soft-bottom dwellers, animals from other tropical communities, and even temperate forms on occasion, particularly if they belong to largely tropical genera or if they are of special evolutionary interest. Throughout the text *A.* = *Actinopyga*, *H.* = *Holothuria*, and *S.* = *Stichopus*, unless otherwise specified.

II. Geological History and Distribution

A. GEOLOGICAL HISTORY

The geological history of holothurians, particularly tropical forms, is little known. This is the result of a paucity of hard parts in many holothurians, intense bacterial activity, relatively high turnover rates of energy at all trophic levels, and disruption of the stratification of sediments by the holothurians themselves (Frizzell *et al.*, 1966; Bakus, 1969). The oldest known holothurian is now apparently *Protocaudina triperforata* Schallreuter from the Middle Ordovician of Sweden (Schallreuter, 1968). The family Holothuriidae, so predominant in the tropics, almost certainly is not Recent in origin. Several fossil sclerites from the Jurassic and later are undoubtedly of the *Holothuria* type.

B. DISTRIBUTION

There are over 1200 species of holothurians, the highest diversity being characteristic of tropical shallow waters (Clark, 1945; D. L. Pawson, personal communication). The tropical genus *Holothuria* alone contains at least 114 species (Rowe, 1969). Their zoogeography and local distributions are discussed primarily in numerous systematics papers and in publications of faunal surveys (e.g., Endean *et al.*, 1956; Macnae and Kalk, 1958; Stephenson *et al.*, 1958). Aspidochirotes are more characteristic of habitats with clear tropical waters (e.g., Eniwetok and other atolls), and dendrochirotes are more characteristic of boreal latitudes (e.g., San Juan Islands, Washington). This phenomenon is related in part to the low standing crops of phytoplankton in tropical oceanic surface waters (Bakus, 1969) and the high plankton densities and numerous organic detritus particles in boreal waters (Bakus, unpublished). Deichmann (1957a) claimed that certain tropical shallow-water forms of presumed older origin have an almost circumtropical range, while the more modern forms, such as the plankton-catching dendrochirotes and the sand- and mud-eating apodous holothurians, have a narrower range and further tend to separate into small local forms. However, other interpretations based on fossils and morphology of present-day forms argue strongly for the primitive nature of plankton-catching dendrochirotes. Holothuriidae and apodous holothurians, although fairly old groups themselves, probably have arisen from more generalized dendrochirote types (Fell and Moore, 1966; Pawson, 1966b). Scheltema (1972) provides evidence to support the suggestion that many tropical species of marine organisms have long-lived larvae and that these act as genetic links between disjunct, geographically isolated populations of benthic marine species.

Random sampling techniques were used in enumeration and zonation of holothurians living across a ½-mile-wide fringing reef flat at Nombur, Gaua Island, New Hebrides (Baker, 1929). *Stichopus chloronotus* Brandt is almost restricted to the innermost (*Montipora*) zone but also occurs in low densities in the boulder zone. *Holothuria atra* Jaeger is principally located in the next (*Porites*) zone, yet occurs in all zones. *Holothuria vagabunda* (now = *H. leucospilota* Brandt) is found only in the boulder-channel zone and *Actinopyga mauritiana* Quoy and Gaimard in the outermost (*Goniastrea*) zone. There are few *S. chloronotus* or *H. atra* where live corals are abundant. This is also characteristic of *H. difficilis* Semper at Eniwetok Atoll, Marshall Islands (Bakus, 1968). Yamanouti (1939) described in detail the distribution of holothurians along a 6-mile traverse in the West Reef of Baberdoobu Island at Arumonogui, Palau Islands.

Many species of cucumbers move shoreward during the breeding season (Deichmann, in Glynn, 1965). During storms, *S. moebii* [now = *Isostichopus badionotus* (Selenka)] of Bermuda retreat to depths of several fathoms, from their places of original exposure to the seas. They also move deeper at nightfall (Crozier, 1918). However, storms may merely dislodge the holothurians and nighttime migrations are rare, if they occur at all (S. Trefz, personal communication). The major benthic factors limiting distribution of holothurians (especially the young) on the shallow sea bottom probably are decomposition products of microorganisms, namely, hydrogen sulfide and methane. The ultimate environmental factors limiting distribution may be waves and currents (Yamanouti, 1939).

III. Population Density

Some authors have stated that holothurians and ophiuroids usually predominate in the tropics, and echinoids and asteroids in temperate and colder waters (Clark, 1919; Gillett and McNeill, 1959; Kalk, 1959;

Frizzell *et al.*, 1966; Pope, 1967a). However, the temperate sea cucumber *Cucumaria elongata* [now = *Leptopentacta elongata* (Düben and Koren)] commonly is found in densities of $>20/m^2$ (Fish, 1967). Echinoids may predominate in certain localities at night when they leave the reef to forage over sand (e.g., Fanning Island, Line Islands and Eniwetok Island, Marshall Islands). There are numerous Caribbean sites where *Diadema* occurs in relatively high densities. *Acanthaster planci* shows high population densities in several regions (Chesher, 1970), as great as $800/900$ ft^2 (Anonymous, 1968). Table I lists the population densities of several species of tropical holothurians. *Holothuria atra* may be the most common tropical sea cucumber (also see Fig. 1). It is the most abundant holothurian at Pearl and Hermes Reef (atoll), Hawaii (Galtsoff, 1933). The population density of *H. vitiens* (sic) [now = *Bohadschia vitiensis* (Semper)] is lowest where living corals are abundant since less sand is present (Yamanouti, 1939). At Eniwetok, Marshall Island, *H. difficilis* occurs individually or in aggregates (≤ 30) during the day. Activity and densities tend to increase at night when they feed (Table I). The population density of *A. mauritiana* is low and individuals are widely scattered (Bakus, 1968). On

Fig. 1. Photograph indicating the density ($5–35/m^2$) of holothurians (predominantly *Holothuria atra* Jaeger) on the reef flat of Aniyaanii Island, Eniwetok Atoll, Marshall Islands.

TABLE I

POPULATION DENSITY OF TROPICAL HOLOTHURIANS

Author	Locality	Species	Density	Remarks
Baker, 1929	Gaua Is., New Hebrides	A. mauritiana Quoy and Gaimard	$\sim$0.5/25 m^2	
	Gaua Is., New Hebrides	H. atra Jaeger	$\sim$7/25 m^2	
Bakus, 1968	Just north of Eniwetok Is., Eniwetok Atoll, Marshall Is.	H. atra Jaeger (with few H. leucospilota Brandt)	1/10 m^2	Estimated
	Aniyaanii Is., Eniwetok Atoll, Marshall Is.	H. atra Jaeger (with few H. leucospilota Brandt)	5–35/m^2	Estimated
Bonham and Held, 1963	Rongelap Atoll, Marshall Is.	H. atra Jaeger	4.5 × 10^6	Estimated for entire atoll
Guppy, 1882	St. Cristoval, Solomon Is.	Probably H. atra Jaeger	$\sim$15–16/rood (1012 m^2) $\overline{<}$5/m^2	
Macnae and Kalk, 1962	Inhaca Is., Mozambique	H. atra Jaeger		
Yamanouti, 1939	Palau Marine Laboratory, Palau Is.	H. atra Jaeger	0.44/m^2	
Bakus, 1968	Eniwetok Is. quarry Eniwetok Atoll, Marshall Is.	H. difficilis Semper	1.4–7/900 cm^2 7–32/900 cm^2 130/m^2 $\overline{>}$200/m^2	Associated with sand Associated with slab rock Maximum diurnal density Estimated nocturnal density, while feeding
Bonham and Held, 1963	Rongelap Atoll, Marshall Is.	H. leucospilota Brandt	1.6 × 10^5	Estimated for entire atoll
Baker, 1929	Gaua Is., New Hebrides	H. vagabunda (now = H. leucospilota Brandt)	$\sim$0.4/25 m^2	
Yamanouti, 1939	Palau Marine Laboratory, Palau Is.	H. vitiens [now = Bohadschia vitiensis (Semper)]	0.072/m^2	
Baker, 1929	Gaua Is., New Hebrides	S. chloronotus Brandt	$\sim$7/25 m^2	

Mozambique Island *H. atra, H. leucospilota* Brandt, *H. difficilis,* and *A. mauritiana* occur in abundance in the midlittoral of a semiexposed rocky shore (Kalk, 1959). Whether the density figures presented here are useful is debatable, since sampling techniques differ for each study. Ideally, comparisons between densities of temperate and tropical holothurians should be made in closely comparable habitats with the same sampling techniques, by the same investigator, and expressed in categories of size, ash-free dry weights, and calories per unit area. If sufficient information is available, it is possible to take a quantitative sample, apply growth curve data and incremental production data to give the rate of production for the population (Buchanan, 1967).

IV. Size, Growth, and Coloration

A. SIZE

Although considerable data on sizes of preserved specimens are available from systematics papers, there is a dearth of information on living holothurians. No generalization can be made regarding a living to preserved size ratio since this varies among the species. *Holothuria atra* has been found from 2 to 60 cm in length and 10 to 2000 gm in weight at Rongelap Atoll, Marshall Islands (Bonham and Held, 1963). *Holothuria arenicola* Semper and *H. pervicax* Selenka measure ≥ 50 cm in length at Inhaca Island, Mozambique (Macnae and Kalk, 1962). *Stichopus variegatus* Semper from the Philippines is reported by Semper to reach 1 m in length and 21 cm in diameter (Hyman, 1955). *Actinopyga mauritiana* averages ~ 30 cm in length and 2800 gm wet weight, whereas *H. difficilis* averages ~ 4 cm in length, 1 cm in diameter, and 2 gm wet weight, the dry weight representing 14% of the wet weight, at Eniwetok, Marshall Islands. *Synapta maculata* Chamisso and Eysenhardt were commonly seen at night in the Eniwetok quarry and once during the day; they measured from 1.8 to 2.4 m in length (Bakus, 1968). Certain specimens may reach 5 m in length (Cuénot, 1948). *Stichopus moebii* of Bermuda has a tendency to be about the same general size in one locality (Crozier, 1918). This phenomenon is common in a number of coral reef holothurians and may be related to reproduction by transverse fission (see Section VI), a complicating factor in the analysis of age structure. It may also explain in part why young holothurians are frequently difficult to locate on reef flats. There has been no attempt to assess in what manner size may be correlated with latitude, either inter- or intraspecifically.

B. GROWTH

Growth rates are available for very few species. A detailed comparison of growth in *H. floridana* Pourtalés with *H. atra* was made by Edwards (1908), emphasizing external and internal morphology and biometrics. *Holothuria floridana* reared in the laboratory increased from 0.33 mm at 5 days of age to 4.00 mm at 75 days. The volume of *H. atra* increases slowly until a body length of 15 cm is attained, thereafter as the cube of the length for sizes 15–25 cm (Bonham and Held, 1963). *Thyone gibber* [now = *Neothyone gibber* (Selenka)] shows the curious phenomenon of coalescing into pairs at Taboga, Panama. This involves fusion of the body wall but not the internal organs. It is not known at which stage of growth the process commences (Deichmann, 1922).

C. COLORATION

Holothurians most frequently are colored brown or gray (Clark, 1945). Black and brown predominate on the Great Barrier Reef (Yonge, 1930); this is typical of many Indo-Pacific reefs. Amoebocytes carry pigment of *H. forskali* Delle Chiaje to the epithelium, as in other echinoderms (Nichols, 1964). Albinism occurs in *S. japonicus* Selenka (Ohshima, 1932). Color variation is reported in many systematics papers; for example, it occurs in *Synapta* (Kent, 1893). Certain *Synapta* have patches of brown, blending like coral, and are reported to be protected from predators by a sudden change of shape (Studer, 1889). No attempt has been made to study the adaptive advantages of color polymorphism in coral reef holothurians. *Stichopus japonicus* occurs in three color phases and is distributed along the entire coast of Japan. A green form lives in sand or mud near bays. A red form lives on reefs and pebble or gravel beds on an exposed shoreline. The body contractility of the red form is remarkable; it forms a ball under mechanical stimulus whereas the green form does not (Choe and Ohshima, 1961; Choe, 1963). This behavior pattern may be related to wave action or predation (see Sections XI and XVI). Mortensen (1917) thought that black coloration on white sand may serve as an aposematic (warning) device since not all species of holothurians with Cuvierian organs are conspicuously colored. He described an "undoubted" case of protective coloration in *Synaptula hydriforme* (sic) [*Synaptula hydriformis* (Lesueur)] (West Indies) in which the animal is green and striped like the algae where it lives. The natural coloration of certain sea cucumbers may be altered by their habit of covering the body with foreign objects such as sand or algae (Östergren, 1897). The adaptive advantage of such behavior is a moot point (see Section XI).

V. Biochemistry

Knowledge of the biochemistry of tropical holothurians is limited except for research on toxins (see Section XV). A chemical analysis was made of *H. floridana* from Puerto Rico. CaO was found to be 5 to 26 times more abundant in the skeleton of *H. floridana* than in the temperate and boreal latitude species that were studied; the calcium is bound in carbonates (Clarke and Wheeler, 1922). Further data on chemical composition of holothurians were presented by Vinogradov (1953), Kaiser and Michl (1958), and Habermehl and Volkwein (1968). *Holothuria scabra* Jaeger has relatively high levels of Ca, P, Na, and protein (Springhall and Dingle, 1967). Periodic acid-Schiff (PAS) reaction was very conspicuous in the body wall of *H. scabra* indicating a variety of carbohydrates: 1-2 glycol groups, acid mucopolysaccharides, muco- and glycoproteins present (Krishnan, 1968). No relationship was suggested with saponins even though *H. scabra* is a toxic species (Halstead, 1965). Most of the epidermal cells of *S. japonicus,* a toxic species (Halstead, 1965), are mucous cells. Mucoid vesicles are generated in the proximal nuclear region of a cell by the Golgi apparatus and arranged in a chain along the long cytoplasm of the cell; this indicates high activity of formation of mucus (Kawaguti, 1966). The possible connection between mucus production and toxicity is discussed in Section XV.

The concentration factor (concentration in animal/concentration in seawater) of certain important radionuclides is relatively high (490–540) for ^{131}I in the intestine of *S. regalis,* exceedingly high (78,000) for ^{55}Fe and ^{59}Fe in the body wall muscle of *S. japonicus,* relatively high (240) in ^{57}Co, ^{58}Co, and ^{60}Co in *S. tremulus* [now =*Parastichopus tremulus* (Gunnerus)], and relatively high (1400) in ^{65}Zn for *S. tremulus* (Ichikawa, 1961).

VI. Reproduction

A. Sexual Reproduction and Larval Development

The act of gamete release has been described for only one tropical holothurian, *H. marmorata* (now =*Bohadschia marmorata* Jaeger) at Ghardaqa (Mortensen, 1937). The male raises the anterior end vertically, spreading it out cobralike; a genital papilla appears, and emits a stream of milky sperm. The female behaves similarly and sheds eggs usually during the evening or night. Sometimes several animals spawn at the same time. The larvae are extraordinarily uniform in shape and color. Gastrulae appear after 18 hours; Table II presents further data from Ghardaqa.

TABLE II

DEVELOPMENT OF HOLOTHURIANS AT GARDAQA, RED SEA[a]

Species	No. days to reach auricularia stage
Actinopyga serratidens Pearson	4
Holothuria arenicola Semper var. *boutani* Hérouard	(Metamorphosis at 4 weeks)
Holothuria scabra Jaeger	2
Holothuria spinifera Théel	3
Stichopus variegatus Semper	4
Synapta reciprocans [now = *Synaptula reciprocans* (Forskål)]	3

[a] Data after Mortensen (1937).

The embryo of *H. floridana* hatches on the sixth day as a larva with five primary tentacles. There is no free auricularia (Edwards, 1909). Holothurian larvae of shallow temperate and boreal waters remain planktonic for up to 6 weeks (Thorson, 1961), but nothing is known about larval life of tropical forms. The fact that certain holothurians are circumtropical suggests that a relatively long larval period may be operational (see Section II). No data are available on mortality rates. *Holothuria scabra* breeds throughout the year with peak intensities in July and October in south India. Although changes in water temperature, particularly increases, induce breeding in some temperate animals, decreased salinity or optimal salinity and to some extent concentration of food, may play this role in the tropics (Krishnaswamy and Krishnan, 1967). A catalog of echinoderm larvae has been prepared by Vannucci (1959 onward). The generalization that tropical holothurians spawn during "winter months" (Frizzell and Exline, 1955) is erroneous.

B. BROODING

Of 30 species of sea cucumbers known to brood their young, only two are tropical species, *Chirodota rotifera* Pourtales and *Synapta vivipara* [now = *Synaptula hydriformis* (Lesueur)], and they are limited to the West Indies (Clark, 1896, 1902; Vaney, 1925; Hyman, 1955).

This characteristic may be a relict from the Pleistocene or earlier times when water surface temperatures were considerably lower than those of today (J. C. Briggs, personal communication, 1969). The colder the water, the higher the percentage of animals having either direct development or a reduced larval stage (Thorson, 1936). The actual adaptive advantage of brooding in holothurians may be related to estuarine conditions in which larvae may not survive in low salinity waters.

The development of *Synapta vivipara* was described by Oerstedt in 1851. Eggs pass via genital ducts to the coelom where they are fertilized and develop to a length of about 2.5 cm. There may be up to 175 young. They leave the parent through a rupture in the body wall, or more often through a perforation in the wall of the intestine (Gerould, 1898; Clark, 1902). *Chirodota rotifera* lives in sand beneath broken coral rock in Jamaica where it broods young, as many as 522 in a parent measuring <50 mm in length. The pentactula larva measures a maximum of 3 mm in length and possesses a maximum of eight tentacles which are in constant motion. The surrounding ciliary collar is equally active. One larva lived >24 hours after removal from the parent (Clark, 1910).

C. Asexual Reproduction and Abnormal Growth

Transverse fission is a well-known mode of asexual reproduction in certain holothurians (Crozier, 1915a; Hyman, 1955). It has been reported in *A. difficilis* (now =*H. difficilis* Semper), *A. parvula* [now =*H. parvula* (Selenka)], *Cucumaria planci* [now =*Pentacucumis planci* (Brandt)], *H. surinamensis* Ludwig (Deichmann, 1922); *Microthele parvula* (now =*H. parvula* Selenka), *Semperothuria surinamensis* (now =*H. surinamensis* Ludwig)(Tikasingh, 1963); and *H. atra* (Bonham and Held, 1963). As mentioned previously, it may be responsible for the dearth of distinct age classes in a locality. It undoubtedly occurs in more species than reported to date. There is no correlation between the stage of development of the gonad and the occurrence of fission in *H. parvula*. Fission may be repeated under natural conditions without the intervention of sexual reproduction (Kille, 1942). The present author has collected a specimen of *H. atra* from Eniwetok which seems to have a bud (Fig. 2). An investigation of the internal anatomy is needed in order to determine whether the specimen is in the process of budding or is abnormal. Clark (1896) and Ohshima (1934) describe holothurians with abnormal growth, such as double larvae, an adult with a double posterior end, and individuals with as many as five sets of tentacles and four digestive tracts.

Fig. 2. Holothuria atra Jaeger with what appears to be a bud. Note the strings of feces near the holothurians.

VII. Osmoregulation, Respiration, and Temperature Tolerance

A. OSMOREGULATION

It is not known whether coral reef holothurians, many of which may live under relatively constant environmental conditions, are physiologically stenotopic. *Opheodesoma spectabilis* Fisher of Hawaii reduces its coelomic fluid content in fresh water by way of the mouth and anus, the body wall being impermeable. This sea cucumber is found in relatively high densities in shallow water about coral reefs but has been collected as deep as 13 m where the seawater is presumably of normal salinity. During heavy rains, the animal is unaffected by low saline water that decimates populations of other reef-dwelling invertebrates. It can tolerate a level as low as 70% seawater. It is suggested that the tolerance to fresh water is incidental (Freeman, 1966).

B. RESPIRATION

The cloacal gas exchange of *H. forskali* accounts for ~60% of the total oxygen uptake. Uptake of oxygen occurs only when pumped water is $\geq$60–70% saturated with air. At lower levels of saturation, there is no gaseous exchange through respiratory trees and no increase in absorption through the general body surface. Three main modes of pumping water are described. The rate of pumping varies inversely with the oxygen level. As the saturation level lowers to 60–70%, pumping ceases. A period of reduced gas exchange is followed by increased uptake of oxygen when pumping is resumed (Newell and Courtney, 1965). *Holothuria difficilis* at Eniwetok has a diurnal–nocturnal respiration rate of 0.053–0.056 ml O_2/(gm wet wt hour). These values are relatively high in part because the organism is so small (Bakus, 1968).

C. TEMPERATURE TOLERANCE

Temperature tolerances are recorded for several holothurians. The temperature sense of *H. surinamensis* is reported to be poorly developed (Crozier, 1915a). It was suggested that the unusual bounding movements of *Astichopus multifidus* (Sluiter) may be an avoidance of high-temperature stress (Glynn, 1965). If this interpretation is valid, it is curious that similar behavioral phenomena have not been reported for the numerous species of holothurians that are temporarily trapped in reef flat tidepools during low water in many tropical regions. *Holothuria atra* can live in pools where the water temperature ranges from 31.1° to 39.4°C (Bonham and Held, 1963). *Holothuria difficilis* tolerates natural ambient temperatures of 28°–31°C. Under experimental conditions, the animal becomes immobile at 36°C, yet the tentacles are capable of moving at 40°C. It will recover from a 10-minute seawater immersion at 38°–40°C, but not at 43°–45°C (Bakus, 1968). For further information on the physiology of holothurians, see Prosser and Brown (1961) and Boolootian (1966).

VIII. Feeding

A. INTRODUCTION

One of the earliest descriptions of feeding in holothurians was that of Jaeger (1833) who erroneously suspected they are carnivores. It is probably true that holothurians are the most important sand-deposit feeders on many coral reefs (Gardiner, 1904; Bonham and Held, 1963). Few, if any, will feed under laboratory conditions initially, although they may feed after a period of starvation or when they are placed in outside aquaria. Holothurians tend to crawl up sides of aquaria and thus remain above the sandy substrate, but if kept on shallow saltwater tables they will feed (S. Trefz, personal communication). Chemical discrimination in food selection is assumed to be poor since certain species in aquaria (e.g., *H. atra*) will reingest their own feces (Mayer, 1917; Crozier, 1918; Trefz, 1956; Choe, 1963; Bakus, 1968).

B. SIZE OF FOOD PARTICLES

A very high positive correlation is reported between the body size of deposit feeders and particle size, regardless of the type of animal concerned. Detritus feeders predominate in the finest sediments and deposit and filter feeders in intermediate grades. A linear relationship is suggested between grain size and the cube root of dry tissue weight (McNulty *et al.*, 1962). Glynn (1965) did not find this correlation in *Astichopus multifidus*, which feeds in part on fine-grained (median 212 μm) calcareous bioclastics.

The size of food particles in holothurians varies with the species as well as the locality. Statements which claim that sediments are appreciably reduced in size by passage through the digestive tract (Gardiner, 1901, 1903, 1904; Henderson, in Kindle, 1919) or that larger particles are segregated from smaller ones are not supported by more critical investigations (Finckh, 1904; Crozier, 1918; Yamanouti, 1939; Trefz, 1956; Bonham and Held, 1963; Bakus, 1968).

Holothuria difficilis consumes particles of which about 80% are <250 μm in diameter; the remaining calcareous fragments measure up to 2 mm (Bakus, 1968). *Holothuria atra* feeds on coral rubble measuring up to 2 cm. Dissolution of ingested anchor spicules of *Opheodesoma spectabilis* by *H. atra* did not occur after passage through the digestive tract. A detailed analysis of feeding habits in five species of Hawaiian sea cucumbers indicated that different holothurians partition substrates of different types and sizes—there seems to be little selection other than suitable size (Trefz, 1956). This phenomenon of size specificity in feeding is not characteristic of the four dominant species of the ophiuroid *Ophiocoma* at Eniwetok (Chartock, 1969).

C. TYPES OF FOOD CONSUMED

Tropical holothurians often feed on living microorganisms and on the organic content of sand, mud, ooze, and detritus. This is even true of some dendrochirotes in Florida, which are deposit feeders in part (Engstrom, personal communication). A few tropical species reportedly feed on plankton, organic matter on rocks, microcrustaceans, and polychaetes (Finckh, 1904; Clark, 1945; Frizzell and Exline, 1955; Macnae and Kalk, 1958). More critical examination of feeding suggests that an array of food items may be typical of quite a number of tropical holothurians. Among these are sand, shell, calcareous (coral) fragments, ooze from sea plants, living and dead filamentous blue-greens and diatoms, red algae, *Halimeda* fragments, foraminiferans, sponge spicules, nematodes, gastropods, fragments of sea urchin spines, holothurian ossicles, copepod exuvia, fish eggs, fish teeth, and detritus (Mayer, 1917; Yamanouti, 1939; Trefz, 1956; Bakus, 1968; Rao, 1968). Trefz (1956) found that diatoms, trochophore larvae, and copepods retained their motility when removed from the posterior end of the intestine of *H. atra*. She suggested that small *Cymatium* and *Morula* (gastropods) are frequently ingested since they were often observed in feces. The interstitial holothurian *Psammothuria ganapatii* Rao from India is considered to be "omnivorous" since it ingests sand, detritus, and living organic matter, including nematodes and copepods (Rao, 1968). Foraminiferans are reported to be dominant food items in several species (Kent, 1893; Crozier, 1915a). In fact, it is claimed that examination of holothurians for the determination of foraminiferans in sediments is more efficient than an analysis of dredged sediments (Barth *et al.*, 1968). Bacteria and Foraminifera may be major sources of food for atoll holothurians (Bakus, 1968). Bacteria are usually abundant when associated with detritus and may occur in highest concentrations in tropical waters (Jørgensen, 1966). The production of bacterioplankton in tropical waters is thought to be a major food source for filter feeders (Sorokin, 1971). Holothurian amoebocytes ingest bacteria which occur in great numbers in sand consumed in Hawaii (Trefz, 1956). Because foraminiferans may pass through the digestive tract little altered, it is now hypothesized that tropical holothurians primarily assimilate bacteria and organic detritus and that their diet is supplemented by active absorption of dissolved organic matter from surrounding waters (see Smith and Greenberg, 1966; Stephens, 1968). There are no studies on changes in diet with age in tropical holothurians. Young individuals of *S. japonicus* feed on microalgae and detritus; the adults are nonselective deposit feeders (Choe, 1963).

D. Feeding Efficiency

Long ago it was presumed that a large number of holothurians and other sand-ingesters live on an extremely small percentage of organic matter in coral reef sands (Gardiner, 1904). This was substantiated by later studies. *Astichopus multifidus* consumes sediments containing only 0.7% organic matter (Glynn, 1965). *Holothuria difficilis* utilizes about 2% of the dry weight of sediment consumed; the ash-free dry weight or approximate organic content of this sediment is 4–10% (Bakus, 1968). Approximately 50% of the nitrogen in sand was utilized by *H. atra* (Trefz, 1956) and 51–57% of organic carbon digested by *S. japonicus* (Choe, 1963). These studies indicate that tropical holothurians are relatively efficient in processing sediments since their assimilation efficiency is approximately 50%.

E. Period of Feeding

The time from ingestion to egestion in seven species of Palau Islands holothurians is 2–5 hours (Yamanouti, 1939). The digestive tracts were 5–35% full at a minimum. *Holothuria atra*, measuring 27–37.5 cm long, pass sand marked with colored shells in 10–36 hours (Trefz, 1956). All *S. moebii* studied in any one Bermudan locality usually had partially filled digestive tracts, the degree of filling varying from locality to locality. They averaged about two intestinal fillings per day throughout the year (Crozier, 1918). It was estimated that *H. difficilis* may take at least 15 hours to pass food (Bakus, 1968). *Stichopus japonicus* feeds from 1.5 to 5 hours and passes food in 30 hours (Tanaka, 1958).

Gardiner (1904) observed that surface forms feed during the night, remaining more or less dormant during the day. Ample observations and experiments indicate that this generalization applies only to certain species (e.g., *H. difficilis* and *H. surinamensis*)(Crozier, 1915a; Bakus, 1968). *Holothuria atra* consumes sediments both day and night (Trefz, 1956; Yamanouti, 1939), contrary to Gardiner (1931) who stated that they feed only during the night. *Holothuria atra, H. edulis* Lesson, and *H. flavomaculata* Semper eat continuously; *H. scabra, H. vitiens, H. bivittata* [now = *Bohadschia bivittata* (Mitsukuri)], *H. lecanora* var., *S. variegatus,* and *S. chloronotus* stop eating at least for one-third of daylight hours. During this time *H. scabra, H. vitiens,* and *H. bivittata* burrow in sand, from before dawn to noon or to the evening. *Holothuria vitiens* has an endogenous feeding rhythm, a change in light is thought to be the environmental cue. *Holothuria flavomaculata, Synapta* sp., *H. lecanora* [now = *Actinopyga lecanora* (Jaeger)], *H. lecanora* var., and an unidentified black sea cucumber feed on ooze from "sea plants" (Yamanouti, 1939). *Stichopus japonicus* stops feeding during summer estivation and its alimentary canal atrophies (Choe, 1963). Estivation also occurs in the temperate latitude species *Cucumaria elongata* (Fish, 1967), but the dormancy phenomenon has not been reported in truly tropical holothurians, so far as is known.

F. AMOUNT OF SEDIMENT PASSED

The amount of sediment passed by tropical holothurians is presented in Table III. *Stichopus moebii* shows a curvilinear relationship between body length and weight of digestive tract contents (Crozier, 1918). Trefz (1958) devised a formula for *H. atra* based on length of the specimen: $t = 5.3 + 0.233 \, L$ for specimens 25–38 cm long, where $t =$ time for passage in hours and $L =$ length in centimeters. Feeding rates vary much during the year in those species undergoing dormancy (Choe, 1963).

TABLE III

AMOUNT OF SEDIMENT PASSED BY TROPICAL HOLOTHURIANS

Author	Species	Dry weight of sediment passed
Guppy, 1882	*H. atra* Jaeger?	18 ft^3 rood^{-1} year^{-1} [a]
Gardiner, 1931	*H. atra* Jaeger	44 gm/day
Yamanouti, 1939	*H. atra* Jaeger	1 gm/17 min
		13.69 kg m^{-2} year^{-1}
Trefz, 1958	*H. atra* Jaeger	1 gm/7 min (30-cm-long holothurian)
Bonham and Held, 1963	*H. atra* Jaeger	1 gm/5–10 min
Bakus, 1968	*H. difficilis* Semper	>1 kg m^{-2} year^{-1} (estimated)
Mayer, 1917	*H. floridana* Pourtalés	72–94 gm/day
Gardiner, 1904	*H. maculata* (now = *H. arenicola* Semper)	layer of sand 4 cm thick/year (in lagoon)
Yamanouti, 1939	*H. vitiens* [now = *Bohadschia vitiensis* (Semper)]	1.91 kg m^{-2} year^{-1}
Mayer, 1917	*S. moebii* [now = *Isostichopus badionotus* (Selenka)]	~25 gm/day
Crozier, 1918	*S. moebii* [now = *Isostichopus badionotus* (Selenka)]	6.8 kg m^{-2} year^{-1} (minimum) 13.6 kg m^{-2} year^{-1} (maximum)

[a] Rood = 1012 m^2.

G. Production of Feces

Holothurians produce feces in pellet form or they may pass sand in a continuous stream (Gardiner, 1904). *Stichopus moebii* usually rapidly voids the entire contents of the digestive tract in a continuous mass (Crozier, 1918). Feces in the form of strings may be carried from the reef flat to the lagoon by unidirectional current flow at Eniwetok, thus contributing to lagoon sediments (Bakus, 1968) (Fig. 2).

IX. Digestion

A. Levels of pH in the Digestive Tract

One of the reasons that doubt is cast on the efficacy of holothurians in altering sediments is that few persons have investigated sediments concomitantly with digestive enzymes. Moreover, pH values vary widely among species (see Table IV). The belief that food organisms change

TABLE IV
LEVELS OF pH IN THE DIGESTIVE TRACT OF HOLOTHURIANS

Author	Species	pH	Remarks
Tanaka, 1958	*Caudina chilensis* [now = *Paracaudina chilensis* (Müller)]	7.3–7.7	—
Yonge, 1931	*H. atra* Jaeger	5.1	Intestine
Trefz, 1956	*H. atra* Jaeger	5.3–7.4	Midgut, starved animals
		5.6–7.4	Midgut, with sand (pH tends to be low in foregut)
Mayer, 1917	*H. floridana* Pourtalés	7.0	Replete with sand
		4.75–7.0	Empty
Yonge, 1931	*H. stellati* Della Chiaje	5.1	Intestine
Yonge, 1931	*H. tubulosa* Gmelin	5.1	Intestine
Tanaka, 1958	*S. japonicus* Selenka	6.1–5.6	During digestion
Mayer, 1917	*S. moebii* [now = *Isostichopus badionotus* (Selenka)]	4.8–5.5	Stomach
Van der Heyde, 1922	*Thyone briarius* [now = *Sclerodactyla briareus* (Lesueur)]	7.6 7.2 8.2	Stomach ($\bar{x}$) Intestine ($\bar{x}$) Rectum ($\bar{x}$)
Yamanouti, 1939	8 spp. tropical holothurians	5.0–6.2 5.5–6.7	Empty Full
Barth *et al.*, 1968	Brazilian holothurians	6.5–7.0	—

little after passing through the digestive tract of holothurians is based on temperate [e.g., *Thyone briarius* (now = *Sclerodactyla briareus* (Lesueur) (see van der Heyde, 1922)] as well as on tropical species. No food remains after a digestive period of 12 hours in *S. japonicus* (Tanaka, 1958). However, Choe (1963) reported a digestive period of 21 hours for *S. japonicus*.

B. Effects of pH and Enzymes on Sediments

The intestine of holothurians contains extracellular protease, amylase, invertase, and lipase, but all enzymes are very weak (Yonge, 1931; Trefz, 1956). Secretion of enzymes occurs only in certain parts of the digestive tract in *H. tubulosa* Gmelin. Absorption takes place at all levels of the digestive tract, but it is more marked in the stomach and intestine. Amoebocytes are the most metabolically active cells in this process (Rosati, 1968); their role was suggested long ago (Yonge, 1931). By sieving analysis, Yamanouti (1939) was able to show that calcareous sands pass through holothurian digestive tracts without appreciable change; only 0–1.2% alteration was found in sediment size categories tested. Thus dissolution may occur by acid but it is slight. However, organic detritus is degraded by extracellular enzymes in *H. atra* (Trefz, 1956). This is apparent from data given previously on organic material removed from sediments (see Section VIII). The effect of temperature on digestion is comparatively weak (Tanaka, 1958).

C. Active Absorption

Holothuria atra and its bacteria take up ^{32}P (H_3PO_4) over the entire body length. The larger the integument the smaller the uptake and concentration per gram of tissue. This may be related to growth rate. The greatest sites of uptake are the integument and the anal–respiratory tree complex, the oral region shows the least uptake. A possible metabolic utilization of phosphorus by the respiratory tree was postulated (Ahearn, 1968).

X. Effects on Coral Reefs

Although biologists have recognized since the last century that holothurians do not eat living corals, contrary to Darwin's often-quoted statement (Guppy, 1882; Thurston, 1895; Gardiner, 1904), some persist in this belief without presenting supporting evidence (Moret, 1940). Despite statements to the contrary (Gardiner, 1901; Mayer, 1918; Galtsoff,

1933), evidence has been presented to deny the existence of any efficacious reduction in the size of coral fragments by holothurians (see,
especially, Yamanouti, 1939). Mayer (1917) maintained a specimen of
S. *moebii* in an outdoor aquarium for 30 days and concluded that it
had caused the dissolution of 380.5 gm of sediment, thus being efficient
in deepening lagoons. This is difficult to accept, particularly because
solution of finer calcareous bioclastics could have occurred and organic
detritus was certainly removed and assimilated. Trefz (1956) concluded
that the buffering action of seawater, the rate of passage of sand through
H. atra, and the near neutrality of much of the digestive tract indicate
that dissolution will not occur. *Holothuria atra* was fed crushed *Pocillopora damicornis*, but no erosion was detected after periods of 5 and
8 weeks.

We come to the question of what effects, if any, do holothurians
have on coral reefs? They move sediments (Crozier, 1918; Yamanouti,
1939; Frizzell and Exline, 1955; Bonham and Held, 1963; Bakus, 1968),
but, more explicitly, they are of major importance in working over sediments with the resultant destruction of initial stratification (Frizzell
et al., 1966). Whether or not this in itself is of significance to the biota
of soft bottoms remains to be tested.

XI. Behavior

A. Coverage of the Body with Extrinsic and Intrinsic Objects

Certain holothurians are covered in varying degrees with extraneous
material. *Holothuria surinamensis* is covered by a thin layer of fine silt
(Crozier, 1915a), *H. cubana* Ludwig by sand grains (Clark, 1942), and
H. floridana and *H. atra* by plant debris, shells, and sand (Edwards,
1908, 1909). Numerous very small pedicels (tube feet) hold the particles.
Specimens of *H. atra* are covered with sand or they may lack sand.
It has been suggested that sand reflects light and retains a slightly lower
body temperature (Bonham and Held, 1963). This is difficult to accept
since many holothurians are bathed in seawater, at least in part, and
it does not account for those species that are active only at night. Pope
(1967b) stated that *H. leucospilota* is exposed by retreating tides. Their
mucous coat may protect them from desiccation or reduce solar radia-
tion; it is sloughed off on the incoming tide.

Psammothuria ganapatii is an interstitial holothurian from beach sands
of Waltair, India. *Leptosynapta minuta* (Becher), the only other known
interstitial sea cucumber lives in the North Sea. It lives in sand with

grains measuring 300–600 μm in diameter, where salinity varies from 20–30 ‰ and temperature from 24° to 30°C. It moves like *Hydra* with its vermiform body. The disposition of spicules in the body is believed to be protective against abrasion (Rao, 1968). *Pseudostichopus trachus* Sluiter, reportedly numerous at a depth of 100 fm in the Sagami Sea, has a dorsal surface covered with sponge spicules. This also occurs in *Pseudostichopus occultatus* Marenzeller and *Meseres hyalegerus* Sluiter (Mortensen, 1917).

B. Nocturnal Activity and Sensitivity to Chemicals

Little attention has been directed to holothurians that are active at night. Gardiner (1904) observed that large synaptids leave overhanging coral masses at night and wander about. This was true of *Synapta maculata* at Eniwetok, although one animal was observed to be active during daylight hours (Bakus, 1968) (see Section XVI). Although numerous experiments have indicated that holothurians react to various chemical stimuli (Crozier, 1915b; Domantay, 1931), the value of such investigations is questionable since there is little or no effort to relate these results to the natural environment.

C. Phototaxis

Phototaxis varies from neutral in *Astichopus multifidus* and *Isostichopus* (Glynn, 1965) to negative in *H. leucospilota* (Bonham and Held, 1963) and *H. captiva* [now = *H. parvula* (Selenka)] (Crozier, 1916). The entire body surface in *H. captiva* is sensitive to light and shading. Photic stimulation depends on the amount of light falling on the surface and is independent of the angle of incidence. The direct action of light, not a change of intensity, furnishes thé stimulating agency (Crozier, 1914, 1916). This species occasionally discharges a few Cuvierian tubules in bright sunlight only during the first 15 minutes of exposure (Crozier, 1915b). *Holothuria leucospilota* also reacts suddenly to shadows (Bonham and Held, 1963), as does *H. surinamensis*. The latter species, which is negatively phototaxic, does not respond to a sudden increase in light intensity but to a sudden decrease. Shade impinging on any part of the body causes a general contraction followed by expansion. To all stimuli tested, the degree of sensitivity is as follows: tentacles > anterior end > posterior end > papillae, podia > midbody surface (Crozier, 1915a). Organized photoreceptors occur in a few synaptids (Hyman, 1955).

D. Thigmotaxis and Geotaxis

Thigmotaxis reportedly ranges from neutral in *Astichopus multifidus* and *Isostichopus* to positive in *H. surinamensis*. All body parts are sensitive to touch in *H. surinamensis*, the least sensitive being the midbody surface, the most sensitive the oral end, followed by the cloacal brims (Crozier, 1915a; Glynn, 1965). In *Holothuria*, locomotory and papillate podia were found to be about equally sensitive but less so than the tentacles (Hyman, 1955). The papillae on tentacles of *Synapta* were thought to be olfactory in function (Cuénot, 1891). The most complicated sense organs are known chiefly in synaptids, where they appear to compensate for lack of podia (Hyman, 1955). *Holothuria atra* and *H. surinamensis* tend to show negative geotaxis in aquaria (Crozier, 1915a; Trefz, 1956). There has been little attempt to relate these behavioral patterns to the animal living under natural conditions. The interstitial *Psammothuria ganapatii* is positively thigmotactic, negatively phototaxic, gregarious, and adheres to the substratum (sand) principally by tentacles (Rao, 1968).

E. Locomotion

Holothurians that move freely (e.g., *S. badionatus* [now =*Isostichopus badionotus* (Selenka)], *A. agassizi* (Selenka), *H. parvula* (Selenka), and *H. mexicana* (Ludwig) have numerous ventral tube feet. Burrowers [e.g., *H. impatiens* (Förskal) and *H. princeps* Selenka] show equal development of podia on the ventrum and dorsum, and the mouth is often terminal. The large apodous species *Euapta lappa* (Müller) usually hides among coral rocks and *H. glaberrima* Selenka, which lives in the surf zone, has a smooth dorsum (Deichmann, 1957b). Hyman (1955) concluded that dendrochirotes are essentially sedentary. This is undoubtedly related to the fact that they are plankton-feeders. *Holothuria atra* and *S. variegatus* wander from 0 to 52 m/day, covering greater distances on "poor" feeding grounds (i.e., coral–seagrass mixture) than on "rich" grounds (Yamanouti, 1939). *Stichopus panimensis* Clark creeps by muscular waves (Hyman, 1955). *Astichopus multifidus* walks, bounds, rolls, and has erect exploratory movements. Cutress reported swimming in this species (in Glynn, 1965). The large sea cucumber *Paelopatides* sp., observed at a depth of about 2000 m south of New England, also swims (H. Sanders, personal communication; see also Mauzey *et al.*, 1968). Horst (1900) maintained that the spicules of many Synaptidae lie too deep in the epidermis to be effective in locomotion and their action would also be hindered by mucus secretion. According to Quatrefages (in Östergren, 1897), anchors of *Synapta* are used for locomotion. They serve as an attachment in crawling since synaptids lack podia (Cuénot, 1891; Clark, 1896; Hyman, 1955).

F. Burrowing Behavior

Little is known about burrowing, behavior common to a number of tropical holothurians (Gardiner, 1904). *Holothuria arenicola* and *H. pervicax* burrow down almost vertically with the anus situated at the surface of the substrate. Characteristic feces are produced at the summits of mounds (Macnae and Kalk, 1962). Burrowing species probably ingest sand while they burrow (Hyman, 1955) and during the early stage of "resting," which is followed by "deep sleep." The "sleep" is interpreted as an adaptation to burial in sand during an 8–13-hour period (Yamanouchi, 1956).

XII. Evisceration and Autotomy

The nature of evisceration and autotomy varies with the morphology of the species. *Synapta* pinches off fragments (autotomy) from the posterior end; young *Synapta maculata* breaks the body into many fragments, older individuals show only partial breaks; *Thyone* ejects viscera (evisceration) through the body wall; *H. atra*, *H. sanguinolenta*, and *S. chloronotus* sever the digestive tract near the cloaca and eject internal organs through the anus (Crozier, 1915a; Domantay, 1931). In *H. atra*, only the left respiratory tree is shed with the digestive tract. The right respiratory tree contains numerous red blood cells, but the left does not. The left respiratory tree may play a role in excretion (Trefz, 1956).

Gardiner (1904) thought that evisceration is a method of ridding the animal of very coarse sand, whereas Domantay (1931), Gillett and McNeill (1959), and Nichols (1962) suggested that it possibly provides a meal for predators. Evisceration is caused by handling, temperature, pH and O_2 (Russell, 1965), electric shock (Kille, 1936), chemicals (Pearse, 1909), direct sunlight (Crozier, 1914), and foul water (Domantay, 1931). *Holothuria difficilis* does not eviscerate when it is placed in seawater which is heated. *Actinopyga mauritiana* will not discharge Cuvierian tubules or eviscerate under intense provocation; it will eviscerate when out of seawater during the night (Bakus, 1968). Strong stimuli which result in a very active or contracted condition do not always induce evisceration (Pearse, 1909). Evisceration in *A. agassizi* does not occur without previous eversion of the Cuvierian organs. High water temperature was the most effective method of causing evisceration; the majority of animals would eviscerate in $\frac{1}{2}$–7 hours with almost 100% survival. Zinc ions also induce evisceration. However, *A. agassizi* rarely eviscerates in nature. Evisceration may be caused by exposure of the holothurian to its own toxin. Casual observation indicates that many animals eviscerate for no readily apparent reason. The role of Cuvierian tubules in evisceration is obscure (Mosher, 1956). Evisceration occurs seasonally in *S. regalis* (Cuvier) and *Parastichopus californicus* (Stimpson) (Mosher, 1965). It can occur without Cuvierian tubule discharge (Crozier, 1914). Evisceration seldom occurs under natural conditions in some holothurians (Kille, 1936; Mosher, 1965). It is unlikely that evisceration is a normal defense response (Glynn, 1965), in part because of the foregoing evidence and the fact that holothurians are rarely consumed by predators in tropical waters (Bakus, 1968). Moreover, some species have toxic viscera (see Section XV). Domantay (1931) suggested that evisceration usually decreases the total amount of metabolism, thus the holothurian may be able to survive until better environmental conditions again arise. The lost organs are rapidly regenerated. The only stimulus invariably producing autotomy in *H. surinamensis* is stagnation of seawater. This is true also for *H. atra* (S. Trefz, personal communication). Visceral autotomy is interpreted as a pathological condition and not absolutely dependent on the presence of a nerve ring (Crozier, 1915a), contrary to the opinion of Pearse (1909). It can be concluded that evisceration is often induced by poor environmental conditions, is probably not defensive, and experimentation under natural conditions is needed to elucidate its true role, one that will undoubtedly be complex in terms of physiology and adaptation.

XIII. Regeneration

A. Regeneration of Viscera and Body Wall

Early stages of regeneration of the digestive tract in *H. floridana* took place 4–8 days after evisceration (Kille, 1937). In the same species and in *H. impatiens* rudiments from the cloacal mesentery and the esophagus began growing toward each other at 10 days. A continuous alimentary canal occurred from 10 to commonly 25 days, although three animals lacked a digestive tract after 36 days. Of 600 individuals of *H. parvula*, 15% were undergoing regeneration after reproduction by transverse fission (Kille, 1936). *Actinopyga agassizi* undergoes rapid initial regeneration of the entire intestine (18 days); at higher temperatures (30°–33°C), a functional intestine develops after 25 days. The general plan of regeneration is the formation of an intestinal rudiment along all of the ragged free edge of remaining mesentery (Mosher, 1956). Mosher discussed histological changes taking place in this process. Later studies showed that *A. agassizi* has a complete intestine after 38 days, a rudimentary rete mirabile after 81 days, and is almost normal after 97 days (Mosher, 1965). Deichmann (1922) stated that holothurians can regenerate either the anal or oral ends after fission, before the animal is full grown. Regeneration of the anterior or posterior end in *H. surinamensis* can take place within 2–3 weeks (Crozier, 1915a). Torelle (1909), who studied regeneration in 550 specimens comprising 12 species of *Holothuria* and 150 specimens consisting of other genera, concluded the following: (1) Regeneration is more rapid in Dendrochirotida than Synaptidae or Aspidochirotida. (2) Body parts posterior to the "lantern" regenerate more readily than parts containing the "lantern." (3) Animals divided longitudinally do not survive. (4) A body wall cut open from the oral to the aboral end will regenerate new tissue to close the wound and will replace missing parts autotomously thrown off. (5) The intestine is usually regenerated from the cloaca or from part of the old intestine near the cloaca. When the body of *Leptosynapta crassipatina* Clark is cut transversely into three equal sections, there is no gradient of survival time along the body in regeneration. Longitudinal sectioning invariably causes death. Preliminary studies suggest that nutrition is the vital factor in survival of posterior ends and that nutrients must be taken up directly (Smith and Greenberg, 1966).

B. Regeneration of the Epidermis

Holothuria grisea Selenka, living in an aquarium, was once observed to cast off its pigment-laden skin (Millott, 1954). During unfavorable environmental conditions, *Isostichopus badionotus* (Selenka) sheds large patches of skin with considerable mucus. The epidermis quickly heals, sometimes overnight (Tikasingh, 1963).

XIV. Cuvierian Tubules

A. Nature of Cuvierian Tubule Discharge

One of the most interesting behavioral traits in certain holothurians is the discharge or ejection of Cuvierian tubules (Cuvierian organs), apparently first noted by Cooper in 1880 (Halstead, 1965). Many biologists consider them primarily organs of defense (Bell, 1884; Cuénot, 1891; Minchin, 1892; Russo, 1899; Cuénot, 1948; Endean, 1957; Matsuno and Ishida, 1969), with some doubts (Ludwig, 1891; Frizzell and Exline, 1955). They have been observed to be effective in snaring crabs (*Carcinus moenas*) (Cuénot, 1898) and lobsters (Minchin, 1892; MacBride, 1906), although it is uncertain if this occurs in nature. Crabs and fishes may be completely immobilized (Ritchie, 1910; Mortensen, 1917; Bakus, 1968), but it is dubious that the holothurian "escapes" from the predator (see Frizzell and Exline, 1955) in view of their sluggish movements. A small spider crab with Cuvierian tubules of *A. parvula* about his legs ate them. Deichmann (1926) made no comment on the reaction of the crab to the tubules, if any. This holothurian is not listed as a toxic species by Halstead (1965). The tubules apparently are seldom if ever used against the inquiline fish *Carapus* since those holothurians with tubules often contain this fish (Hipeau-Jacquette, 1967), the protective mechanism being unknown (see Section XVII). Mosher (1956) suggested that the Cuvierian organ possibly prevents poisoning of sea cucumbers by their own toxin, but this is highly unlikely.

B. Distribution of Cuvierian Tubules and Their Evolution

Cuvierian tubules are almost restricted to tropical holothurians (e.g., certain *Actinopyga* and *Holothuria*), only a few species with Cuvierian organs having invaded temperate latitudes (Mosher, 1956; Halstead, 1965). Their occurrence may be related to predation (see Section XVI). The fact that many species lack Cuvierian organs contradicts the idea that they represent a morphological rudiment of an organ that formerly had some very different function. They are racemose or undifferentiated from the respiratory trees in certain holothurians, in others they are highly specialized. It is suggested that Cuvierian organs are simply a portion of the viscera especially modified for ejection. It is assumed that Cuvierian organs originally had a respiratory function. Mucus-secreting cells increased their unpalatability and they became passively offensive followed by the evolution of aggressive offense (Minchin, 1892).

C. Behavior of Cuvierian Tubule Discharge

Many holothurians with Cuvierian tubules are highly sensitive to touch (Ritchie, 1910; Crozier, 1915b; Macnae and Kalk, 1958; Tikasingh, 1963), and some characteristically direct their anus toward the stimulus and then accurately discharge tubules. The tubules are cast out the cloaca along with or without part of the intestine depending on species and circumstances (Barthels, 1897; Crozier, 1915b; Deichmann, 1926; Bakus, 1968). Many species have sticky Cuvierian organs but they do not adhere to the body of the holothurian (Minchin, 1892). The tubules of *H. niger* (now = *H. forskali* Delle Chiaje) elongate 12 times their original length and swell 7 times in diameter. Six tubules supported a suspended weight of 800–1000 grains (52–65 gm) (Bell, 1884). Several to many tubules are discharged at a time and discharge can occur up to four times in succession in *H. difficilis*. Tubule discharge was circadian in April–May at Eniwetok. No tubule discharge occurs in heated seawater (Bakus, 1968). Ejected tubules reportedly are not regenerated, the basal vesicles remain as vestigial remnants (Frizzell and Exline, 1955). In contrast, Hyman (1955) and Bennett (1967) stated that the tubules are readily regenerated. This latter conclusion would be in accord with their true function (see above). The discharged Cuvierian organs of *A. agassizi* are not sticky, they do not elongate; they are toxic (Hyman, 1955; Russell, 1965), more so than other body parts (Halstead, 1965). However, Mosher (1956) claimed that the Cuvierian organ of *A. agassizi* is not toxic. This is clearly erroneous (see Nigrelli and Jakowska, 1960).

D. Physiology of Cuvierian Tubule Discharge

Early experiments indicated that a rise of pressure in the coelom precedes and accompanies the discharge of tubules. Undischarged tubules removed from the body of *H. nigra* (now = *H. forskali* Delle Chiaje) can be made to elongate in a manner exactly resembling normal discharge by injecting them with seawater or other fluid (Mines, 1912). Crozier (1915b) found that inorganic acids, phenol, turpentine, essential oils, increased temperature, or fresh water did not cause discharge of tubules. Discharge or even partial discharge was rarely accompanied by increased internal pressure. Crozier concluded that normal discharge includes action of the nervous system, though perhaps only indirectly. The mechanism of tubule ejection was elucidated by Endean (1957). When a tubule of *H. leucospilota* is stretched in seawater, cells of the outer layer split and their contents (proteinaceous angular bodies) form an amorphous mass which has strong adhesive properties. Tubules stick to most objects but not the sea cucumber body wall. It is suggested that water in the lumen of respiratory trees must burst through blind ends of extensions of the lumen of respiratory trees found in the papillae. Water must be forced into the tubules before they are ejected via the anus. Ejection occurs when the cloacal wall tears. Isolated tubules will swell if placed in seawater, possibly the result of the two muscular systems present. Tubules are released by contraction of rings of muscle at the papillae. Collagen fibers are their major structural components. Their ability to resist tensile forces enhances the effectiveness of tubules as organs of defense.

XV. Toxicity

A. Physiology and Biochemistry of Holothurin

Nigrelli and Yamanouchi independently discovered that certain holothurians contained a toxin; both named it holothurin (Halstead, 1965). Nigrelli and Jakowska (1960) and others (e.g., Sobotka, 1965; Friess *et al.*, 1968) studied the physiological effects on a variety of organisms and the biochemical nature of holothurin; we will consider a select few. Holothurin is a saponin (steroid saponin or steroid glycoside) found in four of five orders in the class Holothuroidea (Nigrelli and Jakowska, 1960). It may be highly concentrated in the body wall, viscera, Cuvierian tubules, in two of these three regions, or in all three. The concentration of holothurin may vary on a seasonal basis (Yasumoto *et al.*, 1966). There may be more than one type of saponin in an individual holothurian. The distribution and biochemistry of echinoderm saponins were reviewed by Tursch (1972; see also Bakus, 1968). Holothurin appears to have a direct effect on muscle contraction. It also has a nerve-blocking effect similar to that of cocaine, procaine, and physostigmine in laboratory animals, but its effects on humans have not been fully determined (Halstead, 1969). There is no method by which one can accurately predict if a species of tropical holothurian will be toxic and where the toxin(s) are located. *Actinopyga agassizi* releases a toxic mucus from the body wall when rubbed (Mosher, 1956); *H. atra* behaves similarly (see below). *Carapus bermudensis*, an inquiline of *A. agassizi*, died in 8 minutes in an extract of 1000 ppm. taken from the holothurian host. Fage (in Arvy, 1954) described the effect of holothurin from *H. tubulosa*, *H. polii* Delle Chiaje, and *H. impatiens* on fishes. Extracts of the body wall of these three species and the Cuvierian tubules of *H. impatiens* are hemolytic. Extracted holothurin killed eight species of marine teleosts and three species of frogs in <30 minutes *in vivo* and *in vitro* (Arvy, 1954). *Stichopus japonicus* contains a steroid glycoside which displays high activity against fungi (Shimada, 1969). Saponin is found in every part of the body of *H. leucospilota,* all organs showing higher concentrations in July. The ovaries and Cuvierian tubules have remarkably high concentrations of saponins in July. A hemolytic index (HI) (rabbit RBC per gram wet organ) was used to describe the effects of the toxin on the hemolysis of red blood cells. The saponin content of the tubules reaches a peak in June to August (HI = 1250), the breeding season, then decreases during winter (HI = 526). The physiological role of these saponins in the Echinodermata is unknown (Matsuno and Ishida, 1969).

B. Effects of Holothurin on Animals and on Man

Yamanouchi (1955) found that holothurin kills marine and freshwater fishes and earthworms (*Eisenia*), but it has no effect on crustaceans or mollusks. Holothurin is considerably stronger than the most powerful hemolytic reagent saponin and it probably enters fishes through the gills. Freshwater fishes are more resistant to holothurin than are marine fishes, probably because gills of the latter are less permeable. Of 27 species of South Sea and Japanese sea cucumbers >80% are toxic. Each species appears to contain chemically different toxins. Glynn (1965) suggested that *Astichopus multifidus* may possibly release trace amounts of holothurin in averting predators. The poison is not released naturally, that is, without physical contact by a person or predator. A body-wall extract of 1000 ppm from the holothurian caused death in a fish in 10 minutes.

There are over 30 species of holothurians that contain holothurin; the present author has discovered numerous additional toxic holothurians and suggests that there may be more than 100 toxic species. Liquid ejected from the visceral cavity of some species may cause contact dermatitis or blindness in man. Ingestion of sea cucumber poison may be fatal. The hemolytic action of holothurin may be the major cause of death in poisoned vertebrates (Halstead, 1965). However, poisoning in man by holothurians is rare. Nausea and vomiting are occasionally reported from eating trepang or bêche-de-mer. Acute conjunctivitis has been reported in persons swimming in water containing tissue extracts of toxic sea cucumbers (Russell, 1965).

Natives of Guam use holothurians to poison coral reef fishes [*H. atra* is possibly used, although S. Trefz (personal communication) found this species ineffective in poisoning a tidepool fish]. They cut the animal and squeeze out its contents underwater. This renders fishes weak and less active. Sea cucumbers are also used on Majuro where they are pounded or pulped in canoes and placed into pools. This method of

fishing is considered to be a recent social phenomenon (Frey, 1951).
Holothuria vagabunda is used as a fish poison in the Tokara Islands,
according to Tokioka (in Yamanouchi, 1955).

C. ECOLOGY OF TOXICITY IN HOLOTHURIANS

Yamanouchi (1955) concluded that fishes may learn by trial and error
to avoid toxic holothurians since they may undergo paralysis if they
bite them, and that holothurian poison has little ecological significance.
In contrast, Bakus (1968) demonstrated that holothurin plays a significant role in protecting sea cucumbers against predators. *Holothuria atra*
releases copious amounts of burgundy-colored toxin when handled (Fig.
3), which kills flatworms and polychaetes. Crabs and blennies emigrate
from poisoned tidepools, *Conus* becomes immobile and *H. difficilis* becomes hyperactive. Four species of Eniwetok holothurians were tested
for toxicity in the laboratory followed by the hand-feeding of body
parts of sea cucumbers to fishes in the natural environment. All body
parts found to be toxic by laboratory research were not consumed by
fishes and seldom was an attempt made even to mouth them. All nontoxic

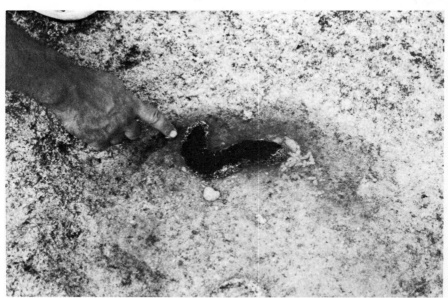

Fig. 3. Touching and rubbing the body wall of *Holothuria atra* Jaeger causes the
release of a pigment and toxin (holothurin) into the surrounding seawater. This
behavior appears to be an effective deterrent against predation.

body parts were readily consumed. These data combined with studies on Cuvierian discharge in *H. difficilis* indicated that holothurin is a very effective deterrent against predation.

XVI. Predation

A. NATURE OF PREDATION ON HOLOTHURIANS

It is generally believed that sea cucumbers have few predators except for an occasional seagull (Frizzell and Exline, 1955; Bonham and Held, 1963; Pawson, 1966a). It is doubtful that lobsters and crabs are holothurian predators (Frizzell and Exline, 1955), and there is no evidence to support this contention. Lack of predators is attributed to a tough integument (Crozier, 1915a) and toxicity (Bakus, 1968). The viscera of *H. nigra,* when fed to sea anemones, was always rejected in a few minutes (Minchin, 1892). Holothurians are rarely consumed by fishes in the Indo-Pacific; sharks will occasionally take specimens of *S. chloronotus,* a toxic holothurian (Bakus, 1968). Eight species of Caribbean fishes eat sea cucumbers, but only in the case of the trunkfish (*Lactophrys bicaudalis*) do holothurians comprise more than 4% by volume of total food ingested (Randall, 1967). In nontropical waters holothurians may comprise a significant part of the diet of some demersal fishes (Graham, 1939; Pawson, 1966a). This is presumably related to the fact that they are nontoxic. Moreover, they are consumed by asteroids in certain regions and the sea cucumber may respond to the predator by swimming (Mauzey *et al.,* 1968). Recently it was discovered that in Jamaica the triton *Charonia variegata* consumes *A. agassizi* and *H.* (*Ludwigothuria*) *mexicana* Ludwig. There is strong evidence that *Isostichopus badionotus* is also attacked by the same snail (Parrish, in Bakus, 1972). At Eniwetok, Marshall Islands, *H. difficilis* is consumed by the tun shell *Tonna.* This occurs at night when the sea cucumbers are exposed and feeding (M. Chartock, personal communication, 1971). In conclusion, there is little doubt that the most important enemy of holothurians is man (Pawson, 1966a). This is particularly true of the tropics. However, it should be noted that nothing is known about predation on larvae, although this must certainly occur.

B. EVOLUTION OF DEFENSIVE MECHANISMS IN HOLOTHURIANS

Frizzell and Exline (1955) suggested that the habit of "hiding" in holothurians, a widespread behavioral trait, strongly implies a search by predators. This conclusion is questionable, and an oversimplification for many sea cucumbers. They stated that camouflage by sand grains, for example, may serve the function of concealment, but this does not explain why one finds both sand-free and sand-covered individuals in a species population. S. Trefz (personal communication) believes that those particles of sand which happen to alight on a sea cucumber are retained. If sand is removed from a holothurian in the laboratory considerable time passes before the animal is recovered. *Pseudostichopus* and *Meseres* are said to cement sharp sponge spicules on the skin as an active defense against fishes, but there seems to be no evidence to support this claim. Bakus (1969) presented a hypothesis in which toxicity plays an overwhelming role in minimizing predation in the tropics, a tough body wall and large size also being effective deterrents. It is assumed that the feeding habits of the diverse predatory fishes associated with coral reefs have resulted in the selection, over a period of geological history, of those species with noxious traits and Cuvierian discharge, followed by the evolution of toxicity, or the influence of predators has led to the formation of holothurian cryptofauna. Today selection is proceeding in the same direction, but relatively few fishes can either tolerate their noxious chemicals or Cuvierian discharge or can reach certain species in recesses. In temperate waters, more species of fish predators may consume holothurians because many of these sea cucumbers are presumably nontoxic and lack Cuvierian organs. This is supported by recent research in the San Juan Islands, Washington (Bakus, unpublished). The paucity of these defense mechanisms is thought to be the result in part of relatively low intensity predation by fishes during recent geological history.

XVII. Biological Associations

A. Types of Interspecific Biological Associations

There are many biological associates of holothurians. Those living on the body surface include bacteria, diatoms, protists, a sponge, polychaetes, gastropods, bivalve mollusks, amphipods, copepods, and ascidians. Both substrate and nutrition are believed to be basic factors favoring surface associations. Internal organisms include gregarines, rhabdocoel turbellarians, copepods, and others. Parasitism is common in these associations. It is thought that the associates of holothurians excluding copepods, parallel those of ascidians (Changeux, 1961). Frizzell and Exline (1955) stated that commensalism in holothurians is developed to a minor extent, but there are many examples of parasitism

The known parasites are limited to relatively few members of diverse phyla, suggesting little host specificity. In strong contrast, Hyman (1955) and Jones and Mahadevan (1965) maintained that holothurians are subject to a long list of both commensals and parasites.

B. Epizooism and Commensalism

Among some of the interesting cases of epizooism and commensalism is a small unidentified calcareous sponge which lives on *Synaptula hydriformis* (Caribbean) and the 20–30 pycnogonids per host [*H. lubrica* var. *moebii*—now = *H. moebii* (Ludwig)] found near the Seto Marine Laboratory in Kii, Japan (Ohshima, 1927). The synaptid *Chondrocloea striata* (Sluiter) is found only on the large sponge *Petrosia testudinaria*, particularly at depths of 17–22 m. The hard sponge is thought to serve as a firm attachment for the 50–60 cm holothurian (Nayar and Mahaderan, 1965). Practically nothing is known concerning the biology of these and other similar associations. In Mozambique, *H. atra* is almost invariably accompanied by the polynoid polychaete, *Gastrolepidia clavigera*, which crawls over its host and matches the host in color. The worm leaves rapidly when the host is picked up (Macnae and Kalk, 1962). This is probably caused by a release of toxin (see Fig. 3). About 30% of *H. atra* in Galle, Ceylon, have commensal (?) polychaetes which match the color of the host. They quickly return to the host if detached. Certain of the same holothurians contain a cryptically colored crab that lives in the cloaca (Pearson, 1915). *Stichopus chloronotus* has a surface annelid (*Gastrolepidia*) adapted in color and form to the host. It also has *Polynoe setosa* which matches the host in color (Sivickis and Domantay, 1928). Kent (1893) described a polynoid polychaete on *S. chloronotus* which has parapodia modified to form suckers. *Actinopyga mauritiana* also has a surface polychaete that matches the host in color. *Ludwigothuria mexicana* (now = *H. mexicana* Ludwig) reportedly contains a commensal gastropod (*Balcis*) and an inquiline fish (*Carapus*). Many individuals have various types of algae on the dorsum, presumably held by papillae and minute tube feet (Tikasingh, 1963). The pea crab *Pinnixa leptosynaptae* lives in association with *Leptosynapta crassipatina* (Wass, 1968). The crab *Lissocarcinus orbicularis* lives near the tentacles of *H. nigra*. It is also found on most *H. atra* in Hawaii, located within tentacles, in the cloaca, or on the body surface. It is black with conspicuous white spots and is well camouflaged on the sandy sea cucumber. The same crab is brown with white spots, on the brown holothurian *A. mauritiana* (S. Trefz, personal communication). A common portunid crab in the Maldives is polymorphic. When on sand-covered *H. atra* they are gray; on sand-free *H. atra* they are black (Bouvier, 1908). No experimental studies have been conducted to relate cryptic coloration to predation, a most likely relationship in these cases, nor is the exact nature of the biological associations known.

C. Inquilinism

Inquilines are often reported from tropical holothurians. In Kakinada Bay, India 50% of *Molpadia* sp. harbor an intestinal hesionid inquiline. There usually is a single worm, occasionally an adult and a young polychaete (Ganapati and Radhakrishna, 1962). Adult *Pinnaxodes floridensis* live in the cloaca and respiratory tree of *Theelothuria princeps* (=*H. princeps* Selenka) where they filter food from water circulated by the host. Juvenile crabs have been recovered from the anterior part of the digestive tract (Wells and Wells, 1961). The pea crab *Pinnotheres deccanensis* occurred in the lower respiratory tree in 10 of 25 *H. scabra* examined. Only females were found; they are restricted to this species of sea cucumber. The crabs benefit by receiving shelter and protection. They occasionally injure the host by piercing the wall of the respiratory tree but the holothurians' capacity for regeneration may negate this effect (Jones and Mahadevan, 1965). Fishes of the genus *Carapus* (pearlfish, Carapidae) live in the cloaca of tropical holothurians and have been noted innumerable times (e.g., Fisher, 1907; Sivickis and Domantay, 1928; Ancona-Lopez, 1956). The fish *Encheliophis gracilis* (Bleeker) is found in Hawaiian holothurians, but is uncommon (S. Trefz, personal communication). *Actinopyga agassizi*, a holothurian with toxic Cuvierian tubules, often contains *Carapus* (Deichmann, 1938, 1957b). The incidence of *C. bermudenis* in *A. agassizi* (four localities) ranged from about 30 to 69%. It was suggested that alternate hosts may be utilized in areas where the primary host is rare (Smith and Tyler, 1969). Yamanouchi (1956) concluded that the occurrence of pearlfish is unrelated with the toxin holothurin but related to the diameter of the cloaca. Two theories have been proposed to explain the holothurian–pearlfish association: (1) The fish simply inhabits the host, using the cloaca as a protective home. (2) The fish consumes the gonads and respiratory organs of the host. Hosts of the Carapidae include bivalve mollusks, holothurians, asteroids, and ascidians. *Carapus homei* is found in several species of holothurians and one species of asteroid. Each of the four stages of development of the fish has a characteristic morphology and behavior. Entry into the holothurian occurs under the influence of several factors, especially a chemical stimulus from the integument of the holothurian. The fish, particularly when young, eat body organs of the host. The gonads are preferred; the association is one of parasitism. The adult can lead an independent life. The fish is morphologically specialized for a parasitic existence in the host (Hipeau-Jacquotte, 1967).

D. PARASITISM

Holothuria scabra is heavily parasitized by *Mucronalia* sp. and by *Odostomia* sp. (gastropods). *Odostomia* is attached to the buccal membrane or to the body. *Mucronalia* (one or more specimens) lie in a gall around the anus; the proboscis penetrates to the respiratory trees of the host. Densities of up to 1 *Mucronalia* per 25 hosts are found in some parts of Inhaca Island, Mozambique (Macnae and Kalk, 1958, 1962). Bivalve mollusks (e.g., *Entovalva*) are often slightly modified, whereas snails (e.g., *Entoconcha, Entocolax*) may be altered almost beyond recognition (Hyman, 1955). Gastropod parasitism was discussed in detail by Vaney (1913). Copepods are commonly endoparasites in holothurians (Humes, 1967, 1968; Humes and Ho, 1969). Virtually nothing is known about the ecology of these relationships. The evolution of parasitism in holothurians is best exemplified in copepods, as follows: (1) The host and associate live in the same regime. (2) A specific positive chemotaxis evolves from the association. (3) Populations of the parasite become isolated followed by divergence. (4) An evolution of stereotaxis occurs, resulting from positive chemotaxis (Changeux, 1961).

XVIII. Economics

A. HOLOTHURIANS AS A HUMAN FOOD RESOURCE

Numerous articles have been published on edible holothurians (trepang or bêche-de-mer) because they are consumed in many tropical localities (e.g., Jaeger, 1833; Thurston, 1895; Galtsoff, 1933; Frey, 1951; Endean, 1965; Krishnaswamy and Krishnan, 1967). The majority of these accounts are either popular or they are principally of local interest. Several comprehensive discussions on trepang fisheries are those of Kent (1893), Koningsberger (1904), Hornell (1917), Sella and Sella (1940), and Panning (1944). The sun-dried body walls of *Holothuria, Stichopus,* and *Thelenota* are frequently used in soups (Nichols, 1962). Some 7.7 thousand metric tons of trepang were landed in 1961 by Japan and

0.4 thousand metric tons by South Korea (Anonymous, 1963). Toxic holothurians are consumed, but those that are relatively less toxic are preferred. For example, *H. atra* was not used as trepang in Ceylon (Pearson, 1915). *Stichopus badionotus* is reportedly unpalatable to most animals and unsuited for the preparation of trepang (Deichmann, 1957b). The Japanese species *S. japonicus* and *Cucumaria japonica* Semper, which are eaten raw, have weaker toxins than the Seto *H. monacaria* [now = *H. gyrifer* (Selenka)] and *H. vagabunda*, both inedible species (Yamanouchi, 1955). Holothurians are seldom utilized in temperate latitudes except in the Orient.

B. HOLOTHURIANS AS A FOOD FOR DOMESTIC ANIMALS

An attempt was made to utilize holothurians as a food resource in the chicken industry. Boiled and dried *H. scabra* were fed to chicks during their first 3 weeks of life. A 3% bêche-de-mer meal was satisfactory when fat was extracted or when an antioxidant was added. Meals with >3% bêche-de-mer resulted in bone weakness, reduced epiphyseal calcification, rubbery beaks, edema, nephrosis, degenerative myopathy, and poor growth. These symptoms are related to imbalances in levels of Ca, P, and Na in the diet. *Holothuria scabra* was found to have relatively high levels of Ca, P, Na, and protein (Springhall and Dingle, 1967).

C. HOLOTHURIANS AND MEDICINE

As mentioned previously, a highly active antifungal steroid glycoside has been isolated from the sea cucumber *S. japonicus* (Shimada, 1969). Nigrelli *et al.* (1967) have discovered antitumoral and neurotropic substances derived from echinoderms.

XIX. Summary

Knowledge of tropical holothurians in terms of ecology, evolution, and experimentation, with few exceptions, is in a preliminary stage of development at the present time.

The geological history of tropical holothurians is little known because of intense biotic activity and disruption of stratified sediments, among other things. There are over 1200 species of holothurians, the highest diversity being characteristic of tropical shallow waters. The tropical genus *Holothuria* contains at least 114 species. Aspidochirotes are more characteristic of habitats with clear tropical waters, and dendrochirotes are more characteristic of boreal latitudes, due in part to the abundances of plankton and organic detritus. The ultimate environmental factors limiting distribution may be waves and currents.

The echinoderm class Holothuroidea often predominates on atolls. Densities as high as 130 holothurians/m² have been reported but the value of density figures is questionable since sampling techniques vary so widely.

Holothurians may attain a length of up to 5 m. No generalization can be made regarding a living to preserved size ratio since this varies between species. The tendency for one size class to occur in a locality may be related to reproduction by transverse fission, a complicating factor in the analysis of age structure. Growth rates are known for very few tropical species. Most coral reef holothurians possess a dull coloration, black, brown, and gray predominating. No attempt has been made to study the adaptive advantages of color polymorphism.

Knowledge on the biochemistry of tropical holothurians is limited except for research on toxins. Certain radionuclides may become highly concentrated in holothurian tissues.

Gamete release has been described for only one species of tropical holothurian. Larvae are very poorly known. Brooding of young occurs in only two tropical species. Transverse fission has been reported in a number of holothurians. Fission may be repeated under natural conditions without the intervention of sexual reproduction.

Osmoregulation, respiration, and temperature tolerance have been little studied in tropical holothurians. It is not known whether coral reef holothurians, many of whom may live under constant environmental conditions, are physiologically stenotopic.

Holothurians probably are the most important sand deposit feeders on many coral reefs. The size of food particles in holothurians varies with the species and locality. Different species partition and consume substrates of different sizes. Coral reef holothurians consume a large variety of living and dead microorganisms. It is hypothesized that many tropical holothurians primarily assimilate bacteria and organic detritus and their diet is supplemented by active absorption of dissolved organic matter from surrounding waters. The few studies made indicate that coral reef sediments often are poor in organic material. The assimilation efficiency of tropical holothurians is relatively high, roughly 50% based on preliminary evidence. Passage of sediments through the digestive tract of holothurians takes from 2 to 36 hours; the amount passed varies among species and localities.

Levels of pH in the digestive tracts of holothurians vary widely within and among species, from 4.75 to 8.2. Digestive enzymes have no appreciable effect on the sizes of calcareous bioclastics but organic detritus is degraded. Holothurians are of major importance in working over sediments with the resultant destruction of initial stratification, but the significance of this process for the biota of soft bottoms remains to be tested.

Although a number of holothurians become covered with a variety of extraneous material, the adaptive significance of this behavior is unknown. Sea cucumbers tend to respond suddenly to shadows, a pattern typical of many invertebrates. The degree of sensitivity to stimuli seems to be as follows: tentacles > anterior end > posterior end > papillae, podia > midbody surface. Some holothurians move up to 52 m/day; a few species are capable of swimming.

Evisceration can be induced experimentally by a large variety of agents, but it seldom occurs under natural conditions, with few exceptions. The most frequent causes of evisceration are poor environmental conditions such as stagnant seawater. The nature of evisceration and autotomy vary with the morphology of the species. Lost organs are rapidly regenerated. A complete digestive tract may be regenerated in 10–38 days.

It is assumed that Cuvierian organs or tubules originally had a respiratory function. There is ample evidence to indicate that they are organs of defense in certain species, but practically no observations have been made on their use under natural conditions. These tubules are largely restricted to tropical holothurians; the presence and nature of the tubules and their ejection varies with the species.

Tropical holothurians often contain a toxin called holothurin, a steroid saponin, which may be concentrated in the body wall, viscera, Cuvierian tubules, or throughout the body. The concentration of holothurin may vary on a seasonal basis, reaching a peak during the warmest months. Holothurin is capable of killing a large variety of invertebrates and vertebrates; it is a very powerful hemolytic agent. Coral reef holothurians have very few predators, owing, in part, to their toxic body wall, large size, and cryptic habits. Holothurin plays an important role in protecting sea cucumbers against predators, particularly coral reef fishes. It is hypothesized that toxicity in holothurians was selected during a period of geological history, in response especially to the high predation intensity of the diverse fishes associated with coral reefs.

Although there are numerous described cases of interspecific biological associations in holothurians, practically nothing is known about their exact relationships. No experimental studies have been conducted to relate cryptic coloration to predation. The inquiline pearlfish *Carapus* is now known to be an endoparasite, particularly as a juvenile.

Certain holothurians continue to be an important food source in southeast Asia and Japan. Toxic species are consumed by man but those that are least toxic are preferred. Toxic sea cucumbers are suitable as a food for domestic animals only when they comprise a very small percentage of meal, and are properly treated. Substances of medical importance derived from holothurians are beginning to be studied in greater detail.

Acknowledgments

I am indebted to Dr. David L. Pawson, Curator, Division of Echinoderms, Smithsonian Institution, for his unstinting interest and help by providing research space, division and personal library, materials and supplies, camaraderie, and for reviewing the manuscript of this paper. Dr. Shirley Trefz, Division of Mathematics and Natural Science, Leeward Community College, Hawaii, was kind enough to criticize the manuscript, for which I am grateful. Dr. Ailsa M. Clark, Division of Echinoderms, British Museum of Natural History provided me with references on certain of the latest publications in echinoderm ecology. Colleagues in the Division of Echinoderms, Smithsonian Institution, are thanked for their interest and companionship throughout the year. Librarians of the Smithsonian National Museum of Natural History were most helpful in locating obscure references and providing xerox copies of certain articles. I am grateful to Linda Gunter for typing the manuscript.

References

Ahearn, G. A. (1968). *Biol. Bull.* **134**, 367.
Ancona-Lopez, A. A. (1956). *Pap. Dep. Zool. Sec. Agr. Sao Paulo* **12**, 389.
Anonymous. (1963). *FAO Bull. Fish. Statist.* **1**, 1.
Anonymous. (1968). *Life (Aust. Issue)* June 24, pp. 35–60.
Arvy, L. (1954). *C. R. Acad. Sci.* **239**, 1432.
Baker, J. R. (1929). *J. Ecol.* **17**, 141.
Bakus, G. J. (1968). *Mar. Biol.* **2**, 23.
Bakus, G. J. (1969). *Int. Rev. Gen. Exp. Zool.* **4**, 275–369.
Bakus, G. J. (1972). *Atoll Res. Bull.* (in press).
Barth, R., Bonel-Ribas, L., and Osorio E Castro, M. L. (1968). *Publ. Inst. Pesqui. Mar.* **9**, 1.
Barthels, P. (1897). *Sitzungsber. Niederrhein. Ges. Natur.- Heilk.* p. 76.
Bell, F. J. (1884). *Nature (London)* **30**, 146.
Bennett, I. (1967). "The Fringe of the Sea." Rigby, Adelaide.
Bonham, K., and Held, E. E. (1963). *Pac. Sci.* **17**, 305.
Boolootian, R. A., ed. (1966). "Physiology of Echinodermata." Wiley (Interscience), New York.
Bouvier, E. L. (1908). *Bull. Mus. Hist. Natur., Paris* p. 503.
Buchanan, J. B. (1967). *Symp. Zool. Soc. London* **20**, 1–11.

Changeux, J.-P. (1961). "Contribution à l'étude des animaux associés aux Holothurides." Hermann, Paris.

Chartock, M. (1969). *Abstr., West. Soc. Nat. 15th Annu. Meet.* p. 14.

Chesher, R. H. (1970). *Science* **167**, 1275.

Choe, S. (1963). Ph.D Dissertation, Pusan National University, Pusan.

Choe, S., and Ohshima, Y. (1961). *Bull. Jap. Soc. Sci. Fish.* **27**, 97.

Clark, H. L. (1896). *J. Inst. Jam.* **2**, 278.

Clark, H. L. (1902). *Rep. Mich. Acad. Sci.* **3**, 83.

Clark, H. L. (1910). *J. Exp. Zool.* **9**, 497.

Clark, H. L. (1919). *Carnegie Inst. Wash., Dep. Mar. Biol.* **13**, 49.

Clark, H. L. (1942). *Bull. Mus. Comp. Zool., Harvard College* **89**, 367.

Clark, H. L. (1945). *Amer. Natur.* **35**, 479.

Clarke, F. W., and Wheeler, W. C. (1922). *U.S., Geol. Surv., Prof. Pap.* **124**, 1.

Crozier, W. J. (1914). *Amer. J. Physiol.* **36**, 8.

Crozier, W. J. (1915a). *Zool. Jahrb.* **35**, 233.

Crozier, W. J. (1915b). *Amer. J. Physiol.* **36**, 196.

Crozier, W. J. (1916). *Science* **43**, 148.

Crozier, W. J. (1918). *J. Exp. Zool.* **26**, 379.

Cuénot, L. (1891). *Arch. Biol.* **11**, 313.

Cuénot, L. (1898). *Bull. Soc. Zool. Fra.* **23**, 37.

Cuénot, L. (1948). *In* "Traité de Zoologie" (P. P. Grassé, ed.), Vol. 11, pp. 82–120. Masson, Paris.

Deichmann, E. (1922). *Vidensk. Medd. Dan. Naturh. Foren.* **73**, 199.

Deichmann, E. (1926). *Stud. Natur. Hist. Iowa Univ.* **11**, 9.

Deichmann, E. (1938). *Proc. Fla. Acad. Sci.* **3**, 128.

Deichmann, E. (1957a). *Geol. Soc. Amer., Mem.* **67**, 1193–1196.

Deichmann, E. (1957b). *Amer. Mus. Nov.* **1821**, 1.

Domantay, J. S. (1931). *Natur. Appl. Sci. Bull.* **1**, 389.

Edwards, C. L. (1908). *Biometrika* **6**, 236.

Edwards, C. L. (1909). *J. Morphol.* **20**, 211.

Endean, R. (1957). *Quart. J. Microsc. Sci.* **98**, 455.

Endean, R. (1965). *Wild. Aust.* **2**, 14.

Endean, R., Kenny, R., and Stephenson, W. (1956). *Aust. J. Mar. Freshwater Res.* **7**, 88.

Fell, H. B., and Moore, R. C. (1966). *In* "Treatise on Invertebrate Paleontology" (R. C. Moore, ed.), Vol. 2, Part U, pp. 108–118. Geol. Soc. Amer., Univ. of Kansas Press, Lawrence.

Finckh, A. E. (1904). "Royal Society Report on Funafuti," p. 125. Royal Society, London.

Fish, J. D. (1967). *J. Mar. Biol. Ass. U.K.* **47**, 129.

Fisher, W. K. (1907). *Smithson. Misc. Collect.* **32**, 637.

Freeman, P. J. (1966). *Pac. Sci.* **20**, 60.

Frey, D. (1951). *Copeia* p. 175.

Friess, S. L., Durant, R. C., and Chanley, J. D. (1968). *Toxicon* **6**, 81.

Frizzell, D. L., and Exline, H. (1955). *Mo., Univ., Sch. Mines Met., Bull.* **89**, 1.

Frizzell, D. L., Exline, H., and Pawson, D. L. (1966). *In* "Treatise on Invertebrate

Paleontology" (R. C. Moore, ed.), Vol. 2, Part U, pp. 641–672. Geol. Soc. Amer., Univ. of Kansas Press, Lawrence.

Galtsoff, P. S. (1933). *Bull. Bishop Mus., Honolulu* **107**, 3.

Ganapati, P. N., and Radhakrishna, Y. (1962). *Curr. Sci.* **31**, 382.

Gardiner, J. S. (1901). *Rep. Brit. Ass., 1900* p. 400.

Gardiner, J. S. (1903). *Rep. Brit. Ass., 1902* p. 654.

Gardiner, J. S. (1904). *Fauna Geogr. Maldive Laccadive Archipelagos* **1**, 12, 146, 313, and 376.

Gardiner, J. S. (1931). "Coral Reefs and Atolls." Macmillan, New York. 181 pp.

Gerould, J. H. (1898). *Amer. Natur.* **32**, 273.

Gillett, K., and McNeill, F. (1959). "The Great Barrier Reef and Adjacent Isles." Coral Press, Sydney, Australia.

Glynn, P. W. (1965). *Biol. Bull.* **129**, 106.

Graham, D. H. (1939). *Trans. Proc. Roy. Soc. N. Z.* **68**, 421.

Guppy, H. B. (1882). *Nature (London)* **27**, 7.

Habermehl, G., and Volkwein, G. (1968). *Naturwissenschaften* **55**, 83.

Halstead, B. W. (1965). "Poisonous and Venomous Marine Animals of the World," Vol. 1. US Govt. Printing Office, Washington, D.C.

Halstead, B. W. (1969). *In* "The Encyclopedia of Marine Resources" (F. E. Firth, ed.), pp. 675–687. Van Nostrand-Reinhold, Princeton, New Jersey.

Hipeau-Jacquotte, R. (1967). *Rec. Trav. Sta. Mar. Endoume Marseille, Suppl.* **6**, 141.

Hornell, J. (1917). *Madras Fish. Bull.* **11**, 1.

Horst, R. (1900). *Tijdschr. Ned. Dierk. Ver.* [2] **6**, 72.

Humes, A. G. (1967). *Beaufortia* **14**, 135.

Humes, A. G. (1968). *Proc. Biol. Soc. Wash.* **81**, 179.

Humes, A. G., and Ho, J.-S. (1969). *J. Parasitol.* **55**, 877.

Hyman, L. H. (1955). "The Invertebrates: Echinodermata. The Coelomate Bilateria," Vol. IV, pp. 1–763. McGraw-Hill, New York.

Hyman, L. H. (1959). "The Invertebrates: Smaller Coelomate Groups. Chaetognatha, Hemichordata, Pogonophora, Phoronida, Ectoprocta, Brachiopoda, Sipunculida. The Coelomate Bilateria," Vol. V, pp. 1–783. McGraw-Hill, New York.

Ichikawa, R. (1961). *Bull. Jap. Soc. Sci. Fish.* **27**, 66.

Jaeger, G. F. (1833). "De Holothuris (Dissertation)," pp. 1–40. Turici, Typis Gessnerianis.

Jones, S., and Mahadevan, S. (1965). *J. Mar. Biol. Ass. India* **7**, 377.

Jørgensen, C. B. (1966). "Biology of Suspension Feeding." Pergamon, Oxford.

Kaiser, E., and Michl, H. (1958). "Die Biochemie der tierischen Gifte." Deuticke, Vienna.

Kalk, M. (1959). *Rev. Biol. (Lisbon)* **2**, 1.

Kawaguti, S. (1966). *Biol. J. Okayama Univ.* **12**, 35.

Kent, W. S. (1893). "The Great Barrier-Reef of Australia; Its Products and Potentialities." Allan, London.

Kille, F. R. (1936). *Carnegie Inst. Wash., Yearb.* **35**, 85.

Kille, F. R. (1937). *Carnegie Inst. Wash., Yearb.* **36**, 93.

Kille, F. R. (1942). *Biol. Bull.* **83**, 55.

Kindle, E. M. (1919). *Amer. J. Sci.* **47**, 431.

Koningsberger, J. C. (1904). *Med. Plantentuin Jena* **71**, 1.

Krishnan, S. (1968). *Mar. Biol.* **2**, 54.

Krishnaswamy, S., and Krishnan, S. (1967). *Curr. Sci.* 36, 155.

Ludwig, H. (1891). *In* "Klassen und Ordungen des Thierreiches" (H. G. Bronn, ed.), Vol. 2, Sect. 3, Nos. 7–16, pp. 383–487. Winter, Leipzig.

MacBride, E. W. (1906). *In* "The Cambridge Natural History" (S. F. Harmer and A. E. Shipley, eds.), pp. 425–623. Macmillan, New York.

Macnae, W., and Kalk, M. (1958). "A Natural History of Inhaca Island, Mozambique." Witwaterstrand, Johannesburg.

Macnae, W., and Kalk, M. (1962). *J. Anim. Ecol.* 31, 93.

McNulty, J. K., Work, M. C., and Moore, H. B. (1962). *Bull. Mar. Sci. Gulf Carib.* 12, 322.

Matsuno, T., and Ishida, T. (1969). *Experientia* 25, 1261.

Mauzey, K. P., Birkeland, C., and Dayton, P. K. (1968). *Ecology* 49, 603.

Mayer, A. G. (1917). *Carnegie Inst. Wash., Yearb.* 16, 186.

Mayer, A. G. (1918). *Carnegie Inst. Wash., Dep. Mar. Biol.* 9, 3.

Millott, N. (1954). *Bull. Mar. Sci. Gulf Carib.* 3, 305.

Minchin, E. A. (1892). *Ann. Mag. Nat. Hist.* (6) 10, 273.

Mines, G. R. (1912). *Proc. Cambridge Phil. Soc.* 16, 456.

Moret, L. (1940). *C. R. Soc. Geol.* p. 11.

Mortensen, T. (1917). *Vidensk. Medd. Dan. Naturh. Foren.* 69, 57.

Mortensen, T. (1937). *Dan. Vid. Selsk. Skr.* [9] 7, No. 3, 1.

Mosher, C. (1956). *Zoologica* 41, 17.

Mosher, C. (1965). *Bull. Mar. Sci. Gulf Carib.* 15, 255.

Nayar, K. N., and Mahadevan, S. (1965). *J. Mar. Biol. Ass. India* 7, 199.

Newell, R. C., and Courtney, W. A. M. (1965). *J. Exp. Biol.* 42, 45.

Nichols, D. (1962). "Echinoderms." Hutchinson, London.

Nichols, D. (1964). *Oceanogr. Mar. Biol. Annu. Rev.* 2, 393.

Nigrelli, R. F., and Jakowska, S. (1960). *Ann. N.Y. Acad. Sci.* 90, 884.

Nigrelli, R. F., Stempien, M. F., Jr., Ruggieri, G. D., Liguori, V. R., and Cecil, J. T. (1967). *Fed. Proc., Fed. Amer. Soc. Exp. Biol.* 26, 1197.

Ohshima, H. (1927). *Proc. Imp. Acad.* (*Tokyo*) 3, 610.

Ohshima, H. (1932). *Annot. Zool. Jap.* 13, 461.

Ohshima, H. (1934). *Annot. Zool. Jap.* 14, 327.

Östergren, H. J. (1897). *Zool. Anz.* 20, 148.

Panning, A. (1944). *Mitt. Hamburg Zool. Mus. Inst.* 49, 2.

Pawson, D. L. (1966a). *In* "Physiology of Echinodermata" (R. A. Boolootian, ed.), pp. 63–71. Wiley (Interscience), New York.

Pawson, D. L. (1966b). *In* "Treatise on Invertebrate Paleontology." (R. C. Moore, ed.), Vol. 2, Part U, pp. 641–646. Geol. Soc. Amer., Univ. of Kansas Press, Lawrence.

Pearse, A. S. (1909). *Biol. Bull.* 18, 42.

Pearson, J. (1915). *Spolia Zeylan* 10, 175.

Pope, E. C. (1967a). *Aust. Natur. Hist.* 15, 310.

Pope, E. C. (1967b). *Aust. Natur. Hist.* 15, 278.

Prosser, C. L., and Brown, F. A., Jr. (1961). "Comparative Animal Physiology." Saunders, Philadelphia, Pennsylvania.

Randall, J. E. (1967). *Proc. Int. Conf. Trop. Oceanogr., 1965*, pp. 665–847.

Rao, G. C. (1968). *Proc. Indian Acad. Sci., Sect. B* 67, 201.

Ritchie, J. (1910). *Ann. Scot. Natur. Hist.* 73, 11.

Rosati, F. (1968). *Monit. Zool. Ital.* 2, 49.

Rowe, F. W. E. (1969). *Bull. Brit. Mus. (Natur. Hist.)*, *Zool.* **18**, 9.
Russell, F. E. (1965). *Advan. Mar. Biol.* **3**, 255.
Russo, A. (1899). *Monit. Zool. Ital.* **10**, 133.
Schallreuter, R. (1968). *Neues. Jahrb. Mineral., Geol. Palaeontol., Monatsh.* **9**, 522.
Scheltema, R. S. (1972). *4th Eur. Symp. Mar. Biol., 1969* (in press).
Sella, A., and Sella, M. (1940). *Thalassia* **4**, 1.
Shimada, S. (1969). *Science* **163**, 1462.
Sivickis, P. B., and Domantay, J. S. (1928). *Philipp. J. Sci.* **37**, 299.
Smith, C. L., and Tyler, J. C. (1969). *Copeia* p. 206.
Smith, G. N., Jr., and Greenberg, M. J. (1966). *Amer. Zool.* **6**, 549.
Sobotka, H. (1965). *Bull. Soc. Chim. Biol.* **47**, 169.
Sorokin, Y. I. (1971). *Mar. Biol.* **11**, 101.
Springhall, J. A., and Dingle, J. G. (1967). *Aust. Vet. J.* **43**, 298.
Stephens, G. C. (1968). *Amer. Zool.* **8**, 95.
Stephenson, W., Endean, R., and Bennett, I. (1958). *Aust. J. Mar. Freshwater Res.* **9**, 261.
Studer, T. (1889). "Die Forschungsreise S.M.S. Gazelle in der Jahren 1874–76," Part III. von Schleinitz, Berlin.
Tanaka, Y. (1958). *Bull. Fac. Fish. Hokkaido Univ.* **9**, 14.
Thorson, G. (1936). *Medd. Groenland* **100**, 1.
Thorson, G. (1961). *In* "Oceanography," Publ. No. 67, pp. 455–474. Amer. Ass. Advance. Sci., Washington, D.C.
Thurston, E. (1895). *Bull. Madras Gov. Mus.* **3**, 1.
Tikasingh, E. S. (1963). *Stud. Fanna Curaçao* **14**, 77.
Torelle, E. (1909). *Zool. Anz.* **35**, 15.
Trefz, S. M. (1956). *Off. Nav. Res. Proj.* NR 165-264, p. 1.
Trefz, S. M. (1958). Ph.D. Dissertation, University of Hawaii.
Tursch, B. T. (1972). V. Echinoderms. Natural Products of Marine Origin (in preparation).
van der Heyde, H. C. (1922). Ph.D. Dissertation, de Boer, Jr., Den Helder, Netherlands.
Vaney, C. (1913). *Bull. Sci. Fra. Belg.* [7] **47**, 1.
Vaney, C. (1925). *Trav. Sta. Zool. Wimereux* **8**, 254.
Vannucci, M. (1959 onwards). *Inst. Paulista Ocean.* pp. 21–73 and 97–102.
Vinogradov, A. P. (1953). *Sears Found. Mar. Res. Mem.* No. 2, p. 1.
Wass, M. (1968). *Tulane Stud. Zool.* **14**, 137.
Wells, H. W., and Wells, M. J. (1961). *Bull. Mar. Sci. Gulf Carib.* **11**, 267.
Yamanouchi, T. (1955). *Publ. Seto Mar. Biol. Lab.* **4**, 183.
Yamanouchi, T. (1956). *Publ. Seto Mar. Biol. Lab.* **5**, 347.
Yamanouti, T. (1939). *Palao Trop. Biol. Stud.* **4**, 603.
Yasumoto, T., Tanaka, M., and Hashimoto, Y. (1966). *Bull. Jap. Soc. Sci. Fish.* **32**, 673.
Yonge, C. M. (1930). "A Year on the Great Barrier Reef." Putnam, New York.
Yonge, C. M. (1931). *J. Cons., Cons. Perm. Int. Explor. Mer* **6**, 175.

II

EARLY LIFE HISTORIES OF CORAL REEF ASTEROIDS, WITH SPECIAL REFERENCE TO *Acanthaster planci* (L.)

Masashi Yamaguchi

I. Introduction

Most zoologists who visit coral reefs are quick to note how conspicuous adult echinoderms are, while their juvenile forms appear to be, as a rule, either very scarce or hidden from view. Mortensen, during his extensive studies on the morphological aspects of tropical echinoderm larvae, referred to the echinoid, *Diadema*, as follows (Mortensen, 1938, p. 11): "With the millions of eggs produced, e.g., by each specimen of *Diadema*, it is an extraordinary fact that young specimens are as a rule a great rarity, though the adult *Diadema* are common and conspicuous enough, usually living in large flocks." Ohshima (1962) mentioned that a similar picture was presented by the asteroid, *Culcita novaeguineae* (Müller and Troschel) in Okinawan waters. Yamaguchi (1969) reported that a starfish, *Protoreaster nodosus* (L.), from Palau occurred in great numbers on seagrass beds of *Enhalus* and *Thalassia* feeding on sediment or detritus in a manner similar to holothurians. The starfish population consisted only of fully grown adults. It has always puzzled investigators how such echinoderms recruit to their populations.

The coral predator *Acanthaster planci* (L.) has recently undergone a mysterious population explosion on some Pacific coral reefs (Barnes, 1966; Chesher, 1969; Pearson and Endean, 1969; Weber and Woodhead, 1970). A number of theories has been proposed to explain the possible causes and processes of the starfish plagues. Because of the fecundity of adult female starfish, which normally produce millions of eggs, most theories are based on a supposed reduction in predation on free-swimming larval stages by corals and other potential predators. Unfortunately, these theories are based on speculation without critical estimations or experimental studies of larval forms and subsequent stages of the microscopic juvenile forms.

It is obviously important to study the early life histories of coral reef organisms not only to understand the significance of the *Acanthaster* population explosion, but also to provide biological and ecological data for the conservation of coral reefs which are being subjected to ever-increasing pressures by human activities, such as tourism and pollution by development of local industries.

The morphology and behavior of larval forms of tropical echinoderms have been studied extensively by Mortensen (1931, 1937, 1938) in the Java Sea, Mauritius, and the Red Sea. His studies embraced the larval forms of 12 species of tropical starfish, including observations on *Acanthaster planci* up to the brachiolaria stage. Metamorphosis of *Acanthaster* larvae was observed recently by Henderson and Lucas (1971) in Australia, as well as by Yamaguchi in Guam as described below. The present author has also raised larvae of two other common asteroids, *Culcita novaeguineae* and *Linckia laevigata* (L.), through metamorphosis.

II. Larval Development and Behavior of Coral Reef Asteroids

A. LARVAL DEVELOPMENT

Three types of embryonic and larval development occur among the species studied by the above authors.

In *Luidia savignyi* (Audouin), *Astropecten polyacanthus* Müller and Troschel, and *Astropecten velitaris* von Martens, there is no brachiolaria stage and metamorphosis takes place directly from the bipinnaria stage without attachment to the substratum (type I). The majority of the rest of the species studied show the normal stages of embryonic development—gastrulae, bipinnariae, brachiolariae, and finally metamorphosis (type II). However, *Fromia ghardaqana* Mortensen and *Echinaster purpureus* (Gray) embryos are formed from large yolky eggs. Their larvae show a reduction in characteristic larval structures and develop without feeding (type III).

Although minor differences occur among species in some larval structures, e.g., size, color, and behavior, larval development is similar in *Archaster typicus* Müller and Troschel, *Culcita novaeguineae* Müller and Troschel, *Culcita schmideliana* (Retzius), *Pentaceraster mammillatus* (Audouin), *Linckia laevigata* (L.), *Linckia multifora* (Lamarck), *Asteropsis carinifera* (Lamarck), and *Acanthaster planci* (L.) (see Table I).

In the above studies, gametes of starfish were obtained by several methods. Mortensen removed the gonads from adults. After waiting for the ova to ripen, he inseminated them artificially. In some species he waited for spontaneous spawning by animals kept in holding tanks. Henderson (1969) and Henderson and Lucas (1971) adopted a method developed by Chaet (1964). They used radial nerve extract on the excised gonads of *Acanthaster*. The present author used injections of 1-methyladenine in seawater (a dose of about 30 μg per adult *Acanthaster*) to induce spawning in the adult starfish. Kanatani (1969; see also Kanatani *et al.*, 1969) found this substance to be the factor which induces meiosis and subsequent spawning in starfish in general.

Spawning reactions of asteroids after being injected with 1-methyladenine vary greatly in time and intensity. However, the gametes which result from this induced spawning appear quite ripe since the percentage of ova with germinal vesicles was always very low and fertilization of eggs so obtained was always successful. Spawning of *Acanthaster* has been observed only occasionally in nature (Pearson and Endean, 1969; Owens, 1971).

The diameters of egg cells of coral reef asteroids usually fall between 0.1 and 0.2 mm, except for *Fromia* and *Echinaster* which produce large yolky eggs (Table I). Although Mortensen did not record the sizes of egg cells in many of the asteroids which he studied, it may be presumed that the sizes of the eggs in these species lie in a similar range. He referred to *Acanthaster* eggs as being small (0.1 mm) and *Asteropsis* eggs as being rather large (~0.2 mm).

I have found that the ripe egg cells of *Acanthaster* are nearly 0.2 mm in diameter, whereas Mortensen (1931) and Henderson (1969)

TABLE I

Embryonic and Larval Development of Coral Reef Asteroids

Species	Type of Development[a]	Diameter of egg cells (mm)[b]	Minimum age to development (days)[b]			Fully grown larval length (mm)[b,c]	Temperature (°C)[b]	Locality	Reference
			Bipinnaria	Brachiolaria	Metamorphosis				
Luidia savignyi	I	*	2	—	12	1.5	*	Red Sea	Mortensen (1938)
Astropecten polyacanthus	I	*	*	—	3	1.0	Around 24?	Red Sea	Mortensen (1937)
Astropecten velitaris	I	*	*	—	5	1.1	Around 24?	Red Sea	Mortensen (1937)
Archaster typicus	II	*	3	8–14	24	0.7	*	Java Sea	Mortensen (1931)
Culcita novaeguineae	II	0.18	3	14	17	1.4	26–30	Guam	Yamaguchi (this paper)
Culcita schmideliana	II	*	*	38?	*	*	*	Mauritius	Mortensen (1931)
Pentaceraster mammillatus	II	0.1	2	16	24	1.4	*	Red Sea	Mortensen (1938)
Linckia laevigata	II	*	3	*	*	*	*	Java Sea	Mortensen (1931)
		0.15	3	16	22	1.3	27–29	Guam	Yamaguchi (this paper)
Linckia multifora	II	0.2	5?	21	27	1.0	*	Red Sea	Mortensen (1938)
Asteropsis carinifera	II	0.1	4	30	*	1.0	Around 24?	Red Sea	Mortensen (1937)
Acanthaster planci	II	0.1	*	16	*	*	*	Java Sea	Mortensen (1931)
			4	23	28	1.0	24–25, 28–29[d]	Australia	Henderson (1969); Henderson and Lucas (1971)
		0.19[e]	4	16	27	1.2	24–25, 27–29[d]	Guam	Yamaguchi (this paper)
			3	11	21	1.2	27–29	Guam	Yamaguchi (this paper)
Fromia ghardaqana	III	1	—	3[f]	16	1.1	*	Red Sea	Mortensen (1938)
Echinaster purpureus	III	*	—	4[f]	*	1.5	*	Red Sea	Mortensen (1938)

[a] Type I, metamorphosis at bipinnaria stage without attachment; type II, regular development, bipinnaria–brachiolaria; type III, reduced embryonic development, without feeding.

[b] Asterisks indicate that there is no description given.

[c] Measurement from specimens in drawings or photographs or from live specimens by Yamaguchi.

[d] Larvae kept initially at the lower temperature and transferred to the higher.

[e] Ripe eggs of *A. planci* are mostly about 0.2 mm in diameter, but eggs of about 0.1 mm were obtained in a few batches.

[f] Reduced form equivalent to brachiolaria.

both recorded the diameter as 0.1 mm. This difference in egg size puzzled the present author, but it may stem from the use of different methods for obtaining the gametes. The two authors mentioned above removed the gonads from the starfish, while I induced semispontaneous spawning. Smaller eggs, almost 0.1 mm in diameter, were indeed found in a few instances and they appeared normal. In addition to variation in size of eggs, their reflected color varied from yellowish to very pale or nearly white among batches from different females of *Acanthaster*.

After fertilization, rapid changes of form in the regularly developing asteroid embryo take place, the embryos passing through morulae, blastulae, gastrulae, and then forming bipinnariae. Hatching of free-swimming embryos as slightly oblong bodies occurs at the early gastrula stage. By the second to fourth day, early bipinnariae begin to complete the digestive tract and begin feeding on suspended particulate matter. The period required for development into each of the larval stages varied among species and also among different batches of the same species (Table I).

The pelagic larvae in type II asteroids attain their full growth as brachiolariae in 3–4 weeks. Their longitudinal axes at this time lie between 0.7 and 1.4 mm. The size of fully grown bipinnariae of type I is 1.0–1.5 mm and the reduced forms of brachiolariae of type III are 1.1–1.5 mm (Table I). Of the species whose embryonic development was studied, all started their juvenile lives as microscopic creatures less than 1 mm in diameter after metamorphosis from pelagic larvae.

B. Behavior of Pelagic Larvae

Swimming of *Acanthaster* gastrulae begins while embryos are inside their egg membrane. Ciliary movement causes them to rotate continuously on their longitudinal axes throughout the pelagic stages, but the speed of rotation decreases as they develop.

After a short pause on the bottom of culture dishes, hatched *Acanthaster* gastrulae swim upward to the surface. Hereafter, the larvae remain close to the surface if kept in still water. Negative geotaxis continues until the brachiolariae settle on the substratum. Similar behavior is exhibited by other asteroid larvae in general, except for *Pentaceraster* larvae, which swim close to the bottom (Mortensen, 1938). A shaker bath (Henderson and Lucas, 1971) or mild aeration via capillary tubes in culture dishes (present author) were used to keep asteroid larvae in better contact with food and to prevent them from clustering on the surface. The strong negative geotaxis exhibited may keep asteroid larvae near the ocean surface. However, because the speed of locomotion, e.g., in the 6-day-old *Acanthaster* bipinnaria, is only about 0.4 mm/sec, their swimming ability may be negated by currents and turbulence.

After the bipinnaria stage, pelagic larvae of *Acanthaster*, as well as those of other species, are sensitive to mechanical stimuli and strong light. Contraction of the anterior part of the body, causing the larvae to bend backward, was observed when they were disturbed by either stimulus. No phototactic behavior has been exhibited by the coral reef asteroid larvae studied.

Fully developed brachiolariae of *Acanthaster* are very sensitive to touch and react by folding their arms tightly around their bodies when disturbed. Similar behavior was shown by advanced larvae of *Linckia multifora* (Mortensen, 1938). The present author has observed the same behavior pattern in *Culcita novaeguineae* and *Linckia laevigata*. Furthermore, *Acanthaster* brachiolariae nearing metamorphosis respond to stimuli by a strong contraction of the whole anterior portion of their body.

Pelagic larvae of asteroids filter suspended particulate matter from seawater. The food passes into the esophagus and is carried into the stomach by rhythmical contractions of the esophagus. A sphincter between the esophagus and the stomach prevents regurgitation of food. The size of particles available to asteroid larvae is limited by the diameter of the esophagus. The inside diameter of the esophagus is about 40–60 μm in larvae of *Acanthaster* and other species. If larger particles are trapped in the mouth, the larvae bend their anterior part backward and expel the particles from the mouth. The feeding behavior and food rejection mechanisms employed by the larvae of asteroids and other echinoderm classes were extensively studied by Strathmann (1971).

Cultured unicellar algae (*Isochrysis galbana*, *Gymnodinium* sp., *Amphidinium* sp., *Cyclotella nana*, and *Dunaliella primolecta* (Henderson and Lucas, 1971); *Nitzschia closterium* and *Chlamydomonas* sp. (present author) have been fed to *Acanthaster* larvae. Mortensen relied only on natural food present in seawater. He frequently transferred larvae into fresh seawater.

C. Growth and Survival in Pelagic Stages

The growth rates of cultured pelagic larvae of asteroids vary greatly not only among species but also among different batches of the same species. Despite similar water temperatures at both localities, *Acanthaster* bipinnariae in northern Australia advanced into brachiolariae in 23 days (Henderson and Lucas, 1971), whereas only 16 days were required in Guam. This 16-day period was further reduced by another 5 days in a batch kept at a higher temperature (Table I).

Growth rates among individuals in the same batch also fluctuated greatly. Frequently when some individuals are undergoing metamorphosis, others are still at the bipinnaria stage. It is apparent that the duration of larval life in asteroids is subject to wide fluctuations even in the same species under the same conditions.

Different environmental conditions, such as different water temperatures, might be responsible for the variation in growth rates observed among the different culture batches, but individual variation under the same conditions is difficult to explain. This phenomenon is also found in cases where larvae do not feed but subsist on the yolk substance of the eggs, as occurs in *Fromia ghardaqana* (Mortensen, 1938). Mortensen noted that some larvae metamorphosed at the age of 16 days, while others continued to swim for an additional 2–4 weeks before attaching prior to metamorphosis.

During repeated attempts to raise *Acanthaster* larvae in July and August 1971, the present author observed that the larvae could not advance into the brachiolaria stage from bipinnariae at water temperatures lower than 25°C, even though they were feeding vigorously. Furthermore, many larvae kept at this temperature, which is slightly below the ambient (i.e., 27°–30°C on Guam), showed regression to an earlier developmental stage. A similar phenomenon was described in a larval culture of *Acanthaster* studied in northern Australia (Henderson and Lucas, 1971). There, larvae completed development at 28°–29°C, but those at 24°–25°C did not advance beyond the early brachiolaria stage. These findings are quite interesting because water temperature in Hawaii, where a large aggregation of *Acanthaster* was reported, is slightly lower than 25°C during April and May when spawning was observed (Branham *et al.*, 1971).

Pelagic *Acanthaster* larvae, as well as those of other asteroids, may be eaten by many kinds of predators, not only by corals and other benthic filter-feeders but also by pelagic carnivores. No observations of such predation have been reported, except for the fish *Abudefduf curacao*, which fed on newly released eggs from a spawning female of *Acanthaster* on Arlington Reef, Australia (Pearson and Endean, 1969).

Several species of planktonic carnivores including a small comb-jelly (*Pleurobrachia* sp.), an ostracod (*Euconchoecia elongata*), and an arrowworm (*Sagitta* sp.) were tested by the present author for predation on asteroid larvae (*Linckia*), but none of them fed on the larvae. However, *Pleurobrachia* activity fed on nauplii of *Artemia salina* in the same dish containing asteroid larvae and the others ignored the larvae.

A reef coral, *Pocillopora damicornis*, was observed to feed on larvae of *Acanthaster planci, Culcita novaeguineae,* and *Linckia laevigata.* Corals may be important predators on pelagic stages of *Acanthaster* as Chesher (1969) pointed out, but this would also apply to other species of asteroids and to closely related larval forms such as those of holothurians.

III. Settlement and Metamorphosis of *Acanthaster* Brachiolariae

When they begin to metamorphose into juvenile starfish, the fully developed brachiolariae of *Acanthaster planci,* as well as those of other regularly developing asteroids (type II), attach themselves to the substratum by means of brachiolar arms and a sucker (or adhesive disc). The brachiolar arms develop on the anterior part in conjunction with the extension of the coelomic cavity. The adhesive disc, or sucker, begins to appear among the three brachiolar arms as they grow.

A series of papillae is formed along each side of the ventral median lobe (one of the brachiolar arms) and a short series forms along the paired brachiolar arms. This arrangement of papillae on the brachiolar arms is different from that found in brachiolariae of *Asterias* which develop the papillae as terminal crowns on each brachiolar arm. The structure of brachiolar arms in *Linckia laevigata* (Fig. 1) and *Culcita novaeguineae* (Fig. 2) is similar to that of *Acanthaster planci* (Fig. 3). Also, brachiolar arms with a similar arrangement of papillae were found in larvae of *Linckia multifora* and *Pentaceraster mammillatus* (Mortensen, 1938). Concomitant with the development of brachiolar arms, the posterior part of *Acanthaster* brachiolariae develop definitive star (future star) and hydrocoel lobes. Five lobes of the definitive star are clearly visible from the side of the brachiolaria at this stage.

The brachiolariae of *Acanthaster* test the substratum with their brachiolar arms as is normal in other asteroid larvae. Henderson and Lucas (1971) reported that they would not settle on the surface of clean glass dishes but would settle on the bottoms of dishes in the presence of encrusting algae and algal detritus, except for one larva which settled on an algal strand on a dead coral (*Pocillopora damicornis*). The present author observed most larvae settling directly on pieces of dead coral encrusted with coralline algae (*Porolithon*) and other epiphytes. The settlement of *Acanthaster* larvae was not encouraged by bleached coral-

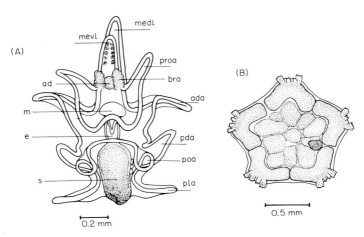

Fig. 1. Larva and juvenile of *Linckia laevigata*. (A) Brachiolaria, 3 weeks old, near metamorphosis; (B) juvenile, 9 weeks after metamorphosis, aboral surface. ada, anterodorsal arm; ad, adhesive disc; ba, brachiolar arm; e, esophagus; medl, median dorsal lobe; mevl, median ventral lobe; m, mouth; pda, posterodorsal arm; pla, posterolateral arm; poa, postoral arm; proa, preoral arm; s, stomach.

line algae or by a small piece of beach rock covered with only filamentous algae. A similar settling behavior of brachiolariae was observed in *Culcita novaeguineae* and *Linckia laevigata*.

Metamorphosis of *Acanthaster* brachiolariae into five-armed juvenile

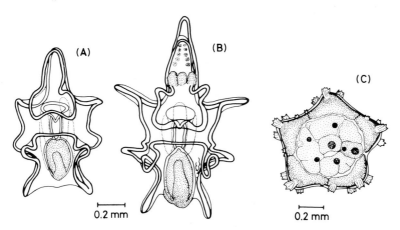

Fig. 2. Larvae and juvenile of *Culcita novaeguineae*. (A) Bipinnaria, 2 weeks old, at lower temperature; (B) brachiolaria, 3 weeks old, near metamorphosis; (C) juvenile, 2 weeks after metamorphosis, aboral surface.

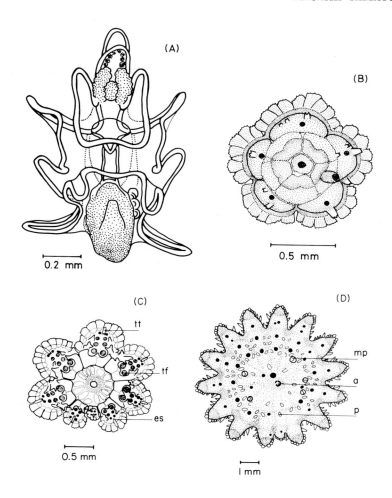

Fig. 3. Larva and juveniles of *Acanthaster planci*. (A) Brachiolaria, 4 weeks old, near metamorphosis; (B) juvenile, 2 weeks after metamorphosis, aboral surface; (C) 7-week-old juvenile, oral surface: note bud of 9th arm between 7th and 8th; (D) 19-week-old juvenile, aboral surface: about 8 mm across, adult structure almost complete. a, anus; es, eye spot; mp, madreporite; p, papula; tf, tube foot; tt, terminal tentacle.

starfish occurred with absorption of the anterior part of larval body and took 2 days. The juveniles were about 0.5 mm (0.3–0.5 mm in Henderson and Lucas, 1971) in diameter and their color was yellowish white. Each arm carried two pairs of tube feet and a primary podium (or a terminal tentacle) with a red eyespot on its basal part. Skeletal plates on the aboral surface were made up of a simple reticulum of calcified tissue and marginal and dorsal spinules were developed.

IV. Growth and Behavior of Juvenile *Acanthaster planci*

A. GROWTH AND MORPHOGENESIS

Juvenile *Acanthaster planci* were kept in aquaria with closed circulating systems driven by airlifts. Plastic petri dishes served as substrata for the juveniles. These dishes had been submerged in the sea for several months and were covered with encrusting algae and sedentary microfauna. Dead bivalve shells with similar encrustations on their surfaces were also used after juveniles had grazed most of the encrusting algae on the petri dishes. Plain surfaces were necessary for monitoring their growth because of the small size of juveniles during their early stages. Dead-shell substrata were renewed repeatedly in order to provide fresh food.

Two batches of larval *Acanthaster* cultures metamorphosed. These cultures were started on August 9 and August 18, 1971, respectively. Two weeks after metamorphosis, 14 individuals from the first batch were selected for monitoring of their growth. Figure 4 indicates the growth of juveniles in an aquarium under the conditions described above. Water temperature in the aquarium ranged between 25° and 30°C but was usually around 27°–28°C. The mean diameter of the juveniles increased from 0.5 mm immediately after metamorphosis to 11.1 mm by the end of January 1972, about 20 weeks after metamorphosis (Fig. 4).

From Fitzroy Island Reef, Great Barrier Reef, 142 juveniles ranging from 15.0 to 79.0 mm (mean 33.8 mm) in diameter were found mostly on the dead basal part of colonies of *Acropora echinata* and numerous feeding scars were noted on their upper living parts (Pearson and Endean, 1969). The mean growth rate of juveniles between 10 and 60 mm in diameter was 11 mm/month (Pearson and Endean, 1969). From the growth data described above and the breeding season known for *Acanthaster* on the Great Barrier Reef (mid-December to mid-January) it may be estimated that the juveniles found at Fitzroy Island Reef in mid-February were approximately 1 year old.

Several juveniles, 60–100 mm in diameter, were collected from the field in Guam and raised to preadults about 200 mm in diameter by the present author. They were fed corals in aquaria provided with closed

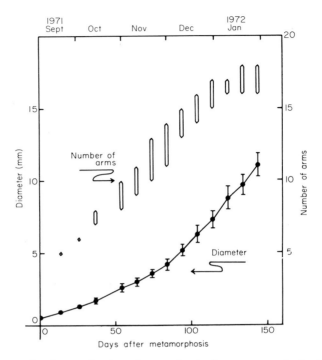

Fig. 4. Growth of juvenile *Acanthaster planci* after metamorphosis. Mean diameter ± standard deviation of 14 individuals. Vertical bars for the number of arms indicate the range, including any recently formed short arms with a terminal tentacle.

circulating systems. Their growth curves were almost linear and the growth rate was 30–40 mm/month in diameter. On the other hand, 10 starfish of slightly larger initial size were caged in the field in Australia, and grew at a rate of 9 mm/month (Pearson and Endean, 1969). Thus, growth data vary under different environmental conditions and for different stages. However, it is estimated that *Acanthaster planci* would reach a size of 30 cm in diameter in at least 2 years from the fertilized eggs.

Signs of development of the first new arm were recognized about 3 weeks after metamorphosis in *Acanthaster* juveniles. New arms appeared one by one, at intervals of 9–10 days, until the total number of arms reached 16 to 18, in about 18 weeks (Fig. 4). During the development of the first few new arms the body color of the juveniles changed to a bright pink and this camouflaged them on the coralline algae substratum of similar color which they normally occupy.

The scheme of formation of new arms is illustrated in Fig. 5. All the new arms developed in a definite order, except for a few individuals which developed one or two extra arms at irregular positions. According to Carpenter's naming system for the five arms (in Hyman, 1955), arm A is that opposite the madreporite and the others occur in alphabetical order, counterclockwise when viewed from the dorsal side. The first new arm appeared between arm B and arm C. Then the majority of juveniles developed the seventh arm, G, between arm C and the sixth arm, F, and the eighth between arm F and arm G. Thus every new arm that followed appeared between the two arms most recently formed. Whenever a bud of a new arm appeared and developed between older arms, the position of the new arm was located just behind the anus (occurring at a corner of the central skeletal plate). A few juveniles developed the seventh arm between arm B and arm F and then the remaining arms between the most recently formed arms (see Fig. 5).

Madsen (1955) speculated that *Acanthaster planci* would begin life

Fig. 5. Scheme of formation of arms in *Acanthaster planci.* a–g, regular pattern; c′ and d′, pattern observed in 2 out of 14 cases, with 7th arm developing between arm B and arm F. Arrows indicate the position where the next new arm will develop.

as a normal five-armed sea star and that the number of arms would increase with increasing size but in no definite order. However, this speculation was based on limited numbers of young specimens housed in museums. These specimens appeared abnormal from his figures and descriptions.

Adults of *Acanthaster* are not only multirayed but also possess from 5 to 16 madreporites (Hyman, 1955). The madreporites of juveniles are hardly recognizable among the numerous nodulated spinules present. When the juveniles grow to about 10 mm in diameter, their madreporites attain a form similar to that of adults. The number of madreporites increases from one, in just metamorphosed juveniles, to four to nine in specimens 10 mm in diameter. As the madreporites change their form, the short spines on the dorsal surface begin to lengthen. First those around the anus lengthen, then others in a circle on the disc and on the arms lengthen.

Soon after metamorphosis, the juveniles possess four to five pairs of marginal spines on each arm. These marginal spines are fan-shaped and function together with the tube feet to resist dislodgement of the juveniles from the substratum (Fig. 3B,C). As the juveniles grow, a series of pointed spines also develops along each side of the arms (Fig. 3D). These spines become orange when the juveniles attain a size of 6 mm in diameter. Papulae on the dorsal surface begin to appear at about the same time.

The number of tube feet increases as the arms grow, from the original 2 pairs to 14 pairs in juveniles 10 mm in diameter. The ratio of the length of arm from the center (R) to the radius of disc (r) was 1.46 at this size, which is much smaller than that of adults ($R/r \sim 2$). Therefore, the juveniles have rather short arms compared with the disc diameter (Fig. 3D).

B. FEEDING

The small size of juveniles and their method of feeding, which involves stomach eversion, made it difficult to determine what kind of organisms were eaten by the earlier juveniles that were sitting on the algal-covered substratum. However, when the juveniles changed their position on the substratum, white circular feeding marks on the reddish coralline algae (*Porolithon*) were apparent and these became distinct as the juveniles grew. The diameters of the marks were similar to the diameters of the juvenile discs.

Glass slides covered with epiphytic diatoms and young sporelings of *Porolithon* were prepared for observation of feeding behavior of juvenile starfish. *Acanthaster* juveniles, observed under a microscope, were seen to evert their stomach over these algae and all the algae covered by the stomach were killed. Some juveniles reared on a substratum covered with epiphytic algae, but without coralline algae, grew at a rate similar to those that fed mostly on coralline algae. However, juveniles preferred coralline algae when available.

From the numbers of feeding marks on the substratum it was determined that juveniles of about 6–7 mm in diameter fed twice a day on an average. The period spent sitting on one spot seemed to vary greatly and feeding seemed not to be a continuous process because frequently no feeding mark was noticed when a juvenile changed position.

Younger juveniles of less than 8 mm in diameter did not attempt to feed on corals even when they were placed in contact with the coral polyps. Furthermore, one coral (*Acropora* sp.) killed the juveniles, wrapping them in extended mesenterial filaments. Corals appear to be a hazard for juveniles of microscopic size.

The transition of feeding behavior from herbivorous (on algae) to carnivorous (on coral polyps) began in some juveniles about 8 mm in diameter, 18 weeks after metamorphosis. However, they continued to feed at this age on algae as long as they remained on the algal substratum.

C. BEHAVIOR AND SURVIVAL

Encrusting coralline algae, *Porolithon*, is normally found on the dead parts of coral colonies and on the under surfaces of coral boulders, etc. The feeding behavior of *Acanthaster* juveniles, as well as the larval settling behavior, is related to the distribution of encrusting coralline algae. *Acanthaster* juveniles rarely move to any great extent when they are on an algal substratum. They usually stay at one location and change position only occasionally.

Speed of locomotion in 2-week-old juveniles, placed in a clean dish without food, is about 1.0 mm/min. They move steadily in one direction and there is no definite photoorientation to directed light, although the juveniles tend to remain in shaded regions. If the algal substratum is illuminated on one side and the other shaded, most juveniles stay on the shaded side and move to the illuminated side only when the algae have been consumed on the shaded side.

Although about 120 fully developed *Acanthaster* brachiolariae went into metamorphosis, a total of only 57 juveniles were recovered from the small pieces of dead coral covered with coralline algae which provided substrata for settlement of brachiolariae. About 50% of larvae disappeared during the course of settlement and metamorphosis. The causes of this loss are unknown. In *Linckia laebigata* and *Culcita novaeguineae* retrieval of juveniles after settlement was very poor.

The dead coral substratum contains many species of small benthic animals such as actinians, free-living nematodes, nemerteans, polyclads, polychaetes, gastropods, and crustaceans. Some of these could not be removed from the material used to induce settlement of asteroid larvae and they might have been predators on the metamorphosing larvae or juveniles immediately after metamorphosis.

No predation or natural death was observed in juvenile *Acanthaster* after the age of 2 weeks when they were transferred to plastic petri dishes encrusted with epiphytic algae and where all possible predators could be controlled. Because of the small number of juveniles surviving, the present author could not test predation by benthic animals systematically. This subject is to be studied later, if and when a mass culture of starfish larvae becomes available.

The smallest juvenile *Acanthaster* collected in the field in the Great Barrier Reef region was 11 mm in diameter (Pearson and Endean, 1969). Several juveniles of similar size have been found on Guam. One of them (15-armed and 10 mm diameter) was found on the underside of a dead coral boulder, 10 m in depth at Tanguisson Beach. No juveniles under this size have been located on the coral reefs.

The finding of the juveniles mentioned above, as well as those found on Fitzroy reef, described in Section IV,A, may suggest that pelagic larvae of *Acanthaster* settle and survive primarily on a substratum of coralline algae. The juveniles then tend to remain in one location as long as food is available.

V. Discussion

Encrusting coralline algae, mostly *Porolithon*, form a predominant substratum on coral reefs. Coralline algae are commonly found on the surface of dead coral skeletons, under boulders, and so forth. It is a reasonable assumption that many kinds of coral reef animals have developed a close relationship with the algae. For instance, planulae of the coral *Pocillopora damicornis* settle predominantly on coralline algae encrustations and rarely on clean surfaces (Yamaguchi, unpublished).

While most shallow water asteroids in the regions of higher latitude are carnivorous, many coral reef asteroids are herbivorous as are the earlier juveniles of *Acanthaster planci*. Most of the comet-forming small asteroids that are abundant on coral reefs, such as *Ophidiaster, Echinaster,* and *Linckia,* seem to feed on encrusting algae and benthic micro-organisms. *Culcita novaeguineae* feed on both corals and algae. A less common asteroid, *Choriaster granulatus* Lütken, is the only species known to be a scavenger-type starfish in the coastal waters of Guam. The paucity of carnivorous asteroids, which feed mainly on mollusks, reflects the fact that there are no great populations of sedentary suspension-feeding mollusks on coral reefs. Bivalve mollusks and cirripeds which are abundant in colder waters, where the seawater carries higher concentration of phytoplankton and suspended organic matter, are usually sparsely represented in tropical waters.

One of the characteristics of larger coral reef asteroids is that the adults develop heavily calcified skeletal plates and stay exposed on the reef all the time. *Acanthaster* is an exception, it usually hides under boulders or in crevices during daytime and comes out to feed on corals at night. The presence of numerous individuals in the field with regenerating arms and wounds suggests that *Acanthaster* is subject to a heavy predation pressure. There are only a few confirmed predator species, but there may be many other organisms which would attack this soft-bodied starfish in the field, even though the spines on the aboral surface protect the animals from attack to some extent.

As was pointed out in an earlier part in this chapter, larvae of coral reef asteroids show a convergence in their sizes which are similar to those of many other larval forms of coral reef echinoderms. The great fecundity of coral reef starfish and the small diameters of eggs produced might be adaptations to the coral reef environment in general. However, the rather long pelagic larval stage, lasting usually several weeks, may be a handicap with regard to recruitment of juveniles to the same location as that of their parent population, although it may help the dispersion of the animals over wide areas. The larval forms in many species of coral reef asteroids are similar, but their adults show a great diversity in structure and behavior. Among them *Acanthaster* is well adapted to the coral reef environment as a predator of reef corals.

The island of Guam is located in the trade wind zone and the coastline is dominated by fringing reefs which are exposed to the open ocean. It is hard to imagine how larvae of coastal animals can manage to stay near shore until settlement. However, it is possible that there is a convergence of coastal water around the island which holds pelagic larvae near shore as was observed to occur near Bermuda by Boden (1952).

It seems reasonable to postulate that environmental conditions affecting the survival of larvae of coral reef asteroids act in a similar manner on each species of the same type. For example, predators would be nonselective toward similar larval forms. If this view is correct, then the factors which control the reduction of pelagic stages of a larval population would not necessarily be specific to *Acanthaster planci*. It is apparent that abundance of food for both juveniles and adults of *Acanthaster* on coral reefs is not, under normal conditions, limiting population size. The specific factors which control the population recruitment of *Acanthaster* to coral reefs should be the subject of further investigation.

Acknowledgments

The original observations reported in the present article have been made at the Marine Laboratory, University of Guam, with the support of a Government of Guam *Acanthaster* research grant. I wish to thank all the staff of the Marine Laboratory for their assistance and encouragement. My thanks are also extended to Dr. R. Hirano of the Department of Fisheries, University of Tokyo, for providing me with algal strains for larval cultures of asteroids and to Dr. H. Kanatani of the Ocean Research Institute, University of Tokyo, for information about the induction of spawning in asteroids by 1-methyladenine. Contribution No. 22, Marine Laboratory, University of Guam.

References

Barnes, J. H. (1966). *Aust. Natur. Hist.* **15**, 257.
Boden, B. P. (1952). *Nature (London)* **169**, 697.
Branham, J. M., Reed, S. A., and Bailey, J. H. (1971). *Science* **172**, 1155.
Chaet, A. B. (1964). *Biol. Bull.* **126**, 8.
Chesher, R. H. (1969). *Science* **165**, 280.
Henderson, J. A. (1969). *Fish. Notes, Dept. Harbours Mar.* **3**, 69.
Henderson, J. A., and Lucas, J. S. (1971). *Nature (London)* **232**, 655.
Hyman, L. H. (1955). "The Invertebrates: Echinodermata." McGraw-Hill, New York.
Kanatani, H. (1969). *Exp. Cell Res.* **57**, 333.
Kanatani, H., Shirai, H., Nakanishi, K., and Kurokawa, T. (1969). *Nature (London)* **221**, 273.
Madsen, F. J. (1955). *Vidensk. Medd. Dan. Naturh. Foren.* **117**, 179.
Mortensen, T. (1931). *Kgl. Dan. Vidensk. Selsk., Skr. Naturvid. Math. Afd., Ser. 9*, **4**, 1.
Mortensen, T. (1937). *Kgl. Dan. Vidensk. Selsk., Skr. Naturvid. Math. Afd., Ser. 9*, **7**, No. 1, 1–65.
Mortensen, T. (1938). *Kgl. Dan. Vidensk. Selsk., Skr. Naturvid. Math. Afd., Ser. 9*, **7**, No. 3, 1–59.

Ohshima, H. (1962). "Sea-cucumbers and Sea-urchins." Uchida-Rokakuho, Tokyo (in Japanese).

Owens, D. (1971). *Fiji Agr. J.* 33, 15.

Pearson, R. G., and Endean, R. (1969). *Fish. Notes, Dep. Harbours Mar.* 3, 27.

Strathmann, R. R. (1971). *J. Exp. Mar. Biol. Ecol.* 6, 109.

Weber, J. N., and Woodhead, P. M. J. (1970). *Mar. Biol.* 6, 12.

Yamaguchi, M. (1969). *In* "Report of Marine Biological Survey at Palau," p. 11. Sci. Exped. Club, Tokyo Univ., Tokyo (in Japanese).

12

POPULATION EXPLOSIONS OF *Acanthaster planci* AND ASSOCIATED DESTRUCTION OF HERMATYPIC CORALS IN THE INDO-WEST PACIFIC REGION

Robert Endean

I. Introduction

During the last decade population explosions of the crown-of-thorns starfish, *Acanthaster planci* (Linné, 1758), have been recorded from many parts of the tropical Indo-West Pacific region (Endean and Chesher, 1973). The starfish preys on coral polyps, and it has become apparent that a massive destruction of hermatypic corals has occurred in some areas as a result of the feeding activities of very large numbers of *A. planci* (Chesher, 1969a,b; Endean, 1969; Pearson and Endean, 1969; Endean and Stablum, 1973a,b). Indeed, Chesher (1969a, p. 283) has put forward the view that coral destruction might continue to the point where the coral fauna cannot recover and has stated that "there is a possibility that we are witnessing the initial phases of extinction of madreporarian corals in the Pacific." Other workers have expressed different ideas. Thus Vine (1970) regarded the starfish population explosions as being merely normal fluctuations in the density of *A. planci* populations on reefs while Walsh *et al.* (1971) considered them to be cyclical phenomena. Weber and Woodhead (1970) considered that *A. planci* was normally far more common than previously thought. These different points of view, as well as the possibility of economic loss as a result of the destruction of corals at some localities, have stimulated research into the biology, particularly the population dynamics, of *A. planci* and have highlighted the need for research into coral reef biology generally.

Although the causes, significance, and ultimate effects of the starfish infestations are in dispute, the occurrence of these infestations has caused some questioning of the generally accepted view that coral reefs are very stable biotic associations (e.g., Margalef, 1968). Other aspects that require examination in the light of the starfish infestations include (1) the roles of "rare" species in the ecology of coral reefs and the factors regulating the abundance of these species; (2) the apparent dearth of juvenile echinoderms generally on coral reefs and factors affecting the recruitment of juveniles; (3) the effects on the fauna and flora generally of the catastrophic destruction of the hard coral cover of reefs; and (4) the rate, manner, and extent of the recovery of reefs from such catastrophic destruction. Then too, the apparent need for control of *A. planci* populations in some areas has aroused the interest of scientists, politicians, and the general public of many countries. All this ensures that the starfish population explosions constitute one of the most fascinating problems of coral reef biology to have emerged in recent years.

II. The Biology of *Acanthaster planci*

A. General Morphology and Distribution

Acanthaster planci (Fig. 1) is a large, multirayed starfish found on coral reefs throughout the tropical Indo-West Pacific region, from the East African coast and the Red Sea in the west to Hawaii and the Tuamotus in the east. The species attains a maximum diameter of approximately 60

Fig. 1. Several specimens of *A. planci* clustered on coral. Keeper Reef, August, 1970. (Courtesy T. W. Brown.)

cm and R is approximately 2r. The number of arms possessed by adult specimens ranges from 9 to 21. However, the mean number of arms possessed by Red Sea specimens is 13 (Campbell and Ormond, 1970), while the mean number possessed by specimens from Guam and the Great Barrier Reef is 16 (Chesher, 1969a; Endean, 1969). The aboral surface is covered with prominent spines, a feature that has given rise to the popular name "crown-of-thorns" applied to this species. The spines range from about 1.5 to 4.5 cm in length and are articulated with pedicels. There is great variation in color with gray, greenish-blue, and brown predominating on the aboral surface of the disc and arms, while the spines are usually tipped with red.

B. Taxonomy

The remarkable appearance of specimens belonging to the genus *Acanthaster* attracted the attention of the early naturalists. In 1705 Rumphius mentioned a starfish obviously belonging to this genus. According to Madsen (1955), a specimen of *Acanthaster* from Goa was described and figured by Plancus and Gualtieri in 1743. The species *Asterias planci* was created by Linné in 1758. It was subsequently placed in the genus *Acanthaster* erected by Gervais in 1841. The synonomy of *A. planci* is listed by Madsen (1955).

Cogeners of *A. planci* are *A. ellisii* (Gray) from reefs in the eastern Pacific and *A. brevispinus* Fisher with a known range extending from the Philippines to southern Queensland, Australia (Fisher, 1919; Bennett, 1958; Endean, 1961). *A. brevispinus* has been found on a muddy bottom off Rockhampton, Queensland (Endean, 1961) and has also been found in Moreton Bay, Queensland, among rocks and corals (Endean, unpublished). In the field, *A. brevispinus* is readily separable from *A. planci* and appears to be a valid species. *A. brevispinus* has not been recorded from reefs of the Great Barrier Reef.

C. Habitat

During the last 20 years remarkably few specimens of *A. planci* have been seen by the present author on reefs of the Great Barrier Reef outside the current limits of the region of starfish infestation. On uninfested reefs most specimens seen were large adults. They were usually found associated with coral pinnacles in lagoons or back-reef areas. During daylight hours specimens were found in crevices, under ledges, or among the basal branches of large acropore colonies. On only two occasions were specimens observed to be feeding (on tabular acropores) during daylight hours, and, on one occasion, a specimen was observed moving across the sandy floor of a coral pool during daylight hours. It would appear that the species is essentially nocturnal.

D. Movements

Adult *A. planci* were found to be capable of moving over bare sand at speeds slightly in excess of 20 m/hour while juveniles 19–70 mm in diameter moved at rates which ranged from 1.4 to 4.0 m/hour (Pearson and Endean, 1969). However, no studies have been made to determine the length of time over which such speeds could be maintained. Specimens marked with anchor tags at Guam moved as far as 250 m/week (Chesher, 1969a).

When present in large numbers on a reef, specimens migrate from one region of the reef to another (Chesher, 1969a; Endean, 1969; Endean and Stablum, 1973a). Chesher (1969b) noted that herds of starfish at Guam could move across poorly developed dead reef areas at a rate of approximately 3 km/month. Migration of adults between reefs of the Great Barrier Reef is also believed to occur (Endean, 1969; Pearson and Endean, 1969; Endean and Stablum, 1973a). Adult *A. planci* have been trawled from a sandy-mud bottom in 40 m of water off Townsville (T. W. Brown, personal communication).

E. Toxicity

The intense pain resulting from contact with the spines of *A. planci* was first mentioned by Rumphius in 1705. Barnes and Endean (1964) and Pope (1964) have discussed human envenomations involving this species.

F. Prey and Feeding Mechanisms

In 1931 Mortensen found that *A. planci* feeds on madreporarian corals. The feeding process has been studied by Goreau (1963). When feeding, the animal everts its stomach through its mouth and the gastric folds are applied to the surface of its coral prey. Digestive enzymes liberated from the stomach digest the soft tissues of the prey, and the products of digestion are then absorbed by the walls of the alimentary canal. It was found by Brauer *et al.* (1970) that eversion of the stomach of *A. planci* can be triggered by seawater extracts of material from the surface of corals. During trials, extracts of some corals found in the Red Sea, such as *Acropora formosa* and *Pocillopora eydouxi*, produced stomach eversion while extracts of others, such as *Porites iwayamaensis* and *P. lutea*, caused an initial aversive response that was subsequently reversed in only two out of eight instances. The authors noted that *P. iwayamaensis* had weak nematocyst defenses and that other factors must be operative to cause acceptance of extracts of some species of coral and rejection of others. The active materials in the extracts seemed to be water soluble, heat-stable substances of low molecular weight. There were indications that the responsiveness to chemical evocation of stomach eversion in *A. planci* was related to the physiological state of the starfish, particularly its nutritional state and the time of day.

Despite the generally aversive response to *Porites* extracts shown by *A. planci*, Campbell and Ormond (1970) found that *Porites* is predated frequently in the Red Sea. They studied the effects of water movements on the feeding behaviour of *A. planci*, and they found that in the most exposed areas studied species of *Acropora* and *Pocillopora* were most predated; in less exposed situations species of *Goniastrea* and *Goniopora* were predated heavily, while in increasingly protected areas a greater proportion of *Porites* was attacked.

On the Great Barrier Reef, *A. planci* appeared to prey on all species of stony madrepore corals. Large as well as small colonies were attacked. Some massive colonies over 2 m in diameter were observed to be killed by the starfish. On some reefs but not on others, very large colonies of massive *Porites* and *Astreopora* were bypassed by the feeding starfish (Endean and Stablum, 1973a). Possibly the presence of strong tidal currents in some reef areas was responsible for this. At Guam, Chesher (1969a) noted that the tops of many of the larger massive coral colonies, such as *Porites lutea* growing in water shallower than 3 m, were alive, but the lower portions had been eaten. It was assumed that *A. planci* could not maintain a hold on the evenly rounded coralla in the presence of substantial surge movements. Barnes *et al.* (.1970) noted that, when climbing onto or over a coral colony, *A. planci* used its arms and spines extensively rather than utilizing its tube feet. They considered that this behavior was a response to the presence of coral nematocysts that seemed to be very effective against the tube feet but ineffective against the stomach of the starfish. At the same time they pointed out that some corals, such as *Acropora formosa*, that have strong nematocyst defences are more easily climbed than the smooth massive growths of *Porites lutea* that has weaker nematocyst defences. These authors also noted that the gastric folds are spread out over a coral surface by means of the tube feet of the starfish.

The feeding scar produced by *A. planci* on corals such as species of *Turbinaria,* species of *Porites,* and *Acropora hyacinthus,* which possess extensive and relatively smooth surfaces, is approximately circular in outline and about half the diameter of the starfish. When feeding on most branching corals the starfish wraps itself around one or more branches and spreads its stomach over the branches inserting gastric folds between adjacent branches (Pearson and Endean, 1969). Sometimes large numbers of *A. planci* attack the same coral colony, and, at such times, the arms of adjacent specimens may overlap, and the colony may be almost completely enclosed by the starfish (Endean and Stablum, 1973a).

Only on rare occasions has *A. planci* been observed to attack alcyonarians, the hydrocoral *Millepora* sp. or the octocoral *Heliopora* sp. Endean, 1969; Endean and Stablum, 1973a). Apart from one record of *A. planci* attacking the exposed adductor muscle of a recently killed bivalve (Pearson and Endean, 1969) there are no records of *A. planci* eating animals other than coelenterates.

When present at low population densities, *A. planci* generally feeds only at night. It often eats only a portion of a coral colony and then moves some distance away before attacking another colony. However, when present at high population density, large numbers of adult *A. planci* have frequently been observed feeding during daylight hours.

G. REPRODUCTION AND SPAWNING

The sexes in *A. planci* are separate with the sex ratio approaching unity (Pearson and Endean, 1969). These authors have estimated that a ripe female, 30 cm in diameter, carries between 12×10^6 and 24×10^6 eggs. Studies of gonad indexes indicated that the breeding season for the starfish on the Great Barrier Reef extended from mid-December to late January. However, breeding starfish were observed in the field on only one occasion. At 1:00 PM on January 10, 1968, starfish were observed on the tips of the branches of a thicket of a species of a staghorn *Acropora* growing in 3 m of water. Gametes were shed directly into the water, and spawning in both sexes lasted about 30 minutes.

Owens (1971) observed an *A. planci* population at Muaivuso, Fiji spawning on February 1, 1970, at 2:00 PM on a falling tide. There was an apparent migration during January, 1970, of individuals from deeper water to water between 0.5 and 4 m deep where they aggregated prior to spawning. Up to 10 starfish per m² were noted at this stage. Chesher (1969a) stated that *A. planci* breeds during November and December in Guam. In Hawaii, Branham *et al.* (1971) found that *A.*

planci spawned in April and May. It should be noted that in all the above cases *A. planci* was present at high population density. Spawning behavior may be different when adults are present at low population densities.

H. Development

Development of the larval stages of *A. planci* has been studied by Mortensen (1931), Henderson (1969), Henderson and Lucas (1971), and Yamaguchi (Chapter 11). Pelagic larval stages typical of asteroids are possessed by *A. planci*, and Yamaguchi has provided a detailed account of their development. Two aspects warrant attention. One is that, although larvae do not develop normally at temperatures below 25°–27°C, they can pass from the egg stage through all developmental stages to the settling and metamorphosing brachiolaria stage within 21 days at 27°–29°C. Another is the finding by Yamaguchi that brachiolariae settle on, metamorphose on, and subsequently feed on coralline algae.

I. Juveniles and Growth

Yamaguchi (Chapter 11) found that immediately after metamorphosis juveniles have only 5 arms but additional ones form rapidly. He noted that juveniles began to feed on corals about 18 weeks after metamorphosis when they were about 8 mm in diameter. Also, he found that about 20 weeks after metamorphosis juveniles were about 11 mm in diameter. The smallest specimen found in the field by Pearson and Endean (1969) was 11 mm in diameter and resembled a miniature adult in external appearance. These authors found 46 specimens ranging from 11 mm to 69 mm (mean 34.7 mm) in diameter in shallow water on Fitzroy Reef, Great Barrier Reef, during January and February 1967. Two specimens were found on the underside of dead coral; the remainder was taken from living corals, principally *Acropora echinata* and *Stylophora mordax*. In early 1968, 142 juveniles ranging from 15 mm to 79 mm in diameter (mean 33.8 mm) were found on Fitzroy Reef on corals in shallow water. Most of the juveniles were found on the dead basal portions of colonies of *Acropora echinata*. Numerous small feeding scars were noted on the upper parts of the colonies.

Endean and Stablum (1973a) found juveniles on reef crests and the tops of coral pinnacles on several reefs of the Great Barrier Reef. The juveniles were feeding mostly on low acropores. At Slashers No. 4 Reef, 102 specimens were found on January 27, 1971, and they ranged from 7 cm to 15 cm in diameter (mean 10.9 cm).

The mean growth rate of juvenile starfish between 2 and 20 cm in diameter was found to be of the order of 1 cm per month by Pearson and Endean (1969). However, juvenile specimens 6–9 cm in diameter were observed to grow at the rate of 3–4 cm per month in Guam by Yamaguchi. The reason for this difference in observed growth rates is not known. Pearson and Endean (1969) found that during the breeding season starfish containing mature gonads were generally larger than 14 cm in diameter. It would appear that, in the main, starfish breeding for the first time are approximately 20 cm in diameter and 2 years of age. However, it is possible that under natural conditions the length of the period between fertilization and metamorphosis varies markedly from one specimen to the next and that growth rates vary markedly also. If allowance is made for these variations, starfish could mature when they were between 1 and 3 years of age inclusive.

J. Predators

The eggs of *A. planci* were observed on one occasion to be preyed on by a species of fish (*Abudefduf curacao*) (Pearson and Endean, 1969), but the importance of this predation is not known. It is to be expected that the pelagic larval stages of the starfish will be preyed on by a variety of predators in the plankton and in shallow water by a variety of benthic predators (Endean, 1969). Yamaguchi (Chapter 11) has shown that at least one coral, *Pocillopora damicornis*, will feed on the planktonic larvae, but other predators of these larvae have not been identified. Predation on the immediate postlarval stages has not been studied but could be heavy.

Larger juveniles as well as adult *A. planci* are preyed on by the giant triton, *Charonia tritonis* (Fig. 2). A total of 50 adult *Charonia tritonis* and 2 large juvenile specimens of *C. tritonis* has been found during visits to numerous reefs in the central region of the Great Barrier Reef during 1966–1971 (Pearson and Endean, 1969; Endean and Stablum, 1973a). Six giant tritons were eating *A. planci* when encountered in the field. It is noteworthy that 5 of the 6 specimens being eaten were about 20 cm in diameter. Starfish of this size are engulfed whole and may be preferred to larger specimens. Twenty-eight of the 52 tritons found were collected, and 7 of those collected subsequently regurgitated *Acanthaster* spines. Thus at least 13 of the 52 tritons seen were preying on or had recently preyed on *A. planci*.

Experiments were carried out in the field to assess the efficiency of *Charonia tritonis* as a predator of *Acanthaster*. It was found that 15

Fig. 2. The giant triton, *Charonia tritonis,* captured while eating a specimen of *A. planci.* Nathan Reef, January, 1970.

tritons consumed 125 adult starfish in 3 months (Pearson and Endean, 1969). Unfortunately, experiments were not carried out with large juvenile starfish, which appear to be preferred to large adult starfish by *C. tritonis.* A specimen of *C. tritonis* about 40 cm in length was observed to eat, within a space of 3 days, one specimen of *A. planci* about 25 cm in diameter and two specimens each about 18 cm in diameter.

Chesher (1969a) found that when confined with large specimens of *Acanthaster planci, Charonia tritonis* actively sought out its prey. However, frequently only portion of a starfish was eaten and the remainder survived and regenerated lost parts. A similar occurrence was not observed during the experiments carried out with tritons and starfish on the Great Barrier Reef. Chesher may have used larger adult starfish at Guam than were used in the Great Barrier Reef experiments.

As well as eating *A. planci, Charonia tritonis* will eat other coral reef asteroids including *Nardoa pauciforis, Linckia laevigata,* and *Culcita novaeguineae.* One triton, 25 cm in length, showed a preference for the smallest starfish present (specimens of *Nardoa pauciforis*) when placed in an aquarium with specimens of *N. pauciforis, Linckia laevigata,* and *Acanthaster planci* (Pearson and Endean, 1969). The experiment should be repeated using starfish of similar size. The giant triton will eat at least two species of holothurians as well as asteroids (Endean and Stablum, 1973a). *Charonia tritonis* has been found on all regions of coral reefs in Great Barrier Reef waters and at all depths ranging from the reef crest to the sea floor. However, it is usually found in water 2–6 m deep. Occasionally, it is found in small caves and under ledges, but usually it lies fully exposed on or among corals and is readily seen by an experienced diver. The species appears to be confined to coral reefs.

A report was received from a shell collector (Endean, 1969) that the giant helmet *Cassis cornuta* is a predator of *A. planci*. However, the reported predation requires confirmation, since it is possible that the collector had confused *A. planci* with the needle-spined sea urchin, *Diadema setosum*, which has been observed to be preyed on by *Cassis cornuta* (Endean, 1972). As far as is known the Cassidae feed exclusively on echinoids.

Many specimens of *A. planci* showed apparent damage to one or more arms. Thus Pearson and Endean (1969) found that 116 of 346 starfish examined possessed one or more rays less than half normal size. It is assumed that these rays had been damaged and were in process of regeneration when the starfish were collected. Nine of 31 specimens of *A. planci* examined in the Red Sea area had damaged arms (Campbell and Ormond, 1970). Pyne (1969) noted that more than 50% of 47 starfish examined from a small reef off Port Moresby, Papua, showed definite signs of arm regeneration, five arms being involved in one individual. However, it is not known how the damage to the arms had arisen, although it is suspected that a fish predator such as the hump headed wrasse, *Cheilinus undulatus*, might be implicated. This species has been found with *A. planci* spines embedded in its mouth tissue (P. Wilson, quoted by Chesher, 1969b), and it has also been observed mouthing a macerated specimen of *A. planci* on a reef of the Great Barrier Reef (Endean and Stablum, 1973a). *Cheilinus undulatus* attains a length of approximately 2 m, and it may be an important predator of *A. planci*. On the other hand, it may rarely eat more than a few rays from specimens of *A. planci* and may not play a major role in controlling populations of *A. planci*. *Cheilinus undulatus* was seen on many reefs of the Great Barrier Reef that were infested with *A. planci*, but the typical population density of this fish is not known.

A small strikingly marked shrimp, *Hymenocera picta*, was observed to eat *A. planci* kept in aquaria (Wickler and Seibt, 1970). After causing the starfish to retract its tube feet by nibbling upon them, the shrimp turned the animal onto its aboral side, cut into the body wall, and devoured the internal tissues. However, it is not known whether *H. picta* preys on *A. planci* in its natural environment.

Another crustacean, *Neaxius glyptocercus*, which inhabits burrows in sandy areas among coral formations at some mainland islands in Queensland waters, has been observed to attack *A. planci*. Some of the starfish attacked were completely devoured, whereas others were only partially eaten and survived (T. W. Brown, personal communication). However, it was noted that the crustacean would attack almost any slow-moving object that passed over the entrance of its burrow; it is not a specific predator of *A. planci*. Moreover, it does not appear to occur commonly on the patch reefs of the Great Barrier Reef.

K. Longevity and Regeneration

The life span of *A. planci* is not known, but it is certainly over 3 years. Chesher (1969a) estimated the life span at about 8 years, but possibly it is greater than this.

A. planci appears capable of regenerating arms, but regeneration is slow (Pearson and Endean, 1969; Owens, 1971). Natural disc schizogony has not been observed, but Chesher (1969a) observed that, when attacked by *Charonia tritonis*, specimens of *A. planci* frequently autotomized the part held by the giant triton, the rest escaping and subsequently regenerating lost parts. Owens (1971) cut a starfish approximately 35 cm in diameter in half. The two halves survived and, after 2 months, the two new individuals so formed were found feeding.

III. Population Explosions of *Acanthaster planci* and Infestations of Reefs

A. Normal Population Density and Population Structure

Available evidence indicates that *A. planci* normally occurs at low population densities on coral reefs. On reefs of the Great Barrier Reef outside the area of *A. planci* infestation, the starfish is rarely seen. Thus Pearson and Endean (1969) reported only eight starfish from six reefs visited north of Lizard Island (lat. 14°40′S), while Vine (1970) did not see a single specimen on twenty-one reefs he visited between Lizard Island and Thursday Island, which lies near the northern end of the Great Barrier Reef. On ten reefs of the Swain Reef Complex, near the southern end of the Great Barrier Reef, Pearson and Endean (1969) found only one specimen of *A. planci*. Likewise, Weber and Woodhead

(1970) found few or no *A. planci* on reefs visited near the southern end of the Great Barrier Reef. Indeed, on reefs of the Great Barrier Reef outside the region of starfish infestation between lat. 15°S and lat. 19°20'S, it is unusual to find more than three or four *A. planci* during an hour's search. One to three seen during 4–5 hour's search would be a typical finding. Moreover, on some reefs no *A. planci* have been seen despite intensive searches in areas that would seem to provide suitable habitats for the starfish.

Chesher (1969b) stated that normal populations of *A. planci* are generally represented by two to three specimens per km² of reef, the specimens usually occurring singly. Occasionally, a small concentration of about 20 specimens was seen on a reef in a situation which Chesher considered to be normal in that the starfish were causing little damage to the corals in their vicinity. The possibility that these aggregations were breeding aggregations was raised.

Campbell and Ormond (1970) found *A. planci* at an average rate of one specimen per $5\frac{1}{4}$ man hours of search on reefs along 125 km of the Sudanese Red Sea coast.

The population structure of *A. planci* at normal population density is not known. Most specimens of *A. planci* seen on uninfested reefs of the Great Barrier Reef by the present author were large adults between 30 and 60 cm in diameter.

B. Rate and Extent of Coral Destruction at Normal Population Density of *A. planci*

It would appear that on uninfested reefs *A. planci* normally feeds at night and tends to be cryptic during the day. As noted by Chesher (1969b), *A. planci* under these conditions frequently attacks only a portion of a particular coral colony, and the remaining portion continues to grow. The starfish does not appear to be territorial but moves about. The overall extent of damage inflicted on corals is negligible and is soon repaired.

C. What Constitutes an Infestation

It is difficult to give precise quantitative expression to an *A. planci* infestation. Chesher (1969b) gave a figure of 20 animals seen per 20 minutes of search as indicative of a possible infestation and 100 seen per 20 minutes of search as indicative of a definite infestation. Pearson and Endean (1969), for the purpose of comparing starfish densities on different reefs, arbitrarily selected a figure of 40 starfish seen per

20 minutes as constituting an infestation. However, on infested reefs of the Great Barrier Reef these authors frequently found hundreds of starfish per 20 minute search. Endean and Stablum (1973a) found the starfish packed so densely at some localities on the Great Barrier Reef that the arms of adjacent specimens overlapped. Even so, it should be appreciated that when present in what may be described as plague proportions starfish are not uniformly distributed on a reef. They usually migrate in large groups forming a number of fronts on a reef, each front leaving a trail of coral skeletons in its wake. Also, if infestation of a reef results from adult invasion, large numbers of starfish first appear in the deep water around the periphery of a reef (Section VI). At first they are cryptic during the day, feeding at night. Subsequently, they ascend the reef slopes killing coral as they ascend prior to invading the reef-flat and back-reef areas where they are readily seen in shallow water since they feed during the day. A few stragglers are usually found in the areas of recently killed coral in the wake of the migrating starfish.

Then again, juvenile starfish may be found in high density in shallow water areas. For example, Endean and Stablum (1973a) collected 700 A. planci with a mean size of 16.4 cm from the top and upper areas of the sides of one coral pinnacle at Nathan Reef on the Great Barrier Reef. However, the aggregation of juveniles appeared to be localized, extensive coral damage being restricted to a small area, and the reef as a whole could not be regarded as infested. Even so, a similar phenomenon has not been observed on reefs of the Great Barrier Reef outside the known region of starfish infestation; it is possible that the aggregation observed represented an incipient infestation.

If present in sufficient numbers, A. planci will clearly overwhelm its coral prey. However, because starfish are cryptic at some stages of an infestation of a reef but not at others, because they are not uniformly distributed on a reef, and because there may be an immigration of adults and/or settling larvae of A. planci to a reef at some stages of an infestation and emigration of adults at other stages, overall numbers of starfish present on a reef are extremely difficult to determine. For practical purposes it would appear necessary to make reference to the extent of coral destruction caused by the starfish as well as reference to starfish numbers if the existence of an infestation is to be demonstrated. Chesher (1969b, p. 90) defined an infestation as "a concentration of A. planci whose combined feeding effort clearly exceeds what can be supported by the existing coral growth and whose survival and recruitment rate are such that migration and dispersion do not result in a balanced condition." However, this definition has its drawbacks. The coral cover at some reef areas is much sparser than at others and obviously fewer starfish would be required to devastate the bulk of the hard coral cover at some reef areas than at others and vice versa. A consideration of mean feeding rates of the starfish present at a particular area of reef under consideration is also required as rates would be related to starfish size, type of coral present, etc. The survival and recruitment rate of an *A. planci* population is extremely difficult to determine. Also, an estimation of the rate of recruitment of new coral colonies and the length of time that these colonies would require to attain a significant size would be required.

In general, if abnormal amounts of freshly exposed coral skeletons are found on a reef and the damage has not obviously been caused by recent storms, freshwater runoff from adjacent land masses, excessive siltation, or emersion, an *A. planci* infestation is possible. A search will reveal hundreds of *A. planci* killing large numbers of coral colonies scattered over hundreds of square meters of reef on some region of the reef if it is infested. It should be noted that it is possible to visit a sector of a reef where coral growth is luxuriant and no *A. planci* are present, yet *A. planci* can be present in very large numbers on other sectors of the same reef.

D. POPULATION STRUCTURES ON INFESTED REEFS

Actual numbers of starfish on infested reefs have not been determined and, for reasons just discussed, would be exceedingly difficult to determine. Occasionally, large numbers of starfish have been observed fully exposed in shallow water on a reef flat. Such an aggregation was observed and photographed (Fig. 3) at the Slasher Reef Complex on the Great Barrier Reef in 1970 (Endean and Stablum, 1973a). It was apparent that tens of thousands of starfish were present, but an actual count was not made. In 1970, 20,000 starfish were counted on a section of a fringing reef at Molokai, Hawaiian Islands (Braham *et al.*, 1971). In 1972 it was estimated that at least 210,000 specimens of *A. planci* were present on reefs near Sesoko Island on the west coast of Okinawa (Nishihira and Yamazato, 1972).

An approach which would yield an approximate figure for the mean number of starfish on a reef during the period for which the reef was infested requires an estimate of the amount of coral killed on a reef and knowledge of the period for which the reef was infested. Experiments carried out by Pearson and Endean (1969) indicated that adult specimens of *A. planci* consume coral at a mean rate of 160 cm^2 per

Fig. 3. Large numbers of A. *planci* feeding on coral. Reef flat, Slashers Reef Complex, August, 1970. (Courtesy of T. W. Brown.)

day. If this rate is maintained throughout the year each starfish would kill about 6 m² of coral per year. On the Great Barrier Reef, the bulk of hard coral on patch reefs, each several square kilometers in extent in flat projection and well covered with coral colonies, was found to be killed within 2–3 years. If each starfish feeds at the rate of 6 m² per year, it is apparent that many tens of thousands of starfish must be responsible for the destruction of such reefs. A tentative estimate of the mean A. *planci* population at Lodestone Reef, Great Barrier Reef, during the 1969–1970 period of infestation was 300,000 (Endean, unpublished).

Another more direct approach is to collect all the starfish in a specified area for a specified time. In 1965–1966 a total of 27,000 starfish was taken from one small area at Green Island Reef on the Great Barrier Reef. During a 2-week period in December, 1969, 13,847 starfish were collected from the fringing reef on the southern shore of Upolu Island in Western Samoa (Garlovsky and Bergquist, 1970). In 10 days in 1970, six divers collected 9860 specimens of A. *planci* from the reef on the Muiavuso area of Fiji (Owens, 1971). In a 20-month period at Guam, 44,000 starfish were killed (Tsuda, 1971). In 1957 more than 220,000 starfish were reported to have been collected during a government-sponsored control program at Miyako Island Reef in the Ryukyus (Endean and Chesher, 1973). It is apparent that tens of thousands of starfish are indeed present on infested reefs.

Specimens of *A. planci* were observed to be aggregated during all seasons of the year on infested reefs of the Great Barrier Reef (Endean and Stablum, 1973a). This observation rules out any possibility that the apparent starfish infestations were merely large breeding aggregations, since Pearson and Endean (1969) have shown that *A. planci* breeds only during the summer months on the Great Barrier Reef.

Although population samples from different infested reefs of the Great Barrier Reef (Endean and Stablum, 1973a) show strong domination by certain size groups, a wide range of sizes was represented within each group. It seems likely that the size groups represent year groups. The wide range within each group encountered could stem from variation in growth rate within each year group or could stem from brachiolariae settling from the plankton at different times or from both causes.

On reefs of the Great Barrier Reef that had been invaded initially by adults, the mean size of the starfish present exceeded 30 cm, but on reefs that appeared to have been invaded initially by larvae, the mean size of the starfish was smaller, the actual figures obtained depending on the time of the year when the samples were taken. Juveniles were restricted to shallow water and tended to stay there until they were at least 12 cm in diameter (1–2 years of age). Subsequently, they moved over the reef but tended to remain together. On some reefs the picture was confused because several year groups had intermingled (Endean and Stablum, 1973a).

Chesher (1969b) found that starfish on infested areas at Guam averaged 24.2 cm in diameter.

E. Rate and Extent of Coral Destruction when a Reef Is Infested with *A. planci*

Pearson and Endean (1969) estimated that an adult starfish is capable of killing about 6 m² of coral per year, but Chesher (1969a) estimated that an adult starfish killed coral at twice this rate. Under natural conditions the actual rate of destruction would be affected by many factors such as reef topography, the extent of coral cover, the species of coral present, the mean size of starfish present, the number of starfish present, the state of infestation of the reef reached, etc. On the Great Barrier

Reef, the bulk of hard coral on patch reefs, each several square kilometers in extent in flat projection, was killed within 2–6 years, sometimes within 2–3 years. On the narrow fringing reef at Guam, Chesher (1969a) estimated that 90% of coral present was killed along 38 km of shoreline in $2\frac{1}{2}$ years.

Sometimes starfish departed from reefs in Great Barrier Reef waters before killing the coral cover in major sectors of the reef. Endean and Stablum (1973b) found that, although most coral colonies in the lee of exposed outer patch reefs were frequently killed by *A. planci*, coral colonies on the windward side were largely untouched. Sometimes, starfish also departed from an inner patch reef before completing destruction of the major part of the coral cover (Pearson and Endean, 1969). Usually, however, only coral colonies in shallow water survived the starfish infestations.

F. How Reefs Become Infested

It is postulated (see Section VI) that the release of large juveniles and adult *A. planci* from predator pressure on a reef results in the gradual build-up of numbers of the starfish on the reef, thereby enabling substantial numbers of breeding adults to come together during the breeding season and produce vast swarms of larvae. The planktonic larvae are then carried by currents to reefs in the same general area where they settle. Initially the juvenile starfish occur in shallow water, but as they mature they gradually spread to other parts of the reef. However, the feeding starfish tend to move in groups.

Chesher (1969b) referred to seed populations (large groups of 500 to 1000 specimens located within a small area) at Guam. Coral damage was moderate to severe within the confines of such a population, but coral in adjacent areas was alive. A seed population, according to Chesher, is the first manifestation of an infestation, and the groups comprising a seed population congregate primarily in shallow water in areas of lush coral growth. It is noteworthy that the specimens in such groups averaged about 24 cm in diameter indicating that they were young adults from 2–3 years of age. Subsequently, the starfish moved to all depth zones in groups comprised of several hundred specimens. Ultimately, very large migratory herds appeared that moved parallel with the shoreline at Guam (Chesher, 1969b).

Endean and Stablum (1973a) have found large numbers of adult starfish on reefs that did not appear to be carrying large numbers of juvenile starfish, and evidence was obtained indicating that many reefs of the Great Barrier Reef infested in recent years were invaded by adults that had migrated across the sea floor from nearby reefs. Coral at the foot of a reef under attack was first affected; then, as numbers of invading adults increased, the starfish ascended the reef slopes and eventually invaded the reef flat.

G. Decline of Population Explosions, Adult Migration, and Residual Populations

Chesher (1969b) noted that after *A. planci* had recently grazed all of the coral on a particular island reef in Micronesia a large population of *A. planci* could still be present. He stated that the starfish may then enter an equilibrium condition with the density of specimens depending on the rate of settlement and growth of corals. Under these conditions he believed the reef would remain impoverished. On the other hand, he maintained that, if an infestation of a reef is so serious that all coral colonies are eaten and recruitment of new coral colonies is inhibited by succession communities, *A. planci* may starve before food corals re-establish themselves. Under these circumstances he believed no residual population of starfish would be found.

It is noteworthy that whereas the fringing reefs and atoll reefs of Micronesia are often separated by deep water, the patch reefs of the Great Barrier Reef in the region of infestation are separated from one another by shallow water averaging about 60 m in depth. Moreover, adjacent reefs in the region are separated by mean distances of about 10 km. The available evidence indicates that, after devastating a reef in Great Barrier Reef waters, the bulk of the adult starfish population departs from the reef and migrates to uninfested reefs (Endean and Stablum, 1973a). However, on some reefs, particularly large reefs infested during the 1960's, residual adult starfish populations were found. Also, *A. planci* larvae settle in shallow areas exposed to wave action, which are usually avoided by adults. Larvae may continue to settle in such areas on a reef after the bulk of adult starfish has departed from the reef, and may effectively constitute a residual population of starfish that would hamper recolonization of the reef by hard corals.

IV. Effects of *A. planci* Population Explosions on Coral Reefs

A. Immediate Effects

After attack by *A. planci* the skeletons of corals are exposed (Fig. 4). For a few days they remain stark white, but within 2–3 weeks the

Fig. 4. A *planci* feeding on a colony of *Montipora foliosa*. The skeleton of the coral exposed as a result of the feeding activities of the starfish is white. Slashers Reef Complex, August, 1970. (Courtesy of T. W. Brown.)

skeletons acquire a film of greenish filamentous algae, principally *Entero-morpha clathrata* (Roth.) Grev. Subsequently the algal coating thickens and darkens, and the coral skeletons become coated with dark tufts of algae (Endean and Stablum, 1973b). From a distance of a few meters the algae-covered skeletons appear dark, almost black, at this stage (Fig. 5). After several months coralline algae become evident among the filamentous algae, and the coral skeletons assumed a grayish rather than a blackish appearance.

Coral-haunting fish such as chaetodons (Chaetodontidae), pullers and humbugs (Chromidae), and damsel fish (Pomacentridae) remain associated with the skeletons of dead corals initially, but disappear when these acquire a coating of filamentous algae (Endean and Stablum, 1973b). Presumably, most of the small organisms associated with living corals attacked by the starfish are killed by the digestive enzymes released by the starfish. At any rate, apart from fish, the freshly exposed coral skeletons appear devoid of organisms normally associated with living corals.

Not all coral colonies on a reef attacked by large numbers of *A.*

planci are killed by the starfish initially. On the Great Barrier Reef, colonies growing on reef crests and in shallow water on the tops of coral pinnacles exposed to considerable wave action usually survived the starfish infestations. Also, corals growing in upper regions of the seaward slopes of the windward sides of exposed inner reefs and on seaward slopes of outer patch reefs exposed to heavy wave surge were not usually attacked by the starfish. Occasionally, patches of coral and, on some reefs, very large specimens of massive corals (particularly species of *Porites* and *Astreopora*) were bypassed by the feeding starfish. Species of the hydrozoan *Millepora* and the octocoral *Heliopora* were usually avoided by the starfish. Sometimes coral colonies belonging to

Fig. 5. Algae covered skeleton of a staghorn acropore attacked by *A. planci* some months earlier. The tips of some of the branches of the coral survived the attack. Keeper Reef, August, 1970. (Courtesy of T. W. Brown.)

various genera were only partially killed by *A. planci*. The tips of some
of the branches or part of one or more branches of branching corals
occasionally survived. Likewise, part of a massive coral sometimes survived. In such cases the pigmented living tissue contrasted strongly
with the white, freshly exposed skeleton or the dark, algae-covered skeleton of the colony. The presence of such partially killed coral colonies
conferred a characteristic facies on reefs devastated by *A. planci*.

There is no question that *A. planci* has caused a catastrophic destruction of the hard coral cover of most of the major reefs lying between
lat. 16°30'S and lat. 19°S on the Great Barrier Reef (Endean and
Stablum, 1973b), and it is likely that a massive destruction of the hard
coral cover of reefs between lat. 15°S and lat. 16°30'S has also occurred.
However, precise figures for the extent of destruction of hard corals
on individual reefs are not available. Estimates that have been made
relate to the percentage of dead coral in the total coral cover in a
sampled area of reef after the reef has been devastated by the starfish
or while the devastation was in progress. These estimates lack precision.
Allowance should be made in these estimates for the amount of recently
killed coral present *in situ* in an area before the starfish attacked the
area. Coral colonies are attacked by a variety of organisms (see Chapter
9). On the Great Barrier Reef a gastropod *Drupella cornus* and
the starfish *Culcita novaeguineae* have been observed to kill small
acropore colonies (Endean, unpublished). However, the amount of recently exposed coral skeletons normally present *in situ* on a reef of
the Great Barrier Reef is small and usually much less than 10% of the
total coral cover (Endean and Stablum, 1973b). Of course, the total
coral cover present varies from one reef to another and from one region
to another of the same reef. It is necessary to determine the percentage
coral cover (surviving coral plus freshly exposed skeletons *in situ*)
present in an area if the significance of coral destruction in the area
is to be assessed. The obtaining of adequate quantitative data over
a large area of a single reef is a time-consuming task and one which
is technically difficult. However, when *A. planci* invades a reef in the
large numbers recently observed at certain reefs of the Great Barrier
Reef and at certain reefs in Micronesia, the results of studies of the
extent of the damage to corals caused by the starfish are unequivocal.
Most coral colonies in the reef area attacked are killed and, as far as
reefs of the Great Barrier Reef are concerned, *A. planci* kills coral
colonies from the sea floor to the reef crest (Fig. 6) and in most sectors
of a reef (Endean and Stablum, 1973a). In the large areas of high
coral mortality, an apparent collapse of typical reef community organiza-

Fig. 6. Portion of Taylor Reef showing massive destruction of many types of coral by *A. planci*. September, 1969. (Courtesy of T. W. Brown.)

tion occurs. There is an obvious dearth of coral-associated animals, and it would appear that a mass exodus of nektonic animals has occurred.

Occasionally, the bulk of starfish departs from a reef leaving the hard coral cover of a sizeable sector of reef intact as was noted to have occurred to Mackay Reef (Pearson and Endean, 1969), but usually only corals growing in regions exposed to heavy wave action survive *en masse* (Endean and Stablum, 1973b).

B. Effects after Lapse of Some Years

Although algae-covered skeletons of tabular corals (*Acropora hyacinthus*) previously killed by *A. planci* had been observed to remain *in situ* for almost 3 years when last observed (Pearson and Endean, 1969), many coral skeletons are eroded by boring and abrading organisms and possibly by microorganisms. Certainly the exposed skeletons of branching corals, in particular, become very friable. On some reefs of the Great Barrier Reef devastated by *A. planci*, Endean and Stablum (1973b) noted that the exposed skeletons of branching acropores were smashed (presumably by wave action) within a few months after exposure and formed piles of rubble. Often, the skeletons of tabular corals broke away from their points of attachment after a few months, and they lay in heaps on ledges and at the bases of coral pinnacles.

Portions of some staghorn and tabular acropore colonies survived the starfish invasions and continued to grow. Algae-covered regions of the skeletons of these colonies did not appear to acquire a new covering of coral polyps as a result of regeneration from surviving portions of the original colony. As many of the algae-covered skeletons will be eroded and ultimately collapse, it is to be expected that the surviving portions of the colonies will, in most cases, be lost. Sometimes, too, destruction of massive coral colonies was incomplete. Again, exposed portions of the skeleton become coated with algae and, in some cases, with other organisms such as alcyonarians. It is not known whether colonies of damaged massive corals will, in time, regenerate a covering of polyps in the damaged regions of the skeletons. If they do, regeneration evidently takes place very slowly.

Within a few months after a reef has been devastated by *A. planci,* an obvious increase in the alcyonarian cover of the reef usually occurs. The soft corals frequently grow over coral skeletons and some areas of reef become carpeted with soft corals (Fig. 7).

Stands of *Millepora* that are in the main avoided by *A. planci* (Pearson and Endean, 1969) increased in extent markedly within 2–3 years after

Fig. 7. A carpet of soft corals (*Lobophytum* sp.) spreading over the skeletons of corals killed by *A. planci.* Beaver Reef, September, 1969. (Courtesy of T. W. Brown.)

devastation of a reef by *A. planci.* Within 3–4 years after starfish had devastated some areas of reef, recently settled hard corals were observed. However, the extent of recolonization was slight, and few species were represented. *Pocillopora damicornis, Seriatopora hystrix, Stylophora pistillata,* and species of *Turbinaria, Porites,* and *Acropora* were prominent among the recolonizers on devastated reefs of the Great Barrier Reef (Endean and Stablum, 1973b). These authors noted an apparent relationship between the rate of recovery of an area of reef and the extent of coral destruction in that area caused by the starfish initially, i.e., the more complete the initial destruction the slower the recovery and vice versa. It was noted that many of the recolonizing corals had settled on the skeletons of tabular corals that may ultimately be eroded and break away from their points of attachment. Many such recolonizers probably will be lost.

C. Long-Term Effects

Recovery of coral reefs devastated by catastrophic events depends primarily on the recolonization of devastated areas by hard coral colonies and the continued growth and reproduction of surviving coral colonies.

Factors affecting the rate of recolonization of a reef by hard corals
have been discussed by Endean (1973). These factors include (1)
the initial magnitude and extent of the coral destruction caused by a
catastrophic event; (2) the proximity of undamaged areas of coral reef
which could provide significant numbers of coral planulae; (3) the presence of favorable water currents for conveying the planulae to
devastated areas; (4) the presence of favorable conditions for settlement
of planulae and for the growth of the coral colonies they initiate. Even
so, full recovery of a devastated reef would require the return of most
or all of those species characteristically associated with flourishing coral
reefs in the geographical region concerned and the reestablishment of
the complex relationships normally existing among the numerous species
comprising the biota of a reef. Stoddart (1969) and Endean (1973)
have provided recent summaries of recorded instances of catastrophic
mortality of corals. It would appear that the recent destruction of corals
on reefs of the Great Barrier Reef and in Micronesia has been on an
unprecedented scale; this may also be true for other localities that have
recently experienced or are currently experiencing A. planci plagues.
Certainly coral destruction caused by A. planci has been far more widespread and severe on the Great Barrier Reef and in Micronesia than
recorded instances of recent coral destruction attributable to other causes.
In view of this, it is probable that recovery of affected reefs will be
long delayed.

Insufficient time has elapsed for recovery to proceed very far on any
reefs devastated during the 1960's. Some recolonization by hard corals
of reefs of the Great Barrier Reef devastated during the mid-1960's
was observed in 1970 and 1971 (Endean and Stablum, 1973b); but
recolonization was not marked, and on many reefs visited it was negligible. Moreover, it is to be expected that many of the recolonizers observed
will be lost since they have settled on unstable substrates. The presence
of an extensive cover of alcyonarians on some reefs and of mats of
filamentous and stalked algae on others must hamper recolonization,
as must the presence of large stands of Millepora on many reefs. It
is also to be expected that there will be a succession of species during
the recovery process, pioneer species being replaced subsequently by
other species in many cases. Among the commonest of the early recolonizers noted on devastated reefs of the Great Barrier Reef were
Pocillopora damicornis, Seriatopora hystrix, and Stylophora pistillata.
These species are known to breed throughout the year. For this reason,
Endean and Stablum (1973b) suggested that they are rapid recolonizers.
At the same time, absence of competition for substratum from other

species of corals may facilitate the spread of the pioneer species, further restricting the amount of substratum available for other species of corals. Because of all these factors, it is apparent that full recovery of devastated reefs will be slow.

Endean (1973) has estimated that a period in excess of 20 years and possibly a period of between 20 and 40 years will be required for full recovery of a reef devastated by *A. planci.* At the same time he pointed out that factors that have caused the current *A. planci* infestations may still be operative, and hence starfish may reinvade reefs as these are recolonized by hard corals. Also, residual populations of *A. planci* are certainly present on at least some devastated reefs of the Great Barrier Reef and on reefs in Micronesia. Thus Cheney (1971) noted that a residual population of *A. planci* at Tumon Bay, Guam, was feeding on new coral growths. The presence of these residual populations might result in reefs remaining impoverished indefinitely. In this connection it is of interest to recall that Goreau (1963) postulated that certain reefs in the Red Sea may be impoverished because of predation by *A. planci.*

V. History of Infestations of Coral Reefs by *A. planci*

A. Prior to 1957

There are a few references in the literature to the abundance of *A. planci* on certain reefs that may indicate that populations greater than normal (Section III) were found on these reefs prior to the 1960's. Thus Domantay and Roxas (1938) stated that the species was "common" in Port Galera Bay and Sabang Cove in the Philippines. Hayashi (1938) found the species "very common" in the Arakabesan region and rare in the Arappu region at the Palau Islands. Mortensen (1931) stated that *A. planci* was found "rather commonly" on the coral reef at the little island of Haarlem off Batavia, near Onrust. Edmondson (1933) noted that whereas *A. planci* was not "common" in Hawaiian waters it was "very common" about Christmas Island in the Line Islands. Later (Edmondson, 1946) he found it "abundant" about Christmas Island. Chesher (1969b) commented that Kuop in the Carolines was reported to be infested with *A. planci* immediately after World War II and that inspection teams, which visited Kuop in 1969, believed that Kuop had been stripped of its living coral many years previously although some coral regrowth had occurred in a few portions of the reef. Vine (1970) stated that a professional diver recalled that there were very large numbers on the southeast side of Lodestone Reef on the Great Barrier Reef (near Townsville) in 1954 and that fishermen with whom he had spoken in the Solomon Islands recalled large concentrations of them there many years ago.

Newman (1970) and Dana (1970) have drawn attention to the possibility that population explosions of *A. planci* have occurred in the past but had gone unnoticed. However, Chesher (1970) stated that there is no compelling evidence that population explosions of *A. planci* had occurred in the past and queried Edmondson's (1946) use of "abundant" to describe the *A. planci* population at Christmas Island. The exact interpretation that a naturalist puts on expressions of abundance could indeed vary from individual to individual. Thus although Domantay and Roxas (1938) stated that *A. planci* was "common" in Port Galera Bay, Domantay (personal communication, 1970) stated that *Acanthaster planci* was never a "pest" in Port Galera Bay. Then again, the professional diver who was quoted by Vine (1970) as reporting large numbers of starfish on Lodestone Reef in 1954 also reported that crown-of-thorns starfish infested the same reef in 1962 but that the reef "had been back to normal within three years" (Australian Broadcasting Commission News of July 19, 1970). However, T. W. Brown (personal communication) who was engaged in research on shark repellents in the Lodestone Reef area during the period 1961–1965 saw no sign of *A. planci* or of marked coral damage at Lodestone Reef. From time to time the present author has received reports about infestations of reefs of the Great Barrier Reef by *A. planci* prior to the 1960's, but in most cases it was apparent that *A. planci* had been confused with another starfish, *Protoreaster nodosus,* or with the needle-spined echinoid, *Diadema setosum.* Likewise, a report of an *A. planci* outbreak at North East Malaita in the Solomon Islands is now believed to have stemmed from the sighting of *Protoreaster nodosus* (J. L. Pepys-Cockerell, personal communication). Although it is possible that localized and transient aggregations of *A. planci* that give the appearance of a population upsurge do occur occasionally on some reefs, particularly during the breeding season of *A. planci,* there is no convincing evidence for the occurrence prior to 1957 of population explosions of *A. planci* similar to those that have occurred on the Great Barrier Reef, at Guam, and many other Pacific reefs since 1957. (The Kuop infestation mentioned above is a special case and is discussed in Section VI.) If massive destruction of corals such as that which has been caused by these population explosions had occurred regularly in the past, it could not have failed to arouse the attention of people in the reef areas concerned. Yet there are no records of such destruction, and accounts of such destruction have not been incorporated into the folklore of the indigenous peoples of coral reef areas. In this connection it should be remembered that native divers have actively sought food and shell ornaments on many Pacific reefs for centuries and that commercial divers have operated in coral reef areas for at least a century. Diving amid the corals of a coral reef for work or pleasure has not been restricted to the period following the development of self-contained underwater breathing apparatus.

B. Infestations since 1957

1. On the Great Barrier Reef

Population explosions of *A. planci* were noted on reefs of the Great Barrier Reef (Fig. 8) in the Cairns region during 1962 and, by early

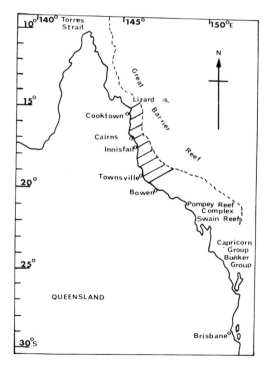

Fig. 8. Map of Queensland showing the region (cross-hatched) of The Great Barrier Reef known to have been infested by large numbers of *A. planci* during the period 1962–1972.

1963, Green Island Reef, near Cairns, was infested with starfish that were causing obvious damage to hard corals on the reef (Barnes and Endean, 1964). The significance of these observations was not understood, but it was decided that the situation should be examined further. The progress of the starfish infestation at Green Island up to 1966 was described by Barnes (1966). In March 1966, a survey of *A. planci* infestations of reefs of the Great Barrier Reef was started at the request of the Queensland government. During the ensuing 3 years it was found that the infestations appeared to be confined to the region of the Great Barrier Reef lying between approximately lat. 15°18′S and approximately lat. 18°58′S (Endean, 1969; Pearson and Endean, 1969). However, within that region 57 patch reefs representing only about a third of the total number present were actually visited. Approximately 50% of those visited yielded starfish counts in excess of 20 starfish per 20 minutes of search and are considered to have been infested when visited. It was noted that infestations were more common on inner than on outer patch reefs. Judging by the extent of coral destruction reported for some reefs visited in 1966, it was apparent that the reefs had been infested for at least several months and some possibly for 2 or 3 years. By late 1967, a decline in starfish numbers occurred on some reefs in the Cairns-Innisfail area, possibly because starfish migrated elsewhere after the bulk of their coral prey was killed.

Between August, 1969 and May, 1971, 82 of the approximately 150 reefs lying between lat. 16°34′S and lat. 19°20′S (Fig. 9) were examined (Endean and Stablum, 1973a,b). It was found that at least 18 and probably 20 of the reefs visited had already been attacked by *A. planci* and that massive destruction had been caused to the hard coral cover of these reefs. Thirty-six of the 82 reefs were carrying large numbers of starfish when visited and destruction of their hard coral cover was in progress. The remaining 26 reefs had not been invaded by starfish, but invasion of some was thought to be imminent because adjacent reefs were infested. Some reefs, such as Britomart and Trunk Reefs, which were not infested when visited in 1966, were infested when visited in 1969. It was found that within approximately 12 months the bulk of the hard coral cover of the seaward slopes of a small reef such as

Fig. 9. Map showing approximate positions and relative sizes of reefs of the Great Barrier Reef lying between lat. 16°34′S and lat. 19°20′S. (Some of the names given to reefs shown are unofficial. The map is based on part of a strip map of the Great Barrier Reef and Adjacent Isles published at the Survey Office, Department of Lands, Brisbane, Queensland and reproduced here with the permission of the Surveyor-General and the Minister for Lands, Queensland. Crown copyright reserved.)

John Brewer Reef (about 8 km² in flat projection) could be killed by large numbers of A. *planci*. Also, it was estimated that the bulk of the hard corals of most reefs in the region of the Great Barrier Reef investigated had been killed within 2–6 years after large numbers of starfish appeared on the reefs.

Recent charts of the Great Barrier Reef show the existence of about 1100 patch reefs. Between lat. 15°S and lat. 19°20'S (the apparent region of infestation) about 240 reefs occur; 117 of these reefs, including most of the larger ones, were visited between mid-1966 and mid-1971, some on more than one occasion (Pearson and Endean, 1969; Endean and Stablum, 1973a). Approximately 60% were found to be infested with A. *planci* at some stage during that period. It is likely that a similar percentage of the 123 reefs that were not visited was also infested at some stage during that period giving a total of approximately 144 reefs infested in the region. Moreover, some of the reefs which were uninfested when first visited were found to be infested on subsequent visits, and it is a reasonable assumption that others that have not been revisited could have become infested subsequent to the initial visits. Thus the total number of reefs infested with A. *planci* in the region could well exceed 144. Only future research will reveal the actual number, but it would seem a reasonable estimate that approximately 14% of the total number of patch reefs comprising the Great Barrier Reef have been infested with A. *planci* in the last decade. At the same time it should be noted that the majority of reefs outside the known area of infestation have not been visited. Of 11 reefs lying between lat. 14°S and lat. 15°S, which were examined by Pearson and Endean (1969), only one (Eye Reef), where 58 A. *planci* were seen in 40 minutes, appeared to be infested. Not a single specimen of A. *planci* was seen by Vine (1970) during visits to 21 reefs lying between Lizard Island (Lat. 14°40'S) and Thursday Island (lat. 10°35'S). A few reefs south of the known region of infestation have been visited. Only one specimen of A. *planci* was found at 10 reefs of the Swain Reefs Complex lying between lat. 20°58'S and lat. 21°43'S visited in 1967 (Pearson and Endean, 1969). No A. *planci* was observed in the Swain Reefs Complex or in the Pompey Reef Complex when reefs in these areas were visited between 1966 and 1969 (Weber and Woodhead, 1970). However, A. *planci* is readily found in lagoons but not on seaward slopes at Lady Musgrave Reef, Boult Reef, Fitzroy Reef, and One Tree Reef in the Capricorn and Bunker Groups at the southern end of the Great Barrier Reef, and occasional specimens have been found at other reefs belonging to these groups (Endean, unpublished).

Endean and Stablum (1973a) believed that the starfish infestations of reefs of the Great Barrier Reef can be traced back to accessible fringing and patch reefs near the major centers of human population on the Queensland coast between Cooktown and Townsville. They considered that *A. planci* population increases occurred almost simultaneously on these accessible reefs during the early 1960's and that, after the bulk of coral had been killed on the reefs first infested, adult starfish had migrated from these primary centers of infestation to adjacent reefs. In 1971, it was apparent that additional reefs were still coming under attack and that there was recruitment to the starfish populations of some reefs. It was not known in 1971 whether overall numbers of starfish were increasing or decreasing, but there was a general tendency for outer patch reefs lying between lat. 16°34'S and lat. 19°S to come under attack and for a southward spread of the infestations to reefs between lat. 19°S and lat. 20°S. It is possible that starfish will encounter unfavorable conditions on the reefs currently infested and that the starfish infestations will attenuate during the 1970's. However, it is equally possible that the infestations will continue. Information obtained in August 1972 reveals that the starfish infestations have spread south of lat. 19°20'S at least as far as Line Reef (lat. 19°45'S).

2. On Reefs of the Indo-West Pacific Region Generally

Chesher (1969a,b) has provided well-documented accounts of infestations at Guam and the Marianas, at the Marshall Islands, the Carolines, and the Palaus. Owens (1971) has discussed infestations of reefs at Fiji, Pyne (1969) has commented on the distribution of *A. planci* on reefs in Papua and New Guinea waters, and Garlovsky and Bergquist (1970) have described *A. planci* infestations of reefs in Western Samoa. Endean and Chesher (1973) have summarized knowledge of *A. planci* populations on these and other reefs throughout the Indo-West Pacific region (Fig. 10). Apart from infestations of reefs in the areas mentioned above, infestations have recently occurred on Towartit Reef off the Sudanese coast, on reefs off the east coast of Ceylon, on reefs off Malaya and Borneo and in the Gulf of Siam, on reefs off Taiwan, in the Ryukyus, at several localities in the Philippines, in the Solomon Islands, in the Cook Islands at the Hawaiian Islands, and at the Society Islands. The first major infestation by *A. planci* apparently occurred in the Ryukyus in 1957 when 220,000 specimens of *A. planci* were collected, followed by the Great Barrier Reef infestations, which began in the early 1960's. Since then, infestations have been reported from numerous areas of the tropical Indo-West Pacific region. There are no indications in the

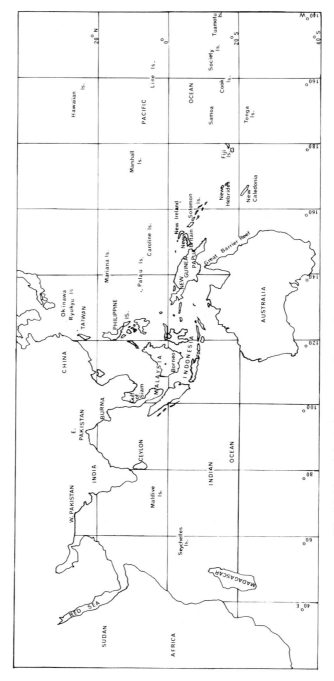

Fig. 10. Map of the Indo-West Pacific area showing localities mentioned in the text.

early 1970's of an attenuation in the extent or severity of the infestations. However, starfish numbers have declined on some reefs where the bulk of the hard coral cover has been killed by the starfish or where control measures have been instituted successfully.

It is perhaps significant that no infestations of reefs remote from human civilization such as those in the central Coral Sea area, those of the Tuamotus, or those in the Indian Ocean lying at a considerable distance from the African coast have been reported. Indeed, the overall picture that emerges is that reefs most readily accessible to humans and hence most frequently visited, particularly those in the vicinity of human population centers, are the ones most commonly infested by *A. planci.*

VI. Possible Causes of the *A. planci* Population Explosions

At the outset, a distinction should be made between primary infestations of reefs involving local increases in starfish numbers on certain reefs owing to the operation of factors peculiar to those reefs or the waters around those reefs and secondary infestations stemming from carriage by currents of large numbers of larvae from the primary centers of infestation to other reefs or from migration of large numbers of adult starfish from devastated reefs to other reefs.

A. PRIMARY INFESTATIONS

1. Normal Event

a. Natural Fluctuations of Breeding Cycle. A high fecundity and planktotrophic larval stages of long duration characterize most marine invertebrates that reproduce by external fertilization following the release of gametes. Sometimes optimal conditions for spawning, fertilization, development, and survival of larvae of a particular species occur, and at such times there is a heavy recruitment into the population of that species in a particular region. Such short-term fluctuations in the abundance of species are well known and have been observed by several workers (e.g., Thorson, 1950; Coe, 1956). Subsequently, compensating mechanisms such as increased predation come into play, and the population returns to normal. Pearson and Endean (1969) discussed the possibility that the current *A. planci* infestations are natural phenomena, and it was suggested by Vine (1970, p. 342) that "we are probably observing natural fluctuations in the population of an animal "[A. planci] which appears to be one of the main predators of coral." However, there is no possibility that the current population explosions on the Great Barrier Reef could be the result of exceptional spatfall in one year or even in 2 or 3 successive years. On infested reefs A. planci population structures are generally polymodal indicating the presence of several age classes. Indeed, infestations of some reefs of the Great Barrier Reef were recorded in the early 1960's (Barnes and Endean, 1964), and in the late 1960's and early 1970's heavy recruitment of juveniles to the A. planci populations of other reefs was still being recorded (Endean and Stablum, 1973a). In any case, the idea that destruction of the bulk of the coral cover on approximately 14% of the reefs of the Great Barrier Reef or 90% of the coral along 38 km of the fringing reef at Guam is a result of a "natural" fluctuation in numbers of A. planci is difficult to accept.

A rise in water temperature of 1°C in eastern Australian waters in 1959 has been suggested as a possible trigger of the starfish infestations on the Great Barrier Reef (Anonymous, 1970). However, population explosions of A. planci have been recorded, almost concurrently, from many areas of the Indo-West Pacific region, most of these areas being separated by hundreds of miles. It is scarcely conceivable that short-term rises in water temperature capable of triggering population explosions of A. planci occurred almost simultaneously at certain widely scattered areas but not at intervening ones. Moreover, there is no evidence that a small rise in water temperature would initiate A. planci population explosions. Ormond and Campbell (1971) have pointed out that normal A. planci populations occur in the Red Sea where extreme water temperatures are encountered.

b. A Cyclic Phenomenon. It has been proposed that the A. planci infestations are periodic events (Walsh et al., 1971). The basis of this hypothesis is obscure as it is completely unsupported by available data. Coral reefs are regarded by most marine biologists as being mature ecosystems possessing very stable biotic associations that are resistant to normal perturbations because of their trophic complexity and multiplicity of homeostatic mechanisms. A. planci population explosions similar to those now being encountered have not been recorded previously in the scientific literature. Nor is their previous occurrence known to the indigenous inhabitants of Indo-West Pacific coral reef areas. Then again, it has been estimated that some of the larger coral heads killed recently at Guam were over 200 years old (Chesher, 1969b). Likewise, massive coral colonies estimated to be aged in excess of 100 years were killed during the 1960's on many reefs of the Great Barrier Reef. Thus, if the population explosions are periodic events, the interval between successive population explosions must be of this order at least. Indeed, Goreau (in Chesher, 1969b) estimated that some of the corals recently devastated at Guam represented at least a thousand years of continuous development. It is difficult to conceive of any factor, or factors, capable of triggering *A. planci* infestations that would operate at intervals of a hundred or a thousand years. Moreover, the cyclic phenomenon hypothesis encounters the major difficulty that *A. planci* population explosions have occurred almost concurrently at localities that are hundreds of miles apart but not at intervening localities. Clearly the hypothesis is untenable.

2. Unique Event

The virtual absence of scientific or historical records relating to previous *A. planci* infestations of coral reefs suggests that the starfish plagues are unique. The catastrophic damage caused by starfish infestations to reefs supports this concept. Affected reefs will, in many cases, probably require decades for complete recovery, if indeed they do recover completely. It is difficult to envisage such wholesale destruction of coral reefs caused by a single species as being a normal phenomenon.

a. Mutant Strain. The possibility that in recent years a mutant of *A. planci* has appeared that has a great potential for reproduction has been raised and rejected (Chesher, 1969b; Endean, 1969).

b. Human Involvement. The distribution of the population explosions of *A. planci* (on accessible reefs near centers of human population) suggests human involvement in initiating them. Features of the *A. planci* populations typical of uninfested reefs are the low population density of adults and the apparent scarcity of juveniles. Neither adults nor juveniles are resource limited as their normal prey is present in abundance, so it would appear that their populations are controlled by other factors, possibly predators. When a primary infestation of a reef occurs, there must be far greater recruitment of *A. planci* to the reef than usual. Such enhanced recruitment would result from a release of predator pressure (Endean, 1969). This is the basis of most theories proposed to explain the starfish population explosions. Differences among hypotheses based on this general theme relate to the type of predator involved, the manner in which the predator numbers are reduced, and the stages in the life cycle of *A. planci* most affected.

Some theories involve the release of predator pressure on eggs and larvae. It was observed that fish (*Abudefduf curacao*) ate eggs of *A. planci* (Pearson and Endean, 1969), and it has been suggested that the removal of such egg-eating fish as a result of human activity would result in more eggs and hence more larvae. Then too, it can be expected that starfish larvae would be subjected to predation by a wide variety of planktonic predators and by a wide variety of benthic predators, including corals. As pointed out by Endean (1969), there must always be a heavy mortality of eggs and larval stages of *A. planci* owing to the activities of such predators, but there is no evidence to indicate that predator pressure on eggs and larval stages has decreased significantly in recent years in the regions from which *A. planci* plagues have been reported. No marked decrease in the numbers of any predator of eggs and larvae of *A. planci* has been recorded. However, Chesher (1969a) has hypothesized that local destruction of reefs by blasting, dredging, and other human activities has provided fresh surfaces free of filter feeders for settlement of larvae that have given rise to seed populations of starfish. On the other hand, Endean and Stablum (1973a) have found that on the Great Barrier Reef small juvenile *A. planci* are confined to shallow water on reef crests and tops of coral pinnacles where the ratio of dead to living coral is normally high. Also, Yamaguchi (Chapter 11) has shown that *A. planci* larvae are normally found in surface waters and metamorphose on coralline algae (common in shallow regions where juvenile *A. planci* are found). Thus there are normally large areas partially free of benthic predators in the preferred region of larval settlement. Then too, severe tropical storms have caused extensive damage to many reefs in the past, and many coral reefs were blasted extensively by high explosive during World War II, but, as far as is known, such reefs did not become infested with *A. planci*.

Mass mortalities of corals as a result of proliferation of an alga *Dictyosphaeria cavernosa* attributable to sewage pollution have been recorded at Kaneohe Bay, Hawaii (Banner and Bailey, 1970), but pollution generally does not appear to have affected benthic organisms on other reefs adversely as yet. On the other hand, it is possible that planktonic predators of starfish larvae, rather than benthic predators, have been selectively killed by pollutants such as persistent pesticides (Chesher, 1969b; Fisher, 1969). However, as Yamaguchi (Chapter 11) pointed out, other coral reef starfish with development phases and planktonic stages similar to those of *A. planci* and with brachiolariae that metamorphose on the same type of substratum as *A. planci* have not shown a marked increase in numbers in recent years. Then again, it is difficult to conceive of a pollutant with the necessary selective toxicity for the predators of *A. planci* larvae being introduced continuously into the waters over reefs in widely separated areas throughout the Indo-West Pacific region. Moreover, the reefs of the Great Barrier Reef where primary infestations of *A. planci* were reported (Endean, 1969; Endean and Stablum, 1973a) are, on the average, about 30 km from the mainland, and there are strong surface currents and tidal water movements in the area, which would tend to disperse pollutants.

It. has been shown by Yamaguchi (Chapter 11) that *A. planci* brachiolariae settle and metamorphose on coralline algae and that small juvenile stages feed exclusively on this type of algae. Predation on these small juveniles could be of great significance. Possibly the microfauna inhabiting coralline algae takes a heavy toll of the recently meta-mophosed larvae, while small carnivorous or omnivorous animals, particularly mollusks and fish (or even herbivores grazing the algae), take a toll of the small juveniles, which remain associated with the algae for about 5 months. Some reduction of the numbers of small molluscan predators (e.g., carnivorous muricids or cymatiids) or grazing mollusks, such as *Trochus niloticus*, the trochus of commerce, could have been brought about by shell collectors and some reduction in the number of small fish by fish collectors at certain localities. However, the actual extent to which predation on the very small juvenile stages of *A. planci* has been affected by human agency is extremely difficult to assess.

The extent to which the wrasse *Cheilinus undulatus* normally predates on juvenile or adult *A. planci* is not known. If this big wrasse is a potent predator of the starfish, it then could be postulated that the spearing by divers of large numbers of *C. undulatus* could have reduced its numbers on some reefs to the point where it could no longer exert any control on *A. planci* numbers.

Predation on larger juvenile and adult *A. planci* by the giant triton, *Charonia tritonis*, has been well documented (Endean, 1969; Pearson and Endean, 1969). Juveniles and small adults are eaten whole (Endean and Stablum, 1973a). It has been frequently stated that specimens of *Charonia tritonis* are not sufficiently common to exert control over *A. planci* populations (Chesher, 1969a; Vine, 1970; Ormond and Campbell, 1970; Weber and Woodhead, 1970), Certainly *C. tritonis* is rare in the region of *A. planci* infestations of the Great Barrier Reef. Only 52 specimens were observed during visits made to 130 reefs (some reefs being visited more than once during the period 1966–1971). Most marked was the dearth of juvenile *C. tritonis*, only two juveniles being seen. However, no studies have been made of the typical population density and population structure of *C. tritonis* on coral reefs uninfested by *A. planci* and where the giant triton has not been heavily collected.

Information has been received (Endean, 1969) indicating that *C. tritonis* has been collected intensively in Queensland waters since World War II, and it is probable that giant tritons have also been collected intensively at many other coral reef areas in the Indo-West Pacific region since that time. Of course, giant tritons have been collected for centuries by the indigenous peoples of many coral reef areas and used as trumpets to call tribes together for pleasure or war. However, after World War II shell collecting became a hobby indulged in by large numbers of people throughout the world. Large showy shells from tropical waters came into great demand and a flourishing shell trade developed. Unfortunately, precise information is not available on the extent to which *Charonia tritonis* has been collected since World War II. Available information indicates that thousands of specimens were collected on reefs of the Great Barrier Reef during the 1950's and sold to tourists at several localities in the Townsville to Cooktown region of the Queensland coast and also sold to the shell trade from Thursday Island, Torres Strait, which was the home base for many trochus luggers which worked Barrier Reef waters. Chesher (1969b) has referred to the intensive collecting of giant triton shells at several islands in the Marianas and Carolines. This collecting is still continuing at many localities. Owens (1971) mentioned that when a ban was placed by the Fijiian government in February, 1970, on the taking or exporting of *C. tritonis* there were a thousand specimens in the Suva market. In 1971, specimens were on sale at several localities on Manus Island (Endean, unpublished). Prices for triton shells have increased markedly during the last decade. In Hawaii, in 1971, medium-sized shells of *C. tritonis* were on sale to the public for $65 each. Increased prices offered for giant tritons appear to have resulted in their collection on remote reefs. In 1970, for example, Taiwanese fishermen were fined by the Australian government for collecting giant tritons on the isolated Swain Reefs near the southern end of the Great Barrier Reef. These reefs are thousands of miles from the home port of the fishermen. It would seem likely that in some areas there has been a marked reduction in population densities of *C. tritonis* as a result of collecting by humans. Also, it might be expected that accessible reefs near the major centers of population or near tourist centers would be the ones where collecting of giant tritons was most intense. These are the reefs from which the majority of recent population explosions of *A. planci* have been recorded.

As well as a reduction in numbers as a result of intensive collecting by humans, the numbers of *Charonia tritonis* on certain reefs could have been reduced as a result of the accumulation in their tissues of toxic residues from pesticides or other pollutants emanating from centers of human population or regions of marked agricultural activity. These residues could have accumulated until levels that were lethal or levels that interfered with reproduction were attained. It should be noted that *C. tritonis* is a predator of high trophic status. In this way pollution could have been a factor in initiating the starfish infestations.

The situation whereby a reduction in the numbers of one species of high trophic status has far-reaching repercussions for a whole community of animals has received theoretical consideration by Paine (1969) in his key species hypothesis. Endean and Stablum (1973a) have postulated that *C. tritonis* is a key species on coral reefs and that normally *A. planci* populations, which are not normally resource limited, are held in check as a result of predation on large juveniles and adults by *C. tritonis*.

On the other hand, it has been suggested that predation by *C. tritonis* on *A. planci* is of little consequence, because Chesher (1969a) has reported that half of a starfish attacked by *C. tritonis* survived and regenerated missing portions of its body. However, none of the numerous starfish observed to be attacked by *C. tritonis* on the Great Barrier Reef survived the attack. Even so, it is possible that large specimens of adult *A. planci* usually survive attacks by *C. tritonis*.

Possibly the large adult specimens of *A. planci* normally seen on an uninfested reef are virtually free from predation because of their large size, armature, and toxicity. Occasionally, they may lose parts of their bodies to specialized predators such as *Charonia tritonis, Hymenocera picta*, or *Cheilinus undulatus*, but they regenerate these parts. Because they are normally present at low population density and are widely dispersed on reefs, breeding may be infrequent. On those occasions when it occurs, there is probably a high mortality of eggs, larvae, and small juveniles owing to the activities of nonspecific predators. Subsequently juveniles are subjected to predation by relatively specific predators, particularly *Charonia tritonis*, during the years of growth that elapse before a specimen, because of its large size, toxicity, and capacity to regenerate parts removed by predators, becomes virtually immune to predation.

If predator pressure on large juveniles and small adult starfish by those relatively specific predators is lowered markedly, it could be expected that a gradual increase in the numbers of *A. planci* present on a reef (the starfish breeds for the first time at about 2 years of age) would occur. Ultimately, the breeding starfish population could be such that enormous numbers of eggs and larvae are produced. Recent evidence (Yamaguchi, Chapter 11) would indicate that a period of at least 3 weeks elapses between egg release and the settling of brachiolariae. Consequently there is ample time for dispersal of larvae by currents, and it would appear unlikely that, as suggested by Endean and Stablum (1973a), juveniles on a reef are usually the progeny of adults on the same reef. However, there could be a closed or semiclosed system of surface currents in an area, or the eggs could be released near the time when currents in the area wane or change direction. As noted by Endean *et al.* (1956), reversals of surface currents occur in central regions of the Great Barrier Reef during the summer months (December–February). This is the period when A. *planci* spawns.

In these ways larvae could settle on the same reef or reefs in the same general area as aggregated starfish constituting the primary centers of infestation. In either case, there could be a positive feedback to the primary centers, and, in the absence of effective compensating mechanisms (predation), an overall buildup in starfish numbers at these centers would occur slowly at first but with explosive rapidity subsequently. It should be noted that the A. *planci* population explosions could have been initiated at a few reefs and that subsequently other reefs could have become infested as a result of invasion by larvae carried in currents or invasion by migrating adults.

B. Secondary Infestations

Because larvae settle in shallow water and tend to remain in shallow water until they are at least 12 cm in diameter (Endean and Stablum, 1973a), secondary infestations of reefs stemming from larval invasion would be characterized initially by the presence of large numbers of juveniles in shallow water and a normal low density adult population in deeper water. Subsequently, if there were progressive recruitment of larvae and compensating mechanisms were inadequate to reduce starfish populations substantially, the bulk of the coral in shallow water habitats would be killed and the coral in deeper water would then come under attack. Sometimes recruitment would be insufficient to maintain a high density population of A. *planci* on a reef, and only a limited amount of damage would then be caused to the reef's coral cover.

There is evidence that in Great Barrier Reef waters adult specimens of A. *planci* migrate from devastated reefs to adjacent uninfested reefs by walking across the intervening sea floor (Pearson and Endean, 1969)

Infestation of new reefs in this case is initiated by migrating adults, which appear first in deep water around the periphery of reefs and subsequently ascend reef slopes (Endean and Stablum, 1973a). Such migrating adults would account for the infestation of reefs that, because of their positions with respect to surface currents, would not receive a quota of *A. planci* larvae from sites of primary infestation. Again, if starfish numbers were sufficiently large and compensating mechanisms were inadequate to reduce substantially the numbers of invading adults, the bulk of coral on the infested reef could be killed by the starfish.

The hypothesis that reduction of predator pressure on large juvenile and small adult *A. planci* owing to the lowering of population densities of *Charonia tritonis* on reefs as a result of human activity has been responsible for the recent population explosions of *A. planci* can be used to provide an explanation of the timing and geographic locations of population explosions recorded in recent years. It could also be used to explain the occurrence of a few devastated reefs in certain areas of the Central Pacific where massive destruction of the hard coral cover, except for species of *Millepora*, appears to have occurred prior to the 1960's but which currently lack concentrations of *A. planci*. Thus Chesher (1969b) noted that Kuop in the Carolines appeared to have been stripped of its living coral some years ago and mentioned that a local chieftain stated that the reef at Kuop was infested with *A. planci* immediately after World War II. Japanese service personnel lived on the atoll during World War II and, as stated by Chesher (1969b, p. 40), they instigated a "major interest in collecting tritons, collecting them for food as well as ornamentation." The presence of many dead patch reefs in the lagoons of Tarawa and Abaiang Atolls in the Gilbert Islands (Weber and Woodhead, 1970) may have stemmed from a similar cause. The hypothesis could also be used to predict the timing and approximate location of future *A. planci* infestations. For example, information has been received about the heavy collection of *Charonia tritonis* in the Manus Island area during the 1960's, and it is predicted that *A. planci* outbreaks will be reported from that area in the near future.

It should be possible to test the validity of the hypothesis by collecting the populations of *Charonia tritonis* from selected reefs in a remote area and observing subsequent changes in *A. planci* populations on reefs in the area. There is a possibility that other human activities have acted synergistically with the collecting of *Charonia tritonis* to produce the *A. planci* infestations, and this possibility should be taken into account when testing the validity of the hypothesis.

The absence of *Charonia* from the west coast of the Americas (Beu,

1970) is noteworthy. Populations of *Acanthaster ellisii* were reported near islands in the southern Gulf of California at an average density that exceeded that given in several definitions of abnormal densities of *A. planci* populations in the Indo-West Pacific region (Dana and Wolfson, 1970). These authors speculated that *Acanthaster* predation, together with other factors, might have contributed significantly to the almost total absence of reef formation in the Gulf of California.

VII. Assessment of the Seriousness of the *A. planci* Problem and of the Need for Control Measures

There is no question that recent *A. planci* infestations have caused massive damage to the hard coral cover of reefs of the Great Barrier Reef and to many reefs in Micronesia. The extent of the damage has been studied in some detail at these localities. It seems likely that severe damage has also been inflicted on many other reefs (e.g., reefs at Fiji, Ceylon, the Philippines, Taiwan, and Okinawa), but a full assessment of the extent of damage at these localities is not yet available. The destruction of coral continues at most localities from where outbreaks have been reported in the 1960's, and reports of new *A. planci* outbreaks at other reefs have been received since the start of the 1970's. It is possible that the *A. planci* infestations will attenuate in the near future as they spread from the primary centers of infestation to other reefs where effective compensating mechanisms are operative. Opposed to this view there is the possibility that the infestations will continue to spread or even snowball during the 1970's. At this juncture nobody knows which of these possibilities will prevail.

Recovery of reefs from the starfish plagues is, on present indications, likely to be a prolonged affair and, because of the presence of residual starfish populations, the possibility exists that affected reefs might remain impoverished indefinitely. The available evidence militates against the infestations being normal phenomena. They appear to be unique and there is strong circumstantial evidence that the plagues are man-induced. Irrespective of the origin of the plagues, the question of their control warrants attention. In regions where the local human population depends on the integrity of the reef for food, it is obviously desirable that *A. planci* plagues be controlled just as locust plagues attacking crops on land warrant control. In other regions, such as Australia's Great Barrier Reef, the destruction of the coral cover of numerous reefs may not have immediate economic implications. Even so, the possibility that the reefs may be impoverished for indefinite periods must arouse concern among responsible scientists, statesmen, and the general public. It would seem wise to control the expanding starfish populations wherever possible while the causes of the population explosions are determined. As pointed out by Chesher (1969b), if subsequent research reveals that the starfish plagues are definitely undesirable, then reefs will have been protected. On the other hand, if research reveals that *A. planci* plagues are a normal part of reef ecology no harm will have been done by the institution of control measures for a brief period. Some reefs are definitely known to have been free of starfish plagues for decades without the biota of these reefs suffering any apparent ill effects (e.g., Green Island and Heron Island on the Great Barrier Reef, Guam in the Marianas). Even if it were found that, in the long term, *A. planci* plagues are beneficial rather than harmful to coral reefs, no permanent change to *A. planci* populations will have been caused by instituting suitable control measures now. These control measures would certainly not endanger survival of the species. *A. planci* is normally sparsely represented on coral reefs, and a reduction of *A. planci* numbers below those normally found on coral reefs would be almost impossible to achieve. In this connection it is interesting to note that *Acanthaster* is not found at all on coral reefs in the Atlantic Ocean.

Although a variety of control measures including quicklime barriers, the dropping of quicklime pellets on coral reefs, electric fences, $CuSO_4$ pipes, suction dredges, electric guns, etc., has been suggested, practical control measures have centered around the manual collection of starfish or their destruction by injecting them with toxic materials such as formalin and ammonia. At Guam and in Micronesia generally, control efforts have met with a large measure of success (Tsuda, 1971). Likewise, manual collection of starfish on reefs in Western Samoa appears to have been successful in reducing starfish numbers markedly (Garlovsky and Bergquist, 1970). The results of collecting programs that have been undertaken at Hawaii, the Ryukyus, Tahiti, and Fiji have still to be evaluated.

The collecting of juvenile and adult starfish, if carried out systematically on a particular reef, should be successful in halting coral destruction by starfish on the reef. Also, it could be used to contain starfish infestations in reef archipelagoes such as the Great Barrier Reef (Endean, 1969). When the bulk of adult starfish is removed from a reef, there should be regular surveillance of the perimeter of a reef to locate any invading adults and an annual inspection of shallow water areas near reef crests and coral pinnacles to locate juveniles. If the causes of the *A. planci* plagues have been correctly assessed and these plagues have stemmed from the removal of *Charonia tritonis* (or other predators of juvenile and adult starfish), long-term control would involve the re-introduction of natural predators such as *Charonia tritonis* and, in the interim, surviving stocks of predators, particularly *C. tritonis*, should be rigidly protected. It is, of course, possible that factors other than depletion of stocks of tritons or other predators of juvenile and adult starfish have been involved in initiating and maintaining the *A. planci* outbreaks. Only further research, which is urgently required, will enable an assessment of the relative importance of these other factors. In the interim, the collection of juvenile and adult starfish would provide temporary protection for reefs until the necessary research is carried out and the most efficacious form of control determined.

Some governments have reacted with commendable speed to protect reefs for which they are responsible; others have not yet taken the necessary action. There is need for international action to coordinate control measures and research on *A. planci*. At the same time, there is a need for the adoption of effective conservation measures for coral reefs in most parts of the world. These reefs have suffered increasingly in recent years from the activities of commercial shell collectors, fish collectors, coral collectors, limestone gatherers, blasting, dredging, toxic chemicals, pollution, and increased freshwater runoff from neighboring land masses as a result of forest removal and agricultural practices.

VIII. Conclusions

It is still too early to provide a reasonably complete picture of the causes, significance, and ultimate effects of the *A. planci* population explosions, but a picture is beginning to emerge. Normally *A. planci* occurs at low population densities (rarely exceeding 2–3 specimens per km² of reef) among coral pinnacles in lagoons and back-reef areas. Most specimens encountered are large adults. Juveniles are rarely seen. Adults feed almost exclusively on madreporarian corals. When present at normal population densities, the species causes negligible damage to reefs and is certainly not resource limited. It has great fecundity, millions of eggs being produced by each female, but it is not known how frequently breeding occurs when *A. planci* is present at normal low population density. However, some breeding must occur periodically, and, if the numbers of *A. planci* on a reef depended primarily on larval success, the marked variation in larval recruitment to the *A. planci* population of a reef, which might be expected from year to year because the species has planktotrophic larval stages, should be reflected in marked fluctuations in the population of adult A. *planci* found on the reef. Such marked fluctuations in adult A. *planci* populations have not been recorded prior to 1957; yet, had they occurred on a large scale prior to 1957, the resultant catastrophic destruction of coral could not have failed to attract attention. Although eggs and planktotrophic larvae of long duration must be subjected to heavy predation by a variety of nektonic, planktonic, and benthic predators (many of which would be relatively nonselective), some larvae must survive and metamorphose on reefs. Obviously, recruitment to the breeding A. *planci* population on a reef must be carefully regulated if the normal low population density on a reef is to be maintained. It is postulated that regulation is achieved as a result of predation on juvenile and young adult A. *planci* by a relatively specific predator, *Charonia tritonis*. This predator is of high trophic status and can be regarded as a key species in the sense used by Paine (1969).

Since 1957, population explosions of A. *planci* have been recorded from certain coral reefs at widely separated localities in the Indo-West Pacific region. Although not uniformly distributed, tens of thousands of A. *planci* are present on infested reefs. When aggregated in such large numbers adult starfish soon overwhelm their coral prey. There is now no question that catastrophic damage can be caused to the hard coral cover of infested reefs. Indeed, the bulk of the hard coral cover of a reef can be killed, resulting in an apparent breakdown of community organization on the reef, with associates of living corals being particularly affected. There is also little doubt that recovery of reefs from the devastation caused by A. *planci* will be retarded by many factors including the development of succession communities. It is estimated that decades will be required for full recovery. Also, there is a possibility that devastated reefs will remain impoverished indefinitely because of the presence of residual starfish populations on some reefs and because the original causes of the starfish infestations may still be operative on other reefs.

There is no convincing evidence for the occurrence, prior to 1957, of A. *planci* population explosions on a scale similar to that reported since 1957, and the population explosions appear to be unique. There is strong circumstantial evidence that recent starfish infestations of reefs are man-induced. To date, the most satisfactory explanations of their origin involves the release from predator pressure of juvenile and small adult A. *planci*. It is postulated that the intensive collecting by humans of *Charonia tritonis*, on reefs readily accessible to humans, has initiated the *A. planci* plagues by enabling the buildup of large breeding populations of *A. planci*. Other reefs have been subjected to secondary infestation by carriage to them on currents of larvae from the primary centers of infestation or as a result of invasion by migrating adults that have left devastated reefs when the availability of coral has become a limiting factor. It is not known whether the *A. planci* infestations will attenuate, increase in extent, or even snowball during the 1970's. However, there is an obvious need to control starfish populations on reefs while the causes of the starfish plagues are determined and their significance evaluated.

Irrespective of whether the *A. planci* plagues are proved to be normal or unique phenomena, it is apparent that *A. planci* is currently the most important biotic factor governing the growth and development of coral reefs. However, it would not be surprising if the *A. planci* plagues are proved to be man-induced and the coral reef ecosystem is shown to be the latest to suffer from overexploitation by humans. As Margalef (1968, p. 48) pointed out "a strong exploitation of very mature ecosystems, like tropical forests or coral reefs may produce a total collapse of a rich organization. In such stable biotopes nature is not prepared for a step backwards."

References

Anonymous (1970). "*Acanthaster planci* (Crown-of-Thorns Starfish) and The Great Barrier Reef." Rep. Aust. Acad. Sci. No. 11.

Banner, A. H., and Bailey, J. H. (1970). "The Effects of Urban Pollution Upon a Coral Reef System. A Preliminary Report," Tech. Rep. No. 25. Hawaii Institute of Marine Biology.

Barnes, D. J., Brauer, R. W., and Jordan, M. R. (1970). *Nature (London)* **228**, 342.

Barnes, J. H. (1966). *Aust. Natur. Hist.* **15**, 257.

Barnes, J. H., and Endean, R. (1964). *Med. J. Aust.* **1**, 592.

Bennett, I. (1958). *Proc. Linn. Soc. N.S.W.* **83**, 375.

Beu, A. G. (1970). *Trans. Roy. Soc. N.Z.* **11**, 205.

Branham, J. M., Reed, S. A., Bailey, J. H., and Caperon, J. (1971). *Science* **172**, 1155.

Brauer, R. W., Jordan, M. R., and Barnes, D. J. (1970). *Nature (London)* **228**, 344.

Campbell, A. C., and Ormond, R. F. G. (1970). *Biol. Conserv.* **2**, 246.

Cheney, D. P. (1971). *In* "Status of *Acanthaster planci* and Coral Reefs in the Mariana and Caroline Islands, June, 1970 to May, 1971" (R. T. Tsuda, ed.), Tech. Rep. No. 2. The Marine Laboratory, University of Guam.

Chesher, R. H. (1969a). *Science,* **165**, 280.

Chesher, R. H. (1969b). "Acanthaster planci: Impact on Pacific Coral Reefs," Doc. No. PB187631. Westinghouse Electric Corporation Report to U.S. Dept. Interior.

Chesher, R. H. (1970). *Science* **167**, 1275.

Coe, W. R. (1956). *J. Mar. Res.* **16**, 212.

Dana, T. F. (1970). *Science* **169**, 894.

Dana, T., and Wolfson, A. (1970). *Trans. San Diego Soc. Nat. Hist.* **16**, 83.

Domantay, J. S., and Roxas, H. A. (1938). *Philipp. J. Sci.* **65**, 203.

Edmondson, C. H. (1933). *Spec. Publ., Bishop Mus.* **22**, 67

Edmondson, C. H. (1946). *Spec. Publ., Bishop Mus.* **22**, 73.

Endean, R. (1961). *Univ. of Queensl. Pap., Dep. Zool.* **1**, 289.

Endean, R. (1969). "Report on Investigations Made into Aspects of the Current *Acanthaster planci* (Crown of thorns) Infestations of Certain Reefs of the Great Barrier Reef." Fisheries Branch, Queensland Dept. of Primary Industries, Brisbane.

Endean, R. (1972). *Chem. Zool.* **7**, 421.

Endean, R. (1973). *J. Mar. Biol. Ass. India* (in press).

Endean, R., and Chesher, R. H. (1973). *Biol. Conserv.* **5**, 87.

Endean, R., and Stablum, W. (1973a). *Atoll Res. Bull.* (in press).

Endean, R., and Stablum, W. (1973b). *Atoll Res. Bull.* (in press).

Endean, R., Kenny, R., and Stephenson, W. (1956). *Aust. J. Mar. Freshwater Res.* **7**, 88.

Fisher, J. L. (1969). *Science* **165**, 645.

Fisher, W. K. (1919). *U.S., Nat. Mus., Bull.* **100**, 1.

Garlovsky, D. F., and Bergquist, A. (1970). *South Pacific Bull.* **20**, 47.

Gervais, P. (1841). *Dict. Sci. Nat., Suppl.* **1**, 461.

Goreau, T. F. (1963). *Sea Fish Res. Sta. Haifa, Bull.* **35**, 23.

Hayashi, R. (1938). *Palao Trop. Biol. Stud.* **1**, 417.

Henderson, J. A. (1969). *Queensl. Fish. Notes, Dep. Harbours Mar.* **3**, 69.

Henderson, J. A., and Lucas, J. S. (1971). *Nature (London)* **232**, 655.

Madsen, F. J. (1955). *Vidensk. Medd. Dan. Naturh. Foren.* **117**, 179.

Margalef, R., ed. (1968). "Perspectives in Ecological Theory" Univ. of Chicago Press, Chicago, Illinois.

Mortensen, T. (1931). *Kgl. Dans. Vidensk. Selsk., Skr. Nat. Math. Afd.* **4**, 29.

Newman, W. A. (1970). *Science* **167**, 1274.

Nishihira, M., and Yamazato, K. (1972). "Brief Survey of *Acanthaster planci* in Sesoko Island and Its Vicinity, Okinawa." Tech. Rep. No. 1. Sesoko Marine Science Laboratory, University of the Ryukyus.

Ormond, R. F. G., and Campbell, A. C. (1970). *Symp. Zool. Soc. London* **28**, 433.

Owens, D. (1971). *Fiji Agr. J.* **33**, 15.

Paine, R. T. (1969). *Amer. Natur.* **103**, 91.

Pearson, R. G., and Endean, R. (1969). *Queens. Fish. Notes, Dep. Harbours Mar.* **3**, 27.

Pope, E. C. (1964). *Aust. Natur. Hist.* **14**, 350.

Pyne, R. R. (1969). *Papua New Guinea Agr. J.* **21**, 128.

Rumphius, G. E. (1705). D'Amboinische Rariteitkamer.

Stoddart, D. R. (1969). *Biol. Rev.* **44**, 433.

Thorson, G. (1950). *Biol. Rev.* **25**, 1.

Tsuda, R. T. (1971). "Status of *Acanthaster planci* and Coral Reefs in the Mariana and Caroline Islands, June 1970 to May 1971." Tech. Rep. No. 2. The Marine Laboratory, University of Guam.

Vine, P. J. (1970). *Nature* (*London*) **228**, 341.

Walsh, R. J., Harris, C. L., Harvey, J. M., Maxwell, W. G. H., Thomson, J. M., and Tranter, D. J. (1971). "Report of the Committee on the Problem of the Crown-of-Thorns Starfish (*Acanthaster planci*)." CSIRO, Melbourne.

Weber, J. N., and Woodhead, P. M. J. (1970). *Mar. Biol.* **6**, 12.

Wickler, W., and Seibt, U. (1970). *Z. Tierpsychol.* **27**, 352.

AUTHOR INDEX

Numbers in italics refer to the pages on which the complete references are listed.

Y

Z

SYSTEMATIC INDEX

A

SUBJECT INDEX

A

Acanthaster
  bipinnariae of, 371, 374
  gastrulae of, 371, 373
  growth rates, variation of in larvae,
      375
  larvae of, 371–386
Acanthaster planci
  breeding season of, 395–396
  distribution of, 391–392
  gonad indexes in, 395
  habitat of, 392, 393
  infestation of reefs by, 389–436
      control of, 432–434
      as cyclic phenomenon, 424–425
      history of, 415–423
      human involvement in, 425–430
      as natural phenomena, 423–424
      primary, 425, 427
      resulting from adult invasion, 402
      secondary, 423, 430–432, 436
      triggered by temperature rise, 424
      as unique events, 425–430
  juveniles of, 396
      behavior of, 382–384
      density of, 402
      growth rate of, 397
      locomotion of, 383
      photoorientation in, 383
      recruitment of, 391, 393
  larval development in, 396
  life history of, 371–386
  locomotion of adult, 393
  long-term effects of devastation by,
      413–415
  longevity of, 400
  metamorphosis of, 396
  migration of adult, 407, 423
  morphology of, 391–392
  movements of, 393
  mutant strain of, 425
  population density, normal of, 400, 401
  population explosion(s) of, 370
      decline of in *A. planci,* 407
      effects of, 407–415
      possible causes of, 423–432
  population structure of
      on infested reefs, 403–405
      normal of *A. planci,* 400–401
  predator pressure on, reduction of,
      425–426, 431–432
  prey of, 393–395
  regeneration of arms of, 399–400
  reproduction in, 395
  sex ratio in, 395
  size groups in, 405
  stomach eversion in, 393, 394
  taxonomy of, 392
  toxicity of, 393
Acansterol, in *Acanthaster planci,* 187
Accretion, rates of in reef assemblages,
    273
Acids, *see* specific compounds
Acrylic acid, 135, 137
Actiniaria, 79, 80
Actinomycetes, 122
Aeroplysinin-1, 150
Aerothionin, 150
Africa, West coast, 283
Age structure, 331
  of corals, 234, 235, 239
Aggregates
  bacterial, 25, 26, 29, 30
  organic, 3, 18, 29
Aggregation, types of, 253
Aggression, hierarchial among corals, 227
Alcyonacea, 78
Alcyonaceans, xeniid, 106
Alcyonarians, 395, 412

464